Financial Reporting

Sixth edition

David Alexander and Anne Britton

THOMSON

™ Australia   Canada   Mexico   Singapore   United Kingdom   United States

Financial Reporting – Sixth Edition

Copyright © 1986, 1990, 1993, 1996, 1999, 2001 D. Alexander and A. Britton
First published by International Thomson Business Press 1996.

The Thomson logo is a registered trademark used herein under licence.

For more information, contact Thomson Learning, Berkshire House, 168–173 High Holborn, London, WC1V 7AA or visit us on the World Wide Web at: http://www.thomsonlearning.co.uk

British Library Cataloguing-in-Publication Data
A catalogue record for this book is available from the British Library

First edition published by Chapman & Hall 1986
Reprinted 1988, 1990
Second edition published by Chapman & Hall 1990
Reprinted 1991
Third edition published by Chapman & Hall 1993
Reprinted 1994
Fourth edition published by International Thomson Business Press 1996
Fifth edition published by International Thompson Business Press 1999
Reprinted 1999
Reprinted 2000 by Thomson Learning
Sixth edition published by Thomson Learning 2001
Reprinted 2002 by Thomson

Produced and typeset by Gray Publishing, Tunbridge Wells, Kent
Printed in Great Britain by TJ International Ltd, Padstow, Cornwall

ISBN 1-86152-672-5

Thomson Learning
Berkshire House
168–173 High Holborn
London WC1V 7AA

http://www.thomsonlearning.co.uk

Contents

Abbreviations

ACT	Advance corporation tax
ASB	Accounting Standards Board
ASC	Accounting Standards Committee
ASSC	Accounting Standards Steering Committee
CC	Current cost
CCAB	Consultative Committee of Accounting Bodies
COSA	Cost of sales adjustment
CPP	Current purchasing power
DV	Deprival value
ED	Exposure draft
eps	Earnings per share
EV	Economic value
FASB	Financial Accounting Standards Board
FIFO	First in, first out
HC	Historic cost
HP	Hire purchase
IASC	International Accounting Standard Committee
LIFO	Last in, first out
MWCA	Monetary working capital adjustment
NBV	Net book value
NPV	Net present value
NRV	Net realizable value
PAYE	Pay As You Earn
PE	Price earnings (ratio)
P&L	Profit and loss
RC	Replacement cost
RPI	Retail prices index
SOI	Statement of Intent
SORP	Statement of Recommended Practice
SSAP	Statement of Standard Accounting Practice
VAT	Value added tax

Preface

This book is about financial reporting. It is about how an accountant should report to people outside a business about the financial events of that business. It is also, in part, about how to 'do' accounting. In other words you will see how to move numbers around the financial reports, in accordance with the regulatory framework, or not as the case may be. Another distinctive feature is the interactive style adopted by the authors to develop your understanding of the ideas put forward.

The presentation is divided into three parts. The first is concerned with ideas. We consider basic questions about what accountants are doing, and for whom; how do they go about their tasks, and what other alternatives are available to them instead? Part Two provides a basic legal framework. What constraints does the law impose on financial reporting? Part Three is the longest part and considers what is known as the regulatory framework – what constraints does the accounting profession itself create? It concludes with two entirely new chapters on the interpretation of accounts. This enables the effects of accounting policy changes to be more thoroughly explored.

This division and sequence is deliberate, and readers should follow it as far as possible. It is not sufficient, for any purposes, simply to try to 'learn' the various standards discussed in Part Three. The accountant of today needs to be flexible, intelligent and critical – both in his or her work and in the examination room. The Accounting and Reporting Standards programme can only be assessed and appraised, and therefore properly understood, with a prior knowledge of the ideas underlying accounting – with some understanding of theories and concepts, if you like. As the emphasis throughout is on ideas and possibilities and not merely on either 'what is done' or 'how it is done', the book will be highly suitable for use on the second and third years of degree courses in accounting and on business studies courses for students choosing the accounting 'stream' or accounting options. It will also be particularly suitable for professional students taking financial accounting examinations and is essential for papers 10, Accounting and Audit Practice and 13, Financial Reporting Environment, in the old ACCA syllabus and papers 2.5 Financial Reporting and 3.6 Advanced Corporate Reporting in the new syllabus.

Similarly, the advanced financial accounting papers of the Institute of Chartered Accountants in England and Wales, and indeed of all the recognized 'accounting bodies', cannot be successfully tackled without a thorough command of the areas covered by this book.

An introduction is provided to all aspects of financial reporting and its problems. The student can then proceed to deeper studies as and when desired. It is our firmly held view that accounting and financial reporting present interesting – yes, even fascinating – problems and issues. When you have read this book, we hope you will think so too.

Many people have contributed in one way or another to the writing of this book. We have learnt much over the years from colleagues and from successive generations of students. We often wonder if students realize the extent to which education is a two-way process. For the faults that the book contains, however, we alone are responsible. All we ask is that if you find them, please let us know.

We are grateful to our publishers, Thomson Learning, for their confidence, encouragement and support. We are grateful to the members of the Accounting Standards Board for not getting it all right yet, and thereby leaving so much of interest to discuss. If the 1980s was the decade of the Accounting Standards Committee (whose task was an extremely hard one), the 1990s the time for the Accounting Standards Board, then the new century will be the time for the International Accounting Standards Committee and its various boards as they move us towards global harmonization. The new century should be most interesting.

Last but certainly not least, we thank our respective spouses and children for their forbearance during creation of both the original volume and of this sixth edition.

David Alexander
The Birmingham Business School
The University of Birmingham

Anne Britton
Leeds Business School
Leeds Metropolitan University

Part One

The conceptual framework

In this first part we look at what financial reporting is all about – what it is trying to achieve and how the accountant sets about achieving it. We also look in some detail at ideas for altering, and hopefully improving, the effectiveness of financial reporting. We consider the criteria for effectiveness – what do we mean by improve – and you are invited to form your own opinion on the suggestions made.

Accounting theory, *or* accounting can be interesting

After reading this chapter you should be able to:
- explain and discuss the scope of accounting in general and of financial accounting in particular
- outline the approach taken by this book.

Introduction

At its simplest level, accounting is about the provision of figures to people about their resources. It is to tell them things such as:

1 what they have got
2 what they used to have
3 the change in what they have got
4 what they may get in the future.

You may have done quite a lot of 'accounting' already. In many cases, this will have consisted largely of technical manipulation – writing up ledger accounts, preparing profit and loss accounts and balance sheets, and so on. Much of the emphasis is likely to have been on 'doing things with numbers'. Given a figure to start with, you can probably record it in a proper double-entry manner and see its effect through onto a balance sheet that actually balances.

But this is only part of the story. Suppose you are not 'given a figure'. Suppose you are given, or have available, a whole variety of figures all related to a particular item or transaction. Which figure or figures should you actually put into the double-entry system? More fundamentally, *how* are you going to decide which ones to put in? In very general terms, we can answer this question by going back to our original simple definition of accounting. Namely that it concerns the provision of figures to people about their resources. Presumably, therefore, the figures that we as accountants should provide to people are the figures that they need to know for their own particular purpose.

So the key question is: what do people want to know about their resources? What use do they wish to make of the figures we as accountants provide? Once we have answered this question, we can go on to say that the figure we should put into our double-entry system is the one likely to be *most useful to the user of our accounting reports*.

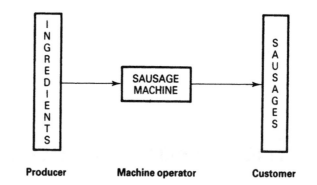

Figure 1.1
Sausage-making.

An analogy – all about sausages

It may help to put the various aspects of financial accounting into context by considering what at first might appear to be a rather unusual analogy. As most of you will know, a sausage is a general word for a long round thing containing meat and several more or less edible additions and flavourings. The possibilities for combining different ingredients are almost endless, but nevertheless we always know a sausage when we see one. If you want to run a sausage-making business, then the first thing to do is to get a sausage-making machine. The second thing to do is to choose and obtain the desired ingredients, and the third thing is to produce and sell sausages of the type or types that our customers actually want. Figure 1.1 shows the process.

Now, what sort of sausage does the customer want? We have to find out by one means or another in order to produce sausages that will sell. Having found this out, how do we vary the taste of the sausages we produce? The answer is obvious – we alter the ingredients. So clearly Fig. 1.1 is incomplete because there is a connection, an information flow, between customer and producer, and this affects the process. A more complete diagram is shown in Fig. 1.2.

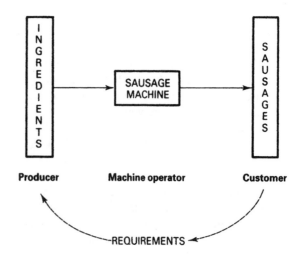

Figure 1.2
Sausage-making and
customer reaction.

To summarize, this is a process containing three major elements:

1 the ingredients, controlled by the producer
2 the sausage machine, controlled by a machine operator
3 the sausages, controlled by the customer.

There is an essential information flow (possibly indirect, i.e. through simply not buying sausages of certain types) from the customer to the producer, i.e. from element 3 to element 1. The crucial point to draw out at this stage is that to provide a different sausage in accordance with the customer's wishes (element 3) we have to alter the ingredients (element 1). There is usually no need to make any alteration at all to the sausage machine itself (element 2).

This analogy could be worked equally well, of course, with other 'general' types of food such as omelettes, or curry.

Activity

How does this sausage analogy relate to the accounting process?

Activity feedback

This all relates back to the accounting process as follows. The central stage in the accounting process, element 2, is the data-recording system. This may be a book-keeping system in the traditional sense, or it may be mechanized or computerized. Whatever its precise form, it is a system for handling and recording data. It is controlled by a book-keeper, machine operator or computer operator, as appropriate. The final stage, element 3, is controlled by the reader or user of accounting statements. The end product of the recording system is accounting statements. Someone, the 'customer', actually uses these – otherwise there is clearly no point in providing them.

But what about the first stage, element 1? That is where we as accountants come in. We have to decide what figures to *put into* the data recording system. If, for example, the

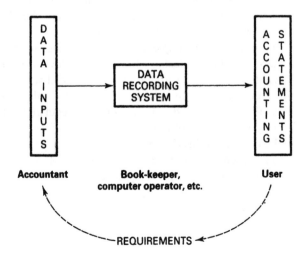

Figure 1.3
The accounting system.

'customer' wishes to know about the cost of the resources held by a business, then the accountant must feed information about *costs* into the data-recording system. But suppose that the 'customer' is a lender to the business. He or she is likely to want to know how much the resources of the business could be sold for, so as to indicate the likelihood of being sure to get their money back. In this case, the accountant will have to feed information about selling (market) prices into the sausage machine in order to produce the required accounting statement about selling prices. We can now redraw our diagram in a proper accounting context (Fig. 1.3).

Once again it is important to note that in order to provide a different financial statement in accordance with a user's particular wishes (element 3), we have to alter the data inputs (element 1). There is not usually any need to make any alteration to the data-recording system.

The focus of the book

Remember our simple opening suggestion that accounting is about the provision of figures to people about their resources. We can now see the need for another vital word to be included. The word is 'useful'. We can thus say that:

Accounting is about the provision of useful figures to people about their resources.
Relating this statement back to the discussion on p. 5, we can suggest that accounting needs:

1 an effective and efficient data handling and recording system
2 the ability to use that system to provide something *useful* to somebody.

This book is essentially concerned with the second of these needs. We have to consider three fundamental issues:

1 *Who* are the users of accounting statements?
2 *What* is the purpose for which each particular type of user requires the information?
3 *How* can we provide the user with the information best suited to their needs?

However, we have to remember also that the accountant and the user have themselves to operate within, and under the control of, the community at large. There is therefore an element of *regulation* that has to be taken into account.

Part One sets out to consider the three fundamental issues stated above. The approach taken is to start from the beginning and steadily build up our ideas in a logical way. We are concerned here with needs and with ideas and possibilities for fulfilling those needs. We shall use frequent simple illustrations to illustrate the various ideas. An important aim of this book is that students should gradually develop their own individual opinions. This book is not merely about learning facts and official statements.

Part Two considers the *legal* regulations within which financial accounting has to work, and Part Three considers the *institutional* regulations. Thus Part Two is concerned with regulations created *outside* the accounting profession, and Part Three is concerned with regulations created *inside*, i.e. by the accounting profession. A continuing theme of Part Two and, especially, Part Three will be the extent to which the various regulations agree with the personal opinions developed in Part One.

Summary

Accounting is an ever-changing and at present rapidly changing profession. The qualified accountant of the future will have the opportunity to influence this process. He or she will also have to live and work with the results. Many important issues in financial accounting are at present in a state of uncertainty or even confusion. After studying this book, you should have your own independent thoughts on these issues that you are capable of defending. If this does not happen then:

1 You will have missed out on a great deal of interest
2 This book will have failed in its most important aim.

Exercises

1 Look up as many definitions of accounting as you can find, noting the source and the date of publication. Appraise them, noting their differences, and look for any trend or change over time. Suggest your own personal definition of 'financial accounting'.
2 Who needs accounting information?
3 Try to provide some accounting information about yourself. Are you better off today than you were a year ago?

The objectives of financial statements and their usefulness to the general user groups

After reading this chapter you should be able to:
- describe the major types of user of published financial information, and discuss the implications of their different needs
- list and discuss the characteristics of accounting information which are likely to maximize its usefulness
- outline both the importance and the difficulty of effective communication.

Introduction

So, how are we going to go about deciding the precise content of the accounts we prepare? We are communicators of information that people will find useful. We, therefore, have to discover who our 'customers' are, and what it is that they want from us. So we have to consider some questions:

1 Who are the users of accounting statements and accountant's reports?
2 What do they want to use them for?
3 What particular information do they need to enable them to use them effectively for their purposes?

The Corporate Report

In 1974 the Accounting Standards Steering Committee (ASSC), operated jointly by the major accounting bodies, appointed a subcommittee to prepare a wide-ranging discussion paper. Its terms of reference were:

> The purpose of this study is to re-examine the scope and aims of published financial reports in the light of modern needs and conditions.
>
> It will be concerned with the public accountability of economic entities of all kinds, but especially business enterprises.
>
> It will seek to establish a set of working concepts as a basis for financial reporting. Its aims will be to identify the persons or groups for whom published financial reports should be prepared, and the information appropriate to their interests.

It will consider the most suitable means of measuring and reporting the economic position, performance and prospects of undertakings for the purposes and persons identified above.

The report was published in 1975 under the title *The Corporate Report*. It is an important document, wide ranging and at times progressive. It is in no way out-dated. It is remarkable how little of what it suggests has actually been implemented. Much of what it proposed for discussion is still being discussed – or even merely still proposed for discussion – today. The increased interest in the idea of creating a broader and more coherent overall accounting framework – discussed later in Chapters 10 and 15 – is at last a welcome sign.

Rather confusingly *The Corporate Report* refers to published accounting statements as corporate reports. Users of corporate reports are defined as:

Those having reasonable right to information concerning the reporting entity...
A reasonable right to information exists where the activities of an organization impinge or may impinge on the interest of a user group.

The user groups

Activity 1

Suggest the major types of user of financial reports. If possible obtain some actual published accounts as a catalyst for your ideas.

Activity 1 feedback

The *Report* identifies seven separate 'user groups', as follows:

1 The equity investor group, including existing and potential shareholders and holders of convertible securities, options or warrants.
2 The loan creditor group including existing and potential holders of debentures and loan stock, and providers of short-term secured and unsecured loans and finance.
3 The employee group including existing, potential and past employees.
4 The analyst–adviser group, including financial analysts and journalists, economists, statisticians, researchers, trade unions, stockbrokers and other providers of advisory services, such as credit-rating agencies.
5 The business contact group including customers, trade creditors and suppliers and in a different sense competitors, business rivals and those interested in mergers, amalgamations and takeovers.
6 The government, including tax authorities, departments and agencies concerned with the supervision of commerce and industry, and local authorities.
7 The public, including taxpayers, ratepayers, consumers and other community and special interest groups, such as political parties, consumer and environmental protection societies and regional pressure groups.

Activity 2

Taking each of these seven groups one at a time, consider first the sort of decisions that they are likely to wish to make using accounting information, and secondly the implications from this as to what information they might need.

Activity 2 feedback

The equity investor group

Essentially this group consists of existing and potential shareholders. This group is considering whether or not to invest in a business: to buy shares, or to buy more shares; or, alternatively, whether or not to disinvest, to sell shares in the business. Equity investors look for one or a combination of two things: income, a money return by way of dividend, or capital gain, a money return by way of selling shares at more than their purchase price. It should be intuitively apparent from common sense that these two are closely related. Indeed the only difference is the time scale. However, the simple theory is made immensely more complex in practice by the effects on share prices of other equity investor's expectations.

For example, share prices for a company may rise because higher dividends are expected to be announced by the company. Alternatively they may rise because other people *believe* dividends will increase. *A* buys some shares in expectation of 'good news'. This causes prices to rise. *B* then buys some shares in expectation of the price rise continuing. This causes the price to rise again – a self-fulfilling prophecy – which brings in *C* as a buyer too. The original hope of 'good news' is soon forgotten. If, however, at a later date the news arrives and turns out to be bad, everyone involved, *A*, *B* and *C*, may want to sell, and the price will come crashing down.

The motivational and psychological arguments involved here are well beyond the scope of this book. It is the information requirements that concern us. If the investor is taking a short-term view then current dividends is the major factor. As the time horizon of our investor lengthens then future dividends become more important, and future dividends are affected crucially by present and future *earnings*. The focus then is on profits, which both determine future dividends and influence the share price.

One obvious point is that investors, both existing and potential, need information about *future* profits. The emphasis in published accounting information is almost wholly on past or more-or-less present profits. These may or may not be a good guide to the future. The need to make the past results useful for estimating (guessing?) the future is an important influence on some of the detailed disclosure requirements we shall explore later. The general trend is to make reported accounting statements as suitable as possible for the investor to make their own estimations. We should note an alternative possibility however. This is that the company itself – through either the management or possibly through the auditors – should make a forecast. After all, the management and the auditor have a much greater insight into possibilities and risks than the external shareholder.

The loan creditor group

This group consists of long, medium or short-term lenders of money. According to the subdivisions suggested by *The Corporate Report*, trade creditors are not included here, but only explicit, i.e. deliberate, loan creditors.

The crucial question an existing or potential loan creditor wishes to consider is obvious: Will he or she get their money back? A short-term loan creditor will primarily be interested, therefore, in the amount of cash a business has got or will very soon get. As a safeguard, they will also be interested in the net realizable value (NRV) of all the assets, and the priority of the various claims, other than their own, on the available resources. Longer-term lenders will clearly need a correspondingly longer-term view of the firm's future cash position. This implies that they cannot restrict their interest to cash. They need to assess, as *The Corporate Report* correctly says, the 'economic stability and vulnerability of the borrower'. Their needs are thus similar to the needs of the equity investor group – they need to estimate the overall strength and position of the business some way into the future.

The employee group

Employees or their representatives need financial information about the business for two main reasons:

1 fair and open collective bargaining (i.e. wage negotiations)
2 assessment of present and future job security.

In these respects they too need to be able to assess 'the economic stability and vulnerability' of the business into the future.

The employees, actual or potential, will have additional requirements as well, however:

1 They will often need detailed information at 'local' level, i.e. about one particular part of the business or one particular factory.
2 They will need information in a clear and simple non-technical way.
3 They will need other information that is inherently non-financial. They will want to know, for instance, about management attitudes to staff involvement in decision-making, about 'conditions of service' generally, promotion prospects and so on. It can thus be seen that the employee group may require particular statements for its own use, and that it may require information not traditionally regarded as 'financial' at all.

The analyst–adviser group

In one sense this is not a separate group. It is a collection of experts who advise other groups. Stockbrokers and investment analysts will advise shareholders, trade union advisers will advise employees, government statisticians will advise the government, and so on. The needs of the analyst–adviser group are obviously essentially the needs of the particular group they are advising. However, being advisers and presumably experts they will need more detail and more sophistication in the information presented to them.

The business contact group

As defined in *The Corporate Report*, this is rather a 'rag-bag' group. It consists, in effect, of all those who have or may have dealings with the business, but who are not included in any other group. It can usefully be divided into three subgroups:

1 *Suppliers and trade creditors* need similar information to that required by short-term loan creditors. But they will also need to form a longer-term impression of the business's future. Regular suppliers are often dependent on the continuation of the relationship. They may wish to consider increasing capacity specifically for one particular purchaser. They will therefore need to appraise the future of their potential customers both in terms of financial viability and in terms of sales volume and market share.
2 *Customers* will wish to assess the reliability of the business both in the short-term sense (will I get my goods on time and in good condition?) and in the long-term sense (can I be sure of after-sales service and an effective guarantee?). Where long-term contracts

are involved, the customer will need to be particularly on his or her guard to ensure that the business appears able to complete the contract successfully.

3 *Competitors and business rivals* will wish to increase their own effectiveness and efficiency by finding out as much as possible about the financial, technical and marketing structure of the business. The business itself will naturally not be keen for this information to become generally available within the industry, and it is generally recognized that businesses have a reasonable right to keep the causes of their own competitive advantage secret. Competitors may also wish to consider a merger or an amalgamation, or a straight takeover bid. For this purpose they need the above information, plus the information required by the equity investor group. They also need information about what they – the bidders – could do with the business. In other words, they need to be able to form an opinion on both:

   (a) what the existing management is likely to achieve; and

   (b) what new management could achieve with different policies.

It is clear that in all three subgroups here the requirements are future oriented, and also go well beyond the limitations of purely *financial* information.

The government

Everybody is aware that governments require financial information for purposes of taxation. This may be the most obviously apparent use by governments, but it is not necessarily the most important. Governments also need information for decision-making purposes. Governments today take many decisions affecting particular firms or particular industries, both in a control sense and in government's capacity as purchaser or creditor. Also, governments need information on which to base their economic decisions as regards the economy as a whole. This information is likely to need to be very detailed, and to go well beyond the normal historic information included in the usual published accounting reports. Again there is an obvious need for future-oriented information.

The public

Economic entities, i.e. businesses in the broadest and most general sense, do not exist in isolation. They are part of society at large and they react and interact with society at every level. At the local level, there will be concern at such things as employment, pollution and health and safety. At the wider level, there may be interest in, for example, energy usage, effective use of subsidies, dealings with foreign governments and contributions to charities in money or kind. Much of this information is non-financial. Indeed some of it cannot be effectively measured at all. Whether it is accounting information is an open question. But it is certainly useful information about business.

Summary of user needs

Several general points emerge from the preceding discussion:

1 Many, though not all, of the informational requirements are essentially forward-looking.

2 Different users, with different purposes, may require *different* information about the *same* items.

3 Different users will require (and be able to understand) different degrees of complexi-

ty and depth.

4 Not all the information required is likely to be included in financial accounts.

Characteristics of useful information

It is useful not only to consider the purposes for which the information is required, but also to consider the *characteristics* of useful information. In fact, what do we mean by 'information'? The first of these issues is considered in *The Corporate Report*. The *Report* first of all summarizes its own conclusion as to the fundamental objective of published accounts:

> The fundamental objective of corporate reports is to communicate economic measurements of and information about the resources and performance of the reporting entity useful to those having reasonable rights to such information.

Activity 3

Make a list of the desirable attributes or characteristics (such as relevance, for example) which financial information should have if it is likely to be useful.

Activity 3 feedback

The Corporate Report suggested seven, although you are likely to have thought of others which could be at least as important. These seven are discussed below.

Relevance

This sounds obvious, but on reflection is difficult to define and therefore to achieve. A report must give the user what he or she wants. As already indicated this presupposes that we as the accountants preparing the report know:

1 who the user is
2 what their purpose is
3 what information he or she requires for this purpose.

Clearly these requirements may change as time goes by.

Understandability

Different users will obviously have different levels of ability as regards understanding accounting information. Understandability does not necessarily mean simplicity. It means that the reports must be geared to the abilities and knowledge of the users concerned. Complex economic activities being reported to an expert user may well require extremely complicated reports. Simple aspects being reported to users with little or no background knowledge will need to be very simple. The problems really arise when we have the task of reporting on complex activities but to the non-expert user.

Reliability

The user should be able to have a high degree of confidence in the information presented to him or her. This does not necessarily mean that the information has to be factually correct, but it should be as credible, as believable, as possible. Preferably, it should be independently verified, e.g. by an independent qualified auditor. However, unverified – or unverifiable – information may be better than no information.

Completeness

The user should be given a total picture of the reporting business as far as possible. The *Report* uses the words 'a rounded picture of the economic activities of the reporting entity'. This is a tall order. It implies large and complex collections of information. It may also imply problems of understandability.

Objectivity

> The information presented should be objective or unbiased in that it should meet all proper user needs and neutral in that the perception of the measurer should not be biased towards the interest of any one user group.

So says *The Corporate Report*. Objectivity is a confused notion, with several different possible meanings. We shall consider the problems in more detail later. The present proposition is that reports should not be biased by the personal perception, the personal opinion, of the preparer of those reports. The stated need is not for reports with no personal opinion, but for reports with unbiased personal opinion.

Timeliness

Essentially, this means that information should be provided to the user in time for use to be made of it. Information presented should be as up-to-date as possible. Approximate information, made available in time to assist with some decision or action, is likely to be more useful than precise and accurate information presented after the decision has already been made.

Comparability

Information about any one business for any one period should be presented so that:

1 it can be easily compared with information about the same business for a different period; and
2 it can be easily compared with information about a different business for the same, or even a different, period.

Clearly consistency of treatment is very important here – the application of generally accepted standards (and generally accepted Standards).

The need for communication

So we have some idea of the various characteristics of useful information. But, more fundamentally, what is information? Remember our earlier suggestion that 'accounting is about the provision of useful figures to people about their resources'. The accountant has to provide figures to the user. But 'provide' does not just mean 'send'. It is not enough to send, to deliver, sheets of paper with words and figures on. There has to be *communication*, there has to be *understanding* by the user. The point about communication, the point about information, is that the receiver is genuinely informed. He or she must become mentally and personally aware. R.J. Chambers put the point as follows:

If effective communication is to take place the language used must be such that the signs employed evoke in others the same response as if those others were to see the object represented instead of the signs.

This is, of course, an idealistic position. A television-news film can never really put the viewer in the same position in every respect as if they were physically present at the actual event filmed. Even less successful is a verbal description by 'someone who was present'. In accounting the means of communication is essentially a few numbers, usually prepared by someone who was not actually involved in the financial events supposedly being portrayed anyway. But it is a useful idea to bear in mind, however impossible to achieve.

Another problem is the likely ignorance of the intended receiver of the information. Accounting 'signs' are highly 'coded'. The accountant knows what he or she means, but does anybody else? And how is the user requiring the information to specify exactly what is wanted from the accountant if they cannot 'speak the language'? Clearly, when we think about it, the accountant has to communicate the main features of the reports in *non-accounting terms*.

Summary

In this chapter we have thought about the users of financial information, and the type and characteristics of information they might need. This is a necessary part of the overall framework of accounting that we need to build up. In the next chapter we explore the accountants' traditional response. What does the financial accountant actually do, in attempting to meet the needs we have considered?

Exercises

1 Consider the relative benefits to accounts users of:
   (a) information about the past
   (b) information about the present
   (c) information about the future.
2 Do you think a single set of financial reports can be designed that will be reasonably adequate for all major users and their needs?
3 Do you think all users actually know what to ask for from their accountant or financial adviser?
4 Are the seven desirable characteristics suggested in *The Corporate Report* in any way mutually contradictory?
5 It has been suggested that published accounting statements should attempt to be relevant, understandable, reliable, complete, objective, timely and comparable.
   Required:
   (a) Explain briefly in your own words, the meaning of these terms as applied to accounting. (12 marks)
   (b) Are there any difficulties in applying all of them at the same time?
   (4 marks)
   (16 marks)
   (ACCA)
6 It has been suggested that, apart from owners/investors, there are six separate user groups of published accounting statements: the loan creditor group, the employee group, the analyst–adviser group, the business contact group, the government and the public.

Required:
(a) Taking any FOUR of these six user groups, explain the information they are likely to want from published accounting statements.   (12 marks)
(b) Are there any difficulties in satisfying the requirements of all four of your chosen groups, given the requirements of other users?

(4 marks)
(16 marks)
(ACCA)

Traditional accounting conventions

After reading this chapter you should be able to:
- describe and apply the traditional conventions applied in financial reporting
- discuss and illustrate the internal coherence or inconsistency of this set of conventions.

Introduction

We have looked at some of the possible things that financial accountants *could* do in order to provide useful figures to people about their resources. We have looked at who the users are, and what sort of information they might want. In this and the following chapters we look at what accountants usually *do* do. Many different words are used in textbooks, articles and statements to describe these ideas – concepts, conventions, assumptions, postulates for example. Some of them are described as being more 'fundamental' than the others. In this chapter we shall simply refer to all of them as 'conventions'. Later in Part Three (Chapter 15) we shall look at how the accounting bodies define and divide them, but here we concentrate on the ideas themselves.

We shall consider twelve separate conventions, as follows: business entity, duality, monetary measurement, cost, realization of revenue, matching, accounting period, continuity (going concern), conservatism (prudence), consistency, materiality and objectivity.

The conventions

Business entity

This states that the business has an identity and existence distinct from its owners. This contrasts with the legal position. From the legal point of view, a limited company and its owner are separate legal entities, able to contract with each other, sue each other, etc. (see Chapter 12). With a sole 'trader', however, the legal position is different. The sole trader and his or her business are legally the same thing. The rights, possessions, privileges and risks of the one are also the rights, possessions, privileges and risks of the other. But the accountant takes a different view. To the accountant, whatever the legal position, the business and the owner(s) are considered completely separately. Thus the accountant can always speak of the business owing the owner money, borrowing money from the owner, owing profits to the owner, and so on. Think of the basic business balance sheet:

Fixed assets	Capital
Current assets	Liabilities
Total	Total

As we know, a properly prepared balance sheet can always be relied upon to balance. Why is this? The simple answer is because capital is the balancing figure. Capital is the amount of wealth invested in the business by the owner, or the amount of money borrowed by the business from the owner, or the amount the business owes the owner. None of these three statements could be made unless the accountant is treating the business as separate from, and distinct from, the owner. The accountant usually prepares the accounts of, i.e. the balance sheet of, the business. Transactions of the business are recorded as they affect the business, not as they affect the owner. In principle, another balance sheet always exists, namely for the owner as an individual. This will contain the owner's investment in the business, shown as one of his or her assets.

Duality

This may be regarded as a formalization of the basis of double-entry. It states that in relation to any one economic event, two aspects are recorded in the accounts, namely:

1 the source of wealth
2 the form it takes (i.e. its application).

In the simplest of terms, **1** is 'where it comes from', and **2** is 'what we have done with it'. The source from where it came will have a claim back on it. Thus, again in balance sheet terms, we can say that the balance sheet shows the array of resources at a point in time (assets), and the claims on those resources (liabilities); it shows the application of what was available (assets) and the source of what is available (liabilities or claims).

Monetary measurement

Accountants regard their job as dealing with *financial* information. This convention states that the accountant only records those facts that are expressed in money terms. Any facts, however relevant they may be to the user of the information, are ignored by the accountant if they cannot conveniently be expressed in money terms. It is often said that the greatest asset an effective and efficient business possesses is its workforce. So why does the workforce never appear on a business balance sheet? The short answer is that it would be extremely difficult to 'put a figure on' the workforce, i.e. to express this asset, this resource, in money terms. So the accountant does not bother to try. Facts and outcomes that cannot be expressed in money terms are ignored. This convention and its limitations are sometimes queried. (See the discussion on social responsibility reporting, p. 121.)

Cost

This convention states simply that resources acquired by the business are recorded at their original purchase price. It follows on from the previous convention in that it tells us *how* the item is actually to be measured. This is the well-known historic cost (HC) convention. It does not always now receive the near-universal support of earlier years.

Accounting period

This very simple convention recognizes that profit occurs over time, and we cannot usefully speak of the profit 'for a period' until we define the length of the period. The maximum length of period normally used is one year. This is supported by legislation normally requiring the preparation of full audited accounts annually. This does not of course preclude the preparation of accounts for shorter periods as well. But the formal 'published accounts' period is nearly always one year.

Continuity (going concern)

This important convention states that in the absence of evidence to the contrary it is assumed that the business will continue into the indefinite future. This convention has a major influence on the assumptions made when evaluating particular items in the balance sheet. For example, the convention allows us to assume that stock will eventually be sold in the normal course of business, i.e. at normal selling prices. Perhaps even more obviously it allows for the principle of depreciation. If we depreciate an item of plant over ten years, then we are assuming that the plant will have a useful life to the business (not necessarily a useful total *physical* life) of ten years. This assumption can only be made if we are first assuming that the business will continue – or keep going – for at least ten years. Notice, incidentally, that the going-concern assumption does not say that the business is going to keep being profitable into the indefinite future. It merely assumes that the business will manage not to collapse altogether.

Conservatism (prudence)

This convention refers to the accounting practice of recognizing all possible losses, but not anticipating possible gains. This will tend to lead to an understatement of profits – to an understatement of asset values with no corresponding understatement of liability.

The accounts are in essence trying to give an indication of the current position (the balance sheet) and of the degree of success achieved through the accounting period (the profit and loss (P&L) account). This convention requires the accountant to attempt to ensure that the position or the degree of success is not overstated. Recognizing that absolute accuracy is not possible, the accountant, according to this convention, should ensure the avoidance of overstatement by deliberately setting out to achieve a degree of understatement. This requires that similar items, some of which are positive and some of which are negative, should not be treated identically or symmetrically.

Activity 1

Give some examples of regular non-symmetrical treatment of positive and negative aspects of otherwise similar items.

Activity 1 feedback

There are many examples to choose from. Two examples are:

1 The treatment of stocks, which are usually shown at cost or NRV if lower (but not at

NRV if higher) – see Statement of Standard Accounting Practice (SSAP) 9 (Chapter 20); and

2 The whole approach to contingent items – see SSAP 18 (Chapter 23).

Consistency

This is the practice of applying the same accounting rules, methods or procedures in each similar case. This convention should:

1 avoid short-term manipulation of reported results
2 facilitate comparisons within the firm over different accounting periods (intrafirm comparisons)
3 facilitate comparison between different entities (interfirm comparisons).

Consistency can of course never overrule the requirements of proper and useful reporting (the 'true and fair view'). But the convention does certainly support the argument that where several alternative treatments or approaches are acceptable, the business should make a decision and then stick to it year by year for all similar items. Depreciation methods for similar assets is an obvious example – see Chapter 16.

Materiality

This is a statistical concept that, in its application to accounting, implies that insignificant items should not be given the same emphasis as significant items. The insignificant items are by definition unlikely to influence decisions or provide useful information to decision-makers, but they may well cause complication and confusion to the user of accounts. Their detailed treatment may also involve a great deal of time and effort – and therefore of money! – for no useful purpose. Many firms, for example, treat smallish items that fulfil all the theoretical requirements of the definition of fixed assets (p. 138), but cost below a defined minimum amount, as simple current expenses. This is not done because it is correct. It is done because it is easier and because it is 'good enough' for practical purposes and for users' informational needs.

Objectivity

This convention refers to an attribute or characteristic of accounting information generally regarded as desirable. This is that accounting measurements and information should permit qualified individuals working independently to develop similar measures or conclusions from the same evidence. In a nutshell, accounting information should be verifiable. Two schools of thought seem to have arisen in recent years over the full implications of this. One argues that the desire for objectivity implies as much factual content as possible. Facts, e.g. the actual cost figure specified in a contract, are easily verifiable. This idea surely corresponds with the everyday meaning of objectivity, i.e. the avoidance of subjectivity, the avoidance of personal opinion.

The second school of thought seems to argue that the degree of objectivity can be indicated not by the amount of formal (factual) verifiability, but by the degree of consensus achieved by several independent opinions. The question of whether a young woman is pretty or a young man is handsome clearly depends on the person giving the opinion ('beauty is in the eye of the beholder'). But this second school of thought would presumably argue that if, say, six people all say that they agree with such a statement, then it becomes objective, becomes a fact ('the majority is always right'?). The reader must make their own mind up. But what is clear in any event is the convention that verifiability is a desirable element in accounting.

Realization of revenue

We have just established the convention that an asset acquired by the business is usually recorded at the original purchase price. It is thus based on a market transaction. It is obvious that, at the latest, when the asset is disposed of by the business, we must record the actual disposal price. So if we buy stock for £30, £30 has to be recorded as having gone, and stock (of £30, cost convention) has to be recorded as being present. If we then sell the stock for £50, then we must record £50 as being present, and stock has to be removed from the accounts. Thus an asset of £30 has been replaced by an asset of £50, giving a profit of £20. Once the £50 is physically in, there is no other possibility than to record an asset of £50. But is there no possibility of recognizing an asset of £50 before, i.e. earlier than, the physical arrival of the money? Suppose we sell the stock on 1 December and receive the money on 10 December. When did assets of £30 turn into assets of £50? Was it 10 December, when we received the money? Or was it 1 December, when we acquired the expectation – indeed the right – to receive the money?

More importantly perhaps what are the *criteria* we are going to use to answer this question? On what *grounds* should we decide when the total asset figure increased, i.e. when the profit was made? This is a very complicated matter. We can first of all state the usual conventional answer: revenue is recognized as soon as, and is allocated to the period in which:

1 it is capable of objective measurement; and
2 the asset value receivable in exchange is reasonably certain.

But this is really rather simplistic, and we need to explore the area in more detail.

Before we do that, we should complete our overview by seeing how the revenue recognition question leads on to the calculation of profit. Since profit is revenue less expenses, we must explore the idea of matching expenses and revenues together.

Matching

Looking back over the conventions we have discussed so far, we have:

1 decided on the basic characteristics of the recording system (**business entity** and **duality**)
2 decided on how we are going to record items entering the business's control (**monetary measurement** and **cost**); and
3 decided on how to record the proceeds from the disposal of such items (**revenue recognition**).

The essential item missing is clearly the mechanism for recording the actual loss of the item – its removal from the financial statements about the business. The question was asked above: when did assets of £30 turn into assets of £50? It is intuitively clear that whenever this did happen (and the revenue recognition convention tells us when), a profit of £20 was made. Thus, if the revenue, the benefit, is £50, then the expense, the amount used or lost, is £30. The matching convention covers this final stage in the process of profit calculation. It states that:

> Income (or profit) determination is a process of matching against revenue the expenses incurred in earning that revenue.

When an asset gets used, it becomes an expense. The question in effect is: at precisely what point does the accountant regard an asset as being 'used'? The answer is: at the point when the related revenue is recognized, so the process of profit calculation can be summarized as follows. First, we determine the point at which the revenue is to be recognized, the time when the proceeds are 'made'. Secondly, we *match* the *expense* against the revenue, i.e. we regard the expense as occurring at the same time as the revenue. So if the revenue from selling an item of stock is recognized on 28 December as £50 then the expense of £30 is also recognized on 28 December. Accounts prepared on 31 December will include profit of £20, and an asset of £50 (debtors or cash). But if the revenue from selling an item of stock is recognized on 2 January, then the expense will also be recognized on 2 January. Accounts prepared on 31 December will include an asset of £30 (stock), no revenue and no expense, and therefore no profit or loss from this transaction.

The **matching convention** is often referred to as the **accruals convention**, although some writers distinguish between them. The accruals convention should be contrasted with the ideas of cash flow accounting (Chapter 27). The essence of the accruals convention is that the time when an item of benefit should be recognized and recorded by the accountant is determined by the reasonably ascertainable *generation* of the benefit – not by the date of the actual (cash) *receipt* of the benefit. Similarly, the time when an item of expense should be recognized and recorded as such by the accountant is determined by the *usage* of the item, not by the date of the acquisition of the item or of the *payment* for the item. The accruals convention is therefore another way of saying that the process of profit calculation consists of relating (matching) together the revenues with the expenses. It is not directly concerned with cash receipts and cash payments.

The revenue recognition problem explored

In a very simplified way we shall look at a complete production cycle for a manufactured product. We assume that only one unit of the product is involved. Each stage in the process occurs at a different, later point in time to the previous stage. We can designate each point in time by T followed by a suffix. This will enable us to plot a simple graph showing the

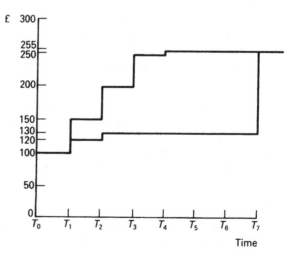

Figure 3.1
Monetary figures
and time scale.

various monetary figures on the vertical axis, and the various time points on the horizontal axis (see Fig. 3.1).

The data are as follows:

At T_0 Mr Jones buys raw materials for £100.

At T_1 He adds labour to the raw material and produces the finished product. The cost of labour is £20, and the item could now be sold on previous experience for £150.

At T_2 He puts the product in an extremely attractive coloured box at a further cost of £10. This raises the estimated selling price to £200.

At T_3 When market conditions for the product have altered, Mr Smith offers to buy the unit for £250, so long as it is in good condition.

At T_4 After some bargaining, Jones agrees to sell, and Smith agrees to buy, for £255.

At T_5 Jones delivers the product to Smith.

At T_6 Smith confirms that he has received the product in good condition.

At T_7 Smith pays Jones £255.

Now remembering our assumption that the business consists of this single production cycle and that the next cycle will not be started until after this cycle is complete (i.e. until after T_7), the overall result is very clear. Jones must have begun at T_0 with £130 available to spend on this product. Equally obviously, at the end of the cycle at T_7, he has £255. These are physical facts – shining bright new £1 coins if you like. Therefore his profit from the complete cycle must be 255 – 130 = £125. Over the total time period from T_0 to T_7, Jones has made a profit of £125. That is no problem. But when, precisely, did he make his profit?

It should be noted that this is by no means an academic question. First, the accountant may *at any time* be asked questions like: 'What is the profit so far this year?', 'How do the last six weeks' profit compare with the corresponding period last year?'. Secondly, the formal end of an accounting period may occur at absolutely any point in the production cycle for a unit of product. At this precise point, a profit figure has to be struck and the balance sheet figure agreed. The third point, related to the second, is the interrelationship between profit figures and balance sheet figures. This section is called 'the recognition of revenue', but it could almost equally be called 'the valuation of assets'.

The problem considered

The obvious procedure for answering the question 'when did Jones make his profit?' is as follows:

1 apply the revenue-recognition convention as defined
2 apply the matching convention appropriately.

We should bear in mind the other conventions, especially perhaps prudence and objectivity. We should also bear in mind the requirements of the users of the accounts.

The convention as defined was: revenue is recognized as soon as, and is allocated to the period in which:

1 it is capable of objective measurement; and
2 the asset value receivable in exchange is reasonably certain.

So there we are. In the context of the Smith and Jones situation when was that?

Activity 2

When was that? Think about this for a few minutes. We have explored lots of hopefully useful conventions. We have then set up what is after all a very simple business situation. What do the conventions tell us we should do, as intelligent accountants, in that situation?

Activity 2 feedback

It is quickly obvious that the convention as stated is not very much help. How 'objective' do we need to be? What on earth does 'reasonably' mean? A strict application of the prudence convention would give us a clear enough answer. At what point can we be absolutely certain of the asset value receivable in exchange? At what point can we be absolutely certain Jones will get his money? The answer is T_7, and not before. Jones cannot be *absolutely* certain he will receive the money until he actually has received it. This would imply that if accounts are drawn up at, say T_6, no revenue has been 'earned' from this production cycle, and therefore that the total asset figure in Jones' balance sheet would be £130. This would presumably have to be called 'stock' although common sense might suggest that the reality of the situation (Smith has agreed to buy it, Smith has physically got it, Smith has confirmed he has received it in good condition) is nearer to the idea of a debtor. But the idea of showing debtors of £130 (i.e. at cost!) when the amount owed is undoubtedly £255, takes some swallowing.

This is not what the accountant usually does. He or she recognizes revenue at an earlier stage than this and does not strictly follow the prudence convention. The accountant says that the asset value receivable in exchange only needs to be *reasonably* certain. At T_6 Smith has confirmed satisfactory possession of the product. T_6 is only a little less certain, therefore, than T_7. Surely recognizing revenue at T_6 is safe enough? At T_5 the physical position is not very different from T_6. Jones knows that he has properly delivered the goods, even if Smith has not yet confirmed it. Surely T_5 is safe enough too! But what about the legal position? At T_4 there is a contract between Smith and Jones. Jones can presumably sue for any losses he suffers caused by Smith. So why not recognize the revenue at T_4? Surely this is 'reasonable'. Surely the amount receivable in exchange is already 'reasonably certain'? Remember also the other element in the stated convention. Is the revenue capable of 'objective measurement' at T_4? Noting the known costs of £130, and the agreed contract of sale for £255, can we 'objectively' say that revenue is £255 and profit £125? Surely this figure is, by the point in time T_4, adequately verifiable? However, all the time we move backwards from T_7, all the time we suggest the recognition of revenue at earlier stages, we are relaxing the application of the prudence convention a little bit more. However small the risks are at T_4 of something 'going wrong', they are larger than they are at T_5, and T_6, and so on. Are we being sufficiently prudent?

One way round the prudence problem is to make some allowance, some reduction in the asset figure, and therefore some allowance in the profit figure, to take account of future risks. Thus we might know, on the basis of past experience, that once stage T_4 is reached there is a 5% risk of not receiving the money, once T_5 is reached the risk falls to 3%, and at T_6 to 1%. Thus, by creating a provision for possible loss, we could record a net asset position at 95% of £255 at T_4 and/or 97% of £255 at T_5, and/or 99% of £255 at T_6, with corresponding net revenue figures accumulated at each stage.

This last idea is what the accountant actually does. Revenue is recognized somewhere about the T_5 mark. In practice the precise date will usually be determined more or less arbitrarily by the date on the documentation. A multicopy document will be prepared containing advice note, delivery note, invoice, copy invoice, and so on, probably somewhere between T_4 and T_5, and the date of these documents will usually be accepted as determining the date of 'sale'. Before this point a revenue of zero, expenses of zero and stock of £130 will be recorded. After this point a revenue of £255, expenses of £130 plus possibly an allowance for 'doubtful debts' and assets of £255 (debtors) less any allowance for doubtful debts will be recorded. This is the usual interpretation of the appropriate response to the somewhat conflicting demands to be reasonably certain, to be prudent, and to be objective. But why cannot we argue for recognition of revenue at an even earlier stage? As accountants we accept the argument that the risks associated with recognizing revenue around the T_4/T_5 stage are not excessive, and can be allowed for if felt material by provisions for possible losses. So why not accept the argument that the risks associated with recognizing revenue at point T_3 are not excessive either. They are clearly not very much greater than at point T_4. After all Smith, an independent person of sound mind, has voluntarily come along and offered £250. So why not recognize an asset of £250 and revenue of £120 at this point? And if the risk of T_3 as compared with T_4 is materially greater we can increase the percentage allowance for the risk of things going wrong, e.g. to 10%. The other £5 of revenue (255 − 250) can then be recognized a little later at T_4. And if this argument is acceptable surely we can extend it further back, and recognize some revenue at T_2?

The compromise solution

It should be abundantly clear from the above discussion that the usual practice as regards revenue recognition is an arbitrary, though convenient, compromise between opposing arguments. Prudence suggests delaying recognition as long as possible, and objectivity perhaps points in the same direction. But reality points the opposite way. In the real world most production does get sold, most customers do pay. The way in which the stated revenue recognition criteria are interpreted by accountants in practice – the interpretation of 'objective measurement' and 'reasonably certain' – is a compromise based on general consensus. Do you agree with it?

Activity 3

A firm produces a standard manufactured product. The stages of the production and sale of the product may be summarized as follows:

Stage	**A**	**B**	**C**	**D**
Activity	Raw material	WIP-I	WIP-II	Finished product
	£	£	£	£
Costs to date	100	120	150	170
Net realizable value	80	130	190	300

Stage	**E**	**F**	**G**	**H**
Activity	For sale	Sale agreed	Delivered	Paid for
	£	£	£	£
Costs to date	170	170	180	180
Net realizable value	300	300	300	300

Required:
(a) **What general rule do accountants apply when deciding when to recognize revenue on any particular transaction?**   (4 marks)
(b) **Apply this rule to the above situation. State and explain the stage at which you think revenue will be recognized by accountants.**   (4 marks)
(c) **How much would the gross profit on a unit of this product be? Why?**
                                                                           (4 marks)
(d) **Suggest arguments in favour of delaying the recognition of revenue until stage H.**   (4 marks)
(e) **Suggest arguments in favour of recognizing revenue in appropriate successive amounts at stages B, C and D.**   (4 marks)
                                                                        (20 marks)
                                                                           (ACCA)

Activity 3 feedback

1 The rule may be stated as follows:
   Revenue is recognized as soon as, and is allocated to the period in which:
   (a) it is capable of objective measurement; and
   (b) the asset value receivable in exchange is reasonably certain.
2 The requirement is to be reasonably certain, not certain. It is normally argued that the agreement with the customer provides objective evidence and adequate certainty, and stage F will be the usual point of revenue recognition. However, the documentary evidence for the agreement will often be the delivery note, and the distinction between stages F and G may in practice be an artificial one.
3 The gross profit is £130, not £120. Gross profit is sales minus cost of sales. Cost of sales includes all costs of making the product sellable, but not costs of selling it. To put it simply it includes carriage in, but not carriage out.
4 The essential argument is prudence (conservatism). Until H has occurred it is always possible that the product will be damaged or the customer fail to pay – either event leading to a significant loss. Earlier recognition could possibly lead to an overstatement of the position, although provisions may attempt to take account of this danger.
5 Probably the major argument is that it could be more useful. If it is 'reasonably' likely to be sold, and we have produced it, why not report the current position? How certain does reasonably certain need to be?

A coherent framework

In the previous sections we considered, separately, twelve conventions. How do they relate together? The idea of an all-embracing framework is discussed more fully in Chapter 10. What we can usefully do at this stage is to look at the 12 conventions discussed above to consider whether they are 'coherent' or consistent with each other.

One of the most problematic conventions is that of prudence, or conservatism. At its most basic this derives from the obviously sensible belief that it is important not to encourage the users of accounts to spend money or to consume resources they haven't got. Consideration of this convention, together with several of the other conventions, gives rise to considerable difficulties.

Activity 4

Suggest pairs of conventions which we have already discussed which are, or may be, contradictory or in opposition to each other, and illustrate the possible problems between them.

Activity 4 feedback

Here are some possibilities we thought of.

1 *Prudence and going concern.* The going-concern convention argues that the firm will 'keep going', e.g. that it will not be forced out of business by competition or bankruptcy. This may be a likely and rational assumption, but it is not necessarily prudent – in certain circumstances it could be decidedly risky.

2 *Prudence and matching.* The matching convention, building on the going-concern convention, allows us to carry forward assets into future periods on the grounds that they will be used profitably later. This obviously makes major assumptions about the future that may not be at all prudent. The contradiction between these two conventions is one of the major problems of accounting practice, and it underlies some of the more problematic SSAPs (e.g. SSAP 13 on research and development, Chapter 17). Pure matching (given also the cost convention as defined above) would require that the asset figure be carried forward until the benefit is received from its use. This is usually modified, by the prudence convention, to the practice of reducing the asset figure (by increasing *current* expenses) so that the maximum amount to be carried forward is the amount of the expected revenue or benefits. But how definite, how certain, does the expectation of revenue or benefit have to be? Should we, when in doubt, emphasize prudence or matching? Should we ensure that we never overstate the position, or should we do our professional best to 'tell it like it is'? Should we report the worst possible position (prudence) or the most likely position (matching)?

3 *Prudence and objectivity.* Objectivity implies certainty and precision. It implies freedom from personal opinion, freedom from bias. Prudence, quite explicitly, implies that we *should* bias the information we choose to report in a certain direction. If accounting information could be genuinely objective, then prudence would be irrelevant by definition, because any bias would be impossible. In practice, of course, since accounting always has to make assumptions about future events, objectivity can never be completely achieved.

4 *Prudence and the cost concept.* This is a particularly interesting pairing of ideas. The cost concept is supported by objectivity (not on the grounds that it is objective, but on the grounds that it usually has a greater objective element than alternative valuation concepts) and is often regarded as being supported by prudence. In some respects, it is.

Prudence suggests that in areas of valid choice, lower asset figures should be incorporated in accounts. In times of rising prices, use of replacement costs (RCs) could therefore be seen as imprudent, as compared with use of HC. But consider the effect on reported profits of using a RC basis rather than HCs (Chapter 5). This splits up the HC profit into operating profit and holding gain, enabling the 'genuine', and therefore safely distributable, operating profit to be distinguished. Nothing could be more imprudent than to distribute resources needed to maintain the business, and HC accounting can easily permit this to happen!

Much fun can be had with some of the other possible pairings of conventions, and some suggestions will be found in the exercises at the end of this and the next chapter. It is already clear, however, that 'coherence' and 'consistency' are lacking.

A useful test of the conventions on a more practical plane is to try to apply them to particular circumstances. Given a particular situation, do the conventions tell us what to do? Take depreciation for example. Consider the following information concerning a fixed asset:

> Bought 1 January, year 1, for £1000
> Estimated physical life, ten years
> Estimated useful life to our business, seven to eight years
> Estimated scrap value after eight years, £25 to £50.

At the end of year 1 we decide on the straight-line basis (matching and going concern) based on a figure of £1000 (cost). We decide on a useful life of seven years (prudence) and scrap value of £25 (prudence) or, more likely, we assume the scrap value to be £nil (materiality). (NB: how objective have we been?) Some further examples again will be found in the exercises.

A third important consideration as regards the conventions is their usefulness. Do they lead to users getting what they need? Look back at the seven suggested desirable characteristics of corporate reports (p. 13), and relate them to the 12 suggested conventions. Only one item appears in both lists – objectivity. It is by no means clear that the desirable characteristics of relevance and completeness are satisfied by the cost and prudence conventions. Nor is it clear that understandability is supplied by the traditional accounting conventions – indeed there is considerable evidence to the contrary (p. 156). We can also suggest that the conventions will be of relatively different importance to different users. Prudence, at least as regards balance sheet figures, may perhaps be important to a short-term creditor. On the other hand, the cost convention is unlikely to be of great relevance to a short-term creditor, the NRV of the assets will surely be much more useful.

Here are two more activities for you to think about. Both are concerned with the inter-relationships between the conventions and with the application of the conventions to particular situations.

Activity 5

'The historical cost convention looks backwards but the going concern convention looks forwards.'

Required:
(a) **Explain clearly what is meant by:**
   (i) the historical cost convention;
   (ii) the going concern convention.   (6 marks)
(b) **Does traditional financial accounting, using the historical cost convention, make the going concern convention unnecessary? Explain your answer fully.**
                                                                              (8 marks)
(c) **Which do you think a shareholder is likely to find more useful – a report on the past or an estimate of the future? Why?**   (4 marks)
                                                                          (18 marks)
                                                                              (ACCA)

Activity 5 feedback

Here are some suggestions:

1 **(a)** *The historical cost convention* is that transactions are recorded in the accounts at the original price. An item then remains in the accounting records at that original figure until disposal. Assets, and therefore expenses, are recorded and evaluated at original cost, and profit is calculated as revenues less original cost of resources used.

   (b) *The going concern convention* is the assumption, in the absence of evidence to the contrary, that the business will continue to trade in the normal way into the foreseeable future. This enables the accountant to assume that stocks will eventually be sold, that fixed assets will continue to be used, and so on.

2 No, traditional financial accounting based on the historical cost convention does not make the going concern convention unnecessary. Traditional and current practice relies heavily on the going concern convention. Stocks are evaluated on the assumption that they will eventually be sold in the ordinary course of business. Fixed assets are depreciated over their estimated useful life to the business, and this requires the assumption that the business will continue to operate over the period of that useful life. Prepayments assume that the firm will operate and use the service acquired. Indeed the whole basis of the accruals convention is that the business is a continuing operation and the going concern convention is therefore crucial to current accounting practice even though that practice is based on the historical cost convention.

3 The reason why a shareholder needs a report at all is because he or she wishes to use the report to influence some future action or decision on their part. If this is not so then the shareholder has no use for the report whatever its contents. However, the above does not strictly answer the question. The shareholder may well find a report on the past events extremely useful as a guide to predicting future outcomes and future trends. Equally, however, the shareholder may find management's estimate of future events to be directly useful to them. Perhaps the short answer to the question is both!

Activity 6

On 20 December 20X7 your client paid £10 000 for an advertising campaign. The advertisements will be heard on local radio stations between 1 January and 31 January 20X8. Your client believes that as a result sales will increase by 60% in 20X8 (over 20X7 levels) and by 40% in 20X9 (over 20X7 levels). There will be no further benefits.

Required:
Write a memorandum to your client explaining your views on how this item should be treated in the accounts for the three years 20X7 to 20X9. Your answer should include explicit reference to at least THREE relevant traditional accounting conventions, and to the requirements of TWO classes of user of published financial accounts.

(17 marks)
(ACCA)

Activity 6 feedback

To: Client
From: Accountant
Treatment of advertising costs
There are a number of possible treatments:

(a) Write off the whole amount in 20X7. This could be justified on the grounds of *prudence* – any return being highly speculative.

(b) Write off the amount in strict proportion to the expected benefits. This would be supported by the *matching* convention, i.e. to allocate the expenses over the period of benefit in proportion to that benefit. This would imply expenses of £0 in 20X7 (as benefit does not commence in 20X7), £6000 in 20X8 and £4000 in 20X9.

(c) The conflict between prudence and matching is usually resolved through compromise, though in areas of real doubt and difficulty prudence should prevail and be given greater emphasis. A reasonable compromise in this case might well be to charge all the £10 000 as an expense in 20X8 – any returns in 20X9 being much more speculative than those expected in 20X8.

(d) The validity of this suggestion would depend on the particular circumstances, advice of advertising and industry experts, your earlier treatment of similar items (*consistency* is an important accounting convention) and also on the *materiality* of the amounts concerned. If the amounts concerned are small in relation to your results as a whole, then it is pointless to spend my time (and your money!) in a lengthy and detailed investigation.

(e) We should perhaps also consider the users of your accounting reports. For example, a *trade creditor* will be particularly interested in your assets and liability position. From this point of view, an asset which exists because of the speculative expectation of higher sales next year is not exactly a safe 'near-cash' security. On the other hand, a *shareholder* will be concerned with the future trend of profits, and application of the matching convention is arguably an essential requirement for showing a fair indication of present profit and current and future trends.

Summary

In this chapter we have explored the traditional ideas of accounting purposes and underlying conventions. We have seen that they certainly provide a methodology for suggesting a possible treatment in any given situation. However, they most certainly do not seem to provide a system for suggesting *the* appropriate treatment in any given situation. Can we get at least somewhat closer to that position?

We explore more recent thinking relating to this whole issue in Chapter 10. However before we do that, we have another big area to explore. We have discussed the question of revenue, and we have seen at least intuitively that revenue recognition is inherently tied up with the asset valuation issue. The whole asset valuation area needs to be explored thoroughly from first principles, and this we do in the next few chapters.

Exercises

1 Which of the suggested conventions do you regard as most important? Why?
2 Which of the suggested conventions do you regard as most useful? Why?
3 Explain the differences, if any, between your answers to questions **1** and **2**.
4 How objective is the traditional HC balance sheet?
5 Completeness is not compatible with the monetary measurement convention. Discuss.
6 'Where the accruals (matching) concept is inconsistent with the prudence concept, the latter prevails' (SSAP 2, para. 14b). Explain with reasons whether you support this view.
7 A firm spends £10 000 developing a new product, and £5000 on an advertising campaign for it. Which conventions will help you in deciding on the appropriate accounting treatment, and what do they imply?
8 Which conventions underlie the usual accounting treatment of stocks and work in progress?
9 'HC accounts are neither objective nor useful.' Discuss.
10 'The normal accounting practice of revenue recognition proves that accountants are prudent.' Discuss.
11 How do accountants decide when to recognize revenue?
12 When do accountants usually recognize revenue?
13 Do your answers to questions **11** and **12** satisfy the objectivity convention?
14 Explain the relationship between revenue recognition and asset valuation.
15 **(a) What do you understand by the term 'revenue recognition'?**   (10 marks)
   (b) Briefly outline a policy on revenue recognition for each of the following:
      (i)   magazine subscriptions received by a publisher   (3 marks)
      (ii) the sale of cars on credit terms   (3 marks)
      (iii) work in progress on a long-term contract.   (4 marks)
                                                            (20 marks)
                                                            (ACCA)
16 'The idea that stock should be included in accounts at the lower of historical cost and net realizable value follows the prudence convention but not the consistency convention.'
   Required:
   (a) Explain clearly what is meant by:
      (i)   historical cost
      (ii) net realizable value
      (iii) prudence convention
      (iv) consistency convention.   (8 marks)
   (b) Do you agree with the quotation?   (4 marks)
   (c) Explain, with reasons, whether you think this idea (that stocks should be included in accounts at the lower of historical cost and net realizable value) is a useful one. Refer to at least two classes of user of financial accounting reports in your answer.   (6 marks)
                                                            (18 marks)
                                                            (ACCA)
17 A scout troop collects subscriptions from its members, and also has to pay 60% of them to central scouting funds. In the year to 31 December 20X8 the troop receives:

for 20X7	£20
for 20X8	£60
for 20X9	£10

It pays to central funds in that year:

for 20X7	£12
for 20X8	£30
for 20X9	nil

Required:
(a) **Produce a summary of the subscription position for the troop for the year 20X8, on**
   (i)   **a receipts and payments basis,**
   (ii) **a revenue and expenses basis.**   (5 marks)
(b) **Outline the advantages and disadvantages of each basis with reference to appropriate accounting conventions. Give the scout troop leader your recommended method, with reasons. Discuss also any difficult decisions you have to make in deciding your answer to (a) above.**   (10 marks)

(15 marks)
(ACCA)

4

Economic valuation concepts

After reading this chapter you should be able to:
- provide an overview and context of the asset valuation debate
- explain definitions and interrelationships of income, capital and value
- describe the variety of alternatives that need to be explored within the parameters of the valuation debate
- outline the concepts of income developed by Fisher and Hicks
- contrast *ex ante* and *ex post* economic income
- outline the scope of economic thinking in this area.

Introduction

Before we can properly consider the various accounting theories relating to asset valuation and income measurement, we need to explore the basic issues and interrelationships. This chapter establishes a framework within which we can then discuss and appraise accounting thinking.

The basic equation

We have already established that a well-behaved balance sheet does not balance just because accountants are good at adding up. It balances because it is *defined* in such a way that it *must* balance. Following from the business entity convention, capital is the balancing figure. Capital is the liability of the business entity to the ownership entity. The business owns a collection of assets, and owes a collection of borrowings to lenders and unpaid suppliers of goods and services. Deducting these borrowings from the assets enables us to say that the business owns a collection of net assets. So the owners own the business and the business owns the net assets. Therefore the owners' investment in the business – i.e. the capital – *must* equal the net assets.

The above is couched in static terms. But we can easily modify the wording to allow for profit or income. To avoid possible confusion, we use profit and income as, in the accounting context, completely synonymous terms. Profit (income) means the positive difference between revenues and expenses for a given period. If a business makes a profit then money or money's worth received or to be received increases by more than money or money's worth consumed. This is a complicated way of saying that its net assets go up by the amount of the profit. But in logic and in book-keeping profit represents an increase in capital. Profit is attributable to owners, is owned by owners, and is therefore owed by the business to the owners.

So the amount of profit equals the amount of the increase in the net assets which in turn equals the amount of the increase in the capital. In practice, drawings or dividends are likely to occur. These obviously represent a withdrawal of money or money's worth and therefore a reduction in net assets. They also mean that the business has paid the owners some of what is owed to them. There is therefore a reduction in what remains owing to them, i.e. a reduction in capital. If drawings in a period equal profits for the period then capital (and net assets) is maintained at its original level. If profit exceeds drawings in a period capital (and net assets) increase.

This can usefully be summarized schematically. Let W_1 be the opening wealth (net assets) of the business and W_2 be the closing net assets. Let P be the profit for the period and D be the (net) drawings. Then

$$W_1 + P - D = W_2$$

Or in more purely accounting terms:

Opening capital plus profit minus drawings equals closing capital.

It is obvious that the $W_1 + P - D = W_2$ equation fits our traditional accounting model. But it is in no way restricted to that model. It is expressed in the most general of terms. It can be reduced to:

$$
\begin{aligned}
& \text{What you had} \\
+\ &\text{What you've added to it} \\
-\ &\text{What you've removed from it} \\
=\ &\text{What you've got.}
\end{aligned}
$$

This is a truism, mere tautology. The unit of measurement could be absolutely anything. But in accounting we take a particular view. First, we measure the elements in money terms. Secondly, we traditionally measure the sums of money in a particular way, following the concepts we considered in Chapter 3. We record assets using the historic cost convention, and we recognize revenue and net asset increases following the realization and accrual conventions. We are so used to this procedure that we tend to do it automatically, without considering the alternatives. We tend to accept normal practice out of sheer habit. Such acceptance will not do.

Income and capital

Activity 1

Go to a library and look up the words 'income' (or 'profit') and 'capital' in (a) a number of accounting texts, (b) a number of economics texts, (c) general dictionaries and encyclopaedias.

Record book titles under these three subheadings, and summarize the definitions given.

Record also book titles which fail to include definitions of either concept (you may wish to avoid these in the future!).

Does a clear consensus and a clear understanding emerge?

Activity 1 feedback

You may have more luck than we did, but likely conclusions are:

1 the terms have a wide variety of different meanings
2 clear definition is extremely difficult
3 many accounting texts evade the difficulties by talking in purely book-keeping terms.

A useful starting point is the work of the economist Irving Fisher (1930). He defines capital as: 'Capital is a stock of wealth at an instant in time.' In contrast to this we can say that: income is a flow of benefits or services arising through time. This is quite consistent with our earlier tautological equation. What you had (capital, stock) plus additions (income, flow) less withdrawals equals what you have got.

In our old edition of Hendriksen (1982) he states that:

> Capital is the embodiment of future services, and income is the enjoyment of these services over a specific period of time. With these definitions it does not seem possible to confuse the two terms.

This last sentence seems at first sight optimistic. Capital is a stock of wealth which generates income. Income is the enjoyment from the use of capital. These seem like circular and therefore inadequate definitions. The way round this difficulty is to distinguish between *capital*, on the one hand, and *the value of capital*, on the other. *Capital* is a stock of assets capable of generating future services. *The value of capital* is dependent on the value of those future services. For example, a field is a stock of wealth, a field is capital. The value of the field, the value of the capital, is dependent on the (net) value of crops to be grown on the field, i.e. on the income.

The above makes income and the value of capital sound like forward-looking concepts. Perhaps they are!

Wealth and value

It should be clear by now that we can talk about evaluating the assets of an entity, we can talk about evaluating the wealth of an entity, and we can talk about evaluating the capital of an entity. Each of these descriptions amounts to exactly the same thing. It amounts to an evaluation of what the entity 'has got'. Whichever way we look at this problem, whichever word we wish to use, the key point is the obvious need for evaluation. We noticed earlier that *any* measuring unit will do. But there must *be* a measuring unit – certainly a generally understandable one, and preferably one generally accepted as a means of exchange (i.e. acceptable as 'money'). You are already familiar with the ways in which accountants usually evaluate different assets in a balance sheet. You are familiar, at least intuitively, with ideas of the 'A is better off than B', or 'this car is worth more than that car' variety. Try the next activity – it may be both more fun and more productive if you try it in a group, but if this is not possible think it over for half an hour whilst doing something else, and then summarize your ideas.

Activity 2

A brief case study
We have an asset, for example a briefcase, and we wish to evaluate it, to attach a monetary value to it. List and describe all the possible ways of doing this you can think of. Illustrate each possible way by making up some simple figures. Which is the best method?

Activity 2 feedback

One of the purposes of this activity is simply the realization that there is a very large number of possible answers. Here are some possibilities grouped into four sections.

1   We could take as our basic figure the amount of money we originally paid for the briefcase:
    (a) We could simply use this base figure as being our 'value'.
    (b) We could reduce it according to the life of the item. Thus, if the briefcase cost £10, is expected to last for ten years and is now eight years old, we could retain the figure of £10 as giving the 'value', but it arguably makes more sense to say that since the briefcase is eight-tenths 'used up', then eight-tenths of the £10 has been 'used up' and therefore the remaining 'value' is £2.
2   We could take as our basic figure the amount of money we would have to pay, today, to buy such a briefcase. Again there are several specific possibilities arising from this basis:
    (a) We could take the cost, today, of buying a new briefcase.
    (b) We could take the cost, today, of buying a second-hand briefcase in this particular condition.
    (c) We could take the cost, today, of buying a new briefcase and reduce it according to the life of our briefcase. Thus, if a new briefcase costs £20, the second-hand cost of an old one is £3, and other information is as above, the alternative figures under this basis would be (a) £20; (b) £3; (c) eight-tenths of £20, i.e. £4.
    A variant of this basis is not to consider the cost of replacing the asset, but rather to consider the cost of replacing its function. Thus, in our example, we would consider the cost of enabling me to carry my bits and pieces if my briefcase was lost, rather than the cost of replacing my briefcase. In situations of rapid technology change, this variant may be the only practical possibility, as the original assets are no longer available.
3   We could take as our basic figure the amount of money we would get if we sold the briefcase in its existing condition – say £1. This should be the net figure after deducting any selling expenses.
4   We could take as our basic figure an evaluation of the future usefulness to us of the briefcase if we keep it and use it. We might say that the value of the use we shall get from the briefcase in the two final years of its life is £3 and £2, respectively. This does not mean that our basic figure would be $3 + 2 = £5$. The question is not: what is the sum of the valuations of the usefulness in each year over the remaining life of the briefcase, but rather: what is the value today of the receipts of usefulness expected in the future. Thus, in our example we need to find the value today of receiving a benefit of £3 in one year's time and a further £2 in two year's time. (Strictly, this assumes that the whole of a year's benefit or usefulness occurs on the last day of the year.)
    The essence of this problem can be considered as follows. Suppose I owe you £80:

If I say 'would you prefer £80 now or £90 in one year', you would probably say you would take £80 now.

If I say 'would you prefer £80 now or £150 in one year'; you would probably prefer the £150 in one year.

There will be some point between 90 and 150, at which you are completely indifferent as between the £80 and the higher figure in one year.

If that point occurs at £100, i.e., you are completely indifferent between £80 now, and £100 in one year, then the rate of discount is 25% (25% × 80 = 20; 100 – 20 = 80).

This enables us to say that £100 expense in one year is the equivalent of £80 expense today, and equally that £100 benefit in one year is only 'worth' £80 benefit today.

Suppose a project involves expenses of £100 p.a. for three years and then benefits of £200 for a further two years. At a 25% discount rate the present 'value' of this project is found as follows:

$$
\begin{array}{llllll}
\text{End year} & 1: & -100 \times 80\% = & & & -80 \\
& 2: & -100 \times 80\% = & 80 \times 80\% = & & -64 \\
& 3: & -100 \times 80\% = & 80 \times 80\% = & 64 \times 80\% & -51 \\
& 4: & +200 \times 80\% = & 160 \times 80\% = & 128 \times 80\% = & \\
& & & & 102 \times 80\% = & +80 \\
& 5: & +200 \times 80\% = & 160 \times 80\% = & 128 \times 80\% = & \\
& & & & 102 \times 80\% = & \\
& & & & 80 \times 80\% = & +64 \\
\hline
& & & & & £-51 \\
\end{array}
$$

Therefore the project, involving net cash inflow of £100, (2 × 200) – (3 × 100), has a net present 'value' (discounted value) of – 51, and is not worth pursuing (unless all available alternatives give even greater negative present values).

The problem, of course, is finding the rate of discount, which is influenced by alternative uses of the resource (e.g. interest on money) and by future expectations, which are of necessity subjective. Even if a discount rate as of now can be found, the implied assumption used above that the rate remains constant is almost certainly false.

If we take the same 25% discount factor as in the above example, then £3 in one year will be evaluated at 80% of £3 today, i.e. £2.40, and £2 in two years will be evaluated at 80% of 80% of £2, i.e. £1.28. Thus the value today of the future usefulness to us of the briefcase would, under these assumptions, be £2.40 + £1.28 = £3.68.

We can give these four evaluation approaches labels, thus:

1 historic cost
2 replacement cost
3 net realizable value
4 net present value, or economic value.

You may of course have thought of other ideas or other combinations. Our suggestions above are restricted in at least two ways. First, we have thought purely in monetary terms. Secondly, we have assumed that money is a perfectly acceptable measuring unit – that we know exactly what one pound means. Both these assumptions require critical consideration.

Activity 3

Analyse and summarize the thought process which made you decide that this book was worth buying.

Activity 3 feedback

These suggestions make the assumption, not necessarily valid, that you did actually buy it. Whatever the price you paid, we can logically deduce that you considered that having the book was worth more to you than having the money. But you do not want the book in order to have the book. You bought the book in order to read it, to learn from it, to enjoy and savour its every word. This cannot be precisely evaluated. Equally, if you had not bought the book it would not be because you wanted to have the money. It would be because you wanted to spend the money on something else *even more advantageous* than ownership of your own copy. This also would not mean that you had evaluated the benefits of this alternative with any precision. There is no need to *evaluate* the benefits of these alternative courses of action, merely to *rank* them. So in order to take this significant investment decision it is not obvious that we necessarily can restrict our thinking to the financially quantifiable. This idea is further explored in Chapter 9.

Activity 4

You need some 'props' for this one. Obtain a pencil, a measuring rule calibrated, if possible, in both inches and centimetres, and an elastic band. Now attempt to measure the length of the pencil (a) with the inches scale of the ruler, (b) with the centimetres scale of the ruler, and (c) with the elastic band.

Activity 4 feedback

Quite! Stupid isn't it. A centimetre is a precisely defined concept. An inch is a precisely defined concept. The relationship between the two is precisely defined. But the idea of measuring a length with an elastic band is nonsensical because of course we do not know how far we have stretched it – it is continually changing by unknown amounts.

But a pound is an elastic concept in just the same way as the elastic band is! In relative terms, for example in relation to the US dollar, the pound keeps changing, as published exchange rates tell us. Even more importantly, the pound keeps changing in absolute terms – indeed, is undefinable in absolute terms – as published inflation rates confirm. The value of a pound is neither clearly defined, nor constant. Yet accountants use it as if it was both! This is another idea requiring detailed analysis, and we return to it in Chapter 7.

An array of value concepts

A fuller and more formal explanation of some possible value concepts is given in a famous book, which every accounting student should read, by Edwards and Bell (1961). We are asked to consider a semifinished asset, i.e. part way through the production process, to enumerate the various dimensions through which we can describe this asset, and thus to calculate and define all the possible permutations arising from this multidimensional consideration.

Three dimensions are suggested:

1 the form (and place) of the thing being valued
2 the date of the price used in valuation
3 the market from which the price is obtained.

We can discuss these one at a time.

The form can be of three types. First, the asset could be described and valued in its present form, e.g. a frame for a chair. Secondly, it could be described and valued in terms of the list of inputs – wood, labour, etc., its initial form. Thirdly, it could be described and valued as the output it is ultimately expected to become, less the additional inputs necessary to reach that stage – a chair less a padded seat for example. This last can be described as its ultimate form.

The date of the price used in valuation, when applied to any of the above three forms, itself gives rise to three possibilities – past, current and future. We can talk about past costs of the initial inputs, current costs of the initial inputs, or future costs of the initial inputs. We can talk about past costs of the present form (i.e. what we *could* have bought it for in the past as bought-in-work-in-progress), about current costs of the present form, or about future costs of the present form. Finally, the prices assigned to the asset in its ultimate form (and to the inputs which must be deducted) could also bear past, current or future dates.

The above yields nine possible alternatives for our asset. But we have still to consider the third dimension – the market from which the price is obtained. Two basic types of market need to be distinguished, the market in which the firm could *buy* the asset in its specified form at the specified time, giving entry prices, and the market in which the firm could *sell* the asset in its specified form at the specified time, giving exit prices. Adding this third dimension with its two possibilities leads to a total of 18 possible alternatives for the asset. Edwards and Bell summarize this in the form of a table (Table 4.1).

Activity 5

Articulate and explain the meaning of each of the eighteen alternatives shown in Table 4.1.

Activity 5 feedback

Your words will undoubtedly be different from ours but your ideas should be somewhat on the following lines.

Initial inputs:

Past, entry	original costs of raw inputs.
Past, exit	past selling prices of those raw inputs in their raw form.

Table 4.1 An array of value concepts

Value date, market	Form and place of asset		
	Initial inputs	Present form	Ultimate form
Past, entry	historic costs	discarded alternatives	irrelevant
Past, exit	discarded alternatives	discarded alternatives	irrelevant
Current, entry	current costs	present costs	irrelevant
Current, exit	irrelevant	opportunity costs	current values
Future, entry	possible replacement costs	possible replacement costs	irrelevant
Future, exit	irrelevant	possible selling values	expected values

Current, entry	cost of those raw inputs.
Current, exit	today's potential selling price of those raw inputs if still in their original form (which they are not!).
Future, entry	expected future costs of those same raw inputs in their original form.
Future, exit	the expected future selling price of the raw inputs if still in their original form (which they are not).

Present form:

Past, entry	the past cost at which the product could have been purchased in its present partially completed form (it was not).
Past, exit	past selling prices at which the product could have been sold in its present partially completed form (but it was not).
Current, entry	the cost at the present time of buying the asset in its present partially completed form.
Current, exit	today's selling price of the product in its present partially completed form.
Future, entry	the expected future cost of buying the asset directly from a supplier in its present partially completed form.
Future, exit	the expected future selling price of the product in its present partially completed form.

Ultimate form:

Past, entry	the past cost at which the product could have been purchased directly from a supplier in its final fully completed form (but it was not).
Past, exit	the past selling price at which the product could have been sold in its final fully completed form (if we had had the product in that form, which we did not).
Current, entry	the cost at the present time of buying the product in its final fully completed form (which we did not).
Current, exit	today's selling price of the product in its final fully completed form.
Future, entry	the expected future cost of buying the product directly from a supplier in its final fully completed form.
Future, exit	the expected future selling price of the product in its final fully completed form.

Activity 6

You may have found Activity 5 rather mind-bending! It is a good example of the type of mental flexibility required if we are going to analyse from first principles without being influenced by prior experience. Now a rather easier task. Select the six alternatives from the total of 18, which you think are most likely to lead to the provision of useful information.

Activity 6 feedback

The six as selected and defined by Edwards and Bell themselves are shown in Table 4.2. It is clear from the feedback to Activity 5 that not all of the other tasks are totally irrelevant (though some of them obviously are). So you may have included one or two different ones. Satisfy yourself, however, that you at least agree that the six alternatives selected

Table 4.2   Edwards and Bell useful valuation possibilities

Exit values:
1 *Expected values* (ultimate, future, exit) – values expected to be received in the future for output sold according to the firm's planned course of action.
2 *Current values* (ultimate, current, exit) – values actually realized during the current period for goods or services sold.
3 *Opportunity costs* (present, current, exit) – values that could currently be realized if assets (whether finished goods, semifinished goods, or raw materials) were sold (without further processing) outside the firm at the best prices immediately obtainable.

Entry values:
1 *Present cost* (present, current, entry) – the cost currently of acquiring the asset being valued.
2 *Current cost* (initial, current, entry) – the cost currently of acquiring the inputs which the firm used to produce the asset being valued.
3 *Historic cost* (initial, past, entry) – the cost at time of acquisition of the inputs which the firm in fact used to produce the asset being valued.

---

in Table 4.2 will indeed provide useful information for decision-making purposes. These six ideas, as developed by later thinking, are all explored in later chapters.

Economic value

We have already met the idea of this in our brief case study (Activity 2). It is mentioned again here in order to point out that the Edwards and Bell exposition of the array of value concepts is clearly incomplete in that it excludes the economic value possibility. To extend their own illustration, one possible course of action with a partly completed chair is to complete it and hire it out for rental, or use it oneself by sitting on it, in either case producing returns over a number of periods capable of being evaluated using the discounting process. Economic value, too, requires proper exploration in a later chapter.

Capital maintenance

We established with our tautology that profit is increase in capital. Turning the argument round, we can suggest that profit is the increase in the closing capital *after having maintained the original capital*. This provides a different but often useful way of looking at problems of income measurement. For each and every *value* concept that we can define, with its corresponding income concept, there is also a clearly definable capital maintenance concept.

Activity 7

Under traditional accounting conventions, based on historic cost, what precisely is the definition of capital which has to be maintained before a profit is reported?

Activity 7 feedback

Traditionally, profit is the numerical quantity of money units generated by the business for the owners over a period. If opening money capital is 100 and closing money capital is 103, then (ignoring dividends and capital infusions) profit is 3. Profit is the excess after having maintained the original 100, so it is the original money capital, the number of pounds originally invested, which has to be maintained under this traditional thinking. If the 100 was in 1896 and the 103 is in 1996, the above statement still applies!

We shall return to the idea of capital maintenance for each of the methods we consider in detail. It will help considerably in appraising the usefulness of the various alternatives.

Criteria for appraising alternative valuation concepts

We discussed the definition and role of accounting together with suggested characteristics of useful information. In essence, accounting communicates useful information for decision-making. We need to analyse each valuation concept to be considered so as to understand in detail the meaning and significance of the information it gives. Different users face different decisions. Users are asking a number of questions. An array of valuation bases is providing a number of answers. If we can match up question with answer then we are being useful. Many valuation bases may be useful, but for different purposes. The question is generally not 'which is the best valuation concept?', but 'which is the best valuation concept to answer this question or help this decision?'. Appraisal is a way of analysing and a way of thinking, never an absolute.

Activity 8

What are the questions, what are the decisions, for which traditional historic cost accounting as outlined in Chapter 3 appears to provide the relevant information?

Activity 8 feedback

One safe answer, following from our discussion on capital maintenance, is that it tells us our gain, our profit, after ensuring the retention of the number of pounds we originally invested. It does not seem obvious, however, that this is very useful information. Investment and expansion decisions as regards future activity require projections into the future based on today's pounds. Reports on past activity related to pounds of the day the business started seem a pretty illogical substitute. But you may, of course, have other ideas!

Fisher and psychic income

The implication of Activity 3 in this chapter was that people buy something, not because of the object itself, but because of what they can do with it. This idea leads us into Fisher's concept of psychic income. People do things because of the satisfaction they derive from so doing. Satisfaction is a mental occurrence, an event of the mind. It is a psychic rather than a physical happening. People act, and make decisions about actions, so as to maximize their personal, mental or psychic satisfaction. Fisher (1930) puts the argument as follows:

> For each individual only those events which come within the purview of his experience are of direct concern. It is these events – the psychic experiences of the individual mind – which constitute ultimate income for that individual. The

outside events have significance for that individual only in so far as they are the means to these inner events of the mind. The human nervous system is, like a radio, a great receiving instrument. Our brains serve to transform into the stream of our psychic life those outside events which happen to us and stimulate our nervous system.

Directors and managers providing income for thousands of people sometimes think of their corporation merely as a great money-making machine. In their eyes its one purpose is to earn money dividends for the stock-holders, money interest for the bond-holders, money wages and money salaries for the employees. What happens after these payments are made seems too private a matter to concern them. Yet that is the nub of the whole arrangement. It is only what we carry out of the market place into our homes and our private lives which really counts. Money is of no use to us until it is spent. The ultimate wages are not paid in terms of money but in the enjoyments it buys. The dividend cheque becomes income in the ultimate sense only when we eat the food, wear the clothes, or ride in the automobile which are bought with the cheque.

The essence of this proposition seems to us to be obviously correct. How do we decide whether to work overtime and earn an extra £20, or to go for a walk in the sunshine? We shall take the decision which we believe (possibly wrongly, of course) will lead to the greater pleasure. Clearly the pleasure to be derived from spending the £20 is relevant in this equation. Equally obviously, such pleasure or satisfaction – enjoyment income as Fisher terms it – cannot be measured directly or objectively. He proposes a series of approximations. The first approximation he calls real income. This involves physical events and material things. A pint of milk and a daily newspaper are both examples of real income. Real income consists

of those final physical events in the outer world which give us our inner enjoyments. This real income includes the shelter of house, the music of a radio, the use of clothes, the eating of food.

In one sense real income is measurable, 'pint' is an objective term (although 'milk' is less so!). But there is no additivity – no standard measuring unit or common denominator. To achieve this we need to move to a second approximation, which Fisher calls the cost of living. This consists of the money paid to obtain the real income – the cost of the pint of milk and the daily newspaper. Fisher's exposition of the argument has something of a period flavour.

So, just as we went behind an individual's enjoyment income to his real income, we now go behind his real income, or his living, to his cost of living, the money measure of real income. You cannot measure in dollars either the inner event of your enjoyment while eating your dinner or the outer event of eating it, but you can find out definitely how much money that dinner cost you. In the same way, you cannot measure your enjoyment at the cinema, but you do know what your house shelter is really worth to you, you can tell how much you pay for your rent, or what is a fair equivalent for your rent if you happen to live in your own house. You cannot measure what it is worth to wear an evening suit, but you can find out what it costs to hire one, or a fair equivalent of its hire if, perchance, the suit belongs to you. Deducing such equivalents is an accountant's job.

> The total cost of living, in the sense of money payments, is a negative item, being outgo rather than income; but it is our best practical measure of the positive items of real income for which those payments are made.

The problem with this as Fisher himself recognizes is that money paid out (outgo) does not seem to make much sense as a measure of income in money terms. We therefore move to a third approximation, that of money income:

> All money received and readily available and *intended* to be used for spending is money income.

We can illustrate Fisher's arguments by considering the eating of a meal. If we wish to eat, we have to go out and earn some money. This means that we have a money income – in this case, wages. This money income, of course, is the idea that corresponds to the everyday use of the words 'income' or 'earnings'. Having some money, we go out to a restaurant where we eat, and pay for, a meal. Here we have real income. We have the 'final physical event', namely the actual eating of the food. This is approximately measured by the 'cost of living', i.e. by the cost of the meal – the amount we pay the restaurant. This idea of taking a cost-based approach is clearly not a new idea to an accountant.

But this is not the end of the story. Fisher argues further. We did not earn money for the sake of it, we ate a meal to receive the satisfaction, the pleasure of having eaten (or to avoid the unpleasantness, the pain, of feeling hungry). This satisfaction, this pleasure, is the 'enjoyment' or 'psychic' income. It may be unmeasurable, at least in a manner that can be recorded, but it is still, argues Fisher, the most important. After all – if it did not exist, we would have had no reason to buy the meal. And without a reason to buy the meal, we have no reason to earn the wages.

Fisher thus distinguishes:

> three successive stages, or aspects, of a man's income:
>
> *Enjoyment* or psychic income, consisting of agreeable sensations and experiences
>
> *Real income* 'measured' by the cost of living
>
> *Money income*, consisting of the money received by a man for meeting his costs of living
>
> The last – money income – is most commonly called income; and the first – enjoyment income – is the most fundamental. But for accounting purposes real income, as measured by the cost of living, is the most practical.

This last statement may seem surprising. Fisher dismisses money income as being unimportant (enjoyment income is the most important, the cost of living is the most practical).

Notice again the definition he gives of money income, emphasis now added:

> All money received and readily available and *intended* to be used for spending is money income.

So if we receive a salary of $10 000 (Fisher's figures, writing in 1930!), save $4000 and put $6000 as available for spending, the significant figure to Fisher is the $6000, not the $10 000. Real income as measured by the cost of living may be more or less than money income. Real income is a closer approximation to ultimate reality (i.e. psychic satisfaction) than money income, so real income is the preferable concept.

A definition of income which satisfies both theory and practice, in both economics and accountancy, must reckon as income in the most basic sense all those uses, services, or living for which the cost of living is expended even though such expenditure may exceed the money income.

What this all boils down to is that Fisher's definitions of income *do not involve a concept of capital maintenance*. It is this point that distinguishes Fisher's ideas from the mainstream of both accounting and economic thinking. Fisher's measure of income is really a measure of consumption.

Psychic income and Frankel's critique

Frankel (1953) attacks the very foundations of Fisher's proposals. The arguments are not easy, and to follow them in detail you should read the article, possibly more than once. In essence Frankel makes two related points. The first is that the distinction Fisher draws between doing something, and enjoying it, is simply misguided. He quotes Gilbert Ryle (1949) as follows:

in describing the workings of a person's mind we are not describing a second set of shadowy operations. We are describing certain phases of his one career; namely, we are describing ways in which parts of his conduct are managed ... When a person talks sense aloud, ties knots, paints and sculpts ... he for a person is bodily active and he is mentally active, but he is not being synchronously active in two different 'places'.

Following this line of thinking, argues Frankel,

This psychic income is not an event or happening which 'occurs' somewhere, i.e. in a person's mind, and is 'caused' by another external event or happening, for example by the receipt of goods and services by that person.

and again,

The agreeable sensations which Fisher would have us believe are the stuff of which ultimate psychic income is made are not things or episodes. It is therefore 'nonsense to speak of observing, inspecting, witnessing, or scrutinizing them'; and it is, I submit, equally nonsense to try, as Fisher would have us try, to 'measure' them, however indirectly, 'since the objects proper to such verbs are things and episodes'.

This line of thinking leads on to Frankel's second major argument. He again quotes Gilbert Ryle:

It does not make sense to speak of my observing, scrutinizing, reporting on, being conscious of, inferring, or *measuring* that I am enjoying the eating of my dinner. If it did, then

it would seem to make sense to ask whether, according to the doctrine, I am not also conscious of being conscious of inferring, that is, in a position to say 'Here I am, spotting the fact that here I am deducing such and such from so and so.' And then there would be no stopping place; there would have to be an infinite number of onion-skins of consciousness embedding any mental state or process whatsoever.

There is a nice parallel here with the business entity convention. The accounting assumption that the business is always a separate entity from the owner mirrors Fisher's assumption that the body is a separate entity from the mind. As Frankel puts it:

> What is significant in Fisher's approach is that to overcome this dichotomy he invents a fiction similar to the one which is usually employed to obtain the symmetry of a double-entry accounting system in connexion with the investment made by the proprietors of a business or venture as something **apart or dissociated** from its proprietors. So Fisher employs, as a last resort, the fiction that the body as a transforming instrument is something **apart or dissociated** from its 'proprietor', namely, 'the mind' to which the 'body' pays out final (or 'true') income, which final income, he argues, is not received until, as subjective income, it emerges into 'the stream of consciousness of any human being'.

But this, argues Frankel, is where Fisher's theory finally collapses. The accountant's system works because he postulates another entity which interrelates with the business entity under consideration. For Fisher's theory to work we have to similarly postulate another layer of consciousness to interact with the mind. But this is not consistent with the notion that the mind is the ultimate consumer, as you cannot go beyond the ultimate!

Activity 9

Briefly appraise Fisher's concept of psychic income and its approximations from the viewpoints of theoretical validity, and of usefulness.

Activity 9 feedback

We would make four points. The first is the rather philosophical one that if all incomes and outgoes except the ultimate (psychic) satisfaction cancel out, then all intermediate balance sheets will balance but not the ultimate one. The only way to make the ultimate balance sheet balance is to postulate a 'post-ultimate' one which is obviously nonsense (Frankel, 1953). Secondly, capital maintenance, i.e. *potential* consumption, *is* of crucial importance. As Kaldor (1969) puts it:

> If we defined income as consumption, we should still require another term to denote as potential income the consumption that would obtain if net savings were zero. Hence, apart from the trivial question of which is the right use of words, it is evident that income and consumption (as ordinarily understood) do not refer to the same thing, but to two different things; and if we reserved the term income for consumption we should still need another term for what would otherwise be called income; and we should still be left with the problem of how to define the latter.

Note also that the words 'real' and 'cost of living' do not have here the same meanings as they will be seen to have in the inflation debate.

Thirdly, there are the obvious practical problems of measurement. No psychic or subjective concept is capable of physical or objective measurement. Therefore for the accountant, the provider of useful figures, it will not do. Fourthly, however, the *logic* of Fisher's fundamental argument, that psychic satisfaction is what matters most in analysing any decision-making process, seems to us obviously correct. It will serve us well as accountants to remember that all information we provide is several stages of approximation removed from the real motivating forces affecting the decision-making process.

Hicks and capital maintenance

We have already seen (Activity 2) that in very general terms economic value is based on a current evaluation of future streams of (net) receipts. It is also obvious that in our earlier equation (p. 34)

$$W_1 + P - D = W_2$$

capital maintenance requires that W_2 is at least equal to W_1. Another way of putting this is that D (= drawing or consumption) cannot exceed P (= profit or income). The classic analysis of the implications of this thinking is by Hicks (1946). The opening of the following quote makes it clear just how fundamental he feels capital maintenance to be.

> The purpose of income calculations in practical affairs is to give people an indication of the amount which they can consume without impoverishing themselves. Following out this idea, it would seem that we ought to define a man's income as the maximum value which he can consume during a week, and still expect to be as well off at the end of the week as he was at the beginning. Thus, when a person saves, he plans to be better off in the future; when he lives beyond his income, he plans to be worse off. Remembering that the practical purpose of income is to serve as a guide for prudent conduct, I think it is fairly clear that this is what the central meaning must be.
>
> However, business men and economists alike are usually content to employ one or other of a series of approximations to the central meaning. Let us consider some of these approximations in turn.

Hicks moves on to attempt to operationalize this 'central meaning'. Like Fisher, Hicks is obviously adopting a forward looking approach to valuation and income measurement. We have seen in Activity 2 that we can operationalize such an approach (once we have invented the raw figures!) by calculating net present value figures for expected receipts. Putting these two ideas together, we can regard capital, wealth, 'well-off-ness' as being the net present value of expected receipts. If we put this notion into the original definition in place of the vague 'as well off', we arrive at a first approximation.

> Income No. 1 is thus the maximum amount which can be spent during a period if there is to be an expectation of maintaining intact the capital value of prospective receipts (in money terms). This is probably the definition which most people do implicitly use in their private affairs; but it is far from being in all circumstances a good approximation to the central concept.

There are several problems with this as an operational concept. First, interest rates may change.

Activity 10

Suppose that at the beginning of the week our individual possesses property worth £10 010, and no other source of income. Then if the rate of interest were one-tenth per cent per week, income would be £10 for the week. For if £10 were spent, £10 000 would be left to be reinvested; and in one week this would have accumulated to £10 010 – the original sum. This is Income No. 1. But suppose that the rate of interest per week for a loan of one week is one-tenth per cent, that the corresponding rate expected to rule in the second week from now is one-fifth per cent, and that this higher rate is expected to continue indefinitely afterwards. What is the individual's income for: (**a**) week 1, (**b**) week 2?

Activity 10 feedback

At the beginning of week 1 the individual is bound to spend no more than £10 010 in the current week, if he is to expect to have £10 010 again at his disposal at the end of the week; but if he desires to have the same sum available at the end of the second week, he will be able to spend nearly £20 in the second week, not £10 only. The same sum (£10 010) available at the beginning of the first week makes possible a stream of expenditures

£10, £20, £20, £20, ...,

while if it is available at the beginning of the second week it makes possible a stream

£20, £20, £20, £20, ...

It is obvious that these two alternative possible expenditure streams do not give equal well-off-ness. One is worth more than the other. If we put the income as £10 for week 1 and £20 for week 2, then we are not 'maintaining intact the capital value of prospective receipts (in money terms)'. The amount the individual can spend each week while still maintaining well-off-ness intact *must*, under these conditions, be the same in week 1 and in week 2 (and subsequent weeks).

> This leads us to the definition of Income No. 2. We now define income as the maximum amount the individual can spend this week, and still expect to be able to spend the same amount in each ensuing week. So long as the rate of interest is not expected to change, this definition comes to the same thing as the first; but when the rate of interest is expected to change, they cease to be identical. Income No. 2 is then a closer approximation to the central concept than Income No. 1 is.

The second problem is that prices may be expected to change. In principle we can deal with this easily by a small addition to the wording.

> Income No. 3 must be defined as the maximum amount of money which the individual can spend this week, and still expect to be able to spend the same amount in real terms in each ensuing week. If prices are expected to rise, then an individual who plans to spend £10 in the present and each ensuing week must expect to be less well off at the end of the week than he is at the beginning. At each date he can look forward to the opportunity of spending £10 in each future week; but at the first date one of the £10s will be spent in a week when prices are relatively low. An opportunity of spending on favourable terms is present in the first case, but absent in the second.

Thus, if £10 is to be his income for this week, according to definition No. 3 he will have to expect to be able to spend in each future week not £10, but a sum greater or less than £10 by the extent to which prices have risen or fallen in that week above or below their level in the first week.

In practice of course the apparent simplicity of this change is false. We need expectations of price changes for every individual for every commodity of projected purchase for every need of each anticipated expenditure!

In addition to this practical difficulty Income No. 3 also has the problem of how to deal with long-term assets, i.e. fixed assets or 'durable consumption goods'.

Strictly speaking, saving is not the difference between income and expenditure, it is the difference between income and consumption. Income is not the maximum amount the individual can spend while expecting to be as well off as before at the end of the week; it is the maximum amount he can consume. If some part of his expenditure goes on durable consumption goods, that will tend to make his expenditure exceed his consumption; if some part of his consumption is consumption of durable consumption goods, already bought in the past, that tends to make consumption exceed expenditure.

It should be noted that we have now come full circle back to an emphasis on consumption. But Hicks is concerned with consumption and capital maintenance, whereas Fisher is only concerned with consumption. We can summarize the basic difference between Fisher and Hicks by realizing that whilst Fisher is concerned with consumption, Hicks, on the other hand, is concerned with the capacity to consume. This is clearly a long-run concept. To take an obvious example, consider the farmer's seed-corn. This is the basis of next year's crops. It is available now, and it could be eaten (consumed). But if it is eaten now then there will be no crop next year and therefore no possibility of consumption next year. Therefore, if we wish to maintain the capacity to consume next year, the seed-corn must not be consumed now. In other words it must be saved. This, to put it mildly, is useful information.

The calculation of economic income

One way of summarizing the above is to say that for Fisher:

$$Income = Consumption,$$

but for Hicks:

$$Income = Consumption \text{ and } Saving,$$

which can be expressed as:

$$Y = C + S$$

Savings can be expressed as $(K_e - K_s)$ where:

$$K_e = \text{value of capital at the end of a period}$$
$$K_s = \text{value of capital at the start of the period}$$

Thus:

$$Y = C + (K_e - K_s)$$

For example if income = £100, capital at the end of the period = £280, and capital at the beginning of the period was £300, then: £100 = 120 + (280 − 300).

This tells us that consumption has exceeded income by £20, because of dis-saving of £20. 'Well-off-ness' has not been maintained.

In the business world rather than the personal consumption world, C is redefined as the realized cash flows of the period. We will illustrate this as simply as possible.

Activity 11

An investment on 1 January year 1 has expected receipts on 31 December each year of £1000 for three years. The discount rate to reflect the time value of money is 10%. Calculate the capital as at 1 January for each of the years 1, 2 and 3.

Activity 11 feedback

On 1 January year 1 the expected receipt on 31 December year 1 needs to be discounted back by one year, the expected receipt on 31 December year 2 needs to be discounted back by two years, and the expected receipt on 31 December year 3 needs to be discounted back by three years.

Thus capital at 1 January year 1 is:

$$\frac{1000}{1.1} + \frac{1000}{(1.1)^2} + \frac{1000}{(1.1)^3}$$

$$= 909 + 826 + 751 = £2486$$

On 1 January year 2 the receipt on 31 December year 1 is now irrelevant. The expected receipt on 31 December year 2 now needs to be discounted back to 1 January year 2, i.e. by *one* year, and the expected receipt on 31 December 03 also needs to be discounted back to 1 January 02, i.e. by two years. Similarly, on 1 January 03 only the expected receipt on 31 December year 3 is of any relevance and this needs to be discounted back to 1 January year 3, i.e. by *one* year. Thus capital at 1 January year 2 is:

$$\frac{1000}{1.1} + \frac{1000}{(1.1)^2}$$

$$= 909 + 826 = £1735$$

and capital at 1 January 03 is:

$$\frac{1000}{1.1} = £909$$

Activity 12

Considering the investment in the previous activity, now suppose that the actual cost of the investment, on 1 January year 1, is £2486. According to the Hicksian way of thinking, what is the income for each year?

Activity 12 feedback

Our formula was:

$$Y = C + (K_e - K_s)$$

so in the year 1:

$$Y = 1000 + (1735 - 2486)$$
$$= 1000 - 751$$
$$= £249$$

In the year 2:

$$Y = 1000 + (909 - 1735)$$
$$= 1000 - 826$$
$$= £174$$

In the year 3:

$$Y = 1000 + (0 - 909)$$
$$= 1000 - 909$$
$$= £91$$

In the year 1, the cash receipts are £1000, but the income is stated as £249. The difference (£751) needs to be reinvested (saved), in order to facilitate *future* spending. This reinvestment of £751 on 1 January year 2 will by itself earn 10% in the year 2, i.e. £75. So total income in year 2 is £174, from the original investment, plus £75 from the reinvestment, i.e. again £249.

In the year 2, the cash receipts from the original investment are £1000, but the income is stated as £174. The difference (£826) again needs to be reinvested. This investment of £826 will itself earn £83 in the year 3, giving total cash receipts in that year of £91 from the original investment, £75 from the first reinvestment, and £83 from the second reinvestment, i.e. £249 once again. Similarly in the year 3, cash receipts will be £1000, but the income is stated as £91. The difference (£909) will be reinvested at 10%, earning itself £91 in each year. Total cash receipts in year 4, all from reinvestments, will therefore be 75 + 83 + 91 = £249, and similarly in year 5 onwards. This of course satisfies our original conditions. The income of year 1 is the amount 'that can be spent while still enabling the income of all future periods to be the same amount'. This has been shown to be £249 under the given assumptions. All these results are summarized in Table 4.3.

The present value of an annual income stream of £249, to infinity, at a 10% discount rate is £2490. This, allowing for rounding errors, gives us our original 'capital' figure of £2486, which of course is what it should do. So the answer may possibly have come as no surprise. But you should still make sure you understand all the logic involved.

Income *ex ante* and income *ex post*

We have assumed that we are in a world of perfect knowledge and perfect foresight – an ideal world in fact. The economic income devised under these assumptions is known as ideal income. It is obviously an unreal oversimplification. We can, however, extend our

Table 4.3 Hick's economic income model

	1	2	3	4	5	6	7	8	9
Year	C	K_e	K_s	Y	Reinvestment	Cumulative reinvestment	Total reinvestment	Income from reinvestments	Total economic income
0	0	2486	0	0	0	0	2486	0	0
1	1000	1735	2486	249	751	751	2486	0	249
2	1000	909	1735	174	826	1577	2486	75	249
3	1000	0	909	91	909	2486	2486	158	249
4	0	0	0	0	0	2486	2486	249	249

Notes: 4 = 1 + 2 − 3
5 = 1 − 4
7 = 2 + 6
9 = 4 + 8.

analysis to allow for estimates of future events, and this leads to two further models, income *ex ante* and income *ex post*. Income *ex ante* means income measured before the event. Income for a period is calculated based on expectations as at the beginning of the period.

Two possibilities for changes exist: in the timing and/or amount of forecast cash flows, and in the appropriate discount rate.

Formally, income *ex ante* can be expressed as

$$Y = C_1 + (K_e^1 - K_s)$$

where C_1 is the expected realized cash flow for the period anticipated at the beginning of the period, K_e^1 is the closing capital as measured (estimated) at the beginning of the period, and K_s is the capital at the beginning of the period as measured (estimated) at the beginning of the period.

Activity 13

Assume the same original information as in the previous two activities. Now suppose that at the end of year 2, the expected return from the investment in the year 3 increases to £1100. Using an *ex ante* approach consider the effects on the calculations for each of the years.

Activity 13 feedback

Using an *ex ante* approach the effects will be:

Year 1 – No change

Year 2 – Still no change. The calculations for the year 2 are based on expectations as at the beginning of the year 2, and they had not altered at that time.

Year 3 – The opening capital K_s will no longer be the same as the closing capital K_e at the end of year 2. It will now be

$$K_s = \frac{1100}{1.1} = £1000$$

This compares with the corresponding figure of £909 for K_s in year 3 under the ideal income calculations. There is therefore a windfall gain of £91 appearing under the *ex ante* way of thinking in the year 3.

Income *ex post* means that income is measured after the event. Income ex post can be expressed correspondingly, as

$$Y = C + (K_e - K_s^1)$$

where C is the actual realized cash flow of the period, K_e is the closing capital measured (estimated) at the end of the period, and K_s^1 is the opening capital measured (estimated) at the end of the period.

Activity 14

Given all the information of the previous activity, reconsider the effects of the change in expectations which occurs at the end of the year 2.

Activity 14 feedback

Again there will be no change in the year 1 but, using an *ex post* approach, there will be a change in the calculations for the year 2, because at the end of the year 2 our expectations had already altered. Capital at 1 January year 2, based on expectations as at the end of the year 2, is:

$$\frac{1000}{1.1} + \frac{1100}{(1.1)^2}$$

$$K_s = 909 + 909 = £1818$$

This compares with the corresponding figure of £1735 for K_s in the year 2 under the ideal income calculations, giving rise to a windfall gain of £83 appearing in the year 2.

For present purposes, it is not considered necessary to pursue the calculations any further as regards recalculation of reinvestment amounts and so on. However, several points should be noted:

1 Income *ex post* is measured after the event, but it is still based on expectations of the future. Income *ex post* for the year 2 is derived from the expectations held as at the end of the year 2, but these expectations relate to the years 3, 4 and so on to infinity. Economic income *ex post* is therefore just as subjective as economic income *ex ante*.
2 Is the windfall gain realized? This is relatively straightforward. The gain becomes realized as the cash flow whose estimation gave rise to it is actually received.
3 Is the windfall gain income or capital, i.e. should it be saved (reinvested) or can it be spent? This is not so clear-cut, as it depends on where we consider our starting point to be. Taking our original example, if our original, and permanent, intention is to maintain the capacity to consume £249 each year to infinity, then it is clear that we have already achieved that requirement without taking account of the windfall gain. The gain is, therefore, 'spare', it need not be reinvested, and so it is available for immediate consumption. Notice carefully that the windfall gain is available for consumption as soon as it is recognized, 'whether or not it has been realized', i.e. in year 2 under the *ex post* method

and in year 3 under the *ex ante* method. Thus the windfall gain could be regarded as a simple one-off increase in possible consumption (do not forget it could be a windfall loss, leading to a one-off decrease in possible consumption).

However, the change in expectations might cause us to amend the permanent annual consumption requirement in some way. We might for example wish to redo the complete calculations taking the year 2 as a new starting point, giving 2 years of cash flow only. Here the windfall gain would not, or not necessarily, be spendable at all (even if it is already realized!).

It is of course possible, taking the original ideal income scenario as our starting point, to consider an almost infinite number of changes in expectations, variable as to timing of the change in expectations, changes in the expected timing of receipts, changes in the expected amounts of receipts, and changes in discount rates. In every case, under both *ex ante* and *ex post* thinking, we need to establish whether the effect of the change is on income or on capital before we can attempt to rework all the calculations, and this depends entirely on the intentions of the decision-maker concerned. If these intentions remain unaltered despite the change in expectations then the windfall will be income.

Refer back to the Hicks' Income No. 3 definition: the maximum amount of money which the individual can spend this week, and still expect to be able to spend the same amount in real terms in each ensuing week. If 'this week' is and remains week 1, then the windfall is income. But if 'this week' means 'the current week', e.g. the week when expectations change, then the windfall affects capital and requires that a new permanently spendable weekly consumption be calculated.

Summary

Income, capital and value are interrelated concepts. Value can be defined and enumerated in a variety of ways, and detailed description, analysis and appraisal of the alternatives is required.

It is suggested that the economic ideas outlined above are:

1 theoretically sound and logically sensible
2 highly subjective in application as regards
   (a) size of future cash flows
   (b) timing of future cash flows
   (c) discount rate to apply to future cash flows
3 problematic as regards windfall gains and losses
4 and therefore, as far as accounting is concerned, they probably represent an unattainable ideal.

Exercises

1 Obtain three sets of published accounts of quoted companies. Look carefully at the consolidated balance sheets, and notes thereto, and read the 'accounting policies'. Taking each item in the balance sheet separately describe how the item is evaluated. Are these evaluations consistent?, i.e. in mathematical terms, do we have genuine additivity?

2 Two retail businesses, A and B, run a similar trade from similar shops in similar areas. A bought its shop in 1950 for £5000 and B bought its shop in 1990 for £105 000. Both busi-

nesses consistently prepare their accounts on historic cost principles, and they have identical operating profits. To what extent do the resulting accounts give a true (and fair) representation of the relative performance of the two businesses?

3 It is never possible to define capital *or* income, only to define capital *and* income. Do you agree?

4 **(a)** Outline Fisher's thinking on the concept of income.
   (b) Outline Hick's thinking on this topic.
   (c) Relate and compare the two.

5 Explain the principles of economic income, carefully distinguishing income *ex ante* and income *ex post*.

6 'Economic income is an unattainable ideal.' Consider and discuss.

7 **(a)** **Describe briefly the theory underlying Hicks' economic model of income and capital. What are its practical limitations?**   (10 marks)

   (b) Spock purchased a space invader entertainment machine at the beginning of year 1 for £1000. He expects to receive at annual intervals the following receipts; at the end of year 1 £400; end of year 2 £500; end of year 3 £600. At the end of year 3 he expects to sell the machine for £400.

   Spock could receive a return of 10% in the next best investment. The present value of £1 receivable at the end of a period discounted at 10% is as follows:

End of year 1	0.909
End of year 2	0.826
End of year 3	0.751

   Required:
   Calculate the ideal economic income, ignoring taxation, and working to the nearest whole pound.

   Your answer should show that Spock's capital is maintained throughout the period and that his income is constant.   (10 marks)
                                                                      (Total 20 marks)
                                                                               (ACCA)

8 The economic income model has three forms: ideal income, *ex ante* income and *ex post* income.
   (a) **Describe each of these three models of income measurement.**
   (b) **Say which of these models you consider to be most relevant to the practice of accounting.**
      Give the reasons for your choice.
                                                                          (20 marks)
                                                                               (ACCA)

Current entry value

After reading this chapter you should be able to:
- explain the effects and implications of using current entry values to record the possession and usage of economic resources
- carry out the necessary technical manipulation
- explain the strengths, usefulness and weaknesses of the resulting information.

Introduction

The ideas of the previous chapter are of fundamental importance. But they are inherently highly subjective to apply. Of crucial importance from the point of view of accounting thinking, they are far removed from the market place. All eighteen of the value concepts considered by Edwards and Bell (see Chapter 4) relate directly to actual or expected market values. One of these, past entry values, i.e. the historic cost (HC) of the initial inputs, is the traditional process which we have covered in Chapter 3.

Four of the remaining five are current values, two being current entry values and two current exit values. We look first at current entry values. Remember that entry values represent a market buying price, i.e. current entry values represent a *cost-based* process (but not a *historic* cost-based process).

Back to basics

Activity 1

On 1 January, Mr Jones starts off in business with 100 pence. His transactions are as follows:

2 January   Buys one bag of sugar for   40p
4 January   Sells one bag of sugar for   50p
5 January   Buys one bag of sugar for   44p

Prepare balance sheets on 2 January and on 6 January, and a P&L account for the intervening period.

Activity 1 feedback

This should not present major problems.

Balance sheet 2 January

Stock	40	Capital	100
Cash	60		
	100p		100p

Balance sheet 6 January

Stock	44	Capital	110
Cash	66		
	110p		110p

Profit and loss

Sales	50
Cost of sales	40
	10p

In terms of our very general equation, $W_1 + P - D = W_2$ (see p. 34)

$$100 + 10 - 0 = 110$$

So Jones has made a profit of 10p. This of course is the usual accounting approach. But it is important to notice that there are really two stages in the progress from 2 January to 6 January. Between 2 January and the evening of 4 January, after the sale was made, Jones has turned 100p into 110p. On 4 January he actually has physically 110p and nothing else. Then between the evening of 4 January and 6 January he has changed 110p plus nothing into 66p plus a bag of sugar. Since the second bag of sugar cost 44p and we are recording all our resources at original, or historical, cost it necessarily follows that we show total resources of 110p on both 4 January and 6 January. The 4 January balance sheet was as follows:

Balance sheet 4 January

Cash	110	Capital	110
	110p		110p

Comparing this 4 January position with the 2 January and 6 January balance sheets confirms that:

1 A profit of 10p was made between 2 January and 4 January and
2 No profit or loss at all was made between 4 January and 6 January.

Jones of course is running a business. He also has to live. So he decides to withdraw the business profit for his own spending purposes.

If he takes 10p out then, by the accountant's definition, he has still left in all the money originally put in. This 10p must therefore be genuine gain, so it can obviously be withdrawn from the business without in any way reducing the resources of the business. So we can rewrite our 6 January sheet, after the withdrawal, as follows:

Balance sheet 6 January

Stock	44	Capital	100
Cash	56		
	100p		100p

Our equation now becomes:

$$100 + 10 - 10 = 100$$

Activity 2

Compare the *physical* possessions of Jones' business on 2 January with those on 6 January, assuming still that Jones withdraws his 10p profit.

Activity 2 feedback

In physical terms the business possesses:

On 2 January:

1 one bag of sugar
2 a pile of 60 shiny bright 1p pieces.

On 6 January:

1 one bag of sugar
2 a pile of 56 shiny bright 1p pieces.

Now, by simple subtraction, we can compare the physical position between 2 January and 6 January in terms both of sugar and of shiny bright 1p pieces. In terms of sugar, we are comparing one bag with one bag. There is no difference. In terms of bags of sugar the business is exactly the same size as it was before. In terms of shiny bright 1p pieces, the business had 60 on 2 January and 56 on 6 January. There is therefore a reduction of four shiny bright 1p pieces. In terms of shiny bright 1p pieces the business has got smaller by four pieces.

Something must be wrong somewhere. The accountant has shown us that there is a 'genuine gain' of 10p over and above the original 100p capital put in. Jones has therefore withdrawn the 10p, and yet the result is **not** that the business is 'back where it started'. The result is that the business has **got smaller** to the tune of 4p.

Surely, either the physical comparison is wrong, or the profit and loss statement prepared in Activity 1 is wrong. If the physical comparison is correct (try it yourself) then the 'genuine gain' of 10% mentioned above is quite simply not genuine! Further thinking is needed. On 4 January we had, in physical terms, as we have already seen, a pile of 110 shiny bright 1p pieces. We have also already seen that the profit of 10p was made by 4 January. It therefore follows that the accountant's statement at 4 January is identical with the actual physical position at that date. The accountant says cash is 110p and profit is 10p. The physical position shows a pile of 110 shiny bright 1p pieces. It is obvious that since the physical position and the accounting position were identical as at 4 January the divergence, the difference between the two, must have occurred after 4 January. But only one event has happened *after* 4 January. This was the purchase of the second bag of sugar on 5 January. So the problem *must* be something to do with the accounting treatment of the second bag.

Question: Why did Jones have to buy a second bag of sugar for 44p? The answer is: because he has sold the first bag of sugar (for 50p). He would not have bought the second bag of sugar if he had not sold the first one. It seems, therefore, that the selling of the first bag of sugar and the buying of the second bag of sugar are really two parts of one complete action. If he does not sell the first bag of sugar and does not buy the second bag of sugar, he obviously ends up with the same amount of cash on 6 January as he had on 2 January, i.e. 60p. If he does sell the first bag of sugar for 50p and *does* buy the second bag of sugar for 44p, he will end up with 6p more cash on 6 January than he had on 2 January. So the result of selling bag 1 and buying bag 2, *as compared with doing neither*, is a gain of 6p.

We can show this as follows:

Sales	50p
Costs incurred as a direct result of making sale	44p
Profit	6p

We are now suggesting a profit of 6p, as compared with the earlier suggestion of 10p. This will presumably reduce the maximum drawing payable by $10p - 6p = 4p$. And remember, we argued earlier that the error, the difference between the original accountant's calculations and physical reality, the amount by which Jones' business had unintentionally 'got smaller' was 4p. We seem to have corrected the error exactly. We have produced an accounting calculation that agrees with actual physical events:

$$W_1 + P - D = W_2$$
$$100 + 6 - 6 = 100$$

The business itself

It is essential to remember the purpose and nature of Jones' business. It is a sugar-selling business. The essence of the conclusion above is a very simple one. It is that the cost of sales figure that we should relate to any particular sale should be calculated as equal to the *cost of the resulting replacement*, assuming that the replacement occurs immediately. The cost of sales figure should not be related to the cost of the item actually sold. This raises a difficulty. In order to be able to transfer this higher replacement figure out of the balance sheet and into the profit and loss calculation, the higher replacement figure must obviously first be recorded in the balance sheet. The complete picture is most easily seen by a series of balance sheets:

1 January

Cash	100	Capital	100
	100p		100p

2 January

Sugar	40	Capital	100
Cash	60		
	100p		100p

3 January

Sugar (1st bag)	44	Capital	100
Cash	60	Gain	4
	104p		104p

4 January

Cash	110	Capital	100
		Gain	4
		Profit	6
	110p		110p

5 January

Sugar (2nd bag)	44	Capital	100
		Gain	4
Cash	66	Profit	6
	110p		110p

Now we must choose our words carefully. It is perfectly correct to say that Jones began his business on 1 January with 100p. But that is not the point. The point is that Jones began the business on 1 January with *60p plus the capacity to buy a bag of sugar.* Jones is setting up in business for the purpose of acquiring, and selling, bags of sugar. Therefore, we need to evaluate his position at any time in terms of his capacity, his ability, to carry out his purpose. In other words, his capacity to acquire and sell sugar.

So on 1 January Jones had the capacity to buy one bag of sugar (for 40p) plus also 60p. On 4 January Jones had 110 pence. More usefully, we can say that on 4 January Jones had the capacity to buy one bag of sugar (for 44p), plus also 66p. Comparing the 4 January position with the 1 January position clearly shows that Jones has:

1 maintained his capacity to buy one bag of sugar; and also
2 gained 6 shiny bright 1p pieces.

This calculation agrees with the real physical events. Jones has:

1 6 more shiny bright 1p pieces; and
2 a statement from his accountant giving a figure for profit of 6p.

On the assumptions that Jones wishes to carry on selling and buying bags of sugar this is obviously the correct answer.

We have solved a major problem. We have shown the accountant how to produce a profit figure that actually makes physical sense, and that Jones can actually believe. But we have created another difficulty. The statement from the accountant showed not only a *profit* of 6p, but also a separate, different *gain* of 4p. This gain of 4p occurred earlier than the profit. The gain was included in the balance sheet of 3 January and the profit did not appear until 4 January. We know that this 'gain' is not the same as profit – the whole point of all this is that the 'total' profit, i.e. the total increase in the capacity of the business to do things, is only 6p. So if the 'gain' is not profit, what on earth is it?

In the most simple of terms it is the double entry for an increase in the recorded figure for an item of stock.

Activity 3

Open T-accounts to reflect Jones' balance sheet on 2 January (as before). Record in these and any other necessary T-accounts the increase in stock figure leading to the 3 January balance sheet, then the full effect of the sales transaction on 4 January.

Activity 3 feedback

We have on 2 January, the stock T-account shows a debit of 40p and on 3 January, a total debit of 44p. In full we have on 2 January:

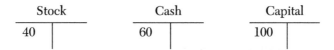

Stock	Cash	Capital
40	60	100

On 3 January we increase the stock so as to bring the recorded figure up to the current level of replacement cost (RC). Thus there is a debit of 4p to stock and a credit of 4p somewhere else. This credit cannot be to cash, nor can it be to capital, so it must be to a new T-account. Now this 4p represents a gain that has arisen as a result of *holding* our stock over a period of time. We did not sell it, but we *held* it over a period during which the replacement cost rose. We shall more formally refer to this gain as a holding gain. So on 3 January:

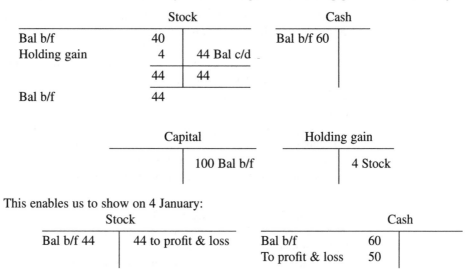

Stock

Bal b/f	40	
Holding gain	4	44 Bal c/d
	44	44
Bal b/f	44	

Cash

Bal b/f 60	

Capital

	100 Bal b/f

Holding gain

	4 Stock

This enables us to show on 4 January:

Stock

Bal b/f 44	44 to profit & loss

Cash

Bal b/f	60	
To profit & loss	50	

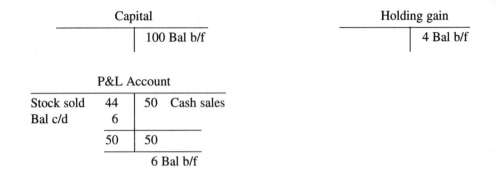

Capital				Holding gain	
	100 Bal b/f				4 Bal b/f

P&L Account

Stock sold	44	50	Cash sales
Bal c/d	6		
	50	50	
		6	Bal b/f

Capital maintenance

Given that we are considering a different profit concept from the traditional historic profit, we are necessarily implying also a different capital maintenance concept from that discussed in Activity 7, Chapter 4.

Activity 4

Define clearly the capital maintenance concept implied by the above T-account calculations.

Activity 4 feedback

Profit could here be defined as the amount generated by the business over and above that necessary to replace the assets. The capital maintenance concept could therefore be said to be the maintenance of the capacity to replace the resources of the business.

A more rigorous analysis

If an item of stock is bought for £10, held until its buying price increases to £12, and then sold for £15 then the HC profit is £15 − £10 = £5. But we know from the discussion above that this can be split into two parts, as follows.

During the time the stock is held, the cost price rises from £10 to £12. There is therefore a holding gain of £2, giving a recorded stock figure immediately before the sale of £12. When the stock is sold, an asset of £12 (stock) is transformed into an asset of £15 (cash) giving rise to a profit from operating of £3. Clearly we have split the HC profit into two elements, namely the operating profit (revenue minus current replacement cost), and the holding gain (current replacement cost minus original purchase cost). In these circumstances both elements would be regarded as 'realized' (see Chapter 3).

More normally, both realized and unrealized gains will be involved, as in the following example:

1 October 20X1	Buy 2 at £30
1 November 20X1	Sell 1 at £50, when RC is £35
31 December 20X1	RC is £38
31 January 20X2	Sell 1 at £60, when RC is £40

The HC profits are:

Year 1   50 – 30 = £20
Year 2   60 – 30 = £30

A fuller analysis gives the following:

1 Between 1 October and 1 November, there has been a holding gain of $2 \times (35 - 30) =$ £10.
2 On 1 November one of the items is sold; therefore on 1 November:
   (a) Half of the holding gain becomes realized (i.e. $1 \times [35 - 30]$), as the item to which it relates has been sold.
   (b) There is a (realized) operating profit of 50 – 35 = £15.
3 On 31 December there is an additional holding gain of 38 – 35 = £3.
      This will be unrealized as the item is still unsold. Between 31 December 20X1 and 31 January 20X2 there has been a holding gain of 40 – 38 = £2.
4 On 31 January the second item is sold, and therefore:
   (a) there is a (realized) operating gain of 60 – 40 = £20
   (b) all the unrealized holding gain related to the second item becomes realized.

To summarize, for the year 1 we have:

Operating profit	£15
Realized holding gain	£5
Unrealized holding gain	£8 (5 + 3, or 38 – 30)

For the year 2 we have:

Operating profit	£20
Realized holding gain	£10
Unrealized holding gain	£0

Note carefully that the £10 holding gain realized in the year 2 includes the £8 holding gain that was *recognized* and *recorded* in the year 1, but which had not become realized in the year 1, as well as the £2 of holding gain recognized in the year 2.

These figures demonstrate that the HC profit consists of two of the three elements involved:

HC profit = Operating profit + Realized holding gains

In the year 1   £20 = 15 + 5
In the year 2   £30 = 20 + 10

Notice that we include all the holding gains realized in the year, whether or not they have been recognized and recorded (as unrealized) in earlier years.

Edwards and Bell (1961) referred to the reported results under a RC system as business income, which they defined as follows:

Business income = Operating profit + Realized holding gain recognized in the period
                             + Unrealized holding gains recognized in the period.

Thus business income in the year 1 is:

$$15 + 5 + 8 = £28$$

and in the year 2 is:

$$20 + 2 + 0 = £22$$

Observe that the proportion of the realized holding gain in the year 2 which had already been included in business income of the year 1 (as an unrealized holding gain) is not included in the year 2. To do so would of course involve double counting.

Examination will show that the differences between accounting (HC) income and business income are caused by different elements of the holding gains being included.

Activity 5

Derive the formal relationship between accounting income and business income, and apply it to the above situation.

Activity 5 feedback

Accounting income includes:

1 realized holding gains of the period recognized in the period; plus
2 realized holding gains of the period recognized in previous periods.

Business income includes:

3 realized holding gains of the period recognized in the period; and
4 unrealized holding gains recognized in the period.

Since (**1**) and (**3**) above are the same, it follows that:

$$\text{Accounting income} - (\mathbf{2}) = \text{Business income} - (\mathbf{4})$$

or:

$$\text{Accounting income} = \text{Business income} - (\mathbf{4}) + (\mathbf{2})$$

as defined above.

> For the year 1 £20 = 28 – 8 + 0, and
> For the year 2 £30 = 22 – 0 + 8

The important thing about all this analysis is that it enables us to discuss and decide which elements we wish to include in our own preferred definition of income. Edwards and Bell, arguing in favour of a current entry (RC) approach, include all the holding gains *recognized* in the period as being included in income. This has been criticized on two grounds. First, it is suggested that no unrealized gains should be included, as this would lack prudence. Secondly, and more importantly, it is suggested that all the holding gains, whether realized or unrealized, need to be retained in the business in order to enable it to replace resources as they are used. Using the terminology we developed earlier on p. 62 the operating profit is the gain after having retained sufficient resources to enable us to do those things which we originally had the capacity to do. If we ask the question: 'How much profit can I remove without impairing the substance, the operating capability of the business?' then the answer is the operating profit. Only the operating profit should be regarded and reported as income. Holding gains, whether realized or not, should be excluded. This objection to the Edwards and Bell conclusion is generally regarded as a valid one and most authors argue that the central profit figure under a current entry value system should consist of the operating profit alone.

Remember the capital maintenance concept as we defined it above in Activity 4, i.e. the maintenance of the capacity to replace the resources of the business. The holding gains represent reserves – i.e. ownership claims on resources – corresponding to the resources which will have to be used in addition to replace existing assets if they are replaced at current prices. Income, within this capital maintenance requirement, therefore excludes all such holding gains.

In practice the changes in cost levels are likely to be approximated to by the use of appropriate price indices. Activity 6 below provides an example of the application of this mechanism to the principles already discussed. Study the activity carefully, and try to at least rough out a solution before you work through the feedback which follows.

Activity 6

Chaplin Ltd's balance sheet on 31 December, year 1, after one year's trading was as follows:

	£		£	£
Capital – £1		Land and buildings at cost		110 000
ordinary shares	200 000	Plant and equipment at cost	40 000	
Profit	26 000	*less* Depreciation	4 000	36 000
	226 000			146 000
Creditors	50 000	Stock	90 000	
Loan	50 000	Debtors	90 000	
				180 000
	326 000			326 000

1 The capital and loan had been contributed in cash and the land and buildings, plant and equipment and opening stock of £60 000 had been purchased on 1 January.
2 Transactions took place evenly during the year. The situation may therefore be treated as if all opening balances were held from 1 January until 30 June, as if all transactions took place on 30 June, and as if all closing balances were held from 30 June until 31 December.
3 Price indices were as follows:

	RPI	Plant	Stock
1 January	100	100	100
30 June	110	105	115
31 December	120	110	130

4 The land and buildings were professionally valued at 31 December at £135 000.
Prepare:
A closing balance sheet on RC lines.

Activity 6 feedback

Chaplin Ltd – RC solution

HC profit			26 000
less Adjustments:			
Depreciation	$4\,000 \times \dfrac{(110 - 100)}{100}$	400	
Stock	$60\,000 \times \dfrac{(115 - 100)}{100}$	9000	9 400
Current operating profit			16 600
Add Holding gains:			
Stock: realized as above			9 000
unrealized	$90\,000 \times \dfrac{(130 - 115)}{115}$	11 740	
Plant and equipment: realized as above		400	
unrealized	$40\,000 \times \dfrac{(110 - 100)}{100} - 400$	3 600	
Land and buildings:			
unrealized	$135\,000 - 110\,000$	25 000	49 740
Business income			£66 340

The general view today is that the holding gains should be shown separately as holding gains, rather than combining all gains of every sort as 'business income'. This leads to the following balance sheet:

Fixed assets:

		£	£
Land and building			135 000
Plant and equipment	$40\,000 \times \dfrac{110}{100}$	44 000	
less depreciation	$4\,000 \times \dfrac{110}{100}$	4 400	39 600
			174 600

Current assets:

		£	£
Stock	$90\,000 \times \dfrac{130}{115}$	101 740	
Debtors		90 000	191 740
			£366 340

	£
Share capital	200 000
Holding gain reserve	49 740
P&L account	16 600
	266 340
Loan	50 000
Creditors	50 000
	£366 340

In checking through Activity 6 note the treatment of the stock gains; it is assumed that the opening stock was all sold on 30 June, so the relevant holding gain is realized, the £90 000 closing stock is treated as being purchased on 30 June and held ever since. Check that you understand the usage of all the index adjustments (and note the irrelevance of the retail prices index (RPI) here). As regards the distinction between realized and unrealized holding gains, note that *only the current operating profit* can be distributed without impairing the ability to replace physical assets.

Replacement cost accounting and depreciation

Activity 7

There is one particular problem with replacement cost (RC) accounting and depreciation that is not revealed by the Chaplin illustration. Consider the following:

> A fixed asset costs £100, has an expected useful life of four years, with zero scrap value, and the RC of a new asset rises by £20 each year. Calculate the profit and loss (P&L) account charge and show the balance sheet position, for each of the first two years, under RC.

Activity 7 feedback

The year 1 position is simple enough. We have:

Cost (RC)	£120
Depreciation (25%) (in P&L a/c)	30
Balance sheet	£ 90

But year 2 is problematic. From a P&L account viewpoint we have an RC figure of £140 and we have had 25% of the benefit, therefore we should have an expense to match of 25% of 140 = £35. This leaves total accumulated depreciation of £65 and a balance sheet figure of £75 (140 − 65). But taking a balance sheet view we have an asset with an RC of £140 that is exactly half used up. Therefore, again following the matching convention, we should have accumulated depreciation of exactly half of £140, leaving a balance sheet figure also of exactly half of £140 to carry forward for future matching. This implies an expense figure in year 2 of £40 (closing depreciation balance 70, opening balance 30, therefore necessary charge for this year £40).

We are obviously in trouble. In year 2 we need a £35 charge in the P&L account (25% × 140) and at the same time a deduction of £40 (70 − 30) in the balance sheet. From a double-entry viewpoint this is somewhat disturbing. This problem is usually solved by the idea of backlog depreciation. The year 2 balance sheet deduction is regarded as consisting of two elements:

1 the proper annual charge (£35)
2 the extra figure necessary to bring the accumulated depreciation at the beginning of year 2 up to what it would have been if the current (end of year 2) RC had been prevailing earlier (£5).

Thus we have a credit of £40 to depreciation provision, a debit of £35 to P&L account, and a debit of £5 to – well, where?

Since the £5 relates in effect to the correction of what we now know with hindsight to have been under-depreciation in earlier years, one possibility would seem to be to reduce the accumulated revenue reserves figure brought forward – like a prior year adjustment. On the other hand, the earlier years' accounts were certainly correct at that time with the matching convention properly applied in the then current circumstances. It could be argued that the problem of this backlog adjustment is covered by the existence and recording of holdings gains. Therefore the £5 could be 'charged to' holding gain account. This last argument is usually followed. This would give year 2 balance sheet entries as follows in our example:

Fixed asset	RC		140
	Depreciation		70
	NBV		70
Holding gain reserve	b/f	20	
	add	20	
	less	5	35

Current entry values, a preliminary appraisal

Activity 8

Prepare a list, in point form, of advantages and disadvantages which you think could reasonably be said to apply to current entry value accounting.

Activity 8 feedback

Possible, but not necessarily exhaustive suggestions are as follows:

Advantages

1 It provides more information in that it splits the total profit into holding gains and operating profit. This permits better appraisal of earlier actions, and provides more useful data for decision-making purposes.
2 By permitting holding gains to be excluded from reported profit, it allows for a proper maintenance of operating capacity – the 'business substance'.
3 It provides a balance sheet based on current value, on figures relevant to the date of the balance sheet.
4 It is consistent with accounting concepts – if holding gains are excluded from reported profit it is more prudent than HC.
5 Holding gains are recognized and reported when they occur.
6 Comparisons over time, and performance analysis, are more valid and meaningful.
7 It is practicable, it has been shown to be feasible in practical application.

Disadvantages

1 It requires more subjectivity (or arbitrary choice between different available indices). It is therefore less 'auditable'.
2 It requires the use of replacement cost figures for assets that the firm does not intend, or perhaps could not possibly, replace.
3 It still fails to give an indication either of the current market value of most assets in their present state, or of the business as a whole.
4 It fails to take account of general inflation, of changes in the purchasing power of money.

You may recall from the array of value concepts analysed by Edwards and Bell (see p. 39) that they suggested that two different concepts of current entry value were worthy of more detailed consideration. They named and defined these as:

1 *Present cost* – the cost currently of acquiring the asset being valued.
2 *Current cost* – the cost currently of acquiring the inputs which the firm used to produce the asset being valued.

So far in this chapter we have ignored this distinction. We would suggest, broadly following the thinking of Edwards and Bell themselves, that the route to making a rational choice between them lies in remembering the underlying arguments for using current entry values in the first place. As we saw in Activity 4 we are seeking the maintenance of the capacity to replace the resources of the business. We are therefore seeking to ensure the continued long-run operation of the business. The approach we need to adopt, therefore, is that which accords with the expected operations of the firm in the ordinary course of its business. Given that the going concern convention applies, and given that the firm is going to continue operations in the long run, it is clear that current cost rather than present cost (both as defined above) will better reflect the reality of transactions and economic events in most cases. To a firm in business to manufacture motorcars and aiming for long-run operations as a manufacturer of motorcars, it is the cost of the replacement inputs which it needs to manufacture motorcars which is the relevant data to ensure the maintenance of operating capacity. The cost to a manufacturer of motorcars of buying in complete motorcars (at present cost) is not normally an operationally relevant figure.

So it is argued that current cost is normally the appropriate current entry value to use, on the grounds of its relevance to normal ongoing business operations. It follows, however, that where this justification ceases to be true, because, for example, the inputs are no longer available, then the conclusion may well no longer be correct. If the firm would as a matter of expected action (not merely should as a matter of efficient management) replace an asset in a more complete state than with the previous raw components, then the appropriate present cost should be used instead.

It could be suggested that in arguing for the relevance of current cost as a useful entry value measure leading to the practical maintenance of operational capability, we are failing to follow properly the logic of the arguments put forward. The essence of the whole thinking is that a firm should charge as an expense the costs of replacing the resources used or consumed. Past (historic) costs are useless for this purpose. But what is theoretically needed is obviously the amount that *will* have to be paid for the replacement items at the time when they are replaced. The *current* cost may or may not be identical to the actual cost when replacement eventually occurs. In many cases current cost will be the same as expected actual cost. But if it is not, should we make some adjustment?

Theoretically, at least from the viewpoint of the income statement and capital maintenance in the operating sense, the answer seems to be yes. But there are at least two arguments against this. The first is the essentially practical one that a considerably greater degree of subjectivity is introduced which may more than outweigh the theoretical advantages. The second argument is that there are perhaps implications for the matching principle and the balance sheet. A current entry value balance sheet can be argued as being consistent within itself, giving proper additivity in the mathematical sense. But a future entry value balance sheet, with the timing implications of the word future being different for different items, is of more suspect validity. And since today's asset figure affects next period's results there are possible implications for future periods too.

Summary

In this chapter we have explored the logic of using current entry values for the preparation of accounting results, analysed the effects and usefulness of the additional information derived, related the approach to capital maintenance, and prepared and interpreted current entry value information.

The main advantages of current entry value accounting lie in its effects on the profit and loss account information given. It can be argued as giving more effective application of the matching and accruals conventions (*current* costs against current revenues), and, through its long-run economically rational capital maintenance concept, of the going-concern convention. It provides important information, at minimum, about those elements of historic cost profit which do not represent increases in economic wealth (given continuing operation). As regards the balance sheet it gives figures based on up-to-date market numbers. However the approach is still clearly to determine profit and loss figures and then to 'stick what is left' in the balance sheet. The balance sheet is still essentially a statement of unexpired expenses, not a list of marketable assets at valuation.

Exercises

1 Explain and demonstrate how RC accounting affects reported profit as compared with HC.
2 Is RC more or less prudent than HC?
3 Which holding gains should be reported as:
   (a) realized
   (b) part of profit
   (c) distributable
   under an RC system? Why?
4 Discuss the problem of back-log depreciation.
5 I.M. Confused, computer dealer.
   From the following information compute
   (a) Profit and loss accounts and closing balance sheets for each of the years 20X1 and 20X2 under historical cost principles.
   (b) Profit and loss accounts and closing balance sheets for each of the years 20X1 and 20X2 under current replacement cost principles.
   Comment briefly on the significance of the results.

Date	Event relating to trading in computers	'Wealth' Computers	£ cash
01/01/X1	Set up business with £10 000 in the bank		10 000
02/01/X1	Buy six computers for £1000 each	6	4 000
01/05/X1	Sell two for £1500 each (RC = £1100)	4	7 000
01/09/X1	Buy two computers for £1200 each	6	4 600
01/10/X1	Pay annual rent of £600	6	4 000
31/12/X1	Financial year-end. Pay tax of £200	6	3 800
03/03/X2	Sell two computers for £1800 each (RC = 1300)	4	7 400
01/10/X2	Pay annual rent £700	4	6 700
01/11/X2	Buy two computers for £1 400 each	6	3 900
31/12/X2	Financial year-end. Pay tax £450	6	3 450

6 Mallard Ltd was formed on 1 January 20X1 with 10 000 issued £1 ordinary shares.
   The same day they obtained a 12% loan of £8000 and bought fixed assets for £9000.
   During 20X1 their purchases and sales of widgets were as follows:

	Purchases		Sales	
3 January	100 at £80	8 000		
1 February			60 at £120	7 200
1 April	110 at £75	8 250		
1 May			90 at £120	10 800
1 July	100 at £85	8 500		
1 August			130 at £120	15 600
1 October	120 at £90	10 800		
1 November			110 at £130	14 300

   (a) Purchases and sales were all paid for in cash.
   (b) The loan interest was paid early in the following year (20X2).
   (c) The buying price of widgets changed on 1 March, 1 June, 1 September and on 1 December (when it was £100).
   (d) The fixed assets are to be depreciated at 10% p.a. At 31 December 20X1 their buying price was £12 600.
   (e) General expenses during the year were £13 200.
      (i) Prepare a balance sheet as at 31 December, 20X1 together with a trading and profit and loss account for the year to 31 December 20X1, on replacement cost lines.

      (ii) What are holding gains? In what circumstances are they distributable?

7 *L and H*

On 1 January, L and H each started a business by investing £100 in cash, and then immediately purchasing one widget.

L sold her widget on 3 March for £110, but on 1 April discovered that she needed to pay this to buy another, which she did.

On 30 June this was sold for £120, and a new one bought on July for £120.

On 29 September this was sold for £130, and a replacement purchased on 30 September for £130.

H had been less active and had merely kept his first widget and read the newspaper.

Both have decided to adopt 30 September as their accounting date, and come to you for accounting services.

All widgets are identical.

(a) How would the above appear under
    (i) historic cost
    (ii) replacement cost.

(b) Which results make more sense, and why?

8 *Stan and Oliver*

On 1 January, Stan and Oliver each started a business by investing £100 in cash, and then immediately purchasing one widget, which at that date could have been resold for £120.

Stan sold his widget on 31 March for £130, but on 1 April discovered that he needed to pay £115 to buy another, which he did.

On 30 June this was sold for £140, and a new one bought on 1 July for £125.

On 29 September this was sold for £150, and a replacement purchased on 30 September for £130, on which date the new one could have been sold for £160.

Oliver had been less active and had merely kept his first widget and read the newspaper.

Both have decided to adopt 30 September as their accounting date, and come to you for accounting services.

All widgets are identical.

Replacement costs changed on 31 March, 30 June, 29 September.

How would the above appear under:

(a) historic cost
(b) replacement cost
(c) net realizable value

(Note: You may find it helpful to do this by using a table with each date on the left and columns for Cash, Stock, Profit, Holding Gains, etc. across the top.)

9 (a) Thomas started in business with capital of £4600. He bought a machine on 1 January 20X2 for £3600. The machine has an expected life of ten years and a nil residual value. On 31 December 20X2 the replacement cost of the machine is £4000. On 1 January 20X1 Thomas bought 100 components at £10 each and sold 80 of these for cash on 31 December 20X2 for £20 each, on which date the replacement cost was £15.

    You are required to prepare historical cost and replacement cost profit and loss accounts and balance sheets for the financial year-ended 31 December 20X2, and show your workings. Ignore taxation. (8 marks)

(b) **Explain the disadvantages of replacement cost accounting.**

(c) 'Petrol retailers raised petrol pump prices from midnight after increases in the Rotterdam spot market for oil prices. An energy spokesperson said the petrol pump increases were unjustified because petrol now being sold to motorists had been bought before oil prices rose.'
    Comment (6 marks)

                                       (14 marks)
                                         (ACCA)

6

Current exit value and mixed values

After reading this chapter you should be able to:
- explain the effects and implications of using current exit values to record the possession and usage of economic resources
- outline the implications of using an *ad hoc* mixture of valuation methods
- define and explain the effects and implications of deprival values as the basis of recording the possession and usage of economic resources
- discuss the overall relevance of current values.

Introduction

In this chapter we look first of all at remaining current values worthy of consideration, current output or exit values. We then explore the possibility of using a combination of different valuation methods in preparing financial reports, and in particular the concept of deprival value. In each case, as in earlier chapters, we seek to investigate both the techniques and logic of calculation, and the meaning and usefulness of the resulting information.

Current exit value accounting

Edwards and Bell suggested two current exit value concepts as worthy of consideration (see p. 41). These were current values and opportunity costs. Current values they defined as 'values actually realized during the current period for goods or services sold'. On reflection, however, it quickly becomes apparent that the idea of substituting current values so defined into our basic equation of $W_1 + P - D = W_2$ does not make a great deal of sense. Values actually realized for goods and services already sold cannot obviously be argued as relevant to resources still possessed at the date or dates under consideration. Rather, of course, these realized values are the basis of revenue flows.

It is the second concept, that of opportunity costs, which we need to develop. Edwards and Bell defined this as 'values that could currently be realized if assets were sold (without further processing) outside the firm at the best prices immediately obtainable'. This is certainly a concept relevant to the resources possessed at the date under consideration. It shows the amount of money we could derive immediately (currently) from the resources held, or to take the alternative viewpoint it shows the amount of money we choose not to derive immediately if we retain the resources for any reason. We can adapt the application of the definition slightly to allow for further unavoidable processing or expenses of disposal, and consider the concept of net realizable value (NRV), i.e. the proceeds after deducting these additional unavoidable expenses of disposal. These ideas are explored further below.

We intend to base our valuation figure on the current market selling price, more precisely on NRV. So if an asset could be sold for £250, but the sale would involve £10 of selling expenses, the NRV is £240. The income under this method is based on the difference between the NRV of all resources at the two chosen dates. Following Edwards and Bell, it is often referred to as realizable income. It can be defined as follows:

$$Y_r = D + (R_e - R_s)$$

where Y_r is the exit value income, D is the distributions (less new capital inputs), R_e is the NRV of the assets at the end of the period and R_s is the NRV of the assets at the start of the period.

In practice, several possibilities exist as to exactly what we mean by NRV.

Activity 1

Consider an item of work in progress that has an NRV today of £10 in its existing state. The finished product (which would require a further £4 of expenses) has an NRV today of £20, but by the time the actual item of current work in progress is finished and sold, it is expected to have an NRV of £22. On a forced sale (e.g. if all the assets have to be sold off at once by a liquidator), the item in its existing state would realize £6.

Suggest possible figures for the exit value, and which one you would normally find it most useful to use.

Activity 1 feedback

Possible figures for the exit value would seem to include £6, £10, £(20 – 4) and £(22 – 4). It is generally agreed that exit values should refer to assets in their existing state, on the assumption that they are sold in an orderly manner, i.e. in the normal course of business. Thus in the above example the exit value for the work in progress would be £10.

It is clear that the exit value capital (R) at any particular date shows the amount of money that the business *could* obtain from its assets as on that date. Turning this round, exit value is seen as an opportunity cost concept – it shows the amount of cash that the business could obtain if it did not keep the asset. The opportunity cost of having an asset is the amount of cash the business sacrifices by retaining the asset instead. Advocates of exit value accounting argue that it is necessary to know the cash resources tied up in a business in order to measure efficiency. The amount of cash potentially available – the 'current cash equivalent' of the resources of a business – also provides a genuinely common measuring unit when comparing different businesses. It is often argued – indeed often merely stated – that exit value accounting does not conform to the going concern convention. Its advocates argue that it is not intended to show what will happen, rather it is intended to show the results of what could happen, in order to assist decision-making and internal appraisal.

We can usefully divide the exit value income (Y_r) into four elements:

$Y_r =$ realized operating gains
+ unrealized operating gains $\quad\Big\}$ i.e. on assets held for resale
+ realized non-operating gains
+ unrealized non-operating gains $\quad\Big\}$ i.e. on assets held for use

Before looking at an example, it is important to understand the effect of exit value accounting on the P&L account. Since the opening and closing balance sheets are now value based, and not cost based, it necessarily follows that the P&L account is also value based and not cost based. For example 'depreciation' is no longer a process of cost allocation under the matching convention. It simply becomes the loss in value of the asset in the period. This is such a fundamental change that it would be better to invent a different word, but unfortunately nobody has yet done so.

Now work through the following example. Remember particularly that an unrealized gain in year 1, reported as such, will become a realized gain in a later year and will need to be reported as a realized gain. Care is needed to ensure that gains are not reported twice, as both unrealized and realized. This of course would be double counting.

Example

A company commences business with capital in cash of £15 000. It buys a fixed asset for £10 000. The following information is available:

	Year 1 £		Year 2 £	
NRV of fixed asset	6 000		4 000	
Sales	20 000		25 000	
Cost of sales	11 000		12 000	
Closing stocks: cost	2 000		3 000	
NRV	2 500		3 800	
Exit value revenue statements				
Sales	20 000		25 000	
Cost of sales	11 000		12 000	
	9 000		13 000	
'Depreciation'	4 000	(1)	2 000	(2)
	5 000		11 000	
less Operating gain included in previous year	—		500	(3)
	5 000		10 500	
add Unrealized operating gain	500	(4)	800	(5)
Realizable income	5 500		11 300	
Exit value balance sheets				
Fixed assets	6 000		4 000	
Stock	2 500		3 800	
Cash	12 000	(6)	24 000	(7)
	20 500		31 800	
Capital	15 000		15 000	
Realizable income	5 500		16 800	
	20 500		31 800	

Notes

1 10 000 – 6000

2 6000 – 4000

3 Included as realized in the 11 000, but already included, as unrealized, in the 5500 for year 1

4 2500 – 2000

5 3800 – 3000

6 15 000 – 10 000 + 20 000 – (11 000 + 2000)

7 12 000 + 25 000 – (12 000 + 1000)

The unrealized gain on stocks is here calculated on an annual basis, stocks during the year being left at cost. It would be possible, although more complicated, to record such unrealized gains more frequently – even daily if desired. Care must be taken, however, to ensure that a previously recorded unrealized gain is not again added into 'realizable income' when it is realized.

Now try the following activity, making a proper attempt before looking at the feedback which follows.

Activity 2

Bonds plc commenced business on 1 January year 7. Let us assume all transactions are by cheque and no credit is given or taken and that Bonds plc deals only in one type of item of stock.

1 January Year 7
Introduced capital of £25 000 and purchased a machine for £9000.
Purchased 500 items of stock for £15 each.

31 December Year 7
Sold 300 items of stock for £30 each.
Paid rent and rates for the year of £1000.
Paid other expenses for the year of £1000.

1 January Year 8
Purchased 400 items of stock for £17 each.

31 December Year 8
Sold 500 items of stock for £33 each.
Paid rent and rates for the year of £1100.
Paid expenses for the year of £1200.

The following information relates to the machine:

	31.12.7 £	31.12.8 £
Replacement cost	10 000	12 000
Realizable value	8 000	6 000
Cost of realization	1 000	1 000

Required:
Produce a set of realizable value accounts for year 7 and year 8.

Activity 2 feedback

Bonds plc Trading and P&L account for the year-ended 31 December

		31.12.7		31.12.8
		£		£
Sales		9 000		16 500
Less cost of sales		(4 500)		(8 100)
Gross profit		4 500		8 400
Rent and rates	1 000		1 100	
Expenses	1 000		1 200	
Depreciation (note (2))	2 000		2 000	
		(4 000)		(4 300)
Gross profit		500		4 100
Holding gain (note (3))		3 000		(1 400)
		3 500		2 700

Balance sheet as at 31 December:

		31.12.7		31.12.8
		£		£
Fixed assets				
Machine at NRV		7 000		5 000
Current assets				
Stock at NRV (note (1))	6 000		3 300	
Bank	15 500		22 900	
		21 500		26 200
		28 500		31 200
Share capital		25 000		25 000
Profit for year		3 500		6 200
		28 500		31 200

Notes

1 *Stock*. The stock is also brought into the balance sheet at the end of each year at its net realizable value.

31.12.7 200 units × £30 = £6000
31.12.8 100 units × £33 = £3300

2 *Depreciation*. The depreciation is the difference between the NRV of the asset at the end of each year less the NRV of the asset at the beginning of the year. Note that the NRV is after deducting the costs of realizing the asset.

Year 1   £7000   £9000
Year 2   £5000   £7000

3 *Holding gain.* In year 7 the holding gain is the unrealized holding gain on the closing stock:

$$200 \text{ units} \times £15 \text{ (i.e. } £30 - £15) = £3000$$

In year 8 the holding gain of year 7 has now been realized (and therefore included in the trading account for year 8) whilst there is an unrealized holding gain on the closing stock of:

$$100 \text{ units} \times £16 \text{ (i.e. } £33 - £17) = £ 1600$$

Therefore, in year 8 the holding gain (loss) is:

	£
Unrealized holding gain in year 8	1600
less: unrealized holding gain from year 7 now realized in year 8	3000
	(1400)

In effect we have a holding loss.

Current exit values, a preliminary appraisal

> ### Activity 3
>
> Prepare a list, in point form, of advantages and disadvantages which you think could reasonably be said to apply to current exit value accounting.

Activity 3 feedback

Advantages

1 It follows the economic 'opportunity cost' principle. It reveals the money sacrifice being made by *keeping* an asset. This permits rational decision-making on the alternative uses of resources.
2 Exit values facilitate comparisons. They provide a genuinely common measure for the value of assets – cash or current cash equivalent.
3 The concept of realizable value is easy for the non-accountant to understand.
4 Useful information about assets is provided to outsiders, e.g. creditors.
5 It is already widely used, e.g. debtors, stocks at lower of historical cost (HC) and NRV, revaluation of land and buildings.

Disadvantages

1 It is highly subjective. Arguably more so than replacement cost (RC) accounting.
2 It fails to follow the going concern assumption, fails to recognize that firms do not usually sell all their assets (the proponents of exit value accounting explicitly deny this charge, arguing that it makes no assumptions either way, it merely provides useful information).

3 It fails to concentrate attention on long-run operational effectiveness.
4 It fails to give realistic information about the internal usefulness of assets – particularly of highly specialized assets that could have a very low NRV on the general market.

You may of course have some slightly different views. One point we should certainly consider is the possible relevance of expected values, which Edwards and Bell suggested to be a concept worth further exploration. They defined expected values (see p. 41) as 'values expected to be received in the future for output sold according to the firm's planned course of action'. Expected values are therefore a future exit rather than a current exit way of thinking. Expected values defined in this way certainly give useful information. In fact they form the raw material for the preparation of both cash and revenue budget statements. However our essential purpose here is to prepare statements of current position, and similar arguments apply to those already considered in relation to future entry values (see p. 40). To use future exit values would introduce greater subjectivity, greater possible inconsistency of evaluation, and could be argued as failing to reflect current reality. Current exit values are suggested as a more useful concept.

It is essential to remember that exit value NRV accounting tends to focus on the balance sheet to a considerably greater extent than current entry value RC accounting. Profit or gain is very much determined by a consideration of changes in output values of resources. The balance sheet under NRV can be regarded as a consistent statement, with all figures on the same basis and as at the same date. This balance sheet is not just a list of 'balances left over' in the sense that a current entry value balance sheet is (see Chapter 5). However, it follows from this that it is the profit and loss calculation which in a sense picks up and contains 'the figures lying around'. Current exit value is essentially a short run concept. It provides valuable information about market values of business resources, and therefore about short-term alternatives and possibilities. This is clearly seen in the capital maintenance concept associated with NRV. This could be expressed as: the maintenance of the NRV, the current cash equivalent, of the resources of the business. But exit value accounting information does not provide us with the information necessary for management to seek to ensure the long-run operational capability of the business.

Mixed values – *ad hoc* methods

As we shall see in detail later on (Chapter 13), companies in the UK have a great deal of flexibility in practice as regards the valuation policy they wish to adopt. There is no requirement for any consistency of approach as between one asset and another. It is in fact extremely common for businesses which broadly follow historical cost accounting principles to revalue some of their fixed assets at intervals (not necessarily annually), sometimes then depreciating on the revalued figure, sometimes not depreciating at all. This may well lead to the provision of more useful information as regards particular resources. For example a current or recent valuation of land or factory is surely more useful than a 50-year-old cost figure. But of course it further increases the inconsistencies within the accounting reports as a whole, making the balance sheet as a statement of resources and the sources thereof ever more difficult to understand, usually influencing the size of expense figures charged, and certainly influencing any interpretational ratios relating return with the resource base being employed.

A particularly apposite example is the statement of accounting policies from the Annual Report and Accounts of the Institute of Chartered Accountants in England and Wales of a

I Convention
The financial statements are prepared under the historical cost convention as modified to include the revaluation of certain assets as detailed below. These statements have been prepared in accordance with applicable Statements of Standard Accounting Practice and having regard to proposed Statements of Standard Accounting Practice. They have also been prepared in accordance with relevant presentational requirements of the Companies Act 1985.

II Freehold property
The freehold properties, Chartered Accountants' Hall, London and Gloucester House, Milton Keynes are stated at their valuations made by Messrs Richard Ellis, Chartered Surveyors, at 31 December 1990 on an open market existing use basis.

After taking advice, Council considers, that the remaining useful life of Chartered Accountants' Hall and Gloucester House will be at least fifty years and twenty five years respectively. Accordingly depreciation is provided on the average of the valuations of the buildings at the beginning and end of the accounting period at 2% on Chartered Accountants' Hall and 4% on Gloucester House. In previous years the depreciation of Chartered Accountants' Hall was based on the value of the whole property, and a remaining useful life of fifty years, with a depreciation rate of 2%, was assumed for both properties.

A transfer is made annually to the Accumulated Fund of the element of the Revaluation Reserve which is deemed to have been realized as a result of the annual depreciation charge.

III Silver collection and antiques
The Institute's silver collection, rare books, period furniture, pictures and sculpture are stated at estimated current replacement cost valuations made by:
Professor Gerald Benney (the Benney silver collection)
William Walter Antiques Limited (other silver)
Messrs Roger McCrow Rare Books (rare books)
Mr Ernest G Albone (period furniture, pictures and sculpture)
In view of the nature of these assets no depreciation is provided.

IV Furniture, computers, and equipment
Items of furniture, computers, and equipment costing more than £5,000 are stated at historical cost. Depreciation is calculated on a straight line basis over the estimated useful lives of the assets ranging from three to ten years. Items costing £5,000 or less are written off to the Revenue Account.

V Leased equipment
Payments in respect of operating lease agreements (being agreements not giving rights approximating to ownership) have been charged to the Revenue Account on a straight line basis.

VI Investments
(a) *Fixed asset investments*
Fixed asset investments are stated at cost and represent holdings in subsidiary companies which the Institute does not intend to dispose of in the foreseeable future.
(b) *Current investments*
British Government securities and sterling fixed and floating interest securities held as short-term investments are included in current assets at market value. Variations in their year-end value are dealt with through the Revenue Account.

VII Stocks
Stocks, including work-in-progress, are valued at the lower of cost and net realizable value.

VIII Policy development costs
The initial costs of policy development in relation to new regulatory functions are treated as pre-payments to be recovered, in not more than three years, from the fees chargeable to Members for authorisation to practice in the areas concerned.

IX Pension fund
The Institute operates a pension scheme providing benefits based on final pensionable pay. The assets of this scheme are held in a separate trustee administered fund. Contributions to the scheme are charged to the Revenue Account so as to spread the cost of pensions over employees' working lives with the Institute.

X Deferred taxation
Deferred taxation is provided on unrealized gains on current investments reduced by expenditure charged to the Revenue Account which will be deductible for corporation tax purposes in future years. The main items of such expenditure are Staff Pensions Fund contributions (note 15), and capital expenditure.

Figure 6.1
Accounting
policies

XI Repairs provision
A provision for repairs was maintained to cover major items of expenditure likely to be incurred in the foreseeable future. The balance of the provision has been released to the Revenue Account.

few years ago. This is reproduced complete as Fig. 6.1. This seems to have virtually everything in it – historical cost, market value together with notional transfers of 'realized' depreciation on the same assets, current replacement cost without depreciation, not to mention costs of policy development as an asset and provisions for future repairs now released to revenue. In economic terms, what does the balance sheet total of 'total assets less current liabilities' really mean?

Mixed values – deprival value

A much more theoretically defensible approach to the idea of using different valuation bases for different assets, or more accurately for using different valuation bases for assets in different circumstances, is the concept of deprival value.

Assume that a business owns an asset. What is that asset 'worth' to the business? The deprival value (DV) approach says that the DV of an asset is the loss that the rational businessman or businesswoman would suffer if he or she were deprived of the asset. This loss will depend on what would rationally have been done with the asset if he or she had not lost (been deprived of) it.

Activity 4

Six people, A to F, are possessors and owners of six assets, U to Z, respectively. The various monetary evaluations (in £) of each asset by its owner are shown in the following table:

Person	Asset	HC	RC	NRV	EV
A	U	1	2	3	4
B	V	5	6	8	7
C	W	9	12	10	11
D	X	16	15	14	13
E	Y	17	19	20	18
F	Z	23	22	21	24

All six people signed a contract with an insurance agent, Miss Prue Dential, under which they shall be reimbursed, in the event of loss of their assets, by 'the amount of money a rationally acting person will actually have lost as a result of losing the asset'.

Put yourself in the position of the rationally acting person, decide what *action* you would take in each circumstance, and then calculate the net effect on your monetary position.

Activity 4 feedback

In each situation the first question to ask is: Would the rationally acting businessman or businesswoman replace the asset or not? He or she will replace it if the proceeds of *either* selling it (NRV), *or* using it (economic value, EV) are higher than the costs of replacing it. If it is going to be replaced, then the loss suffered is clearly the cost of replacement. Thus, in situations where the rationally acting businessman or businesswoman would replace the asset, DV is RC. If he or she would not replace it then the loss suffered is given by the value of the benefits that *would have derived* from the asset but which he or she will now never receive. Being rational, the intention must have been to act so as to derive the high-

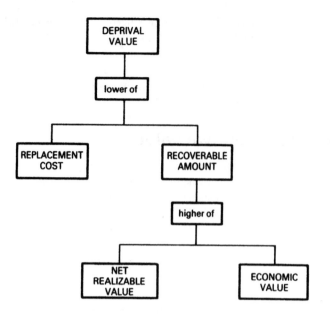

Figure 6.2
Relationship
between DV, RC,
NRV and EV.

est possible return, i.e. the higher of NRV and economic value (EV). Therefore, in situations where the rationally acting businessman or businesswoman would not replace the asset if deprived of it, DV is the higher of NRV and EV. This last element, the higher of NRV and EV, is known as the 'recoverable amount'.

So we can formally state that DV is the lower of RC and recoverable amount, where recoverable amount is the higher of NRV and EV (see Fig. 6.2). Given three different concepts (RC, NRV and EV) there are in fact only six possible different rankings:

EV	>	NRV	>	RC
NRV	>	EV	>	RC
RC	>	EV	>	NRV
RC	>	NRV	>	EV
NRV	>	RC	>	EV
EV	>	RC	>	NRV

The example contains all six of these alternatives. The DV in each situation is as follows:

Person	DV	Reason
A	2	Cost of replacement
B	6	Cost of replacement
C	11	EV not received
D	14	Realizable value not received
E	19	Cost of replacement
F	22	Cost of replacement

Make sure that you understand why, in the context of the logic of the DV definition (and notice the irrelevance of the HC figures).

Deprival value (DV) – an appraisal

DV formed the basis of the recommendations of the Sandilands Report, i.e. of **current cost accounting**. Because the DV arguably takes account of the intentions, or at least the logical actions of the business concerned, it is often termed the 'value to the business' of an asset. It is this latter term that was usually used by the Accounting Standards Committee (ASC).

Value to the business was defined by the ASC in Statement of Standard Accounting Practice SSAP 16 in a slightly different way, but the effect is that the two expressions mean the same:

42   The value to the business is:
   (a)   net current replacement cost;
         or, if a permanent diminution to below net current replacement cost has been recognized,
   (b)   recoverable amount.

43   The recoverable amount is the greater of the net realizable value of an asset and, where applicable, the amount recoverable from its further use.

What about capital maintenance? Profit is here being regarded as the excess after maintaining the 'value to the business' of its assets. The value to the business is clearly seen to be related to actual operations (what the business would do). Following from this, we can say that DV seeks to maintain the business' capacity to do things, usually expressed as the **operating capacity** or **operating capability**. We saw above that in four of the six possible rankings, DV equals RC. In the practical business situation, the chances of replacement cost being higher than both NRV and EV will generally be relatively small, so the other two rankings will in practice not occur frequently. This means that in a practical business context, DV usually comes back to RC.

Theoretically therefore it can be suggested that deprival value provides an improvement and refinement on current replacement cost accounting. It reduces itself to replacement cost when the economically logical action is to replace, and uses the more relevant benefit foregone figure in those situations where replacement would logically not occur. Notice of course that it is not strictly a completely *current* concept at all, as the EV possibility is a future orientation. Another way to look at the implications of the above discussions would be to take the more practical line of arguing that deprival value shows that replacement cost is relevant most of the time. In other words deprival value thinking positively explores the possibilities of refining replacement cost thinking, and shows that in most situations the refinements introduce difficulty and subjectivity, for very little benefit in terms of extra relevance of information.

As a final thought, what about additivity? Is deprival value a separate concept, leading to a balance sheet consistently valued in deprival terms? Or is deprival value merely a formula for choosing which of the three (RC, NRV, EV) valuation bases to use in any particular situation? Under the latter way of thinking deprival value obviously leads to a variety of bases in the balance sheet and therefore to a lack of additivity.

Activity 5

Prepare a list, in point form, of advantages and disadvantages which you think could reasonably be said to apply to deprival value accounting.

Activity 5 feedback

Advantages

1 All of the advantages of RC accounting can be claimed here also.
2 As a 'mixed value' system it is more realistic and relevant than either RC or NRV. It values resources at RC if it is profitable to replace them and at the expected proceeds if they would not be replaced.

Disadvantages

1 Disadvantages **1**, **3** and **4** of RC accounting can be claimed here too.
2 It is more subjective than RC.
3 If the balance sheet is expressed in 'mixed values', what do the asset and capital employed totals mean? Can mixed values be validly added at all?
4 Firms are not in practice being continually deprived of their assets.

Current values, some overall thoughts

Later in this section we summarize and explore the practical proposals made in recent years, although we still have some further issues of principle to explore first. However we have now finished our review of the major 'pure' concepts of valuation. In Chapter 3 we revised and developed the traditional historical cost model. This is backwards looking and relatively objective (remember the relatively!). In Chapter 4 we considered the thinking of important economists in this area, the psychic theories of Fisher – unmeasurable in money terms by very definition but properly recognizing that only human beings take decisions, and that they are the ultimate consumers, and the more quantifiable work of Hicks with its important capital maintenance implications. These economic-based ideas are properly forward-looking and logically relevant to the decision-making process, but they are highly subjective. Current values lie in the middle of this spectrum both in terms of their time relationship (in between past and future), and in terms of their degrees of objectivity/subjectivity. In this sense they are clearly worth exploring as a compromise between relevance and verifiability.

There are stronger claims that can be made, however. The usual financial reporting statements essentially claim to report on the position at a (current) date and on the results ending on that date. Current values can properly claim to provide information consistent with this approach. The question follows, of course, which current value? The discussions in this and the previous chapter suggest that each of the suggested bases has particular merits. All of them provide useful information. All of them give good and relevant answers to *some* questions. One obvious suggestion to follow from this is that the preferable method in any situation depends on the particular situation itself – in other words the abstract question 'Which is the best method?' has no answer and indeed is simply a silly question. We should be prepared to use different valuation methods and different reporting methods for different purposes.

A second suggestion is a thought for you to take away and think about. The practice and application of double-entry channels us unthinkingly into the assumption that the balance sheet and the income statement are two elements in the same system, and that they therefore have to be fully compatible with each other. But our basic purpose is to produce meaningful reports, and there is no logical reason why they should be in any way constrained by data recording systems. Perhaps we should consider producing smaller more *ad hoc* statements, using *combinations* of valuation bases depending on the purpose of each statement.

Summary

In this chapter we have analysed the logic and implications of current exit value accounting and prepared accounting statements on a current exit (NRV) basis. We then explored the possibility of *ad hoc* mixtures within the framework of traditional accounting reports, and analysed the logic and implications of deprival value accounting. Finally, we asked ourselves to consider the usefulness of current values generally and individually.

Exercises

1 Explain the principles of exit value accounting, providing a simple made-up illustration.
2 Explain the principles of deprival value accounting, providing a simple made-up illustration.
3 Discuss the proposition that businesses should be required to publish their P&L statement on replacement cost lines and their balance sheet on net realizable lines.
4 Deprival value removes significant disadvantages of replacement cost, whilst retaining its advantages. Discuss.
5 (a) **Briefly describe the current value exit model of income measurement and asset valuation (also known as realizable value accounting).**

(10 marks)

(b) **What are said to be the advantages of the current value exit model?**

(10 marks)

(20 marks)

(ACCA)

6 (a) **Provide a definition of the deprival value of an asset.**   (2 marks)

(b) **For a particular asset, suppose the three bases of valuation relevant to the calculation of its deprival value are (in thousands of pounds): £12, £10 and £8. Construct a matrix of columns and rows showing all the possible alternative situations and, in each case, indicate the appropriate deprival value.**

(6 marks)

(c) **Justify the use of deprival value as a method of asset valuation, using the matrix in (b) above to illustrate your answer.**   (12 marks)

(20 marks)

(ACCA)

7 Steward plc commences business on 1 January year 1. Let us assume all transactions are by cheque and no credit is given nor taken and that Steward deals only in one type of item of stock.

1 January Year 1
Introduced capital of £30 000.
Purchased machine for £10 000.
Purchased 1000 items of stock for £10 each.

31 December Year 1
Sold 800 items of stock for £15 each.
Paid expenses for the year of £1000.
The NRV of the machine is £9000.

1 January Year 2
Purchased 800 items of stock for £13 each.

31 December Year 2
Sold 500 items of stock for £20 each.
Paid expenses for the year of £1200.
The NRV of the machine is £8000.

Produce profit and loss accounts and balance sheets relating to years 1 and 2 using NRV accounting.

8 (a) **Give a brief summary of the current value replacement cost accounting system (entry values).**   (6 marks)
   (b) **Give a brief summary of the current value net realizable value accounting system (exit values).**   (6 marks)
   (c) **To what extent to do you consider it would be useful to prepare financial statements which used entry values for the profit and loss account and exit values for the balance sheet and why?**   (8 marks)
                                                                    (20 marks)
                                                                       (ACCA)

9 **With regard to income measurement and the maintenance of capital, explain the main differences between the traditional accounting income model, the economic income model and the current value income model.**

                                                                    (20 marks)
                                                                       (ACCA)

7

Current purchasing power accounting

After reading this chapter you should be able to:
- explain the concept of general inflation and its implications for accounting measurement
- explain the mechanisms for taking account of general inflation in financial reporting especially, but not exclusively, in the context of historical cost accounting
- discuss theoretical arguments, and practical considerations, for and against current purchasing power accounting.

Introduction

In our discussions so far we have considered various methods of 'putting a monetary figure on something'. There are many ways of deriving a figure with a £ sign in front that we must consider and appraise. But we have not yet stopped to consider what we mean by the £ sign. What is a pound? It is a unit of money – and money is of no use by itself. Money has no intrinsic value. Its value is related to what we can get with it, what we can do with it. When most prices are rising, then we can obtain gradually less and less with any given number of pounds. This means that if, under any particular valuation basis, we have maintained our capital appropriately defined in terms of numbers of pounds, we have not necessarily maintained our capital in terms of the purchasing power of those pounds. **Current purchasing power** (CPP) accounting attempts to take account of this.

The measuring unit problem

There are many examples of difficulties with measuring units, particularly in the UK. Litres and gallons, or inches and centimetres are classic examples. But in these cases the use of different measuring units may be a nuisance, but the problems are capable of rapid and objective solution. An inch has a precise or standard specification. A centimetre has a precise or standard specification. It follows of course that the relationship between the two also has a precise or standard specification. We can very exactly convert one to the other, and, even more significantly, the conversion factor is fixed and constant between different people, between different places, and between different times.

None of this is true of money as a measuring unit. A unit of money is an artificial construct. It is related to spending power, and spending patterns, and these are personal and individual. It follows that a unit of money is not fixed as between different people, is not fixed between different places, and, crucially for accounting, it is not fixed between different times. We need a conversion factor between our altering measuring units. But since our units (pounds) are not fixed in inherent valuation, it follows that the conversion factor cannot be fixed either. The solution (or evasion) which current purchasing power provides to this problem is to use averages as an approximate surrogate for the theoretically unique conversion factor required. The pound is converted, or adjusted, by means of general indices.

Current purchasing power

It is vital to understand that current purchasing power (CPP) is a general purchasing power concept. We are concerned with general inflation, usually expressed as the average rise in the cost of living, i.e. with inflation in the politicians' sense. In the UK, it is usually measured by the RPI. If inflation in the last year is 10%, then £100 last year has the same general (i.e. average) purchasing power as £110 this year. This means that in order to know what we are talking about we have to 'date' all our pounds. Pounds at different dates can no longer be regarded as the same, as a common measuring unit. In order to return to the position, essential for proper comparison, of having a common measuring unit, we have to convert pounds of one date's purchasing power into pounds of the other date's purchasing power. This needs illustrating!

Basic figures (all at 31 December) are:

20.1   £200
20.2   £250

The general inflation index stood at 300 in 20.1 and 330 in 20.2 (i.e. inflation in the year was 10%).

Over the year 200 20.1 pounds have been changed into 250 20.2 pounds. We can express this as $£_{20.1}$ 200 and $£_{20.2}$ 250. How much better off are we?

Activity 1

Well. How much better off are we?

Activity 1 feedback

To answer this, we need to calculate the equivalent in $£_{20.2}$, of $£_{20.1}$ 200. In terms of general purchasing power this will be:

$$200 \times \frac{330}{300} = £_{20.2}\ 220$$

So in terms of a common measuring unit ($£_{20.2}$) we have an increase in well-off-ness of $250 - 220 = £_{20.2}$ 30.

The description 'basic figure' used above is deliberately vague. The idea of CPP adjustments can be superimposed on *any* valuation basis. The practical proposals made in the

UK in recent years for the introduction of CPP have assumed a HC basis, and for the present we will discuss and illustrate the ideas under this assumption.

It is important to distinguish, when considering CPP accounting, between monetary and non-monetary items. Monetary items are items fixed by contract, custom or statute in terms of numbers of pounds, regardless of changes in the general price level and the purchasing power of the pound. Examples are cash, debtors and creditors, and longer-term loans. Non-monetary items are all items not so fixed in terms of number of pounds, for example land, buildings, plant, stock, shares held as investments.

Suppose I held a monetary asset in 20.1 of £200 (i.e. $£_{20.1}$ 200). If I still hold this asset, untouched and unchanged, a year later, it will be worth £200. It might even be a pile of 200 physical £ coins, though it could equally be a debtor or a loan. But in 20.2 what sort of pound is it worth 200 of? The answer is 20.2 pounds. By definition the item is fixed in terms of number of pounds. So I have turned $£_{20.1}$ 200 into $£_{20.2}$ 200. But we know that in terms of general purchasing power $£_{20.2}$ is worth less than $£_{20.1}$ was. Therefore, in maintaining my position in terms of the number of pounds of my monetary asset, I have failed to maintain my position in terms of purchasing power.

On the other hand suppose we borrow £100 in 20.1 and repay the loan, £100, one year later. We have borrowed $£_{20.1}$ 100 and repaid $£_{20.2}$ 100. We have repaid the same number of pounds that we borrowed, but each pound is of lower purchasing power. Therefore, in terms of (general) purchasing power we have repaid less than we borrowed, so we have gained. (We shall also have to pay interest of course, which may have attempted to take account of the effects of inflation.) These gains and losses on monetary items are an important part of the argument in favour of CPP accounting – it is suggested that such gains and losses should be calculated and reported.

With monetary items, then, when considering two sets of accounts at different dates, no *adjustment* to the £ figure reported is needed, but care must be taken in interpretation. However, when *comparing* two sets of accounts of the same business at different dates it is necessary to adjust *all* the contents of one balance sheet into the measuring unit (dated pound) of that of the other. The question may be: what is the current (today) purchasing power of the £100 I held one year ago (and still hold)? The answer is 100 of today's pounds. But the question might be: If I have £200 today and I had £100 one year ago, how much better off am I in terms of purchasing power? The answer, in terms of today's pounds, is:

$$200 - 100 \times \frac{\text{(RPI today)}}{\text{(RPI 1 year ago)}}$$

For example:

$$200 - 100 \times \frac{(330)}{(300)}$$
$$= 200 - 110$$
$$= £ \text{ today } 90$$

This process leads to a good deal of confusion. Study the following example carefully.

Example

Given: All the information of Chaplin Ltd, as on p. 65.
Prepare: A closing balance sheet under CPP principles.

Chaplin Ltd – CPP solution

		£	£
Capital	$200\,000 \times \dfrac{120}{100}$		240 000
Operating profit			21 382
			261 382
Gain on net monetary liabilities			2 000
			263 382
Loan			50 000
Creditors			50 000
			£363 382
Land & buildings	$110\,000 \times \dfrac{120}{100}$		132 000
Plant & equipment: cost	$40\,000 \times \dfrac{120}{100}$	48 000	
depreciation	$4000 \times \dfrac{120}{100}$	4 800	43 200
Stock	$90\,000 \times \dfrac{120}{110}$	98 182	175 200
Debtors		90 000	188 182
			£363 382

Notes

1 *Operating profit*. Balancing figure, or provable as follows:

Per HC results		26 000
Less Depreciation adj.	$4000 \times \dfrac{110 - 100}{100}$	400
Stock sold adj.	$60\,000 \times \dfrac{110 - 100}{100}$	6 000
Adjusted profit as *30 June prices*		19 600
Adjusted profit at 31 December prices	$19\,600 \times \dfrac{120}{110}$	£21 382

2 *Gain on net monetary liabilities.*

   (a) In total this is easily provable as follows:

      Net monetary liabilities 1 January £10 000 (loan 50 000 less cash 40 000).

      Net monetary liabilities 31 December £10 000 (loan 50 000 plus creditors 50 000 less debtors 90 000).

      Therefore gain is $10\,000\left(1 - \dfrac{120}{100}\right) = £2000$ (at 31 December prices).

   (b) More generally, however, the figures should be considered individually:

      Debtors – arose on 30 June, remained until 31 December:

$$90\,000\left(1 - \frac{120}{100}\right) = \text{Loss} \qquad\qquad\qquad £8\,181$$

      Creditors – arose on 30 June, remained until 31 December:

$$50\,000\left(1 - \frac{120}{110}\right) = \text{Gain} \qquad\qquad\qquad £4\,545$$

      Loan – arose on 1 January, remained until 31 December:

$$50\,000\left(1 - \frac{120}{100}\right) = \text{Gain} \qquad\qquad\qquad £10\,000$$

      Cash – arose on 1 January, remained until 30 June:

$$40\,000\left(1 - \frac{110}{100}\right) = \text{Loss} \qquad\qquad\qquad £4\,000$$

      But this loss on holding cash is expressed in 30 June pounds. This figure must be converted to 31 December pounds i.e.:

$$4000 \times \frac{120}{110} = \text{Loss} \qquad\qquad\qquad\qquad £4\,364$$

      So in summary, we have:

Losses of 8181 + 4364	£12 545
Gains of 4545 + 10 000	£14 545
Giving a net gain on net monetary liabilities of:	£ 2 000

      Is this £2000 gain distributable? Is it realized? In fact as the practical businessman or businesswoman might say, where is it?

3 *Indices used.* Study carefully which index number is used where, and make sure you see why. Remember the simplifying assumption that all sales, purchases and associated payments occurred on 30 June, and also that monetary items need no adjustment for balance sheet purposes. Note the irrelevance of the plant and stock indices.

4 *Complexity.* This example is highly simplified yet the numbers, and more important the logic, are not at all easy.

5 *Comparatives.* Next year this balance sheet will be used as a comparative for next year's results. For this purpose it will need, next year, to be multiplied by:

$$\frac{\text{(RPI at 31 December next year)}}{120}$$

This will need to be done to every figure, whether monetary or non-monetary. Thus, for example, the loan figure at the end of the year 2 will be 50 000 year 2 pounds. If the RPI is then 150, then the comparative figure from year 1, as updated to year 2 pounds, will be:

$$50\,000 \times \frac{150}{120} = £62\,500$$

This cannot, of course, mean that the loan has been reduced in monetary amount by £12 500. What it does mean is that the loan has reduced in value in terms of year 2 pounds (i.e. there has been another gain on monetary liabilities).

Now try the following activity. A suggested solution follows, but we strongly suggest that you make a serious attempt at your own solution first.

Activity 2

Mushroom Ltd was established on 1 January 20X4. Its opening balance sheet (on this date) was as follows:

	£
Land	6 000
Equipment	4 000
Stock	2 000
Equity	12 000

During 20X4, the company made the following transactions:

(a) purchased extra stock £10 000
(b) sold stock for £11 000 cash, which had an historical cost value of £9000
(c) closing stock on 31 December 20X4 had an historical cost of £3000 and was bought when the RPI index was 115 (average)
(d) the equipment has an expected life of four years, and nil residual value. The straight-line method of depreciation is used
(e) the general price index stood at:

100 on 1 January 20X4
110 on 30 June 20X4
120 on 31 December 20X4

You should assume that purchases and receipts occur evenly throughout the year. There are no debtors or creditors.
Required:
Calculate the CPP profit for 20X4 and prepare the CPP balance sheet as at 31 December 20X4.

Activity 2 feedback

		£CPP	£CPP
Sales	11 000 × 120/110		12 000
Opening stock	2 000 × 120/100	2 400	
Add purchases	10 000 × 120/110	10 909	
		13 309	
less closing stock	(3 000 × 120/115)	3 130	
			10 179
			1 821
less depreciation			1 200
			621
Loss on holding monetary assets (cash)*			91
CPP profit			530

*If cash accrues evenly over the year, the loss is

$$£(1000 × 120/110) – £1000 = £91$$

The historical cost profit (£11 000 – £9000 – £1000 for depreciation = £1000) and the CPP profit can be reconciled as follows:

	£
Historical cost profit	1000

Stock
Additional charge based on restating the cost of stock at the beginning and end of the year in pounds of current purchasing power, thus taking the inflationary element out of the profit on the sale of stock.
Opening stock + 400 minus closing stock – 130 ... (270)

Depreciation
Additional depreciation based on cost, measured in pounds of current purchasing power of fixed assets £1200 – £1000 ... (200)

Monetary items
Net loss in purchasing power resulting from the effects of inflation on the company's net monetary assets ... (91)

Sales, purchases and all other costs
These are increased by the change in the index between the average date at which they occurred and the end of the year. This adjustment increases profit as sales exceed the costs included in this heading ... 91

CPP profit ... 530

*The historical cost profit is based on:

	£	£$_{CPP}$	Difference £
Sales	11 000	12 000	1000
Purchases	10 000	10 909	(909)
		Net difference	91

Calculation of balance sheet items, and reconciliation of profit figure with balance sheet:

1 Value of equity, 1 January 20X4 £12 000
Revalued in terms of £$_{CPP}$ at 31 December 20X4
(£12 000 × 120/100) £$_{CPP}$ 14 400

2 Mushroom Ltd
CPP Balance Sheet as at 31 December 20X4

		£$_{CPP}$	£$_{CPP}$
Land	6 000 × 120/100		7 200
Equipment	4 000 × 120/100	4 800	
less depreciation	1 000 × 120/100	1 200	
			3 600
			10 800
Stocks	3 000 × 120/115	3 130	
Cash	(11 000 – 10 000)	1 000	
			4 130
			14 930
Financed by equity and reserves			14 930
CPP profit = £CPP (14 930 – 14 400) =		£$_{CPP}$	530

Combination of methods

As already stated, CPP thinking can be applied to any valuation basis, not just historical costs. It is often suggested that CPP adjustments could and indeed should be applied to replacement cost calculations. It is important to remember that:

1 RC accounting deals with *specific* price rises only
2 CPP accounting deals with *general* price rises only; and
3 both types of change are in fact occurring at the same time.

Thus to take the simplest of examples, if HC = 10, and a year later RC = 13, there is a holding gain of £3. But if the RPI has increased by 10% then (10 × 110/100) = £1 of that holding gain of 3 (closing date) pounds is not 'real' because it cannot be translated into increased purchasing power. The 'real' holding gain is arguably only 2 (3 – 1) (closing date) pounds. This combined approach, known as **stabilized accounting**, is shown for Chaplin Ltd in the example opposite.

Example

Chaplin Ltd – stabilized (RC plus CPP) solution

	£
Capital (per CPP answer)	240 000
Operating profit	18 328
	258 328
Real holding gain	8 012
	266 340
Loan	50 000
Creditors	50 000
	£366 340
Land and building (per RC answer)	135 000
Plant and equipment (per RC answer)	39 600
Stock (per RC answer)	101 740
Debtors	90 000
	£366 340

Notes

1 *Operating profit:*

Per HC answer	$26\,000 \times \dfrac{120}{110}$	=	28 364

Depreciation	RC 30 June	4 200
Depreciation	*less* HC	4 000

	$200 \times \dfrac{120}{110}$	=	(218)

Cost of sales (per RC answer)	$9000 \times \dfrac{120}{110}$	=	(9 818)
			18 328

2 *Real holding gain:*

Gain on net monetary items (per CPP answer)			2 000

Land and buildings	$110\,000 \times \left(\dfrac{135}{110} - \dfrac{120}{100} \right)$	=	3 000

Plant and equipment:

Cost	$40\,000 \times \left(\dfrac{115}{100} - \dfrac{120}{100} \right)$	=	(4000)

Depreciation $\left(400 \times \dfrac{105}{100}\right) \times \left(\dfrac{110}{105} - \dfrac{120}{100}\right)$ = $\underline{182}$ (3 818)

$\overline{1\,181}$

Cost of sales:

Opening stock $\left(60\,000 \times \left(\dfrac{115}{110} - \dfrac{110}{100}\right)\right) \times \dfrac{120}{110}$ = 3 273

Closing stock $90\,000 \times \left(\dfrac{130}{115} - \dfrac{120}{110}\right)$ = $\underline{3\,557}$ $\underline{6\,830}$

$\underline{\underline{£8\,012}}$

Current purchasing power – what does it really mean?

It is most important when thinking about CPP accounting to be fully aware of exactly what it is doing and what it is not doing. The crucial point is that it is not producing a current valuation of the item concerned in any sense. What it is doing, in general terms, is to re-express in terms of current pounds, the figures as originally calculated under the original measurement basis, whatever that was. It does not alter the basis of valuation. It alters the measuring unit which is being applied to the original basis of valuation.

Activity 3

Look at the figure of £132 000 for land and buildings shown in the Chaplin CPP example on p. 90, and think about it carefully. What does it mean?

Activity 3 feedback

We would suggest it means something like: the number of current pounds that would have to be spent today to buy the land and buildings if all economic circumstances were exactly unaltered from when the original purchase was made. Since all economic circumstances will most certainly not be unaltered from when the original purchase was made, it is not obvious that this is particularly useful information.

The other point that could be made concerns the assumption that a **general** adjustment to purchasing power is of relevance even when viewed in measuring unit terms to the **particular** user of the **particular** set of accounts of the **particular** business being considered. Can the spending or purchasing power of a pound coin be equated as between a retail shop and a chemical manufacturer? Can the spending or purchasing power of a pound coin be equated as between a non-smoking pensioner and a smoking teenager? Is general purchasing power so general that it is not really relevant to any particular user?

Activity 4

Prepare a list, in point form, of advantages and disadvantages which you think could reasonably be said to apply to current purchasing power accounting.

Activity 4 feedback

Advantages

1 All necessary figures are stated or restated in terms of a common measuring unit (CPP units). This facilitates proper comparison.
2 It distinguishes between gains or losses on monetary liabilities and assets, on the one hand, and 'real' gains or losses through trading activities.
3 It requires only a simple objective adjustment to HC accounts. Easily auditable.

Disadvantages

1 It is not clear what CPP units are. They are not the same as monetary units.
2 **General** purchasing power, by definition, has no direct relevance to any **particular** person or situation.
3 When CPP is applied to HC-based accounts, the resulting figures necessarily contain all the disadvantages of the original HC accounts.
4 It fails to give any sort of meaningful 'value' to balance sheet items, although it gives the impression to non-accountants that it has done precisely that.
5 It is extremely difficult to understand and interpret.

Summary

In this chapter we have explored the concept of general inflation and current purchasing power adjustments, and seen how the figures are calculated. Finally, we attempted to consider the meaning and usefulness of the resulting accounts and statements.

Exercises

1 From the following historic cost accounts of Page plc, prepare a set of CPP accounts for the year-ended 31.12.8.

		31.12.7 £000		31.12.8 £000
Fixed assets				
Cost (purchased 1.1.5)		500		500
less depreciation		300		400
		200		100
Current assets				
Stock (purchased 31.10)	100		150	
Debtors	200		300	
Bank	150		350	
	450		800	
less Current liabilities	300		400	
		150		400
		350		500

Share capital	100	100
Reserves	250	400
	350	500

Profit and loss account for the year-ended 31 December year 8:

		£000
Sales		1850
Cost of goods sold		
opening stock	100	
purchases	1350	
	1450	
less closing stock	150	
		1300
		550
Gross profit		
Expenses	300	
Depreciation	100	
		400
Net profit		150

The movement on the retail price index has been as follows:

1 January year 5	180
1 January year 7	200
Average for year 7	210
31 October year 7	215
31 December year 7	220
Average for year 8	230
31 October year 8	235
31 December year 8	240

Assume all sales, purchases and expenses accrue evenly throughout the year.

2 What do CPP adjustments do, and how do they do it?

3 Are general indices more or less useful in financial reporting than specific price changes?

4 (a) **Explain the primary objective of current purchasing power accounting and outline the basic technique.** (8 marks)

(b) **What do you consider are the advantages and disadvantages of current purchasing power accounting as a method of adjusting financial statements for price level changes?** (12 marks)

(20 marks)

(ACCA)

5 (a) **Explain the following terms used in financial accounting.**
        Matching
        Prudence
        Inflation
        Price changes
        Going concern
        Objectivity   (18 marks)
   (b) **Should price changes be taken into account during the matching process?**
        Give reasons for your answer.   (7 marks)
                                                                   (25 marks)
                                                                        (ACCA)

6 Look at the figure of £240 000 for capital shown in the Chaplin CPP example on p. 90, and think about it carefully. What does it mean?

The UK position: past, present and future?

After reading this chapter you should be able to:
- explain and illustrate, in its historical context, attempts at regulation in the UK in the area of accounting for inflation and price changes
- outline the current position
- place current thinking in its international context, and suggest pointers forwards both for practical development and for you the reader.

Introduction

In earlier chapters we explored the various theoretical aspects and alternatives of income measurement; perhaps we should say of progress measurement in order to fully embrace the cash flow measurement alternative. In this chapter we survey the attempts at practical application of some of these ideas in the UK since the early 1970s, and in particular Current Cost Accounting, derived from Deprival Value, as introduced by SSAP 16. We then try to summarize the position and attitudes today. Finally, we note the relevance to the UK position of international trends, and also the importance, frequently forgotten, of the purposes, users and uses of financial reporting. Rigorous theorizing is an essential element in the improvement of practical usefulness. It does not necessarily follow, however, that the most coherent and attractive theories are the most useful in the real world of today. Finally, but crucially, we ask the obvious question. Where are we, or rather where are you the reader, going next?

The background to SSAP 16

In the early 1970s inflation in the UK was rising, and there was a widespread view that something should be done about it. Majority view in the accounting profession was that whatever was done should be as objective as possible, and as close as possible to historical cost accounting and to traditional practice. This view encouraged a preference for general indexation. We could prepare all our traditional accounts in the traditional way, and then all we would have to do would be to make a few adjustments. Since these adjustments would be based on published indices they could easily be checked, and so the life of the auditor could go on very much as before.

In May 1974, SSAP 7 had been issued: *Accounting for Changes in the Purchasing Power of Money*. This recommended CPP adjustments to HC based accounts. (In fact it was issued as PSSAP 7, a Provisional Standard. It was therefore mandatory on accountants, but only provisionally so – whatever that means!)

However the government, represented as much by the civil service as by the politicians, was not keen on the idea of general indexation, more for fear that the process would fuel inflation than for logically based criticism of the methodology itself. A committee was appointed, known as the Sandilands Committee after the name of its chairman. The Sandilands Report, published in 1975, not only proposed a completely different approach based on specific price changes, but actually opposed, with considerable violence, any form of general indexation adjustment of any sort. The accounting profession was rather upset. The *general* reaction in the profession was to accept the Sandilands proposals as far as they went, but to argue that they did not go far enough. This reaction was expressed in two ways:

1 the Sandilands proposals failed to take account of *general* inflation
2 the Sandilands proposals failed to take account of gains and losses on monetary items.

These two arguments are obviously related, and there was a widespread view that the Sandilands proposals should be added to so as to 'do something about monetary items'. The process to a full-blown Standard was as follows:

November 1976	Issue of ED18	Withdrawn after strong opposition from practising (particularly chartered) accountants
November 1977	Issue of interim recommendations (the 'Hyde Guidelines')	
April 1979	Issue of ED24	
March 1980	Issue of SSAP 16	

The Sandilands Report proposed in essence that two adjustments should be made to HC profit, namely:

1 a stock, or cost of sales adjustment
2 a depreciation adjustment.

These adjustments are designed to increase the total expenses charged (i.e. to reduce the reported profit) as compared with the HC profit, by:

1 the difference between the 'value to the business' of the stock used, as at the date of sale, and its HC
2 the difference between the 'value to the business' of the fixed assets 'used up' (under the appropriate depreciation assumptions) and the HC depreciation charge.

Thus if 'value to the business' of the appropriate assets is the RC this process will in principle give an operating profit identical to that under a pure RC basis.

ED18 proposed only the two original Sandilands adjustments. The Hyde Guidelines proposed a third, the gearing adjustment, and ED24 added a fourth, the monetary working capital adjustment. The essence of these two adjustments is considered below.

SSAP 16 and current cost accounting

SSAP 16 required assets to be recorded (and therefore expensed), at their 'value to the business'. It is clear from the definitions given in the SSAP itself that value to the business is in essence the same as deprival value, as discussed earlier (p. 81).

> *Value to the business*
> **42** The value to the business is:
> > **(a)** net current replacement cost or, if a permanent diminution to below net current replacement cost has been recognised
> > **(b)** recoverable amount.
>
> *Recoverable amount*
> **43** The recoverable amount is the greater of the net realisable value of an asset and, where applicable, the amount recoverable from its further use.

The profit calculation is divided into two stages. The first stage is to arrive at the current cost operating profit.

> **40** The current cost operating profit is the surplus arising from the ordinary activities of the business in the period after allowing for the impact of price changes on the funds needed to continue the existing business and maintain its operating capability, whether financed by share capital or borrowing. It is calculated before interest on net borrowing and taxation.

This is calculated by starting from the historical cost profit and then making three adjustments. These are the depreciation and cost of sales adjustments and the monetary working capital adjustment. All three will usually, though not universally, be debits.

The second stage is to calculate the current cost profit attributable to shareholders.

> **41** The current cost profit attributable to shareholders is the surplus for the period after allowing for the impact of price changes on the funds needed to maintain their proportion of the operating capability. It is calculated after interest, taxation and extraordinary items.

This is calculated by starting from the current cost operating profit and then making the gearing adjustment. This will normally be a credit.

The methodology of the depreciation adjustment and the cost of sales adjustment will be exactly the same as for replacement cost accounting as considered earlier (see Chapter 5). The only difference is that the calculations will be based on the 'value to the business', which is usually the replacement cost, rather than on the replacement cost, which of course is always the replacement cost. The other two adjustments require more detailed consideration.

Monetary working capital adjustment

If profit is revenue less expenses, and the HC profit is correctly calculated to include all expenses, then adjustments for cost of sales and depreciation would seem to be all that is necessary to update the reported profit figure. Incidental expenses can reasonably be assumed to be 'current' already (e.g. administrative wages, the telephone bill, and so on). An alternative argument, however, points out that rising costs will, other things being equal, have an effect on working capital needs as a whole, not just on stocks. Rising costs of inputs will lead to higher cash payments, and these cash payments are not replaced in cash terms until the debtors resulting from the eventual sale actually pay. Therefore the amount of cash the firm needs to finance from its own resources is increased because of the rise in the replacement cost of the inputs. Rising costs therefore lead to an increased burden because of rising debtors. Conversely, creditors will tend to protect the business to some extent because the business will lag behind current prices in its rate of payment.

For example, if stock costing £100 is bought and not paid for, and then stock costing £110 is bought and not paid for, but the first stock is now paid for, then the business has not, at this point, had to pay any extra money because of the rise in cost levels. The amount of extra finance needed to support the level of activity has arguably not increased. Therefore the unfavourable stock (cost of sales) adjustment of £10 can be offset by a favourable monetary working capital adjustment (MWCA) of £10.

There are several problems arising from this idea:

1 How do we determine which monetary items are part of monetary *working* capital? It should include trade creditors, trade debtors, cash floats necessary in operating the business, any items of stock not included in the cost of sales adjustment (COSA), and any part of bank balances or overdrafts relating to fluctuations in stock, debtors or creditors. It should not include loans, idle money, or any 'non-operating' items. In practice, this obviously leads to difficult distinctions.

2 Which index should be used? It is usually argued that a specific cost index is often used as for the COSA. However, it could be argued that a selling price index should be used – if selling price goes up 15% and input costs go up 10% then the money tied up in debtors, the money the firm would have already had if debtors had paid immediately, has gone up by 15% not 10%. Alternatively, it could be suggested that a general index should be used on the grounds that money is by definition available for any purpose, and anything other than a general index makes unjustified assumptions about intentions.

3 Why regard an 'amount of money' as an expense? The MWCA does not reduce profit by the cost of the extra finance. It reduces profit by the *amount* of the extra finance. It could therefore be suggested that it confuses expenses with increases in necessary investment. This, of course, brings us back to the capital maintenance concept of operating capability.

MWCA is a difficult concept, and opinions differ as to its desirability. Both elements of this statement are even more true of the gearing adjustment.

The gearing adjustment

In essence, the argument for a gearing adjustment can be stated very simply. The depreciation and COSAs, and the MWCA if present, have, by definition, related to the business as a whole. The depreciation entries relate to all the fixed assets, and so on. This is obviously necessary, as the whole point of the operation is to maintain the operating capability (of the business as a whole). But for the gearing adjustment we take a different standpoint.

We consider how the total assets of the business (regarding net working capital as 'an asset' for this purpose) have been financed. The assets have generally been financed from two sources:

1 shareholders equity – capital and reserves of all kinds
2 loans and borrowings from non-shareholders.

So, we have adjusted (generally reduced) profit by a series of adjustments that relate to all the assets. But we are reporting primarily to shareholders, and therefore what we *should* be doing is adjusting profit by adjustments that relate to those assets financed by the shareholders. Therefore we have over-adjusted, and we need to 'add a bit back again' – to adjust the adjustments, in fact!

To calculate the gearing adjustment the basic procedure is as follows:

1 Add the adjustments made in arriving at current cost operating profit.
2 Calculate the gearing proportion. The gearing proportion is the relationship between the average net borrowing (L), and the average total capital employed figure (the ordinary shareholders equity S, + L), i.e.:

$$\text{Gearing proportion} = \frac{L}{L + S}$$

3 Multiply the total arrived at in **1**, by the proportion arrived at in **2**.

This procedure arrives at the gearing adjustment, which then reduces the effect of the 'operating' adjustments. In the general case where the operating adjustments reduce profit (i.e. are debits) the gearing adjustment will be a credit. Using the terminology of SSAP 16, we have:

HC profit		X
less Depreciation adjustment	X	
COSA	X	
MWCA	X	
	X	
CC operating profit		X
plus Gearing adjustment		X
CC profit attributable to shareholders		X

The double entry for these adjustments goes into the revaluation reserve, now called **current cost reserve**, on the balance sheet.

The example below shows the replacement cost (RC) solution to Chaplin, reworked to include a MWCA and a gearing adjustment. Study it carefully.

Example

Chaplin – SSAP 16 accounts

	£	£
HC profit		26 000
less Adjustments		
Depreciation	400	
Stock	9 000	
MWCA	4 615	14 015
CC operating profit		11 985

add back gearing adjustment
(not applicable to shareholders)
$18\% \times 14\,015$ 2 524

CC profit attributable to shareholders 14 509

Balance sheet:

	£		£
Share capital	200 000	Assets (per RC answer)	366 340
Profit	14 509		
Holding gains	51 831		
	266 340		
Loan	50 000		
Creditors	50 000		
	366 340		366 340

	£	
Holding gains:	Per RC answer	49 740
	+ MWCA	4 615
	Less Gearing	(2 524)
		51 831

Notes

1 *Calculation of MWCA:*

	Actual	Mid-year	£
Opening MWC	$0 \times \dfrac{115}{100} =$		0
Closing MWC	$40\,000 \times \dfrac{115}{130} =$		35 385
Increase	40 000		35 385

This mid-year increase is the 'real' increase, therefore the 'price effect' increase must be $40\,000 - 35\,385 = £4615$

2 *Calculation of gearing adjustment*

Closing capital, on a current cost basis, equals closing assets on a current cost basis less closing liabilities:

366 340	(as RC solution)
−100 000	(50 000 + 50 000)
£266 340	

Opening capital = £200 000

$$\text{Average capital} = \frac{200\,000 + 266\,340}{2} \quad = £233\,170$$

$$\text{Gearing proportion} = \frac{50\,000}{50\,000 + 233\,170} = 18\%$$

The idea of the gearing adjustment is difficult and controversial. If we look at the business as a whole, as an entity in itself, then a gearing adjustment seems unnecessary. This is known as the 'entity view'. In order to maintain the operating capability, and assuming that the assumptions made in calculating value to the business adjustments are valid, *all* of the appropriate operating adjustments must be made to HC profit. Gains on borrowing are not represented by cash inflows to the business, and they are not available for distribution as dividends without reducing the business's 'well-off-ness'.

This means that the 'CC profit attributable to shareholders' does *not* generally show the amount that can be paid out as dividends without reducing the operating capacity of the business. This maximum amount of dividend that can be paid out without defeating the stated capital maintenance concept of operating capacity is given by the CC operating profit.

Alternatively we can take what is known as the 'proprietary view'. This suggests that we should look at the company through the eyes of the shareholders; we should look at the business as it affects the shareholders, and not as an entity in itself. This would seem to support the idea of a gearing adjustment. It is additionally argued by supporters of this viewpoint that the business, although admittedly unable to distribute the gearing adjustment from its own resources, can always borrow the additional cash necessary for this distribution without increasing (worsening) the gearing proportion. This argument is technically correct, but the relevance of a *financing* argument to a *profit* calculation is not universally accepted. A second major problem is that the gearing adjustment as illustrated here is closely related to the operating adjustments, and the logic of this can be criticized. First, it can be criticized as being too conservative. Consider the treatment of the plant and equipment in the Chaplin CC accounts (p. 104). The CC reserve has been increased by £4000, the debit being to the balance sheet. Arising from this, £400 has been deducted from profit as depreciation adjustment, the credit being to the balance sheet. This £400 adjustment is usually regarded as realized. Our gearing adjustment has increased profit attributable to shareholders by the gearing proportion of the (realized) depreciation adjustment, i.e. by 18% of the £400. But the total gain is £4000. Since 18% of this £4000 can clearly be deemed to be financed by borrowing, why not increase profit attributable to shareholders by 18% of the whole £4000? Certainly it cannot be argued as being realized, but remember that even 'realized' gains are not necessarily distributable anyway.

Additionally, remember that what the gearing adjustment does is to 'do something about monetary items'. We have argued earlier that gains or losses on monetary items are perhaps best measured in terms of purchasing power – the fall in the value of money. This implies the use of a *general* index, and that any gearing adjustment must be calculated completely independently of the operating adjustments. If we are focusing our attention on the assets, which are financed by borrowing, perhaps a specific asset index is suggested. If we are focusing our attention on the borrowings of the business and on opportunity costs and future effects, perhaps a general index is indicated.

Activity 1

Blue Ltd was formed on 1 January 20X1 with share capital of £10000 and loan capital of £10000. £10000 was used to purchase stock and £4000 to purchase fixed assets.

At 31 December, the following HC balance sheets were prepared:

		20X1		20X2
Fixed asset	4 000		4 000	
Less Depreciation	1 000	3 000	2 000	2 000
Stock		18 000		21 000
Debtors		4 000		6 000
		25 000		29 000
Share capital		10 000		10 000
Profit		5 000		9 000
		15 000		19 000
Loan capital		10 000		10 000
		25 000		29 000

The following price changes took place:

	RPI	Fixed assets	Stocks
1 January 20X1	100	80	80
1 January 20X2	100	100	80
Average 20X2	110	120	100
31 December 20X2	121	144	125

Required:
Redraft the accounts for 20X2 in accordance with SSAP 16, making whatever simplifying assumption you feel appropriate.

Activity 1 feedback

Blue Ltd
Assumptions – all goods bought 1 January, sold 30 June and held till year-end
COSA

$$\text{Opening stock } \left(18\,000 \times \frac{100}{80}\right) - 18\,000 \qquad = \qquad 4\,500$$

Closing stock – already at mid-year prices per assumption

$$\text{Depreciation } 1000 \times \frac{144}{80} = 1800 - 1000 \qquad = \qquad 800$$

	Actual		**Mid-year**

MWCA

$$\text{Debtors – Creditors} \quad \textbf{(a)} \text{ Opening } 4000 \times \frac{100}{80} \qquad = \qquad 5\,000$$

(b) Closing $6000 \times \dfrac{100}{125}$ $=$ $\underline{4\,800}$

Increase   2000   (200)
(b) – (a)
i.e. real **decrease** = 200

Price effect = $\underline{2\,200}$
– Total CC adjustments excluding gearing $\underline{7\,500}$

$$\text{Gearing*} = \frac{\text{Average net loans} \times 100}{\text{Average NL} + \text{Average CC equity}}$$

Average net loans = 10 000
Average CC capital: Requires calculation of CC of assets
  less liabilities per closing balance sheet = £25 850 (see below) and per opening balance sheet

= 15 000 + Net holding gain on fixed assets $=$ 15 000

$+ 4000 \times \dfrac{100}{80} - 4000$ $=$ 1 000

Less Depreciation: $1000 \times \dfrac{100}{80} - 1000$ $\dfrac{(125)}{15\,875}$

$\therefore$ Average Cap $= \dfrac{15\,875 + 25\,850}{2} = 20\,862$

$\therefore$ Gearing % $= \dfrac{10\,000}{10\,000 + 20\,862} = 32\%$

Blue Ltd: CC Balance Sheet
Net Assets

Fixed assets $\left(4000 \times \dfrac{144}{80}\right)$ 7 200

Less Depreciation $\left(2000 \times \dfrac{144}{80}\right)$ $\underline{3\,600}$

3 600

Stock $\left(21\,000 \times \dfrac{125}{100}\right)$ 26 250
Debtors $\underline{6\,000}$

$\underline{32\,250}$
$\underline{35\,850}$
Less Long-term loan $\underline{10\,000}$
$\underline{\underline{25\,850}}$

Funded by

Shares	10 000
Reserves (see below)	15 850
	25 850

Reserves

Operating profit

HC profit (9000 – 5000)	4 000
Less CC adjustments (see above)	7 500
	(3 500)
Add back Gearing adj. (32% × 7500)	2 400
	(1 100)

Holding gains

Fixed assets (see above)	3 200
Opening stock (see COSA above)	4 500
Closing stock (see above)	5 250
MWCA	2 200
	15 150

But last year's depreciation was charged at HC – it is now in the balance sheet at CC. The difference (i.e., debit to reserves)

= 1 000 × 144/80 – 1 000 =	(800)
	14 350
Profit brought forward (is this distributable?)	5 000
Gearing adjustments (see above)	(2 400)

Reserves = 14 350 + 5 000 – 2 400 – 1 100 = 15 850

The array of possibilities

Turn back and look again at Table 4.2. This suggested the six valuation methodologies which Edwards and Bell regarded as worthy of development and consideration. It is interesting to relate their views to the detail of the propositions covered in the later chapters. It is clear that many of their thoughts have been refined and tightened considerably. Broadly speaking current exit values (Chapter 6) are close to the opportunity cost concept of Table 4.2, and current entry values (Chapter 5) are close to the current cost concept of Table 4.2. The mixed value argument of deprival value (leading on to value to the business and SSAP 16) is in essence, at least by the time we reach SSAP 16, a refinement of the current entry value thinking. Superimposed on this whole debate of course is the issue of general indexation and purchasing power adjustments. By now you should have your own theoretical preferences.

But it is not sufficient simply (?) to appraise all this in theoretical terms. Think back to the work you did on the purposes of accounting and the consideration of users and their needs. Bearing in mind these considerations as well as our theoretical thoughts, what do you think of the major practical proposals described earlier in this chapter? Are either of them satisfactory? Are both of them satisfactory but for different purposes? Or is any system which does not embrace cash flow thinking bound to be unsatisfactory?

UK practice

We have already implied that SSAP 16 was unnecessarily complicated. Whether or not its complications were logically necessary, they were certainly offputting to preparers (and users) of accounts. As the rate of inflation and the speed of price changes tended to fall through the 1980s criticism of SSAP 16 became ever stronger, and the degree of compliance became ever smaller. After much uncertainty and confusion SSAP 16 was first suspended and then withdrawn. Its use is now rare, though not unknown. The only point of significant theoretical interest from the various abortive attempts at the time to replace or amend SSAP 16 was a proposed greater flexibility in the treatment of gearing adjustment. This proposal (three paragraphs of the ill-fated ED 35) was as follows:

18   A gearing adjustment is needed to recognize the effect of debt capital. Various types of gearing adjustment have been suggested. As there is less agreement on how the gearing adjustment should be calculated than the other current cost adjustments, this statement gives a choice of three methods for calculating the gearing adjustment. The method selected must be explained and applied consistently. The first form of gearing adjustment indicates the extent to which the additional cost of business maintenance recognized by the current cost adjustments outlined in paragraphs 15–17 is regarded as being attributable to debt capital, measured by the extent to which a proportion of the net operating assets may be deemed to be financed by borrowing. It may be regarded as an abatement of the current cost adjustments for the year to the extent that they fall upon providers of loan capital rather than equity, and is calculated by applying the average gearing ratio in the year to the aggregate of the other current cost adjustments for the year. This is the form of gearing adjustment required by SSAP 16 'Current cost accounting'.

19   The second type of gearing adjustment represents those parts of the other current cost adjustments and the unrealized revaluation surpluses arising in the year that may be regarded as being financed by borrowing. If operating capability is to be maintained, an amount equal to this gearing adjustment could be borrowed and the gearing ratio would remain unchanged.

20   A gearing adjustment of a different nature can be calculated to reflect the effect of general price changes on the net borrowing (or net monetary assets other than those included in monetary working capital). When combined with the net charge or credit for interest paid or received during the year in money terms, it shows the net interest charge or credit for the year in real terms. This type of gearing adjustment is calculated by applying the rate of increase in general prices to the average net borrowing (or net monetary assets other than those included in monetary working capital) during the year.

The Accounting Standards Board (ASB) seems to take the view that historical cost accounting is clearly unsatisfactory but that they are not likely to be able, in the foreseeable future, to do much about it as regards formal regulatory requirement.

A significant recent trend is the increasing importance of the concept of fair value. This can be defined as 'the amount for which an asset could be exchanged, or a liability settled, between knowledgeable, willing parties in an arm's length transaction'. This is, in effect, the market price in a theoretically perfect market. It is important to notice that fair value is not identical to net realizable value. Net realizable value is the expected sales proceeds reduced by any future transaction costs of the selling process. Fair value is the expected gross exchange value, without any reduction for transaction costs. The importance of fair value seems likely to increase further on the international scene over the next few years, although this may well create tension and disagreement. It will require a change in attitude in many countries, but the ASB in the UK seems supportive of the principle. Follow the debate!

Summary

In this chapter we have outlined the various practical attempts to introduce some form of alternative to historical cost accounting in the UK since the early 1970s. We have seen that none of them have lasted. Finally, we reminded ourselves that the theoretical issues and practical needs remain. What *should* the future UK position on these issues be?

Exercises

1 The complexities of SSAP 16 were justified in terms of its increased usefulness and relevance. Discuss.
2 Is some form of gearing adjustment necessary?
3 What should the ASB recommend in the area of income measurement and asset valuation methods?
4 Explore the statements, either explicit or implicit via press leaks and inspired speculation, made by the ASB in the area of income measurement and asset valuation since the publication of this book.
5 You are required to discuss the advantages and disadvantages of using historical cost accounting in preparing financial statements which are presented to shareholders.   (15 marks)
(CIMA)
6 From the following information produce a set of current cost accounts as per SSAP 16. Calgary plc had the following historic cost profit and loss account for the year-ended 30 June:

		Year 4
		£000
Sales		7000
Profit before interest and taxation		1560
Interest	140	
Taxation	300	
		440
Profit attributable to shareholders		1120
Dividends		300
Retained profit for the year		820
Balance brought forward		1420
Balance carried forward		2240

Balance sheet as at 30 June:

	Year 3 £000	Year 4 £000
Fixed assets		
Land at cost (purchased 1 July year 2)	1500	1500
Plant and machinery at cost (purchased 1 July year 2)	1200	1200
Less depreciation	(240)	(480)
	2460	2220

Current assets			
Stock (purchased 30 April)	650		900
Debtors	830		1300
Bank	10		620
	1490		2820
Less Current liabilities			
Creditors	790		1060
		700	1760
		3160	3980
Share capital		1040	1040
Profit and loss		1420	2240
		2460	3280
Loan capital		700	700
		3160	3980

The following index numbers are applicable.

	RPI	Land	Stock	Plant and machinery
1 July year 2	120	213	412	610
30 April year 3	125	232	423	639
30 June year 3	131	241	431	649
31 December year 3	139	263	442	661
30 April year 4	148	278	456	678
30 June year 4	158	289	462	691

7 You are the management accountant of a manufacturing company where production is capital-intensive using machinery that is estimated to have a five-year life. The present machinery is now approximately three years old. Whilst raw material stocks have a low turnover due to supply problems, finished goods are turned over rapidly and there is minimal work-in-progress at any one time. The technology incorporated in the means of production is thought to be stable.

In recent years, it has not been possible to increase the price of the company's outputs beyond the rate of general inflation without diminishing market share, due to keen competition in this sector. The company does not consider that it has cash-flow problems. The company is all equity financed. Although a bank overdraft is a permanent feature of the balance sheet this is primarily due to customers being given a 60-day credit period, whilst most suppliers are paid within 30 days. There is always a positive balance of short-term monetary assets.

In the previous financial year, net profit after taxation on a strict historic cost basis was considered very healthy, and the directors felt that they could prudently distribute a major portion of this by way of dividend. The directors are considering whether, and if so how, to reflect price-level changes in their financial statements. They are concerned that this would affect their profit figure and therefore the amount they could distribute as dividend.

The following price-level changes have been brought to the attention of the directors:

	Retail price index	Index for company's machinery	Raw materials stock index
3 years previously	100	100	100
2 years previously	104	116	102
1 year previously	107	125	108
Present	112	140	120

You are required to prepare a report for your directors setting out in general terms how to explain to the shareholders the likely impact on the historic cost profit of possible methods of accounting for price-level changes. **(15 marks)**

(CIMA)

8   A manager in your firm has read the following quotation from an article in *Management Accounting* by David Allen, concerning accounting for changing price levels:

'What was required was a comprehensive system which calculated

(i) the capital maintenance provision by reference to the fall in the value of money; but

(ii) unrealized holding gains by reference to the changes in the specific prices of the particular assets employed by an enterprise.'

You are required to write a report to the manager in your firm

(a) explaining the above statement in relation to published financial statements

(10 marks)

(b) giving a short, numerical example to illustrate your explanation.

(5 marks)

(15 marks)

(CIMA)

Some possible extensions to the accounting framework

After reading this chapter you should be able to:
- identify the need for additional statements to be included in a reporting package
- outline, and comment on the importance of, a variety of possible additional statements and reports which could be included in a reporting package.

Introduction

The earlier chapters have considered a wide range of alternative ways of evaluating financial events. However, in terms of the basic statements that are to be used for presentation to the users of the accounting information nothing fundamentally new has been discussed. It has been implicitly assumed throughout that two essential statements are to be created:

1 some form of position statement (balance sheet)
2 some form of income statement (P&L account).

Several possible extensions or alternatives have been suggested in recent years, and we will consider some of these here.

The need for additional statements

All of the very varied analysis of the last few chapters has been based on the concepts of income and value. We have been thinking about different ways of producing a statement of wealth, and about different ways of producing a statement of income, i.e. of change in wealth over time. All of these methods and methodologies, even when reporting on past periods, contain significant assumptions and estimates, and it can be argued that this makes them all less than satisfactory.

Even the traditional accounting process is, as we have seen, an uncertain and complex process. Not only is profit determination complex, it is potentially misleading. In any accounting year, there will be a mixture of complete and incomplete transactions. Transactions are complete when they have led to a final cash settlement and these cause no profit-measurement difficulties.

Considerable problems arise, however, in dealing with incomplete transactions, where the profit or loss figure can only be estimated by means of the accruals concept, whereby revenue and costs are:

> matched with one another so far as their relationship can be established or justifiably assumed, and dealt with in the profit and loss account of the period to which they relate.

Thus, the profit for the past year is dependent on the validity of many assumptions about the *future*, e.g. the future life of assets is estimated in order to calculate the depreciation charge for the past year.

The greater the volume of incomplete transactions, the greater the degree of estimation and, accordingly, the greater the risk that investors could turn out to have been misled if actual outcomes deviate from estimates.

Thus, one possible extension to the accounting framework would be to provide information on cash inflows and outflows for a business. This is considered further in Chapter 27.

Possible additional financial reporting statements

Activity 1

Make a list of further statements of information, additional to profit and loss, balance sheet and some form of cash or funds statements, which might be significantly useful to one or more of the user groups.

Activity 1 feedback

The Corporate Report discussion paper we quoted from earlier (p. 8) suggests six additional statements and we will deal with them below. The *Report* stated:

> We recommend that, where appropriate, corporate reports contain the following statements in addition to those now current:
>
> **(a)** A statement of value added, showing how the benefits of the efforts of an enterprise are shared between employees, providers of capital, the state and reinvestment. This statement will assist users to evaluate the economic performance of the entity.
>
> **(b)** An employment report, showing the size and composition of the work-force relying on the enterprise for its livelihood, the work contribution of employees and the benefits earned. This report will assist users in assessing the performance of the entity, evaluating its economic function and performance in relation to society, assessing its capacity to make reallocations of resources and evaluating managerial performance, efficiency and objectives.
>
> **(c)** A statement of money exchanges with government, showing the financial relationship between the enterprise and the state. This statement will assist users to assess the economic function of the entity in relation to society.
>
> **(d)** A statement of transactions in foreign currency showing the direct cash dealings of the reporting entity between this country and abroad. This statement will assist users to judge the economic functions and performance of the enti-

ty in relation to society and the national interest. It may also provide information of assistance in assessing the stability and vulnerability of the reporting entity and in estimating its capacity to make future cash payments.

(e) A statement of future prospects, showing likely future profit, employment and investment levels. This statement will assist users to evaluate the future prospects of the entity and assess managerial performance.

(f) A statement of corporate objectives showing management policy and medium-term strategic targets. This statement will assist users to evaluate managerial performance, efficiency and objectives.

In addition to these six statements the concept of social reporting has gained prominence in recent years. Indeed it was briefly mentioned in the *Report*. Also mentioned in the *Report* was segmental reporting.

Statement of value added (value added statements)

Value added is the wealth that a business has been able to create by its own and its employees' efforts. It is defined as 'sales income less materials and services purchased'. In rough and ready terms then, it consists of the sales proceeds, reduced by resources forked out to other parties not connected with the business. In this context employees, providers of capital and the government are regarded as connected with the business. This thinking enables the second half of the statement to show how the total value added is shared out between employees, providers of capital, the state (government) and finally the business itself for reinvestment. 'This statement would show how value added has been used to pay those contributing to its creation.'

The Corporate Report recommends that a value added statement should, as a minimum, contain the following information:

1 turnover
2 bought-in materials and services
3 employees' wages and benefits
4 dividends and interest payable
5 tax payable
6 amount retained for reinvestment.

The *Report* gives an illustration, which is reproduced as the example below.

Example

A manufacturing company – statement of value added:

	Year to 31 Dec. £m	Preceding year £m
Turnover	103.9	102.3
Bought-in materials and services	67.6	72.1
Value added	**£36.3**	**£30.2**

Applied the following way:

To pay employees:

Wages, pensions and fringe benefits		25.9	17.3

To pay providers of capital:

Interest on loans	0.8		0.6
Dividends to shareholders	0.9		0.9
		1.7	1.5

To pay government:

Corporation tax payable		3.9	3.1

To provide for maintenance and expansion of assets:

Depreciation	2.0		1.8
Retained profits	2.8		6.5
		4.8	8.3
Value added		£36.3	£30.2

A value added statement does not give any information that is not already available in traditional published accounts. What it does do is to rearrange that information and present it from a different perspective. The emphasis on shareholders inherent in the P&L account is removed. Instead, attention is focused on the wealth created by the business as a whole, as an economic unit, and on how that created wealth has been split up for various subgroups of the community as a whole. It is therefore arguable that a much more rounded picture is presented, both of the business as a whole and of the interrelationships between the various essential inputs that make the business operations possible.

There are no formal requirements from any source on the necessity to include a value added statement in the reporting package – no legal or stock exchange requirement, and no statement or even exposure draft from the ASB. In spite of this, many public companies have published a statement of this type in the past although few companies do so currently. This may, of course, be because a statement that shows very large sums being paid to employees as wages and to the government as taxes, and *relatively* small sums being paid to shareholders, is more politically (though not of course Politically) attractive than the P&L format! Unfortunately this lack of any formalized requirement leads to a lack of consistency in presentation. One particular question mark hangs over *The Corporate Report* treatment of depreciation. It is not immediately obvious that depreciation exists to 'provide for the *maintenance* of assets'. Perhaps even more importantly it can be argued that the maintenance of assets must be taken care of before we can talk about value *added*. This would suggest showing depreciation as a deduction from turnover, along with bought-in materials and services. The resulting lower value added figure is perhaps a better indication of economic wealth 'created'.

Employment report

Employees are obviously closely involved in business. They have to make many important decisions for themselves that will be heavily influenced by the activities, actions and prospects of business organizations. It could be argued that they have much more to lose than many shareholders or lenders, particularly as they are unable to 'spread their risks'. Employees almost always have to put their faith in one firm; they cannot involve themselves with large numbers, as investors or lenders can.

Employees certainly need some indication of future profitability, as do other users, but they also need additional information. Some of this may be financial, e.g. relating to the profitability of their own particular plant, but much of it will not be best presented in financial terms at all. In spite of this, many accountants would regard the provision of information useful to employees as being a necessary component of the total reporting package. This was certainly the view of *The Corporate Report*, which recommended that reporting statements should include an employment report containing the following information:

1 numbers employed, average for the financial year and actual on the first and last day
2 broad reasons for changes in the numbers employed
3 the age distribution and sex of employees
4 the functions of employees
5 the geographical location of major employment centres
6 major plant and site closures, disposals and acquisitions during the past year
7 the hours scheduled and worked by employees giving as much detail as possible concerning differences between groups of employees
8 employment costs, including fringe benefits
9 the costs and benefits associated with pension schemes and the ability of such schemes to meet future commitments
10 the cost and time spent on training
11 the names of unions recognized by the entity for the purpose of collective bargaining and membership figures where available, or the fact that this information has not been made available by the unions concerned
12 information concerning safety and health including the frequency and severity of accidents and occupational diseases
13 selected ratios relating to employment.

Statement of money exchanges with government

Part of the purpose of this idea is to emphasize the extent to which businesses provide governments with money, and therefore to show the importance of business organizations to the community as a whole. *The Corporate Report* states that the:

> purpose of the statement of money exchanges with government is to present the direct flow of money between enterprises and government with the object of demonstrating the degree of interdependence between the enterprise and the state. It does not purport to reflect the full extent of the direct and indirect benefits derived by entities from social services and public facilities provided by government.

The *Report* recommends that economic entities should:

> include in their corporate reports a statement of money exchanges with local and central government (distinguishing where appropriate between home and overseas governments). Such statements should include the following information

(which should be reconcilable to the funds flow statement and should distinguish between amounts collected and paid over in the capacity of agent and those directly borne by or benefiting the entity):

(a) PAYE collected and paid over.

(b) VAT collected and paid over.

(c) Corporation tax and similar taxes paid over and borne by the entity.

(d) Rates and similar levies paid over to local authorities and borne by the entity.

(e) Other sums paid to government departments and agencies including social security, training levies and duties.

(f) Money receipts from government including grants and subsidies.

Statement of transactions in foreign currency

The Corporate Report recommends that economic entities:

should present, as part of their corporate reports, a statement of cash transactions in foreign currency during the reporting period containing at least the following information:

(a) UK cash receipts for direct exports of goods and services.

(b) Cash payments from the UK to overseas concerns for direct imports distinguishing between imports of a capital nature (e.g. plant and machinery for use rather than resale) and those of a revenue nature (e.g. raw materials and services).

(c) Overseas borrowings remitted to or repaid from the UK.

(d) Overseas investments and loans made from or repaid to the UK.

(e) Overseas dividends, interest or similar payments received in the UK or UK dividends, interest or similar payments remitted overseas.

Contributions to the balance of payments, and the needs of users to assess the additional risks involved in overseas trade, are suggested as two reasons supporting this requirement. These reasons do not perhaps seem very compelling, and such statements are not common.

Statement of future prospects

Two points are absolutely clear. First, many users want to assess a business entity's future prospects. Secondly, any such assessment of future prospects involves a high degree of uncertainty. *The Corporate Report* is well aware of the problems:

It is important to recall that forecasts are projections rather than predictions. They do not so much predict the future as set out, in a logical and systematic manner, the future implications of past and present known facts adjusted by reference to estimates of likely future developments. Such projections may be judged to have different degrees of probability attached to them: but rarely is their probability so sure that they could be termed predictions. It is the certainty of uncertainty that makes entities unwilling to make public projections, though all those acquainted with such exercises are perfectly familiar with the limits on reliability which are inherent in them. The fear is that those less instructed will misunderstand and be misled.

The objections to publishing such forecasts include:

(a) Forecasts are concerned with the future and are therefore inherently uncertain. But unless carefully presented, users may regard forecasts as presenting facts rather than best estimates.

(b) Management will be judged by how well it has met its forecasts and may be encouraged to lower its targets by publishing only conservative forecasts which it knows are wholly attainable and to accept results which meet those forecasts.

(c) The provision of forecasts by enterprises suffering from financial difficulties may result in the withdrawal of support and thus precipitate an otherwise avoidable collapse.

However, forecasts are certainly desired by users (and competitors). And, in general, management and the accountants, with their inside knowledge and experience, are likely to be able to make better and more rational projections, which can then be reported, than the external users can make for themselves. *The Corporate Report* recommended that:

> While we would encourage the publication of more information about projections, we regard it as unrealistic to suggest that the publication of precisely quantified forecasts could form a standard part of corporate reports at the present time. Our recommendation is that corporate reports as a minimum include a statement of future prospects for the year following the balance sheet date. Such a statement should include information concerning:
> **(a)** Future profit levels.
> **(b)** Future employment levels and prospects.
> **(c)** Future investment levels.
> It should also include a note of the major assumptions on which the statement has been based.

Forecasts are required in a prospectus when a company is seeking a quotation on a stock exchange. Profit forecasts are often issued, usually as a defensive measure, in takeover bids. Again the assumptions underlying them are of crucial importance. The only formal requirement affecting annual accounts is for the directors' report to give an indication of future prospects or developments. Such an indication is unlikely to be quantified, and is usually couched in the vaguest of terms.

Statement of corporate objectives

It can be argued that the objectives being pursued by a business need to be publicized for two reasons. First, so that users can see the extent to which management objectives differ from their own, and, secondly, so that management's ability to achieve the stated objectives can be assessed. *The Corporate Report* recommended:

> that corporate reports of entities falling within our tests of significance should include a statement of corporate objectives including a statement of general philosophy or policy and information concerning strategic targets in the following policy areas:

   (a) Sales.
   (b) Added value.
   (c) Profitability.
   (d) Investment and finance.
   (e) Dividends.
   (f) Employment.
   (g) Consumer issues.
   (h) Environmental matters.
   (i) Other relevant social issues.

Again, of course, there is a distinct danger that management will declare objectives that it feels it can be almost certain of achieving.

Social accounting

In addition to the six specific proposals for additional statements that we have just considered, two other aspects are briefly considered in *The Corporate Report*. Social accounting is one of these. The comments in the *Report* are here reproduced in their entirety:

> Through legislation, society is imposing duties on business enterprises to comply with anti-pollution, safety and health and other socially beneficial requirements. Legislation of this type seems likely to increase in the future.
>
> Such regulations impose new costs, formerly borne by the community generally, on individual enterprises. There is good reason therefore for requesting such compulsory expenditure to be reported. Equally good arguments can be put forward for disclosing expenditure of this nature undertaken voluntarily.
>
> It is tempting to propose that entities disclose information which will show their impact on and their endeavours to protect society, its amenities and environment. In our opinion such a proposal would be impractical at the present time since the necessary generally agreed measurement techniques are not available.
>
> We believe that social accounting (the reporting of those costs and benefits, which may or may not be quantifiable in money terms, arising from economic activities and substantially borne or received by the community at large or particular groups not holding a direct relationship with the reporting entity) will be an area of growing concern to the accounting profession and one in which it has an opportunity to help develop practical reporting techniques.
>
> We recommend that further study be conducted into methods of social accounting but that no obligation to report on social and environmental issues be imposed until acceptable, objective and verifiable measurement techniques have been developed which will reveal an unbiased view of both the positive and negative impact of economic activities. Individual enterprises, as hitherto, will show the way. Where expenditure can be identified as relating primarily to projects undertaken to protect the environment or to benefit society it is likely that entities will wish to disclose the amounts involved for public relations purposes.

Remember the date of this publication – 1975. A certain amount of experimentation has been done, mainly in the United States. For example, an attempt has been made to work out a figure for pollution 'costs' caused by employees driving to work. The calculation used was number of employees times average journey length times 1 cent. The usefulness of this is doubtful to put it mildly – the 1 cent is obviously a purely arbitrary figure, and the implication that the employer is in some way to blame if the employee lives a long way away is hard to swallow. Perhaps the problem is that as accountants we tend to insist on translating everything into financial terms.

The definition of social accounting given by the *Report* quite correctly points out that the costs and benefits of interest here 'may or may not be quantifiable in money terms'. If accounting is defined as dealing with financial information, then it can be argued that social accounting or social reporting has nothing to do with accountants as such. Today, however, some accountants would certainly reject this restriction. The attention of the community is increasingly focused on the 'quality of life' rather than money, and if accountants do not attempt to produce useful information in this area then someone else will.

We must measure up to this challenge if we are to fulfil our duty as a profession to promote the public interest – so stated Sir Michael Lickiss, then President of the Institute of Chartered Accountants in England and Wales, in *Accountancy* (p. 6, January 1991). Have we measured up to this challenge? The 1990s has seen an extensive growth in environmental reporting and environmental legislation which has forced companies to begin to assess their environmental liabilities and risks. Shell plc has recently discovered the pressure that environmental groups can assert, as they were forced to abandon their attempts to dump the Brent Spar oil platform at sea. Users of Shell's financial statements may now demand a great deal more information in respect of Shell's environmental risks and liabilities.

Several research initiatives into social and environmental accounting have been established, in particular a centre has been established at the University of Dundee. The ACCA has also established an award for environmental reporting but as yet no standard setting authority has taken up the challenge in the UK. The Canadian Institute has produced a discussion paper on social and environmental reporting.

Social and environmental reporting is gaining in importance politically, for example the European Union has produced a regulation – Community Eco-management and Audit Schemes (EMAS) – where participating companies must establish environmental goals and report on their performance in meeting those goals. These reports will require external verification. A job for auditors surely! The Canadian Institute formed a study group in 1992 to look at environmental reporting and to clarify the term 'environmental audit'. They defined it as a 'systematic process of objectively obtaining and evaluating evidence regarding a verifiable assertion about activities and events to ascertain the degree of correspondence between the assertion and established criteria and then communicating the results [of the process] to interested users.'

Most environmental reporting both in the UK and elsewhere tends to be narrative and descriptive with companies using the document as a public relations exercise rather than as a true measure of the environmental risks and liabilities they carry. This is due to the inherent difficulties of measurement of environmental factors and of applying accounting concepts to these factors.

Activity 2

Traditionally accounting is based around the concepts of money measurement, going concern, accruals and prudence. Identify whether environmental issues are taken into account in the application of these concepts to a business and if not why not.

Activity 2 feedback

Money measurement requires that only those facts that can be recorded in monetary terms with some objectivity are taken account of even if other facts are extremely relevant (see Chapter 3). Environmental factors are very difficult to measure in monetary terms. How, for example, do you place a monetary measure on the damage being done to the environment through car exhaust emissions of employees travelling to work?

The going concern convention states that in the absence of evidence to the contrary it is assumed that the business will continue into the future. This convention is principally concerned with solvency and financial performance not with the impact of environmental factors. For example, in assessing going concern for Shell, little regard will be had as to whether pressure groups could ever force them out of business, but the problems of Brent Spar may well have had an effect on their sales.

Accruals requires a matching of expenses used up in generating revenues. However, companies make no assessment of the expense of environmental factors such as their contribution to global warming through the emission of carbon dioxide or to acid rain from the emission of sulphur and nitrogen oxides.

Prudence is the concept of recording all possible losses, but not anticipating gains. The concept rarely includes environmental losses as they are difficult to quantify or sometimes even anticipate! Business entity is also possibly relevant as losses which cannot be 'charged' to the entity itself are ignored.

The Institute of Chartered Accountants in England and Wales (ICAEW) environment steering group produced a discussion draft on reporting environmental liabilities, but excluded decommissioning of nuclear power stations from its discussion! Is this prudent?

Environmental performance reports (EPR) are in their infancy and there is no standard format. BT state that the primary objective of their EPR is:

■ to publish a balanced, open and honest view of the environmental performance of BT
■ to record progress (or otherwise) towards BT's environmental policy commitments
■ to demonstrate continuous improvement in environmental performance through the publication of specific targets
■ to identify areas for future improvement
■ to contribute to the global debate on environmental management and sustainable development
■ to contribute to the development of recognized methods and standards of environmental reporting.

They also state:

> that whilst every effort has been made to ensure that the information is neither incomplete nor misleading it cannot be considered to be as reliable as the financial information published in the annual accounts.

The report provides lots of data and statistics, for example, the amount of fuel used, distances travelled, number of plastic cups and cans recycled, but rarely do we see a pound sign in respect of environmental liabilities and risks. But then this is understandable given the problems of measurement we have already identified.

However, environmental information is becoming essential for many businesses and its users. Indeed some organizations, which see environmental issues as important, are becoming market leaders, for example, Body Shop. Businesses are becoming 'greener' and must develop accounting systems to enable environmental performance reporting to take place.

The view of one writer on environmental reporting is reproduced below from an article in *Accountancy* (p. 98, October 1994) by Chris Hibbitt:

> From a positive perspective, the environmental challenge represents a golden opportunity for the profession to serve management, shareholders, governments and other stakeholders. But it requires, in return, a willingness to undergo a major re-assessment of conventional accounting theory, the role and purpose of financial reporting and of the way accountants think, learn and apply their knowledge and skills. As part of this process, they will have to be prepared to sacrifice the false idol of objectivity. It may also involve throwing away most of the present set of concepts and standards and developing new ones that are more relevant to the present and future needs of management, governments and society.
>
> The ASB can start this process by setting up a task force to address accounting for sustainable development. The Auditing Practices Board should do the same in relation to environmental auditing standards. All of us can and must contribute to the environmental challenge. The profession's raison d'être, as the assurer of the integrity of financial information, depends on it. Public trust demands it.

It is also worthy of note that BT and Touche Ross have attempted to take a leading role in environmental reporting. Touche Ross were appointed as the external verifiers of the BT EPR in 1994 and 1995. Touche Ross state the reasons for verification as being:

■ to underpin the credibility of the EPR
■ to provide the reporting company's management with a level of comfort that its reporting systems are adequate and that it has begun to address all the key environmental impacts and risks of its operations
■ to provide a degree of assurance that the company is not unknowingly publishing erroneous performance data.

We reproduce below for you the verification report by Touche Ross on BT's EPR:

> *Report by Touche Ross & Co. to British Telecommunications plc*
> We have reviewed the Environmental Performance Report for the year-ended 31 March 1994 set out on pages 2 to 43. The report is the responsibility of, and has been approved by, the Directors.
>
> The report has been prepared on the basis described under 'BT's Environmental Report in Context' on page 2. The inherent limitations in completeness and accuracy of data are set out therein.
>
> The report contains:
> (i)   data and information, highlighted in blue type, in respect of BT's significant environmental impacts; and
> (ii) other data included to indicate the scale of BT's environmental issues.
>
> In respect of (i), our review consisted of making enquiries of management responsible for compiling the data, an examination of relevant supporting schedules, and a review of the work performed and enquiries made by BT's internal audit division. In respect of (ii), our review was limited to enquiries made of BT's internal auditors.

On the basis of our review, in our opinion BT has made reasonable endeavours to:

- identify its significant environmental impacts
- give a fair and balanced disclosure of all available information relevant to those impacts where material.

Environmental reporting and the international scene

The international scene in respect of environmental reporting is also developing. FEE, the Federation des Experts Comptables Europeens, has established an environmental task force to review the current body of IASs and to recommend improvements in those standards to IASC (International Accounting Standards Committee). A report by UNCTAD (United Nations Conference on Trade and Environment) Secretariat: Environmental Financial Accounting and Reporting at the Corporate Level has also been issued on 19th November 1997. This report aims to identify 'best practice' for reporting and communicating environmental performance both in terms of reporting costs of environmental liabilities and in presenting non-financial information. The report was actually synthesized from two other papers:

- Accounting and reporting for environmental liabilities and costs within the existing financial reporting framework (David Moore, Canadian Institute of Chartered Accountants, 1997) and
- Linking environmental and financial performance: a survey of best practice techniques (Roger Adams, ACCA, 1997).

The findings of the report were that Financial Sector investors were placing increasing importance on environmental data in forming their investment decisions, although no obvious causal mechanism could be identified.

It also makes recommendations on potential environmental disclosures in annual reports:

Annual report element	Recommended environmental disclosure(s)
Chairman/CEOs report	■ corporate commitment to continuous environmental improvement ■ significant improvements since last report
Business segment	■ segmented environmental performance data (if not provided in the environmental review (see below) ■ improvements in key areas since previous report
Environmental review	■ scope of the review ■ corporate environmental policy statement ■ extent of world-wide compliance ■ key environmental issues facing the company ■ organizational responsibilities ■ description of environmental management systems for international standards (e.g. ICC/ISO/EMAS) ■ segmental performance data based around: energy use, materials use emissions (CO_2, CFCs, NO_x, SO_2, etc.) and waste disposal routes

	■ sector-specific data including industry agreed EPIs (including eco-efficiency based EPIs)
	■ financial data on environmental costs (energy, waste reme-diation, staffing, exceptional charges and write downs, fines and penalties, green taxes paid, capital investment)
	■ financial estimates of savings and benefits flowing from pro-environment efforts
	■ cross-reference to other environmental reports
	■ independent verification statement
Operating and financial review/MD & A	■ key environmental issues facing the company
	■ short/medium term plans for addressing these
	■ progress in addressing changes required by future legal requirements
	■ actual and projected levels of environmental expenditure
	■ legal matters pending
Report of the Directors	■ environmental policy statement (if not provided elsewhere)
Accounting policy	■ estimation of provisions and contingencies
disclosure	■ capitalization policies
	■ impairment policies
	■ de-commissioning and land remediation policies
	■ depreciation polices
Profit and loss account	■ exceptional environmental charges (e.g. for remediation, de-commissioning or impairment charges)
	■ other environmental costs and benefits (if not disclosed in separate environmental review – see above)
Balance sheet	■ environmental provisions
	■ de-commissioning provisions
	■ environmental costs capitalized
	■ expected recoveries
Notes to the accounts	■ contingent environmental liabilities plus explanations
Other	■ Environmental data can also be put in the summary finan-cial statements (e.g. Body Shop, Scottish Hydro)

and in stand-alone reports.

Improving the quality of stand-alone environmental performance reports:

■ clearer statements regarding the key environmental issues facing the reporting entity
■ more use could be made of the sort of segmental reporting techniques used for consol-idated financial reporting purposes
■ a clearer statement of the completeness of the environmental reporting should be made
■ a statement of the number of contaminated sites, the current state of remediation at each site, and the likely timing and cost of future remediation procedures
■ the provision of industry relevant and industry accepted benchmarked environmental per-formance indicators
■ the provision of externally verified third-party opinions based on accepted and tested verification procedures
■ increased experimentation with development of sustainable development indicators.

Recommendations for future work were made in the following areas:

- agreeing financial accounting definitions in respect of environmental costs and revenues
- development of standardized environmental performance indicators
- acceptance of a standard format of presentation for environmental reporting both within financial statements and stand alone
- development of qualitative conceptual framework
- improving the credibility by formalizing audit of the process.

Activity 3

The following are extracts in respect of environmental issues taken from financial statements:

Delta annual report and accounts 1997

Environmental policy

The Group is committed to best environmental practice and has clear management responsibilities to ensure full compliance. The Group's overall policy forms the basis of further detailed policies that are appropriate to the individual operating businesses.

It is Group policy to manage its activities so as to give benefit to society; this entails ensuring they are acceptable to the community and that any adverse effects on the environment are reduced to a practicable minimum.

It is also Group policy to:

- Encourage and promote the interchange of environmental information and technology among its companies.
- Provide information to enable Group processes, when used under licence, to be operated without unacceptable effects on the environment.
- Encourage its companies to establish and implement for themselves environmental policies and environmental management systems.

The managing director of each business area is responsible to the Chief Executive (who is in turn responsible to the Delta plc Board) for ensuring adherence to the above Group policy and for an organisational structure within his business area to ensure adherence. Overall policy is coordinated by the Company Secretary.

The Group requires the following objectives and targets at all operating companies. This, of course, is not an exhaustive list, but they are corporate objectives and targets which have been given a high priority by the Group.

The implementation of these objectives must be at local level, but any change of policy or corporate implementation will be from the Company Secretary.

The objectives are:

- To promote an environmental awareness in all employees and thereby develop a well motivated and environmentally proactive workforce.
- To eliminate the use of ozone depleting substances (ODS).
- To set targets for reduction of electricity, gas, oil and water consumption.

- To encourage waste management programmes which encourage recycling and provide environmental incentives to employees.
- The environmental probity of suppliers and sub-contractors will be investigated.
- To ensure compliance with all environmental legislation.
- To reduce and prevent emissions to air, discharges to water and deposits to land.

The targets for reaching each of the above objectives will be set by each operating company within the Group. Each of the targets will be audited within the Group Environmental Audit.

The Group has appointed external consultants to initiate an environmental review covering its sites worldwide.

Ladbrokes Group plc report and accounts 1997

Environment

Ladbroke Group recognises the importance of improving its environmental performance, and efficiencies in energy and waste management are sought across its operating divisions worldwide.

As a founder member of the International Hotel Environment Initiative ('IHEI'), part of the Prince of Wales Business Leaders Forum, Hilton International is committed to environmentally sound practices. A central group oversees the development of environmental strategy and practices which are then issued to our hotels for implementation. All general managers and their staff are encouraged to introduce environmentally-friendly best practice into their hotels.

One example is the Sandton Hilton in South Africa which opened on 1st November 1997. Hilton International has, from the outset, taken steps to ensure the hotel becomes an environmental showcase for the company by incorporating sound environmental practice in the structure, planning and management of the hotel. High building specifications were set and, in line with IHEI guidelines, the hotel worked closely with the Hilton Technical Services team with monthly site visits to track the process. This has resulted in a low rise hotel which enhances the surrounding residential area with grounds that have been planted with indigenous trees and shrubs. Natural products such as wool carpets have been used throughout the hotel and a hot water storage system installed which allows water to be heated during off peak times and stored until required. In addition, an in-house 'Green Team' has been created to manage environmental issues on an ongoing basis.

TI Group plc annual report 1997

Environment

TI Group's environmental policies are implemented by its global Environmental Co-ordination Panel which reports to a main Board Director. It is tasked with ensuring that all TI businesses execute the Group's environmental policies through the implementation of environmental management systems.

Specfic objectives have been developed for TI Group's main business groups which have active programmes for the management of scarce resources, reducing discharges to the air, waste management and energy conservation. TI Group's commitment is endorsed by senior management and environmental issues are an integral part of managerial responsibilities at every level.

The Panel has undertaken a global audit of TI Group's businesses and is implementing regular reporting against agreed objectives. TI Group has begun working towards the international environmental standard ISO 14001 in all its worldwide businesses.

TI Group's businesses are used to operating in the most demanding legislative environment. As proof of this, the Group has won Environmental Awards in the UK, the USA and Continental Europe and is a member of environmental organisations in these regions.

Compare these statements with the recommendations from the UNCTAD report in respect of environmental reporting in annual reports and state whether or not they meet these recommendations.

Activity 3 feedback

The obvious answer is that these statements make little contribution to the achievement of these recommendations. For example, it is very laudable of Ladbrokes to state they are committed to environmentally sound practices but we are given no substantial data to assess this, nor is the statement independently verified, nor are we given actual and projected levels of environmental expenditure.

United Biscuits annual report 1997 provides the following statement in respect of the environment:

Environment

Our latest environmental audit confirms that we have further reduced the impact of our operations on the environment. Specific examples are as follows.

Atmosphere. Detailed monitoring and maintenance have reduced emissions from vehicles and plant, and prevented microbiological emissions. The small remaining amounts of CFCs and asbestos are being eliminated.

Water. We have made marked progress in this area. Reductions in water consumption at many sites included 60% at Harlesden, 70% at Halifax and 66% at Deventer. Okehampton is making savings worth £10 000 a year and our Teesside crisps factory has cut consumption per tonne of product by 35%.

Energy. Harlesden has cut boiler fuel usage by 60% and improvements at Manchester should save around £250 000 a year. In China, our most recent oven incorporates more effective insulation to improve efficiency.

Packaging. Our factories continue to reduce wastage, and the use of stronger but lighter board has reduced costs by 5% at Okehampton.

Waste. Various waste reduction projects have reduced transport energy costs and landfill requirements. Wherever feasible, we sell edible waste as animal feed. Savings achieved through better understanding and control of processes include £200 000 a year on Hula Hoops production.

Noise. Improved soundproofing and quieter new plant have reduced the effects of noise on employees and neighbours alike. Relocation of the factory entrance at Tolicross has reduced the impact of vehicles on the community.

Wildlife. Young's has signed the Statement of Intent of the Marine Stewardship Council, a new body set up to accredit sustainable fishing.

There are some data here but it is mostly about informing users how much the company has saved or will save rather than providing full environmental disclosure as recommended by the report.

It seems there is a long way to go before companies reach the level of reporting required. However, the number of UK companies producing environmental stand-alone reports continues to grow, 30 out of the FT top 100 did so in 1997 according to a survey by KPMG. Indeed, Shell has bowed to public pressure and in April 1998 published its first social responsibility report, and in June 1998 a health, safety and environmental report fully audited. Powergen in their financial statements for the year-ended March 1998 state that their 1997 Environmental Report; 'is the most comprehensive yet! As well as containing environmental information from all of the company's locations, it features a range of articles on recent environmental initiatives such as the company's progress towards the international environmental management standard, ISO 14001'. In fact the report itself runs to 44 pages and includes:

- an environmental policy statement
- statement on achieving environmental management standard ISO 14001
- external verification statement
- performance data in terms of emissions and chemical release calendar
- details of individual power stations.

What is impossible to find in the report though is one single pound sign! Other notable publications in the environmental accounting area are:

- *An Exploration of the Business Conceptions of Sustainability and its Implications for Accounting* (Bebbington and Thompson, ACCA, 1996)
- *Environmental Accounting Case Studies: Full Cost Accounting for Decision Making at Ontario Hydro* (United States Environmental Protection Agency, 1996)
- *Full Cost Accounting From an Environmental Perspective* (CICA, 1997).

In conclusion to the discussion on environmental accounting we return to Hicks and the theory of capital maintenance that was dealt with in Chapter 4. On p. 47 the following quote from Hicks was provided:

> The purpose of income calculations in practical affairs is to give people an indication of the amount which they can consume without impoverishing themselves.

This can be applied to the environment as if we continue to consume the environment we will impoverish, perhaps not ourselves, but certainly future generations. Economic activity affects the environment as natural resources are depleted or polluted through for example usage, the effects of global warming and acid rain. There is a need to look forward, as the theory of maintenance of capital does (see Chapter 4), to ensure natural wealth – the environment – is maintained and therefore a system of stewardship and maintenance of this natural wealth is a necessity. Reporting in respect of stewardship and maintenance of assets is the accountants domain; remember in Chapter 2, p. 13, accounting was identified as the provision of useful figures to users about their resources. It will be seen later when considering the Statement of Principles produced by the ASB that they define the objectives of financial statements to be to provide information about the financial position, performance and adaptability of an enterprise for assessing the stewardship of management and for making economic decisions. In the view of many financial statements need to incorporate the issue of environmental reporting to meet this objective. This will not be an easy task as systems will be difficult to design but as is stated in *Accounting and the Challenge of the Nineties* edited by Dave Owen, p. 269:

> Accountants through their training are ideally placed to play a leading role in environmental reporting. Some, including the author of this chapter (Brian Ing) would argue it is their duty to undertake this role.

Activity 4

Obtain an environmental report for any company of your choice and assess whether it fulfils the requirements identified by the UNCTAD report for stand-alone reports.

Activity 4 feedback

Difficult to provide so we suggest you do your own!

Disaggregation or segmental reporting

The Corporate Report states:

> The problem of disaggregation (i.e. the analysis of general corporate information between separate divisions or classes of business which are individually of economic significance, sometimes called segment or site reporting) arises in the context of the degree of disclosure appropriate in basic financial statements. The problem is found at its most extreme in organizations of vast size and spread such as nationalized industries and multinational companies.
>
> Our suggestion is that the basis of division of activities selected should be the one which in the opinion of the management will most fairly represent the range and significance of the entity's activities. The division could be based on groups of products or services, group companies, operating or geographic divisions, markets served or any combination of these items which would assist fair presentation.
>
> We consider it desirable that the following information (the preparation of which may involve some arbitrary apportionments) should be disclosed about each main class of activity:
>
> **(a)** Turnover.
> **(b)** Value added.
> **(c)** Profits or losses before tax.
> **(d)** Capital employed.
> **(e)** Employment information.

The basis of division into classes of activity should be stated as should, where appropriate, other bases for internal and special purpose reporting. There should also be disclosed, insofar as they will assist in forming a view of the entity's financial position and will not be damaging to its interests, significant changes during the year in principal products, services or markets as classified in the corporate report.

Segmental reporting is one of the ideas from *The Corporate Report* which have been taken up to some extent both nationally and internationally. The UK regulatory requirements are discussed at length in Part Three, Chapter 26.

More (or less) information?

There is a school of thought that more information is always, provided it is properly presented, a good thing. The list of possibilities is almost endless: details of expenses, breakdowns of existing figures in various ways, more statements, presentation of statements on several different bases, and so on. But there is a danger here that the purpose of the whole operation gets forgotten. We are trying to produce information that the typical user can actually *use*. What evidence there is tends to suggest that many users are not able to understand the information they are already getting. It could be argued that the priority for accountants should be to improve their ability to communicate understanding, rather than to increase the detail and complexity of their reports. Is the graph or the pie chart more useful than the beautifully balanced balance sheet? Is the 'chatty' chairman's statement of more use than the precisely detailed and carefully audited accounts and voluminous notes? Is the EPR of more use than the segmental report even if it does lack a degree of reliability, a primary characteristic of useful information? And how can we audit the chairman's chatty statement and EPR? As a profession, if we put all our trust in figures, especially subjective figures, we do so at our peril.

Summary

In this chapter we have outlined a wide variety of possible developments and extensions to the accounting framework and to reporting practice. All involve additional effort and therefore additional cost. But if the advantages to some of the users or potential users outweigh those costs, then we should presumably produce them.

Exercises

1 The matching (accruals) convention is essential if accountants are to satisfy the needs of the users of accounting reports. Discuss.

2 In the last analysis, financial reporting is about numbers. Discuss.

3 (a) **Who were considered to be the potential users of financial reports in *The Corporate Report?*** (8 marks)

(b) **What do you consider to be their information needs?** (8 marks)

(c) **How would you expect a consideration of user needs to influence financial reporting?** (9 marks)

(25 marks)

(ACCA)

4 The discussion document issued by the Accounting Standards Committee entitled *The Corporate Report* recommended that companies should include the following four statements in their annual published reports:

(a) **Money exchanges with the government.** (5 marks)

(b) **Transactions in foreign currency.** (5 marks)

(c) **Future prospects.** (5 marks)

(d) **Corporate objectives.** (5 marks)

You are required to explain the purpose and outline some of the possible contents of each statement. **(20 marks)**

(ACCA)

5 'An objective of financial statements is to provide information useful for the predictive process. Financial forecasts should be provided when they will enhance the reliability of users' predictions.'

What do you consider would be the advantages and disadvantages of including a financial forecast as part of a company's published financial statement?

(20 marks)

(ACCA)

6 'The fundamental objective of corporate reports is to communicate economic measurements of and information about the resources and performance of the reporting entity useful to those having reasonable rights to such information.'

The Corporate Report

Required:

Analyse the above quotation and discuss each part in relation to financial reporting. **(20 marks)**

(ACCA)

7 (a) **Define social responsibility accounting.** (7 marks)

(b) **To what environmental aspects should companies draw attention in their annual reports?** (6 marks)

(c) **Why has the traditional model of income measurement failed to account for the impact of business activities on the environment?** (7 marks)

(20 marks)

(ACCA)

8 It has been suggested that shareholders find the written information in the chairperson's and directors reports more useful than the quantitative information in the full financial statements.

You are required to discuss this statement in the context of the usefulness of company reports. **(20 marks)**

(ACCA)

9 (a) **Give FOUR examples of items that could be included in an employee report and state for each how this information might be useful to an employee.**

(12 marks)

(b) **Do you consider that entities should produce employee reports? Why? List the advantages and disadvantages of producing employee reports.**

(8 marks)

(20 Marks)

(ACCA)

10 'The simplest way of putting profit into perspective *vis-à-vis* the whole enterprise as a collective effort is by presentation of a statement of value added.'

The following five-year financial summary has been extracted from the annual report of Ovett Holdings plc for the year-ended 30 June 20X5. Ovett Holdings' principal activity is to weave the cloth used on the rollers of paper making machines.

	Years ended June				
	20X1	20X2	20X3	20X4	20X5
	£m	£m	£m	£m	£m
Nets assets employed:					
Fixed Assets	37	42	53	71	69
Current assets	28	10	46	67	72
Current liabilities	13	15	16	31	37
Net current assets	15	25	30	36	35
Long-term liabilities	(1)	(3)	(5)	(14)	(11)
	51	64	78	93	93
Financed by:					
Issued ordinary shares	3	3	3	3	3
Reserves	34	41	29	34	36
	37	44	32	37	39
Issued preference shares	–	–	22	22	22
Total shareholders' funds	37	44	54	59	61
Minority interest	14	20	24	34	32
	51	64	78	93	93
Turnover	71	89	103	125	138
Costs of sales					
Material	20	29	36	78	88
Labour	10	11	14	12	12
Depreciation	6	7	9	7	7
Increase in finished stocks and WIP	(4)	(6)	(7)	(12)	(9)
	(32)	(41)	(52)	(85)	(98)
Gross profit	39	48	51	40	40
Other net operating expenses					
Wages and salaries	4	4	4	8	8
Employees' profit share	–	1	1	–	1
Depreciation	2	2	3	4	4
Legal fees on reorganization	–	–	–	3	–
Other	19	21	19	2	2
	(25)	(28)	(27)	(17)	(15)
Operating profit	14	20	24	23	25
Interest payable	(2)	(1)	(1)	(3)	(4)
Profit on ordinary activities before taxation	12	19	23	20	21
Share of profit of associated companies	4	6	7	7	7
Taxation	(1)	(3)	(5)	(1)	(4)
Share of taxation of associated companies	(1)	(2)	(2)	(2)	(2)
Profit on ordinary activities after taxation	14	20	23	24	22
Minority interest	(7)	(10)	(12)	(17)	(14)
Profit attributable to members of Ovett Holdings plc	7	10	11	7	8
Extraordinary charges	–	(1)	(2)	–	(2)
Profit for the financial year	7	9	9	7	6
Preference dividends	–	–	(1)	(2)	(2)
Ordinary dividends	(1)	(2)	(3)	(3)	(3)
Profit retained transferred to reserves	6	7	5	2	1
Average number of employees	1819	1837	1901	1936	1796

Required:
(a) Draft value added statements of Ovett Holdings plc and its subsidiaries for each of the five years 20X1–20X5. (8 marks)
(b) Describe and justify alternative treatments for:
   (i) depreciation
   (ii) PAYE and national insurance contributions in the preparation of value added statements. (4 marks)
(12 marks)
(ACCA, adapted)

11 'When users are asked what they want from corporate environmental statements, there appears to be the usual mix of that which is deliverable, that which would be nice if only the accountants could find a way of delivering it and that which will never be deliverable – available or not – because of commercial sensitivity.'

Roger Adams *Accountancy Age* (p. 16, May 1994).

Is this pessimistic or realistic? Discuss and illustrate.

Towards a general framework

After reading this chapter you should be able to:
- state and discuss definitions of the major classes of items found in financial statements
- explain the concept and viability of a conceptual framework for financial reporting
- outline and discuss the International Accounting Standards Committee (IASC) framework
- state and defend your own preferred improvements to financial reporting principles and practices.

Introduction

The first purpose of this chapter is to explain and define the major items that appear in financial accounting. There is a gap between the general principles we have been discussing so far, and the detail of many SSAPs and FRSs. SSAP 12 on depreciation, for example, defines depreciation in the context of 'fixed assets'. However, it makes no attempt to define 'fixed assets', or even 'assets'!

The second purpose of this chapter is to provide a historical and logical basis for the consideration of current thinking about the creation of a more general framework. The recent work by the Accounting Standards Board (ASB) in this area is discussed in Part Three, Chapter 15. Here we build up the picture from the earlier American thinking, and explore the work of the International Accounting Standards Committee (IASC), on which much of the ASB material is based.

The idea of a completely coherent set of accounting conventions relating together to form a single unified theory gained considerable support in the United States in the mid-1970s. The main American Accounting Standards authority, the Federal Accounting Standards Board (FASB), instituted an extremely lengthy and expensive research project, known as the Conceptual Framework project. This project has produced numerous reports and publications. In 1981, a report was prepared by Professor Macve for the ASC in the UK on the desirability and practicality of developing an agreed conceptual framework. Its terms of reference were:

> To review critically current literature and opinion in the US, UK and elsewhere with a view to forming preliminary conclusions as to the possibilities of developing an agreed conceptual framework for setting accounting standards and the nature of such a framework; and to identify areas for further research.

A conceptual framework has been defined by the FASB as:

> A constitution, a coherent system of interrelated objectives and fundamentals that can lead to consistent standards and that prescribes the nature, function and limits of financial accounting and financial statements.

In general terms, to quote Macve, it is 'a basic structure for organizing one's thinking about what one is trying to do and how to go about it'.

The basic conclusions of Professor Macve's report were first that such a coherent framework was unattainable, and secondly that the process of attempting to find one was highly beneficial in that it was an important educational process aiding understanding and clarification of thought, objective and definition. The subtlety of this distinction was too much for the accountants of the early 1980s and the report was widely interpreted as giving a general 'thumbs down' to the whole concept. However, interest in the concept has returned from several quarters in more recent years.

This chapter uses a publication from the original US project as a starting point to consider formal definitions of the major classes of accounting items. We then discuss the more recent moves.

The elements of accounting

The word 'elements' comes from a publication by the American FASB as part of their *Conceptual Framework Project, Elements of Financial Statements of Business Enterprises* (December 1980). This publication is used as the basis for this section merely as a convenient starting point. We shall consider the ten 'elements' defined there and expand discussion as necessary for our purposes.

'Elements' are defined in the report as follows:

> Elements of financial statements are the building blocks with which financial statements are constructed – the class of items that financial statements comprise. The items in financial statements represent in words and numbers certain enterprise resources, claims to those resources, and the effects of transactions and other events and circumstances that result in changes in those resources and claims.

Given any particular transaction, we need some workable definitions in order to determine which 'classes of items' in financial statements (American for accounts) are affected.

The balance sheet

Assets

Assets are probable future economic benefits obtained or controlled by a particular entity as a result of past transactions or events. Thus an asset should:

1 give probable future benefit
2 be possessed or controlled by the business
3 have arisen from some earlier transaction or event.

Activity 1

Consider whether each of the following are assets, giving reasons for your answers.

1 A heap of rusty metal worth £10 as scrap but costing £20 to transport to the scrap dealer.
2 A municipal or trades union social or welfare centre outside the factory that substantially improves the overall working conditions of a firm's employees.
2 The benefits derived from next year's sales.

Activity 1 feedback

None of the above are assets because

1 has no probable future benefit
2 is not possessed or controlled by the business
3 there is no earlier transaction or event.

It must be noted that throughout this chapter we are concerned with definition, not with measurement. The question here is: 'Is there an item to put in the assets section of the accounts?' If the answer is yes, then we can consider the appropriate valuation or measurement approach – cost concept, NRV, or whatever.

Assets are always divided into **fixed assets** and **current assets**. The definition of fixed assets is often misunderstood. A fixed asset is not an asset with a long life. The essential criterion is the *intention* of the owner, the intended *use* of the asset. A fixed asset is an asset that the firm intends to *use* within the business, over an extended period, in order to assist its daily operating activities. A current asset, on the other hand, is usually defined in terms of time. A current asset is an asset likely to change its form, i.e. likely to undergo some transaction, within twelve months. Consider two firms, A and B. Firm A is a motor trader. It possesses some motor vehicles that it is attempting to sell, and it also possesses some desks used by the sales staff, management and so on. Firm B is a furniture dealer. It possesses some desks that it is attempting to sell, and it also possesses some motor vehicles used by the sales staff and for delivery purposes. In the accounts of A, the motor vehicles are current assets and the desks are fixed assets. In the accounts of B, the motor vehicles are fixed assets and the desks are current assets. Note incidentally that a fixed asset which, after several years' use, is about to be sold for scrap, remains in the fixed asset part of the accounts even though it is about to change its form.

These two definitions, because they are based on different criteria (one on use and one on time), are not mutually exclusive. It is possible to think of assets that do not conveniently appear to be either fixed or current. Investments, for example, or goodwill. At one time the UK Companies Act recognized a category of assets that are 'neither fixed nor current', but this is no longer the case.

Liabilities

Liabilities are probable future sacrifices of economic benefits arising from present obligations of a particular entity to transfer assets or provide services to other entities in the future as a result of past transactions or events. Thus a liability should:

1 involve probable future sacrifice

2 arise from present obligations to act in the future

3 be as a result of past transactions or events.

So, for example, a firm will have a liability arising from a guarantee extending into next year given on this year's sales. However, the firm does not have a liability, today, to pay for next week's purchases or for next week's wages. This last point is, in fact, rather problematic. The firm cannot avoid paying next week's wages under UK employment legislation – either in the normal way or as payment in lieu of notice and redundancy pay. But next week's wages are still not treated as a liability. This is presumably on the grounds that next week's work has also not been done. The important 'event' is regarded as the doing of the work, which is a future event, not as the signing of the employee's contract – which would be a past event.

Liabilities are usually divided into current liabilities and long-term liabilities. Here the distinction is simply one of time. Current liabilities are those likely to be settled within twelve months. Long-term liabilities are those items regarded as long-term sources of finance for the business. Current liabilities are regarded as part of working capital (a negative part). Long-term liabilities are regarded as part of capital employed (a positive part – see the formats in Chapter 13). Even here, however, there can be problems of distinction. How should taxation payable in fifteen months' time be regarded?

Equity

Equity is the residual interest in the assets of an entity that remains after deducting its liabilities. In a business enterprise, the equity is the ownership interest.

This is straightforward. The ownership interest – equity, or capital – is the net of assets and liabilities. It is the balancing figure in the balance sheet.

Investments by owners

Investments by owners are increases in net assets of a particular enterprise resulting from transfers to it from the entities of something of value to obtain or increase ownership interests (or equity) in it.

Distributions to owners

Distributions to owners are decreases in net assets of a particular enterprise resulting from transferring assets, rendering services, or incurring liabilities by the enterprise to owners. Distributions to owners decrease ownership interest (or equity) in an enterprise.

These two are also fairly straightforward. The essential point is to distinguish between:

1 transactions affecting the amount of owners' equity caused by the transfer of money or money equivalent *between* the business and the owners – investments or distributions depending on the direction of movement; and

2 transactions affecting the amount of owners' equity caused by business activity leading to an alteration in the assets less liabilities (net assets) of the business – comprehensive income as defined below.

Profit and loss

Comprehensive income

Comprehensive income is the change in equity (net assets) of an entity during a period from transactions and other events and circumstances from non-owner sources. It includes all changes in equity during a period except those resulting from investments by owners and distributions to owners. This 'total income' is broken down into four subgroups, as follows:

Revenues

Revenues are inflows or other enhancements of assets of an entity or settlements of its liabilities (or a combination of both) during a period from delivering or producing goods, rendering services, or other activities that constitute the entity's ongoing major or central operations.

Expenses

Expenses are outflows or other using up of assets or incurrences of liabilities (or a combination of both) during a period from delivering or producing goods, rendering services, or carrying out other activities that constitute the entity's ongoing major or central operations.

Gains

Gains are increases in equity (net assets) from peripheral or incidental transactions of an entity and from all other transactions and other events and circumstances affecting the entity during a period, except those that result from revenues or investments by owners.

Losses

Losses are decreases in equity (net assets) from peripheral or incidental transactions of an entity and from all other transactions and other events and circumstances affecting the entity during a period except those that result from expenses or distributions to owners.

Revenues and expenses clearly relate together. They are the items, positive and negative, respectively, arising from the business's major or central operations. They are the every-day operational inflows and outflows of assets (not of money). They are to be distinguished from gains and losses. These, as defined, are all alterations to owners' equity except:

1 those caused by investments/distribution; and
2 those caused by revenues/expenses.

This threefold distinction, capital adjustments, operating items, non-operating items, is of fundamental importance. That is not to say, however, that the definitions given here are easy to apply or that the distinctions are easy to make. In particular we have to define exactly what the 'ongoing major or central operations' are. But the principles are clear enough. Capital adjustments are simply transfers between business and owner, and of themselves do not affect the wealth of the owners. Operating items, revenues and expenses, are clearly P&L account items. Gains and losses, as defined, are the incidental events affecting business resources. Their treatment is less clear, except to say that they must be treated differently from the other two.

These elements are defined at a high level of generality. In terms of operational usefulness, the definitions are perhaps not specific enough. Are holding gains on stock revenue (enhancement of assets related to ongoing central operations), or are they gains (businesses exist to sell stock, not to hold it!)? But the above discussion does highlight the importance of such basic questions and distinctions.

A conceptual framework for the millennium?

In recent years there has been a gradual but significant increase in interest in the conceptual framework concept. It is hard to pinpoint the origin of this, but it seems to have two essential strands. The first is an emerging recognition that detailed specific regulation is ineffective. The letter of specific regulation can be avoided by changing the form of any particular transaction. To prevent this it is necessary to establish general underlying principles which permeate and underpin any specific transaction or chain of transactions which exists or which may be invented at a later date. The second strand is a whole spate of formal proposals from various bodies and individuals seeking to provide or move towards an all-embracing theory.

We concentrate here on the International Accounting Standards Committee (IASC) publication, as it is the most 'balanced' and considered likely to turn out the most authoritative.

The current UK thinking is considered in more detail in Part Three (Chapter 15).

The IASC framework

The framework, after earlier appearance in exposure draft form, was published in July 1989. It is not itself a standard and indeed its exact status is rather unclear. Its declared purposes are to:

1 (a) assist the Board of IASC in the development of future International Accounting Standards and in its review of existing International Accounting Standards;

(b) assist the Board of IASC in promoting harmonization of regulations, accounting standards and procedures relating to the presentation of financial statements by providing a basis for reducing the number of alternative accounting treatments permitted by International Accounting Standards;

(c) assist national standard setting bodies in developing national standards;

(d) assist preparers of financial statements in applying International Accounting Standards and in dealing with topics that have yet to form the subject of an International Accounting Standard;

(e) assist auditors in forming an opinion as to whether financial statements conform with International Accounting Standards;

(f) assist users of financial statements in interpreting the information contained in financial statements prepared in conformity with International Accounting Standards; and

(g) provide those who are interested in the work of IASC with information about its approach to the formulation of International Accounting Standards.

The overall scope of the document covers

5 (a) the objective of financial statements;

(b) the qualitative characteristics that determine the usefulness of information in financial statements;

(c) the definition, recognition and measurement of the elements from which financial statements are constructed; and

(d) concepts of capital and capital maintenance.

6 The framework is concerned with general purpose financial statements (hereafter referred to as 'financial statements') including consolidated financial statements.

The framework first of all outlines the users of accounting information in a manner broadly similar to *The Corporate Report* (Chapter 2):

9 (a) *Investors.* The providers of risk capital and their advisers are concerned with the risk inherent in, and return provided by, their investments. They need information to help them determine whether they should buy, hold or sell. Shareholders are also interested in information which enables them to assess the ability of the enterprise to pay dividends.

(b) *Employees.* Employees and their representative groups are interested in information about the stability and profitability of their employers. They are also interested in information which enables them to assess the ability of the enterprise to provide remuneration, retirement benefits and employment opportunities.

(c) *Lenders.* Lenders are interested in information that enables them to determine whether their loans, and the interest attaching to them, will be paid when due.

(d) *Suppliers and other trade creditors.* Suppliers and other creditors are interested in information that enables them to determine whether amounts owing to them will be paid when due. Trade creditors are likely to be interested in an enterprise over a shorter period than lenders unless they are dependent upon the continuation of the enterprise as a major customer.

(e) *Customers.* Customers have an interest in information about the continuance of an enterprise, especially when they have a long-term involvement with, or are dependent on, the enterprise.

(f) *Governments and their agencies.* Governments and their agencies are interested in the allocation of resources and, therefore, the activities of enterprises. They also require information in order to regulate the activities of enterprises, determine taxation policies and as the basis for national income and similar statistics.

(g) *Public.* Enterprises affect members of the public in a variety of ways. For example, enterprises may make a substantial contribution to the local economy in many ways including the number of people they employ and their patronage of local suppliers. Financial statements may assist the public by providing information about the trends and recent developments in the prosperity of the enterprise and the range of its activities.

10 While all of the information needs of these users cannot be met by financial statements, there are needs which are common to all users. As investors are providers of risk capital to the enterprise, the provision of financial statements that meet their needs will also meet most of the needs of other users that financial statements can satisfy.

It then goes on to summarize the overall objectives of financial statements. This is pretty standard stuff and can be briefly extracted here:

12 The objective of financial statements is to provide information about the financial position, performance and changes in financial position of an enterprise that is useful to a wide range of users in making economic decisions.

13 Financial statements prepared for this purpose meet the common needs of most users. However, financial statements do not provide all the information that users may need to make economic decisions since they largely portray the financial effects of past events and do not necessarily provide non-financial information.

15 The economic decisions that are taken by users of financial statements require an evaluation of the ability of an enterprise to generate cash and cash equivalents and of the timing and certainty of their generation. This ability ultimately determines, for example, the capacity of an enterprise to pay its employees and suppliers, meet interest payments, repay loans and make distributions to its owners. Users are better able to evaluate this ability to generate cash and cash equivalents if they are provided with information that focuses on the financial position, performance and changes in financial position of an enterprise.

19 Information about financial position is primarily provided in a balance sheet. Information about performance is primarily provided in an income statement. Information about changes in financial position is provided in the financial statements by means of a separate statement.

20 The component parts of the financial statements interrelate because they reflect different aspects of the same transactions or other events. Although each statement provides information that is different from the others, none is likely to serve only a single purpose or provide all the information necessary for particular needs of users. For example, an income statement provides an incomplete picture of performance unless it is used in conjunction with the balance sheet and the statement of changes in financial position.

Next the framework discusses the various 'assumptions and characteristics' of accounting statements. These correspond closely to the conventions of Chapter 3 and *The Corporate Report* characteristics of Chapter 2, but they are arranged in a series of subgroups with various headings and subheadings which give interesting nuances of degrees of relative significance and importance. In order to give the full flavour of this the framework is quoted here at some length.

Underlying assumptions

Accrual basis

22 In order to meet their objectives, financial statements are prepared on the accrual basis of accounting. Under this basis, the effects of transactions and other events are recognized when they occur (and not as cash or its equivalent is received or paid) and they are recorded in the accounting records and reported in the financial statements of the periods to which they relate. Financial statements prepared on the accrual basis inform users not only of past transactions involving the payment and receipt of cash but also of obligations to pay cash in the future and of resources that represent cash to be received in the future. Hence, they provide the type of information about past transactions and other events that is most useful to users in making economic decisions.

Going concern

23 The financial statements are normally prepared on the assumption that an enterprise is a going concern and will continue in operation for the foreseeable future. Hence, it is assumed that the enterprise has neither the intention nor the need to liquidate or curtail materially the scale of its operations; if such an intention or need exists, the financial statement may have to be prepared on a different basis and, if so, the basis used is disclosed.

Qualitative characteristics of financial statements

24 Qualitative characteristics are the attributes that make the information provided in financial statements useful to users. The four principal qualitative characteristics are understandability, relevance, reliability and comparability.

Understandability

25 An essential quality of the information provided in financial statements is that is it readily understandable by users. For this purpose, users are assumed to have a reasonable knowledge of business and economic activities and accounting and a willingness to study the information with reasonable diligence. However, information about complex matters that should be included in the financial statements because of its relevance to the economic decision-making needs of users should not be excluded merely on the grounds that it may be too difficult for certain users to understand.

Relevance

26 To be useful, information must be relevant to the decision-making needs of users. Information has the quality of relevance when it influences the economic decisions of users by helping them evaluate past, present or future events or confirming, or correcting, their past evaluations.

27 The predictive and confirmatory roles of information are interrelated. For example, information about the current level and structure of asset holdings has value to users when they endeavour to predict the ability of the enterprise to take advantage of opportunities and its ability to react to adverse situations. The same information plays a confirmatory role in respect of past predictions about, for example, the way in which the enterprise would be structured or the outcome of planned operations.

28 Information about financial position and past performance is frequently used as the basis for predicting future financial position and performance and other matters in which users are directly interested, such as dividend and wage payments, security price movements and the ability of the enterprise to meet its commitments as they fall due. To have predictive value, information need not be in the form of an explicit forecast. The ability to make predictions from financial statements is enhanced, however, by the manner in which information on past transactions and events is displayed. For example, the predictive value of the income statement is enhanced if unusual, abnormal and infrequent items of income or expense are separately disclosed.

Materiality

29 The relevance of information is affected by its nature and materiality. In some cases, the nature of information alone is sufficient to determine its relevance. For example, the reporting of a new segment may affect the assessment of the risks and opportunities facing the enterprise irrespective of the materiality of the results achieved by the new segment in the reporting period. In other cases, both the nature and materiality are important, for example, the amounts of inventories held in each of the main categories that are appropriate to the business.

30 Information is material if its omission or misstatement could influence the economic decisions of users taken on the basis of the financial statements. Materiality depends on the size of the item or error judged in the particular circumstances of its omission or misstatement. Thus, materiality provides a threshold or cut-off point rather than being a primary qualitative characteristic which information must have if it is to be useful.

Reliability

31 To be useful, information must also be reliable. Information has the quality of reliability when it is free from material error and bias and can be depended upon by users to represent faithfully that which it either purports to represent or could reasonably be expected to represent.

32 Information may be relevant but so unreliable in nature or representation that its recognition may be potentially misleading. For example, if the validity and amount of a claim for damages under a legal action are disputed, it may be inappropriate for the enterprise to recognise the full amount of the claim in the balance sheet, although it may be appropriate to disclose the amount and circumstances of the claim.

Faithful representation

33 To be reliable, information must represent faithfully the transactions and other events it either purports to represent or could reasonably be expected to represent. Thus, for example, a balance sheet should represent faithfully the transactions and other events that result in assets, liabilities and equity of the enterprise at the reporting date which meet the recognition criteria.

34 Most financial information is subject to some risk of being less than a faithful representation of that which it purports to portray. This is not due to bias, but rather to inherent difficulties either in identifying the transactions and other events to be measured or in devising and applying measurement and presentation techniques that can convey messages that correspond with those transactions and events. In certain cases, the measurement of the financial effects of items could be so uncertain that enterprises generally would not recognize them in the financial statements; for example, although most enterprises generate goodwill internally over time, it is usually difficult to identify or measure that goodwill reliably. In other cases, however, it may be relevant to recognize items and to disclose the risk of error surrounding their recognition and measurement.

Substance over form

35 If information is to represent faithfully the transactions and other events that it purports to represent, it is necessary that they are accounted for and presented in accordance with their substance and economic reality and not merely their legal form. The substance of transactions or other events is not always consistent with that which is apparent from their legal or contrived form. For example, an enterprise may dispose of an asset to another party in such a way that the documentation purports to pass legal ownership to that party; nevertheless, agreements may exist that ensure that the enterprise continues to enjoy the future economic benefits embodied in the asset. In such circumstances, the reporting of a sale would not represent faithfully the transaction entered into (if indeed there was a transaction).

Neutrality

36 To be reliable, the information contained in financial statements must be neutral, that is, free from bias. Financial statements are not neutral if, by the selection or presentation of information, they influence the making of a decision or judgement in order to achieve a pre-determined result or outcome.

Prudence

37 The preparers of financial statements do, however, have to contend with the uncertainties that inevitably surround many events and circumstances, such as the collectability of doubtful receivables, the probable useful life of plant and equipment and the number of warranty claims that may occur. Such uncertainties are recognised by the disclosure of their nature and extent and by the exercise of prudence in the preparation of the financial statements. Prudence is the inclusion of a degree of caution in the exercise of the judgements needed in making the estimates required under conditions of uncertainty, such that assets or income are not overstated and liabilities or expenses are not understated. However, the exercise of prudence does not allow, for example, the creation of hidden reserves or excessive provisions, the deliberate understatement of assets or income, or the deliberate overstatement of liabilities or expenses, because the financial statements would not be neutral and, therefore, not have the quality of reliability.

Completeness

38 To be reliable, the information in financial statements must be complete within the bounds of materiality and cost. An omission can cause information to be false or misleading and thus unreliable and deficient in terms of its relevance.

Comparability

39 Users must be able to compare the financial statements of an enterprise through time in order to identify trends in its financial position and performance. Users must also be able to compare the financial statements of different enterprises in order to evaluate their relative financial position, performance and changes in financial position. Hence, the measurement and display of the financial effect of like transactions and other events must be carried out in a consistent way throughout an enterprise and over time for that enterprise and in a consistent way for different enterprises.

40 An important implication of the qualitative characteristic of comparability is that users be informed of the accounting policies employed in the preparation of the financial statements, any changes in those policies and the effects of such changes. Users need to be able to identify differences between the accounting policies for like transactions and other events used by the same enterprise from period to period and by different enterprises. Compliance with International Accounting Standards, including the disclosure of the accounting policies used by the enterprise, helps to achieve comparability.

41 The need for comparability should not be confused with mere uniformity and should not be allowed to become an impediment to the introduction of improved accounting standards. It is not appropriate for an enterprise to continue accounting in the same manner for a transaction or other event if the policy adopted is not in keeping with the qualitative characteristics of relevance and reliability. It is also inappropriate for an enterprise to leave its accounting policies unchanged when more relevant and reliable alternatives exist.

42 Because users wish to compare the financial position, performance and changes in financial position of an enterprise over time, it is important that the financial statements show corresponding information for the preceding periods.

Constraints on relevant and reliable information

Timeliness

43 If there is undue delay in the reporting of information it may lose its relevance. Management may need to balance the relative merits of timely reporting and the provision of reliable information. To provide information on a timely basis it may often be necessary to report before all aspects of a transaction or other event are known, thus impairing reliability. Conversely, if reporting is delayed until all aspects are known, the information may be highly reliable but of little use to users who have had to make decisions in the interim. In achieving a balance between relevance and reliability, the over-riding consideration is how best to satisfy the economic decision-making needs of users.

Balance between benefit and cost

44 The balance between benefit and cost is a pervasive constraint rather than a qualitative characteristic. The benefits derived from information should exceed the cost of providing it. The evaluation of benefits and costs is, however, substantially a judgmental process. Furthermore, the costs do not necessarily fall on those users who enjoy the benefits. Benefits may also be enjoyed by users other than those for whom the information is prepared; for example, the provision of further information to lenders may reduce the borrowing costs of an enterprise. For these reasons, it is difficult to apply a cost-benefit test in any particular case. Nevertheless, standard-setters in particular, as well as the preparers and users of financial statements, should be aware of this constraint.

Balance between qualitative characteristics

45 In practice a balancing, or trade-off, between qualitative characteristics is often necessary. Generally the aim is to achieve an appropriate balance among the characteristics in order to meet the objective of financial statements. The relative importance of the characteristics in different cases is a matter of professional judgement.

True and fair view/fair presentation

46 Financial statements are frequently described as showing a true and fair view of, or as presenting fairly, the financial position, performance and changes in financial position of an enterprise. Although this framework does not deal directly with such concepts, the application of the principal qualitative characteristics and of appropriate accounting standards normally results in financial statements that convey what is generally understood as a true and fair view of, or as presenting fairly such information.

It is worth studying the above with some care. It should be compared with Chapters 2 and 3. It should also be remembered and related to the detailed existing Standards in the UK as you work through Part Three. In particular note that the accruals basis (= matching convention more or less) is given the status of an underlying assumption – one of only two. On the other hand, prudence is reduced to a subcharacteristic of reliability. The underlying assumptions are a main heading whilst prudence is two stages down as a sub-sub-heading. This contrasts sharply with the evenhandedness of earlier thinking and even more sharply with the explicit statement in the SSAP 2 (see Chapter 15) 'where the accruals concept is inconsistent with the prudence concept, the latter prevails'. Note also the appearance of substance over form as a concept in its own right. This idea now influences much of the ASB's thinking (see Part Three, especially Chapter 18).

The IASC framework continues with a lengthy consideration of the 'elements of financial statements'. This corresponds to the discussion of the various definitions earlier in this chapter. Included here are merely the bare bones of the definitions they suggest. The general point to note is that the definitions are very general and the substance over form concept permeates them and their interpretation.

The framework very logically first of all defines them, secondly discusses their recognition and finally discusses their valuation. Key definitions are:

49 (a) An *asset* is a resource controlled by the enterprise as a result of past events and from which future economic benefits are expected to flow to the enterprise.
(b) A *liability* is a present obligation of the enterprise arising from past events,

the settlement of which is expected to result in an outflow from the enterprise of resources embodying economic benefits.

(c) *Equity* is the residual interest in the assets of the enterprise after deducting all its liabilities.

50 The definitions of an asset and a liability identify their essential features but do not attempt to specify the criteria that need to be met before they are recognized in the balance sheet. Thus, the definitions embrace items that are not recognised as assets or liabilities in the balance sheet because they do not satisfy the criteria for recognition discussed in paragraphs 82 to 98. In particular, the expectation that future economic benefits will flow to or from an enterprise must be sufficiently certain to meet the probability criterion in paragraph 83 before an asset or liability is recognised.

51 In assessing whether an item meets the definition of an asset, liability or equity, attention needs to be given to its underlying substance and economic reality and not merely its legal form.

70 (a) *Income* is increases in economic benefits during the accounting period in the form of inflows or enhancements of assets or decreases of liabilities that result in increases in equity, other than those relating to contributions from equity participants.

(b) *Expenses* are decreases in economic benefits during the accounting period in the form of outflows or depletions of assets or incurrences of liabilities that result in decreases in equity, other than those relating to distributions to equity participants.

74 The definition of income encompasses both revenue and gains. Revenue arises in the course of the ordinary activities of an enterprise and is referred to by a variety of different names including sales, fees, interest, dividends, royalties and rent.

75 Gains represent other items that meet the definition of income and may, or may not, arise in the course of the ordinary activities of an enterprise. Gains represent increases in economic benefits and as such are no different in nature from revenue. Hence, they are not regarded as constituting a separate element in this framework.

76 Gains include, for example, those arising on the disposal of non-current assets. The definition of income also includes unrealised gains; for example, those arising on the revaluation of marketable securities and those resulting from increases in the carrying amount of long term assets. When gains are recognised in the income statements, they are usually displayed separately because knowledge of them is useful for the purpose of making economic decisions. Gains are often reported net of related expenses.

78 The definition of expenses encompasses losses as well as those expenses that arise in the course of the ordinary activities of the enterprise. Expenses that arise in the course of the ordinary activities of the enterprise include, for example, cost of sales, wages and depreciation. They usually take the form of an outflow or depletion of assets such as cash and cash equivalents, inventory, property, plant and equipment.

79 Losses represent other items that meet the definition of expenses and may, or may not, arise in the course of the ordinary activities of the enterprise. Losses represent decreases in economic benefits and as such they are no different in nature from other expenses. Hence, they are not regarded as a separate element in this framework.

80 Losses include, for example, those resulting from disasters such as fire and flood, as well as those arising on the disposal of non-current assets. The definition of expenses also includes unrealised losses, for example, those arising from the effects of increases in the rate of exchange for a foreign currency in respect of the borrowings of an enterprise in that currency. When losses are recognised in the income statement, they are usually displayed separately because knowledge of them is useful for the purpose of making economic decisions. Losses are often reported net of related income.

Capital maintenance adjustments

81 The revaluation or restatement of assets and liabilities gives rise to increases or decreases in equity. While these increases or decreases meet the definition of income and expenses, they are not included in the income statement under certain concepts of capital maintenance. Instead these items are included in equity as capital maintenance adjustments or revaluation reserves.

Once we have established that an element exists within the above definitions we have to decide whether to recognize it, i.e. whether to record it in the accounting system and in the financial statements.

82 Recognition is the process of incorporating in the balance sheet or income statement an item that meets the definition of an element and satisfies the criteria for recognition set out in paragraph 83. It involves the depiction of the item in words and by a monetary amount and the inclusion of that amount in the balance sheet or income statement totals. Items that satisfy the recognition criteria should be recognised in the balance sheet or income statement. The failure to recognise such items is not rectified by disclosure of the accounting policies used nor by notes or explanatory material.

83 An item that meets the definition of an element should be recognised if:

(a) it is probable that any future economic benefit associated with the item will flow to or from the enterprise; and

(b) the item has a cost or value that can be measured with reliability.

84 In assessing whether an item meets these criteria and therefore qualifies for recognition in the financial statements, regard needs to be given to the materiality considerations discussed in paragraphs 29 and 30. The interrelationship between the elements means that an item that meets the definition and recognition criteria for a particular element, for example, an asset, automatically requires the recognition of another element, for example, income or a liability.

88 An item that possesses the essential characteristics of an element but fails to meet the criteria for recognition may nonetheless warrant disclosure in the notes, explanatory material or in supplementary schedules. This is appropriate when knowledge of the item is considered to be relevant to the evaluation of the financial position, performance and changes in financial position of an enterprise by the users of financial statements.

The document goes on to discuss the application of these principles to the four elements of assets, liabilities, expenses and revenues, but this adds nothing of importance. As regards the final stage in this logical process, that of deciding what figure to use to record the recognition of the elements, the framework is brief and purely descriptive.

99 Measurement is the process of determining the monetary amounts at which the elements of the financial statements are to be recognised and carried in the balance sheet and income statement. This involves the selection of the particular basis of measurement.

100 A number of different measurement bases are employed to different degrees and in varying combinations in financial statements. They include the following:

(a) *Historical cost.* Assets are recorded at the amount of cash or cash equivalents paid or the fair value of the consideration given to acquire them at the time of their acquisition. Liabilities are recorded at the amount of proceeds received in exchange for the obligation, or in some circumstances (for example, income taxes), at the amounts of cash or cash equivalents expected to be paid to satisfy the liability in the normal course of business.

(b) *Current cost.* Assets are carried at the amount of cash or cash equivalents that would have to be paid if the same or an equivalent asset was acquired currently. Liabilities are carried at the undiscounted amount of cash or cash equivalents that would be required to settle the obligation currently.

(c) *Realisable (settlement) value.* Assets are carried at the amount of cash or cash equivalents that could currently be obtained by selling the asset in an orderly disposal. Liabilities are carried at their settlement values; that is, the undiscounted amounts of cash or cash equivalents expected to be paid to satisfy the liabilities in the normal course of business.

(d) *Present value.* Assets are carried at the present discounted value of the future net cash inflows that the item is expected to generate in the normal course of business. Liabilities are carried at the present discounted value of the future net cash outflows that are expected to be required to settle the liabilities in the normal course of business.

101 The measurement basis most commonly adopted by enterprises in preparing their financial statements is historical cost. This is usually combined with other measurement bases. For example, inventories are usually carried at the lower of cost and net realisable value, marketable securities may be carried at market value and pension liabilities are carried at their present value. Furthermore, some enterprises use the current cost basis as a response to the inability of the historical cost accounting model to deal with the effects of changing prices of non-monetary assets.

The final section of the IASC framework discusses the essentials of alternative capital maintenance concepts. This is an extremely clearly worded summary of a complex area and no apologies are made for quoting it in full.

Concepts of capital

102 A financial concept of capital is adopted by most enterprises in preparing their financial statements. Under a financial concept of capital, such as invested money or invested purchasing power, capital is synonymous with the net assets or equity of the enterprise. Under a physical concept of capital, such as operating capability, capital is regarded as the productive capacity of the enterprise based on, for example, units of output per day.

103 The selection of the appropriate concept of capital by an enterprise should be based on the needs of the users of its financial statements. Thus, a financial concept of capital should be adopted if the users of financial statements are primarily concerned with the maintenance of nominal invested capital or the purchasing power of invested capital. If, however, the main concern of users is with the operating capability of the enterprise, a physical concept of capital should be used. The concept chosen indicates the goal to be attained in determining profit, even though there may be some measurement difficulties in making the concept operational.

Concepts of capital maintenance and the determination of profit

104 The concepts of capital in paragraph 102 give rise to the following concepts of capital maintenance:

(a) *Financial capital maintenance.* Under this concept a profit is earned only if the financial (or money) amount of the net assets at the end of the period exceeds the financial (or money) amount of net assets at the beginning of the period, after excluding any distributions to, and contributions from, owners during the period. Financial capital maintenance can be measured in either nominal monetary units or units of constant purchasing power.

(b) *Physical capital maintenance.* Under this concept a profit is earned only if the physical productive capacity (or operating capability) of the enterprise (or the resources or funds needed to achieve that capacity) at the end of the period exceeds the physical productive capacity at the beginning of the period, after excluding any distributions to, and contributions from, owners during the period.

105 The concept of capital maintenance is concerned with how an enterprise defines the capital that it seeks to maintain. It provides the linkage between the concepts of capital and the concepts of profit because it provides the point of reference by which profit is measured; it is a prerequisite for distinguishing between an enterprise's return on capital and its return of capital; only inflows of assets in excess of amounts needed to maintain capital may be regarded as profit and therefore as a return on capital. Hence, profit is the residual amount that remains after expenses (including capital maintenance adjustments, where appropriate) have been deducted from income. If expenses exceed income the residual amount is a net loss.

106 The physical capital maintenance concept requires the adoption of the current cost basis of measurement. The financial capital maintenance concept, however, does not require the use of a particular basis of measurement. Selection of the basis under this concept is dependent on the type of financial capital that the enterprise is seeking to maintain.

107 The principle difference between the two concepts of capital maintenance is the treatment of the effects of changes in the prices of assets and liabilities of the enterprise. In general terms, an enterprise has maintained its capital if it has as much capital at the end of the period as it had at the beginning of the period. Any amount over and above that required to maintain the capital at the beginning of the period is profit.

108 Under the concept of financial capital maintenance where capital is defined in terms of nominal monetary units, profit represents the increase in nominal money capital over the period. Thus, increases in the prices of assets held over the period, conventionally referred to as holding gains, are, conceptually, profits. They may not be recognised as such, however, until the assets are disposed of in an exchange transaction. When the concept of financial capital maintenance is defined in terms of constant purchasing power units, profit represents the increase in invested purchasing power over the period. Thus, only that part of the increase in the prices of assets that exceeds the increase in the general level of prices is regarded as profit. The rest of the increase is treated as a capital maintenance adjustment and, hence, as part of equity.

109 Under the concept of physical capital maintenance when capital is defined in terms of the physical productive capacity, profit represents the increase in that capital over the period. All price changes affecting the assets and liabilities of the enterprise are viewed as changes in the measurement of the physical productive capacity of the enterprise; hence, they are treated as capital maintenance adjustments that are part of equity and not as profit.

110 The selection of the measurement bases and concept of capital maintenance will determine the accounting model used in the preparation of the financial statements. Different accounting models exhibit different degrees of relevance and reliability and, as in other areas, management must seek a balance between relevance and reliability. This framework is applicable to a range of accounting models and provides guidance on preparing and presenting the financial statements constructed under the chosen model. At the present time, it is not the intention of the Board of IASC to prescribe a particular model other than in exceptional circumstances, such as for those enterprises reporting in the currency of a hyper-inflationary economy. This intention will, however, be reviewed in the light of world developments.

The basic principles of these capital maintenance alternatives are well illustrated in the following simple example, taken from an ASC publication called *Capital Maintenance Concepts: The Choice* issued during the death throes of SSAP 16.

Example

Let us assume that a company begins with share capital of £100 and cash of £100. At the beginning of the year one item of stock is bought for £100. The item of stock is sold at the end of the year for £150, its replacement cost at that time is £120 and general inflation throughout the year is 10%. Profit measured using each of the capital maintenance concepts mentioned earlier would be as shown below.

Financial capital maintenance

	(1) Money capital (historical cost accounts)	(2) Maintenance of general purchasing power of financial capital	Operating capacity capital maintenance
	£	£	£
Sales	150	150	150
less Cost of sales	(100)	(100)	(120)
Operating profit	50	50	30
less Inflation adjustment	—	(10)	—
Total gain	50	40	30

Column 1 shows the gain after ensuring the maintenance of the shareholders' opening capital measured as a sum of money. Column 2 shows the gain after ensuring the maintenance of the shareholders' opening capital measured as a block of purchasing power. Both of these are concerned, under different definitions, with the maintenance of financial capital – in terms either of its money amount or of its general purchasing power. Column 3 shows the gain after ensuring the maintenance of the company's initial operating capacity, and is therefore of a completely different nature.

Conclusions

In general, the IASC framework represents an admirable attempt to be both logical and coherent on the one hand, and undogmatic and non-prescriptive on the other (although we should note the use of the word 'requires' in paragraph 106). The David Solomons monograph by contrast comes out strongly in favour of current cost accounting, and the Institute of Chartered Accountants of Scotland publication (doubtless heavily influenced by Professor Tom Lee) argues for exit value balance sheets.

The Accounting Standards Committee issued its own foreword to the English version of the IASC framework. This indicated strong support for the IASC document.

1 The Accounting Standards Committee (ASC) welcomes the publication by the International Accounting Standards Committee (IASC) of its Framework for the Preparation and Presentation of Financial Statements.

2 One of the stated purposes of the Framework is to assist national standard setting bodies in developing their own standards. ASC believes that the publication of the Framework for use in this way will mark a significant step forward in the process of furthering the international harmonisation of financial reporting.

3 ASC is committed to supporting the work of IASC and its initiative to promote such harmonisation. ASC has agreed to recognise the Framework as a set of guidelines to assist it in its work of developing proposals for new standards and revisions to existing standards in the UK and Republic of Ireland.

4 ASC proposes to use the Framework as the benchmark against which future proposals will be measured. However, in some cases it may be judged necessary to recommend standards that are at variance with aspects of the Framework. In such cases, ASC will explain any departures from the Framework in such explanatory material as is published when the standard is issued.

7 In its present form, the Framework identifies the different measurement bases and the different concepts of capital and capital maintenance that may be adopted in the preparation of financial statements, the selection of which will determine the accounting model used. It is intended to be applicable to a range of models and to provide guidance on the preparation and presentation of financial statements under whichever model is chosen. It does not recommend the adoption of a particular model.

8 In this respect, ASC believes that in due course it may be necessary to develop the Framework further, to indicate the appropriate model that should form the conceptual basis of financial accounting and reporting in the future. ASC hopes that, through its experience of applying the Framework and its own work programme, it can contribute to that process in a positive and active way.

In parallel with its framework document the IASC issued, early in 1989, an exposure draft on 'Comparability of Financial Statements'. This proposed to remove certain free choices of accounting treatments at present permitted in International Accounting Standards. The ASC both welcomed this International Exposure Draft, and indicated that it did not accept the idea of requiring UK companies to disclose departures from International Accounting Standards. These two actions do not appear to be over-consistent with each other. But by the late 1990s there were clear signs of closer cooperation. The IASC and the ASB are working more closely together, and a greater spirit of cooperation between different standard setting bodies generally is in the air.

The international dimension and the whole question of its influence in (and from) the UK is considered further in Chapter 11. The IASC framework may at last represent the early signs of a move towards genuine international cooperation, coherence and harmonization. But we should not underestimate the difficulties. These are not only conceptual but also regional and attitudinal. The UK is by definition involved in European accounting harmonization and there are clear signs that this is not moving in identical directions to the implications of the IASC document. Substance over form is regarded as a highly unnatural concept in some quarters, for example. But a momentum is beginning. Hopefully some readers will themselves later maintain and increase the rate of progress.

Towards a critical review

After studying the preceding chapters, we should be in a position to review our achievements as a profession and as a discipline. How are we doing?

The crunch questions!

It is abundantly obvious that we have no reason for smug self-satisfaction. We claim to operate by a series of conventions that are themselves contradictory (Chapter 3), or that turn out to mean whatever we want them to mean. We undoubtedly put high emphasis on ease of preparation and confirmation of figures (objectivity) and less emphasis on relevance and usefulness. Refer back to the seven 'user' classes discussed on pp. 9–12 and the seven desirable characteristics discussed on pp. 13–14. These desirable characteristics were relevance, understandability, reliability, completeness, objectivity, timeliness and comparability. To what extent does traditional accounting satisfy these characteristics?

How could we improve? Empirical research suggests, for example, that the average non-expert reader of published accounts does not understand most of it – in fact that he or she doesn't even read most of it!

The HC basis is widely felt to be logically irrelevant. Should we therefore change the basis of financial reporting to some form of current – or even future – oriented approach that might be both more relevant and easier to understand? Or should we argue that it is the accountant's job to report the facts as far as possible, leaving the user, the customer to provide the subjective interpretation and implications for himself?

In either event, we surely need somehow to educate the users of accounts better as to what we accountants do actually do. The reader of accounts must understand what our figures do and do not mean. Keynes once said that it is better to be vaguely right than precisely wrong (could this be an argument against the HC convention?). Perhaps we could paraphrase this and suggest that it is better to be approximate, but understood, than to be exact and incomprehensible.

Amongst the many which could be suggested, we should perhaps ask ourselves the following questions:

1 Do our normal actions and conventions make theoretical sense?
2 Do they adequately provide our customers (whoever they are) with whatever they need (whatever that is)?
3 Do any of the alternative models available:
   (a) make more theoretical sense;
   (b) seem set to provide at least some of our customers with more useful information?
4 What empirical evidence is available to help us answer these questions, and what are its implications?
5 What alternative or additional steps can we take to make ourselves 'more useful'?

We have suggested some ideas in relation to the fifth question in Chapter 9. You should not of course regard these as in any way exhaustive. As regards the fourth question we have already established that reference ought to be made to user needs in order to determine the appropriate reporting framework. It would be pleasing to report that the users of accounting information had clear ideas of what they wanted and definite opinions on what they are presently provided with. Unfortunately there is convincing and consistent evidence that many users neither understand nor read the accounting data in financial reports, preferring instead to rely upon the chairman's report or even to use alternative information from newspapers or professional advisers.

There is another body of opinion, again based on empirical research, that would suggest that accounting numbers really do not matter anyway. Proponents of the efficient markets hypothesis contend that by the time companies issue their financial reports most of the information contained therein has already been impounded into the share price and that the reports therefore have little significant informational value. The evidence in support of this hypothesis is impressive.

The message from all this is fairly clear. Empirical research suggests that accountants are not producing particularly useful information, and it does not appear to be used as extensively as it should be. Is this a problem of lack of understanding of our reports, or is it because our reports contain the wrong information? Whichever is the case, how can we improve? As a profession, we have to find answers to these questions if we wish to justify our long-term future.

So what about the first three questions? What practical suggestions would you wish to introduce into financial reporting based on – or for that matter not based on – all the ideas we have been exploring?

Activity 2

How would you alter and improve the conventions and practices of financial reporting in order to increase the usefulness of our accounting role?

Activity 2 feedback

This one is up to you.

Summary

In this chapter we first of all looked at definitional issues and problems concerning the major elements of financial statements. We considered the idea of a wide-ranging or all-embracing framework for our activities. We then explored the IASC framework in considerable detail, using it in effect both as reminder and revision of many of the ideas of earlier chapters and of further investigation of the interrelationships between the various aspects. Finally, we recognized the need and importance of a critical review of the whole accounting position and scene – your critical review, not ours!

Exercises

1 Explain, in terms understandable to a non-accountant, the following terms:
   (a) asset
   (b) fixed asset
   (c) liability
   (d) revenue
   (e) expense
   (f) capital.
2 **The equity investor group are major users of financial statements. Identify the general nature of the 'information needs' of this group of users. Describe the likely specific uses of company financial information by investors and give examples of information which may be relevant to each of these uses.** (20 marks)
   (ACCA)
3 The Accounting Standards Board are currently attempting to develop a 'conceptual framework'.
   Required
   (a) What is generally understood by the term 'a conceptual framework'?
   (4 marks)
   (b) What advantage(s) might arise from using a 'conceptual framework'?
   (8 marks)

(c) **What do you consider are the difficulties in trying to develop a conceptual framework in the UK?** (8 marks)

(20 marks)

(ACCA adapted)

4 **You are required to briefly explain the following five accounting concepts *and* to discuss for each the implications for financial statements if that concept was abandoned.**

(a) **the entity concept**

(b) **the money measurement concept**

(c) **the time interval concept**

(d) **the stable monetary unit concept**

(e) **the substance over form concept.** **(20 marks)**

(ACCA)

5 (a) **If a conceptual framework of accounting were to be developed, what would its principal components be?** (10 marks)

(b) **List and explain the advantages and difficulties which could result from the development of an agreed conceptual framework.**

(10 marks)

(20 marks)

(ACCA)

The international dimension

After reading this chapter you should be able to:
■ outline the general developments in international and European accounting thinking and regulation
■ discuss the interrelationships between the UK scenario on the one hand, and the European and international situations on the other.

Introduction

This book is about UK accounting. So why have a chapter called 'The international dimension'? The reason of course is that, as business operations become ever more international, accounting inevitably becomes more and more international too. Remember that financial reporting seeks to provide useful information. Useful information for international business or international investment activities must be internationally understandable information. To compare the performance of a British company with a German company requires as a necessary (though perhaps not sufficient) condition that the information is or can be presented in a properly comparable manner.

This book makes no attempt to tackle this large but fascinating subject in any detail. But it is essential to appreciate the trends and influences which are at work. UK accounting is being significantly influenced by both actions and arguments on the European and wider international scene. UK accounting and the more broadly based Anglo-Saxon tradition are also a significant force in international debates and progress. If you wish to understand UK financial reporting, and to be involved in its development and progress then you must be aware of this two-way and increasing interaction.

The International Accounting Standards Committee (IASC)

The International Federation of Accountants (IFAC) is the world-wide umbrella organization of accountancy bodies. It is independent of government or pseudo-government control. Its stated purpose is to develop and enhance a coordinated world-wide accountancy profession with harmonized standards. IFAC was created in 1973 and its constitution formally approved in 1977. Perhaps the most important aspect of IFAC so far has been its relationship with the International Accounting Standards Committee (IASC). This was also created in 1973, and all member bodies of IFAC are automatically members of IASC. IASC is independent and has total autonomy in the setting of international accounting standards. Its main objectives are:

1 to formulate and publish in the public interest accounting standards to be observed in the presentation of financial statements, and to promote their world-wide acceptance and observation.
2. to work generally for the improvement and harmonization of regulations, accounting standards and procedures relating to the presentation of financial statements.

The IASC has issued an important series of accounting standards (IASs). These in many ways parallel the topics, and often though not always the approach, of the UK SSAPs (Statements of Standard Accounting Practice) and FRSs (Financial Reporting Standards) which you will explore at such enjoyable length in Part Three. However, where there is any conflict the national standards will prevail, and indeed this is the situation in all countries.

The IASC has operated throughout its existence in the knowledge that when the crunch came, it and its IASs had no formal authority. They therefore have had to rely on persuasion and the quality of their analysis and argument. As a general comment, this can be seen to have had two major effects. First, the quality of logic and discussion in their publications has generally been high, and their conclusions – if sometimes of course debatable – feasible, and clearly articulated. Secondly, however, the conclusions and recommendations of many of the published IAS documents have often had to accommodate two or more alternative acceptable treatments, simply because both or all were already being practised in countries which were members of IASC and were too significant to be ignored.

The disadvantages of this state of affairs are obvious and were well recognized by the IASC itself. Towards the end of the 1980s the IASC decided it would attempt a more proactive approach, and early in 1989 published an exposure draft (E32) on comparability of financial statements. This proposed the elimination of certain treatments permitted by particular IASs, and the expression of a clear preference for one particular treatment even where two alternatives were still to be regarded as acceptable.

There are also signs of closer cooperation between IASC and the International Organization of Securities Commissions (IOSCO). IOSCO has indicated its support for mutually acceptable accounting standards, and clearly any suggestion, however gently expressed, that quoted companies failing to follow standards would be investigated by stock exchange authorities, can only strengthen movements towards greater acceptance of such standards.

Most of the proposed changes announced in E32 in 1989 have now been confirmed and incorporated in revised IASs already published and operative for financial statements covering periods beginning on or after 1 January 1995. These changes, substantially in accordance with the R32 proposals, are summarized in Table 11.1.

Three issues proved rather more difficult. Table 11.2 sets out the proposals made by IASC on these issues in 1989. Table 11.3 gives the revised proposals made by IASC in 1991. Table 11.4 gives the actual requirements of the new IASs operative from 1 January 1995.

Comparison of Tables 11.2–11.4 will show that in two of the three cases, that is, assignment of costs to inventories and treatment of borrowing costs, the final proposals are the same as the orginal (1989) proposals, and in only one case, the treatment of development costs, does the revised 1991 proposed persist. It appears that minds have changed several times.

It is important to put these apparently considerable changes and inconsistencies of atti-

Table 11.1 *IASC Proposals 1991*

Issues	Required or benchmark treatment	Allowed alternative treatment	Treatment eliminated
Correction of fundamental errors and omissions, and adjustments resulting from accounting policy changes	• Adjust opening retained earnings (subject to certain exceptions) • Amend comparative information	• Include in income of the current period. • Present amended pro forma comparative information	
Recognition of revenue and net income on construction contracts	• Percentage of completion method • When the conditions for profit recognition are not met, recognize revenue to the extent of costs incurred that are recoverable		• Completed contract method
Measurement of property, plant, and equipment	• Measure at cost	• Measure at revalued amounts	
Measurement of property, plant, and equipment acquired in exchange for another assets	• Fair value for dissimilar assets acquired • Net carrying amount of asset given up for dissimilar assets acquired		• Net carrying amount of asset given up for similar assets acquired • Fair value for similar assets acquired
Recognition of a revaluation increase relating to a revaluation decrease previously charged to income	• recognize in income of the current period		• Recognize in shareholders' interests
Recognition of revenue on transactions involving the rendering of services	• Percentage of completion method • When the outcome of the contract cannot be reliably estimated, recognize revenue to the extent of costs incurred that are recoverable		• Completed contract method
Determining the cost of retirement benefits	• Accrued benefit valuation methods	• Projected benefit valuation methods	
Use of projected salaries in determining the cost of retirement benefits	• Incorporate an assumption about projected salaries		• Do not incorporate an assumption about projected salaries

Table 11.1 (continued)

Issues	Required or benchmark treatment	Allowed alternative treatment	Treatment eliminated
Recognition of past service costs, experience adjustments and the effects of changes in actuarial assumption	• Recognize systematically over a period approximating the average of the expected remaining working lives of participating employees (subject to certain exceptions)		• Recognize in income of the current period as they arise
Recognition of foreign exchange gains and losses in long-term on monetary items	• Recognize in income of the current period unless hedged		• Defer and recognize in income of current and future periods
Recognition of foreign exchange losses on the acquisition of an asset that result from a severe devaluation against which there is no practical means of hedging	• Recognize in income of the current period	• Recognize as part of the cost of the asset	
Exchange rate for use in translating income statement items of foreign entities	• Exchange rates at the dates of the transactions (or average rate)		• Closing exchange rates
Treatment of differences on income statement items translated at other than the closing rate	• Recognize in shareholders' interests		• Recognize in income of the current period
Subsidiaries operating in hyper-inflation economies	• Restate financial statements in accordance with IAS 29, 'Financial Reporting in Hyperinflationary Economies', before translation		• Translate financial statements without prior restatement
Exchange differences on foreign operations integral to those of the parent	• Recognize in income of the period unless hedged	• Recognize as part of the cost of an asset when they result from a severe devaluation against which there is no practical means of hedging	• Defer and recognize in income of current and future periods
Accounting for business combinations	• Purchase method for acquisitions		• Pooling of interests method for acquisitions

Item	Benchmark		Allowed alternative
	• Pooling of interests method for uniting of interests		• Purchase method for uniting of interests
Positive goodwill	• Recognize as an asset and amortize to income on a systematic basis over its useful life. The amortization period should not exceed 5 years unless a longer period can be justified, which should not, in any case, exceed 20 years		• Adjust immediately to shareholders' interests
Negative goodwill	• Allocate over individual non-monetary assets. After such an allocation, if negative goodwill remains, treat as deferred income and recognize in income on a systematic basis as for positive goodwill	• Treat as deferred income and recognize in income on a systematic basis for positive goodwill	• Adjust immediately to shareholders' interests
Measurement of minority interest arising on a business combination	• Measure at preacquisition carrying amounts		• Measure at post-acquisition fair values
Measurement of investment properties	• Measure at cost with depreciation	• Measure at revalued amounts	• Measure at cost without depreciation
Recognition of a realized gain previously recognized in revaluation surplus	• Transfer to retained earnings		• Recognize in income of the current period

From IASC Statement of Intent, 1991.

Table 11.2 *Some IASC proposals in 1989 (extracted from E32)*

Issues	Required or benchmark treatment	Allowed alternative treatment	Treatment eleminated
Assignment of costs to inventories	• FIFO and weighted average cost formulas	• LIFO formula	• Base stock formula
Development costs	• Recognize immediately as expenses	• Recognize as assets when they meet specified criteria	
Borrowing costs	• Recognize immediately as expenses	• Recognize as part of the cost of an asset if it takes a substantial period of time to get it ready for its intended use or sale	

Table 11.3 *Some revised IASC proposals, 1991 from IASC Statement of Intent 1991*

Issues	Required or benchmark treatment	Allowed alternative treatment	Treatment eleminated
Assignment of costs to inventories	• FIFO and weighted average cost formulas		• LIFO and base stock formulas
Development costs	• Recognize as assets when they meet specified criteria and as expenses when they do not meet criteria		• Recognize developments that meet the specified criteria as expenses
Borrowing costs	• Recognize as part of the cost of an asset if it takes a substantial period of time to get it ready for its intended use or sale; recognize as expense in other circumstances		• Recognize borrowing costs meet criteria for capitalization as expenses

tude into context. First, as Table 11.1 shows, the majority of changes were agreed on and maintained. Second, these are complicated issues from a theoretical perspective, and genuine alternative arguments exist. Third, and perhaps most importantly, we must not forget that the board, that is, the IASC, is not as such a decision-making mechanism. It is the *members* of IASC who collectively make the decisions, if necessary by voting when consensus cannot be reached. From 1 January 2001, the structure and membership, have been changed in a complicated way, in an attempt to make it less controlled by accounting professionals.

Table 11.4 *IASC changes to the proposed changes to the E32 changes*

Issues	Required or benchmark treatment	Allowed alternative treatment	Treatment eliminated
Assignment of costs to inventories	• FIFO and weighted average cost formulas	• LIFO formula	• Base stock formula
Development costs	• Recognize assets when they meet specified criteria and as expenses when they do not meet criteria		• Recognize developments that do meet the specified criteria as expenses
Borrowing costs	• Recognize immediately as expenses	• Recognize as part of the cost of an asset if it takes a substantial period of time to get it ready for its intended use or sale	

Extracted from revised IASs issued 1993, operative from 1 January 1995

Activity 1

We have spent consierable time and effort in thinking about the various accounting conventions in Chapters 3 and 10. We have seen that they are often in conflict, and that choices will often have to be made between them. Look again at Table 11.1; taking a broad brush approach rather than spending too much time on the gory detail, which conventions seem to have been given most prominence in deciding which treatments should be proposed for elimination?

Activity 1 feedback

This is surely an interesting but difficult exercise. On the whole it seems to us that the proposals summarized in Table 11.1 give considerable importance to prudence or conservatism.

In 1995, the IASC entered into an agreement with the International Organization of Securities Commissions (IOSCO) to complete a 'core set' of IASs by 1999. This was achieved with the issuing of IAS 39 *Financial Instruments: Recognition and Measurement* in March 1999. With regard to the agreement, IOSCO's Technical Committe stated that completion of 'comprehensive core standards acceptable to the Technical Committee' would allow it to 'recommend endorsement' of those standards for 'cross-border capital raising in all global markets.' This position led to a potential conflict between IOSCO and IASC on the one hand and the US Securities and Exchange Commission (SEC) and Federal Accounting Standards Board (FASB) on the other, insofar as 'all global markets' include the US markets that are under the SEC's jurisdiction and have the FASB as their accounting standardsetter. The SEC happens, however, to be a very influential member of IOSCO. In practice, therefore, rather than a conflict, the result is pressure on the IASC to satisfy a set of criteria laid down by the SEC.

The SEC's position has ostensibly been one of qualified support for the IOSCO/IASC core standards project, but a close reading of its conditions for accepting IASs suggests that the Commission was in fact reserving its position. First, the core set must include enough standards to be considered a 'comprehensive, generally accepted basis of accounting.' Second, the standards must be of 'high quality.' This appears to mean that the standards must result in financial statements that are 'comparable and transparent to users and provide for adequate disclosure.' Finally, the standards must be 'rigorously interpreted and applied.' The SEC expressed the intention that, once the core set of IASs had been completed, it would *consider* allowing the use of IASs in the financial statements of foreign companies registering with the SEC (in order to obtain a US listing) without the current requirement of reconciling reported earnings and shareholders' equity to US generally accepted accounting principles (GAAP).

In February 2000, the SEC issued a lengthy *Concept Release* that 'framed the discussion of how acceptance of IAS might be accommodated in the SEC's rules in the context of a number of inter-related questions on how IASC standards are interpreted and applied in practice' (IASC Insight, March 2000). *The Concept Release* also sets out five elements of what the SEC believes to be 'a high quality financial reporting structure':

- high-quality accounting standards
- high-quality auditing standards
- audit firms with effective quality controls
- profession-wide quality assurance
- active regulatory insight.

In May 2000, the Technical Committee of IOSCO issued a report of 115 pages, *IASC Standards*, in which it 'recommends to IOSCO members use of 30 selected IASC standards [the IASC 2000 standards] for cross-border listings and offerings by multi-national enterprises, as supplemented in the manner described in this report (i.e. reconciliation, supplemental disclosure and interpretation [and in exceptional cases waiver]), where necessary to address outstanding substantive issues at a national or regional level'. In substance, as officially announced at the IFAC 2000 Conference in Edinburgh, Scotland on 25 May 2000, IOSCO accepted the 'IASC 2000' core standards, subject however to some non-trivial qualifications. The 'outstanding substantive issues at a national or regional level' relate particularly to US reservations about various IAS standards. Moreover, the resolution passed by the IOSCO Presidents' Committee, included in the report, included the following statement: 'IOSCO expects to survey its membership by the end of 2001 in order to determine the extent to which members have taken steps to use the IASC 2000 standards, subject to the supplemental treatments described above. At the same time IOSCO expects to continue to work with the IASC, and will determine the extent to which IOSCO's outstanding substantive issues, including proposals for future projects, have been addressed appropriately'.

The IOSCO's *IASC Standards* report was produced by its Working Group No. 1, headed by one of the SEC's top staff members. The impression created by this and the SEC's *Concept Release* is that, in effect, the SEC has taken the IASC firmly under its wing, which it is able to do because of the pre-eminence of the US capital markets and the highly-developed US system for the regulation of financial reporting.

A final point is that IASC's relationship with IOSCO has meant that IASC is an accounting standardsetter for corporations that seek or aim to seek capital in the international capital markets. Its original concerns with providing international accounting standards for a broader clientele, including companies in emerging economies that do not necessarily seek an international capital market listing, have perforce been abandoned.

The European dimension

The UK is of course a full member of the European Union (EU), and has been so since 1974. So far as the members of the EU are concerned, accounting harmonization is an integral part of the development of the Union into a single 'economic space'. In this connection a distinction needs to be made between two objectives of accounting harmonization. One is the establishment of a 'level playing field' for enterprises competing within the single market, and the others is the promotion of an efficient, integrated capital market for the Union.

According to the principle of the 'level playing field', enterprises within the EU should be able to compete throughout the region on equal terms so far as the legal and regulatory environment is concerned, being neither favoured nor disfavoured by particular requirements in individual member states. The application of this principle to financial reporting implies a need for the harmonization of financial reporting requirements – but not necessarily for the standard of financial reporting within the EU to be 'levelled upwards'.

By contrast, the promotion of an efficient, integrated capital market has implications for the quality and quantity of financial disclosure provided by firms seeking capital in that market, so that arguably a need for 'levelling upwards' is implied. Much research has been carried out, both in order to measure the extent to which actors in capital markets derive information from published financial reports, and to evaluate the effects of differences in accounting and reporting practices on this process. The evidence suggests that, while in many cases information contained in published financial reports may already be known to the market from other sources (such as analysts' reports), in some circumstances published financial reports do convey new information about capital market participants. The crucial role of financial reporting lies in the reduction of information asymmetries which may inhibit the entry of new participants into the market. The better the information provided in published financial reports, the more effective it can be in removing these information asymmetries and promoting market efficiency.

Hence, in seeking to promote capital market integration, the harmonization programme is concerned not just with the reduction of heterogeneity, but with 'levelling up'.

The coordinating organization for the accountancy profession in Europe is the Fédération des Experts Comptables Européens, known as FEE. FEE formally began on 1 January 1987 and was formed by the merger of two earlier organizations, the Union Européene des Experts Comptables, Economiques et Financiers (UEC), founded in 1951, and the Groupe d'Etudes des Experts Comptables de la CEE (Groupe d'Etudes), founded in 1961.

The main objectives of FEE have been stated as follows:

1 to work generally towards the enhancement and harmonization of the practice of accountancy in the broadest sense
2 to promote cooperation among the professional accountancy bodies in Europe in relation to issues of common interest in both the public and private sectors
3 to represent the European accountancy profession at the international level
4 to be the sole consultative organization of the European accountancy profession in relation to the EU authorities.

The members of FEE are formally national professional bodies. The FEE is gradually increasing its role and influence as the 'spokesperson' for European professional accounting bodies, and therefore for European accountants. Thus, its represents a regional grouping within the International Federation of Accountants (IFAC). The FEE does not intend to act as standard setting body, but proposes to promote accounting harmonization in line with the policies of IFAC. The speed with which the FEE emerges as a heavyweight influence in its own right depends, of course, on the extent to which the member national accounting bodies are prepared to give up their own individual attempts at direct influence.

Influences on accounting in Europe

Four very general strands can be considered all of which influence (and explain) differences in specific practice and regulation.

The relative importance of law

The point at issue here is the extent to which the 'law of the land' determines the details of accounting and financial reporting. Tradition in the UK, for example, is that the law specifies general principle only, while in countries heavily influenced by Roman law tradition the law tends to include more detail. Germany is often quoted as an example of the latter approach.

Prescription or flexibility

If regulation is not specified in full and gory detail in legislation, then there are still two alternatives available. First, regulation might be created in detail by professional accounting bodies. Secondly, the broad regulation, whether created by legislation or by professional accounting bodies, may be explicitly designed on the assumption that the *individual* expert, in each unique situation, can and should choose the appropriate course of action, within the broad parameters laid down. The principle of a 'true and fair view' exemplifies this approach.

The providers of finance

The roots of most of the accounting practices discussed in this book predate the arguments of recent years that accounting statements have to satisfy the needs of a wide variety of users. Generally the suppliers of finance to business were the only users seriously considered until late in the twentieth century (sometimes very late). Different countries have very different financial institution structures and finance-raising traditions. It follows that accounting practice will have been adapted to suit the local dominant sources of finance. In some countries tradition tends to focus on the shareholder, and therefore on profit and on the matching of expenses and revenues. Some other countries have more active banking sectors and less shareholder investors. Accounting there will tend to focus on creditors, and therefore on the balance sheet and on the convention of prudence. Germany and Switzerland are often quoted as examples of this second approach.

A more obvious, but less often quoted, example of the influence of finance provision on financial reporting can be seen by considering the systems of eastern Europe, as they begin to emerge from a half-century during which all finance was provided by the state.

The influence of taxation

The general point here is that the scope and extent of the influence of taxation law on financial statements varies considerably. Perceptions of this are often simplistic and extremist. In reality no country can justly claim that tax considerations do not influence published results, and no country can be accused of blindly taking tax-based results and publishing them just as they are. But within these non-existent extremes lies a very real variety of tradition and practice. It is common in many countries, for instance, for some tax allowances to be claimable only if the identical figure from the tax computation is also used in the published financial statements.

The EU directives

For many years the major method of engendering change across the EU has been by means of directives. Once agreed (a process which can and has taken over 20 years), a directive is a binding agreement by all the member states of the EU that they will introduce national legislation. It is important to clarify precisely what this means and what it does not mean. It does mean that all member states are required to implement the directives. It does not mean that citizens or institutions within a member state are required to follow the directive, unless and until the contents of the directive are enacted by legislation within the state. Another important point is that each directive exists not just in one language version, but in each of the nine EU languages. It is the language version applicable to a particular member state which is to be enacted into the law of that country. There may not be perfect semantic equivalence between different language versions of the directives. Furthermore where the contents of the national legislation following from a directive differ from that directive (either by restricting allowed options or by going against the terms of the directive itself), it is only the national legislation which has to be followed within that state.

The fundamental EU directive relating to financial reporting is the Fourth Company Law Directive of 25 July 1978. This relates to the accounts of limited companies. It was followed by the Seventh Company Law Directive of 13 June 1983, which extends the principles of the Fourth Directive to the preparation of consolidated (group) accounts. The Fourth Directive seeks to provide a minimum of coordination of national provisions for the content and presentation of annual financial accounts and reports, of the valuation methods used within them, and of the rules for publication. It applies to 'certain companies with limited liability' – broadly all those above defined minimum-size criteria, and aims to ensure that annual accounts disclose comparable and equivalent information.

It is important to place the Fourth Directive into its historical context. It was drafted and debated over a period of some ten years, beginning when the EU had six members and ending when it had ten. The pre-directive national characteristics of the accounting practices of the member states were significantly different, both in degree of sophistication and in direction. When appraising the success (or otherwise) of this directive we must measure its achievements against those at times startlingly diverse existing practices.

Crucial to the content of the Fourth Directive is the requirement that published accounts should show a 'true and fair view'. The implications and origin of the phrase are discussed in some detail in Part Two, Chapter 13. Briefly, however, this is a classic example of the cultural divide between the common law tradition and the tradition of codified law. In the former, definitions of such concepts are typically provided by courts in relation to specific situations, rather than by legislative texts intended to apply to many different situations. In the latter, the converse is true; the courts have a role of interpretation and clarification of legislative texts, but not of providing situationally appropriate legal definitions. Thus, the tradition of economic liberalism of the English-speaking countries, the faith in markets and the suspicion of technocracy, go hand-in-hand with an essentially pragmatic common law tradition and a belief that the accounting profession can largely lay down its own rules in the form of 'generally accepted accounting principles'. By contrast, the countries of continental Europe have less historical attachment to economic liberalism, more faith in technocracy, and a preference for explicit legal texts, which extends to the framing of accounting rules. Harmonization of accounting within the EU has involved bringing these two traditions into some degree of harmony, and it is in this respect that the inclusion of the 'true and fair' requirement in the Fourth Directive was both crucial and controversial.

One school of thought about the 'true and fair view' prevalent in some European countries, argues that it represents the totality of all the detailed regulations. The opposite school of thought argues that the 'true and fair view' represents precisely that extra element resulting from the integration of the various separate regulatory strands into a coherent whole. In other words, professional judgement about whether financial statements fairly represent that which they purport to represent can transcend particular regulatory requirements about the applications of accounting principles; thus substance prevails over form. The UK tradition, embodied in the wording of the final version of the Fourth Directive, is firmly in the latter camp: correct following of every detailed regulation cannot, of itself, be relied on to give the adequate (true and fair) overall picture. Such a concept is alien to centuries of culture and tradition in some other areas of Europe.

The UK, European and international dimensions

We have pointed out that pre-EU accounting practices in the member states varied widely. The Fourth and Seventh Directives set out to harmonize these practices as far as possible, given the situation at the time. The extent to which practice had been harmonized by the late 1990s is highly debatable. It has frequently been suggested that the Directives were always, and necessarily, seen very much as a first step. In retrospect, and given the divergences of previous practice and attitude, the point seems obvious, but the difficulties of going beyond this first step are also apparent.

Given that there is increasing recognition that the current EU accounting harmonization is obviously less than total in surface appearance, and where it does exist is often only skin deep, what is the way forward? This is a complicated issue, and the following brief sketch attempts to outline the major elements in general terms in a way that will not date too quickly.

It is generally recognized that formal Directives are not an effective way of moving forward. They are too cumbersome in approach and too time-consuming in development. As an alternative mechanism, a European Accounting Forum has been set up under the auspices of the EU Commission. This is intended as a gathering together of all major interested parties – the EU Commission, accounting standard setting bodies, regulatory and government organizations, and business interest groups. The effectiveness of this forum seems to be highly uncertain, as perhaps was its original purpose.

One fundamental issue causing considerable uncertainty and aggravation concerns the relationship between *European* accounting and harmonization, and *international* accounting and harmonization. One school of thought would argue that to attempt further harmonization at the European level is merely to introduce an unnecessary and distracting middle layer into a wider movement toward greater international harmonization and comparability. The other school of thought, to which the European Commission once belonged, takes the view that Europe, consistent with its emergence as a single economic market, needs a single accounting and reporting framework within that market. The European Commission's current position is discussed below.

In April 1997, European Commissioner Mario Monti outlined what he termed 'the Action Plan and Accounting Priorities' as follows. The Action Plan 'covers all measures necessary to ensure that the full benefit of the Single Market is achieved before the introduction of the Single Currency in January 1999'. Key problems to be addressed were 'the incorrect or incomplete transposition of Community law into national law and the excessively complex nature of some national legislation', which are 'two major factors in the Single Market's current inability to realize its full potential'.

With regard to accounting, the Commissioner drew attention to a 'new approach' adopted by the Commission in late 1995, with a view to 'helping Europe's major companies gain access to capital on the world's markets'. This new approach has as a principal objective keeping the Accounting Directives and IASs in line, so that companies operating at the global level can rely on one set of accounts throughout the world, an outcome that depends on the success of the IASC/IOSCO core standards project described above.

The approach is being pursued through closer cooperation and coordination, avoiding new European legislation as far as possible, but with a willingness to amend the Directives where necessary so that they are compatible with existing and new IASs. The European Commission has recently proposed amendments to the Accounting Directives (but, significantly, excluding both the Bank and the Insurance Accounts Directives) to permit the use of fair values as required by various IAS standards.

In May 2000, the European Commission sent a twelve-page letter of reply to the SEC's February 2000 *Concept Release*. This letter was very supportive of the IASC.

A further significant development took place in June 2000, when the Commission published a ten-page Communication entitled *EU Financial Reporting Strategy: the way forward,* and a three-page Memo *Update of the Accounting Strategy: Frequently Asked Questions*, in order to update its 1995 'New Accounting Strategy' position on IAS. These publications gave reasons why the EU should look to the IASC rather than US GAAP as a basis for further harmonisation within the EU, but also state the need for an 'endorsement mechanism' at EU level 'because it would not be wise to delegate accounting standard setting unconditionally and irrevocably to a private organisation over which the EU has no influence ... [and] it is important to create legal certainty by identifying the standards which listed companies will have to apply in the future'. They also note that the endorsement mechanism will examine whether the standards adopted by the IASC conform with EU public policy concerns, and comment that '[b]ecause the endorsement mechanism will have an important pro-active role, it can be expected that the new standards adopted by IASC will also be acceptable in an EU environment'. The main goal of this updated accounting strategy is that, subject to the endorsement mechanism, all corporations whose shares are listed on a regulated market in the EU should prepare consolidated accounts in accordance with IAS by 2005.

This proposed requirement does not extend to the 'national statutory individual accounts', for which 'regulatory and tax requirements could make the use of IAS inappropriate or even invalid'. However, the Member States are to be encouraged to promote or even require the use of IAS for individual accounts whenever possible.

If this process works as the European Commission evidently hopes it will, then all corporations listed on stock exchanges in the EU will, by 2005, be preparing consolidated financial statements using IASC standards in a manner consistent with EU Directives (as revised if necessary), and not using national GAAP for this purpose. The future of national GAAP would be limited to national statutory individual accounts, subject to member states opting to use IASs for this purpose whenever possible. It is too early to say how effectively the 'endorsement mechanism' will work to iron out discrepancies between IASs, present and future, and the EU Directives. The European Commission has indicated a willingness to amend the Directives so as to permit the use of fair values for balance sheet items, as required in many cases by IASs. However, the Commission has not proposed that such amendments would be made to the Bank Accounts Directive or the Insurance Accounts Directive, although banks and insurance undertakings are among the heaviest users of financial instruments, which IAS GAAP require to be carried at fair value in most cases. There are also other exclusions which would leave problems for EU corporations in applying IAS GAAP.

It is also not clear from the above to what extent the process of cooperation and coordination between the European Commission and the IASC will be a two-way one, with the IASC making efforts to accommodate a 'European' perspective in framing IASs. In particular, the IASC's need to satisfy the criteria laid down by the SEC, as indicated above, would imply that the US perspective will largely predominate over the European one in cases where the two differ. The European Commission seems to be hoping that its 'endorsement mechanism' will give it some leverage so that the EU perspective receives consideration, but that remains to be seen. Given the increasing acceptance of the view that financial reporting of listed corporations should respond to the requirements of the capital markets, the EU perspective itself may increasingly converge with that of IOSCO and IASC. Corporate governance from an EU perspective has tended to consider a broader set of stakeholders than capital market participants and creditors. However, the financial reporting implications of this perspective on corporate governance have neither been successfully operationalized nor reconciled with the growing emphasis on capital markets.

Conclusions

As we suggested at the beginning of this chapter, we intend no more than to ensure some awareness of the issues. Financial reporting is crucially related to the economic environment in which it operates. As that environment changes and the national barriers become less important, for both economic and political reasons, accounting must and will change too. Individual attitudes, being inherently culture-based, do not of course change so quickly and the future of practical as opposed to nominal harmonization is highly uncertain.

Activity 2

Do you think European accounting harmonization, left to its own devices and without direct influence from other parts of the world, would move in the same directions as the IASC appears to be doing?

Activity 2 feedback

A difficult one, but we would guess not. The general strength of the legal, prescriptive (and taxation) influence is typically stronger in Europe than in the world as a whole, and the importance of the independent investor much smaller. Note therefore that the UK is perhaps untypical of Europe as a whole. On the other hand, the closer inter-relationships in trade and finance between all countries of the world, and the IASC/IOSCO developments discussed above, may mean that Europe is unable to make its own decisions in accounting issues. The progress of accounting development on the European and international scene is therefore a crucial issue affecting future UK developments!

Summary

In this chapter we have outlined the institutional and attitudinal factors on the European and international accounting scene which impinge on UK developments. We have seen how the IASC is seeking to narrow the range of acceptable alternatives (and to increase its own influence). We also touched on the tensions that perhaps exist between 'typical' IASC thinking and 'typical' European thinking. The UK in this sense is generally nearer to the international than to the European. Accounting is culture related, and the implications of this cannot be ignored.

Exercises

1 In essence, is accounting economics based or law based?
2 If accounting is culture based, and national and indeed local cultures are different, international harmonization will obviously be impossible. Discuss.
3 **What are the objectives of the International Accounting Standards Committee and to what extent have these been fulfilled? State your reasons.** **(20 marks)**
   (ACCA)

4 **You are required:**
   (a) to summarize the objectives of the International Accounting Standards.
   (5 marks)
   (b) to describe the different ways in which the International Accounting Standards Committee attempts to bring about a common international approach. (10 marks)
   (15 marks)
   (CIMA)

5 **You are required to discuss the influence on the published financial statements of British companies of the International Accounting Standards Committee and the European Union.** **(15 marks)**
   (CIMA)

Part Two

The legal framework

In this part we consider the legal framework, the legal constraints, imposed on financial reporting. What does the law require accountants to do, and how does it influence financial reporting generally?

Limited liability companies

> After reading this chapter you should be able to:
> - describe and discuss the implications of limited liability for owners and creditors
> - outline the uncertainties involved in defining distributable profits in the limited company situation
> - state and apply the current legal position relating to distributable profits in the limited company situation.

Introduction

Many skills, inventions and resources contributed to the rise of England as an industrial and imperial power. In particular, the new industries required large amounts of capital to create and, later, feed them. Small individual sums of capital are the hallmark of an agrarian society; an industrial country requires a vehicle that pools the small individual capitals into a common fund from which large enterprises may be sponsored. The limited liability company was such a vehicle, and consequently was one of the great engines of the English industrial revolution.

Two notions are basic to the concept of the limited liability company. One is the idea of **corporate** entity, which merely means that a company (or corporation, to give it its proper description) is a separate legal person completely distinct from the human beings who form the membership. Thus, if four human beings **incorporate** themselves into a company, five legal persons exist – the company itself and its four human contributors of capital, known as **shareholders**. The shareholders can change through transfer of their shares, but the company 'lives' on.

Limited liability

The second notion accommodates those, the majority, who do not wish to risk all of their assets. A **limit of liability** to contribute to the creditors of the enterprise, should it fail, is given to the members of the company. The liability is usually measured by a yardstick of shares and nominal value thereof; thus a member holding 100 shares of 25p nominal value does not contribute more than £25 to the defunct enterprise and nothing at all if he or she had already furnished £25 to the company.

It is difficult, and unnecessary, to point to a precise date on which the two notions were fused in harmony; one may take the first Companies Act of 1862 as the starting point.

Companies Act (until recently) consolidated, but did not codify, the law (see Chapter 13), thus allowing the law to operate in a flexible manner with difficulties being resolved by the courts. Unfortunately, 35 years were to elapse before the Victorian courts fully appreciated the intent of the Act of 1862. The notion of the company itself being a separate legal entity is easy to grasp, but some of the ramifications are not. Further, although everyone easily appreciates that a shareholder in a limited liability company has a *maximum* contribution to the assets of the company, it is easy to overlook that the shareholder has also a *minimum* liability. The two liabilities are the same; the shareholder purchases immunity from liability beyond the nominal amount of the share on the understanding that he or she will contribute, and not evade, his or her basic liability of nominal value. This principle of *minimum* liability may be referred to as the 'sanctity of capital' and is why shares may never be issued, either directly or indirectly, at a discount. The 'sanctity' notion means that a company's capital is a sacred fund that, apart from unsuccessful trading, will never be depleted (except under strict legal supervision) and will remain for the satisfaction of creditors until the cessation of the enterprise. The early nineteenth-century merchants had a suspicion of limited liability arising from the disastrous South Sea Bubble and the unfortunately drafted Bubble Act of 1720 which followed. Consequently, the development of limited liability has always gone hand in hand, although somewhat imperfectly, with the safeguarding of a company's creditors.

Since a company is a separate legal person quite distinct from its constituent members, a creditor has an immense advantage over the creditor of a partnership. The latter must join together all the partners in his or her action for debt – a practical difficulty if the partners are numerous. The former sues the company as a legal person in itself, i.e. only the company is a party to the action. A company creditor has several remedies, the ultimate being the forcing of the company into liquidation, whereupon a liquidator is appointed to rescue and apportion the company assets between the various claimants.

It is essential to realize that the small businessperson is of relatively little economic importance. The nineteenth and twentieth centuries in England belonged to the collectivization of capital, originally by the *laissez-faire* entrepreneurs beloved of Adam Smith and subsequently by state intervention, where private ownership was impossible or undesirable (e.g. the armed services, the police force). The future will certainly belong to the legal, political, taxation and social aspects of the multinational corporation which knows no frontier and no allegiance other than to profit.

The principle established

The confusion in the legal mind over corporate status is highlighted in the bedrock company law case of *Salomon v. Salomon & Co. Ltd* (1897). It must be realized that, had the House of Lords not made the momentous decision here described, commercial cooperation of capitalists would have developed in a different, and probably stranger way than the corporate organization.

Facts of the case

Salomon, a leather merchant, decided to transfer his sole trader's business to a limited company formed for that purpose. Accordingly, he promoted and incorporated Salomon & Co. Ltd. He, his wife, daughter and four sons each took one share in the company to provide the minimum seven members required by the Companies Act of 1862. Salomon grossly overvalued his sole trader's business at £39 000 and, on transfer to the company received a consideration of:

20 000	Shares of nominal value £1
10 000	Debentures
9 000	Cash
39 000	

The original debentures were cancelled and reissued to a person called Broderip and the equitable (deserving) title lay in Salomon. The effect was that Broderip and Salomon could appropriate the assets of the company in repayment of the debentures in priority over ordinary creditors of the business if the company found itself in financial difficulty, which it subsequently did.

Eventually, the trade creditors pressed the company into liquidation. In liquidation, Salomon and Broderip, using their debentures, seized all the company assets, and the unsecured trade creditors were left with nothing.

This happy position (for Salomon and Broderip) would have continued if the company were a separate legal entity distinct from Salomon; although creditors could sue the *company*, they were defeated if the assets had been extracted. Conversely, if Salomon and his company were the same thing, Salomon would have had to pay the creditors from his private purse until his last penny (i.e. in his capacity as shareholder, not in his capacity as debenture holder). Thus, the case turned on whether the company was a separate legal person from Salomon, even though the latter held 20 001 of the 20 007 shares in issue.

Activity 1

Stop and think about this situation for a few minutes. What do you think the judgement should be, and why?

Activity 1 feedback

In the divisional (lower) court, Justice Vaughan Williams had difficulty in grasping the notion of a corporate person. He seemed to follow the Victorian philosophy (that one should pay one's debts) to an extreme conclusion; he found for the creditors, describing the company as an 'alias, sham, agent' of Salomon, who remained the real satisfaction of the creditors.

Salomon appealed to the Court of Appeal. This court found for the creditors, but on a different ground, finding the Salomon company structure to be 'contrary to the true intent of the 1862 Act'. It seems that the court was much disturbed by the grossly unbalanced shareholding in Salomon & Co. Ltd, believing that the 'new' companies were only a kind of partnership, in which there was normally a 'balance of power'.

Salomon appealed to the House of Lords, which unanimously reversed the decisions of the lower courts. The decision may be summarized in three parts:

1 Salomon & Co. Ltd. was validly formed; the 1862 Act merely required at least seven persons holding at least one share each. Thus, the 'unbalanced' shareholding was irrelevant.

2   It is unnecessary for members to:
   (a)   be independent – thus a 'family' company is legal
   (b)   take a substantial interest in the organization (note the modern public company could not exist if this were otherwise)
   (c)   hold a balance of power; and
   (d)   it is irrelevant that a member is under the moral suasion and mental domination of another. Thus, for example, a 'husband-and-wife' company is legal.
3   The leather business belonged to the company and, if there was any question of agency, *Salomon was the agent of the company* and not the converse, as Justice Williams had suggested.

Conclusions and comments

1   For the first time (1897) it was made clear that the law will show no distinction between a large public company and a small company where one person is, in reality, the controller.
2   It is the creditors who are at risk in company operation. Companies are now required to file, in a public registry, numerous documents, usually on an annual basis, so that the public may be informed with regard to the company's progress.

   It thus behoves creditors to inspect the public documents on an annual basis, and certainly before treating with a corporate body.

   In a large company, the largest body of creditors will be employees for wages earned, but not yet paid; employees remunerated by yearly commission, bonus, etc., and conceivably, employees with statutory redundancy claims.
3   The grossly overvalued price that Salomon received from the company he formed was irrelevant, *as the price had been brought to the attention of the prospective members.* This rule still applies on the transfer of assets to a private company, but, in a public company, there are safeguards to prevent sharp practice by promoters transferring their own assets to the company. An independent valuation is now required.
4   It is commonplace for sole traders and partners to copy Salomon and form 'family' companies to which their assets are transferred. The intent of the Companies Act is thus often distorted. That intent was that companies should be controlled by their shareholders on democratic principles. However, in small companies the shareholdings, apart from the 'owner', are usually nominal. This reality will be recognized in law by the introduction of the single member private company.

   In public companies, the small investor is swamped by the large institutional investor. Moreover, it is a current practice for the shareholders to delegate their powers to the board of directors (in so far as they are, by law, allowed so to do) and abdicate from their responsibility of supervising the directors. The average shareholder displays little interest in company meetings.

   The theory of company control by members is, therefore, unreal. Ownership (members) and control (directors) are therefore divorced.
5   Until the Companies Act of 1981, no type of company (except unlimited companies) could take back its share from the members, furnishing them with cash or assets in exchange. This arose from the idea of the sanctity of capital, the notion that capital is irreducible. Even now, the general rule is that any distribution to members in respect of shares taken back by the company must be out of past profits. A private company may

now distribute capital to members, but only if past profits have been exhausted and only, in effect, if the directors take upon themselves the burden of paying creditors if the distributions prove irresponsible.

6 The idea of a nominal value for a share is peculiar to English law and nowadays is absurd. Probably the idea arose out of a desire to buttress the notion of sanctity of capital. Many continental and US companies have dispensed with nominal value, issuing shares of no par value. One great advantage is that the dividend declared is the actual yield of the share and it would eliminate the artificial rule for the treatment of a share premium.

It will now be realized that the notions of corporate entity, limited liability of members and the idea of sanctity of a company's capital (for the protection of creditors) are fundamental.

Sanctity of capital – the 'interim' accounting problem

In origin, the profit or loss of any organization was found by comparing the net assets of the owner at the time of commencement of trade with the net assets at the time of ceasing of trade. This is still the legal way of ascertaining 'profit', and is used by accountants to ascertain profit or loss where financial records have been accidentally destroyed (e.g. by magnetic disturbance of computer memories) or wilfully destroyed (e.g. by directors anxious to avoid a tax investigation). The method is also extensively used to determine tax assessments where no records, or incomplete records, have been kept.

The method was confirmed in *The Spanish Prospecting Co. Ltd* (1911) and is illustrated as follows:

Date	1 January 20X1	1 January 20X2	1 January 20X3
Assets			
Valuation of building	10 000	10 500	15 000
Valuation of machinery	5 000	4 000	3 500
Valuation of stock-in-trade	4 300	5 421	1 632
Monies in bank account	1 000	2 000	1 500
	20 300	21 921	21 632
Liability			
Claim of creditor	800	200	2 219
Net assets	£19 500	£21 721	£19 413

Thus from 1 January 20X1 to 1 January 20X2
the profit is 21 721 – 19 500   =   2 221

And from 1 January 20X1 to 1 January 20X2
the loss is 19 413 – 21 721   =   (2 308)

During the existence of the business
(1 January 20X1 to 1 January 20X3)
the overall loss is 19 413 – 19 500   =   (87)

This method may startle anyone accustomed to finding profit or loss through the traditional trading and P&L account. Nevertheless, it is the basic method, and the superstructure of manufacturing account, trading account, etc., are refinements to enable costing and other useful information to be ascertained. The true ultimate profit or loss of an enterprise cannot, of course, be found until it ceases; all balance sheets presented during the life of a company are only approximate, interim statements with valuations based on certain conventions, and all realistic accountants accept them as such.

The convention adopted for the valuation of assets will affect an 'interim' balance sheet, as we discussed at length in Part One. A balance sheet containing a factory valued at the HC of purchase may be grossly different from a balance sheet containing the same asset at its realizable value or its replacement price.

The legal response

Almost from the commencement of the Companies Act of 1862, accountants have attempted to accommodate this fundamental divergence with the political accountancy problems of the day, while striving to present a 'true and fair view'. Many political accountancy battles have been fought and some won.

Nevertheless, the thrust and intent of modern company legislation is clear – company operation is no longer the mere domestic interest of shareholders; the public and the government have great interest and concern.

Accountants now simplify the fundamental problem by assuming two notions; the division of assets into **fixed** assets and **current** assets and the notion of separating income and expenditure into two classes, **revenue** and **capital**.

In the long term, there is no distinction between fixed and current assets and no difference between capital and revenue expenditure and income. For the interim statements of profit/loss, etc., the notions must, however, be accepted.

Assets retained for a considerable time with the intent of using them for economic profit are termed fixed assets; money is fixed or sunk in them on a long-term basis. Assets that change their nature in the process of earning profit are termed current assets; the money in them circulates through stock, debtors, bank account and creditors. This is shown in Fig. 12.1.

The excess of assets over liabilities at any given time is described by a variety of names, e.g. capital, net worth or 'equity'. It belongs to the owners of the business; hence the description of ordinary shareholders as 'equity' shareholders – they are entitled to all the net assets after any preference shareholders.

For business convenience, the equity may be analysed between the capital initially contributed by the original shareholders and the subsequent profits. The latter may be subapportioned between revenue (sometimes called 'free') reserves and capital reserves.

The Companies Act of 1948 defined a revenue reserve in terms of opinion; it is one that is considered 'free' for distribution through the P&L account. A capital reserve was not defined at all, but is taken to mean one that in prudence should not be distributed to shareholders in the short term.

The distinction between capital and revenue is thus one of short-term business convenience; in the long term it is irrelevant. The distinction arises because of the need to maintain capital for the protection of creditors of the limited liability company (the notion of 'sanctity capital') and the practical requirement of calculating interim profit for taxation and dividend purposes. In public limited companies the idea of sanctity of capital is but-

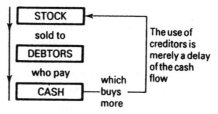

Figure 12.1
Circulation of money.

tressed by the requirement that these companies must now have a minimum amount of capital before proceeding to business. The directors are also required to convene a shareholders' meeting should the company lose half its capital, although a banking creditor would, in practice, have intervened long before that point was reached.

The accounting convention of HC values fixed assets at their original purchase price to the company; if the distance of time is too remote, a past valuation may be taken. The CC concept values fixed assets at their supposed value at a point of time, with consequential adjustments to accumulated depreciation. The Companies Act of 1981 accommodated both bases of valuation, and also provided for selective revaluation of fixed assets. Thus a set of accounts may now have any concept of value between original HC and full CC accounting!

Current assets are valued at what they will realize in the normal course of business, although stock-in-trade will be valued at cost, if that is lower. It is difficult to decide the amount of overhead to include in cost, but, since the closing stock of one period of account is merely the opening stock of the next period of account, short-term aberrations are smoothed and, provided the cost and overhead basis is applied consistently, taxation and dividend requirements are met.

Restrictions affecting capital

Company law attempts to ensure, particularly in the case of public limited companies, that capital is properly raised from the public and properly transferred to the company without promoters and other third parties siphoning funds off for themselves. Once established with capital, the company must not dissipate the fund in unauthorized pursuits, and there must be no return of capital to the company subscribers unless creditors have been paid off or given security.

There are numerous provisions to ensure, in particular, that:

1 Capital is furnished to the company in cash and not in kind – or, in the cases where kind is permitted, a proper valuation of the consideration is made.
2 The company commences with sufficient funds for business – the most common cause of small bankruptcies is initial underfunding.
3 The issue and dealing of shares does not constitute a reduction or discount, directly or indirectly, in the capital fund. Shares may not be issued at a discount, and the legal intent cannot be avoided by issuing shares already partly paid or by the issue of convertible debentures. Conversely, the law does not forbid the issue of shares at a premium over their nominal value (a device for obtaining capital on which dividends need not be declared) but stipulates that the premium shall be retained as capital and not distributed as dividend (as it was pre-1948).

4 The capital fund of the company is used only in the adventures that the members intended to undertake or such altered adventures that they may authorize by special resolution. The objects clause of the Memorandum of Association not only defines but confines the use of the members' money. In practice, objects clauses are now drafted in such a wide manner that the protection given to members is illusory, a fact recognized by the Companies Act of 1989.

5 The recent (1981) provisions, whereby a company can redeem its own shares that are expressed to be redeemable and whereby the company may purchase its own shares, are of restricted use.

Further, since it is a proviso that the returned capital must be replaced with a fresh issue of shares or the capitalization of free reserves, creditors are unlikely to be in jeopardy. After the exhaustion of free reserves, private companies may resort to capital to repay money to the members but, in effect, the directors undertake to indemnify the creditors personally.

Distributable profits, the case law background

Ensuring that the capital fund remains intact is meaningless unless there are further provisions to prevent the excessive payment of dividend to members. Dividend may always be paid out of profit; but a 'dividend' using part or all of the capital fund is merely a colourful return of capital to the members that reduces or extinguishes funds available for the satisfaction of creditors.

The determination of 'profits available for dividend' thus turns on three things:

1 the calculation of profit
2 the protection of creditors
3 the extent to which capital profits are available for dividend.

The Victorian courts had, to the modern eye, a somewhat surprising view of 'profit'. The case of *Verner v. General and Commercial Investment Trust* (1894) rightly pointed out that depreciation must always be provided on circulating (current) assets; put simply, the current assets must be correctly valued. Both the Verner case and the case of *Lee v. Neuchatel Asphalte Co.* (1889), however, stated depreciation need not be provided on fixed or wasting assets and that, in such case, the members would realize that their dividends were, in part, a return of capital. Justice Lindley did point out that such a course might be commercially imprudent, and it is doubtful whether the average company investor appreciated the nuances of the Verner decision. Justice Lindley also pointed out, in the Lee decision, that the reckoning of profit is not a statutory matter, but is left to men of business.

Eady LJ later pointed out (*Ammonia Soda Co. Ltd. v. Chamberlain* (1918)) that past depreciation may be written back to create a current profit and, startlingly, that current profits may be distributed as dividend without making good the losses of past years. *Stapley v. Read* (1924) went further and stated that current profits could be created by a *bona fide* revaluation of goodwill and hence, by analogy, other fixed assets.

The case of *Lubbock v. British Bank of South America* (1892) sensibly stated that a dividend may be paid out of a capital profit that has actually been realized (and thus has improved the liquidity of the company). The decision in *Dimbula Valley (Ceylon) Tea Co. Ltd. v. Laurie* (1961) disturbed the subsequent Jenkins Committee in stating that an unrealized capital profit was available for dividend, but note that Justice Buckley, in that case, was primarily concerned with the class rights of preference shareholders and did sound a cautionary note that the procedure he advocated in the Dimbula case might be completely inappropriate in another.

By the early 1960s the law regarding divisible profits had become so confused and convoluted that statutory intervention became inevitable; the present law is contained in Section 263 and 276 of the Companies Act of 1986.

From the earliest times of company operation, it was agreed by all (and so stated in the Verner and Lee cases) that the protection of creditors is paramount and that no dividend or distribution can be made that would result in a reduction of company funds so as to jeopardize the fund left for creditors.

The Articles, of course, when operating restrictively, overrule the statutory provisions. The members, via the Articles, often prescribe the fund out of which dividends can be paid, and it may be provided that the directors may set sums aside to reserve before arriving at the fund available for dividend; such an article effectively allows directors to decide whether a dividend is paid or not – although directors of a public listed company will always come under pressure from institutional shareholders if the company is run so capriciously that an adequate level of dividend cannot be maintained.

The Companies Act of 1985

After the passage of the Companies Act of 1985, it is clear that dividends and other distributions can only be funded from realized profits after offsetting realized losses.

Section 263 states that (our emphasis):

> A company's profits available for distribution are its *accumulated*, realized profits (not previously distributed or capitalized) less its *accumulated*, realized losses (not previously used in a reduction or reorganization of capital).

The use of the word 'accumulated' ensures that the P&L account is now treated as a continuous account and not merely taken, in isolation, year by year, as was done in the Ammonia Soda case. It is made clear (schedule 4, paragraph 91, Companies Act of 1985) that 'realized profits' are to be determined by the principles of accounting thought current at the time. The onus is thus on the accountancy profession and its learned bodies to pronounce, from time to time, their definition of 'realized profit'.

The basic legal requirements are, in full:

1 Only profits realized at the balance sheet date shall be included in the profit and loss account (schedule 4, paragraph 12(a)).
2 It is hereby declared for the avoidance of doubt that references in this schedule to realized profits, in relation to a company's accounts, are to such profits of the company as fall to be treated as realized profits for the purposes of those accounts in accordance with principles generally accepted with respect to the determination for accounting purposes of realized profits at the time when those accounts are prepared (schedule 4, paragraph 91).

In a statement issued by the six accounting bodies in 1982 it was made clear that there are three major elements contributing to the meaning of the phrase 'principles generally accepted' at any particular time. These are:

1 statutory requirements – especially the five 'accounting principles' of Schedule 4 (p. 228).
2 SSAPs – headed by SSAP 2
3 the overriding true and fair view requirement (Chapter 13).

The definition of 'realized' is therefore ever-changing, as accounting thinking changes! A particularly interesting example of the problems this approach can sometimes bring is discussed in Chapter 20 on long-term contract work in progress.

Section 263 expressly states that if directors are in doubt after 'making all reasonable enquiries' as to whether a profit arising before 22 December 1980 is realized or unrealized, it may be treated as realized. Conversely, a loss arising before 22 December 1980, whose realizability is in doubt, may be treated as unrealized. The Act is not discouraging directors from declaring dividends!

Section 280 defines 'profit' and 'losses' as including all such items, irrespective of whether they arise from capital or revenue, emphasizing the fact that, in the long term, there is no difference between capital and revenue. The company's own Articles, may, of course, prohibit the distribution of a capital profit and may also be more restrictive than the statutory provisions.

Schedule 4 now insists on the depreciation of fixed assets that have only a 'limited useful economic' life, and section 275 includes such depreciation charges in 'realized losses'. Moreover, if assets are revalued and a deficit arises on revaluation, such deficit must be treated as a 'realized loss' except in two cases, namely:

1 where the deficit offsets a previous unrealized profit *on the same asset* (the deficit is then treated as an 'unrealized loss')
2 where the deficit arises on a revaluation of *all the fixed assets*. The deficit is then treated as an 'unrealized loss'. Goodwill, for this purpose, need not be treated as a fixed asset (although the accounting formats of the 1985 Act require goodwill to be shown as a fixed asset).

The law requires the balance sheets of companies to show a true and fair view of the affairs of the company, and businesses should not be discouraged from showing an appreciation of fixed assets by the revaluation thereof and the carriage of the concomitant unrealized capital surplus to revaluation reserve. The increased depreciation charge by virtue of revaluation may now be treated as realized profit, in effect treating it as available for distribution as profit. Table 12.1 makes this clear.

The revaluation of fixed assets has thus not compromised the dividend policy of the directors.

Distributable profits

At the same time as the guidance statement referred to above, the six accounting bodies issued a second statement entitled *The Determination of Distributable Profits in the Context of the Companies Act*. The legal provisions there referred to were originally part of the 1980 Act, but in the extracts from the guidance notes that follow they have been referenced to the 1985 consolidating Act.

The provisions of the Act are summarized as follows:

Table 12.1 *Effect of revaluing assets on dividend*

	Cost £	Revaluation £	Difference £
Fixed assets	2 000	5 000	3 000
Depreciation, on straight-line basis at 20% per annum	400	1 000	600
Profits before depreciation	10 000	10 000	
less Depreciation	400	1 000	
Available for dividend *add back* Depreciation difference due to revaluation	9 600 –	9 000 600	
Total available for dividend	9 600	9 600	

3 A distribution is defined (263(2)) as every description of distribution of a company's assets to members of the company, whether in cash or otherwise, except distributions made by way of:
   (a) an issue of shares as fully or partly paid bonus shares
   (b) redemption or purchase of any of the company's own shares out of capital (including a new issue of shares) or out of unrealized profits
   (c) reduction of share capital; and
   (d) a distribution of assets to members of the company on its winding-up.
4 A company may only make a distribution out of profits available for that purpose (263(1)). A company's profits available for distribution are stated to be its accumulated, realized profits (so far as not previously distributed or capitalized) less its accumulated, realized losses (so far as not previously written off in a reduction or reorganization of its share capital).
   Realized losses may not be offset against unrealized profits. Public companies are subject to a further restriction (see **6** below).
5 A company may only distribute an unrealized profit when the distribution is in kind and the unrealized profit arises from the writing up of the asset being distributed.
6 A further restriction is placed on distributions by public companies (264). A public company may only make a distribution if, after giving effect to such distribution, the amount of its net assets (as defined in 264) is not less than the aggregate of its called up share capital and undistributable reserves. This means that a public company must deduct any net unrealized losses from net realized profits before making a distribution, whereas a private company need not make such a deduction.

Thus, in a private company, the profits available for distribution need only be the accumulated realized profits (capital + revenue) less the accumulated realized losses (capital + revenue). Since unrealized capital profits cannot be included in the P&L account anyway (schedule 4, paragraph 12(a)), the difference between a private and public company now lies only in the matter of unrealized capital losses that must be taken into account in arriving at the profits available for distribution of a public company (section 264).

The undistributable reserves are defined (section 264) as:

1 share premium account
2 capital redemption reserve
3 aggregate accumulated unrealized profits less aggregate accumulated unrealized losses
4 any reserve whose distribution is prohibited by law (other than the Companies Act)
5 any reserve whose distribution is prohibited by the Memorandum or Articles of the company itself.

Although section 264 only applies to public companies, the student should be aware that the reserves referred to are not distributable by private companies either. Section 264 merely established a minimum figure below which a distribution cannot be made.

A distribution means any distribution of a company's assets to its members, the exception only being for purposes laid down in the Companies Act itself (e.g. an issue of bonus shares). Thus, if the directors were to sell the company's stock to themselves at less than normal retail price, the distribution would consist of the difference between the actual selling price and the normal retail selling price.

It must be remembered that, whereas loss of value of current assets must always be provided, depreciation of fixed assets is only required if the asset is of limited useful economic life or the loss is permanent. Thus, land would not normally be depreciated. Fluctuations in long-term investments (e.g. in related companies) may be ignored in the case of a private company, but not necessarily in the case of a public one; for a fall in value might constitute an unrealized loss (which section 264 requires us to take into our calculations in the case of a public company). Adventurers in private companies are presumed to know that their dividends may, in part or whole, be a return of capital (a point often overlooked by Victorian shareholders in mining companies where the chief asset, a mine, was often of uncertain value). The protection of creditors is, of course, paramount and, in practice, banks lending to a private company usually require a personal guarantee from the directors.

Certain expenditure may not now be treated as assets. Expenses of formation of the company, for example, must now be treated as a realized loss, and development costs of some new process or adventure may only be carried in the balance sheet if the directors expressly consider that expenditure to be of value (section 269). Moreover, only goodwill that has been purchased (as opposed to goodwill created by the activities of the company) may be treated as an asset, and then only if it still represents genuine value to the company.

The figures from which the calculation of profits available for dividend is itself made are found by scrutiny of relevant accounts, these usually being the last set of balance sheet and P&L account agreed by the members in general meeting (section 270) and delivered to the registrar for public information. Oddly, by a strict reading of section 270(2) it would seem the directors are only required to look at the figures in the account and not necessarily at any cautionary note appended thereto. Since the directors will usually have appended such note at the behest of the auditor, whose unqualified report on the account is mandatory (section 271), this seems a rather strange drafting of the law. The accounts themselves must have been properly prepared in accordance with the Companies Act and must give a true and fair view (section 271).

The accounts themselves may be prepared by reference to any kind of accounting convention, provided the chosen convention is consistently applied (schedule 4, sections B and

C). Accounts may always be drawn up in the HC convention by simple extraction from the company's book-keeping records. Supplementary accounts based on the CC convention or the selective revaluation convention (both accommodated in the 1985 Act) may also be furnished to the shareholders. Any difference shown in profits available for dividend by virtue of different conventions may be of relevance. It will usually constitute an increase in unrealized profit on the revaluation of assets; the later revaluation requiring a revised charge for depreciation (schedule 4, section C, paragraph 32).

No law, of course, compels directors to declare a dividend, and no shareholder would insert such an absurd clause in the Articles. Public listed companies tend to be controlled in dividend policy by their institutional investors (and institutional creditors). Excessive payment of dividend is only likely in the small private company where shareholders and directors are the same persons.

Activity 2

Try your hand at the following question, taken from a professional body examination paper (ACCA).

1 **What is the general rule for determining distributable profits as stated in the Companies Act of 1985?**
   (Candidates are not required to discuss the special provisions relating to investment and insurance companies.)   (5 marks)
2 **State whether each of the following are realized or unrealized profits (or losses) for the purpose of calculating distributable profits:**
   (a) Depreciation charged on a revalued fixed asset.   (3 marks)
   (b) Development expenditure in the profit and loss account which was previously capitalized in the balance sheet.   (3 marks)
   (c) The share of profits from an associated company to an investing company which does not prepare consolidated financial statements.   (3 marks)
   (d) The profit on the disposal of a fixed asset which had been revalued in a previous year.
                                                                                       (3 marks)
   (e) A provision for libel damages in a forthcoming court case.   (3 marks)
                                                                                    (20 marks)

Activity 2 feedback

1 The general rule is that distributable profits consist of accumulated realized profits less accumulated realized losses. Realized profits and losses are determined by reference to generally accepted accounting principles at the time the financial statements are prepared. There is a further restriction for public limited companies which may only make a distribution if the net assets immediately after the distribution are not less than the total share capital plus undistributable reserves.
2 **(a)** Depreciation on a fixed asset is a realized expense, but where the fixed asset has been revalued the depreciation on the revalued portion may be treated as a realized profit which is available for distribution.
   (b) Development expenditure capitalized in the balance sheet and subsequently charged to the P&L account is a realized loss in the year the expense appears in the P&L account not when the cost was incurred.
   (c) The share of profits from an associated company to an investing company which

are not included in consolidated financial statements are not considered to be realized profits; only the dividends received are considered realized.

(d) The profit on disposal of a fixed asset which has been revalued will be the difference between the proceeds and the valuation of the asset. However, the excess of the valuation over net book value will not have been treated as realized profit in the year of valuation and so in the year of disposal the whole of the profit (proceeds less net book value) will be treated as realized.

(e) The fact that the provision appears in the balance sheet and not as a note to the balance sheet concerning a contingent liability, clearly indicates that the directors expect to pay damages. This decision is probably based on legal advice and in accordance with SSAP 2 *Disclosure of Accounting Policies* has been provided for in the accounts. In these circumstances this would be regarded as a realized loss.

Summary

In this chapter we have investigated the meaning and significance of limited liability, and briefly explored some of the case law background. We reminded ourselves from a more legal perspective of the importance of capital maintenance which we discussed from an economic angle in Part One. Finally, we looked in some detail at the legal position regarding the distributability of profits, and explored the practical application of the rules.

Exercises

1 What are realized profits?
2 Outline the rules for determining distributable profits.
3 Explain the difference between realized profits and distributable profits. Why is the rule not simply that 'all realized profits are distributable'?
4 Camwe Ltd/plc

Balance sheet as at 30 September			£000
Fixed assets			
Land and buildings (Note)		100	
Plant and machinery		130	230
Current assets			
Stock	140		
Debtors	70		
Cash	15	225	
less Current liabilities: Creditors			
(less than one year)		(45)	
Net current assets			180
Total assets less current liabilities			410
Creditors (more than one year)		(150)	
Provisions for liabilities and charges		(10)	(160)
			250
Capital and reserves			
Called up share capital			150
Share premium account			65

Revaluation reserve	(25)
P&L account	60
	250

Note: Professionally valued at 30 September giving rise to revaluation deficit of £25 000
Required:
Calculate the distributable profit for (a) Ltd, (b) plc in the following cases:
(a) Proposed dividend of £50 000 plus a clean auditor's report.
(b) Proposed dividend of £50 000 – plus the following extract from the auditor's report: 'unable to obtain all the information and explanations necessary to satisfy ourselves as to the existence of the stock quantities valued at £140 000 at 30 September.'

5 The summarized accounts of Withdrawals Ltd are as follows:

Share capital	40 000	Freehold land	10 000
Reserves	–	Leasehold property	20 000
		Stock	15 000
Creditors	30 000	Debtors	12 000
		Cash	13 000
	70 000		70 000

(a) Consider (individually), the amount that the shareholders should be permitted to withdraw by way of dividend as a result of each of the following seven transactions, giving your reasons.
(b) In the case of transactions 6 and 7 calculate and comment on the implications of the Companies Act of 1985, on the assumption that the company is:
   (i) private
   (ii) public.
Transactions
(1) Stock costing £5000 has been sold on credit for £10 000.
(2) Stock costing £5000 has been revalued at £10 000. This item is imported, and the world price has doubled since the stock was purchased.
(3) Freehold land costing £10 000 has been sold for £15 000.
(4) Freehold land has been revalued at £15 000 (after a professional revaluation).
(5) Freehold land costing £10 000 has been sold for £15 000; the leasehold property has been written down by £5000; stock costing £5000 has been found to be worthless; stock costing £10 000 has been sold for £20 000.
(6) Stock costing £10 000 has been sold for £20 000 cash; the freehold land has been written down to £5000.
(7) Stock costing £3000 has been sold for £6000 cash; the freehold land has been revalued at £12 000.

6 In connection with distributable profits as defined in the provisions of the Companies Act of 1985:
   (a) What is the general rule for the determination of distributable profits?
   (Candidates are not expected to discuss the special provisions relating to investment and insurance companies.) (4 marks)
   (b) What do you understand by the term 'relevant accounts', which is used in the Companies Act of 1985 in connection with distributable profits? How might such accounts inhibit the payment of a dividend? (6 marks)
   (c) Which of the following items do you consider to be realized or unrealized profits and losses?

(i) profits on long-term contracts in progress, where the requirements of SSAP 9 Accounting for Stocks and Work in Progress have been followed

(ii) depreciation calculated on a revalued fixed asset

(iii) undistributed profits in a subsidiary

(iv) capitalized development expenditure, where the requirements of SSAP 13 Accounting for Research and Development have been followed

(v) the current cost reserve, where a company adopts current cost accounts as its main accounts. (10 marks)

(20 marks)

(ACCA)

7 You are required to answer the following questions on distributable profits as defined by the Companies Act 1985.

(a) **What is the general rule for determining distributable profits?**

(Candidates are not required to discuss the special provisions relating to investment and insurance companies.) (4 marks)

(b) **State whether each of the following are realized or unrealized profits or losses. Briefly explain the reason for your answer.**

(i) A charge to the profit and loss account as a provision for bad debts.

(ii) The final dividend receivable from a subsidiary in respect of an accounting period ending before the end of the parent company's financial year.

(iii) Foreign exchange gains or losses on unsettled short-term monetary items when the temporal method of foreign currency translation is used.

(iv) Surpluses arising on revaluation of assets (before sale). (8 marks)

(c) **The summarized balance sheet at 30 September 20X6 of Global Sports, a limited company, is set out below:**

	£000
Authorized share capital	
250 000 ordinary shares of £1 each	250
Called up share capital	
200 000 ordinary shares of £1 each	200
Share premium account	175
Revaluation reserve (net deficit)	(175)
Other reserves	
Capital redemption reserve	125
General reserve	100
Profit and loss account	200
	625
Fixed assets	400
Net current assets	225
	625

Notes:

1 The deficit on the revaluation reserve arose as a result of a revaluation of all the fixed assets.

2 The articles of association state that the general reserve is non-distributable.

What are the legally distributable profits of Global Sports if:

(i) **it is a private company?**

(ii) **it is a public company?**

(iii) **what difference, if any, would it make to your answers in (c)(i) and (c)(ii) above if the deficit on the revaluation reserve had arisen on the revaluation of an individual asset?**

Explain your workings   (8 marks)

(20 marks)

(ACCA)

8 Why is the sanctity, or preservation, of capital important?

9 Explain carefully in non-technical terms what is meant by 'limited liability'.

10 'Limited liability is by definition unfair on business creditors.' Discuss.

The Companies Act and published accounts

> After reading this chapter you should be able to:
> ■ state and discuss the key Companies Act requirements as to the preparation of published accounts
> ■ describe and apply the specified formats permitted for published accounts
> ■ outline requirements relating to notes to the accounts, directors' reports, etc., and the sources of other requirements affecting companies.

Introduction

Since the major Companies Act of 1948, there were a number of new Acts, each broadly adding further requirements to what had gone before. In 1985 the resulting confusion was largely swept aside by the Companies Act 1985, which consolidated the surviving elements of the 1948 and subsequent Acts into a single coherent whole. Good intentions do not always last, however and within four years the 1989 Act was added, changing and amending as well as complementing the 1985 Act, and renumbering some of the sections in a particularly confusing way.

The true and fair view

Before looking in detail at the disclosure requirements for published company accounts as specified in the Companies Act 1985 we must look briefly at the situation before 1985. As already mentioned, the Companies Act 1948 was the basis of modern company legislation. It contained several detailed disclosure requirements, but, most importantly, it had the overriding requirement to show 'a true and fair view'.

This is now expressed in section 226 of the 1985 Act, as inserted by the 1989 Act:

> **226** Duty to prepare individual company accounts
> **(1)** The directors of every company shall prepare for each financial year of the company –
>> **(a)** balance sheet as at the last day of the year, and
>> **(b)** a profit and loss account
>> Those accounts are referred to in this Part as the company's 'individual accounts'.

(2) The balance sheet shall give a true and fair view of the state of affairs of the company as at the end of the financial year; and the profit and loss account shall give a true and fair view of the profit or loss of the company for the financial year.
(3) A company's individual accounts shall comply with the provisions of Schedule 4 as to the form and content of the balance sheet and profit and loss account and additional information to be provided by way of notes to the accounts.
(4) Where compliance with the provisions of that Schedule, and the other provisions of this Act as to the matters to be included in a company's individual accounts or in notes to those accounts, would not be sufficient to give a true and fair view, the necessary additional information shall be given in the accounts or in a note to them.
(5) If in special circumstances compliance with any of those provisions is inconsistent with the requirement to give a true and fair view, the directors shall depart from that provision to the extent necessary to give a true and fair view.

Particulars of any such departure, the reasons for it and its effect shall be given in a note to the accounts.

Auditors are given a corresponding duty to report on this requirement, stating whether in their opinion (note the subjectivity implied by this phrase) the accounts have been properly prepared in accordance with the Acts, and whether in their opinion a true and fair view is given. It should be noted carefully that section 226, subsections (2) and (3) are separate requirements. Since both must explicitly be attempted, it follows that they are independent and that either one could be achieved without the other. In particular:

1 complying with all detailed requirements of the Acts does not necessarily lead to a true and fair view
2 where such a conflict arises, it is the true and fair requirement which is the more important.

Activity 1

The meaning of 'a true and fair view' is obviously of crucial importance. What does it mean? First of all try to express your ideas in your own words. Then, if possible, use a library to explore other people's views.

Activity 1 feedback

The short answer is that it means whatever the accounting profession currently thinks it means. This is perhaps a rather startling thought, and it needs explaining. Parliament had deliberately decided, following centuries of historical and legal tradition, that the precise definition of what is necessary in order to give a proper impression of the financial results and position of a business is a technical accounting matter and should therefore be left to accountants. Parliament would lay out guidelines, and would establish certain minimum requirements, but would leave the 'fine tuning' to the accounting profession, either through published recommendation or by general practice.

In general, therefore, a firm of accountants could safely certify that in their opinion a true and fair view was given provided that they had done what any other firm of accountants would have done, and that the accounts contained only characteristics that any other firm of accountants would also have found to be satisfactory. It is clear that this approach leads to the precise meaning of a true and fair view being different at different times. The 'normal' view becomes by definition the 'acceptable' view. Of course, this does not necessarily prevent change and progress – attitudes and opinions gradually change within the profession. Case law will also push change from time to time.

An interesting example of the true and fair view in operation concerns depreciation. Surprisingly perhaps, the 1948 Act (and for that matter the 1967 and 1976 Acts) did not require fixed assets to be depreciated. But depreciation and the necessity for it were already firmly ingrained in the practices and beliefs of the accounting profession. Accounts not providing depreciation on tangible fixed assets would not have been regarded as showing a true and fair view.

The introduction of accounting standards into the UK accounting regulatory system has created the need to try and clarify the precise relationship between the standards and the law in general and the true and fair view requirement in particular. Expert legal counsel has twice been given on this question, in 1983 and again, following the changes introduced in the 1989 Companies Act, in 1993. The essence of the argument of the later report, by Mary Arden QC, is well shown by the following extract.

> The changes brought about by the Companies Act 1989 will in my view affect the way in which the Court approaches the question whether compliance with an accounting standard is necessary to satisfy the true and fair view requirement. The Court will infer from Section 256 that statutory policy favours both the issue of accounting standards (by a body prescribed by regulation) and compliance with them: indeed Section 256(3)(c) additionally contemplates the investigation of departures from them and confers power to provide public funding for such purpose. The Court will also in my view infer from paragraph 36A of Schedule 4 that (since the requirement is to disclose particulars of non-compliance rather than of compliance) accounts which meet the true and fair requirement will in general follow rather than depart from standards and that departure is sufficiently abnormal to require to be justified. These factors increase the likelihood, to which the earlier joint Opinions referred, that the Courts will hold that in general compliance with accounting standards is necessary to meet the true and fair requirement.

The issue is a very complicated one, and the logic of counsel's argument is sometimes suspect. The views expressed in that opinion have not been tested in any court, and one should not be oversurprised that a lawyer is happy to see the power of the force of law increased at the expense of the independent professionalism of the individual.

The variability and uncertainty in the practical meaning of the true and fair view concept merely underlines the point made earlier about subjectivity. Fairness, opinion and the idea of a flexible definition all point to a subjective approach, based on personal thought and kept in check only by the need for a general consensus. There is much to be said for such a philosophy. Accounting matters can be decided by the experts (i.e. we hope, accountants). Change, when made necessary by changing circumstances, can be rapid, and need not await the clumsy and ponderous progress of Parliament. It also permits the appropriate exception to the general rule, i.e. an unusual situation can be treated in an unusual way. There are disadvantages, however. In particular there will tend to be a lack of consistency and therefore a lack of comparability. The casual reader will not be able to assume the detailed approach made in a set of accounts. He or she will have to explore them in detail in order to discover precisely what has been done and what has been assumed.

The continental influence

All this subjective flexible approach contrasts very strongly with the traditional practice on the mainland of Europe. Here, as exemplified by, for example, France and particularly Germany, the emphasis was not on giving the appropriate ('fair') impression. The emphasis was on confirming that legal requirements have been followed.

This different approach led to two major differences as compared with the UK which we shall illustrate using Germany as an example. The first is the corresponding requirement to the 'true and fair view' idea. This was stated in the German Companies Act of 1965 (section 149(1)), as being to show the 'Möglichst Sicheren Einblick', the most certain view, of the company's financial position. The emphasis here is clearly on truth, not on truth and fairness. The second difference concerns the detailed disclosure requirements of the German companies act. These, as compared with the UK 1948–67 Acts, are much more specific and much more detailed. The content both as regards calculation and valuation principle, and as regards layout or format, is closely defined and specified. The clear assumption is that provided all these detailed requirements are precisely met, the resulting accounts *must* be all right.

All the members of the European Union are committed to the harmonization of their company laws. A general statement of framework was agreed and published by the European Commission in 1978 (the Fourth Directive). The writers of this statement were faced with the interesting problem of trying to bring together these two very different attitudes and approaches. As regards the importance or otherwise of the 'fairness' concept, the UK view has clearly in the end been given precedence. The three major drafts of the relevant section ('Article') are shown below:

1971 Draft (Art. 2) **1** The annual accounts shall comprise the balance sheet, the profit and loss account and the notes on the accounts. These documents shall constitute a composite whole.

2 The annual accounts shall conform to the principles of regular and proper accounting.

3 They shall be drawn up clearly and, in the context of the provisions regarding the valuation of assets and liabilities and the layout of accounts, shall reflect as accurately as possible the company's assets, liabilities, financial position and results.

1974 Draft (Art. 2) **1** (As 1971 Draft.)

2 The annual accounts shall give a true and fair view of the company's assets, liabilities, financial position and results.

3 They shall be drawn up clearly and in accordance with provisions of this Directive.

1978 Final (Art. 2) **1** (As 1971 Draft.)

2 They shall be drawn up clearly and in accordance with the provisions of this Directive.

3 The annual accounts shall give a true and fair view of the company's assets, liabilities, financial position and profit and loss.

4 Where the application of the provisions of this Directive would not be sufficient to give a true and fair view within the meaning of paragraph 3 additional information must be given.

5 Where in exceptional cases the application of a provision of this Directive is incompatible with the obligation laid down in paragraph 3, that provision must be departed from in order to give a true and fair view within the meaning of paragraph 3. Any such departure must be disclosed in the notes on the accounts together with an explanation of the reasons for it and a statement of its effect on the assets, liabilities, financial position and profit or loss. The Member States may define the exceptional cases in question and lay down the relevant special rules.

The 1971 draft, which was in fact prepared by a German before the UK joined the EU, clearly follows the German 1965 companies act approach. The 1974 draft, affected by UK influence, introduces the true and fair requirement, and gives it in effect equal importance with 'the provisions of the directive' (i.e. with the detailed requirements). The final 1978 version clearly gives the true and fair requirement the greater overriding importance present in the UK ever since 1948.

However, when we look at the other major difference between the two traditions, i.e. the close and precise definition of content and layout, the German and central European influence has come through to a very considerable extent. The 1981 UK Companies Act, which brought the contents of the Fourth Directive on to the UK statute book, specified content and format to a much higher degree of precision than previously. Content, layout, form and sequence are now precisely defined, though with some alternatives and in consequence the direct influence of company law on published UK accounts has substantially increased.

It is beyond our scope here to consider how the more detailed format requirements have affected the actual attitudes of the UK accounting profession (or how the introduction of the overriding true and fair requirement have affected attitudes on the Continent). Our task, armed now with some understanding of the background to, and influences on, the 1985 Act, is to look at its disclosure requirements in detail.

The specified formats

The Act gives two alternative formats for the balance sheet. Format 1 is essentially a vertical format, deducting liabilities from assets. Format 2 is a horizontal format with all assets on one side and all liabilities on the other. UK companies will generally use format 1, following the trend in the UK in recent years. Format 1 is shown in its entirety below together with the notes included in the Act (schedule 4, paragraph 8):

A.   Called up share capital not paid (1)
B.   Fixed assets
    I   Intangible assets
        1 Development costs

      2 Concessions, patents, licences, trade marks and similar rights and assets (2)

      3 Goodwill (3)

      4 Payments on account

II Tangible assets

      1 Land and buildings

      2 Plant and machinery

      3 Fixtures, fittings, tools and equipment

      4 Payments on account and assets in course of construction

III Investments *Financial assets*

      1 Shares in group undertakings

      2 Loans to group undertakings

      3 Participating interests

      4 Loans to undertakings in which the company has participating interest

      5 Other investments other than loans

      6 Other loans

      7 Own shares (4)

C. Current assets

  I Stocks

      1 Raw materials and consumables

      2 Work in progress

      3 Finished goods and goods for resale

      4 Payments on account

  II Debtors (5)

      1 Trade debtors

      2 Amounts owed by group undertakings

      3 Amounts owed by undertakings in which the company has a participating interest

      4 Other debtors

      5 Called up share capital not paid (1)

      6 Prepayments and accrued income (6)

  III Investments

      1 Shares in group undertakings

      2 Own shares (4)

      3 Other investments

  IV Cash at bank and in hand

D. Prepayments and accrued income (6)

E. Creditors: amounts falling due within one year

      1 Debenture loans (7)

      2 Bank loans and overdrafts

      3 Payments received on account (8)

      4 Trade creditors

      5 Bills of exchange payable

      6 Amounts owed to group undertakings

      7 Amounts owed to undertakings in which the company has a participating interest

      8 Other creditors including taxation and social security (9)

    9   Accruals and deferred income (10)

F.   Net current assets (liabilities) (11)

G.   Total assets less current liabilities

H.   Creditors: amounts falling due after more than one year
- **1**   Debenture loans (7)
- **2**   Bank loans and overdrafts
- **3**   Payments received on account (8)
- **4**   Trade creditors
- **5**   Bills of exchange payable
- **6**   Amounts owed to group undertakings
- **7**   Amounts owed to undertakings in which the company has a participating interest
- **8**   Other creditors including taxation and social security (9)
- **9**   Accruals and deferred income (10)

I.   Provisions for liabilities and charges
- **1**   Pensions and similar obligation
- **2**   Taxation, including deferred taxation
- **3**   Other provisions

J.   Accruals and deferred income (10)

K.   Capital and reserves
- **I**   Called up share capital (12)
- **II**   Share premium account
- **III**   Revaluation reserve
- **IV**   Other reserves
  - **1**   Capital redemption reserve
  - **2**   Reserve for own shares
  - **3**   Reserves provided for by the articles of association
  - **4**   Other reserves
- **V**   Profit and loss account

A total would normally be made of items A to J inclusive, balancing with item K.

Notes

1 *Called up share capital not paid*
   This item may be shown in either of the two positions given.
2 *Concessions, patents, licences, trade marks and similar rights and assets*
   Amounts in respect of assets shall only be included in a company's balance sheet under this item if either:
   (**a**) the assets were acquired for valuable consideration and are not required to be shown under goodwill; or
   (**b**) the assets in question were created by the company itself.
3 *Goodwill*
   Amounts representing goodwill shall only be included to the extent that the goodwill was acquired for valuable consideration.
4 *Own shares*
   The nominal value of the shares held shall be shown separately.
5 *Debtors*

The amount falling due after more than one year shall be shown separately for each item included under debtors.

6 *Prepayments and accrued income*

This item may be shown in either of the two positions given.

7 *Debenture loans*

The amount of any convertible loans shall be shown separately.

8 *Payments received on account*

Payments received on account of orders shall be shown for each of these items in so far as they are not shown as deductions from stocks.

9 *Other creditors including taxation and social security*

The amount for creditors in respect of taxation and social security shall be shown separately from the amount for other creditors.

10 *Accruals and deferred income*

The two positions given for this item in Format 1 at E.9 and H.9 are an alternative to the position at J, but if the item is not shown in a position corresponding to that at J it may be shown in either or both of the other two positions (as the case may require).

11 *Net current assets (liabilities)*

In determining the amount to be shown for this item any amounts shown under 'prepayments and accrued income' shall be taken into account wherever shown.

12 *Called up share capital*

The amount of allotted share capital and the amount of called up share capital which has been paid up shall be shown separately.

13 *Creditors*

Amounts falling due within one year and after one year shall be shown separately for each of these items and their aggregates shall be shown separately for all of these items.

No less than four alternative formats are given for the P&L account, two vertical and two horizontal. Again UK companies will generally use the vertical ones, and we will consider them here. They are shown below (the numbers in parentheses refer to the notes on p. 202).

Format 1 (17)

1 Turnover.
2 Cost of sales (14).
3 Gross profit or loss.
4 Distribution costs (14).
5 Administrative expenses (14).
6 Other operating income.
7 Income from shares in group undertakings.
8 Income from participating interests.
9 Income from other fixed asset investments (15).
10 Other interest receivable and similar income (15).
11 Amounts written off investments.
12 Interest payable and similar charges (16).

13 Tax on profit or loss on ordinary activities.
14 Profit or loss on ordinary activities after taxation.
15 Extraordinary income.
16 Extraordinary charges.
17 Extraordinary profit or loss.
18 Tax on extraordinary profit or loss.
19 Other taxes not shown under the above items.
20 Profit or loss for the financial year.

Format 2

1 Turnover.
2 Change in stocks of finished goods and in work in progress.
3 Own work capitalized.
4 Other operating income:
5 (a) raw materials and consumables
  (b) other external charges.
6 Staff costs:
  (a) wages and salaries
  (b) social security costs
  (c) other pension costs.
7 (a) Depreciation and other amounts written off tangible and intangible fixed assets
  (b) Exceptional amounts written off current assets.
8 Other operating charges.
9 Income from shares in group undertakings.
10 Income from participating interests.
11 Income from other fixed asset investments (15).
12 Other interest receivable and similar income (15).
13 Amounts written off investments.
14 Interest payable and similar charges (16).
15 Tax on profit or loss on ordinary activities.
16 Profit or loss on ordinary activities after taxation.
17 Extraordinary income.
18 Extraordinary charges.
19 Extraordinary profit or loss.
20 Tax on extraordinary profit or loss.
21 Other taxes not shown under the above items.
22 Profit or loss for the financial year.

Both formats sum arithmetically downwards. Some of the items are themselves subtotals, for example in format 1 turnover (1) minus cost of sales (2) equals gross profit (3). 'Profit or loss on ordinary activities before taxation' would be inserted before item 13 (format 1) or before item 15 (format 2).

Notes

14 *Cost of sales: distribution costs: administrative expenses*
These items shall be stated after taking into account any necessary provisions for depreciation or diminution in value of assets.

15 *Income from other fixed asset investments: other interest receivable and sim-*

ilar income

Income and interest derived from group companies shall be shown separately from income and interest derived from other sources.

16 *Interest payable and similar charges*

The amount payable to group companies shall be shown separately.

17 *Format 1*

The amount of any provisions for depreciation and diminution in value of tangible and intangible fixed assets falling to be shown under item 7(a) in format 2 shall be disclosed in a note to the accounts in any case where the profit and loss account is prepared by reference to format 1.

Observe the differences between formats 1 and 2. Format 1 analyses the expenses by the purpose, or function of the expense. Format 2 analyses the expenses by the type of each expense. Items 7–20 (format 1) and 9–22 (format 2) are identical.

The rules for operating the formats are precisely stated in schedule 4. Paragraph 1(1) reads:

1 (1) Subject to the following provisions of this Schedule:
 (a) every balance sheet of a company shall show the items listed in either of the balance sheet formats set out below in section B of this Part; and
 (b) every profit and loss account of a company shall show the items listed in any one of the profit and loss account formats so set out; in either case in the order and under the headings and subheadings given in the format adopted.

So the basic requirement is that the exact sequence and the exact wording of every item in the format must be used. Other points include the following (all references are to the fourth schedule):

1 The letters and numbers included in the formats need not be included (paragraph 1(2)).

2 The chosen formats shall be used consistently; the reasons for any change must be included in a note to the accounts (paragraph 2).

3 Any item may be shown in greater detail than specified (paragraph 3(1)).

4 Any item not covered in the formats may be inserted as a separate item, 'but the following shall not be treated as assets in any company's balance sheet:
 (a) Preliminary expenses
 (b) Expenses of and commission on any issue of shares or debentures, and
 (c) Costs of research.'

5 For items with arabic numbers (e.g. '2') the directors 'shall adapt the arrangement and headings and sub-headings' if the nature of the company's business requires it (paragraph 3(3)). This is taken to mean that such items may be shown in notes to the accounts, rather than on the face of the balance sheet or profit and loss account. These items may also be combined if not individually material (paragraph 3(4)).

6 *Any* item may be omitted if its value for the current and preceding years are both zero (paragraph 3(5) and 4(3)).

7 Every P&L account must show separately:
 (a) the amount of the company's profit or loss before taxation
 (b) any amount set aside or proposed to be set aside to, or withdrawn or proposed to

  be withdrawn from reserves and

  (c) the aggregate amount of any dividends paid and proposed (paragraphs 3(6) and 3(7)).

8 Amounts in respect of items representing assets or income may not be set off against amounts in respect of items representing liabilities or expenditure (as the case may be), or vice versa (paragraph 5).

Note the rather strange literal implications of this as regards the P&L account. Three items must be shown (point 7 above) even though none of these items are included in the formats. Conversely *every* item in the P&L formats is preceded by an arabic numeral, i.e. it can be relegated to the notes to the accounts!

In the midst of all this detail do not lose sight of one very important point. All the items included in the balance sheet format identified by letters (e.g. B) or by roman numerals (e.g. II) must be stated, in sequence, and with the exact headings given in the Act. They can only be omitted if both current and comparative figures are zero. (They cannot be omitted on the grounds that the figures, though positive, are not material.) This high degree of legal specification of detail is very much a departure from the previous UK tradition.

Other Companies Act requirements

This book makes no claims to give comprehensive cover of UK company law. As far as possible, the detailed requirements of the 1985 Act as amended have been discussed in the appropriate places in Part Three of this book. This enables a proper bringing together and comparison of the professional attitudes (by SSAP and FRS) and the legal attitudes (by the Companies Act) to each problem area. The purpose of the following sections of this chapter is to give an overview of the relevant portions of the Act as a whole, and to outline the important points.

Schedule 4 is entitled 'Form and Content of Company Accounts'. Part I covers the 'General Rules and Formats'. This has already been discussed above.

Part II is entitled 'Accounting Principles and Rules' and is divided into three sections. Section A, 'Accounting Principles', is fully dealt with in Chapter 15 along with SSAP 2. Section B is called 'Historical Cost Accounting Rules', and Section C is called 'Alternative Accounting Rules'. Not surprisingly, B and C are alternatives and one or the other has to be followed. Section B requires the use of HC accounting:

  16 Subject to Section C of this Part of this Schedule, the amounts to be included in respect of all items shown in a company's accounts shall be determined in accordance with the rules set out in paragraph 17 to 28.

The section refers exclusively to assets, but in effect, of course, this determines the contents of the entire accounts. The basic requirements for fixed and current assets are given separately:

  17 Subject to any provision for depreciation or diminution in value made in accordance with paragraph 18 or 19 the amount to be included in respect of any fixed asset shall be its purchase price or production cost.

  22 Subject to paragraph 23, the amount to be included in respect of any current asset shall be its purchase price or production cost.

  23 (1) If the net realizable value of any current asset is lower than its purchase price or production cost the amount to be included in respect of that asset shall be the net realizable value.

(2) Where the reasons for which any provision for diminution in value was made in accordance with subparagraph (1) have ceased to apply to any extent, that provision shall be written back to the extent that it is no longer necessary.

The fixed asset rules are discussed in more detail in Chapter 16 on depreciation, Chapter 17 on research and development, and Chapter 16 on goodwill. The current asset items are discussed in Chapter 20 on stocks.

Section C permits departures from HC accounting in certain specified directions, as follows:

31 (1) Intangible fixed assets, other than goodwill, may be included at their current cost.

(2) Tangible fixed assets may be included at a market value determined as at the date of their last valuation or at their current cost.

(3) Investments of any description falling to be included under item B. III of either of the balance sheet formats set out in Part I of this Schedule may be included either:

(a) at a market value determined as at the date of their last valuation; or

(b) at a value determined on any basis which appears to the directors to be appropriate in the circumstances of the company;

but in the latter case particulars of the method of valuation adopted and of the reasons for adopting it shall be disclosed in a note to the accounts.

(4) Investments of any description falling to be included under item C. III of either of the balance sheet formats set out in Part I of this Schedule may be included at their current cost.

(5) Stocks may be included at their current cost.

Note the considerable degree of flexibility which this gives! Paragraph 32 provides, oddly, that even under one of these alternative valuation bases, depreciation charged in the P&L account may be under the HC basis, provided that the amount of any difference between this figure and the figure resulting from the alternative basis is 'shown separately in the profit and loss account or in a note to the accounts'. Other paragraphs provide that the notes to the accounts must in effect include sufficient figures to enable the HC accounts to be reconstructed. Net credits resulting from revaluations under the alternative rules must be credited to a revaluation reserve. Amounts can only be transferred from this reserve to profit and loss account if either:

1 the amount in question was previously charged to that account; or
2 it represents realized profit.

The Act continues to specify detailed contents of:

1 the directors' report
2 the notes to the balance sheet
3 the notes to the P&L account.

These requirements are outlined in the following sections.

Additionally, the preparation of 'modified accounts' is allowed for by small and medium-sized companies. These simplified accounts may be filed with the Registrar of Companies instead of the full accounts. This means that less information is on public record. However, the *full* accounts must always be sent to all shareholders. Note the total absence of any reference to, or requirement for, any form of cash flow statement. Schedule 4A, introduced by the 1989 Companies Act, gives the form and content of group accounts.

Directors' report

Statute requires a report by the directors to be attached to every balance sheet and to be despatched to all those entitled to receive notice of a general meeting. The auditors are now required to consider whether the information contained in the directors' report is consistent with that which is in the accounts, and if not to report the inconsistency. All that is contained in the directors' report must amount to a 'fair review' of the development of the company (section 235), which is perhaps consistent with the 'true and fair' approach.

The contents of the directors' report are detailed by statute (schedule 7 to the 1985 Act) and include the following:

1 Particulars of any significant changes in the fixed assets of the company and its subsidiaries during the financial year.
2 For interests in land, if the market value differs from the balance sheet figure, and if in the opinion of the directors this is significant, details must be given.
3 The principal activities of the company and any significant changes thereto.
4 Names of directors at any time in the year, and details of any interests they had in the shares or debentures of the business.
5 Political and charitable gifts in excess of £200, stating the recipient and the amount if for political purposes.
6 Particulars of any important post-balance sheet events.
7 An indication of likely future developments in the business of the company and of any research and development activities.
8 Details of any purchase by a company of its own shares.
9 For companies employing at least 250 people in the UK, a statement relating to the employment of disabled persons, and of the provision of information to employees about the performance of the company.
10 Details of the company's policy as regards health and safety at work for its employees.

Activity 2 (without feedback)

Obtain a set of published accounts and read the directors' report carefully. Are all these points covered? Is the report actually useful and informative?

Notes to the accounts (schedule 4, part III, 1985 Act)

Disclosure of accounting policies

These are required to be stated explicitly, including policies with respect to the depreciation and diminution in value of assets.

Information supplementing the balance sheet

1 Share capital and debentures – details of:
   (**a**) authorized share capital, and of shares allotted including class and of additional allotments during the year
   (**b**) dates and details of redemption if the shares are issued as redeemable
   (**c**) details of any debentures issued during the financial year and of any redeemed debentures that can be reissued.
2 Fixed asset details (Chapter 16).
3 Investments (both fixed and current) – details of listed investments, showing the aggregate market value where this differs from the amount in the balance sheet, and unlisted.
4 Reserves and provisions – details of movements in each category of reserves and provisions, and particulars of each material provision included in 'other provisions' in the balance sheet and of the amount of any provision for taxation other than deferred taxation.
5 Indebtedness (creditors) – details of:
   (**a**) The aggregate amount of any debts repayable more than five years hence, distinguishing these repayable by instalments, and details or an indication of the terms of repayment and interest payable.
   (**b**) Any arrears of fixed cumulative dividends.
6 Guarantees and other financial commitments – details of (Chapter 23).
7 Dividends – show the aggregate amount that is recommended for distribution by way of dividend.

Information supplementing the P&L account

1 Separate statement of certain items of income and expenditure – details of:
   (**a**) interest payable on loans, and overdrafts repayable distinguishing between those other than by instalment repayable before the end of five years, and those so payable, and loans of any other kind made to the company
   (**b**) amounts set aside for redemption of above capital and loans
   (**c**) the amount of income from listed investments, and from rent from land if substantial
   (**d**) amounts charged for hire of plant and machinery
   (**e**) auditors' remuneration.
2 Particulars of tax – disclose:
   (**a**) basis of computation of UK tax
   (**b**) particulars of special circumstances affecting the tax liability
   (**c**) details of the UK tax charge, showing tax on extraordinary items separately.
3 Particulars of turnover – differentiating between substantially different business activities, substantially different geographical markets and giving an analysis of profit before tax in each case.
4 Particulars of staff – the average number of persons employed, and the average number employed within each category, stating the aggregate amounts of wages and salaries, social security costs and other pension costs (unless these are stated in the P&L account itself).
5 Extraordinary items – particulars of any extraordinary income or charges arising in the year.

6 Exceptional items – the effect shall be stated of any transactions that are exceptional by virtue of size or incidence although they fall within the ordinary activities of the company.

Stock Exchange requirements

Companies that obtain a Stock Exchange listing must comply with certain disclosure requirements additional to those imposed by legislation or the accounting profession. They must also agree to issue annual reports within six months of the end of the accounting period. The requirements for disclosure of additional information in company reports cover the directors' report and the preparation of a half-yearly interim report.

Directors' report

The additional information to be included in the directors' report is:

1 statement of reasons for departure from accounting standards
2 explanations of material differences between actual trading results and forecasts
3 analysis of turnover by geographical area and contributions to trading results from operations outside the UK
4 principal country of operation of each subsidiary
5 in respect of each company in which an equity holding of at least 20% is held:
   (a) principal country of operation
   (b) particulars of issued shares and loan capital
   (c) percentages of categories of loan capital in which an interest is held.

Interim report

The half-yearly interim report must be issued to all holders of securities issued by the company, or must be published, as a paid advertisement, in at least two 'leading' daily newspapers. The information to be included is as follows:

1 group turnover
2 group profit or loss before tax and extraordinary items
3 taxation
4 minority interests
5 group profit or loss to shareholders before extraordinary items
6 extraordinary items
7 group profit or loss attributable to shareholders
8 dividend rates
9 earnings per share (in pence per share)
10 comparative figures
11 any supplementary information the directors consider necessary for a reasonable appreciation of the results
12 provisional figures or those subject to audit should be qualified.

In September 1997 the Accounting Standards Board published a Statement on interim reporting. This is not a Standard and is not mandatory. It presents the Board's 'recommendations as best practice in the reporting of interim information'.

Two alternative approaches are possible to interim reporting calculations. The Board explains them, and its preference, as follows.

> One of the major issues, from a theoretical viewpoint, is whether the period on which an interim report is made should be treated as a distinct, stand-alone reporting period in its own right (the discrete method) or as part of the larger annual reporting period (the integral method). The Board believes that the key principle should be that the same measurement and recognition bases are used at the interim reporting date as are used at the year-end. This ensures that the definitions of the elements of the financial statements – assets, liabilities, revenues and expenses – apply equally to interim reports, and has the added advantages of consistency and understandability.
>
> Under this approach, as adopted in the Statement, expenses and revenues are recognised in their proper period and matched where appropriate. Unlike the integral method, it does not aim to smooth the results across the year. Instead, any volatility in the interim report, for example as a result of seasonality or a large one-off expenditure at the beginning of the year, needs to be explained in the narrative commentary. This helps users' understanding of the business, so enhancing their ability to assess the financial performance and position of the company.
>
> The consequence is that the Statement adopts the discrete method, whilst recognising that this incorporates elements of the integral method for certain annually determined items. This approach reflects the fact that, whatever the length of the accounting period chosen, it would rarely be an entirely independent period in that some items of income or expense will always be incomplete. Calculating the interim tax charge by performing a full tax computation on the interim period, for example, could result in a meaningless number because it does not take into account all the factors influencing the level of taxation being charged for that period in the context of the year's events.
>
> The Board recommends that an interim report should include a narrative commentary, summarised profit and loss account, statement of total recognised gains and losses, summarised balance sheet and summarised cash flow statement.
>
> Significant events and trends mentioned in the commentary should be supported by the underlying figures given either on the face of the primary statements or by way of note. Sufficient supplementary information should be given, where appropriate, to the nature of the company's business and as the directors see fit, to permit an understanding of the significant items contained within the primary statements. For example, in certain cases it may be useful to analyse fixed assets into component parts, provide more detail about the company's borrowings, or state the equity and non-equity interests in shareholders' funds, in accordance with FRS 4 'Capital Instruments'.
>
> The information should be presented in a concise manner, should be consistent and comparable with that previously reported (the annual report) and should facilitate comparison between like companies.
>
> As regards key financial statements the Board recommends disclosure as follows.

An interim report should include a summarised profit and loss account that includes the following information where relevant (with separate identification of amounts relating to associates and joint ventures):

- Turnover
- Operating profit or loss
- Interest payable less interest receivable (net)
- Profit or loss on ordinary activities before tax
- Tax on profit or loss on ordinary activities
- Profit or loss on ordinary activities after tax
- Minority interests
- Profit or loss for the period
- Dividends paid and proposed.

A summarised balance sheet (together with comparatives) should highlight significant movements in key indicators of the company's financial position. For consistency, similar classifications to those used in the annual financial statements should be adopted. It is recommended that, for example, a Schedule 4 company or Schedule 4A group should give the following balance sheet information:

- Fixed assets
- Current assets
  - Stocks
  - Debtors
  - Cash at bank and in hand
  - Other current assets
- Creditors: amounts falling due within one year
- Net current assets (liabilities)
- Total assets less current liabilities
- Creditors: amounts falling due after more than one year
- Provisions for liabilities and charges
- Capital and reserves
- Minority interests.

Information on the amounts and sources of cash flows provides an additional perspective to the performance of a company through the interim period. Total amounts for the categories of cash flows specified by FRS 1 (Revised 1996) 'Cash Flow Statements' should be presented as follows:

- Net cash inflow/outflow from operating activities
- Returns on investments and servicing of finance
- Taxation
- Capital expenditure and financial investment
- Acquisitions and disposals
- Equity dividends paid
- Management of liquid resources
- Financing
- Increase/decrease in cash.

In July 1998 the ASB issued another Statement, on preliminary announcements. The status of this document is identical to the one on interim reports discussed above, and the requirements are extremely similar.

Summary

In this chapter we have explored the major legal requirements relating to the content of company accounts. This included consideration of the 'true and fair view' requirement and of the specified formats, requirements for notes, contents of directors' report, and other specifications.

Exercises

1 What is meant by a 'true and fair view'?
2 Do you think the level of format specification first introduced by the Companies Act 1981 is a good thing or a bad thing?
3 Which items required to be shown in:
   (a) the directors' report
   (b) the notes to the P&L account
   (c) the notes to the balance sheet
   do you think are genuinely useful? Why?
4 In the last analysis, accountants must decide what information has to be published, not lawyers. Do you agree?
5 The information to be disclosed in the directors' report of a listed company is prescribed by the Companies Act 1985 and the Stock Exchange. **Say why you think each of the following are included in these disclosure requirements:**
   (a) directors' interest in shares   (4 marks)
   (b) contracts with substantial shareholders   (4 marks)
   (c) reasons for significant departure from Statements of Standard Accounting Practice
                                                                                       (4 marks)
   (d) consultations with employees   (4 marks)
   (e) political and charitable donations.   (4 marks)
                                                                                 (20 marks)
                                                                                      (ACCA)
6 What extra disclosure requirements are necessary for companies quoted on the Stock Exchange? Are these extra requirements important?

Part Three

The regulatory framework

In this final part we look in detail at the rules that accountants have created for themselves to govern financial reporting. In an effort to improve effectiveness and consistency – and their public image – accountants have created a whole series of regulations for themselves. What do they say and what is their effect? Do they achieve what they are setting out to do when considered individually? Do they make sense, when looked at as a whole? As with Part One, you are invited to form your own opinion on 'the story so far'.

14

The accounting standard setting process

After reading this chapter you should be able to explain the accounting standard setting process by:
- describing the events which led to the current standard setting process
- describing the operating process of the Accounting Standards Board (ASB)
- discussing the ASB statement of aims
- outlining the process leading to the issue of a financial reporting standard (FRS)
- explaining the ASB exposure draft – foreword to accounting standards
- describing the role played by the Urgent Issue Task Force and Financial Reporting Review Panel.

Introduction

For many years the Institute of Chartered Accountants in England and Wales (ICAEW) issued a series of *Recommendations on Accounting Principles*, starting in 1942. These were generally summaries of existing practice, and they were not mandatory on the members of the ICAEW. By the 1960s it was becoming all too apparent that the practical results of this approach were not acceptable. Different firms in similar circumstances were following different accounting policies, leading to different and incompatible results, all with the approval of their accountants. In several cases when takeovers occurred, different accountants were seen to produce startlingly different results for the same firm. Accountants and their profession were being publicly criticized and derided for this.

The response of the ICAEW was to set up the Accounting Standards Steering Committee (ASSC) early in 1970. Four other bodies joined shortly afterwards: the Scottish and Irish Chartered Institutes, the Association of Certified Accountants (as it then was) and the Institute of Cost and Management Accountants (as it then was). In 1976 the Institute of Public Finance and Accountancy (as it then was) also joined, and the ASSC was reconstituted. It became a joint committee of the six member bodies collectively acting as the Consultative Committee of Accounting Bodies (CCAB) and was renamed the Accounting Standards Committee (ASC).

Accounting Standards Committee

The ASC was responsible for preparing draft standards, and the CCAB bodies for approving them, unanimity being required. Enforcement was a matter between the individual bodies and their members.

In the 'Explanatory Foreword to Accounting Standards', as revised in 1986, the ASC stated that:

5 In applying accounting standards, it will be important to have regard to the spirit of and reasoning behind them. They are not intended to be a comprehensive code or rigid rules. They do not supersede the exercise of an informed judgement in determining what constitutes a true and fair view in each circumstance. It would be impracticable to establish a code sufficiently elaborate to cater for all business situations and innovations and for every exceptional or marginal case. A justifiable reason may therefore exist why an accounting standard may not be applicable in a given situation, namely when application would conflict with the giving of a true and fair view. In such cases, modified or alternative treatments will require to be adopted.

12 The accountancy bodies, through appropriate committees, may enquire into apparent failures by members to observe accounting standards or to ensure adequate disclosure of significant departures.

Need for reform

The threat contained in paragraph 12 above failed completely in its objective and cases of accountants supporting or ignoring departures from standards were commonplace. This tendency increased the extent in later years to which the ASC looked for practical acceptance, rather than logical acceptability, in its pronouncements. You can appraise the results of this for yourself as you read the following chapters pertaining to SSAPs.

In general the ASC was criticized for the following reasons:

- difficulty of ensuring compliance with standards
- absence of any conceptual framework
- the allowance of alternative treatments within accounting standards
- the general nature of standards rather than detailed procedures
- the time involved in setting standards
- the need for unanimous approval by the six CCAB bodies
- the difficulties faced by small companies in meeting standards.

Dearing Committee

Concern about this situation eventually led to the creation of another committee. This committee, known as the Dearing Committee after its chairman, was set up in 1987 with the following terms of reference:

1 To review the development of the standard setting process in Great Britain and Ireland and in other major industrial countries.

2 To outline the basic purpose of accounting standards and their future bearing in mind the attitude of both government and the public towards regulation of the corporate sector and in the light of major changes in the financial markets and in the approach by preparers of accounts to financial reporting.

3 In the light of the above to make recommendations on:
   (**a**) the most appropriate form which accounting standards should take
   (**b**) the position of standards in relation to company law
   (**c**) procedures for ensuring compliance with standards
   (**d**) the identification of topics for consideration
   (**e**) the need for, and nature of, public consultation about proposed standards
   (**f**) the funding of the cost of standard setting
   (**g**) the composition and powers of any body responsible for standard setting.

The Dearing Committee reported in November 1988 and proposed radical and fundamental changes. The report proposed that the ASC should be abolished and replaced by a two-tier structure. The top tier, the Financial Reporting Council, would determine broad policy and direction. This would consist of about twenty nominated members chosen from as wide a variety of (relevant) backgrounds as possible. The second tier would be an Accounting Standards Board. This would consist of nine members appointed effectively by the Financial Reporting Council. The board would issue standards in its own right (not through the individual CCAB members) and, in order to avoid compromise solutions, a majority of two-thirds would suffice for a standard to be approved. This proposal would be beneficial as regards the speed with which new standards could be introduced or existing standards amended and would also serve to enhance the status of the Accounting Standards Board.

The report explicitly recommended that the movement towards the development of a general conceptual framework (Chapter 10) should be encouraged. The committee also clearly hoped that its suggested requirement of a two-thirds majority rather than unanimity would encourage the development of precise and explicit standard requirements rather than the woolly compromises so often found in recent years.

The final important area tackled by the Dearing Committee's report, perhaps the most important of all, is the question of compliance with SSAPs. It was recommended that a review panel be established to examine any identified or alleged material departures from accounting standards which, in its view, involved an issue of principle or which might result in the accounts in question not giving a true and fair view. The panel would only be concerned with the accounts of large companies. Its constitution would be determined by the same committee as that responsible for determining membership of the Accounting Standards Board. It was proposed that each departure from a standard would be examined by a tribunal whose membership would vary but who would be drawn from a central pool of experts by the chairman of the review panel. Where a company failed to amend its accounts along the lines suggested by the review panel it was suggested that, under a new statutory power under civil law, the directors be required by the court to circulate additional/revised information to all those entitled to receive the accounts so as to ensure compliance with the requirements of the Companies Act or with the true and fair requirement. The necessary statutory power would only be available to the Stock Exchange, the review panel and to the secretary of state.

In general, the report of the Dearing Committee was well received, and most of the recommendations were taken on board.

Accounting Standards Board

In 1990 the Accounting Standards Board (ASB) was set up as a subsidiary of the Financial Reporting Council (FRC) as envisaged by Dearing.

The FRC oversees the arrangements for the standard setting process and has a duty to support the ASB in its task and seek support for it wherever the FRC has influence. An annual review is to be issued by the FRC and the first of these was in November 1991 and stated that:

> There is no place whatever for accounts fit only for fair weather, undermining the credibility of the good reporting for which our country has earned a world-wide reputation. With the initiatives now in hand we seek accounts that may be relied upon to give good service to boards, shareholders, creditors and employees – indeed all who use accounts.

Noble sentiments indeed!

ASB statement of aims

This was issued in July 1991 as follows: 'The aims of the ASB are to establish and improve standards of financial accounting and reporting for the benefit of users, preparers and auditors of financial information.'

This is fundamentally different from the ASC statement of aims which was concerned with defining accounting concepts, narrowing differences of financial accounting reporting and codifying generally accepted best practice.

The ASB's aims are to be achieved by:

- developing principles to guide it in establishing standards and to provide a framework within which others can exercise judgement in resolving accounting issues
- issuing new accounting standards, or amending existing ones, in response to evolving business practices, new economic developments and deficiencies being identified in current practice
- addressing urgent issues promptly.

The ASB's statement of aims also requires that it follows certain guidelines in conducting its affairs:

1 to be objective and to ensure that the information resulting from the application of accounting standards fairly represents the underlying commercial activity and is free from bias
2 to ensure accounting standards are clearly expressed and supported by a reasoned analysis of the issues
3 to determine what should be incorporated in accounting standards based on research, public consultation, careful deliberation and regular communication
4 to ensure consistency both from one financial reporting standard to another and between financial reporting standards and company law
5 to issue standards only when expected benefits exceed the perceived costs.

Activity 1

The first four guidelines can be associated with a specific characteristic of useful information as discussed in Chapter 2. For each guideline identify the characteristic.

Activity 1 feedback

1 Objectivity
2 understandability
3 completeness
4 comparability.

The Board will assess the need for standards in terms of the significance and extent of the problems being addressed and will choose the standard which appears to be the most effective in cost-benefit terms. Also they will take account of the desire of the financial community for evolution rather than revolution.

The ASB discusses the trade-offs between relevance, reliability, timeliness and other characteristics in its statement of principles, discussed in Chapter 15.

Financial Reporting Review Panel

This is also a subsidiary of the FRC and together with the Department of Trade and Industry has procedures for receiving and investigating complaints regarding the accounts of companies in respect of apparent departures from the accounting requirements of the Companies Act. This includes, in particular, the requirement to show a true and fair view.

The review panel can in fact apply to the courts for a declaration that the annual accounts of a company do not comply with requirements of the Companies Act and obtain an order requiring the directors of the company to prepare revised accounts. Action through the courts is often costly and there will, of course, be an appeals procedure for companies. For this reason it was very important that the ASB had sufficient finance when it was set up. The review panel should not, therefore, be inhibited from taking action by the absence of funds available for court proceedings. At the date of writing the Financial Reporting Review Panel (FRRP) has not as yet resorted to court proceedings, but has managed to threaten or persuade companies to review and amend accounts where necessary.

An early example was the FRRP investigation into the accounts of Shield plc 1991 where a prior year adjustment of £3 528 000 was made in respect of the reduced values of properties and investments. This treatment did not comply with SSAP 6 (see Chapter 26) which required such provisions to be regarded as part of the loss for the current year. Shield plc, at the panel's request, re-stated in their interim report, published on 31 January 1992, their P&L account for the year-ended 31 March 1991 in accordance with SSAP 6 and thus the FRRP decided to take no further action.

A more recent example involves the engineering group RMC. RMC had included a contingent liability of £5m in fines in its 1994 group accounts but not in its 1995 group accounts as it was deemed not material. It had however included the liability in the 1995 subsidiary accounts. The FRRP has ruled that the accounts must be restated to include the £5m as it was material on the grounds of nature and circumstances of the times. The FRRP thus judges materiality in terms of quality not just quantity. Several of the large accounting firms are surprised at the FRRP's view of materiality.

Guardian Royal Exchange Insurance Company has also been required by FRRP to restate its profit figure for 1996 in the 1997 statements. The requirement, by the FRRP, to include equalization reserves in the 1996 accounts reduces the profit for GRE by £33m. Other examples of the FRRP's work follow:

- the 1995 accounts of Butte Mining were criticized for treating as realized a profit the panel considered unrealized
- Reckitt and Coleman accounts for 1995 were investigated and the directors agreed to the change requested
- Burn Stewart Distillers plc accounts for year-ended 30 June 1996 have been amended and the amendment circulated to shareholders. The issue involved was disclosure requirements of FRS 5
- Strategem Group plc include in their 1997 accounts a note in respect of a fair value adjustment in respect of 1996 accounts
- Reuters Holdings plc who adopted FRS 10 early in their accounts for the year-ended 31 December 1997 fell foul of the Panel as they showed the amortization of goodwill below operating profit whereas according to the panel it should have been included as part of operating charges. Reuters agreed to make the amendment in the 1998 accounts.

According to the *Annual Report* of the FRC, 1997 saw a significant fall-off in cases coming before the Panel but in recent years it has come close to exercising its statutory powers to apply to the courts to get defective accounts remedied. In fact the panel has incurred extensive costs in instructing counsel and other lawyers and the preparation of papers but companies involved have always backed down in the end.

A new chairman was appointed to the FRRP on 15 September 1997, Peter Goldsmith QC, who has taken over from Edwin Glasgow QC.

Procedure leading to the issue of standards by the ASB

The standards issued by the ASB will be known as Financial Reporting Standards (FRS). All SSAPs issued by the ASC and still in force have been adopted by the ASB. Topic areas for discussion by the ASB can come from either the ASB's own research or from external sources including interested parties.

When a topic is identified by the ASB as requiring the issue of a standard then the board commissions its staff to undertake a programme of research and consultation. This programme is undertaken within the overall framework of relevant conceptual issues, existing pronouncements and practice and the legal and practical implications of the introduction of particular accounting requirements. After the ASB has debated the topic a discussion draft is produced and circulated to interested parties who have registered their interest to the board. An exposure draft is then published to allow an opportunity for all interested parties to comment on the proposals and for the board to gauge the appropriateness and level of acceptance. The exposure draft (ED) is then refined in the light of feedback and if necessary another ED is issued. Finally, an FRS is issued, but although the ASB weigh carefully the views of the interested parties the ultimate content of an FRS is determined by the board's judgement based on research, public consultation and careful deliberation about the benefits and costs of providing the resulting information. So, if the ASB take the view that there should be a different system to that of historical cost accounting in operation, and we are not saying they would, then an FRS will be issued to this effect and the FRRP will have to enforce it.

ASB foreword to accounting standards

This was issued in July 1991 and covers: authority, scope and application of standards, procedures of issue, and relationship of FRSs to international accounting standards.

Authority

The Companies Act requires accounts to state whether they have been prepared in accordance with applicable accounting standards and to give particulars of material departures from these standards. FRSs issued by the ASB now form part of these applicable accounting standards. The CCAB expects all its members, whether they be directors or other officers of a company, to ensure that accounting standards are fully understood by fellow directors and officers. They must also use their best endeavours to ensure that accounting standards are observed and that significant departures are adequately disclosed and explained in financial statements. Where members act as auditors or reporting accountants they should be in a position to justify significant departures to the extent that their concurrence is stated or implied. So it would appear that all CCAB members have a duty to bring discrepancies to the attention of the FRRP.

Scope and application

Accounting standards are applicable to any reporting entity intending its financial statement to give a true and fair view. However, they need not be applied to immaterial items or to financial statements prepared overseas for local purposes.

Relationship of FRSs to International Accounting Standards

FRSs are to be formulated with due regard to international development. Within the process leading to the issue of FRSs International Accounting Standards (IASs) will be considered within the overall framework. The foreword to accounting standards states that the board supports the IAS committee in its aim to harmonize international financial reporting, and thus in most cases compliance with an FRS will automatically ensure compliance with the relevant IAS. Where the requirement of an FRS and an IAS differ then UK entities are required to follow the FRS.

Urgent Issue Task Force

The ASB has another body to assist it in its aims and that is the Urgent Issue Task Force (UITF). It comprises a number of people of major standing in the field of financial reporting. Its role is to assist the ASB in areas of reporting where potential problems are likely to appear, where there may be areas of conflicting interpretation or where a very quick response on an issue is required.

Under the auspices of the ASC these areas were often covered by technical releases which brought the areas to the attention of auditors and accountants, but lacked any formal authority. All pronouncements from the UITF have the full backing of the ASB and the FRRP will provide the monitoring of these pronouncements. In other words financial statements, if a clean bill of health is to be given by the FRRP, will have to accord with UITF pronouncements.

Operation of UITF

The UITF operates by seeking a voluntary consensus of its members about the accounting treatment that should be adopted for a particular area of controversy. This voluntary consensus requires that not more than two UITF members have voted against the proposed accounting treatment within a quorum of eleven members. As the UITF works within the ASB's aim of relying on principles rather than detailed prescription, then the UITF will be concerned with serious divergencies of current practice or with major developments likely to create serious divergencies in the future. Nothing in the UITF pronouncements will, however, be allowed or construed as amending or overriding the accounting standards or other statements issued by the ASB.

When the UITF was set up in September 1990 it was not envisaged that consultation on issues with industry would form part of their method of operation. However, many industrialists have since complained that they have been taken by surprise by the UITF's announcements and that these rulings are perceived as being 'grossly unfair and against natural justice'. In response to this the UITF has agreed to increase its level of communication with industry by issuing regular information sheets. These, according to David Tweedie (the chairman of ASB), 'will give people the opportunity to write in and say what they think'.

By its very nature, the UITF can produce statements at short notice, and there is no pattern in the topics it chooses to address. Its recommendations are also likely to be gradually incorporated in new or revised standards if the problem is seen to be a continuing one.

The accounting standard setting process

Up to summer 2000 the UITF has issued consensus statements (abstracts) on the following subjects:

1   Convertible bonds – supplementary interest/premium.
2   Restructuring costs (already replaced by a new standard).
3   Treatment of goodwill on disposal of a business.
4   Presentation of long-term debtors in current assets.
5   Transfers from current assets to fixed assets.
6   Accounting for post-retirement benefits other than pensions.
7   True and fair override disclosures.
8   Repurchase of own debt.
9   Accounting for operations in hyperinflationary economies.
10   Disclosure of directors' share options.
11   Capital instruments: issuer call options.
12   Lessee accounting for reverse premiums and similar incentives.
13   Accounting for employee share ownership plan trusts.
14   Disclosure of changes in accounting policy.
15   Disclosure of substantial acquisitions.

16 Income and expenses subject to non-standard rates of taxation.

17 Employee share schemes.

18 Pension costs following the 1997 tax changes in respect of dividend income.

19 Tax on gains and losses on foreign currency borrowings that hedge an investment in a foreign enterprise.

20 Year 2000 issues: accounting and disclosure.

21 Accounting issues arising from the proposed introduction of the euro.

22 The acquisition of a Lloyd's business.

23 Application of the Transitional Rules in FRS 15.

24 Accounting for Start-up Costs.

25 National Insurance Contributions on Share Option Gains.

As can be deduced from the titles, many of these statements are involved with technical detail but the majority are also quite brief. For example, UITF abstract 14, issued 21 November 1995, is only four paragraphs long, one side of A4. The issue that UITF 14 addresses concerns the disclosure required when there is a change in accounting policy. FRS 3 requires that the effect this change of policy has on the preceding period must be disclosed but remained silent on whether the effect on the current year should be disclosed. FRS 3 did require though that the figures displayed in the financial statements should be based on the new accounting policy. UITF 14 makes it clear that disclosure should also be made of the effect the accounting policy change has had on the current year's figures.

Summary

Within this chapter we have discussed the regime for setting and monitoring accounting standards. We have briefly looked at the role of the FRC, ASB, FRRP and UITF and outlined their aims and objectives.

Exercises

1 A director of your company has recently taken an interest in accounting and has asked you, the trainee accountant with the company, to explain to her the following abbreviations: ASB, FRC, FRRP, UITF and FRS.

2 The Accounting Standards Committee (ASC) was criticized heavily prior to its replacement by the Accounting Standards Board (ASB). The principal intention of the ASC was to create greater uniformity in the preparation of financial reports in order that there should be more comparability between the results of different companies. Many commentators felt that the ASC failed to achieve their intentions and criticized the role of the ASC because of the following reasons:

    (a) A failure to develop an agreed conceptual framework and to specify user needs.

    (b) The composition of the ASC. The ASC had little representation from independent user groups, with the majority of its members coming from the accounting profession.

    (c) The inadequate enforcement of standards. Some writers criticized the ASC for limiting the enforcement of standards to the qualification of the audit report.

    (d) The ASC was too open to pressure from various interested groups who had a direct interest in the work of the committee. This led to political interference in the standard setting process.

    (e) A failure to respond quickly to emerging issues.

When the Dearing Committee's recommendations on a whole new structure to replace the ASC were adopted, it was hoped that the new structures would lead to the elimination of the above criticisms. However, there are those who feel that there is no need for a standard setting body, and that there is no need for accounting standards. In contrast, others feel that standards should be set by the government and be incorporated in the law.

Required:
    (a) Explain why there is a need for regulation of financial information in the form of accounting standards. (7 marks)
    (b) Discuss to what extent you feel that the criticisms of the ASC set out above apply also to the new structure for regulating accounting standards.
                                                                 (12 marks)
                                                                    (19 marks)
                                                                      (ACCA)

Accounting principles (SSAP 2, FRS 18)

After reading this chapter you should be able to:
- describe and apply the requirements of SSAP 2, 'Disclosure of Accounting Policies'
- appraise the adequacy of SSAP 2
- outline attempts to create a more comprehensive statement of principles by the Accounting Standards Board
- appraise the ASB Statement of Principles
- discuss the proposals in FRED 21, 'Accounting Policies' and the requirements of FRS 18, 'Accounting Policies'
- discuss whether the various conventions and assumptions which underlie accounting thought do have a clear-cut logical heirarchy.

Introduction

The situation regarding accounting principles in the UK is, as we write, rather complicated. It is also in a state of rapid development, although the timing is unclear. First of all, the reader should recall the traditional accounting conventions discussed in Chapter 3, and the discussion on a general framework in Chapter 10. Chapter 10 made it clear that a coherent general framework for accounting, in a scientific sense, does not exist. It also suggested, illustrated in detail from the IASC Framework of 1989, that a set of generally agreed, if at times inconsistent, notions can provide a very useful insight into how accounting thinking often works, and therefore into how to approach particular accounting issues.

In the UK, formal movement towards the establishment of agreed accounting principles has been generally slow and hesitant. Four aspects can be distinguished, three of them accompanied by documents from the UK standard-setting body. These are as follows:

1 The issue of SSAP 2, Disclosure of Accounting Policies, in 1971. At the time of writing this is still in force as a full Standard, though see **3** below.
2 The issue, after a long and difficult gestation period, of a UK Statement of Principles, agreed by the ASB in 1999. This is closely based on the IASC Framework of 1989, but goes into considerably more detail.
3 The decision to replace SSAP 2 by a new standard, to be called: Accounting Policies. An exposure draft, FRED 21, was issued in December 1999. This seeks to update and develop SSAP 2, in the light of changes in general thinking over the 30 years since SSAP 2 was first issued, and in particular to ensure its consistency with the Statement of Principles (SoP). When a Standard emerges from FRED 21, SSAP 2 will be withdrawn.
4 The possibly very rapid, and potentially highly significant, international developments announced in the summer of 2000, referred to in Chapter 11.

This chapter discusses the four aspects listed above, beginning with SSAP 2.

SSAP 2

SSAP 2 is widely regarded as the 'basic' Statement of Standard Accounting Practice (SSAP). It is certainly the one that should have come first, as it deals with how to 'report' the treatments proposed by the other SSAPs. But it must be noted that it does not provide in any sense a coherent body of theory – nor is it intended to. This is not an attempt at an 'agreed framework'. Indeed the reason why detailed disclosure of assumptions made it so necessary is precisely because there is no 'agreed framework'.

The standard distinguishes between three types of accounting idea:

- fundamental accounting concepts
- accounting bases
- accounting policies.

Fundamental accounting concepts

These are defined as 'the broad basic assumptions which underlie the periodic financial accounts of business enterprises'. The SSAP suggests and defines four of them as having 'general acceptability' as follows:

14 (a) The 'going concern' concept: the enterprise will continue in operational existence for the foreseeable future. This means in particular that the profit and loss account and balance sheet assume no intention or necessity to liquidate or curtail significantly the scale of operation.

(b) The 'accruals' concept: revenue and costs are accrued (that is, recognized as they are earned or incurred, not as money is received or paid), matched with one another so far as their relationship can be established or justifiably assumed, and dealt with in the profit and loss account of the period to which they relate; provided that where the accruals concept is inconsistent with the 'prudence' concept (paragraph (d) below), the latter prevails. The accruals concept implies that the profit and loss account reflects changes in the amount of net assets that arise out of the transactions of the relevant period (other than distributions or subscriptions of capital and unrealized surpluses arising on revaluation of fixed assets). Revenue and profits dealt with in the profit and loss account are matched with associated costs and expenses by including in the same account the costs incurred in earning them (so far as these are material and identifiable).

(c) The 'consistency' concept: there is consistency of accounting treatment of like items within each accounting period and from one period to the next.

(d) The concept of 'prudence': revenue and profits are not anticipated, but are recognized by inclusion in the profit and loss account only when realized in the form either of cash or of other assets the ultimate cash realization of which can be assessed with reasonable certainty; provision is made for all known liabilities (expenses and losses) whether the amount of these is known with certainty or is a best estimate in the light of the information available.

Referring back to Chapter 3 will show that these definitions are consistent with the generally accepted notions. As we have already seen they are not consistent with each other, and the SSAP clearly recognizes this. It accepts that the relative importance of the four concepts will 'vary according to the circumstances of the particular case'. And we should note the explicit statement, 'where the accruals concept is inconsistent with the prudence concept, the latter (i.e. prudence) prevails'. The question of how strongly it should prevail has caused much difficulty in the preparation of several later SSAPs.

The fundamental accounting concepts, says the standard, are so fundamental that their use can be assumed:

> They have such general acceptance that they call for no explanation in published accounts and their observance is presumed unless stated otherwise (paragraph 2).

So the formal disclosure requirement for accounting concepts is as follows:

17 If accounts are prepared on the basis of assumptions which differ in material respects from any of the generally accepted fundamental concepts defined in paragraph 14 above, the facts should be explained. In the absence of a clear statement to the contrary, there is a presumption that the four fundamental concepts have been observed.

So silence tells us that these fundamental concepts have been validly observed (although it tells us nothing about how the inconsistency between accruals and prudence has been handled).

Accounting bases

The next type of accounting idea is the accounting base, defined as follows:

15 *Accounting bases* are the methods developed for applying fundamental accounting concepts to financial transactions and items, for the purpose of financial accounts, and in particular:

  (a) for determining the accounting periods in which revenue and costs should be recognized in the profit and loss account; and

  (b) for determining the amounts at which material items should be stated in the balance sheet.

Thus, accounting bases are the alternative available methods of applying the fundamental concepts to particular items to be included in the accounts. They have evolved 'in response to the variety and complexity of types of business and business transactions' (paragraph 3). In general, there will therefore be several acceptable accounting bases for any particular problem area. With depreciation, for example, we have straight-line method, reducing balance method, etc.; with stock we have FIFO, LIFO, weighted average, and so on. For any particular business, we have to choose the appropriate accounting bases for the various areas – those that are 'appropriate to the circumstances and are best suited to present fairly the concern's results and financial position' (paragraph 10).

This leads us on to the third type of accounting idea distinguished in the standard: accounting policies.

Accounting policies

16 *Accounting policies* are the specific accounting bases selected and consistently followed by a business enterprise as being, in the opinion of the management, appropriate to its circumstances and best suited to present fairly its results and financial position.

Since there is a choice of accounting policies in most areas (i.e. there are several acceptable bases), disclosure of the policy adopted is clearly necessary in order properly to understand and interpret the published figures. The formal disclosure requirement is:

18 The accounting policies (as defined in para. 16 above) followed for dealing with items which are judged material or critical in determining profit or loss for the year and in stating the financial position should be disclosed by way of note to the accounts. The explanations should be clear, fair, and as brief as possible.

So a business should have a section in its published accounts giving details of the policies used. For example: depreciation, based on the cost of fixed assets modified by the revaluation of freehold buildings, is calculated on the straight-line basis. The annual rates used are:

Freehold property	1%
Leasehold property	2%, or over the lease period if less than 50 years
Plant and machinery	10–25%, as appropriate

In practice these statements of accounting policies are not always quite so helpful as they should be.

Activity 1

Study the accounting policies section of some recently published sets of company accounts. To what extent do they genuinely tell you exactly what has been done?

Activity 1 feedback

They won't! But some will be better than others, at least in some respects. Think precisely what you *do* need to know in greater detail than presented to you, and how that greater clarity might be achieved.

The Companies Act 1985

The 'fundamental concepts' are specifically referred to in the UK Companies Act of 1985 and also in the International Accounting Standard (IAS) 1. The Companies Act provisions in effect incorporate the four definitions of the concepts given in SSAP 2. They also add a fifth, which is given equal status. The five items are referred to in the Act as 'accounting principles'. They are as follows (schedule 4, paragraphs 10–14):

1 The company shall be presumed to be carrying on business as a going concern. (Going concern.)

2 Accounting policies shall be applied consistently from one financial year to the next. (Consistency.)

3 The amount of any item shall be determined on a prudent basis, and in particular:

(**a**) only profits realized at the balance sheet date shall be included in the profit and loss account; and

(**b**) all liabilities and losses that have arisen or are likely to arise in respect of the financial year to which the accounts relate or a previous financial year shall be taken into account, including those that only became apparent between the balance sheet date and the date on which it is signed on behalf of the board of directors. (Prudence.)

4 All income and charges relating to the financial year to which the accounts relate shall be taken into account, without regard to the date of receipt or payment. (Accruals.)

5 In determining the aggregate amount of any item the amount of each individual asset or liability that falls to be taken into account shall be determined separately.

This last principle is intended to prevent the netting out of assets and liabilities into a single net composite figure.

Departure from these five principles is permitted in certain circumstances (schedule 4, paragraph 15):

> If it appears to the directors of a company that there are special reasons for departing from any of the principles stated above in preparing the company's accounts in respect of any financial year they may do so, but particulars of the departure, the reasons for it and its effects shall be given in a note to the accounts.

This very vaguely worded provision seems likely to be frequently used. See, for example, SSAP 20 (Chapter 25).

Activity 2

Try the following examination question.

SSAP 2 'Disclosure of Accounting Policies' states that there are four fundamental accounting concepts which have general acceptability.

Required:

(a) **State and briefly explain each of these four fundamental concepts.**

(8 marks)

(b) **State and briefly explain three other accounting concepts.** (6 marks)

(c) **In what circumstances might you abandon one of the concepts stated in either part (a) or part (b) when preparing a financial statement?** (6 marks)

(20 marks)

(ACCA)

Activity 2 feedback

SSAP 2 'Disclosure of Accounting Policies' lists the four fundamental concepts as:

1 *Going concern.* This is the assumption that the business will continue in operational existence for the foreseeable future.

2 *Accruals concept.* Revenue and costs are recognized on an accruals basis and not a cash basis, matched where possible, and dealt with in the profit and loss account of the period to which they relate.

3 *Consistency.* Similar items are dealt with consistently both within each accounting period and between accounting periods.

4 *Prudence.* Revenue and profits are not anticipated; provision is made for all known liabilities.

You have a wide variety to choose from here. Four possible examples follow.

1 *Business entity.* This is the assumption that the business can be separately identified from its owners and that financial statements are prepared from this perspective.

2 *Money measurement.* Only those assets and liabilities capable of being expressed in monetary terms are included in financial statements.

3 *Objectivity.* Financial statements should be free from bias and capable of verification.

4 *Stable monetary unit.* This is the assumption that changes in the general purchasing power of money may be ignored.

Again we give here four possible ideas.

1 *Consistency.* The abandonment of this concept between accounting periods may be justified where a firm changes an accounting policy. This will necessitate a note to the accounts.

2 *Accruals concept.* The abandonment of this concept may be justified where its use would be inconsistent with the prudence concept. For example, the accruals concept may suggest research and development be carried forward but the prudence concept may require the expenditure to be written off in the present period.

3 *Prudence.* This concept may be abandoned where a firm values a highly specialized fixed asset at cost, even though the net realizable value may be considerably lower. This practice may be justified by the going concern concept.

4 *True and fair view.* You might and indeed should abandon any concept if it is necessary to do so in order to give a true and fair view. But under exam conditions you should perhaps explain what you think this means.

Activity 3

How important is the concept of prudence?

Activity 3 feedback

Clearly there are a number of different directions which an answer to this activity could take. Important for what? This certainly requires some consideration before you can get very far. Broadly, we would suggest that prudence in the sense of not making optimistic estimates of future operational outcomes is an essential and central requirement of accounting practice and attitude. But prudence as an end in itself is in a sense by definition undesirable, as it fails to reveal information about likely outcomes. It represents a distortion of the information, a bias, and as such will typically give a picture away from the likely norm of economic reality. But you should have your own views on this.

The ASB Statement of Principles

The Statement of Principles, (SoP), has given the ASB a great deal of difficulty. The first draft was prepared gradually and laboriously between 1991 and 1995, and eventually issued as a complete exposure draft, containing seven chapters, in November 1995. This draft met with a great deal of criticism, essentially on the grounds that it was held to focus on the balance sheet rather than on the profit and loss account, thereby, it was said, sacrificing the importance of the matching principle and the calculation and reporting of earnings. Following much prevarication and discussion, not all of it well-informed, the SoP was issued as a definitive document late in 1999, now containing an introduction and eight chapters.

The motivation behind the SoP is not entirely clear. As indicated in Part One of this book, the US has something rather similar, and the IASC Framework has clearly been taken as the starting point, being followed word for word in some places. Perhaps the possession of some such document was seen as inherent in being perceived as an 'advanced' accounting country. However, the UK SoP is a much longer and more complicated document than the IASC Framework, covering broadly the same principles, but also adding much detail.

The introduction states that the primary purpose of publishing the SoP is to provide a coherent frame of reference to be used by the Board in the development and review of accounting standards and by others who interact with the Board during the standard-setting process. Such a frame of reference should clarify the conceptual underpinnings of proposed accounting standards and should enable standards to be developed on a consistent basis by reducing the need to debate fundamental issues each time a standard is developed or revised. The SoP should also help preparers and auditors faced with new or emerging issues to carry out an initial analysis of the issues involved in the absence of an existing accounting standard.

Although the SoP is in a sense more fundamental than the standards, it is clear that if there is any conflict between the SoP and an FRS, then the standard must be followed. As paragraph 5 of the Introduction unequivocally states:

> The Statement of Principles is not an accounting standard, nor does it have a status that is equivalent to an accounting standard. It therefore does not contain requirements on how financial statements should be prepared or presented.

Appropriate genuflection is made to the true and fair view principle, the development of which concept the SoP 'may be expected to contribute to'. Perhaps more interesting is the explicit declaration that 'the SoP has not been developed within the constraints imposed by legislation'. It follows from this that a particular standard may be influenced by the law rather than by the SoP , in the event of a conflict, ie the standard might be inconsistent with the SoP.

We now outline the major points of each of the eight 'chapters' of the SoP.

Chapter 1: The objective of financial statements

The key principles can be quoted directly.

- The objective of financial statements is to provide information about the reporting entity's financial performance and financial position that is useful to a wide range of users for assessing the stewardship of the entity's management and for making economic decisions.
- That objective can usually be met by focusing exclusively on the information needs of present and potential investors, the defining class of user.

- Present and potential investors need information about the reporting entity's ability to generate cash (including the timing and certainty of its generation) and in assessing the entity's financial adaptability.

The SoP elaborates on this at some length, without adding much that is new. Note that the SoP follows the IASC Framework in its cheerful assumption that, at least in practice, the needs of investors are the only necessary consideration. We are entitled to presume that (paragraph 1.12):

(a) information that is needed by investors will be given in either the financial statements or some other general purpose financial report; and

(b) information that is not needed by investors need not be given in the financial statements.

Chapter 2: The reporting entity
The principles are as follows.

- An entity should prepare and publish financial statements if there is a legitimate demand for the information that its financial statements should provide and it is a cohesive economic unit.
- The boundary of the reporting entity is determined by the scope of its control. For this purpose, first direct control and, secondly, direct plus indirect control are taken into account.

To have control, an entity must have both the ability to deploy the economic resources involved, and the ability to benefit (or to suffer) from their employment. It is evident that the whole issue of control, which is not covered in the IASC Framework, is in essence a matter of group accounting principles, covered in Chapter 24, and we do not repeat the issues here. Given the stated nature and purpose of the SoP, it is not obvious why a chapter on a specific and detailed matter such as this has been included.

Chapter 3: The qualitative characteristics of financial information
This is a rather more significant chapter, both in its subject matter and for the nuances of some of the statements made. The principles are relatively lengthy, as they embrace the major conventions one at a time. It is worth stating them in full.

- Information provided by financial statements needs to be relevant and reliable and, if a choice exists between relevant and reliable approaches that are mutually exclusive, the approach chosen needs to be the one that results in the relevance of the information provided being maximised.
- Information is relevant if it has the ability to influence the economic decisions of users and if provided in time to influence those decisions.
- Information is reliable if:
  (a) it can be depended on by users to represent faithfully what it either purports to represent or could reasonably be expected to represent, and therefore reflects the substance of the transactions and other events that have taken place;
  (b) it is free from deliberate or systematic bias and material error and is complete; and

(c) in its preparation under conditions of uncertainty, a degree of caution has been applied in exercising the necessary judgements.

- Information in financial statements needs to be comparable.
- As an aid to comparability, information in financial statements needs to be prepared and presented in a way that enables users to discern and evaluate similarities in, and differences between, the nature and effects of transactions and other events over time and across different reporting entities.
- Information provided by financial statements needs to be understandable, although information should not be excluded from the financial statements simply because it would not be understood by some users.
- Information is understandable if its significance can be perceived by users that have a reasonable knowledge of business and economic activities and accounting and a willingness to study with reasonable diligence the information provided.
- Information that is material needs to be given in the financial statements and information that is not material need not be given.
- Information is material to the financial statements if its misstatement or omission might reasonably be expected to influence the economic decisions of users.

The ASB gives a diagram suggesting the relationships between the qualitative characteristics, which we reproduce as Figure 15.1.

These terms are all familiar, and we do not need to discuss them all again here, although the SoP does go through them one at a time. Some of the suggested interrelationships are interesting enough to warrant comment, however. It is noteworthy that the word 'prudence' does not appear in the summarised 'Principles'. It is in fact masquerading as point (c) of reliability. The SoP defines prudence (paragraph 3.19) as:

> the inclusion of a degree of caution in the exercise of the judgements needed in making the estimates required under conditions of uncertainty, such that gains and assets are not overstated and losses and liabilities are not understated.

The conflict of principle between neutrality and prudence is explicitly recognised. However the practical problems are dismissed and we are told that when there is uncertainty (when is there not uncertainty in accounting?) then the competing demands of neutrality and prudence 'are reconciled' (not may be reconciled) by finding a balance which 'ensures' that the deliberate and systematic understatement of gains and assets or overstatement of losses and liabilities does not occur. This seems to be a rather coded way of saying that the importance of prudence must not be overestimated. 'Ensures' is a strong word. Notice the sharp change in tone and implication of this section of the SoP as compared with the explicit emphasis on prudence in the old SSAP 2.

The other point worth emphasising is the conflict between relevance and reliability. The first 'principle' stated above clearly suggests that relevance is more important than reliability, but a later paragraph (3.34) states that where this conflict exists, then it will usually be appropriate to use the information which is the most relevant 'of whichever information is reliable'. This seems to imply the opposite, as it suggests that information must be reliable before its relevance can even be considered. It is further stated in paragraph 3.35, in regard to a possible conflict between reliability and timeliness, that 'financial information should not be provided until it is reliable'.

THE QUALITATIVE CHARACTERISTICS OF FINANCIAL INFORMATION

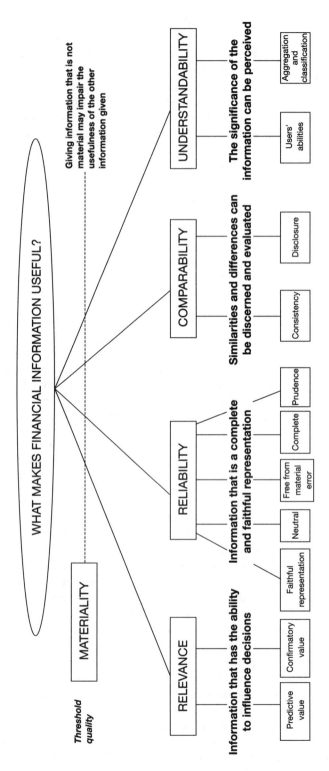

WHAT MAKES FINANCIAL INFORMATION USEFUL?

Threshold quality

MATERIALITY

Giving information that is not material may impair the usefulness of the other information given

RELEVANCE

Information that has the ability to influence decisions

- Predictive value
- Confirmatory value

RELIABILITY

Information that is a complete and faithful representation

- Faithful representation
- Neutral
- Free from material error
- Complete
- Prudence

COMPARABILITY

Similarities and differences can be discerned and evaluated

- Consistency
- Disclosure

UNDERSTANDABILITY

The significance of the information can be perceived

- Users' abilities
- Aggregation and classification

Figure 15.1

Perhaps the real conclusion to be drawn here is one which we have suggested in various places already in this book, ie that the attractive sounding conventions of financial reporting are often inconsistent, and cannot lead to clearcut unarguable solutions (or Standards).

Chapter 4: The elements of financial statements

This chapter defines and discusses the elements, or building blocks as the ASB describes them, with which financial statements are constructed, ie the major classes of items into which financial statement items are divided. The issues have been extensively discussed in Part 1. The ASB definitions are very similar, but not identical, and we need to reproduce them in full.

- The elements of the financial statements are:
  - **(a)** assets
  - **(b)** liabilities
  - **(c)** ownership interest
  - **(d)** gains
  - **(e)** losses
  - **(f)** contributions from owners
  - **(g)** distributions to owners.
- Assets are rights or other access to future economic benefits controlled by an entity as a result of past transactions or events.
- Liabilities are obligations of an entity to transfer economic benefits as a result of past transactions or events.
- Ownership interest is the residual amount found by deducting all of the entity's liabilities from all of the entity's assets.
- Gains are increases in ownership interest not resulting from contributions from owners.
- Losses are decreases in ownership interest not resulting from distributions to owners.
- Contributions from owners are increases in ownership interest resulting from transfers from owners in their capacity as owners.
- Distributions to owners are decreases in ownership interest resulting from transfers to owners in their capacity as owners.

The SoP proceeds to discuss these definitions at some length, but nothing new is added beyond our earlier discussions. Note carefully that gains includes revenues, but is a much wider term. Similarly, losses includes expenses but again has a much broader meaning.

Chapter 5: Recognition in financial statements

Once a transaction or event has given rise to an element, as defined in chapter 4, then in general that element needs to be recognised in the financial statements. However certain criteria need to be met in order for recognition to take place. This chapter of the SoP considers these criteria. The principles are as follows.

- If a transaction or other event has created a new asset or liability or added to an existing asset or liability, that effect will be recognised if:
  - **(a)** sufficient evidence exists that the new asset or liability has been created or that there has been an addition to an existing asset or liability; and

>   **(b)** the new asset or liability or the addition to the existing asset or liability
>   can be measured at a monetary amount with sufficient reliability.
> ■ In a transaction involving the provision of services or goods for a net gain,
>   the recognition criteria described above will be met on the occurrence of the
>   critical event of the operating cycle involved.
> ■ An asset or liability will be wholly or partly derecognised if:
>   **(a)** sufficient evidence exists that a transaction or other past event has elim-
>   inated all or part of a previously recognised asset or liability; or
>   **(b)** although the item continues to be an asset or a liability, the criteria for
>   recognition are not met.

The SoP contrives to discuss the above at considerable length. Much of what they say consists of statements of the obvious, but a few points are worthy of note. As the principles quoted above make very clear, the whole process is inherently uncertain. Uncertainty arises at two
stages in the recording process. The first stage is element uncertainty, where there may be
doubt about whether the definition of an element (as in chapter 4 of the SoP) has been met.
The second stage is measurement uncertainty, where there may be doubt about the appropriate monetary amount with which to record the item. Prudence must not be ignored, but the
SoP repeats the warnings of its chapter 3 that prudence must not be overplayed.

    Much of the debate and criticism surrounding the drafting of the Statement of Principles
has arisen over the relative importance of the profit and loss account and its preparation,
and the balance sheet and its preparation. Chapter 5 makes it explicit that the matching concept can only be applied if any resulting balance sheet items meet the definitional and measurement criteria for asset, liability or ownership interest.

> This means that the Statement does not use the notion of matching as the main
> driver of the recognition process. Nevertheless, the Statement envisages that;
> **(a)** if the future economic benefits embodied in the asset are eliminated at a sin-
>   gle point in time, it is at that point that the asset will be derecognised and a
>   loss recognised; and
> **(b)** if the future economic benefits are eliminated over several accounting periods
>   – typically because they are being consumed over a period of time - the cost
>   of the asset that comprises the future economic benefits will be recognised
>   as a loss in the performance statement over those accounting periods.

    The statement that the critical event of the operating cycle is crucial does not actually
get us very far. The SoP explains that the critical event in an operating cycle is the point
at which 'there will usually be sufficient evidence that the gain exists and it will usually
be possible to measure that gain with sufficient reliability'. Since that quotation contains
the words 'usually' and 'sufficient' twice each in one sentence, this is clearly not a great
advance. Common sense and business reality must in the end be the order of the day.

Chapter 6: Measurement in financial statements

This chapter consists of a brief introduction to the whole issue of historical cost accounting and its alternatives, which we have discussed at considerable length in Part One. The
earlier drafts of the Statement of Principles were heavily criticized from some quarters for
implying an attack on the historical cost principle. This final version goes out of its way to
deny any hidden agenda, and contents itself with a few comments about the weaknesses

of historical cost accounting (which includes, as the SoP sees it, the possibility of reducing assets to recoverable amount and the use of current exchange rates for foreign currency monetary items. ie it is not strictly 'pure' historical cost which is referred to).

The principles of Chapter 6 are summarized as follows.

- In drawing up financial statements, a measurement basis – either historical cost or current value – needs to be selected for each category of assets or liabilities. The basis selected will be the one that best meets the objective of financial statements and the demands of the qualitative characteristics of financial information, bearing in mind the nature of the assets or liabilities concerned and the circumstances involved.
- An asset or liability being measured using the historical cost basis is recognised initially at transaction cost. An asset or liability being measured using the current value basis is recognised initially at its current value at the time it was acquired or assumed.
- Subsequent remeasurement will occur if it is necessary to ensure that:
  - (a) assets measured at historical cost are carried at the lower of cost and recoverable amount;
  - (b) monetary items denominated in foreign currency are carried at amounts based on up-to-date exchange rates; and
  - (c) assets and liabilities measured on the current value basis are carried at up-to-date current values.
- Such remeasurements, however, will be recognised only if:
  - (a) there is sufficient evidence that the monetary amount of the asset or liability has changed; and
  - (b) the new amount of the asset or liability can be measured with sufficient reliability.

Chapter 7: Presentation of financial information

This chapter, as some of the earlier sections have been, is essentially a common sense discussion – on the characteristics of useful financial statements in this case. For completeness, we quote the stated principles.

- Financial statements comprise primary financial statements and supporting notes that amplify and explain the primary financial statements. The primary financial statements themselves comprise the statement of financial performance, the statement of financial position or balance sheet, and the cash flow statement.
- The presentation of information on financial performance focuses on the components of that performance and on the characteristics of those components.
- The presentation of information on financial position focuses on the types and functions of assets and liabilities held and on the relationships between them.
- The presentation of cash flow information will show the extent to which the entity's various activities generate and use cash, and will distinguish in particular between those cash flows that result from operations and those that result from other activities.
- Disclosure of information in the notes to the financial statements is not a substitute for recognition and does not correct or justify any misrepresentation or omission in the primary financial statements.

Chapter 8: Accounting for interests in other entities

This chapter seems to be intended as a summary of some of the issues which underly the preparation of consolidated accounts. We do not consider that it adds anything of usefulness to the contents of the relevant Standards, which we cover in Chapter 24.

The Statement of Principles – a preliminary appraisal

We would make three brief comments, at this early stage in the existence of the definitive document. First, the existence of such a document is beneficial in that it establishes general ways of thinking, and should facilitate the preparation of future standards, and reduce the likelihood of fundamantal inconsistencies between them. Secondly, a careful reading of it really only emphasises the subjective nature of most of the issues that matter. The application of the SoP to the preparation of standards, and the application of the standards to the preparation of financial statements, requires common sense and professionalism. The SoP is a thought process, not a blueprint. Finally, we rather wonder what all the fuss was about. The SoP breaks little new ground, and where it does add to the coverage of the IASC Framework, which we discussed in Part One, adds little of substance.

FRED 21; Accounting policies

FRED 21 was issued in December 1999, at the same time as the definitive version of the Statement of Principles. It is intended to replace SSAP 2. On the whole, it does not attempt very radical changes. However, as indicated earlier in this chapter, and indeed in our more general discussions in Part One, the relative importance of the accounting conventions covered in SSAP 2 has changed significantly over the three decades since it was issued. FRED 21, like the SoP, is influenced by general international thinking, as represented by the IASC Framework of 1989 which we considered in Chapter 10, and accordingly the sections on accounting concepts are significantly different from SSAP 2. Beyond that, the changes are mainly concerned with points of extension or clarification.

The purpose of the FRED is to ensure that accounting policies adopted are appropriate, are amended when necessary, and are adequately disclosed for user purposes. Three definitions are given, as follows.

- Accounting policies are the specific principles, bases, conventions, rules and practices applied by an entity in order to reflect the effects of transactions and other events through recognising, selecting measurement bases for, and presenting assets, liabilities, gains, losses and changes to shareholders' funds. Accounting policies do not include estimation techniques.
- Estimation techniques are the methods and estimates adopted by an entity to arrive at monetary values, corresponding to the measurement bases selected, for assets, liabilities, gains, losses and changes to shareholders' funds.
- Measurement bases are those monetary attributes of the elements of financial statements – assets, liabilities, gains, losses and changes to shareholders' funds – that are reflected in financial statements. Measurement bases fall into two broad categories, those that reflect current values, and those that reflect historical values.

The distinction between accounting policies and estimation techniques is important. One might sum this up by suggesting that different accounting policies seek to present different pictures of a particular set of facts, whereas different estimation techniques are different ways of arriving at the particular picture which has been chosen. Care is needed when an accounting change involves both a change in presentation and a change of estimation technique. The former is a change in accounting policy whereas the latter is not. To give two examples, a change in depreciation method from straight line to reducing balance is a change in estimation tchnique, not a change in accounting policy. However, a change from including some overheads in cost of sales to including those same overheads in administration expenses is a change in presentation, and accordingly does represent a change in accounting policy.

In a deliberate extension to SSAP 2, the FRED explicitly requires that an entity should adopt accounting policies that are, in the opinion of the directors, most appropriate for giving a true and fair view, and are consistent with the requirements of accounting standards and company legislation. However, if in exceptional circumstances compliance with the requirement of an accounting standard is inconsistent with the requirement to give a true and fair view, that requirement must be departed from to the extent necessary to give a true and fair view.

This proposed requirement represents, of course, an explicit statement of the true and fair over-ride, discussed in Chapter 13. It is logically unnecessary here, as the over-ride in the Companies Act already applies without limit. It is presumably restated here to give emphasis to the ASB's support for the principle.

Four factors should be considered when judging the appropriateness of accounting policies to any particular circumstances. These are relevance, reliability, comparability and understandability. In applying these factors, the need for an appropriate balance between the four factors must be considered, as must cost-benefit considerations concerning the resulting information. Two other factors are regarded as more fundamental, namely the going concern convention and the accruals convention (note that this ranking of importance exactly follows that in the IASC Framework and in IAS 1). Once selected, an entity's accounting policies must be reviewed regularly to ensure that they remain the most appropriate. If not, they must be changed.

Estimation techniques should be selected in the same way, and against similar criteria. That is, they should be the most appropriate, taking into account the factors and considerations mentioned in the previous paragraph. Estimation techniques should also be reviewed regularly, and amended if necessary.

The proposed disclosure requirements are important, and quite extensive. Accounting policies for all material items must be disclosed; estimation techniques must be described whenever the use of such technique is material, and where the effect of a change in an estimation technique is material, the effect and a description of the change must be given. Details of changes in accounting policies compared with the preceding year must be disclosed, including an explanation of why the new policy is considered more appropriate, and, 'where practical' the effect of a prior period adjustment on the results of the preceding year, and an indication of the effect of the change in accounting policy on the results of thie current year.

Any departure from the going concern assumption or the accruals convention must be stated prominently, together with an explanation. In the event of a departure from the requirement of any accounting standard or companies legislation, in order to give a true and fair view, detailed disclosures are proposed. This should include a clear statement that the departure has taken place, a description of both the required treatment and the one actually adopted, and an explanation of why the required treatment would fail to give a true and fair view. The effect of the change should be described, normally with quantification of that effect. If the departure continues for more than one accounting period, full disclosure is required on every occasion.

Despite its relatively uncontroversial contents, FRED 21 seems to be taking some time in turning into a Standard. This may be as much due to the changes in the membership of the ASB as to any intrinsic difficulties with the material itself. Another possible cause of uncertainty may be the possibly very rapid advent of International Accounting Standards as a requirement for all listed companies.

Financial accounting standard for smaller entities

The issue

The Companies Act requirements (see Chapter 13) have for many years made a distinction between large and small companies such that small companies are given exemption from some of the disclosure requirements of Schedule 4 of the Act and they have not been required to prepare group accounts. In addition, small companies are exempt from mandatory audit unless the company involves a public interest or is part of a group. A small company is currently defined as a company which does not exceed two or more of the following criteria in a year:

Turnover	£2.8m
Balance sheet total	£1.4m
Average number of employees	50.

With the above in mind, questions were raised by standard setters as to the applicability of accounting standards to small companies. In particular there was a need to debate whether small companies were unduly burdened by having to comply with accounting standards. The issue was first debated in 1986 by a working party of the ASC and they concluded that there was no evidence to suggest an undue burden. However in 1989 the ASC issued a technical release accepting that in special circumstances it was appropriate to exempt some entities by virtue of their size from the requirements of SSAP 13 Research and development and SSAP 25 Segmental reporting. In the early nineties the momentum to reduce the burden of bureaucracy on business continued and a working party was established by the ASB resulting in a consultative document in November 1994. December 1995 saw the issue of a draft FRSSE (frizzy) and this became a standard in November 1997.

Since then, the FRSSE has been revised several times, mainly to update it in relation to newly issued FRSs. The latest revision is effective from March 2000. It is likely that regular annual revisions will appear for the forseeable future, which again will update the coverage, without significantly altering the existing material or the general principles underlying the FRSSE.

The standard

The objective of FRSSE is 'to ensure that reporting entities falling within its scope provide in their financial statements information about the financial position, performance and financial adaptability of the entity that is useful to users in assessing the stewardship of management and for making economic decisions, recognising that the balance between users' needs in respect of stewardship and economic decision making for smaller entities is different from that for other reporting entities (page 9 FRSSE, ASB). Here the ASB makes an assumption that significant public interest is not shown in smaller entities' financial statements and that in general managers will be directors and shareholders or that at least there will not be wide share ownership. As such the users of small companies' financial statements require them to be shown in a simple manner so that they can understand the underlying transactions. The FRSSE is a single accounting standard for small companies which provides accounting guidance on how small companies should prepare their financial statements.

True and fair view

It could be presumed, at this stage, that there are two true and fair views as one set of standards exists for large companies and one for small. However, the meaning of true and fair view develops over time and as accounting issues are debated and standards issued this true and fair view will adapt and change. It is possible that a true and fair view of small companies is more appropriately given by use of the FRSSE. The statement itself states the following:

Para 2.1   The financial statements should present a true and fair view of the results for the period and of the state of affairs at the end of the period. To achieve such a view, regard should be had to the substance of any arrangement or transaction, or series of such, into which the entity has entered. To determine the substance of a transaction it is necessary to identify whether the transaction has given rise to new assets or liabilities for the reporting entity and whether it has changed the entity's existing assets or liabilities.

Para 2.2   Where there is doubt whether applying provisions of the FRSSE would be sufficient to give a true and fair view, adequate explanation should be given in the notes to the accounts of the transaction or arrangement concerned and the treatment adopted.

Conclusions

This has been quite a long chapter to write, and maybe also to read. Much is changing, but it is changing in a complicated and sometimes confusing way. There is considerable repetition or near-repetition between the various documents, such as the UK SoP and the UK FRED 21, between the IASC Framework and IAS 1, between the IASC Framework and the UK SoP, and, to a lesser extent, between IAS 1 and FRED 21. In a sense, the UK documents, both the SoP and FRED 21, are largely catchup documents, formalising the trends of recent years induced by the international thinking. It should not be assumed that the process of change has stopped.

In particular, it should be remembered that all the ASB thinking which we discuss here, including the recent FRED 21, has been conducted on the assumption that UK accounting, notwithstanding international cooperation, is and will remain a matter for the UK, and for the ASB in particular. As discussed in Chapter 11, it is possible that within a very few years, the financial statements of all enterprises listed on the London Stock Exchange will have to be prepared under IASC standards and not under ASB standards. How will the ASB react?

Summary

In this chapter we have explored the ASB thinking on the issue of the meaning, and the disclosure, of accounting policies. This has involved consideration of SSAP 2, issued three dacades ago, the Statement of Principles, and FRED 21 as a draft replacement for SSAP 2. Thinking has changed significantly over the period. We have also noted the role of the financial reporting standard for smaller entities.

Addendum

In December 2000, the ASB turned FRED 21 into a Financial Reporting Standard, FRS 18, Accounting Policies. In its broad thrust, this follows FRED 21 quite closely. FRS 18 reiterates that the main reason for the creation of the FRS, and the consequent withdrawal of the old SSAP 2, is simply to deal with changes of attitude over the three decades since SSAP 2, and in particular to ensure that Standard practice is consistent with the newly issued Statement of Principles. The Board does not see FRS 18 as a fundamental shift away from the ideas of SSAP 2.

There are only really two issues of particular interest in FRS 18. The first is that a clear distinction is attempted between accounting policies and estimation techniques, which is discussed below.

The second interesting point, already mentioned in the chapter in relation to FRED 21, appears rather small and subtle, but may well turn out to be of some significance, especially as FRS 18 differs from the recently revised IASC Standard, IAS 1 (revised 1997). This is that an entity's accounting policies are not merely required to be acceptable. They are not even merely required to be policies that will give a true and fair view. They are explicitly required to be the policies judged to be 'most appropriate in its particular circumstances for the purpose of giving a true and fair view'. This wording at one and the same time imposes a tight rein on the opportunities available to preparers of financial statements, but also strongly emphasizes the ultimately individual nature of accounting policy choice. There is no hint of an approval of accounting uniformity here.

FRS 18 applies to all financial statements intended to give a true and fair view, except those entities to which the Financial Reporting Standard for Smaller Entities applies. With the exception of the references to SORPs, FRS 18 is required practice for accounting periods *ending* on or after 22 June 2001. The references to SORPs are required in respect of those periods *beginning* on or before 23 December 2001.

To update the chapter, we give the official wording of the main requirements here. The Standard contains a number of definitions.

Accounting policies

Those principles, bases, conventions, rules and practices applied by an entity that specify how the effects of transactions and other events are to be reflected in its financial statements through:

- recognizing;
- selecting measurement bases for; and
- presenting

assets liabilities, gains, losses and changes to shareholders' funds. Accounting policies do not include estimation techniques.

Accounting policies define the process whereby transactions and other events are reflected in financial statements. For example, an accounting policy for a particular type of expenditure may specify whether an asset or a loss is to be recognised; the basis on which it is to be measured; and where in the profit and loss account or balance sheet it is to be presented.

Estimation techniques

The methods adopted by an entity to arrive at estimated monetary amounts, corresponding to the measurement bases selected, for assets, liabilities, gains, losses and changes to shareholders' funds.

Estimation techniques implement the measurement aspects of accounting policies. An accounting policy will specify the basis on which an item is to be measured; where there is uncertainty over the monetary amount corresponding to that basis, the amount will be arrived at by using an estimation technique. Estimation techniques include, for example:

(a) methods of depreciation, such as straight-line and reducing balance, applied in the context of a particular measurement basis, used to estimate the proportion of the economic benefits of a tangible fixed asset consumed in a period;

(b) different methods used to estimate the proportion of trade debts that will not be recovered, particularly where such methods consider a population as a whole rather than individual balances.

Measurement bases

Those monetary attributes of the elements of financial statements – assets, liabilities, gains, losses and changes to shareholders' funds – that are reflected in financial statements.

Monetary attributes fall into two broad categories – those that reflect current values and those that reflect historical values. Some monetary attributes will be suitable for use in financial statements only in conjunction with others. A monetary attribute, or combination of attributes, that may be reflected in financial statements is called a measurement basis.

The FRS discusses the practicalities of distinguishing between accounting policies and estimation techniques at some length, and gives a series of examples in an appendix. We have already discussed this area in the chapter in relation to FRED 21. Here is another ASB illustration, well demonstrating the subtlety and possible complexity of the distinction.

Example A
Discounting

An entity has previously reported deferred tax on an undiscounted basis. However, the norm in its industry is to report deferred tax on a discounted basis.

It concludes, for reasons of comparability, that it should adopt the normal industry approach.

Does this involve a change to:

Recognition?	✗
Presentation?	✗
Measurement basis?	✓

Explanation: FRS 19 allows entities to report deferred tax on either a discounted or an undiscounted basis. These are two different measurement bases, and it is a matter of accounting policy which an entity chooses to adopt.

Conclusion: This is a change of accounting policy.

Example B
Discounting

An entity has previously measured a particular provision on an undiscounted basis, in accordance with FRS 12 'Provisions, Contingent Liabilities and Contingent Assets' as the effect of discounting was not material. However, in 2000 it has revised upwards its estimates of future cash flows associated with the provision and, as a result, the effect of discounting is now material. FRS 12 therefore requires it to report the provision at the discounted amount.

Does this involve a change to:

Recognition?	✗
Presentation?	✗
Measurement basis?	✗

Explanation: FRS 12 requires entities to report provisions at the best estimate of the expenditure required to settle the present obligation at the balance sheet date. Where that estimate is based on future cash flows, it is permissible to use undiscounted amounts only where the effect of the time value of money is not material. In such circumstances, the use of undiscounted future cash flows is, in effect, an estimation technique for arriving at the present value.

Conclusion: This is not a change of accounting policy.

The Standard proceeds to consider accounting policies in detail.

An entity should adopt accounting policies that enable its financial statements to give a true and fair view. Those accounting policies should be consistent with the requirements of accounting standards, Urgent Issues Task Force (UITF) Abstracts and companies legislation. If in exceptional circumstances compliance with the requirements of an accounting standard or UITF Abstract is inconsistent with the requirement to give a true and fair view, the requirements of the accounting standard or UITF Abstract should be departed from to the extent necessary to give a true and fair view. In such circumstances, disclosure should be provided.

An entity will not depart from the requirements of an accounting standard or UITF Abstract where a true and fair view can be achieved by additional disclosure. In such circumstances, the requirements of the accounting standard or UITF Abstract are not inconsistent with the requirement to give a true and fair view.

Where it is necessary to choose between accounting policies, an entity should select whichever of those accounting policies is judged by the entity to be most appropriate to its particular circumstances for the purpose of giving a true and fair view.

An entity should prepare its financial statements on a going concern basis, unless

(**a**) the entity is being liquidated or has ceased trading, or
(**b**) the directors have no realistic alternative but to liquidate the entity or to cease trading

in which circumstances the entity may, if appropriate, prepare its financial statements on a basis other than that of a going concern. When preparing financial statements directors should assess whether there are significant doubts about an entity's ability to continue as a going concern.

Note that SSAP 2 said that going concern should be presumed in financial statements unless it was stated to the contrary. SSAP 2 did not actually say that an entity *should* assume a going concern unless ...

An entity should prepare its financial statements, except for cash flow information, on the accrual basis of accounting.

The objectives against which an entity should judge the appropriateness of accounting policies to its particular circumstances are:

(**a**) relevance;
(**b**) reliability;
(**c**) comparability; and
(**d**) understandability.

The constraints that an entity should take into account in judging the appropriateness of accounting policies to its particular circumstances are:

(**a**) the need to balance these different objectives; and
(**b**) the need to balance the cost of providing information with the likely benefit of such information to users of the entity's financial statements.

These four objectives, with which readers should by now be thoroughly familiar, are discussed at length in FRS 18.

An entity's accounting policies should be reviewed regularly to ensure that they remain the most appropriate to its particular circumstances for the purpose of giving a true and fair view. However, in judging whether a new policy is more appropriate than the existing policy, an entity will give due weight to the impact on comparability.

Estimation techniques are regulated as follows.

Where estimation techniques are required to enable the accounting policies adopted to be applied, an entity should select estimation techniques that enable its financial statements to give a true and fair view and are consistent with the requirements of accounting standards, UITF Abstracts and companies legislation.

Where it is necessary to choose between estimation techniques, an entity should select whichever of those estimation techniques is judged by the entity to be most appropriate to its particular circumstances for the purpose of giving a true and fair view.

A change to an estimation technique should not be accounted for as a prior period adjustment, unless:

(a) it represents the correction of a fundamental error, or

(b) another accounting standard, a UITF Abstract or companies legislation requires the change to be accounted for as a prior period adjustment.

The disclosure requirements are extensive. The following information should be disclosed in the financial statements:

(a) a description of each of the accounting policies that is material in the context of the entity's financial statements

(b) a description of those estimation techniques adopted that are significant

(c) details of any changes to the accounting policies that were followed in preparing financial statements for the preceding period, including:

(i) a brief explanation of why each new accounting policy is thought more appropriate;

(ii) where practicable, the effect of a prior period adjustment on the results for the preceding period, in accordance with FRS 3 'Reporting Financial Performance'; and

(iii) where practicable, an indication of the effect of a change in accounting policy on the results for the current period.

Where it is not practicable to make the disclosures described in (ii) or (iii) above, that fact, together with the reasons, should be stated.

(d) where the effect of a change to an estimation technique is material, a description of the change and, where practicable, the effect on the results for the current period.

Where an entity's financial statements fall within the scope of a SORP, the entity should state the title of the SORP and whether its financial statements have been prepared in accordance with those of the SORP's provisions currently in effect. In the event of a departure, the entity should give a brief description of how the financial statements depart from the recommended practice set out in the SORP, which should include:

(a) for any treatment that is not in accordance with the SORP, the reasons why the treatment adopted is judged more appropriate to the entity's particular circumstances, and

(b) details of any disclosures recommended by the SORP that have not been provided, and the reasons why they have not been provided.

The following information should be disclosed in the financial statements in relation to the going concern assessment required:

(a) any material uncertainties, of which the directors are aware in making their assessment, related to events or conditions that may cast significant doubt upon the entity's ability to continue as a going concern.

(b) where the foreseeable future considered by the directors has been limited to a period of less than one year from the date of approval of the financial statements, that fact.

(c) When the financial statements are not prepared on a going concern basis, that fact, together with the basis on which the financial statements are prepared and the reason why the entity is not regarded as a going concern.

For any material departure from the requirements of an accounting standard, a UITF Abstract or companies legislation, particulars of the departure, the reasons for it and its effect should be disclosed. The information disclosed should include:

(**a**) a clear and unambiguous statement that there has been a departure from the requirements of an accounting standard, a UITF Abstract or companies legislation, as the case may be, and that the departure is necessary to give a true and fair view.

(**b**) a statement of the treatment that the accounting standard, UITF Abstract or companies legislation would normally require in the circumstances and a description of the treatment actually adopted.

(**c**) a statement of why the treatment prescribed would not give a true and fair view.

(**d**) A description of how the position shown in the financial statements is different as a result of the departure, normally with quantification, except where

(**i**) quantification is already evident in the financial statements themselves; or

(**ii**) the effect cannot reasonably be quantified, in which case the directors should explain the circumstances.

Where a departure continues in subsequent financial statements, the disclosures should be made in all such subsequent statements, and should include corresponding amounts for the previous year. Where a departure affects only the corresponding amounts, the disclosures should be given for those corresponding amounts.

Where companies legislation requires an entity to make a statement of whether its financial statements have been prepared in accordance with applicable accounting standards, that statement should either include or cross-reference any disclosures, required by points (a)–(d) above.

Where companies legislation requires disclosure of particulars of a departure from a specific statutory requirement, the reasons for it and its effect, disclosures equivalent to those set out above should be provided.

Exercises

1 What is the objective of SSAP 2, and why has it become out of date?
2 Is the Statement of Principles necessary?
3 Is FRED 21 a significant improvement on SSAP 2?
4 Do the Statement of Principles and FRED 21 give sufficient emphasis to the prudence principle?
5 Does the Statement of Principles give sufficient emphasis to the matching (accruals) principle?

Fixed assets and goodwill

After reading this chapter you should be able to:
- discuss and apply the principles, concepts and major methods of providing for depreciation
- explain what depreciation does and does not do
- explain the issues involved in determining appropriate treatments for government grants
- describe, apply and appraise the requirements of SSAP 4 relating to government grants
- describe, apply and appraise the requirements of FRS 15 on accounting for depreciation
- describe company law requirements relating to depreciation
- describe, apply and appraise the requirements of SSAP 19 on accounting for investment properties
- outline the contents of FRS 15 'Tangible Fixed Assets'
- explain what goodwill is
- differentiate between purchased and non-purchased goodwill
- consider ways of evaluating goodwill
- describe possible ways of accounting for goodwill
- explain the Companies Act requirements in respect of goodwill
- explain the requirements of FRS 10 'Goodwill and Intangible Assets'
- discuss the requirements of FRS 10
- explain the requirements of FRS 11 'Impairment of Fixed Assets and Goodwill'.

Introduction

This long chapter brings together a variety of topics which are now inter-linked by the documents issued by the ASB. We begin with the relatively familiar aspects of 'straightforward' fixed assets and depreciation, and then explore some of the ramifications which arise. We then move on to consider the issues of goodwill and intangible assets. Finally we look at the latest thinking from the ASB on the question of 'impairment' of fixed assets and goodwill.

The area is perhaps a good example of how accounting regulation is becoming more complex and more detailed. In our view this is not good for anybody, be they practitioners, textbook writers or students. But it seems to be the way of the world. As you read this chapter, think whether this trend could be avoided.

Depreciation

The first major problem with depreciation, perhaps surprisingly, is to agree on what it is, and what it is for. The generally agreed view nowadays is that it is in essence a straightforward application of the matching, or accruals, convention. With a fixed asset (p. 138) the benefit from the asset is spread over several years. The matching convention requires that the corresponding expense be matched with the benefit in each accounting period. This does not simply mean that the total expense for the asset's life is spread over the total beneficial life. It means, more specifically, that the total expense for the asset's life is spread over the total beneficial life *in proportion to the pattern of benefit*. Thus, to take a simple example, if a fixed asset gives half of its benefit, or usefulness, in year 1, one third in year 2, and one sixth in year 3, and the total expenses arising are £1200, then the matching convention requires the charging of £600 in year 1, £400 in year 2, and £200 in year 3, in the annual profit calculation. This charge is known as the **depreciation charge**.

In order to calculate a figure for this charge it is necessary to answer four basic questions:

1 What is the cost of the asset?
2 What is the estimated useful life of the asset to the business? (This may be equal to, or may be considerably less than, its technical or physical useful life.)
3 What is the estimated residual selling value ('scrap value') of the asset at the end of the useful life as estimated?
4 What is the pattern of benefit or usefulness derived from the asset likely to be (not the *amount* of the benefit)?

It is perfectly obvious that the second, third and fourth of these involve a good deal of uncertainty and subjectivity. The 'appropriate' figures are all dependent on future plans and future actions. It is important to realize that even if the first figure, the cost of the fixed asset, is known precisely and objectively, the depreciation calculation as a whole is always uncertain, estimated and subjective. The estimates should, as usual, be reasonable, true and fair, and prudent (whatever precisely this implies!).

But the first figure is often not at all precise and objective, for several reasons.

Activity 1

Suggest reasons why the cost of a particular fixed asset may be difficult to determine with precision.

Activity 1 feedback

1 Incidental expenses associated with making the asset workable should be included, e.g. installation costs carried out by the business's own staff, probably including some overhead costs.
2 The fixed asset may be constructed within the business by its own workforce, giving rise to all the usual costing problems of overhead definition and overhead allocation.
3 Depending on the accounting policies used by the firm generally, the 'basic' figure for the fixed asset may be revalued periodically. Additionally, if land is not depreciated but the building on the land is, then this requires a split of the total cost (or value) figure for the land and buildings together into two necessarily somewhat arbitrary parts.
4 Major alterations/improvements may be made to the asset part way through its life. If these appear to increase the benefit from the asset over the remaining useful life, and perhaps also to increase the number of years of the remaining useful life, and are material,

then the costs of these improvements should also be capitalized (i.e. treated as part of the fixed asset from then on). However, maintenance costs, including a major overhaul that does not occur frequently, are 'running' expenses and should be charged to P&L account as incurred. In practice, this distinction is itself difficult to make with precision.

The Companies Act of 1985 (schedule 4, paragraph 26) states:

(1) The purchase price of an asset shall be determined by adding to the actual price paid any expenses incidental to its acquisition.

(2) The production cost of an asset shall be determined by adding to the purchase price of the raw materials and consumables used the amount of the costs incurred by the company which are directly attributable to the production of that asset.

(3) In addition, there may be included in the production cost of an asset:

   (a) a reasonable proportion of the costs incurred by the company which are only indirectly attributable to the production of that asset, but only to the extent that they relate to the period of production; and

   (b) interest on capital borrowed to finance the production of that asset, to the extent that it accrues in respect of the period of production; provided, however, that the inclusion of the interest in determining the cost of that asset and the amount of the interest so included is disclosed in a note to the accounts.

(4) In the case of current assets distribution costs may not be included in production costs.

The total figure to be depreciated, known as the **depreciable amount**, will consist of the cost of the asset less the scrap value. This depreciable amount needs to be spread over the useful life in proportion to the pattern of benefit. Once the depreciable amount has been found, with revision if necessary to take account of material improvements, several recognized methods exist for spreading, or allocating, this amount to the various years concerned. The more important possibilities are outlined below. It is essential to understand the implicit assumption that each method makes about the pattern of benefit arising, and therefore about the appropriate pattern of expense allocation.

Methods of calculating depreciation

Straight-line method

The depreciable amount is allocated on a straight-line basis, i.e. an equal amount is allocated to each year of the useful life. If an asset is revalued or materially improved then the new depreciable amount will be allocated equally over the remaining, possibly extended, useful life.

Activity 2

Using the straight-line method calculate the annual depreciation charge from the following data.

Cost ('basic' value figure)	£12 000
Useful life	4 years
Scrap value	£2000

Activity 2 feedback

$$\text{Annual charge} \quad = \frac{£12\,000 - £2000}{4}$$

$$= £2500$$

This is by far the most common method. It is the easiest to apply, and also the preparation of periodic, e.g. monthly, accounts for internal purposes is facilitated. This method assumes, within the limits of materiality, that the asset is equally useful, or beneficial, each year. Whether this assumption is as frequently justified as the common usage of the method suggests, is an open question.

Reducing-balance method

Under this method, depreciation each year is calculated by applying a constant percentage to the NBV brought forward from the previous year. (Note that this percentage is based on the cost less depreciation to date.) Given the cost (or valuation) starting figure, and the useful life and 'scrap' value figures, the appropriate percentage needed to make the net book value at the end of the useful life exactly equal to the scrap value can be found from a formula:

$$d = {}^{n}\sqrt{S/C}$$

where d is the depreciation percentage, n is the life in years, S is the scrap value and C is the cost (or basic value).

This formula is rarely used. In practice, when this method is used a standard 'round' figure is usually taken, shown by experience to be vaguely satisfactory for the particular type of asset under consideration. Notice, incidentally, that the formula, and the method, both fail to work when the scrap value is zero, and produce an extreme and obviously distorted allocation when the scrap value is very small.

Activity 3

Using the data of the previous activity, and assuming a depreciation percentage of 40%, calculate the depreciation charge for each of the four years using the reducing balance method.

Activity 3 feedback

Year 1	Cost	£12 000
	Depreciation 40%	4 800
Year 2	NBV	7 200
	Depreciation 40%	2 880
Year 3	NBV	4 320
	Depreciation 40%	1 728
Year 4	NBV	2 592
	Depreciation 40%	1 037
	NBV	£1 555

If the estimated scrap value turns out to be correct, then a 'profit' on disposal of £445 would be recorded also in year 4. This is an example of a reducing-charge method, or of an accelerated depreciation method. The charge is highest in the first year and gradually reduces over the asset's life. Several arguments can be advanced for preferring this approach to the straight-line method.

Activity 4

Suggest, and critically consider, arguments in favour of using the reducing balance method rather than the straight-line method.

Activity 4 feedback

Here are some possible thoughts.

1 It better reflects the typical benefit pattern, at least of some assets.
2 It could be argued that, where the pattern of benefit is assumed to be effectively constant, the appropriate 'expense', which needs to be correspondingly evenly matched, is not the pure depreciation element, but the sum of:
   (a) the pure depreciation element; and
   (b) the maintenance and repair costs.
   Since (b) will tend to increase as the asset gets older, it is necessary for (a) to be reduced as the asset gets older, in the hope that the total of the two will remain more or less constant. This may be a valid argument in the most general of terms, but of course there is no reason why an arbitrary percentage applied in one direction should even approximately compensate for flexible and 'chancy' repair costs in the other.
3 It better reflects the probable fact that the value (i.e. the market or resale value) of the asset falls more sharply in the earlier years. This argument, often advanced, is invalid in principle. Depreciation is concerned with appropriate allocation of expense, applying the matching convention. It is not concerned with an annual revaluation of the fixed assets, so whether or not a particular method is good or bad from this viewpoint is, or should be, irrelevant. So long as the original estimate of future benefit is still valid, the fact that current market value is small, at an intermediate time, is not of concern.

Some less common alternatives

Sum of the digits method

This is another example of a reducing-charge method. It is based on a convenient 'rule of thumb', and produces a pattern of depreciation charge somewhat similar to the reducing-balance method.

Using the same figures as before, we give the four years weights of 4, 3, 2 and 1, respectively and sum the total weights. In general terms we give the n years weights of n, $n - 1$, ..., 1, respectively, and sum the total weights, the sum being $n(n + 1)/2$. The depreciable amount is then allocated over the years in the proportion that each year's weighting bears to the total.

Activity 5

Use the sum of the digits method to calculate annual depreciation charges for the data in the earlier activities.

Activity 5 feedback

$4 + 3 + 2 + 1 = 10$ (the 'sum' of the 'digits')
Depreciable amount = £12 000 − £2000 = £10 000
Depreciation charges are:

Year 1 $4/10 \times 10\,000 = £4000$
      2        $3/10 \times 10\,000 = £3000$
      3        $2/10 \times 10\,000 = £2000$
      4        $1/10 \times 10\,000 = £1000$

This gives NBV figures in the balance sheet of £8000, £5000, £3000 and £2000 for year-ends 1–4, respectively.

Output or usage method

This is particularly suitable for assets where the rate of usage or rate of output can be easily measured. For example, a motor vehicle might be regarded as having a life of 100 000 miles, rather than a life of four years. The depreciable amount can then be allocated to each year in proportion to the recorded mileage, e.g. if 30 000 miles are covered in year 1, then 3/10 of the depreciable amount will be charged in year 1. The life of a machine could be defined in terms of machine hours. The annual charge would then be:

$$\text{Depreciable amount} \times \frac{\text{Machine hours used in the year}}{\text{Total estimated life in machine hours}}$$

Revaluation or arbitrary valuation

This approach is occasionally used with minor items such as loose tools. An estimated or perhaps purely arbitrary figure for the NRV of the items (in total) is chosen at the end of each year. Depreciation is then the difference between this figure and the figure from the previous year. Strictly, of course, this is not a method of depreciation at all, but a lazy alternative to it.

All of the above methods can be criticized on the grounds that they ignore the fact that the resources 'tied up' in the fixed asset concerned have an actual cost to the business in terms of interest paid, or an implied (opportunity) cost in terms of interest foregone. This could well be regarded as an essential expense that should be matched appropriately against the benefit from the asset. The 'actuarial' methods that attempt to take account of interest expense are complicated to apply and in financial accounting are hardly ever used.

Some misconceptions underlined

It must be remembered that depreciation is a process of matching expenses in proportion to benefits. Given that the depreciable amount has been agreed, the annual charge is based on actual or implied assumptions as to the pattern of benefit being derived, and nothing else. In simple book-keeping terms, all that is happening is that a transfer is being made from the fixed assets section in the balance sheet to the expenses section in the P&L account. And it is the expense that is being positively calculated, not the reduction in the fixed asset figure. It follows from this that:

1 The fixed asset figure for an intermediate year has no very obvious or useful meaning. It can only be defined in a roundabout way. For example, under historical cost (HC) accounting, it is the amount of the original cost not yet deemed to have been used, or not yet allocated. This intermediate figure is often called 'net book value', but it is *not* a value at all within the proper meaning of the word.

2 Depreciation has nothing to do with ensuring that the business can 'afford' to buy another asset when the first one becomes useless. This is true even if we ignore the likelihood of rising price levels. Depreciation does not increase the amount of any particular asset, cash or otherwise.

3 However, depreciation, like any other expense figure, does have the effect of retaining *resources* (or total assets) in the business. By reducing profit we reduce the maximum dividend payable (which would reduce resources) and therefore increase the 'minimum resources remaining' figure. This is, in fact, a particular illustration of the idea of capital maintenance discussed earlier (Chapter 3).

Activity 6

In the year to 31 December, Amy bought a new fixed asset and made the following payments in relation to it:

	£	£
Cost as per supplier's list	12 000	
less agreed discount	1 000	11 000
Delivery charge		100
Erection charge		200
Maintenance charge		300
Additional component to increase capacity		400
Replacement parts		250

Required:

(a) **State and justify the cost figure which should be used as the basis for depreciation.** (5 marks)

(b) **What does depreciation do, and why is it necessary?** (4 marks)

(c) **Briefly explain, without numerical illustration, how the straight-line and reducing balance methods of depreciation work. What different assumptions does each method make?** (5 marks)

(d) **Explain the term objectivity as used by accountants. To what extent is depreciation objective?** (5 marks)

(e) **It is common practice in published accounts in Germany to use the reducing balance method for a fixed asset in the early years of its life, and then to change to the straight-line method as soon as this would give a higher annual charge.**
   What do you think of this practice? Refer to relevant accounting conventions in your answer. (6 marks)

(**25 marks**)
(ACCA)

Activity 6 feedback

1 This figure should be the total cost of making the fixed asset usable, excluding all costs of actually using it. Therefore

$$11\,000 + 100 + 200 + 400 = £11\,700.$$

The additional component is cost of machine as it enhances the revenue earning capacity of the asset but the replacement parts are cost of using machine – hence the difference in treatment between the two. Maintenance is obviously a cost of usage.

2 Depreciation spreads the cost (or value) of an item over its useful life, in appropriate proportion to the benefit (usefulness). It is necessary in accordance with the matching convention – allocating expense against corresponding benefit, as part of the profit calculation.

3 The straight-line method charges a constant percentage of the cost (or value) each year. The reducing balance method charges a constant percentage of the net book value (cost less accumulated depreciation brought forward). Thus the straight-line method has a constant charge but the reducing balance method has a charge reducing each year of the asset life. The two methods therefore make different assumptions about the usefulness, the trend or pattern of benefit, of the fixed asset concerned.

4 Objectivity implies lack of bias. It removes the need for, and the possibility of, subjectivity, of personal opinion. For an accounting figure to be objective, it must be expected that all accountants would arrive at the same figure. Clearly the figure stated on an invoice has a high degree of objectivity. However, the calculation of depreciation is based on estimates of future life and future usefulness and is therefore highly subjective.

5 This practice can claim the advantage of greater prudence, as the expense is always the higher of the two possibilities. However, it seems to lack consistency. Perhaps more importantly, it obviously fails to attempt to follow the matching convention. It makes no attempt to make the trend of expenses consistent with the trend of benefit or usefulness. If the profit figure, or profit trend, is regarded as important, then it seems an unsatisfactory practice – at least to Anglo-Saxon eyes!

Government grants (SSAP 4)

Government grants represent one particular aspect of the problem of determining the 'cost' of fixed assets. They are the subject of a separate standard, SSAP 4. This was first issued in 1974, but a revised version appeared in 1990. This tended to be more explanatory, and involved a change in requirement which is discussed below.

The definitions given are very broadly based and indicate the intended generality of the SSAP.

> 21 *Government includes* government and inter-governmental agencies and similar bodies whether local, national or international.
>
> 22 *Government grants* are assistance by government in the form of cash or transfers of assets to an enterprise in return for past or future compliance with certain conditions relating to the operating activities of the enterprise.

Some 'basic concepts' are suggested, as follows:

> 4 The 'accruals' concept requires that revenue and costs are accrued, matched

with one another so far as their relationship can be established or justifiably assumed, and dealt with in the profit and loss account of the period to which they relate. Government grants should therefore be recognized in the profit and loss account so as to match them with the expenditure towards which they are intended to contribute.

5 The 'prudence' concept requires that revenue and profits are not anticipated, but are recognized by inclusion in the profit and loss account only when realized in the form either of cash or of other assets the ultimate cash realisation of which can be established with reasonable certainty. Accordingly, government grants should not be recognized in the profit and loss account until the conditions for their receipt have been complied with and there is reasonable assurance that the grant will be received.

6 In many cases, the grant-making body has the right to recover all or part of a grant paid if the enterprise has not complied with the conditions under which the grant was made. On the assumption that the enterprise is a going concern, the application of the prudence concept does not normally require postponement of the recognition of the grant in the profit and loss account solely because there is a possibility that it might have to be repaid in the future. The enterprise should consider regularly whether there is a likelihood of a breach of the conditions on which the grant was made. If such a breach has occurred, or appears likely to occur, and it is probable that some grant will have to be repaid, provision should be made for the liability.

In addition the SSAP points out that the application of paragraph 4 should not be influenced by the tax treatment. A grant taxed as income is not automatically income for accounting purposes.

Government grants may be of two types, revenue based and capital based. Revenue-based grants are intended to cover some of the costs of everyday 'revenue expenditure', for example usage costs. They present no accounting difficulties at all. They should simply be credited to the P&L account in the same period in which the relevant expenses are debited, using estimated figures if necessary. Capital-based grants are grants to cover some of the cost of a capital expenditure, i.e. they relate to fixed assets.

The original standard distinguished four possible ways of dealing with such grants in published accounts as follows:

1 to credit to P&L account the total amount of the grant immediately
2 to credit the amount of the grant to a non-distributable reserve
3 to credit the amount of the grant to revenue over the useful life of the asset by:
   (a) reducing the cost of the acquisition of the fixed asset by the amount of the grant; or
   (b) treating the amount of the grant as a deferred credit, a portion of which is transferred to revenue annually.

The first two methods were rejected on the grounds that they 'provide no correlation between the accounting treatment of the grant and the accounting treatment of the expenditure to which the grant relates'. The first method would increase the profits in the first year by the entire amount of the grant, failing to associate the grant with the useful life of the asset. It thus ignores both the prudence convention and the matching convention. The second method means that the grant will *never* affect the profit figure. It also therefore ignores the matching convention, and additionally leaves the 'non-distributable reserve' stuck in the balance sheet, presumably for ever!

The third and fourth methods are both acceptable, as they both follow and apply the matching convention. They both have exactly the same effect on reported annual profits, the differences only being concerned with balance sheet presentation.

Activity 7

Illustrate the effect of each of these acceptable methods, using the information below. Show the effect on profit, and on the balance sheet by means of relevant balance sheet extracts.

Cost of asset	£12 000
Expected useful life	4 years
Expected residual value	Nil
Government grant	£2000
Annual profits before depreciation and grants	£20 000

Activity 7 feedback

Method 3(a) (see p. 256)	£	£	£	£
Profit before depreciation, etc.	20 000	20 000	20 000	20 000
Depreciation	(2 500)	(2 500)	(2 500)	(2 500)
Profit	17 500	17 500	17 500	17 500
Balance sheet extract at year-end				
Fixed asset at (net) cost	10 000	10 000	10 000	10 000
Depreciation	(2 500)	(5 000)	(7 500)	(10 000)
NBV	7 500	5 000	2 500	0
Method 3(b) (see p. 256)				
Profit before depreciation, etc.	20 000	20 000	20 000	20 000
Depreciation	(3 000)	(3 000)	(3 000)	(3 000)
Grant released	500	500	500	500
Profit	17 500	17 500	17 500	17 500
Balance sheet extract at year-end				
Fixed asset at cost	12 000	12 000	12 000	12 000
Depreciation	3 000	6 000	9 000	12 000
NBV	9 000	6 000	3 000	0
Deferred credit				
Government grant	1 500	1 000	500	0

Activity 8

Which of these seems the more useful method, and why?

Activity 8 feedback

The third method (**3(a)**) has the obvious advantage of simplicity. No entries, and no thought, are required in the second and subsequent years. The fourth method, however (**3(b)**) does have some potential benefits, as outlined in the original 1974 SSAP:

The arguments in favour of the second alternative (crediting the amount of the grant to a deferred credit account, and releasing it to revenue over an extended period) are:

1 assets acquired at different times and locations are recorded on a uniform basis regardless of changes in government policy
2 control over the ordering, construction and maintenance of assets is based on the gross value
3 as capital allowances for tax purposes are normally calculated on the cost of an asset before deduction of the grant, adjustments of the depreciation charge shown in the accounts are avoided when computing the amount of deferred taxation.

We are now in a position to read and understand the actual required standard practice as stated in the revised 1990 version of the SSAP.

23 Subject to paragraph 24 of this statement, government grants should be recognized in the profit and loss account so as to match them with the expenditure towards which they are intended to contribute. In the absence of persuasive evidence to the contrary, government grants should be assumed to contribute towards the expenditure that is the basis for their payment. To the extent that grants are made as a contribution towards specific expenditure on fixed assets, they should be recognized over the expected useful economic lives of the related assets. Grants made to give immediate financial support or assistance to an enterprise or to reimburse costs previously incurred should be recognized in the profit and loss account of the period in which they become receivable. Grants made to finance the general activities of an enterprise over a specific period or to compensate for a loss of current or future income should be recognized in the profit and loss account of the period in respect of which they are paid.

24 The foregoing requirements are subject to the proviso that a government grant should not be recognized in the profit and loss account until the conditions for its receipt have been complied with and there is reasonable assurance that the grant will be received.

25 Where the recognition in the profit and loss account of part or all of a grant that has been received is deferred, the amount so deferred should be treated as deferred income. To the extent that the grant is made as a contribution towards expenditure on a fixed asset, in principle it may be deducted from the purchase price or production cost of that asset. The CCAB has received Counsel's opinion, however, that the option to deduct government grants from the purchase price or production cost of fixed assets is not available to companies governed by the accounting and reporting requirements of the Companies Act 1985, as outlined in paragraph 34.

26 Grants relating to leased assets in the accounts of lessors should be accounted for in accordance with the requirements of SSAP 21 'Accounting for leases and hire purchase contracts'.

27   Potential liabilities to repay grants either in whole or in part in specified circumstances should only be provided for to the extent that repayment is probable. The repayment of a government grant should be accounted for by setting off the repayment against any unamortised deferred income relating to the grant. Any excess should be charged immediately to the profit and loss account.

The disclosure requirements of the standard are as follows:

28   The following information should be disclosed in the financial statements:
   (a)   the accounting policy adopted for government grants
   (b)   the effects of government grants on the results for the period and/or the financial position of the enterprise
   (c)   where the results of the period are affected materially by the receipt of forms of government assistance other than grants, the nature of that assistance and, to the extent that the effects on the financial statements can be measured, an estimate of those effects.

29   Potential liabilities to repay grants in specified circumstances should, if necessary, be disclosed in accordance with paragraph 16 of SSAP 18 'Accounting for contingencies'.

The wording of paragraph 25 is interesting. It is clear that 'in principle' the ASC regarded both the methods discussed and illustrated above as acceptable (as did the original 1974 version). Indeed in the explanatory note section of the 1990 SSAP the ASC explicitly state that 'it is considered that both treatments are acceptable and capable of giving a true and fair view'. However, the requirement of paragraph 25 is quite specific that only one method, the deferred income method (3(b) in the activity), is allowed under the standard.

The nearest we get to a detailed justification for this is in paragraph 34, part of the section dealing with the company law requirements. In full this section reads as follows:

32   The balance sheet formats in Schedule 4 require that accruals and deferred income should be shown either under the heading 'Creditors' or separately as 'Accruals and deferred income'. This is relevant to the disclosure of deferred income in relation to government grants. (Standard paragraph 25.)

33   Paragraph 12 of Schedule 4 requires that the amount of any item shall be determined on a prudent basis and, in particular, that only profits realized at the balance sheet date shall be included in the profit and loss account. (Paragraph 91 of the Schedule defines realized profits in relation to a company's accounts as 'such profits of the company as fall to be treated as realized profits for the purposes of those accounts in accordance with principles generally accepted with respect to the determination for accounting purposes of realized profits at the time when those accounts are prepared'.) (Standard paragraph 24.)

34   Paragraph 17 of Schedule 4 requires that, subject to any provision for depreciation or diminution in value, the amount to be included in the balance sheet in respect of any fixed asset shall be its purchase price or production cost. Paragraph 26(1) states that the purchase price of an asset shall be determined by adding to the actual price paid any expenses incidental to its acquisition. The CCAB has received Counsel's opinion that these paragraphs have the

effect of prohibiting enterprises to which the legislation applies from accounting for grants made as a contribution towards expenditure on fixed assets by deducting the amount of the grant from the purchase price or production cost of the related asset. (Standard paragraph 25.)

35 Paragraph 50(2) of Schedule 4 provides that 'The following information shall be given with respect to any other contingent liability not provided for:

(a) the amount or estimated amount of that liability

(b) its legal nature; and

(c) whether any valuable security has been provided by the company in connection with that liability and if so, what'. (Standard paragraph 29.)

It seems to us that paragraph 34 represents a very narrow-minded view of the position – a typical legal perspective dare one say? – surely a purchase price can have negative elements and adjustments as well as positive ones. If you pay £100 and receive £20 how much is the 'actual price paid'? However you should make your own mind up about this. Just as importantly, make sure you are quite clear about what the SSAP says and means.

Depreciation and FRS 15

The first standard dealing with depreciation was SSAP 12 'Accounting for depreciation' first issued in 1977 by the ASC. This was further amended in 1981 and superseded by a completely revised version, SSAP 12 (revised), in 1987. SSAP 12 (revised) was withdrawn in February 1999 on the issue of FRS 15 'Tangible Fixed Assets' which is effective for AP beginning on or after 23.3.2000. SSAP 12 was generally regarded as broadly satisfactory by the ASB but it was felt that several requirements of the SSAP needed further clarification. The opportunity was also taken to collect together in one standard accounting rules for initial recognition, valuation and depreciation of tangible fixed assets excepting investment properties.

The changes from SSAP 12 to FRS 15 in the area of depreciation were mainly concerned with the issues of:

- Depreciation of tangible fixed assets increasing in value. Several companies, holding tangible fixed assets that were increasing in value were not depreciating them, which the ASB deemed to be against the spirit of depreciation.
- Split depreciation. Several companies were charging depreciation on the historical cost of the asset to the profit and loss account and that part relating to any upward valuation of the asset to the reserves. The ASB obtained legal opinion that this was prohibited by the EU 4th Directive.
- Estimate of useful economic life and residual value. The ASB reiterated the need for these estimates to be reviewed regularly, for changes in life to be accounted for prospectively over the remaining life and residual value to be based on prices prevailing at acquisition or latest revaluation date.
- Non-depreciation of tangible fixed assets particularly property. A practice had arisen whereby tangible fixed assets that were maintained or refurbished regularly, thereby extending significantly the useful economic life or maintaining the residual value need not be depreciated. The ASB deemed that this maintenance and refurbishment did not negate the need for depreciation to be charged.

We will deal with all of these issues in more detail as we work through the standard in respect of depreciation.

Scope

FRS 15 applies to all tangible fixed assets, with the exception of investment properties which we will deal with later. Thus intangible fixed assets such as research and development and goodwill are not covered by this standard. In addition entities applying the Financial Reporting Standards for Smaller Entities (FRSSE) are exempt.

Definitions

FRS 15 defines *depreciation* as:

> The measure of the cost or revalued amount of the economic benefits of the tangible fixed asset that have been consumed during the period. Consumption includes the wearing out, using up or other reduction in the useful economic life of a tangible fixed asset whether arising from use, effluxion of time or obsolescence through either changes in technology or demand for the goods and services produced by the asset. (para. 2 FRS 15).

Activity 9

The definition of depreciation given in SSAP 12 (revised) was:

> The measure of the wearing out, consumption or other reduction in the useful economic life of a fixed asset whether arising from use, effluxion of time or obsolescence through technological or market changes.

Identify the changes in the definition of depreciation from SSAP 12 to FRS 15.

Feedback 9

The key change in the definition is to make it quite clear that depreciation is about matching and the accruals technique. It is not about deciding on a new value for the asset but about identifying the economic benefits consumed. In addition the SSAP 12 definition seemed to be indicating that depreciation should be measured in years – 'the measure of the reduction in the useful economic life'! Note that this change in economic life has now been moved to aid the description of consumption. The latest definition clearly focuses on the consumption of economic benefits.

Useful economic life is now defined as 'the period over which the entity expects to derive economic benefit from that asset' (para 3). The key change from the old definition here is that entity has been substituted for 'present owner'. This accords with the ASB's emphasis on substance over form as it is not necessarily the owner who will be recording the tangible fixed asset in his balance sheet but that entity who in substance has the risks and rewards associated with it in accordance with FRS 5.

Residual value of a tangible fixed asset is defined as 'the net realisable value of an asset at the end of its useful economic life. Residual values are based on prices prevailing at the date of acquisition (or revaluation) of the asset and do not take account of expected future price changes' (FRS 15 para 3). This is virtually the same as the SSAP 12 definition but emphasises the fact that future price changes must not be taken on board in the residual value. It must be based on prices prevailing when this estimate is being made.

The last definition to deal with here is *Depreciable Amount* which is defined as 'the cost of a tangible fixed asset (or, where an asset is revalued, the revalued amount) less its residual value' (FRS 10 para 2).

Accounting treatment of depreciation

This is dealt with in paragraphs 77 to 96 of FRS 15. Paragraph 78 identifies that the fundamental objective of depreciation 'is to reflect in operating profit the cost of the use of the tangible fixed asset (i.e. amount of economic benefits consumed) in the period. This requires a charge to operating profit even if the asset has risen in value or been revalued. Note here the emphasis on consumption of economic benefits again and that an asset rising in value must still be depreciated. This is the ASB's response, in part, to the first issue we identified regarding the changes from SSAP 12 to FRS 15.

Activity 10

Two companies each purchase an equivalent tangible fixed asset on 1.1.20X1 costing £1m. Accounting year ends for reporting are 31st December. On the 1.1.20X3 company B revalues the asset to £2m in accordance with FRS 15. Show the depreciation charges in the financial reports of both companies for all years from 20X1 to end of 20X3. Both companies estimate the useful economic life as 50 years and the residual value as zero and charge depreciation on a straight-line basis. The revaluation of the asset by company B does not change these two estimates.

Feedback activity 10

	A £000	B £000
Depreciation charge end 20X1	20	20
Depreciation charge end 20X2	20	20
Depreciation charge end 20X3	20	41.7

The depreciation charge for company B in year 3 is calculated by dividing the depreciable amount i.e. the revalued amount, £2m, less estimated residual value, £0, over the remaining useful economic life, 48 years. This is made quite clear in paragraph 79 of the standard: 'where an asset has been revalued the current period's depreciation charge is based on the revalued amount and the remaining useful life'. Note that due to the revaluation of the asset, company B will be reducing its profits by £21 700 more than company A. This could be regarded as a disincentive to revalue assets. One method of dealing with this disincentive in the past has been to use a method of split depreciation. This is where that part of the depreciation charge that corresponds to the revaluation movement is charged to the Statement of Recognized Gains and Losses (STRGL) and thus, the part relating to the original historical cost only is charged to the profit and loss account. Thus in the example above, company B would try to charge £21 700 to the STRGL and £20 000 only to the profit and loss account as per company A. Several companies have used the technique of split depreciation but FRS 15 makes it quite clear that this is prohibited by articles 33.3 and 35.1 (c)(cc) of the EU Fourth Directive. Curiously the Companies Act 1985 seems to permit split depreciation:

'The amount of the provision for depreciation may be the historical cost amount instead of the adjusted amount, provided that the amount of any difference between the two is shown separately in the profit and loss account or in a note to the accounts.' (para. 32(3))

We noted in our discussion of depreciation on p. 249 that three factors in the calculation of the depreciation charge required us to make estimates: pattern of consumption (depreciation method), useful economic life and residual value of the asset. We need to be aware of how to deal, in accounting terms, with changes in these estimates but first it would be worth while considering the factors that could indicate a change in any of these. Paragraph 80 of FRS 15 states:

Consequently all the following factors need to be considered in determining the useful economic life, residual life and depreciation method of an asset:
- the expected usage of the asset by the entity, assessed by reference to the asset's expected capacity or physical output
- the expected physical deterioration of the asset through use or effluxion of time; this will depend upon the repair and maintenance programme of the entity both when the asset is in use and when it is idle
- economic or technological obsolescence from changes or improvements in production, or a change in the market demand for the product or service output of that asset
- legal or similar limits on the use of the asset, such as the expiry dates of related leases.

Change in method

Accounting requirements for a change in method of providing depreciation are dealt with very thoroughly in paragraph 82 of the standard. There is one requirement that has to be met before we can make the change, and that is that the new method must give a fairer presentation of the results and of the financial position. This is of course a subjective decision. The carrying amount of the tangible fixed asset is then depreciated using the revised method over the remaining useful economic life, beginning in the period in which the change is made. The ASB do not define carrying amount but we will interpret this as being the net book value on the balance sheet.

Activity 11

A tangible fixed asset purchased on 1.1.X1 for £250 000 has an estimated useful life of 5 years, a residual value of £26 840 and is to be depreciated using the reducing balance method. On the 2.2.X3 the directors of the entity take the view that the use of the straight-line method to depreciate the asset would better reflect the consumption of economic benefits. Show the charges to the profit and loss for the asset over its useful life, assuming life and residual value do not change. Accounting period ends on the 31 December each year.

Feedback 11

Using the reducing balance method formula given at p. 251 gives a depreciation percentage of 36%. By the 2.2.X3 the carrying amount of the asset in the books will be £102 400 i.e. £250 000 – £90 000 (dep. X1) – £57 600 (dep. X2). The remaining life of the asset is now 3 years and residual value remains at £26 840, thus depreciation on a straight-line basis for the next 3 years will be £25 187pa.

The FRS requires a disclosure in connection with the change in method as follows:

> Where there has been a change in the depreciation method used, the effect, if material, should be disclosed in the period of change. The reason for the change should also be disclosed. (para. 102).

Note particularly that FRS 15 does not regard a change in depreciation method as a change in accounting policy within the terms of SSAP 2 (Chapter 15). The change does not therefore give rise to a prior year's adjustment within the terms of FRS 3 (Chapter 26).

Useful lives

The ASC was particularly concerned with the failure of companies to use realistic estimates of useful lives of fixed assets. Many companies had developed the habit of deliberately underestimating asset lives, therefore artificially reducing profits in the earlier years of the asset's realistic life (and increasing profit at the end). This habit was ostensibly justified on the grounds either of prudence or of being a rough and ready way of reducing profits in the early years by an additional amount to take account of rising prices. The revised SSAP12 therefore stated, 'it is essential that asset lives are estimated on a realistic basis'. FRS 15 is much more explicit on this issue as para. 93 shows: 'The useful life of a tangible fixed asset should be reviewed at the end of each reporting period and revised if expectations are significantly different from previous estimates. If a useful life is revised, the carrying amount of the tangible fixed asset at the date of revision should be depreciated over the revised remaining useful economic life.' Thus if we do change the useful economic life of an asset we carry on depreciating from where we are but with a new life. There is no prior year adjustment required.

Residual values

Similar requirements are given for residual values.

> Where the residual value is material it should be reviewed at the end of each reporting period to take account of reasonably expected technological changes based on prices prevailing at the date of acquisition (or revaluation). A change in its estimated residual value should be accounted for prospectively over the asset's remaining useful economic life, except to the extent that the asset has been impaired at the balance sheet date. (Note we will deal with impairment later at p. 293). Again we will carry on depreciating from where we are but with a new residual value in the calculation.

Disclosure requirements in respect of the above are:

> where material, the financial effect of a change during the period in either the estimate of useful economic lives or the estimate of residual values.

It is worth noting here that the ASB still requires that the reassessed residual value be at price levels that existed when the asset was purchased or revalued, and that if this is not possible, then current values should be used. Thus residual value based on prices at the reassessment date can only be used if the current price is below the original estimate of residual value. Thus if the residual value at purchase was £1000, on reviewing residual values five years after purchase the value was £2000, but at prices prevailing at that point, it would not be correct to revise the residual value to £2000. Price increases over the five years would have to be deducted from the new estimate. If the price base when the asset was bought was 100 and is now 150 then the residual value would be recorded as £1333 (2000 × 100/150).

Depreciation of land and buildings

A good deal of debate and controversy has arisen in the last few years over the question of depreciation on land and buildings. SSAP 12 contained a major change from the practice followed in many company accounts, in that it required depreciation of all buildings (though not of all land they stood on). This caused considerable controversy at that time especially with regard to properties held for investment purposes rather than for use within the business. These are now dealt with in a separate standard, SSAP 19, which we consider later (page 276).

The treatment of freehold land has not changed from SSAP 12 to FRS 15, which states that 'with certain exceptions, such as sites used for extractive purposes or landfill, land has an unlimited life and therefore is not depreciated'. That seems clear enough but then so did the statement in SSAP 12 that all buildings should be depreciated. However after the issue of SSAP 12 many companies still did not depreciate buildings on the grounds that they were increasing in value or were being maintained to such a level that their useful economic life was infinite and therefore no depreciation was required. The increase in value issue has already been covered (refer Activity 10). The FRS had the following to say on the maintenance issue:

> Subsequent expenditure on a tangible fixed asset that maintains or enhances the previously assessed standard of performance of the asset does not negate the need to charge depreciation. That seems clear enough! Depreciate all buildings. However companies are still likely to be able to make the following statement in their accounting policies:
>
> In the case of freehold and long leasehold properties annual depreciation would not be material in these accounts and hence no depreciation is provided.

Activity 12

Identify the circumstances where the depreciation charge on property would be immaterial.

Feedback 12

The depreciation charge depends on the cost or valuation of the property, estimated residual value and useful economic life. Thus the depreciation charge is likely to be immaterial where the residual value estimate is fairly close to the cost or valuation of the property or the asset has a long life.

FRS 15 at paragraph 90 states that the only grounds for not charging depreciation are on the basis of immateriality, but both the depreciation charge for the year and accumulated charge have to be immaterial. The depreciation is immaterial if it would not reasonably influence the decisions of a user of the accounts. We wait to see what company reporting practice will be in this area.

Disclosure requirements for depreciation

These are quite straightforward and cover:

> Method used; useful economic lives or depreciation rates used; total charge for the period; and the cumulative amount.

Initial measurement and tangible fixed assets

It is perhaps surprising, but prior to the issue of FRS 15 there was no standard that dealt with the issue of the initial recognition and measurement of tangible fixed assets. Practice had arisen that permitted companies to measure these assets at cost or a revalued amount, which was acceptable under the Companies Act. However differences had arisen in what constituted cost, how often revaluations should be revised, if at all, whether all assets should be revalued or could the company 'cherry pick' those assets it wished to revalue. All in all the information that appeared in a company's fixed asset schedule was a confusing mixture of values that rendered comparison over years and between companies somewhat difficult if not misleading.

FRS 15 gives us some useful definitions as follows:

> Tangible fixed assets:- assets that have physical substance and are held for use in the production or supply of goods or services, for rental to others, or for administrative purposes on a continuing basis in the reporting entity's activities
>
> Class of tangible fixed assets:– a category of tangible fixed assets having a similar nature, function or use in the business of the entity.

However FRS 15 does not define cost (the exposure draft to FRS 15, FRED 17 did). It actually takes the standard 13 paragraphs, 4 pages, to identify what cost is. Basically a tangible fixed asset has to be measured at its initial cost, which can only include costs that are directly attributable to bringing the asset into working condition.

Activity 13

Identify costs that are directly attributable to bringing an asset into working condition.

Feedback 13

A fairly difficult task.

- The first cost to identify is the purchase price but is this before or after discounts – FRS 15 states after trade discounts and rebates.
- Other costs would be stamp duty, import duties, purchase taxes (but not refundable VAT), delivery costs (transport and handling charges for example), installation costs, professional fees of lawyers, architects, engineers, accountants, etc.

- Once acquired the asset will probably need siting so we can also include site pre-paration and clearance costs and if a legal obligation or contractual responsibility exists then also the costs of dismantling and removing the asset and restoring the site are part of cost. Legal obligation and contractual responsibility are dealt with under Chapter 23.

- A question then arises over administration and other general overheads and the test here is whether these costs would have been avoided if this specific asset had not been bought. In general these costs can be regarded as not directly attributable but the decision is some-what subjective.

- For a self-constructed asset directly attributable labour costs etc would need including as would incremental costs to the entity that would have been avoided if the tangible asset had not been constructed.

- Abnormal costs such as design errors, industrial disputes, idle capacity, wasted materi-als, are not regarded as part of cost according to FRS 15. It appears we have to assume a normal/ordinary acquisition or self-construction where every aspect runs smoothly. These abnormal costs are not to be regarded as directly attributable to bringing the asset into working condition for its intended use.

- Commissioning costs and start up costs are acceptable as long as we can make the judge-ment that without such costs the asset would be incapable of operating at normal lev-els. Another subjective decision.

- Finance costs can also be viewed as directly attributable and therefore part of cost as, if we hadn't constructed this asset, these costs would have been avoided.

Overall the judgement of what constitutes cost is dependent on our view of those costs that could have been avoided if we hadn't acquired or self-constructed the asset.

Finance costs

However the FRS, having identified those items above as part of cost, then becomes schiz-ophrenic as it states:

> an entity *need not* capitalise finance costs. However, if an entity adopts a policy of capitalisation of finance costs, then it should be applied consistently to all tan-gible fixed assets where finance costs fall to be capitalized in accordance with the FRS.

This will lead to a lack of comparability between those entities that do capitalize and those that don't. The reasons given for capitalizing finance costs are:

- These costs can clearly be demonstrated to be a directly attributable cost, they would be avoided if the asset had not been constructed. We quite agree but then so would finance costs incurred on the acquisition of an asset and these according to the FRS cannot be capitalized as they do not relate to the construction of an asset. Capitalization of finance costs for acquired assets is also prohibited by the requirement in para. 12 of the FRS:

> Capitalisation of directly attributable costs should cease when substantially all the activities that are necessary to get the tangible fixed asset ready for use are complete, even if the asset has not yet been brought into use.

- The inclusion of finance costs in cost aids comparability between those assets that are bought and those that are self-constructed. This is because, presumably, a sensible businessman who is selling an asset will have included his finance costs, but he will also have included his overheads and a profit element so the argument of comparability fails somewhat.

■ The accounts are more likely to reflect the true success or failure of the project, because once capitalized the finance cost will then be depreciated, and matched with the future benefits achieved whereas immediate charge of the finance cost to the profit and loss account would not provide a true and fair view.

The main reason the ASB did not mandate the capitalisation of borrowing costs was because, in theory, this would also require the capitalisation of notional interest costs. Finance costs are generally not clearly identifiable to one project and where this is the case a notional interest per project would have to be identified.

Separate components

FRS 15 provides us with a definition of a fixed asset that appears quite straightforward. However para. 83 of the standard suggests that what we might think of as one fixed asset can actually be two or more.

> Where the tangible fixed asset comprises two or more major components with substantially different useful economic lives, each component should be accounted for separately for depreciation purposes and depreciated over its individual useful economic life.

One such example of an asset is a building where the land and the building itself are treated as separate assets but this paragraph permits further division of assets. For example, from the initial purchase of an aircraft we can separate out a portion as overhaul costs and depreciate these over say 3 years with the rest of the cost depreciated over 25 years. This issue of separate components is highly relevant when we consider subsequent expenditure on a fixed asset.

Subsequent expenditure

The issue here concerns the differentiation between repairs and improvement expenditure. If subsequent costs of a tangible fixed asset can be regarded as an improvement to the asset then a case can certainly be made for capitalizing these costs and thus avoiding a charge to the P&L account in the current year of spending. Prior to the issue of FRS 15 it was felt that companies were arbitrarily deciding on what was repair or improvement spending depending on where they wanted the expense charged: repair, charge to P&L in one year; improvement, spread charge over future P&L accounts by means of depreciation. The FRS requirements in this area are:

> Paragraph 34 'Subsequent expenditure to ensure that the tangible fixed asset maintains its previously assessed standard of performance should be recognised in the profit and loss account as it is incurred'. This is what we would regard as repairs and covers such items as routine painting and overhaul without which the useful economic life or residual value of the asset would be reduced thus increasing the depreciation charge.
>
> Paragraph 36 'Subsequent expenditure should be capitalised in three circumstances:
>
> (a) where the subsequent expenditure provides an enhancement of the econom-

ic benefits of the tangible fixed asset in excess of the previously assessed standard of performance

(b) where a component of the tangible fixed asset that has been treated separately for depreciation purposes and depreciated over its individual useful economic life, is replaced or restored

(c) where the subsequent expenditure relates to a major inspection or overhaul of a tangible fixed asset that restores the economic benefits of the asset that have been consumed by the entity and have already been reflected in depreciation.'

Activity 14

Identify whether the following items of expenditure should be charged to the P&L account in the year or capitalized in accordance with FRS 15

1 Service costs relating to a loading shovel.
2 Overhaul of a concrete pan mixer.
3 Replacement of the lining of a blast furnace treated as a separate component when the asset was first purchased.
4 Replacement of the factory roof identified as a separate asset 5 years ago.
5 Replacement of a factory roof not identified as a separate component.
6 Repainting of building.
7 Installation of new processes on the production line that result in substantial reductions in operating costs.
8 New machinery parts that give rise to no improvement in quality of output.

Activity 14 feedback

1 This is repairs and maintenance, charge to P&L, as presumably the asset will only be maintained to its previous standard of performance.
2 Again repairs and maintenance, charge to P&L, unless the overhaul restores economic benefits previously consumed.
3 Improvement, capitalize as this was recognized as a separate component.
4 Improvement, capitalize for the same reason as 3.
5 This cannot be capitalized as the component was not separately identified when the asset was first capitalized. If the replacement of the roof is to a higher standard than previously and it will enhance the economic benefits received from the asset over and above the assessed standard at the start of its life then capitalization is permitted.
6 Repairs and maintenance.
7 Improvement with enhanced economic benefits therefore capitalize.
8 Repairs and maintenance as no enhancement in economic benefits.

Note that many of the answers to the above activity depend on the separate identification of components when the asset was first capitalized. The following activity illustrates this further.

> # Activity 15
>
> An aircraft is required by law to be overhauled every three years and without this overhaul the aircraft cannot fly. The overhaul expenditure is estimated at £300 000 every three years. How should the overhaul costs be treated in accordance with FRS 15?

Activity 15 feedback

From the initial cost of the aircraft, £300 000 can be treated as a separate component and will need to be depreciated over 3 years. The remainder of the cost of the aircraft will be capitalized and depreciated over its useful economic life. After three years the overhaul cost is then capitalized again and depreciated. If the £300 000 had not been recognized as a separate component originally then the overhaul costs would not be capitalized but charged to the P&L account in the year.

Revaluation of tangible fixed assets

The FRS covers this issue in 20 paragraphs and we would suggest that if you want the full details you read the FRS. The main points covered in the FRS are as follows:

- Tangible fixed assets should be revalued only where the entity adopts a policy of revaluation. The ASB have thus left revaluation optional and the user will have to be aware when making any comparisons.
- Revaluation need only be applied to a class of tangible fixed assets not all classes. A class of tangible fixed assets is defined as a category of tangible fixed assets having a similar nature, function or use in the business of the entity. This means that a company could, if it wished, revalue its land and no other asset.
- The revaluation amount or carrying amount should be the current value of the asset as at the balance sheet date. Current value is the lower of replacement cost and recoverable amount and we would reference you here back to p. 81 as this is actually deprival value!
- The FRS does not insist on annual valuations but suggests that at least for properties a full valuation should take place every 5 years with an interim in year 3 or for non-specialized properties a rolling basis can be used over a five year cycle. Other assets can be updated by the use of appropriate indices where these are judged to be reasonably reliable by the directors.

The above requirements of the FRS are an improvement in that companies, once they have chosen a policy of revaluation, must now keep their asset values up to date and they cannot 'cherry pick' individual assets to revalue, they must revalue a whole class. However because the ASB did not mandate a policy of revaluation we are left with problems of comparability between companies.

The FRS is quite detailed on the valuation basis that should be used for properties. Basically it separates property into three elements and attaches a different valuation base to each. Thus specialized properties, which cover oil refineries, power stations, hospitals, schools, museums, etc. should be valued at depreciated replacement cost, non-specialized properties at existing use value (EUV), and properties surplus to requirement at open market value (OMV). EUV is defined in the FRS and supposedly most closely approaches replacement cost and should reflect the replacement of the service potential rather than alternative uses. In general, i.e. for non-specialized properties EUV should be less than or equal to OMV as the OMV will reflect alternate uses.

Gains and losses on revaluation and disposal

This is another difficult area within the FRS and is problematical because gains and losses need to be allocated between the P&L account and the STRGL. The prime aim of the FRS here is to ensure that revaluation gains are only recognized in the P&L account if they reverse previous revaluation losses on the same asset that were recognized in the P&L account. The amount of gain that can be recognized however is reduced by the amount of depreciation that would have been recognized over the period without the revaluation loss. The following example illustrates this complicated issue.

Example

An asset original cost £100, useful economic life 10 years, residual value £0 is depreciated on a straight-line basis. At the beginning of year 3 the current value is assessed as £60 and at the end of year 4 it is assessed at £65. Show the entries in the P&L account and the STRGL over the life of the asset.

Answer

For year 1 and 2 there will be a depreciation charge of £10 to P&L.
NBV at end of year 2 = £80.
Beginning of year 3 asset revalued to £60, the impairment of £20 charged to P&L.
Depreciation charge year 3 = 60/8 = £7.5
NBV end of year 3 = £52.5
Depreciation charge year 4 = £7.5
NBV end of year 4 = £45
But current value end of year 4 assessed as £65 = revaluation gain of £20
NBV of asset at end of year 4 assuming no impairment at year 3 = £60. On revaluation to £65 this would represent a gain of £5.
Thus STRGL £5, P&L £15 (i.e. the revaluation gain of £20 is reduced by the further depreciation of $2 \times (10 - 7.5) = 5$ that would have been required without impairment)
In other words a gain is shown in the STRGL equal to the difference between current value now and what the NBV of the asset would have been without the previous impairment.

The FRS states the following in respect of losses:

> All revaluation losses that are caused by a clear consumption of economic benefits should be recognised in the profit and loss account. Other revaluation losses should be recognised:
> (a) in the statement of total recognised gains and losses until the carrying amount reaches its depreciated historical cost: and
> (b) thereafter, in the profit and loss account unless it can be demonstrated that the recoverable amount of the asset is greater than its revalued amount, in which case the loss should be recognised in the statement of total recognised gains and losses to the extent that the recoverable amount of the asset is greater than its revalued amount.' (para. 65). We have to remember here that recoverable amount is the higher of net realisable value and value in use.

Activity 16

A company purchases two pieces of land each for £10 000. After 2 years one piece is revalued to £20 000 and after a further 2 years the carrying amount of both assets is assessed at £7000. Identify how the above movements on the assets would be recorded in the company's books in accordance with FRS 15.

Activity 16 feedback

		Land 1		Land 2
		£000		£000
Historical cost		10		10
Revaluation (recognized in STRGL)		0		10
Carrying amount year 3		10		20
Carrying amount year 5		7		7
Loss		3		13
Historical cost		10		10
Loss recognized	P&L	3	thus STRGL	10
			P&L	3

The above is in accordance with FRS 15 unless it can be demonstrated that the recoverable amount of the asset is greater than its revalued amount.

Activity 17

Assume in the above activity that the recoverable amount of both assets is £8000 at the end of year 5. Identify where the loss of £3000 and £13 000 would be recognized in accordance with FRS 15.

Activity 17 feedback

For the first piece of land £1000 can be recognized in the STRGL, the difference between recoverable amount and revalued amount. The other £2000 is recognized in the P&L account. For the second piece £11 000 will be recognized in the STRGL and £2000 in the P&L account.

A more complicated example of reporting of revaluation gains and losses is included in the FRS and we reproduce it here for you.

Example – reporting revaluation gains and losses
Assumption

A non-specialised property cost £1 million and has a useful life of 10 years and no residual value. It is depreciated on a straight-line basis and revalued annually. The entity has a policy of calculating depreciation based on the opening book amount. At the end of years 1 and 2 the asset has an EUV of £1 080 000 and £700 000, respectively. At the end of year 2, the recoverable amount of the asset is £760 000 and its depreciated historical cost is

£800 000. There is no obvious consumption of economic benefits in year 2, other than that accounted for through the depreciation charge.

Accounting treatment under modified historical cost

	Year 1 £000	Year 2 £000
Opening book amount	1000	1080
Depreciation	(100)	(120)*
Adjusted book amount	900	960
Revaluation gain (loss)		
• recognized in the STRGL	180	(220)
• recognized in the profit and loss account	—	(40)
Closing book amount	1080	700

*As the remaining useful economic life of the asset is nine years, the depreciation charge in year 2 is 1/9th of the opening book amount (£1 080 000/9 = £120 000).

In Year 1, after depreciation of £100 000, a revaluation gain of £180 000 is recognized in the statement of total recognized gains and losses, in accordance with paragraph 63.

In Year 2, after a depreciation charge of £120 000, the revaluation loss on the property is £260 000. According to paragraph 65, where there is not a clear consumption of economic benefits, revaluation losses should be recognized in the statement of total recognized gains and losses until the carrying amount reaches its depreciated historical cost. Therefore, the fall in value from the adjusted book amount (£960 000) to depreciated historical cost (£800 000) of £160 000 is recognized in the statement of total recognized gains and losses.

The rest of the revaluation loss, £100 000 (i.e. the fall in value from depreciated historical cost (£800 000) to the revalued amount (£700 000)), should be recognized in the profit and loss account, unless it can be demonstrated that recoverable amount is greater than the revalued amount. In this case, recoverable amount of £760 000 is greater than the revalued amount of £700 000 by £60 000. Therefore £60 000 of the revaluation loss is recognized in the statement of total recognized gains and losses, rather than the profit and loss account – giving rise to a total revaluation loss of £220 000 (£60 000 + £160 000) that is recognized in the statement of total recognized gains and losses. The remaining loss (representing the fall in value from depreciated historical cost of £800 000 to recoverable amount of £760 000) of £40 000 is recognized in the profit and loss account.

Reporting gains and losses on disposal

FRS 15 states the following on this issue:

> The profit and loss on the disposal of a tangible fixed asset should be accounted for in the P&L account of the period in which the disposal occurs as the difference between the net sale proceeds and the carrying amount, whether carried at historical cost (less any provisions made) or at a valuation.

This was a change from FRED 17 which proposed amending the carrying amount of the disposed asset immediately prior to disposal to its disposal proceeds and accounting for the resulting gain or loss in accordance with the previous section.

Activity 18

Show the entries to be made in the accounts in accordance with FRS 15 for the disposal of two pieces of land both sold for £110 000. Both pieces had been bought at £100 000 but one had been revalued to £200 000. Comment on the accounting result.

Activity 18 feedback

The non-revalued piece of land will show on disposal a gain of £10 000 which will be recorded in the P&L account for the period in which the disposal occurred.

The revalued piece of land will show a loss of £90 000 which again will be recognized in the P&L account for the period in which the disposal occurred.

The above appears inequitable but the FRS ensures that companies keep asset values up to date or they will have an increased loss to take to the P&L account in the period of disposal. The company, for the second piece of land, should have revalued the asset at the end of the previous year to say £120 000, and charged the £80 000 loss in value to the STRGL, as this reverses a previous upward revaluation, and then only £10 000 would be charged as a loss to the P&L account of the period of disposal.

Disclosures

Where any class of tangible fixed asset has been revalued disclosure details are required in relation to the valuer, the basis of the valuation, date and amount, and the depreciated historical cost.

Renewals accounting

This method of accounting is permitted by FRS 15 for infrastucture systems or networks. An example of such a system or network is the electricity supply system. Several assets within the system, such as power stations, relay stations, etc. can be identified as separate assets and capitalized and depreciated in accordance with their economic useful life to the entity, but the system also consists of wires and other small components without which the system would be useless. It would appear sensible to capitalize the expenditure on such items in the system but the essential question is at what value. Renewals accounting is a technique whereby the steady state expenditure required to maintain the operating capability of the system is treated as the annual depreciation charge for the year. The actual expenditure on the system per annum is the amount capitalized each year. Several commentators argue that renewals accounting does not reflect the economic benefits of the asset consumed in the year. We leave you to ponder this and the fact that the ASB have restricted the use of renewals accounting to situations where:

- the system or network is maintained at a specified level of service
- the level of expenditure required to maintain the operating capacity or service capability of the system or network is calculated from an asset management plan that is certified by a person who is appropriately qualified and independent
- the network or system is in a mature state.

The Companies Act 1985

It was only in 1981 that the Companies Act made the provision of depreciation compulsory. The 1981 Act introduced several other requirements. All were incorporated in the 1985 Act. Schedule 4, paragraph 18, contains the requirement to provide depreciation:

18   In the case of any fixed asset which has a limited useful economic life, the amount of:

(**a**)   its purchase price or production cost; or

(**b**)   where it is estimated that any such asset will have a residual value at the end of the period of its useful economic life, its purchase price or production cost less that estimated residual value shall be reduced by provisions for depreciation calculated to write off that amount systematically over the period of the asset's useful economic life.

Paragraph 19 deals with fixed assets that have 'diminished in value'. This refers to the situation where the 'recoverable amount', i.e. the maximum monetary benefit derivable from it, is less than the current NBV. In such circumstances, provisions for diminution in value *may* be made, and shall be made if the reduction in value is expected to be permanent. Any such reduction should be 'shown' in the P&L account or 'disclosed' in the notes to the accounts. Where the reasons for any such provision have ceased to apply, then that provision *shall* be written back to the extent that it is no longer necessary, with similar disclosure in the P&L account or the notes.

Paragraph 25 permits tangible fixed assets that are constantly being replaced to be included in the accounts at a fixed quantity and value, provided that:

1   their overall value is not material; and

2   they are not subject to material variation in amount.

This means that the annual expense charge would be the amount spent on such assets in the year.

Where the 'alternative accounting rules' are applied, then the appropriate value or CC is substituted for the HC or production cost. However, schedule 4, paragraph 32, states that the amount charged in the P&L account may be based on either the historic figure or on the new valuation figure, provided in the former case that the 'amount of any difference between the two is shown separately in the P&L account or in a note to the accounts'. This seems surprising, as it allows businesses using a CC approach not to reduce profits sufficiently to take account of current costs! (Note that this paragraph only makes any sense if 'shown' means 'disclosed' rather than 'charged'.)

The disclosure requirements specified in schedule 4, paragraph 42, require notes to the balance sheet showing, for each item of fixed assets:

1   The amount of fixed assets (before any provision for depreciation) at the beginning of the financial year.

2   Any revision to this amount relating to revaluations or current cost increases.

3   Acquisitions of fixed assets during the year.

4   Disposals of fixed assets during the year.

5   Transfers of assets to and from each item during the year.

6   The corresponding amount of fixed assets at the end of the financial year.

For each of these six items, the following information about depreciation must be given:

1   The cumulative provision for depreciation as at the beginning of the financial year.

2 The depreciation provision made in the year.
3 The amount of adjustments made to the cumulative provisions in respect of assets disposed of during the year.
4 The amount of any other adjustments made to the provisions during the year.
5 The cumulative provision for depreciation as at the end of the financial year.

Accounting for investment properties (SSAP 19)

The ASC accepted an argument put forward by the property investment lobby that to apply SSAP 12 to such properties did not make sense. The essential point of their argument was that such assets were not held for consumption in the business, and the disposal of these assets would not materially affect any manufacturing or trading operations. They are held as investments, and, therefore:

1 The matching convention is arguably not relevant, as they are not being used for benefit, at least in the operating sense.
2 The current values of such investments, and any change thereof, are of prime importance and relevance.

The standard applies to all investment properties, except those owned by charities. It applies whether or not the properties are held by a company whose main business is the holding of investments. Investment properties are defined as follows:

7 For the purposes of this Statement, but subject to the exceptions in paragraph 8 below, an investment property is an interest in land and/or buildings:
   (a) in respect of which construction work and development have been completed; and
   (b) which is held for its investment potential, any rental income being negotiated at arm's length.
8 The following are exceptions from the definition:
   (a) A property which is owned and occupied by a company for its own purposes is not an investment property.
   (b) A property let to and occupied by another group company is not an investment property for the purposes of its own accounts or the group accounts.

It is interesting that this definition does not state whether or not investment properties are fixed assets. Paragraph 2 of the SSAP, part of the 'explanatory note', explicitly makes it clear that the ASC do regard them as fixed assets, and they do not appear to have considered any other possibility. But the assumption that they are fixed assets is not obviously correct. Compare the definition given (p. 138), with the arguments of the investment lobby (1 and 2 above).

The essential requirements of the SSAP are that investment properties should usually be shown at valuation, but that revaluation should be taken to a revaluation reserve account, not to P&L account. These requirements are stated more fully as follows:

10 Investment properties should not be subject to periodic charges for depreciation on the basis set out in SSAP 12, except for properties held on lease which should be depreciated on the basis set out in SSAP 12 at least over the period when the unexpired term is 20 years or less.

11 Investment properties should be included in the balance sheet at their own open market value.

12 The names of the persons making the valuation, or particulars of their qualifications, should be disclosed together with the bases of valuation used by them. If a person making a valuation is an employee or officer of the company or group which owns the property this fact should be disclosed.

13 Subject to paragraph 14 below, changes in the value of investment properties should not be taken to the profit and loss account but should be disclosed as a movement on an investment revaluation reserve, unless the total of the investment revaluation reserve is insufficient to cover a deficit, in which case the amount by which the deficit exceeds the amount in the investment revaluation reserve should be charged in the profit and loss account. In the special circumstances of investment trust companies and of property unit trusts it may not be appropriate to deal with such deficits in the profit and loss account. In such cases they should be shown prominently in the financial statements.

This is the original paragraph 13 taken from SSAP 19. However, this was amended in July 1994 when amendment to SSAP 19 – 'Accounting for Investment Properties' was issued. This now requires that:

> changes in the market value of investment properties should not be taken to the profit and loss account but should be taken to the statement of total recognised gains and losses (being a movement on an investment revaluation reserve), unless a deficit (or its reversal) on an individual investment property is expected to be permanent, in which case it should be charged (or credited) in the profit and loss account of the period.

The following example illustrates the change. Brit plc valued its investment properties in its balance sheet as at 31 December 1994 at £1m and a related investment property revaluation reserve at £0.1m. As at 31 December 1995 these investment properties are valued at £0.5m.

The original SSAP 19 would require the following accounting treatment for the year-ended 31 December 1995:

Balance sheet value investment properties	£0.5m
Investment property revaluation reserve	£0
Charge to current year P&L	£0.4m

The amendment to SSAP 19 would suggest the following accounting treatment if the diminution in value was regarded as temporary:

Balance sheet value investment properties	£0.5m
Investment property revaluation reserve	£0
Charge to current year profit and loss	£0

The £0.4m will appear in the statement of total recognized gains and losses which we will deal with in Chapter 26. Note that if the fall in value was regarded as permanent then the accounting treatment would be as the original SSAP 19.

This amendment to SSAP 19 now accords with the Companies Act which only requires a charge to the P&L account when the fall in value in fixed assets is permanent. Given the impact on the P&L account of the above, which is dependent on a subjective judgement of whether or not a fall in value is permanent or temporary, we might have expected some guidance in the amended SSAP on the distinction between the two. However, it was only with FRS 11, not issued until 1998 (see below), that the ASB addressed this issue.

Continuing with the original SSAP 19 requirements we have:

14 Paragraph 13 does not apply to the financial statements of pension funds and the long-term business of insurance companies where changes in value are dealt with in the relevant fund account.

15 The carrying value of investment properties and the investment revaluation reserve should be displayed prominently in the financial statements.

One wonders whether the P&L account is an adequate indicator of a 'true and fair view', without the valuation adjustments – particularly given the words of the standard itself that the current value of these investments is of prime importance. Also if property investments are required to be shown at open market value, why not other investments too?

The ASC accepted without argument that SSAP 19 conflicts with the Companies Act requirement to provide depreciation on any fixed asset with a limited useful economic life. This is perhaps surprising, as they could have got round this problem by arguing that investment properties are not actually fixed assets at all. (Propositions a good deal more suspect than that one have been argued elsewhere, e.g. see SSAP 20 on foreign currencies.)

Activity 19

'It is relatively common now for companies not to charge depreciation on property.'
In what circumstances do you consider a policy of not depreciating property can be justified? State when it cannot be justified. State your reasons.   **(20 marks)**
(ACCA)

Activity 19 feedback

FRS 15 'Accounting for Depreciation' requires companies to depreciate freehold property, but not the land. Since buildings have a finite life they need to be depreciated and the cost of the buildings spread over their useful economic life. It has been suggested that because the market value of property may be in excess of its cost, depreciation is not necessary. This fails to recognize that although the market value of an asset at a point in time may be in excess of cost, nevertheless the asset does not have an infinite life and at some future time the asset will have no value.

FRS 15 requires buildings to be depreciated over their useful life. This is defined as the economic life to the entity which is not necessarily the whole life of the asset. Where it is not intended to hold the asset for all its life, and the residual value on disposal will approximate the cost, then the depreciation charge will be immaterial or even nil. This can also occur where the amount spent on repairs is sufficient to maintain the value of the property.

A policy of not providing depreciation may be justified for investment property. An investment property can be defined as a building which is held for its investment potential and where any rental income is negotiated at arm's length. Such assets are not held for consumption and do not form part of the operating capability of a business. It is not therefore necessary to have a systematic charge for depreciation, but rather recognition of the change in the value of the asset. Investment properties, by definition, are held as an investment rather than for use and as such do not need to be depreciated over their life.

The only exception to this rule on investment properties is where an investment property is held on a lease with a relatively short unexpired term, say 20 years. In these circumstances it is necessary to recognize the annual depreciation in the financial statements to avoid the situation whereby a short lease is amortized against the investment revaluation reserve whilst the rentals are taken to the P&L account.

Transfers from fixed assets to current assets

In July 1992 the UITF (see p. 222) issued a statement (abstract 5) on the transfer of assets from fixed assets to current assets. Companies had thought of the rather clever idea of transferring assets from current assets to fixed assets (justified by a stated change in intention as to the purpose of the asset) at a figure above net realizable value. Once they have become fixed assets any later writedown could be debited to revaluation reserve. This means that the loss which had actually accrued while the items were current assets can eventually be written off without ever affecting reported earnings, as the loss never passes through the P&L account.

The UITF reached a consensus that where assets are transferred from current to fixed, the current asset accounting rules should be applied up to the effective date of transfer, which is the date of management's change of intent. Consequently the transfer should be made at the lower of cost and net realizable value, and accordingly an assessment should be made of the net realizable value at the date of transfer and if this is less than its previous carrying value the diminution should be charged in the P&L account, reflecting the loss to the company while the asset was held as a current asset.

Whether assets are transferred at cost or at net realizable value, fixed asset accounting rules will apply to the assets subsequent to the date of transfer. In cases where the transfer is at net realizable value, the asset should be accounted for as a fixed asset at a valuation (under the alternative accounting rule of the ASC) as at the date of the transfer; at subsequent balance sheet dates it may or may not be revalued, but in either event the disclosure requirements appropriate to a valuation should be given.

Issues concerning intangibles

The brand valuation controversy exploded onto the ASC's agenda during 1988. A brand is simply the name, in effect the label, by which a product or series of products is known and sold. It is self-evident that a well-known brand is worth a great deal of money. One of the cases bringing the brand issue to the fore was the battle of Nestlé trying to take over Rowntree. The (eventually unsuccessful) defence put up by Rowntree was based, not on the accounts or on profits trends, but on a document called 'Our Brands Speak for Themselves'. This included the statement 'This letter has described the enormous value of Rowntree's brands. The strength of our company's brands, their market power, and their international growth potential belong to you, not to Nestlé's shareholders.' Rowntree's accounts did not include any figures for any of these brands. It could be suggested therefore that Rowntree's accounts were (to put it mildly) misleading. Surely they could not possibly be said to show a true and fair view?

As always, the argument is not so one-sided as the previous paragraph might imply. Remember first of all the cost and money measurement conventions which we discussed in Chapter 3. These suggest that whilst the purchase of a brand-name should be recorded, the existence of a brand-name created over a period with no direct cost should not be so recorded. Further, they suggest that a purchased brand-name should be recorded at its purchase price and not revalued. Secondly, the original purchased asset will arguably get 'used up' like any other asset and should therefore be depreciated, eventually disappearing from the balance sheet. It will perhaps be replaced by self-generated brand loyalty, but this has not been 'bought', has no cost, and therefore apparently cannot be recorded. Thirdly, and perhaps most fundamentally, we are entering the whole debate about what a balance sheet is supposed to be for anyway. If stocks are shown generally at cost, if motor cars are shown based on cost, should we show brands on a different basis?

It was not only in a take-over situation that companies became interested in changing their accounting policies and seeking to value (meaning revalue!) their brand-names on the balance sheet. Such a valuation or revaluation has a significant effect (if material) on the whole shape and appearance of the balance sheet. In essence, owners' equity and capital employed will be increased, and the gearing proportion will be reduced, purely by two strokes of the accountant's quill. (Make up your own illustration, with simple numbers to demonstrate this if you do not immediately see why.) This makes it sound an attractive proposition particularly to companies with heavy borrowings. Return on capital employed will be reduced, but earnings per share will not be – unless of course depreciation is then charged on the revalued assets.

It should be clear by now that the question of the appropriate treatment of brand-names, whether or not acquired externally, is both important and difficult. The principles involved are no different from those needed in considering the treatment of any other intangible asset – and in many respects are similar to the arguments about the treatment of *any* asset. FRS 10, discussed below, at last attempts a comprehensive treatment.

Goodwill

Introduction

The value of a business is often greater than the value of its separable net assets; the difference being known as goodwill. Our problems are should we recognize this goodwill in our accounts, if so what is its value and finally should it remain in the accounts indefinitely? Read on and let's see if we or the ASB can answer these questions.

What is goodwill?

FRS 10 gives the following definitions:

Purchased goodwill
The difference between the cost of an acquired entity and the aggregate of the fair values of that entity's identifiable assets and liabilities. Positive goodwill arises when the acquisition cost exceeds the aggregate fair values of the identifiable assets and liabilities. Negative goodwill arises when the aggregate fair values of the identifiable assets and liabilities of the entity exceed the acquisition cost.

Identifiable assets and liabilities

The assets and liabilities of an entity that are capable of being disposed of or settled separately, without disposing of a business of the entity.

Fair value is not, surprisingly, defined here, but may be taken as 'the amount for which an asset (or liability) could be exchanged in an arm's length transaction'.

Activity 20

A business is sold for £100 000. Its identifiable individual assets have fair values as follows:

	£000s
Buildings	20
Plant and machinery	25
Net current assets	10
Patents and trademarks	10
Furniture and fittings	5

What is the value for goodwill?

Activity 20 feedback

The rather obvious answer is £30 000 (100 000 − 70 000). Note, however, that even though patents and trademarks are intangible fixed assets they are separable net assets as they can be sold separately.

In fact the idea of goodwill is a difficult one to put into words. There are really two separate questions:

1 Why does it occur – what does it represent?
2 How should we evaluate it?

These questions need to be considered separately.

Why does goodwill exist?

Goodwill can be said to exist because there are many items of benefit to a business, and therefore of value to it, that are not included as assets in conventional accounts. A highly skilled and experienced workforce is one obvious example. Regular customers, a well-known brand-name, even a vague idea such as 'a good reputation' are others. A new business cannot be successfully created overnight simply by buying another collection of definable (or separable) assets.

How should we evaluate goodwill?

The simple answer is that we should:

1 value the business
2 value the separable net assets, in total
3 calculate the difference.

But if we accept the 'fair value' concept as defined above, how should we value the business? The usual theoretical answer would be on a NPV basis – estimating the future net revenue stream and discounting back. Sometimes the future net revenues are regarded as consisting of two elements:

1 the normal element – the return on the separate assets
2 the abnormal element – the return on the goodwill.

This latter element is known as the 'superprofits', and when discounted back to a NPV would give a figure for goodwill directly. But this distinction is really rather artificial. Market value may also obviously be an indication of the value of the business as a whole, but estimates of this are fraught with difficulty.

The standard says the following:

1 It is usual for the value of a business as a whole to differ from the value of its separable net assets. The difference, which may be positive or negative, is described as goodwill.
2 Goodwill is therefore by definition incapable of realization separately from the business as a whole; this characteristic of goodwill distinguishes it from all other items in the accounts. Its other characteristics are that:
   (a) the value of goodwill has no reliable or predictable relationship to any costs which may have been incurred
   (b) individual intangible factors which may contribute to goodwill cannot be valued
   (c) the value of goodwill may fluctuate widely according to internal and external circumstances over relatively short periods of time; and
   (d) the assessment of the value of goodwill is highly subjective.

Thus, any amount attributed to goodwill is unique to the valuer and to the specific point in time at which it is measured, and is valid only at the time, and in the circumstances then prevailing.

Activity 21

Company A is considering selling its wholly owned subsidiary B but is having difficulty in valuing B for sale. The projected profits of the next four years of company B are £43 000, £35 000, £27 000 and £25 000. The separable net assets of the business are valued at £150 000 and normal expected rate of return on capital by company A is 12%. The director asks you, the newly qualified accountant with the company, to provide a valuation for goodwill of company B.

Activity 21 feedback

Normal profits can be estimated as £150 000 at 12% = £18 000. Thus superprofits are £25 000, £17 000, £9000 and £7000 and their NPVs, discounting by the appropriate number of years at 12%, are £22 325, £13 549, £5724 and £3969 = £45 567 which is the value of goodwill using the superprofits method.

Purchased goodwill and inherent goodwill

It is clear from the above discussion that goodwill is in existence all the time. Its value is both difficult to define, and is constantly changing. (Note that its value can be negative, or possibly zero.) But goodwill is always there, it is inherent in the business. This is often referred to as **inherent goodwill**, **non-purchased goodwill** or **internally generated goodwill**. It is contrasted with purchased goodwill. This contrast is not for reasons of principle, but purely for the practical reason that purchased goodwill has a convenient cost figure. There has been a transaction, the cost convention can be applied, we have a figure capable of being audited. If we buy a business for £100 000 and the net separable assets have fair value of £60 000 then we can certainly say that goodwill is, or at least at that instant, was worth £40 000.

Accounting for goodwill

The problem

It is very easy to ignore non-purchased goodwill. Since there is no transaction, it need never enter the accounting system at all unless we positively want it to. This is not true of purchased goodwill. We have bought it. There has therefore been an unavoidable credit entry somewhere, e.g. cash, bank, creditor or whatever. Since we have a credit entry we are forced, whether we like it or not, to have a debit entry. We are forced to record purchased goodwill as an asset. This forces us to answer another question. Having recorded it as an asset, on the purchase, what should we do with it after that? ED 30 (paragraph 12) suggested six possibilities:

> The principal possible methods of accounting for purchased goodwill are as follows:
> (**a**) carry it as an asset and amortize it over its estimated useful life through the profit and loss account
> (**b**) carry it as an asset and amortize it over its estimated useful life by writing off against reserves
> (**c**) eliminate it against reserves immediately on acquisition
> (**d**) retain it in the accounts indefinitely, unless a permanent reduction in its value becomes evident
> (**e**) charge it as an expense against profits in the period when it is acquired; and
> (**f**) show it as a deduction from shareholder's equity (and either amortize it or carry it indefinitely).

Notice that a seventh possibility, regular revaluation to incorporate later non-purchased goodwill, is not even listed.

Activity 22

Of the six possible methods of accounting for purchased goodwill given above, state, giving reasons which you would consider most appropriate in accordance with accounting principles.

Activity 22 feedback

Several of the six suggestions can be fairly quickly dismissed. According to ED 30, paragraphs 14 and 15:

> ASC rejects method (**b**) on the grounds that if an item is being carried as an asset and amortised over a period, the process of amortization implies that the item is an expense; as such it should be charged in the profit and loss account, not against

reserves. Method (**e**) may be considered, not as a separate method in its own right, but as a special case of (**a**) in which the goodwill is amortised in one accounting period. Method (**f**) is rejected on the grounds of ambiguity; it is tantamount to writing off purchased goodwill against reserves while implying that the goodwill remains available as a form of asset. For this reason it may be subjected to the same criticisms as method (**d**) as set out below. In addition, under the Companies Act, the offset of a liability against an asset is not permitted, and if purchased goodwill is treated as an asset in the accounts of an individual company it must be depreciated.

ASC considers that purchased goodwill should not be retained as an asset indefinitely (method (**d**)), as in its view the value of purchased goodwill diminishes through effluxion of time following an acquisition; it may be replaced, to a greater or lesser extent, by non-purchased goodwill, but non-purchased goodwill is not accounted for and its existence should not be used to justify the indefinite retention of purchased goodwill. Method (**d**) is also contrary to the requirements of the Companies Act for purchased goodwill in the accounts of an individual company.

Method (**f**) requires some explanation. It is known as the **dangling debit method**. The figure appears as a debit, but not on the 'net assets' side of the balance sheet. Rather, it appears as a deduction from shareholders' equity, thus reducing the capital employed figure. It can be argued that this facilitates comparison with other businesses that have no purchased goodwill. Distinguish carefully between method (**f**), where goodwill is deducted from shareholders' equity (and so shown every year) and method (**c**), where it is eliminated against reserves (i.e. shareholders' equity).

Two acceptable possibilities

Two methods are thus left for serious consideration, (**a**) and (**c**) from the ED 30 list, i.e.:

1 creating a fixed asset that is then amortised through the P&L account – following the matching convention
2 writing off purchased goodwill immediately against reserves.

Let us identify the effect that each of these two methods has on the profits and capital employed of a company.

Activity 23

On the purchase of another company £100 000 of goodwill is identified. The directors are unsure how to account for this goodwill and ask you, the accountant, to outline the effect on the company of either (**a**) accounting for goodwill in accordance with matching and (**b**) in accordance with prudence. It is suggested that the goodwill would need to be matched over the next four years. Profits for the next five years are estimated to be £35 000 per annum and capital employed is £200 000 after purchase of the company, including reserves of £125 000. All profits are retained in the business.

Activity 23 feedback

The effects can easily be shown in a table as follows.

Method (**a**) create a fixed asset and amortize through the P&L account:

Year	Profits after amortization	Reserves	Capital employed	Average R on C E end of year
	£000s	£000s	£000s	%
1	10 (35 – 25)	135 (125 + 10)	210 (200 + 10)	4.9
2	10	145	220	4.7
3	10	155	230	4.4
4	10	165	240	4.3

Method (**b**) write off to reserves

1	35	60 (125 – 100 + 35)	135 (200 – 100 + 35)	20.9
2	35	95	170	23
3	35	130	205	18.7
4	35	165	240	15.7

Thus, we can see that compared with elimination against reserves, the method of capitalization and then amortization will have two effects on return on capital employed calculations. It will result in:

1 a higher capital employed figure (more net assets); and
2 a lower return figure (more expenses).

Both of these effects will worsen the return on capital employed picture. On the other hand, businesses whose reserves are not adequate to 'absorb' the goodwill may prefer to choose the capitalization method so as to keep the capital employed (and net assets) figures from appearing dangerously small. It should also be noted that writing off large amounts of goodwill against reserves makes owners' equity smaller and therefore makes the gearing proportion higher (i.e. 'worse').

The Companies Act and goodwill

Goodwill is required to be shown in a balance sheet by itself, under the heading of intangible fixed assets. It may only be included to the extent that the goodwill was acquired for valuable consideration (schedule 4, formats and notes thereto). Depreciation written off 'tangible and intangible fixed assets' must be separately disclosed in the P&L account. The general rules on the depreciation of fixed assets (p. 260) naturally apply to goodwill. In addition schedule 4, paragraph 21, provides that:

> The amount of the consideration for any goodwill acquired by a company shall be reduced by provisions for depreciation calculated to write off that amount systematically over a period chosen by the directors of the company.
>
> The period chosen shall not exceed the useful economic life of the goodwill in question.

In any case where any goodwill acquired by a company is shown or included as an asset in the company's balance sheet the period chosen for writing off the consideration for that goodwill and the reasons for choosing that period shall be disclosed in a note to the accounts.

The balance sheet formats in Schedule 4 require purchased goodwill, to the extent that it has not been written off, to be included under the heading of intangible fixed assets, and shown separately from other intangible assets. Note (3) to the formats states that amounts representing goodwill should be included only to the extent that the goodwill was acquired for valuable consideration. Internally generated goodwill may not be capitalized.

Paragraph 5 of Schedule 4 states that amounts in respect of items representing assets may not be set off against amounts in respect of items representing liabilities. For this reason, the FRS requires negative goodwill to be shown separately from positive goodwill on the face of the balance sheet. Paragraph 31(1) of Schedule 4 prohibits the revaluation of goodwill.

SSAP 22 and after

The ASB has had enormous difficulty in resolving the whole goodwill issue. In the old ASC days, ED 30, referring to methods (a) and (c) (see p. 283) proposed to permit 'either method to be employed'. SSAP 22, although permitting either to be used, expressed a very strong preference for method (c), the immediate write-off against reserves, and the acceptance of method (a), amortization through the P&L account, was extremely grudging. The SSAP openly admitted that a major factor in its preference for immediate write-off against reserves was the fact that most businesses preferred to treat it that way! This was despite the fact that the matching convention obviously supports the alternative method, i.e. that expenditure should be matched, as an expense, against the benefit deriving over the years as a result of such expenditure.

In February 1990 another exposure draft on accounting for goodwill was issued, ED 47. This represented a fundamental reappraisal of the ASC's view. ED 47 proposed to ban altogether the preferred option of SSAP 22! Under ED 47 elimination of purchased goodwill against reserves would not be acceptable, and all purchased goodwill would have to be depreciated through the P&L account as an ordinary expense over the useful economic life. The useful economic life should not exceed 20 years 'except in rare circumstances where it can be demonstrated ... that a period in excess of twenty years would be more appropriate', and should never exceed 40 years. This treatment would of course have the effect of reducing reported earnings.

At the same time the ASC issued a technical release which stated that brands are almost inseparable from goodwill, and therefore should be treated in the same way. The ASC now claimed to regard it as 'more important that purchased goodwill should be treated consistently with other purchased intangible and tangible fixed assets than that purchased and non-purchased goodwill should be treated consistently'.

It was at this point in the saga that the ASC handed the whole problem over to the ASB. It is surely not unfair to say that the ASB was being presented with a complete mess. SSAP 22 demonstrably failed to standardize, was widely criticized for illogicality, was out of step with many other countries, and had in effect, through ED 47, been disowned by the ASC.

The IASC issued a revised international accounting standard effective for financial periods beginning on or after 1 January 1995. This carries the unequivocal requirement that positive goodwill on acquisition should be capitalized and amortised over its useful life, i.e. as an expense charged in arriving at the earnings figure. The ASB issued a discussion memorandum in 1993. This gave some support to two methods, i.e. writing goodwill off to a separate goodwill reserve, and capitalizing it and expensing it over a predetermined useful life. The memorandum also argued that intangible assets were largely indistinguishable from goodwill and should be subsumed within it. This last proposal was heavily criticized.

In 1995 the ASB issued another working paper, with yet different proposals. The ASB had now withdrawn its argument that goodwill and other intangibles are indistinguishable one from another, and it proposed to allow the recognition of intangibles separately from purchased goodwill provided their fair value can be measured reliably. Secondly, the ASB had come off the fence regarding the treatment of positive goodwill (negative goodwill is not discussed), and the working paper proposed that all goodwill with a finite life should be capitalized and depreciated over that useful life, while goodwill with an indefinitely long life would not be depreciated. All balances for goodwill and intangibles, whether being depreciated or not, would be subject to annual 'impairment tests' and the balance sheet carrying value reduced via an immediate expense.

This working paper was followed by an exposure draft, FRED 12, in June 1996, and at last a new standard in December 1997, FRS 10, 'Goodwill and Intangible Assets', both of which broadly followed the thinking of the 1995 working paper.

FRS 10 'Goodwill and Intangible Assets'

It is important to note straight away that the FRS deals with both goodwill and intangible assets, but that it does carefully distinguish between them. The general philosophy behind the ASBs approach is outlined in the opening summary.

> The accounting requirements for goodwill reflect the view that goodwill arising on an acquisition is neither an asset like other assets nor an immediate loss in value. Rather, it forms the bridge between the cost of an investment shown as an asset in the acquirer's own financial statements and the values attributed to the acquired assets and liabilities in the consolidated financial statements. Although purchased goodwill is not in itself an asset, its inclusion amongst the assets of the reporting entity, rather than as a deduction from shareholders' entity, recognises that goodwill is part of a larger asset, the investment, for which management remains accountable.
>
> An intangible item may meet the definition of an asset when access to the future economic benefits that it represents is controlled by the reporting entity, either through custody or legal protection. However, intangible assets fall into a spectrum ranging from those that can readily be identified and measured separately from goodwill to those that are essentially very similar to goodwill. The basic principles set out for initial recognition, amortisation and impairment of intangible assets that are similar in nature to goodwill are therefore closely aligned with those set out for goodwill.

In addition to those definitions already quoted on p. 280, the FRS gives some other significant definitions, as follows:

Intangible assets

Non-financial fixed assets that do not have physical substance but are identifiable and are controlled by the entity through custody or legal rights.

An identifiable asset is defined by companies legislation as one that can be disposed of separately without disposing of a business of the entity. If an asset can be disposed of only as part of the revenue-earning activity to which it contributes, it is regarded as indistinguishable from the goodwill relating to the activity and is accounted for as such.

Class of intangible assets

A category of intangible assets having a similar nature, function or use in the business of the entity.

Licences, quotas, patents, copyrights, franchises and trade marks are examples of categories that may be treated as separate classes of intangible assets. Further subdivision may be appropriate, for example, where different types of licence have different functions within the business. Intangible assets that are used within different business segments may be treated as separate classes of intangible assets.

Impairment

A reduction in the recoverable amount of a fixed asset or goodwill below its carrying value.

Net realisable value

The amount at which an asset could be disposed of, less any direct selling costs.

Readily ascertainable market value

The value of an intangible asset that is established by reference to a market where:

(**a**) the asset belongs to a homogeneous population of assets that are equivalent in all material respects; and
(**b**) an active market, evidenced by frequent transactions, exists for that population of assets.

Intangible assets that meet those conditions might include certain operating licences, franchises and quotas. Other intangible assets are by their nature unique: although there may be similar assets, they are not equivalent in all material respects and so do not have readily ascertainable market values. Examples of such assets include brands, publishing titles, patented drugs and engineering design patents.

Recoverable amount

The higher of net realisable value and value in use.

Residual value

The net realisable value of an asset at the end of its useful economic life. Residual values are based on prices prevailing at the date of acquisition (or revaluation) of the asset and do not take account of expected future price changes.

Useful economic life

The useful economic life of an intangible asset is the period over which the entity expects to derive economic benefit from that asset. The useful economic life of purchased goodwill is the period over which the value of the underlying business acquired is expected to exceed the values of its identifiable net assets.

As regards the initial recognition of positive goodwill and of intangible units, the requirements of the FRS are both clear and reasonably unequivocal.

Initial recognition of positive goodwill and intangible assets

Goodwill

7 Positive purchased goodwill should be capitalised and classified as an asset on the balance sheet.

8 Internally generated goodwill should not be capitalised.

Intangible assets

9 An intangible asset purchased separately from a business should be capitalised at its cost.

10 An intangible asset acquired as part of the acquisition of a business should be capitalised separately from goodwill if its value can be measured reliably on initial recognition. It should initially be recorded at its fair value, subject to the constraint that, unless the asset has a readily ascertainable market value, the fair value should be limited to an amount that does not create or increase any negative goodwill arising on the acquisition.

13 If its value cannot be measured reliably, an intangible asset purchased as part of the acquisition of a business should be subsumed within the amount of the purchase price attributed to goodwill.

14 An internally developed intangible asset may be capitalised only if it has a readily ascertainable market value.

The requirements for amortization are equally clear.

15 Where goodwill and intangible assets are regarded as having limited useful economic lives, they should be amortised on a systematic basis over those lives.

17 Where goodwill and intangible assets are regarded as having indefinite useful economic lives, they should not be amortised.

19 There is a rebuttable presumption that the useful economic lives of purchased goodwill and intangible assets are limited to periods of 20 years or less. This presumption may be rebutted and a useful economic life regarded as a longer period or indefinite only if:

(a) the durability of the acquired business or intangible asset can be demonstrated and justifies estimating the useful economic life to exceed 20 years; and

(b) the goodwill or intangible asset is capable of continued measurement (so that annual impairment reviews will be feasible).

24 Where access to the economic benefits associated with an intangible asset is

achieved through legal rights that have been granted for a finite period, the economic life of the asset may extend beyond that period only if, and to the extent that, the legal rights are renewable and renewal is assured. The amount of the asset that is treated as having the longer useful economic life should exclude those costs that will recur each time the legal right is renewed.

28   In amortising an intangible asset, a residual value may be assigned to that asset only if such residual value can be measured reliably. No residual value may be assigned to goodwill.

30   The method of amortisation should be chosen to reflect the expected pattern of depletion of the goodwill or intangible asset. A straight-line method should be chosen unless another method can be demonstrated to be more appropriate.

33   The useful economic lives of goodwill and intangible assets should be reviewed at the end of each reporting period and revised if necessary. If a useful economic life is revised, the carrying value of the goodwill or intangible asset at the date of revision should be amortised over the revised remaining useful economic life. If the effect of the revision is to increase the useful economic life to more than 20 years from the date of acquisition, the additional requirements of the FRS that apply to goodwill and intangible assets that are amortised over periods of more than 20 years or are not amortised become applicable.

Negative goodwill remaining 'after the fair values of the acquired assets and liabilities have been checked' should be treated as required in paragraphs 48–51. In essence this means that negative goodwill should be recognized and separately disclosed on the face of the balance sheet, immediately below the goodwill heading. It should be recognized in the profit and loss account in the periods in which the non-monetary assets acquired are depreciated or sold. Any negative goodwill in excess of the values of the non-monetary assets should be written back in the profit and loss account over the period expected to benefit from that negative goodwill.

As we have already indicated, the ASB has been moving for some time towards the idea of impairment tests. The definitions given above (pp. 287–289) show that an impairment test involves comparing the carrying value, i.e. the net balance sheet figure brought forward, with the recoverable amount, i.e. the higher of net realizable value and value in use.

An asset is regarded as impaired if its recoverable amount falls below its carrying value. Impairment reviews should be performed to ensure that goodwill and intangible assets are not carried at above their recoverable amounts. Where goodwill and intangible assets are amortised over a period that does not exceed 20 years, impairment reviews need be performed only at the end of the first full financial year following the initial recognition of the goodwill or intangible asset and, in other periods, if events or changes in circumstances indicate that its carrying value may not be recoverable in full. Where goodwill and intangible assets are not amortised, or are amortised over a period exceeding 20 years, impairment reviews should be performed each year.

More or less in parallel with FRS 10, the ASB had also been developing FRS 11, 'Impairment of Fixed Assets and Goodwill'. FRED 15, issued in June 1997, was published as the FRS in July 1998. The situation overall is frankly a little confusing, but broadly FRS 11 apparently seeks to give more detail on how impairment tests should be carried out, whereas FRS 10 seeks to establish the principle of impairment tests. However it is most important that you fully appreciate that FRS 10 applies to 'goodwill and intangible assets', where the FRS defines intangible assets (see p. 288) in such a way that they can only be fixed assets. FRS 11 however applies to 'fixed assets and goodwill', i.e. FRS 11 applies to **all** fixed assets (plus goodwill), whereas FRS 10 applies only to **intangible** (fixed) assets (plus goodwill). We shall deal with FRS 11 shortly (hopefully in both senses of the word!)

The key FRS 10 requirements for impairment of positive goodwill and intangible assets are as follows:

34 Goodwill and intangible assets that are amortised over a finite period not exceeding 20 years from the date of acquisition should be reviewed for impairment:
   (a) at the end of the first full financial year following the acquisition ('the first year review'); and
   (b) in other periods if events or changes in circumstances indicate that the carrying values may not be recoverable.

39 Except as permitted in paragraph 40, impairment reviews should be performed in accordance with the requirements of FRS 11 'Impairment of Fixed Assets and Goodwill'.

40 The first year impairment review required by paragraph 34(a) may be performed in two stages:
   (a) initially identifying any possible impairment by comparing post-acquisition performance in the first year with pre-acquisition forecasts used to support the purchase price; and
   (b) performing a full impairment review in accordance with the requirements of FRS 11 only if the initial review indicates that the post-acquisition performance has failed to meet pre-acquisition expectations or if any other previously unforeseen events or changes in circumstances indicate that the carrying values may not be recoverable.

41 If an impairment loss is recognised, the revised carrying value, if being amortised, should be amortised over the current estimate of the remaining useful economic life.

42 If goodwill arising on consolidation is found to be impaired, the carrying amount of the investment held in the accounts of the parent undertaking should also be reviewed for impairment.

Paragraphs 43–47 discuss the issue of revaluations and restoration of past impairment losses. They may be summarized as follows:

Intangible assets with readily ascertainable market values may be revalued by reference to those market values.

The reversal of a past impairment loss may be recognized only if it can clearly and demonstrably be attributed to the unforeseen reversal of the external event that caused the recognition of the original impairment loss. Past impairment losses may not be restored when the restoration in value is generated internally.

There are few disclosure requirements other than those normally required for any type of fixed asset. Significant additional disclosure requirements include requirements to explain:

- the bases of valuation of intangible assets
- the grounds for believing a useful economic life to exceed 20 years or to be indefinite

- the treatment adopted for negative goodwill.

These additional disclosure requirements are given in detail in paragraphs 52–64 of the Standard.

Consideration of FRS 10

Activity 24

The preferred method of accounting for purchased goodwill under SSAP 22 was immediate elimination against reserves. Outline the arguments for and against this previous treatment.

Activity 24 feedback

The principal rationale for this treatment was that it was consistent with the accepted practice of not including internally generated goodwill on the balance sheet. It can further be argued that goodwill is not an asset that should be recognized by a reporting entity since it is not a right to future economic benefits controlled by the entity.

However, the practice of eliminating goodwill against reserves has weaknesses:

- immediate elimination of goodwill gives the impression that the acquirer's net worth has been depleted or even eliminated
- the problem of equity depletion has encouraged companies to reduce amounts attributed to purchased goodwill by separately valuing brands and similar intangible assets at the date of purchase. Given that such intangible assets are very similar in nature to goodwill and the allocation of value between the two can be subjective, it is widely thought to be inappropriate that the goodwill should be accounted for differently
- management is not held accountable for the amount that it has invested in goodwill: it is not taken into account when measuring the assets on which a return must be earned, and there is no requirement to disclose a loss if the value of the goodwill is not maintained
- although there is consistency in the balance sheet treatment of purchased and internally generated goodwill, there is no consistency in the profit and loss account treatment: the costs that can be attributed to building up internally generated goodwill are offset against profits in the profit and loss account, whereas the costs of acquired goodwill are not charged against profits in this way unless the acquired business is sold
- this inconsistency serves to make companies that grow by acquisition appear more profitable than those that grow organically.

It should also be remembered that the IASC had already issued a new International Standard which refused to accept the preferred SSAP 22 treatment in any circumstances. As soon as the proposal in ED 47 to move away from elimination against reserves (as long ago as 1990 remember!) appeared, it began to be heavily criticized.

Those opposing the proposals argued primarily that, where large sums were spent on maintaining and developing the value of an acquired business, a requirement to amortize a significant part of the investment over an arbitrary period had no economic meaning.

Many of the respondents opposed to amortization of purchased goodwill agreed that it should be capitalized but thought that it should subsequently be written down only if and to the extent that the carrying value of the goodwill was not supported by the current value of goodwill in the acquired business.

This approach is based on the premise that purchased goodwill is neither an identifiable asset like other assets nor an immediate loss in value. Rather, it represents the balance of the purchase consideration that remains after recognizing all the identifiable assets and liabilities in the consolidated financial statements. Essentially, it forms a bridge between the cost of the investment shown as an asset in the acquirer's individual financial statements and the identifiable assets and liabilities recognized in the consolidated financial statements of the combined entities. Although purchased goodwill is not in itself an asset, its inclusion amongst the assets of the reporting entity, rather than as a deduction from shareholders' equity, recognizes that goodwill is part of a larger asset, the investment, for which management remains accountable.

This method ensures that the financial statements reflect management's success in maintaining the value of the goodwill and generating a return from its investment. It can be criticized for treating purchased goodwill differently from internally generated goodwill, although this is true for all methods of accounting for purchased goodwill. Other issues are that:

- impairment reviews, which rely on forecasts of future cash flows, can be subjective
- impairment reviews are onerous and may not be feasible on an annual basis. Where goodwill has a finite life, amortization may provide a much simpler, yet adequate, method of reflecting the depletion in value of the goodwill
- amortization of goodwill is required by companies legislation.

In effect, of course, the final requirements of FRS 10 combine the amortization and impairment options. The theoretical validity of this is something we leave you to think about. The practical effectiveness of the proposals remains to be seen.

The proposals are not without problems. The direct clash with the IASC Standard on Goodwill, IAS 22, has been removed, but IAS 22 does not require impairment tests or adjustments. However recent IASC exposure drafts (e.g. E60 and E61) propose moves in the direction already followed by FRS 10.

A second problem is the clash with the Companies Act. This is quickly dealt with in the FRS by reference to the good old 'true and fair view' override discussed in Chapter 13. The ASB puts it succinctly in their official summary of the Standard.

> Companies legislation requires goodwill to be amortised over a limited period. Hence, where the financial statements of a company include goodwill that is not amortised, they should explain that the departure from this specific requirement is necessary for the overriding purpose of providing a true and fair view, also detailing the reasons for and the effect of the departure.

Finally, one member of the ASB disagrees with its whole approach, arguing in a 'dissenting view' that goodwill should be deducted from shareholder's equity, without amortization.

FRS 11 'Impairment of Fixed Assets and Goodwill'

FRS 11 was developed for two reasons. First, it supports the new approach to accounting for goodwill and intangible assets now required by FRS 10, 'Goodwill and Intangible

Assets': it permits them to be carried without amortization in the balance sheet, but requires unamortised amounts to be reviewed for impairment each year. The approach relies on the impairment reviews being reliable and robust, and FRS 11 gives detailed guidance designed to achieve this.

Second, there have been difficulties in interpreting the legal requirement to write down fixed assets for any permanent (but not temporary) diminution in value. It is inherently very difficult to judge whether a fall in a fixed asset's value will be temporary or permanent. This has meant an inconsistency of views and, in some cases, users of financial statements have not been made aware of losses in value because the company's directors have judged the losses to be temporary. Even when impairment losses have been reported in the accounts, there have been inconsistencies in the way they have been measured.

FRS 11 requires all reductions in the values of fixed assets and goodwill below their carrying amounts to be regarded as permanent. The assets must be written down to their 'recoverable amount' – the higher of the amount that could be achieved from their sale and their value in use within the business. Value in use is measured by forecasting the future cash flows that will be generated by using the asset, and discounting them to their present value.

One complication is that, typically, cash flows are generated not by individual assets but by a group of assets and liabilities used together within a business. So the FRS requires that, where the value in use cannot be calculated for an individual asset, it is calculated for the group of assets and liabilities that all work together to generate income. The FRS calls such groups 'income-generating units'. The value in use of the income-generating unit is compared with the aggregate carrying values of the assets and liabilities in the unit. Any impairment is then allocated against the carrying amounts of the assets in the unit, starting with the goodwill and intangible assets.

Since FRS 11 was explicitly developed to give detailed guidance, rather than to establish principles as in, for example, FRS 10, it reads as a rather technical and, in a sense uninspiring, set of regulations. We are writing a textbook not a detailed operational manual, and if you need every nuance you should read the whole Standard carefully.

The FRS gives a set of definitions, many of them identical to those already given in FRS 10. New ones are as follows:

Income-generating unit
A group of assets, liabilities and associated goodwill that generates income that is largely independent of the reporting entity's other income streams. The assets and liabilities include those directly involved in generating the income and an appropriate portion of those used to generate more than one income stream.

Tangible fixed assets
Assets that have physical substance and are held for use in the production or supply of goods or services, for rental to others, or for administrative purposes on a continuing basis in the reporting entity's activities.

Value in use
The present value of the future cash flows obtainable as a result of an asset's continued use, including those resulting from its ultimate disposal.

The coverage of the FRS is stated as follows:

5 The requirements of the FRS apply to purchased goodwill that is recognised in the balance sheet and all fixed assets, except:

   (**a**) fixed assets within the scope of the FRS addressing disclosures of derivatives and other financial instruments;

   (**b**) investment properties as defined in SSAP 19 'Accounting for investment properties';

   (**c**) an entity's own shares held by an ESOP and shown as a fixed asset in the entity's balance sheet under UITF Abstract 13 'Accounting for ESOP Trusts'; and

   (**d**) costs capitalized pending determination (i.e. costs capitalized while a field is still being appraised) under the Oil Industry Accounting Committee's SORP 'Accounting for oil and gas exploration and development activities'.

The Standard requires that:

8 A review for impairment of a fixed asset or goodwill should be carried out if events or changes in circumstances indicate that the carrying amount of the fixed asset or goodwill may not be recoverable.

9 Impairment occurs because something has happened either to the fixed assets themselves or to the economic environment in which the fixed assets are operated. It is possible, therefore, to rely on the use of indicators of impairment to determine when a review for impairment is needed.

Activity 25

Suggest examples of events and changes in circumstances which indicate that impairment may have occurred.

Activity 25 feedback

The FRS itself suggests the following examples:

10 Examples of events and changes in circumstances that indicate an impairment may have occurred include:

   • a current period operating loss in the business in which the fixed asset or goodwill is involved or net cash outflow from the operating activities of that business, combined with either past operating losses or net cash outflows from such operating activities or an expectation of continuing operating losses or net cash outflows from such operating activities

   • a significant decline in a fixed asset's market value during the period

   • evidence of obsolescence or physical damage to the fixed asset

   • a significant adverse change in:

      – either the business or the market in which the fixed asset or goodwill is involved, such as the entrance of a major competitor

      – the statutory or other regulatory environment in which the business operates

> – any 'indicator of value' (for example turnover) used to measure the
> fair value of a fixed asset on acquisition
> - a commitment by management to undertake a significant reorganisation
> - a major loss of key employees
> - a significant increase in market interest rates or other market rates of return
> that are likely to affect materially the fixed asset's recoverable amount.

The overall point of the whole Standard is stated in paragraph 14.

> **14** The impairment review should comprise a comparison of the carrying amount
> of the fixed asset or goodwill with its recoverable amount (the higher of net
> realisable value and value in use). To the extent that the carrying amount
> exceeds the recoverable amount, the fixed asset or goodwill is impaired and
> should be written down. The impairment loss should be recognised in the prof-
> it and loss account unless it arises on a previously revalued fixed asset, in
> which case it should be recognised as required by paragraph 63.
>
> **63** An impairment loss on a revalued fixed asset should be recognised in the
> profit and loss account if it is caused by a clear consumption of economic
> benefits. Other impairments of revalued fixed assets should be recognised in
> the statement of total recognised gains and losses until the carrying amount
> of the asset reaches its depreciated historical cost and thereafter in the prof-
> it and loss account.

Example in respect of para. 63

A fixed asset was purchased for £1m several years ago and revalued after 5 years to £2m.
At this stage a revaluation reserve of £1m would have been created. In the current year an
impairment review is undertaken and the recoverable amount of the asset is found to be
£0.8m. The impairment of £1.2m will be accounted for as follows:

- £1m will be written off the revaluation reserve
- £0.2m will be charged to the profit and loss account.

Much of the Standard, paragraphs 24–46, is concerned with the problem of calculating the
value in use. The most important of these paragraphs are the following:

> **24** The value in use of a fixed asset should be estimated individually where rea-
> sonably practicable. Where it is not reasonably practicable to identify cash
> flows arising from an individual fixed asset, value in use should be calcu-
> lated at the level of income-generating units. The carrying amount of each
> income-generating unit containing the fixed assets or goodwill under review
> should be compared with the higher of the value in use and the net realis-
> able value (if it can be measured reliably) of the unit.
>
> **25** The value in use of a fixed asset is the present value of the future cash flows
> obtainable as a result of the asset's continued use, including those resulting
> from its ultimate disposal. In practice, it is not normally possible to estimate
> the value in use of an individual fixed asset: it is the utilisation of groups of
> assets and liabilities, together with their associated goodwill, that generates cash
> flows. Hence value in use will usually have to be estimated in total for groups
> of assets and liabilities. These groups are referred to as income-generating units.

26 Because it is necessary to identify only material impairments, in some cases it may be acceptable to consider a group of income-generating units together rather than on an individual basis.

27 Income-generating units should be identified by dividing the total income of the entity into as many largely independent income streams as is reasonably practicable. Except as permitted by paragraph 32, each of the identifiable assets and liabilities of the entity, excluding deferred tax balances, interest-bearing debt, dividends payable and other items relating wholly to financing, should be attributed to (or apportioned between) one (or more) income-generating unit(s).

32 If it is not possible to apportion certain central assets meaningfully across the income-generating units to which they contribute, these assets may be excluded from the individual income-generating units. However, an additional impairment review should be performed on the excluded central assets. In this review, the income-generating units to which the central assets contribute should be combined and their combined carrying amount (including that of the central assets) should be compared with their combined value in use.

The FRS gives a number of examples to illustrate the application (and also the complexity) of these requirements. We give just one of these illustrations here, concerning the identification of income-generating units.

Example in respect of income-generating units

An entity comprises three stages of production A (growing and felling trees), B (creating parts of wooden furniture) and C (assembling the parts from B into finished goods). The output of A is timber that is partly transferred to B and partly sold in an external market. If A did not exist, B could buy its timber from the market. The output of B has no external market and is transferred to C at an interval transfer price. C sells the finished product in an external market and the sales revenue achieved by C is not affected by the fact that the three stages of production are all performed by the entity.

A forms an income-generating unit and its cash inflows should be based on the market price for its output. B and C together form one income-generating unit because there is no market available for the output of B. In calculating the cash outflows of the income-generating unit B+C, the timber received by B from A should be priced by reference to the market, not any internal transfer price.

As always, the calculation of a discount rate is fraught with difficulty and uncertainty. The FRS tries to be as prescriptive as it can.

41 The present value of the income-generating unit under review should be calculated by discounting the expected future cash flows of the unit. The discount rate used should be an estimate of the rate that the market would expect on an equally risky investment. It should exclude the effects of any risk for which the cash flows have been adjusted and should be calculated on a pre-tax basis.

42 Estimates of this market rate may be made by a variety of means including reference to:

(**a**) the rate implicit in market transactions of similar assets;

(**b**) the current weighted average cost of capital (WACC) of a listed company whose cash flows have similar risk profiles to those of the income-generating unit; or

(**c**) the WACC for the entity *but only if* adjusted for the particular risks associated with the income-generating unit.

43 If method (c) is used the following matters are of note.

■ Where the cash flow forecasts assume a real growth rate that exceeds the long-term average growth rate for more than five years, it is likely that the discount rate will be increased to reflect a higher level of risk.

■ The discount rates applied to individual income-generating units will always be estimated such that, were they to be calculated for every unit, the weighted average discount rate would equal the entity's overall WACC.

44 The WACC will be a post-tax rate from the entity's point of view, whereas the required discount rate will be a pre-tax rate.

When it is established that impairment losses exist, they should be allocated as follows.

47 The carrying amounts of the income-generating units under review should be calculated as the net of the carrying amounts of the assets, liabilities and goodwill allocated to the unit.

48 To the extent that the carrying amount of the income-generating unit exceeds its recoverable amount, the unit is impaired. In the absence of an obvious impairment of specific assets within the unit, the impairment should be allocated:

(**a**) first, to any goodwill in the unit;

(**b**) thereafter, to any capitalised intangible asset in the unit; and

(**c**) finally, to the tangible assets in the unit, on a pro rata or more appropriate basis.

49 In this allocation, which aims to write down the assets with the most subjective valuations first, no intangible asset with a readily ascertainable market value should be written down below its net realisable value. Similarly, no tangible asset with a net realisable value that can be measured reliably should be written down below its net realisable value.

Paragraphs 67–73 give details of presentation and disclosure. In general, full details of treatment and assumptions are required.

67 Impairment losses recognised in the profit and loss account should be included within operating profit under the appropriate statutory heading, and disclosed as an exceptional item if appropriate. Impairment losses recognised in the statement of total recognised gains and losses should be disclosed separately on the face of that statement.

In summary, FRS 11 requires us to identify carrying amount (CA), value in use (VIU) and net realizable value (NRV) for all assets that are likely to have become impaired, and if:

- CA > NRV > VIU then impairment has occurred and the asset is written down to its NRV
- CA > VIU > NRV then impairment has occurred and the asset is written down to its VIU
- CA < VIU or NRV no impairment.

Summary

In this complicated chapter we have explored the problems, the arguments, and the thinking of the ASC and ASB on a variety of aspects of the accounting treatment of fixed assets. Make sure you have an adequate knowledge and understanding of SSAPs 4, and 19, and FRSs 10, 11 and 15. Just as important, make sure you understand the underlying issues which they seek to resolve. How successful are they?

Exercises

1 Outline four different depreciation methods, and appraise them in the context of the definition and objectives of depreciation.
2 Do you think depreciation is too subjective in calculation to be useful?
3 Outline the arguments and conclusions of SSAP 4.
4 FRS11–*Impairment of fixed assets and goodwill* requires that all fixed assets and goodwill should be reviewed for impairment where appropriate and any impairment loss dealt with in the financial statements.

   The XY group prepares financial statements to 31 December each year. On 31 December 1998 the group purchased all the shares of MH LTD for £2 million. The fair value of the identifiable net assets of MH Ltd at that date was £1.8 million. It is the policy of the XY group to amortize goodwill over 20 years. The amortisation of the goodwill of MH Ltd commenced in 1999. MH Ltd made a loss in 1999 and at 31 December 1999 the net assets of MH Ltd – based on fair values at 1 January 1999 – were as follows:

	£000
Capitalized development expenditure	200
Tangible fixed assets	1300
Net current assets	250
	1750

An impairment review at 31 December 1999 indicated that the value in use of MH LTD at that date was £1.5 million. The capitalized development expenditure has no ascertainable external market value.

Requirements:

(a) **Describe what is meant by 'impairment' and briefly explain the procedures that must be followed when performing an impairment review.** (12 marks)

(b) **Calculate the impairment loss that would arise in the consolidated financial statements of the XY group as a result of the impairment review of MH Ltd at 31 December 1999.** (4 marks)

(c) **Show how the impairment loss you have calculated in (b) would affect the carrying values of the various net assets in the consolidated balance sheet of the XY group at 31 December 1999.** (4 Marks)

(20 marks)
CIMA (9) MAY00

5 Outline and appraise SSAP 19. Do you regard investment properties as fixed assets?

6 How (if at all) should valuable brand-names be treated in the published accounts of trading companies?

7 The following extract has been taken from the balance sheet of MG plc as at 30 September

Fixed assets	*£m*
Intangible assets – brands	9 268
Tangible assets	15 024
Investments	856
	25 148

The accounting policy of MG plc was as follows. Significant acquired owned brands, the value of which is not expected to diminish in the foreseeable future, are recorded in the balance sheet as fixed intangible assets. No amortization is provided on these assets, but their value is reviewed annually by the directors and the cost written down as an exceptional item where permanent diminution in value has occurred.

Required:

(a) **Explain why a company such as MG plc may have included purchased brands as fixed assets in their balance sheet.**   (4 marks)

(b) **Explain the criteria that should be met if a purchased brand is to be recognized as an asset in the balance sheet.**   (4 marks)

(c) **Explain the justification for including non-purchased brands in the balance sheet and how they should be valued.**   (8 marks)

(d) **Explain the steps taken by the profession to regulate this accounting treatment.**   (4 marks)

(20 marks)

8 (a) Provide a definition of an asset which is broad enough to include all items that may be found under the heading of 'assets' in a balance sheet. Say why you think your definition includes all that is necessary to define an asset.

(10 marks)

(b) **State three criteria which you could use in practice to include all fixed asset expenditure, and to exclude all other expenditure.**   (6 marks)

(c) Sticky Labels plc, a printing firm, has decided to import from abroad a new type of large printing machine for use in producing labels.

List the items that are likely to make up the capitalized cost of the machine in the balance sheet of Sticky Labels plc.   (4 marks)

(20 marks)

(ACCA)

9 You are required to explain the accounting policies below and state whether you agree with them, giving your reasons.

(a) The following note appears in the accounting policies of a company in the water industry.

Infrastructure assets comprise a network of systems. Expenditure on infrastructure assets relating to increases in capacity or improvements of the network is treated as additions, which are included at cost after deducting related grants and contributions. Expenditure on maintaining the operating capability of the network in accordance with defined standards of service is charged as an operating cost. No depreciation is charged on infrastructure assets because the network of systems is required to be maintained in perpetuity and therefore has no finite economic life.

Charges for infrastructure renewals expenditure take account of planned expenditure on maintaining the operating capability of infrastructure assets in accordance with the operational policies and standards underlying the group's investment programme. The timing of the investment programme and other operational considerations may result in uneven patterns of infrastructure renewals expenditure. Charges to the profit and loss account are adjusted by way of accruals or deferrals, as appropriate, to take account of any significant fluctuations between actual and planned expenditure.

(12 marks)

(b) The following note appears in the accounting policies of a football club.

The cost of players' registrations are capitalized and, after allowing for estimated residual values, are amortised over the period of the players' contracts.

Note: the cost of players' registrations are commonly refered to as transfer fees.

(8 marks)

(20 marks)

(ACCA)

10 (a) Explain how the requirements of SSAP 4 'Accounting for Government Grants' are consistent with the accounting concepts of SSAP 2 'Disclosure of Accounting Policies'. (8 marks)

(b) Describe how the grant-related aspects of the following events should be accounted for with respect to a limited company:

(i) A grant of 20% towards the cost of a fixed asset, the economic life of which is estimated to be ten years, and which is financed by a five-year loan.

(4 marks)

(ii) A grant towards revenue expenditure in one year, on the condition that if certain requirements were not met in the next five years, all or part of the grant might be repayable. (5 marks)

(iii) A grant towards consultancy costs to design and install a standard costing system. (3 marks)

(20 marks)

(ACCA)

11 Your managing director has heard about a building company which has capitalized its interest costs in the cost of its assets.

You are required to write a report to your managing director explaining

(a) the alternative accounting treatments of interest costs (5 marks)

(b) the arguments for and against the capitalization of interest costs.

(10 marks)

(15 marks)

(CIMA)

12 'A case can be made for putting brands on to the balance sheet to disclose to shareholders and others the true value of the assets in the business.' (Pizzey – *CIMA Student*, August, 1990).

You are required to discuss the arguments for and against including a value for brand-names in the balance sheet. **(15 marks)**

(CIMA)

13 The managing director of your company has always been unhappy at depreciating the company's properties because he argues that these properties are in fact appreciating in value.

Recently he heard of another company which has investment properties and does not depreciate those properties.

You are required to write a report to your managing director explaining

(a) the consequence of not depreciating the company's existing properties

(2 marks)

(b) the meaning of investment properties (5 marks)
(c) the accounting treatment of investment properties in published financial statements. (8 marks)
(15 marks)
(CIMA)

14 **You are asked to state, giving your reasons, whether the accounting policies set out below are in accordance with UK generally accepted accounting practices. Where they are not, you are required to recommend an acceptable accounting policy.**

(a) interest paid on capital employed on land awaiting development and on the construction and major redevelopment of hotels and restaurants was capitalized as part of the construction costs (4 marks)

(b) a prior-year adjustment was made to restate the accounts of the previous year to reflect the reduced carrying value of certain properties (4 marks)

(c) no depreciation was provided on freehold properties or on equipment which was part of the buildings. (4 marks)
(12 marks)
(ACCA adapted)

15 **Queries raised by Tofalt Ltd's financial accountant.**
The company's accountant (unqualified) has asked your professional advice on the correct accounting treatment in the 1992 annual accounts of the following transactions/situations.

(a) Fixtures and fittings are normally depreciated on a straight-line basis, assuming a ten-year life with a nil residual value. In June 1991, the directors of Tofalt Ltd decided that fittings acquired in 1989 at a cost of £60 000 and on which £12 000 depreciation had been provided to 31 March 1991, should be replaced in April 1993 but could be sold for £4000. Query: How should the depreciation charge to the 1992 final accounts be calculated and treated?

(b) A piece of land included under premises at its cost (£5000) is required by the local authority to enable an access road to be built for a housing development. The price offered at 31 March 1992 has been fixed by the district valuer at £3000. If Tofalt Ltd refuses to sell the land, the local authority will acquire it compulsorily at the valuation figure of £3000. Query: What should the accounting treatment of this situation be in the 1992 final accounts?

(c) Tofalt Ltd's main site is included under premises at cost, £350 000. Up to 31 March 1991 nineteen years' accumulated depreciation of £76 000 had been provided. In March 1992 the site was revalued by a firm of qualified valuers, at a figure of £450 000. The revaluation was to be incorporated into the accounts immediately as land (£200 000) and buildings (£250 000) with a fifty-year life.

Queries: **(i)** How should the effects of the revaluation be dealt with in the 1992 final accounts and what disclosures would have to be made? **(ii)** What would be the effect (if any) on distributable profits in 1993?

(ACCA adapted)

16 What is goodwill?
17 What does negative goodwill mean?
18 A firm has purchased some goodwill. Write a memorandum to the accountant including:
(a) a list of the possible accounting treatments available
(b) summaries of the advantages and disadvantages of each possibility
(c) your own reasoned recommendation.
19 List separately the arguments for and against the inclusion of inherent (non-purchased) goodwill in published accounts.
20 The EU Fourth Directive recommends an absolute maximum writing-off period for good-

will of five years (though individual parliaments can increase this as the UK have done). Is this a good idea? Defend your answer.

21 **(a) How would you define goodwill?** (5 marks)
   (b) Three accounting treatments of goodwill are:
      (i) retain goodwill as an asset to be amortised over its estimated useful life
      (ii) retain goodwill as an asset indefinitely
      (iii) write off goodwill to reserves at the time of acquisition.
   Discuss briefly the principles underlying each of these three approaches.
   (15 marks)
   (20 marks)
   (ACCA)

22 **(a) List three methods of accounting for purchased goodwill and briefly state the arguments in favour of each of the three.** (12 marks)
   (b) What are the main characteristics of goodwill which distinguish it from other intangible assets? To what extent do you consider that these characteristics should affect the accounting treatment of goodwill?
   State your reasons.
   (8 marks)
   (20 marks)
   (ACCA)

23 Do you believe that positive goodwill should always be amortised over a fixed period?

24 O'Leary Ltd acquired a controlling interest in O'Neill Ltd as from 1 April 19X1. The fair value of O'Neill's assets acquired on 1 April X1 were:

	£000s
Fixed assets	448
Stock	154
Debtors	245
Creditors	
amounts due within one year	(232)
amounts due after one year	(175)
	440

The fair value of the purchase consideration given was £336 000. The fixed assets of O'Neill will be depreciated over ten years. The accounting year-end of the O'Leary group is 31 December X1.

Required:
Calculate the amount of purchased goodwill in the above acquisition, show how the goodwill will be treated and presented in the group statements of O'Leary Ltd.

25 Identify the circumstances under which goodwill would incur a limited and a full impairment review, and describe each of these reviews.

26 Discuss whether FRS 10 represents an improvement, on balance, over SSAP 22.

27 Hamilton plc owns the leasehold on a large 12-storey office block in the City area of London, which it purchased on 1 April 1995 for £3 million. On that date the lease had a remaining life of 25 years. The building has been available for sub-letting, which on average over the three years since its acquisition has been 70% occupied. The building is currently classified in Hamilton plc's balance sheet as an investment property under SSAP 19 'Accounting for Investment Properties', and not depreciated. Hamilton plc does not intend to sell the property.

   Platonic and Company, a firm of Chartered Surveyors has revalued the office block annually since acquisition on an open market value basis. The values have been:

year-ended 31 March	1996	1997	1998
	£3.2 million	£3.6 million	£3.6 million

Hamilton plc has adopted these values as the balance sheet carrying value of the property. Included in the report on the valuation for the current year-end (31 March 1998) the surveyors noted that over the next few years there is expected to be a surplus of rented property space in the City and sub-lease rentals are expected to fall. This in turn is expected to lead to a serious decline in the value of properties like Hamilton plc's.

In view of this the directors of Hamilton plc sought further advice from Platonic and Company as to the future use of the property. They were advised that the future anticipated levels of occupancy and rental income would be unlikely to cover the financing and running costs of the property. They suggested that Hamilton plc should consider using the building for the company's administration and as the registered office. They should then change the classification of the office block from an investment property to a leasehold building and this would avoid having to recognize any future revaluation movements on the property as it could then be carried at 'cost'.

During the year the audit manager has made the following notes in the working papers:

- an article in *Accountancy Update* reported that an important paper in the *Journal of Valuation Surveyors* had reported dramatic falls averaging 25% in the value of office property in the City during the last six months of Hamilton plc's current accounting year
- the Managing Director of Hamilton plc is called Mr Moon, and this is the same surname as the signatory on the valuation report from Platonic and Company
- the Managing Director has refused a suggestion by the audit manager that another firm of surveyors should give an opinion on the value of the office block. The refusal was made on the basis that a second valuation would be an unnecessary cost as the fee would be 2% of the valuation
- the draft profit and loss account for the year to 31 March 1998, treating the office block as an investment property, shows only a small after tax profit of £60 000. No dividends have been paid in the year to 31 March 1998.

Required:
(a) **Describe the circumstances in which companies are normally permitted to change their accounting policies; and consider whether the change in the classification of Hamilton plc's office block would represent a change in accounting policy.** (7 marks)
(b) **Explain the accounting implications of Hamilton plc using the office block as a leasehold property rather than an investment property; and, assuming the proposed change of use is from 1 April 1998, quantify the effect on the Financial Statements for the year to 31 March 1998 and 1999:**
   (i) **if Platonic and Company's current valuation is correct and the value of the property will fall by 25% (to £2.7m) in the year to 31 March 1999; and**
   (ii) **if the value of the property had already fallen by 25% during the year to 31 March 1998.** (8 marks)
   (15 marks)
   (ACCA)

28 Accounting practices for fixed assets and depreciation can be said to have developed in a piecemeal manner. The introduction of FRS 11 'Impairment of Fixed Assets' has meant that a standard on the measurement of fixed assets was required to provide further guidance in this area. FRS 15 'Tangible Fixed Assets' deals with the measurement and valuation issue.

Required:
Describe why it was important for a new accounting standard to be issued on the measurement of fixed assets. (6 marks)

(b) Aztech, a public limited company, manufactures and operates a fleet of small aircraft. It draws up its financial statements to 31 March each year.

Aztech also owns a small chain of hotels (carrying value of £16 million), which are used in the sale of holidays to the public. It is the policy of the company not to provide depreciation on the hotels as they are maintained to a high standard and the economic lives of the hotels are long (20 years remaining life). The hotels are periodically revalued and on 31 March 2000, their existing use value was determined to be £20 million, the replacement cost of the hotels was £16 million and the open market value was £19 million. One of the hotels included above is surplus to the company's requirements as at 31 March 2000. This hotel had an existing use value of £3 million, a replacement cost of £2 million and an open market value of £2.5 million, before expected estate agents and solicitors fees of £200 000. Aztech wishes to revalue the hotels as at 31 March 2000. There is no indication of any impairment in value of the hotels.

The company has recently finished manufacturing a fleet of five aircraft to a new design. These aircraft are intended for use in its own fleet for domestic carriage purposes. The company commenced construction of the assets on 1 April 1998 and wishes to recognise them as fixed assets as at 31 March 2000 when they were first utilized. The aircraft were completed on 1 January 2000 but their exterior painting was delayed until 31 March 2000.

The costs (excluding finance costs) of manufacturing the aircraft were £28 million and the company has adopted a policy of capitalising the finance costs of manufacturing the aircraft. Aztech had taken out a three year loan of £20 million to finance the aircraft on 1 April 1998. Interest is payable at 10% per annum but is to be rolled over and paid at the end of the three year period together with the capital outstanding. Corporation tax is 30%.

During the construction of the aircraft, certain computerized components used in the manufacture fell dramatically in price. The company estimated that at 31 March 2000 the net realisable value of the aircraft was £30 million and their value in use was £29 million.

The engines used in the aircraft have a three year life and the body parts have an eight year life; Azetch has decided to depreciate the engines and the body parts over their different useful lives on the straight line basis from 1 April 2000. The cost of replacing the engines on 31 March 2003 is estimated to be £15 million. The engine costs represent thirty per cent of the total cost of manufacture.

The company has decided to revalue the aircraft annually on the basis of their market value. On 31 March 2001, the aircraft have a value in use of £28 million, a market value of £27 million and a net realisable value of £26 million. On 31 March 2002, the aircraft have a value in use of £17 million, a market value of £18 million and a net realisable value of £18.5 million. There is no consumption of economic benefits in 2002 other than the depreciation charge. Revaluation surpluses or deficits are apportioned between the engines and the body parts on the basis of their year end carrying values before the revaluation.

Required:
(i) **Describe how the hotels should be valued in the financial statements of Aztech on 31 March 2000 and explain whether the current depreciation policy relating to the hotels is acceptable under FRS 15 'Tangible Fixed Assets'.** (6 marks)

(ii) **Show the accounting treatment of the aircraft fleet in the financial statements on the basis of the above scenario for the financial years ending on:**
  (a) 31 March 2000; (4 marks)
  (b) 31 March 2001, 2002. (6 marks)
  (c) 31 March 2003 before revaluation. (3 marks)
  (25 marks)
  ACCA FRE JUNE 2000

Research and development (SSAP 13)

After reading this chapter you should be able to:
- discuss the nature of research and development expenditure
- explain how this should be accounted for in accordance with accounting conventions
- describe the accounting treatment recommended by SSAP 13 'Accounting for Research and Development'
- describe the Companies Act requirements in relation to research and development expenditure.

Introduction

Before a business actually produces a product or a range of products, it has to decide on what it should produce, how it should produce it, what technical characteristics it should have, and so on. The business may also be carrying on more basic investigation into scientific and technical possibilities on the one hand, and future marketing trends on the other.

The expenditure on such matters comes generally under the heading of research and development (R&D) expenditure. The nature and the importance of such expenditure will vary greatly between different industries, but in some cases it will be a very large absolute amount, and its accounting treatment will have a material effect on the reported results of the business.

The problem

From our knowledge of accounting conventions generally, how should such expenditure be treated? It is reasonable to assume that a business is suffering this expenditure in order to produce benefits for itself, at least in the long run. By the very nature of R&D, some of the expenditure will not produce results. But then we can reasonably assume that when the time is reached when a successful outcome appears unlikely, then expenditure in that particular direction will promptly cease. So, remembering our earlier statement (p. 137) that an asset is something that will:

1 give probable future benefit
2 be possessed or controlled by the business
3 have arisen from some earlier transaction or event

it seems that R&D is, in principle, an asset.

Following on with this line of reasoning, when the asset starts to be 'used', i.e. when the benefit actually begins to occur, we shall need to apply the matching convention. The asset figure will need to be charged to the P&L account over the period of benefit, in approximate proportion to the benefit pattern. In effect we would have a fixed asset that would require depreciating. And since there is likely to be a gap, perhaps of several years, between expenditure and eventual benefit in terms of production and sales, it follows that the expense or depreciation may be zero for one or more accounting periods. If the benefit has not begun to appear yet, then under the matching convention we should not yet begin to write off the asset as an expense.

The above arguments are entirely logical but can they be criticized?

Activity 1

State with reasons which accounting conventions the above treatment of R&D is inconsistent with.

Activity 1 feedback

It can be suggested that the above treatment is inconsistent with the prudence convention. R&D expenditure is by definition speculative and, particularly with more basic investigation, the outcome is highly uncertain. It is perhaps difficult to argue that the existence of future benefit, of greater amount than the expenditure, can be established with 'reasonable certainty'. It is even harder to argue that the *relationship* to the revenue or benefit in any particular future period can be established with 'reasonable certainty'. It must also be remembered that a successful profitable outcome is crucially dependent on the validity of the going concern convention.

R&D, as an asset, is intangible (i.e. it is not physical) and it may often be difficult to sell by itself. There is therefore no back-up value if things go wrong. Where there is a conflict between the matching convention, SSAP 2 is quite clear on the outcome: prudence should prevail (p. 226). (However, note the changes now made to the 'status' of prudence by FRS 18 and S of P.) Our general conclusion should perhaps be that with many cases of R&D expenditure, the chances of eventual benefit and profit are not sufficiently foreseeable to justify matching as opposed to prudence. But we should recognize that circumstances could arise where capitalization and matching may be justifiable.

It is appropriate at this point to consider the effect on financial statements of treating R&D expenditure, first in accordance with matching principles and secondly in accordance with prudence principles.

Activity 2

Devero plc has an annual turnover of £13 million and a profit after taxation but before charging R&D expenditure of £1 million. The number of ordinary shares Devero has in issue is two million. During the year £500 000 is spent on R&D. Show the effect on the eps for Devero plc of:

1 accounting for R&D in accordance with 'matching' and thereby treating the expenditure as an asset
2 accounting for R&D in accordance with 'prudence'.

Activity 2 feedback

1 If we apply matching and capitalize the expenditure and presuming that no benefit has yet appeared from the expenditure then no charge will be made to the profit for the year. Thus

$$\text{eps} = \frac{100\,000\,000\text{p}}{2\,000\,000} = 50\text{p}$$

2 If we apply the prudence concept at its strictest then all the R&D expenditure should be written off to the P&L account. Thus

$$\text{eps} = \frac{50\,000\,000\text{p}}{2\,000\,000} = 25\text{p}$$

The two results of 50p and 25p above are both extremes and it is probable that the most useful way of dealing with the expenditure would be to capitalize some of it for future matching but charge the remainder to the P&L account in accordance with prudence. The question is how easy it is to make a judgement on which expenditure should be capitalized, and on what precise grounds.

The SSAP's proposals

The ASC had considerable difficulty in producing a standard in this area. Two different EDs were issued, and the eventual standard differed in one important respect from both of them. A revised standard was issued in January 1989, but the only significant difference between this and the original relates to the disclosure requirements. All references are to the revised version. The key definition is as follows:

21 The following definition is used for the purpose of this statement: Research and development expenditure means expenditure falling into one or more of the following broad categories (except to the extent that it relates to locating or exploiting oil, gas or mineral deposits or is reimbursable by third parties either directly or under the terms of a firm contract to develop and manufacture at an agreed price calculated to reimburse both elements of expenditure):
(a) pure (or basic) research: experimental or theoretical work undertaken primarily to acquire new scientific or technical knowledge for its own sake rather than directed towards any specific aim or application;
(b) applied research: original or critical investigation undertaken in order to gain new scientific or technical knowledge and directed towards a specific practical aim or objective;
(c) development: use of scientific or technical knowledge in order to produce new or substantially improved materials, devices, products or services, to install new processes or systems prior to the commencement of commercial production or commercial applications, or to improve substantially those already produced or installed.

Notice that the standard does not apply to mineral deposits and, in particular, therefore does not apply to the currently very important area of oil and natural gas exploration. This is discussed separately at the end of the chapter. In practice, the distinction between the two types of research (pure and applied), between applied R&D, and also between development and actual production cost, is often very difficult to determine. The standard tries to clarify the distinctions as far as possible:

5 Research and development activity is distinguished from non-research based activity by the presence or absence of an appreciable element of innovation. If the activity departs from routine and breaks new ground it should normally be included; if it follows an established pattern it should normally be excluded.

6 Examples of activities that would normally be included in research and development are:
   (a) experimental, theoretical or other work aimed at the discovery of new knowledge, or the advancement of existing knowledge
   (b) searching for applications of that knowledge
   (c) formulation and design of possible applications for such work
   (d) testing in search for, or evaluation of, product, service or process alternatives
   (e) design, construction and testing of pre-production prototypes and models and development batches
   (f) design of products, services, processes or systems involving new technology or substantially improving those already produced or installed
   (g) construction and operation of pilot plants.

7 Examples of activities that would normally be excluded from research and development include:
   (a) testing and analysis either of equipment or product for purposes of quality or quantity control
   (b) periodic alterations to existing products, services or processes even though these may represent some improvement
   (c) operational research not tied to a specific research and development activity
   (d) cost of corrective action in connection with break-downs during commercial production
   (e) legal and administrative work in connection with patent applications, records and litigation and the sale or licensing of patents
   (f) activity, including design and construction engineering, relating to the construction, relocation, rearrangement or start-up of facilities or equipment other than facilities or equipment whose sole use is for a particular research and development project
   (g) market research.

Activity 3

Distinguish between the following in accordance with paragraph 21 of SSAP 13, as applied to a manufacturer of cleaning compounds.

1 £25 000 spent on identifying whether customers prefer powder or liquid detergent.
2 £100 000 spent on identifying an addition to detergent to enable cold washing.

3 £150 000 spent on producing a new concentrated bleach that is highly marketable.
4 £95 000 spent on a subcontract to develop a dry cleaning fluid.
5 £250 000 spent on exploring the possibility of an oil find on land the company owned in the United States.

Activity 3 feedback

1 This is an example of market research and therefore outside the definition of R&D.
2 An example of applied research activities.
3 This would appear to be development expenditure.
4 As this is subcontract work then it is outside the scope of SSAP 13.
5 Again mineral deposits are outside the scope of SSAP 13.

Accounting treatment of R&D

23 The cost of fixed assets acquired or constructed in order to provide facilities for research and development activities over a number of accounting periods should be capitalised and written off over their useful lives through the profit and loss account.

This obviously refers to tangible fixed assets, although it does not say so. They should be treated like any other tangible fixed asset, and not considered as R&D expenditure at all for this purpose.

24 Expenditure on pure and applied research (other than that referred to in paragraph 23) should be written off in the year of expenditure through the profit and loss account.

The distinction between pure and applied research is therefore irrelevant from the point of view of accounting treatment.

25 Development expenditure should be written off in the year of expenditure except in the following circumstances when it may be deferred to future periods:
(a) there is a clearly defined project, and
(b) the related expenditure is separately identifiable, and
(c) the outcome of such a project has been assessed with reasonable certainty as to:
  (i) its technical feasibility, and
  (ii) its ultimate commercial viability considered in the light of factors such as likely market conditions (including competing products), public opinion, consumer and environmental legislation, and
(d) the aggregate of the deferred development costs, any further development costs, and related production, selling and administration costs is reasonably expected to be exceeded by related future sales or other revenues, and
(e) adequate resources exist, or are reasonably expected to be available, to enable the project to be completed and to provide any consequential increases in working capital.

No less than six conditions have to be satisfied before development expenditure can be carried forward in accordance with the matching convention. They are clearly explained in paragraph 25 quoted above. It is particularly important to notice that if all six conditions are satisfied then the development expenditure *may* be deferred to future periods. This is the point that gave the ASC so much difficulty and uncertainty. The first ED, ED 14, although containing all the distinctions and conditions contained in the eventual SSAP, nevertheless concluded that all R&D expenditure should be written off as incurred. This proposal was strongly objected to by those industries, particularly aerospace and electronics, who spent a particularly large proportion of their resources on R&D. ED 14 was then replaced by ED 17, which proposed that if the six conditions as regards development expenditure were met then development expenditure *should, as a standard requirement*, be deferred against future revenue, i.e. that it should be capitalized in the year of the expenditure. This compulsory element also met some objection, and so the ASC compromised and replaced the word 'should' with the word 'may' as shown in paragraph 25 quoted earlier. SSAP 13 therefore does not standardize the treatment of development expenditure. Development expenditure that meets all six conditions *may*:

> be deferred to the extent that its recovery can reasonably be regarded as assured.

Where development expenditure is to be deferred, the following points apply.

27 If an accounting policy of deferral of development expenditure is adopted, it should be applied to all development projects that meet the criteria in paragraph 25.

28 If development costs are deferred to future periods, they should be amortised. The amortisation should commence with the commercial production or application of the product, service, process or system and should be allocated on a systematic basis to each accounting period, by reference to either the sale or use of the product, service, process or system or the period over which these are expected to be sold or used.

29 Deferred development expenditure for each project should be reviewed at the end of each accounting period and where the circumstances which have justified the deferral of the expenditure (paragraph 25) no longer apply, or are considered doubtful, the expenditure, to the extent to which it is considered to be irrecoverable, should be written off immediately project by project.

Let's look at some examples of R&D expenditure and see how we would account for them in accordance with SSAP 13.

Activity 4

1 A company spent £200000 on acquiring new plant and machinery for its R&D unit.

2 In previous years the company had spent £2 million on developing a cure for influenza. This had previously been capitalized in accordance with the criteria laid down in SSAP 13. However, circumstances have changed and the product is viewed as no longer viable. £100000 had already been spent in the current year.

3 The company has spent £500000 in previous years which had been capitalized and £20000 in the current year on a drug to prevent nausea in pregnancy. The drug was successfully launched half-way through the current year and is expected to achieve profits for

five years from its launch. Sales are expected to be £1 million per annum in the first two years from the date of launch and then increase to £2 million per annum for the next two before falling back to £1 million. Sales are achieved evenly throughout a year.

4   £250 000 spent on trying to achieve a cure for AIDS. No marketable product has yet been identified.

Activity 4 feedback

1   These are tangible fixed assets acquired for R&D activities and as with all other tangible fixed assets should be capitalized and depreciated over their useful life.

2   The previous £2 million and the current £100 000 must both be written off as the product is no longer viable. This will have a marked effect on the current year's P&L account. Note the £2 million previously capitalized is not a prior year adjustment as it is not a change in accounting policy or a fundamental error. It is also highly unlikely that the write off of £2 million could be described as extraordinary. It may, however, be viewed as exceptional depending upon its materiality.

3   The expenditure of £520 000 meets the criteria laid down in SSAP 13 therefore can be capitalized and amortized over the life of the product. Amortization will commence with the current year as the product has been sold for six months of the current year.

Amortization calculation: total sales £7 million

$$\text{amortization current year } \frac{520\,000}{7} \times \frac{1}{2} \text{ (as only six months)}$$

$$= £37\,143$$

4   This must be written off in the current year, as research.

Development costs written off

The original version of SSAP 13 specifically prohibited the write-back of any development costs previously written off. The revised standard removes this restriction thus allowing matching to prevail over prudence again. Thus we can apply Companies Act regulations relating to provisions for diminution in value which are no longer necessary and reinstate previously capitalized development expenditure that had been written off.

It is also interesting to note that it is possible to reinstate development costs written off even if they were not previously capitalized. This can be done as a prior year adjustment but only if the expenditure could have been deferred at the time it was incurred.

Disclosure requirements

The disclosure requirements of the standard are:

30   The accounting policy on research and development expenditure should be stated and explained.

31   The total amount of research and development expenditure charged in the profit and loss account should be disclosed, analysed between the current year's expenditure and amounts amortised from deferred expenditure.

32   Movements on deferred development expenditure and the amount carried forward at the beginning and the end of the period should be disclosed. Deferred

development expenditure should be disclosed under intangible fixed assets in the balance sheet.

The requirement in paragraph 31 to disclose details of the P&L account charge for R&D expenditure is the only important change in the revision of 1989. Previously the UK was out of step with most of the other European countries in not requiring the P&L charge to be disclosed. However, there are still some exemptions from this requirement as paragraph 22 makes clear:

> **22**   This standard applies to all financial statements intended to give a true and fair view of the financial position and profit or loss, but, except in the case of Republic of Ireland companies, the provisions set out in paragraph 31 regarding the disclosure of the total amounts of research and development charged in the profit and loss account need not be applied by an entity that:
>
> **(a)**   is not a public limited company or a special category company (as defined by Section 257 of Companies Act 1985) or a holding company that has a public limited company or a special category company as a subsidiary; and
>
> **(b)**   satisfies the criteria, multiplied in each case by 10, for defining a medium-sized company under Section 248 of the Companies Act 1985, as amended from time to time by statutory instrument and applied in accordance with the provisions of Section 249 of the Act.

The Companies Act

The Companies Act makes it clear that capitalized (deferred) development costs should be shown as fixed assets, but also states (schedule 4, paragraph 20) that 'an amount may only be included in a company's balance sheet in respect of development costs in special circumstances'. The Act does not define 'special circumstances', but these are generally taken to refer to the six conditions required by SSAP 13. Where development costs are included in the balance sheet, then a note to the accounts is required, showing (schedule 4, paragraph 20):

1   the period over which the amount of those costs originally capitalized is to be written off; and

2   the reasons for capitalizing the development costs in question.

For the purposes of the calculation of distributable profits under Sections 263 and 264 (p. 188), all amounts shown as an asset under the heading of development costs must be treated as realized losses (section 269), unless the directors can justify otherwise. Thus for distributable profits purposes, development costs should be treated as realized losses whether or not they have been treated as expenses in the P&L account!

Oil and gas exploration costs

The question of the appropriate treatment of exploration costs for oil and natural gas companies has been discussed at length in recent years. Two basic models have been developed. The first model is the **successful efforts method**. This regards each well as a separate entity and therefore as a separate cost centre. This means that broadly speaking the thinking behind SSAP 13 should be applied to each particular well. Until we can be 'reasonably certain' that a well will be profitable, we must therefore write off all costs associated with the drilling operation of that well immediately to profit and loss. It is in the nature of the industry that some wells will be very profitable but many wells will not produce any revenues at all. Given both the uncertainties and the high proportion of unsuccessful drillings this is clearly a very conservative method.

The second model is known as the **pooling of interests method**. This allows the costs of large numbers of wells to be lumped together into one big pool. The costs of the 'pool' can then be matched against the revenues from the 'pool'. This is less prudent than the first method, but is arguably better matching. In its pure form the 'pool' would be world-wide, but this can be narrowed to the creation of a number of 'pools' defined by geographical or geological areas. The oil industry created a SORP for itself on this issue, 'franked' by the ASC. The SORP – wait for it – allows both methods. When the pooling method is used the pool should be defined 'at the discretion of the company, having regard to its organizational, operational and financial development'. Pools 'should not normally be smaller in size than a country but are not subject to a maximum limit'. This statement seems to put emphasis on geographical rather than geological boundaries which is perhaps less than logical. However, given the enormous flexibility in the SORP, and the fact that by definition it does not purport to be mandatory on anybody, it is obvious that accounting practice in this area is not going to become significantly more consistent and comparable.

Summary

R&D is a difficult area to 'regulate'. Each reader will have his or her own idea of the relative importance of the matching and prudence conventions. You may think that the restrictions on deferral implied by the six conditions are excessively constrictive. You may feel that on balance the dangers of allowing any deferral are excessive. What is certainly questionable is the validity, in a SSAP, of allowing the freedom to defer or not as the fancy takes. It is also instructive to consider briefly the process of arriving at the eventual standard. The ASC allowed its views to be materially altered by the views, not of accountants, but of businesses affected by its proposals. It was obviously positively looking for an outcome that no one would particularly criticize. Whether this is pragmatism and sensible consensus leadership, or dereliction of their leadership role, is an open question.

The ASB adopted SSAP 13 (revised) without any changes and to date have no plans to amend it. Allan Cook, technical director of the ASB, has stated 'We have other, rather more urgent projects to deal with first although if people think we should look at it we might consider it'. One of the first calls for the review of the standard has come from the Institute of Chartered Accountants Scotland who believe that the definitions of research and development are too limiting in the current innovative age. The ICAS suggest a new term should be added to the standard – innovation, which is broadly defined as 'the successful exploitation of new ideas'.

Exercises

1 Distinguish between:
   (a) pure research expenditure
   (b) applied research expenditure
   (c) development expenditure
   (d) operating expenditure.
   How should each be treated according to the ASC?

2 Has SSAP 13 got the appropriate balance between prudence and the matching convention?

3 Is the element of choice in the treatment of development expenditure given by the SSAP justified?

4 Prepare extracts from the P&L account of Bleco plc for year-ended 31 August 20X1 and from the company's balance sheet at that date, to incorporate the financial effects of the R&D expenditure.

   Your answer should comply with the requirements of SSAP 13 (revised) ('Accounting for Research and Development'). Detailed workings for each item must be shown. (33 marks)

Information on the R&D activities of Bleco plc.

All projects are given designatory prefixes to indicate their nature:

PR = pure research
AR = applied research
D = development

At 1 September 20X0, the balance brought forward as development costs consisted of:

	£
Project:	
D363	198 300
D367	242 700
D368	nil

During the year-ended 31 August 20X1:
   (a) Project D368 satisfied the SSAP 13 (revised) deferment criteria. In previous years, a total of £47 830 expended on this project had been written off to P&L account. The directors have resolved to defer, by capitalization, the aggregate of the current year's expenditure together with the reinstated figure from previous years.
   (b) An applied research project, AR204, was converted into a development project and redesignated D369, but all expenditure up to this point is to be written off.
   (c) Two more development projects were instituted, D370 and D371. This latter project was commissioned by Lytax Ltd under a contract for full reimbursement of expenditure; to date, £24 000 has been received from Lytax Ltd.
   (d) It has become apparent that the technical feasibility and commercial viability of project D370 are doubtful.
   (e) All other development projects satisfy the SSAP 13 deferment criteria.
   (f) Project D363 entered full commercial production and is to be amortized on a straight-line basis over six years.

Bleco Ltd depreciates fixed assets on a straight-line basis, assuming no residual value, at the following rates:

	% per annum on cost
Laboratory buildings	10
Laboratory equipment	20

A full year's depreciation is charged in the year of acquisition.

(g) Expenditure was incurred as follows:

	PR119 £	AR187 £	AR204 £	D367 £	D368 £	D369 £	D370 £	D371 £	Unallocated £
Wages, salaries and related charges	35 100	27 300	15 260	2 090	16 480	34 070	29 800	27 500	3 300
Materials	810	520	290	340	410	1 560	2 650	3 400	4 070
Direct expenses (other)	250	210	180	170	230	640	690	710	2 240
Production overheads	1 240	3 600	2 950	3 540	4 650	6 980	6 010	6 420	7 070
Fixed assets:									
Experimental laboratory buildings		200 000							
Testing laboratory buildings						310 000			
Laboratory equipment		170 000				472 000			
Related selling and administrative overheads									76 200
Market research									55 600

(ACCA)

5 An analysis of the expenditure written off by Hood plc in the year-ended 31 March 20X1 showed the costs had been incurred on the following activities:

(a)	legal and administrative work in connection with patent applications	£30 000
(b)	relocation of the research department	£55 000
(c)	quality control on product which went into production in 20X1	£15 000
(d)	operating costs of a pilot plant.	£125 000

(In 20X0 the company wrote off £100 000 which had been incurred as operating costs of this pilot plant.)

The finance director of Hood plc now proposes that there should be a change of accounting policy and that each of these items of expenditure should be capitalized in the 20X1 accounts. He further proposes that the operating costs of the pilot plant of £100 000 which were written off in the 20X0 accounts should be capitalized in the 20X1 balance sheet.

Critically discuss the proposed accounting treatment for R&D expenditure with reference to the provision of Companies Act and SSAP 13.

(ACCA)

6 In connection with SSAP 13 'Accounting for Research and Development':

(a) define 'applied research' and 'development' (4 marks)

(b) why is it considered necessary to distinguish between 'applied research' and 'development' expenditure and how does this distinction affect the accounting treatment?

(8 marks)

(c) State whether the following items are included within the SSAP 13 definition of R&D, and give your reasons.

(i) market research (2 marks)

(ii) testing of pre-production prototypes (2 marks)

(iii) operational research (2 marks)

(iv) testing in search of process alternatives (2 marks)

(20 marks)

(ACCA)

18

Substance over form

After reading this chapter you should be able to:
- describe the meaning and significance of the substance over form concept
- discuss applications of substance over form suggested by the Accounting Standards Board or elsewhere.

Scope of the chapter

In Chapter 10 we looked at ideas of forming a general and all-embracing framework. There and elsewhere we have come across the concept of **substance over form**. This is the idea that a transaction should be treated for accounting purposes in accordance with its underlying commercial substance, even if this means ignoring or going against its technical legal form.

The ASC had been moving further and further down this road for a number of years before its demise. This movement is certainly supported in principle by the ASB. In the draft of chapter two of its statement of principles which we referred to in Chapter 15 the following paragraph appears:

> **30** If information is to represent faithfully the transactions and other events that it purports to represent, it is necessary that they are accounted for and presented in accordance with their substance and economic reality and not merely their legal form. The substance of transactions and events is not always consistent with that which is apparent from their legal form, especially if that form is contrived. For example, an enterprise may dispose of an asset to another party in such a way that the documentation purports to pass legal ownership to that party: nevertheless, when the circumstances are looked at as a whole, it may be found that arrangements exist that ensure that the enterprise continues to enjoy the future economic benefits embodied in the asset, or to suffer the obligations of a liability. In such circumstances, the reporting of a sale would not be a valid description of the transaction entered into (if, indeed, there were a transaction).

As an aside it is instructive to compare this paragraph in detail with the corresponding paragraph of the IASC framework discussed in Chapter 10 (see p. 146). The wording is remarkably close. One might infer from this that the ASB is doing little more than pinching and occasionally refining the IASC ideas. One might also infer, to take a very different perspective, that the IASC ideas appear to be largely British – or at least Anglo-Saxon – and are therefore not properly *international* at all.

In the last months of the old ASC a flurry of exposure drafts appeared, several of them relating closely to the substance over form attitude.

In several cases the ideas of the ASC have already been bypassed and the problems tackled elsewhere. An example of this is the problem of defining 'subsidiaries' much more tightly to prevent non-consolidation of what is in reality group indebtedness. This has now been dealt with by the Companies Act 1989 and FRS 2 (see Chapter 24).

FRS 5 'Reporting the Substance of Transactions'

FRS 5 was issued in April 1994 with the following general statement:

> The FRS will not change the accounting treatment and disclosure of the vast majority of transactions. It will mainly affect those more complex transactions whose substance may not be readily apparent. The true commercial effect of such transactions may not be adequately expressed by their legal form and, where this is the case, it will not be sufficient to account for them merely by recording that form.

Its main aim was to address the issue of off-balance sheet financing. The standard itself is fairly brief but then contains several application notes which describe the application of the standard to transactions with certain features, that is consignment stock, sale and repurchase agreements, factoring, securitized assets and loan transfers.

The objective of FRS 5 is to:

> ensure that the substance of an entity's transactions is reported in its financial statements. The commercial effect of the entity's transactions, and any resulting assets, liabilities, gains or losses, should be faithfully represented in its financial statements.

Interestingly the definitions of assets and liabilities given in the standard are the same as those in the conceptual framework (Chapter 3), which was only in discussion form! It certainly appears as though some of the conceptual framework is being approved by the ASB piecemeal through its FRS statements.

Substance of a transaction

According to FRS 5 the substance of a transaction is determined by identifying:

- whether the transaction has given rise to new assets or liabilities for the reporting entity and whether it has changed the entity's existing assets or liabilities
- evidence that an entity has an obligation to transfer benefits (and hence a liability) is given if the entity is exposed to the risk inherent in the benefits, taking into account the likelihood of those risks having a commercial effect in practice
- evidence that an entity has an obligation to transfer benefits (and hence has a liability) is given if there is some circumstance in which the entity is unable to avoid, legally or commercially, an outflow of benefits.

Recognition of an item

Once having decided whether an asset or liability exists for a particular entity we then need to determine if and how we recognize the asset or liability in the balance sheet of the entity. The FRS states that

> the item should be recognised in the balance sheet if there is sufficient evidence of the existence of the items and if it can be measured at a monetary amount with sufficient reliability.

Partial derecognition occurs when the transaction involves:

- a transfer of only part of the item in question
- a transfer of all of the item for only part of its life
- a transfer of all of the item for all of its life but where the entity retains some significant right to benefits or exposure to risk.

Activity 1

Identify at least one example for each of the three cases given above where a transaction would be partially derecognized and identify the accounting treatment for the recognized part of the transaction.

Activity 1 feedback

The standard provides several examples.

A transfer of only part of an item could occur when part of a building is sold, a part interest in a racehorse is sold or a part interest in a loan receivable is sold. In all these cases the entity would cease to recognize that part of the asset that has been transferred but would continue to recognize the remainder. However, a change in the description of the asset may be required to convey to the user the part ownership.

A transfer of all the item for only part of its life could occur for example if property is sold with the agreement to repurchase in the future. In this case the asset will only be recognized at the entity's interest in its residual value and the liability to repurchase will also be recognized.

An example of the last case is the sale of an item subject to warranty. The seller will cease to recognize the asset, but would recognize a liability to the warranty.

The last possible outcome for derecognition is linked presentation. This involves the offset of asset with liability for certain transactions which appears to be in conflict with the Companies Act requirement of separate recognition of assets and liabilities. However, the ASB do not agree. They state that:

> linked presentation does not constitute offset of an asset and a liability but rather it is the provision of additional information about an asset, the net amount, which is necessary in order to give a true and fair view.

The linked presentation is limited to certain non-recourse finance arrangements and several criteria have to be met before it can be used. These circumstances occur when an asset is financed in such a way that

- the finance will be repaid only from proceeds generated by the specific item it finances (or by transfer of the item itself) and there is no possibility whatsoever of a claim on the entity being established other than against funds generated by that item
- there is no provision whatsoever whereby the entity may either keep the item on repayment of the finance or re-acquire it at any time.

The criteria which have to be met for linked presentation are as follows:

1 the finance relates to a specific item (or portfolio of similar items) and, in the case of a loan, is secured on that item but not on any other asset of the entity
2 the provider of the finance has no recourse whatsoever, either explicit or implicit, to the other assets of the entity for losses and the entity has no obligation whatsoever to repay the provider of finance
3 the directors of the entity state explicitly in each set of financial statements where a linked presentation is used that the entity is not obliged to support any losses, nor does it intend to do so
4 the provider of the finance has agreed in writing (in the finance documentation or otherwise) that it will seek repayment of the finance, as to both principal and interest, only to the extent that sufficient funds are generated by the specific item it has financed and that it will not seek recourse in any other form, and such agreement is noted in each set of financial statements where a linked presentation is used
5 if the funds generated by the item are insufficient to pay off the provider of the finance, this does not constitute an event of default for the entity; and
6 there is no provision whatsoever, either in the financing arrangement or otherwise, whereby the entity has a right or an obligation either to keep the item upon repayment of the finance or (where title to the item has been transferred) to re-acquire it at any time. Accordingly:
   (a) where the item is one (such as a monetary receivable) that directly generates cash, the provider of the finance will be repaid out of the resulting cash receipts (to the extent these are sufficient); or
   (b) where the item is one (such as a physical asset) that does not directly generate cash, there is a definite point at which either the item will be sold to a third party and the provider of the finance repaid from the proceeds (to the extent these are sufficient) or the item will be transferred to the provider of the finance in full and final settlement.

Activity 2

Is the following a circumstance where linked presentation may be used? A portfolio of debts is transferred from company A to another company B, who pay a non-returnable fee plus a further amount dependent on whether or not the debts are fully realized.

Activity 2 feedback

Company A does not have a liability to repay the non-returnable fee nor does it have an asset of the debts. However, it does have a new asset, the right to future benefits depending on whether or not the debts are fully realized. The circumstances exist for linked presentation and if all the criteria are satisfied then the linked presentation will be as follows in A's books:

> debts subject to financing arrangements
>> debts (after providing for expected bad debts)   X
>> less non-returnable amounts received   Y   X – Y

This linked presentation shows that A retains significant benefits and risks relating to all the debts, and that the claim of the provider of finance is limited strictly to the funds generated by them.

Quasi-subsidiary

We stated previously in this chapter that one area of off-balance sheet financing, that of consolidation of subsidiaries, was dealt with in FRS 2. However, FRS 5 introduces a quasi-subsidiary. This is defined by the standard as:

> a company, trust, partnership or other vehicle that, though not fulfilling the definition of a subsidiary, is directly or indirectly controlled by the reporting entity and gives rise to benefits for that entity that are in substance no different from those that would arise were the vehicle a subsidiary.

If a quasi-subsidiary exists then FRS 5 requires that:

> the assets, liabilities, profits, losses and cash flows of a quasi-subsidiary should be included in the group financial statements of the group that controls it in the same way as if they were those of a subsidiary. Where an entity has a quasi-subsidiary but no subsidiaries and therefore does not prepare group financial statements, it should provide in its financial statements consolidated financial statements of itself and the quasi-subsidiary, presented with equal prominence to the reporting entity's individual financial statements unless the interest in the quasi-subsidiary is held exclusively with a view to subsequent resale.

Activity 3

Alpha Ltd, a property company, sells half of its buildings to Beta Ltd, a company financed by bank loans on which normal interest is paid. Beta Ltd is set up for the sole purpose of owning these buildings. Alpha Ltd manages the buildings for Beta Ltd and is paid a management fee for this service by Beta Ltd. It is proposed to set the scale of the management fee in one of two ways:

(a) at a level which will absorb all the profit of Beta Ltd after payment of interest on the bank's finance. If any of the buildings are sold by Beta Ltd this must be with the approval of Alpha Ltd and all gains and losses on sale revert to Alpha Ltd

(b) at a specific fee not related to Beta Ltd's profits and Beta Ltd can sell the buildings without recourse to Alpha Ltd.

   In which case would Beta Ltd be a quasi-subsidiary of Alpha Ltd?

Activity 3 feedback

Beta Ltd is a quasi-subsidiary of Alpha Ltd in (a) as here Alpha Ltd controls all of the profits of Beta Ltd; the bank only receiving interest but no profits.

Application notes

The application notes to FRS 5 discuss five common forms of off-balance sheet transactions and how to deal with them. They also cover some thirteen pages of the standard! We do not intend to deal with all these application notes in detail, but the following example and activity should provide you with a flavour of these notes.

Consignment stock example

Consignment stock occurs frequently in the motor industry when a dealer obtains stock from a manufacturer on the basis of sale or return. The stock is generally held on the dealer's premises, thus the manufacturer avoids holding costs. Generally legal title to the stock does not pass from the manufacturer until either the stock is sold to a third party, or the dealer uses it as a demonstration model or has held the stock for a period of time. Legally, therefore, the consignment stock is an asset of the manufacturer, but what is the substance of the transaction?

An analysis of the substance of the transaction requires a judgement on where the risks and rewards associated with the stock lie.

The benefits of consignment stock are according to FRS 5:

- future cash flows associated with the sale of the stock
- insulation from changes to prices charged by the manufacturer
- the right to use as a demonstration model.

The risks of consignment stock are:

- retention of unsaleable stock
- increased finance costs and holding costs due to slow movement.

The substance of the transaction is determined by assessing where the greatest benefit and risk lies, the dealer or the manufacturer. If a dealer is able to legally resist requests made by the manufacturer to return the goods or transfer to another dealer or, if on such transfer, the dealer is compensated then this would indicate that the stock was in substance an asset of the dealer.

If on the other hand a dealer has a legal right to return unsold stock to the manufacturer without incurring an obsolescence risk, then the dealer does not have an asset. In determining the substance of consignment stock transactions a detailed investigation into the actual risks and rewards and where they lie is essential.

The following activity demonstrates another of the application notes contained in the standard.

Activity 4

Tobemor plc, a whisky blending company, sells half of its maturing stock of whisky to a bank for £2 million on 1 April 20X0 and agrees to buy it back one year later for £2.2 million. Note that the whisky never moves from Tobemor's premises. How should the above transaction be accounted for?

Activity 4 feedback

Tobemor plc has not transferred the risks and rewards of ownership of the whisky to the bank. What it has done is to raise a loan of £2 million using the stock of whisky as security. An interest payment of £0.2 million is due at the end of the loan period, one year. The substance of the transaction is therefore that of a loan. The asset of stock of whisky will not change in the books unless, of course, net realizable value falls below cost.

The accounting treatment in Tobemor's books would be as follows:

		Debit £m	Credit £m
01.04.20X0	Cash	2	
	Loan		2

Being the receipt of monies from the bank in respect of whisky.

		Debit £m	Credit £m
31.03.20X1	Profit and loss	0.2	
	Interest payable		0.2

Being the charge for interest on loan to the bank

		Debit £m	Credit £m
01.04.20X1	Loan	2	
	Interest payable	0.2	
	Cash		2.2

Being the payment of cash to the bank for the return of the whisky and the charge for interest on the loan.

FRS 5 is complex and long but does attempt to deal with the problem of off-balance sheet finance by establishing the principle of substance over form. However, the business world is complicated and ever-changing and the ASB cannot hope to have covered all complex transactions in its application notes. We wait to see whether the spirit of the standard will be followed or whether companies will attempt to find loopholes in it so as to account for transactions in a beneficial way to themselves.

Capital instruments

The balance between substance and form is also considered in respect of accounting for capital instruments. Capital instruments are issued by an entity to raise finance. They include shares, debentures, options, warrants, etc. Problems arise with capital instruments in respect of their classification – are they debt or equity? The distinction is important as it will affect the gearing ratio and other financial performance and position indicators. The distinction at first glance appears clear-cut in that if shares are issued then these are equity, if debentures or loans then these are long-term liabilities. However, from the early 1980s innovative forms of finance have been developed and it is now less clear as to whether these capital instruments are debt or equity.

For example:

- is a debenture that is convertible into shares at a given date debt or equity?
- should redeemable preference shares be treated as debt given that their substance is similar to debentures in terms of interest and redemption?
- if preference shares are equity then should we classify them with ordinary shares?

In addition to the above we have the added problem that, once having classified a capital instrument as debt or equity, what exactly is the value it should be shown at? The capital instrument of deep discounted bonds illustrates this problem.

Deep discounted bonds

These are bonds issued for a fixed period at a large discount over face value, and bearing a small or non-existent rate of interest. An example might be a bond issued at £50 bearing no interest at all, repayable at £100 after ten years. The commercial substance is clearly that interest of £50 (100 − 50) is payable over the ten years, but how should this be charged to the P&L account? Should it be charged on the basis of cash paid or over the relevant period in proportion to capital plus unpaid 'interest' at each point in time.

The balance sheet treatment is even more problematic. When the bond in the example above is issued do we have a liability of £50, or do we on the other hand have a liability of £100 and an asset of £50? If the former, the double entry for the debits to profit and loss will be credits to the liability account. If the latter, the double entry for the debits will be credits to the asset account. The former seems much the more logical. First, at this point in time the business has borrowed £50 and not £100, and secondly it seems extremely hard to justify that the debit of £50 falls within the definition of an asset. It has been suggested that the fact that the Companies Act 1985 forbids the netting out of assets and liabilities *requires* the recording of both debit and credit in the balance sheet. This does not follow, however, as the suggestion confuses debits with assets. If we do not have an asset, then the issue of whether we can net it off can never arise.

FRS 4 'Capital Instruments'

In December 1993 the ASB issued FRS 4 'Capital Instruments' to ensure that

financial statements provide a clear, coherent and consistent treatment of capital instruments in particular as regards the classification of instruments as debt, non-equity shares or equity shares.

Its other objective was to

ensure that costs associated with such capital instruments were dealt with in a manner consistent with their classification.

The distinction in the standard between debt and equity is based on the definition of a liability from the ASB's Statement of Principles chapter three. Again the ASB seemed to be pre-empting the approval of the statement of principles. The definition of a liability was as follows:

a liability is an entity's obligation to transfer economic benefits as a result of past transactions or events.

Thus, any capital instrument with an obligation to transfer economic benefits is debt.

Activity 5

A company has in issue £2 million redeemable preference shares. Given the criterion above for classifying capital instruments state whether these redeemable preference shares should be shown as debt or equity.

Activity 5 feedback

Using the criterion would suggest debt as there is an obligation to transfer economic benefits – the redemption value. However, FRS 4 states that the requirement to classify capital instruments as debt if they contain an obligation to transfer economic benefits does not apply to shares, as to classify them as debt would be in breach of Companies Act! The use of substance over form seems to be at the ASB's discretion.

The ASB does require shares to be classified into either equity or non-equity shares, the latter being those shares which are similar to debt.

Definition of shares

FRS 4 provides the following definitions in respect of shares:

- equity shares – shares other than non-equity shares
- non-equity shares – shares possessing any of the following characteristics:
  - (a) any of the rights of the shares to receive payments (whether in respect of dividends, in respect of redemption or otherwise) are for a limited amount that is not calculated by reference to the company's assets or profits or the dividends on any class of equity share
  - (b) any of their rights to participate in a surplus in a winding up are limited to a specific amount that is not calculated by reference to the company's assets or profits and such limitation had a commercial effect in practice at the time the shares were issued or, if later, at the time the limitation was introduced
  - (c) the shares are redeemable either according to their terms, or because the holder, or any party other than the issuer, can require their redemption.

Activity 6

A company issues participating preference shares which are shares carrying a fixed dividend plus a proportion of the dividends paid on equity shares. State whether these shares should be classified as equity or non-equity.

Activity 6 feedback

Part of the dividend payment is calculated by reference to profits and the dividend on equity shares; therefore the definition given by the ASB would seem to suggest they should be treated as equity as the dividends in total are not limited. However, the ASB disagree with this analysis. The application notes to FRS 4 tell us that these participating preference shares are non-equity as they contain a restricted entitlement to a share in profits in the form of a fixed part dividend payment. The definition seems somewhat less than clear!

Finance costs

Finance costs are defined in FRS 4 as:

> the difference between the net proceeds of an instrument and the total amount of the payments (or other transfer of economic benefits) that the issuer may be required to make in respect of the instrument.

Accounting practice

The standard accounting practice for capital instruments prescribed by FRS 4 is as follows:

23   All capital instruments should be accounted for in the balance sheet within one of the following categories:
  - liabilities
  - shareholders' funds
  - in the case of consolidated financial statements, minority interests.

24   Capital instruments (other than shares, which are addressed at paragraphs 37–45 below) should be classified as liabilities if they contain an obligation to transfer economic benefits (including a contingent obligation to transfer economic benefits). Capital instruments that do not contain an obligation to transfer economic benefits should be reported within shareholders' funds.

Debt

Convertible debt

25   Conversion of debt should not be anticipated. Convertible debt should be reported within liabilities and the finance cost should be calculated on the assumption that the debt will never be converted. The amount attributable to convertible debt should be stated separately from that of other liabilities.

26   When convertible debt is converted, the amount recognised in shareholders' funds in respect of the shares issued should be the amount at which the liability for the debt is stated as at the date of conversion. No gain or loss should be recognised on conversion.

Carrying amount and allocation of finance costs

27   Immediately after issue, debt should be stated at the amount of the net proceeds.

28   The finance costs of debt should be allocated to periods over the term of the debt at a constant rate on the carrying amount. All finance costs should be charged in the profit and loss account, except in the case of investment companies, which are addressed in paragraph 52.

29   The carrying amount of debt should be increased by the finance cost in respect of the reporting period and reduced by payments made in respect of the debt in that period.

30   Accrued finance costs may be included in accruals rather than in the carrying amount of debt to the extent that the finance costs have accrued in one accounting period and will be paid in cash in the next. Any such accrual should be

included in the carrying amount of the debt for the purposes of calculating finance costs and gains and losses arising on repurchase or early settlement.

31 Where the amount of payments required by a debt instrument is contingent on uncertain future events such as changes in an index, those events should be taken into account in the calculation of the finance costs and the carrying amount once they have occurred.

Allocation of finance costs

The allocation of finance costs is illustrated in the following example:

Example

Convertible debt is issued on 1 January 1996 for £1000 and is to be redeemed at the same amount on 31 December 2001. It carries interest of £59 a year for the first two years, after which the rate rises to £141 a year.

Finance costs must be allocated according to paragraph 28 therefore:

	Balance at start of year £	Costs 10.3% P&L £	Cash paid during year £	Balance at end of year £
31.12.96	1000	103	59	1044
31.12.97	1044	108	59	1093
31.12.98	1093	113	141	1065
31.12.99	1065	110	141	1034
31.12.00	1034	107	141	1000 redeemed

Paragraph 41 of the standard also requires finance costs for non-equity shares to be calculated on the same basis as those for debt.

Activity 7

Fifty thousand non-equity shares of £1 are issued at a premium of 5p and issue costs total £1000. The shares have a dividend payable of 4% annually and are redeemable in five years at a premium of 10%. Calculate the finance costs involved in this non-equity issue and allocate them over the life of the shares. (Note: take the definition of finance costs given earlier, and assume that the net proceeds is the fair value of consideration received after deduction of issue costs.)

Activity 7 feedback

Finance costs = total amount of payments − net proceeds

total payments = dividends 4% × 50 000 × 5 =	10 000
capital redemption	50 000
premium on redemption	5 000
	65 000
net proceeds = 50 000 + 2500 − 1000 =	51 500
finance costs	13 500

Allocation

Year	Balance of net proceeds	Finance costs 5.11%	Dividend	Balance c/f
	£	£	£	£
1	51 500	2 632	2 000	52 132
2	52 132	2 664	2 000	52 796
3	52 796	2 698	2 000	53 494
4	53 494	2 735	2 000	54 229
5	54 229	2 771	2 000	55 000
		13 500	10 000	

The future of substance over form

The documents emerging from the ASC and the ASB in the last few years make it clear that they are very much following a general attitude that the important element in any transaction or situation is the commercial substance and not the legal form. The economic effect should be followed, not the legal description. This attitude is by no means strongly supported by the legal profession, and a certain amount of tension emerges here from time to time. It must also be understood that this preference for the commercial substance is not equally strongly supported in some other areas of the world.

The root of the substance over form attitude lies in the UK legal tradition of common law and case law. It is strongly supported by the 'true and fair view' requirement and by the philosophy underlying it that Parliament cannot generally legislate successfully for commercial detail. Whilst substance over form is very much a 'vogue' term and approach, it has not suddenly appeared out of the blue.

The danger of substance over form when combined with the true and fair philosophy is that it does rely for success on the adequacy of the accounting profession to interpret sensibly commercial reality in a whole variety of different situations, but according to consistent conventions and tenets. By now you should be forming a view on how the accounting profession has faired in this respect in recent years! However, the principle of seeking to report the commercial substance is not going to go away.

FRS 13 'Derivatives and Other Financial Instruments: Disclosures'

The reporting implications of financial instruments in general, and of the more complicated examples of financial instruments like derivatives in particular, raise problems which the ASB and the other major world standard setting bodies regard as urgent and important. However, they have also generally discovered that financial instruments raise accounting problems which are seemingly intractable. Progress has been difficult and slow. Following an earlier discussion draft the ASB issued FRED 13 in April 1997 followed by a later amendment which recognized the need to deal with banking institutions separately. FRS 13 followed in September 1998.

In recognition of the difficulties involved and of the general world-wide failure so far to arrive at coherent solutions, FRS 13 claims to deal only with disclosure, leaving issues of measurement to be dealt with later. Since FRS 13 explicitly requires numerical as well as discursive disclosures, this is a little disingenuous.

The general approach taken by the ASB is well shown by quoting an extract from Appendix VII (yes it is a long and complicated Standard!)

> The FRS is based on the premise that, in order to be able to make assessments about the financial performance and financial position of an entity, users of financial statements need information on the main aspects of the entity's risk profile and an understanding of how this risk profile is being managed. Since financial instruments contribute to this risk profile and are often used to manage it, they need to be dealt with fully in the disclosures provided. Although some disclosures are already required for financial instruments, they do not represent a coherent set of requirements that cover all the main risks involved. The main purpose of the FRS is therefore to build a set of such requirements.
>
> In developing the FRS, the Board has taken the view that the most meaningful form in which the information can be provided is through a structured mixture of narrative and numerical disclosures. The narrative disclosures will explain the entity's chosen risk profile, including its risk-management policies, and the numerical disclosures will show how these policies were implemented in the period and will provide information to enable significant or potentially significant exposures to be evaluated. Taken together, the disclosures are intended to give a broad overview of the risks arising on financial instruments, focusing on those instruments and risks that are of greatest significance. The approach, in particular, seeks to avoid requiring a mass of detail.
>
> In framing the disclosure requirements, the Board has drawn on the work of other financial reporting standard-setters with the result that the FRS is broadly consistent with present international practice. However, the Board recognises that this is a developing area and it intends to review the FRS in the light of experience and in the context of its proposals on measurement and hedge accounting.

Examples of 'disclosures already required' before FRS 13 would be in FRS 4, and SSAP 21 on leases.

The FRS gives a considerable number of definitions, including the following.

Capital instruments

All instruments that are issued by reporting entities as a means of raising finance, including shares, debentures, loans and debt instruments, options and warrants that give the holder the right to subscribe for or obtain capital instruments. In the case of consolidated financial statements the term includes capital instruments issued by subsidiaries except those that are held by another member of the group included in the consolidation.

A *commodity contract* is a contract that provides for settlement by receipt or delivery of a commodity.

A cash-settled commodity contract is a commodity contract (including a contract for the delivery of gold) which, though having contract terms that require settlement by physical delivery, is of a type that is normally extinguished other than by physical delivery in accordance with general market practice.

Derivative financial instrument

A financial instrument that derives its value from the price or rate of some underlying item.

Equity shares
Shares other than non-equity shares.

Fair value
The amount at which an asset or liability could be exchanged in an arm's length transaction between informed and willing parties, other than in a forced or liquidation sale.

A *financial instrument* is any contract that gives rise to both a financial asset of one entity and a financial liability or equity instrument of another entity.

A financial asset is any asset that is:
(a) cash;
(b) a contractual right to receive cash or another financial asset from another entity;
(c) a contractual right to exchange financial instruments with another entity under conditions that are potentially favourable; or
(d) an equity instrument of another entity.

A *financial liability* is any liability that is a contractual obligation:
(a) to deliver cash or another financial asset to another entity; or
(b) to exchange financial instruments with another entity under conditions that are potentially unfavourable.

An *equity instrument* is an instrument that evidences an ownership interest in an entity, i.e. a residual interest in the assets of the entity after deducting all of its liabilities.

Floating rate financial assets and financial liabilities
Financial assets and financial liabilities that attract an interest charge and have their interest rate reset at least once a year.

Functional currency
The currency of the primary economic environment in which an entity operates and generates net cash flows.

Non-equity shares
Shares possessing any of the following characteristics:
(**a**) any of the rights of the shares to receive payments (whether in respect of dividends, in respect of redemption or otherwise) are for a limited amount that is not calculated by reference to the company's assets or profits or the dividends on any class of equity share.
(**b**) any of their rights to participate in a surplus in a winding-up are limited to a specific amount that is not calculated by reference to the company's assets or profits and such limitation had a commercial effect in practice at the time the shares were issued or, if later, at the time the limitation was introduced.
(**c**) the shares are redeemable either according to their terms, or because the holder, or any party other than the issuer, can require their redemption.

Short-term debtors and creditors
Financial assets and financial liabilities that meet all of the following criteria:
(**a**) they would be included under one of the following balance sheet headings if the entity was preparing its financial statements in accordance with Schedule 4 of the Companies Act 1985

  (**i**) debtors;
  (**ii**) prepayments and accrued income;
  (**iii**) creditors; amounts falling due within one year, other than items that would be included under the 'debenture loans' and 'bank loans and overdrafts' subheadings;
  (**iv**) provisions for liabilities and charges; or
  (**v**) accruals and deferred income;

(**b**) they mature or become payable within 12 months of the balance sheet date; and

(**c**) they are not a derivative financial instrument.

Trading in financial assets and financial liabilities

Buying, selling, issuing or holding financial assets and financial liabilities in order to take advantage of short-term changes in market prices or rates or, in the case of financial institutions and financial institution groups, in order to facilitate customer transactions.

Many derivatives are simple in operation, but even specialized derivatives are based on basic building blocks. When those components are identified it is generally possible to compute a fair value for even the most complex instruments. The approach adopted to determining their fair values will depend on the type and nature of the components of the transaction.

Derivatives can be sub-divided on the basis of the liquidity of the market on which they are traded, and they can be further sub-divided into whether the underlying transactions are certain to occur, or are contingent on some subsequent event. It is the latter (i.e. options) which require more detailed special consideration, but in practice particularly complex options are rare.

The trading arrangements for the more common types of derivatives are shown in the table below:

Derivatives	Traded and relatively liquid	Non-traded and relatively illiquid
Forwards	Forward foreign exchange	Interest rate swaps
	Future rate agreements	Currency swaps
	Interest rate futures	
	Foreign exchange rate futures	
	Commodity futures	
Options	Currency traded options	Interest rate traded options
	Interest rate caps	Interest rate collars

The problem of finding a rational fair value for the non-traded examples is of course a very significant one.

The Standard is divided into three parts. Part B is for banks, part C is for financial institutions other than banks, and part A is for other reporting entities. Only part A is dealt with here.

More fully, part A requires disclosures in:

all financial statements that are intended to give a true and fair view of the reporting entity's financial position and profit or loss (or income and expenditure) for a period and are prepared by a reporting entity that has any of its capital instruments listed or publicly traded on a stock exchange or market, except that it does not apply:

(**a**) if the entity is:
  (**i**) a financial institution or financial institution group;

(ii) an equity that is applying the Financial Reporting Standard for Smaller Entities (FRSSE); or

(iii) an insurance company or group.

(b) to a parent's own financial statements when those statements are presented together with the parent's consolidated financial statements.

Financial instrument disclosure requirements

As already stated, FRS 13 requires both narrative and numerical disclosures. The summary to the FRS described these requirements as follows.

Narrative disclosures

The FRS requires an explanation to be provided of the role that financial instruments play in creating or changing the risks that the entity faces in its activities. The entity should also explain the directors' approach to managing each of those risks, including a description of the objectives, policies and strategies for holding and issuing financial instruments. Where the directors decide, before the balance sheet date, to change these objectives, policies or strategies, that change should also be explained.

The narrative disclosures are mandatory, although the FRS permits them to be given in a statement accompanying the financial statements (such as the operating and financial review or the directors' report) provided that they are incorporated into the financial statements by a suitable cross-reference.

Numerical disclosures

Although all entities within the scope of the FRS are required to provide the same type of narrative disclosures, the FRS requires different numerical disclosures for each of:

- entities that are not financial institutions
- banks and similar institutions
- other types of financial institution.

These different disclosures reflect differences in the significance of the main risks that arise from financial instruments.

The FRS requires specified numerical disclosures to be provided about:

- interest rate risk
- currency risk
- liquidity risk (except for banks and similar institutions, which are covered by existing requirements)
- fair values
- financial instruments used for trading (including, for banks and some other financial institutions, information on the market price risk of their trading book)
- financial instruments used for hedging
- certain commodity contracts.

To avoid the numerical disclosures becoming so detailed that their message is obscured, the FRS encourages, and in some cases requires, a high degree of aggregation.

The FRS gives a number of illustrations of how the disclosure it requires might look in practice. By way of example, two extracts are given, in Tables 18.1 and 2, from the illustration for a 'simpler'(!) company.

The FRS is, overall, very detailed and rather complicated. Although the reporting of financial instruments is a major issue for some businesses, it is perhaps rather esoteric from the viewpoint of the average company. Don't forget, behind all this fuss, that it is only *disclosure* that is covered by the FRS, not measurement. This was the easy bit!

Table 18.1 *Fair values of financial assets and financial liabilities. Set out below is a comparison by category of book values and fair values of the Group's financial assets and liabilities as at 31 December 20X1*

	Book value £m	Fair value £m
Primary financial instruments held or issued to finance the Group's operations:		
Short-term financial liabilities and current portion of long-term borrowings	(215)	(223)
Long-term borrowings	(400)	(370)
Financial assets	7	8
Derivative financial instruments held to manage the interest rate and currency profile:		
Interest rate swaps	–	15
Forward foreign currency contracts	–	(5)

The fair values of the interest rate swaps, forward foreign currency contracts and sterling denominated long-term fixed rate debt with a carrying amount of £250m have been determined by reference to prices available from the markets on which the instruments involved are traded. All the other fair values shown above have been calculated by discounting cash flows at prevailing interest rates.

Table 18.2 *Gains and losses on hedges. The Group enters into forward foreign currency contracts to eliminate the currency exposures that arise on sales denominated in foreign currencies immediately those sales are transacted. It also uses interest rate swaps to manage its interest rate profile. Changes in the fair value of instruments used as hedges are not recognized in the financial statements until the hedged position matures. An analysis of these unrecognized gains and losses is as follows*

	Gains £m	Losses £m	Total net gains/(losses) £m
Unrecognized gains and losses on hedges at 1.1.X1	9	12	(3)
Gains and losses arising in previous years that were recognized in 20X1	8	9	1
Gains and losses arising before 1.1.X1 that were not recognized in 20X1	1	3	(2)
Gains and losses arising in 20X1 that were not recognized in 20X1	18	6	12
Unrecognized gains and losses on hedges at 31.12.X1	19	9	10
Of which:			
Gains and losses expected to be recognized in 20X2	12	6	6
Gains and losses expected to be recognized in 20X3 or later	7	3	4

If you insist on all the detail, read the standard in its entirety. The proposals have not been universally well received, for complexity and general cost versus benefit reasons. Additionally, as already indicated, international attempts to resolve some of the issues and problems will no doubt continue, even if only slowly. The future is uncertain in this area more than in most.

Summary

In this chapter we have investigated the concept of substance over form and outlined the proposals in FRS 4 and 5. Both FRSs are lengthy with a great deal of illustrations as to the substance of transactions. We have also seen the ASB introducing into these standards some of the definitions from the Statement of Principles which were not yet approved. Substance over form will remain a difficult area as businesses continue to attempt to find capital instruments and transactions that provide accounting advantage in terms of balance sheet presentation and/or earnings per share. In the end the desirability of the concept is probably related to our view of what accounting is trying to achieve. We have also explored some of the mysteries of FRS 13 which covers the disclosure, but not the measurement, of derivatives and other financial instruments.

Exercises

1   The doctrine of substance over form, which gives precedence to economic fair presentation rather than to legal creativity, is clearly essential to the provider of financial information. Discuss.

2   Industrial Estates plc is a company that was formed in 1962 to build and sell industrial units. Its share capital and reserves totalled £500 million at 31 December 2002.

During the three years 2000–2, sales turnover fell as a result of financial lending institutions restricting the amount they were prepared to lend to prospective purchasers to 60% of the sales price of an industrial unit.

In 2003 the company was building standard units at a cost of £1 million to be sold for £1.25 million each; and, in order to overcome the decline in sales, it introduced a new scheme which was to be offered as an option to outright purchase whereby

(a)   the company transferred the legal ownership of an industrial unit on payment by the purchaser of £750 000 being 60% of the sales price

(b)   the purchaser gave a second charge over the industrial unit as security for the amount outstanding of £500 000 being 40% of the sales price

(c)   the purchaser paid no annual interest on the £500 000, but in the event of a resale to a third party, would pay the company 40% of the market value as at the date of the resale in full settlement of the amount outstanding; and

(d)   the company agreed to repurchase the unit in the event that the purchaser ceased trading on payment of the market price as at the date of cessation less the £500 000 balance unpaid.

The auditors, Messrs Uptodate & Co, ascertained on reading the agreement relating to the new scheme that the conditions relating to repurchase were not as the company had stated in the information given in the question. The actual terms were that on a repurchase the company would pay the original purchaser 60% of the market value.

As auditors, write a letter to the chief accountant, explaining the effect of this on the treatment of the five units built and sold in 2003 in the P&L account and balance sheet of Industrial Estates plc as at 31 December 2003.

(ACCA adapted)

3 C & R plc is a large company which operates a number of retail stores throughout the United Kingdom. The company makes up financial statements to 30 September each year.

On 1 October 2000 the company purchased two plots of land at two different locations, and commenced the construction of two retail stores. The construction was completed on 1 October 2001.

Details of the costs incurred to construct the stores are as follows:

	Location A	Location B
	£000	£000
Cost of land	500	700
Cost of building materials	500	550
Direct labour	100	150
Site overheads	100	100
Fixtures and fittings	200	200

The construction of the stores was financed out of the proceeds of issue of a £10 million zero coupon bond on 1 October 2000. The bond is redeemable at a price of £25937000 on 30 September 2010. This represents the one and only payment to the holders of the bond.

Both stores were brought into use on 1 October 2001. The store at Location A was used by C & R plc but, due to a change of plan, the store at Location B was let to another retailer at a commercial rent.

It is the policy of C & R plc to depreciate freehold properties over their anticipated useful life of fifty years, and to depreciate fixtures and fittings over ten years. The cost of such properties (including fixtures and fittings) should include finance costs, where this is permitted by the regulatory framework in the United Kingdom.

Required:

(a) **Compute the amounts which will be included in fixed assets in respect of the stores at Locations A and B on 30 September 2001. Give full explanations for the amounts you have included.** (11 marks)

(b) **Compute the charge to the profit and loss account for depreciation on the fixed assets at the two locations for the year to 30 September 2002, stating clearly the reasons for your answers.** (9 marks)

(20 marks)

(CIMA)

4 The overriding requirement of a company's financial statements is that they should present a true and fair view, and represent faithfully the underlying transactions and other events that have occurred. To achieve this, transactions have to be accounted for in terms of their 'substance' or economic reality rather than their legal form. This principle is included in the Accounting Standards Board (ASB) 'Statement of Principles for Financial Reporting', and it is also used in many Standards, in particular FRS 5 'Reporting the Substance of Transactions' and SSAP 21 'Accounting for Leases and Hire Purchase Contracts'.

Required:

(a) **Describe why it is important that substance rather than legal form is used to account for transactions, and describe how financial statements can be adversely affected if the substance of transactions is not recorded.** (5 marks)

(b) **Describe, using examples, how the following features may indicate that the substance of a transaction is different from its legal form:**

(i) **separation of ownership from the beneficial use of an asset;**

(ii) **linking of transactions including the use of option clauses;**

(iii) **when an asset is sold at a price that differs from its fair value.** (9 marks)

(c) On 1 April 2000 Forest plc had a stock of cut seasoning timber which had cost £12 million two years ago. Due to shortages of this quality of timber its value at 1 April 2000 had risen to £20 million. It will be a further three years before this timber is sold to a manufacturer of high-class furniture. On 1 April 2000 Forest plc entered into an arrangement to sell Barret Bank the timber for £15 million. Forest plc has an option to buy back the timber at any time within the next three years at a cost of £15 million plus accumulated interest at 2% per annum above base rate. This will be charged from the date of the original sale. The base rate for the period of the transactions is expected to be 8%. Forest plc intends to buy back the timber on 31 March 2003 and sell it the same day for an expected price of £25 million.

Note: the above does not constitute a long-term contract under SSAP 9, and you are to ignore any storage costs and capitalization of interest that may relate to stocks.

Required:
Assuming the above transactions take place as expected, prepare extracts to reflect the transactions in the profit and loss accounts for the years to 31 March 2001, 2002 and 2003 and the balance sheets (ignore cash) at those year-ends:
(i) if Forest plc treats the transactions in their legal form; and
(ii) if the substance of the transactions is recorded.

Comment briefly on your answer to (c) above   (11 marks)
                                                                   (25 marks)
                                                                   (ACCA)

5 Outline the objectives of FRS 13 and discuss whether it is likely to achieve them.
6 FRS 13 claims to focus on disclosure not measurement. Explain whether you think this has meant that the ASB has evaded the major issues.

Leases and hire purchase contracts (SSAP 21)

After reading this chapter you should be able to:
- consider the issues surrounding leased assets
- look at different forms of lease agreements
- outline the Accounting Standards Board solution to leased assets – SSAP 21
- itemize the Companies Act requirements in respect of leased assets
- identify the benefits of SSAP 21
- consider any problems still remaining in respect of accounting for leases.

Introduction

A company can acquire an asset for use in its business activities by various ways:

1 outright (cash) purchase
2 purchase through a normal credit sale agreement
3 hire purchase (HP)
4 leasing.

With methods **1** and **2**, legal ownership of the asset passes on purchase, whereas with method **3** ownership does not pass until a final payment has been made by the purchaser at the end of the HP agreement, and with method 4, legal ownership may in certain circumstances never pass over.

Hence, in method **2**, the seller's remedy in the case of default in payment by the buyer would be to sue for the outstanding debt, whereas default on the part of the acquirer of the asset under methods **3** and **4** would lead to repossession of the asset involved. It is these differences between the first two methods and the latter two which provide the underlying case for a standard on this topic.

Activity 1

A company obtains the use of two identical assets costing £100 000 by obtaining one asset on a credit sale agreement and the other on a lease. Assuming fixed assets are only recorded on a company's balance sheet when it has legal ownership show the adjustments that would be necessary to the company's accounts and identify the problems, if any, with this method of accounting.

Activity 1 feedback

	£
Fixed assets	100 000
Creditors	100 000

Under this method of accounting only one asset would be shown under fixed assets and only the liability to pay for one asset would be shown.

The fact that the company has the use of another fixed asset and that they have the liability outstanding for lease payments is not shown and this could be considered misleading to shareholders.

Let us consider the above activity in the light of the IASC qualitative characteristics of accounting information discussed in Chapter 10, see p. 144, and being closely followed by the ASB, see Chapter 15, p. 232. One of the characteristics for information to be useful, according to this statement, is that of relevance: 'Information has the quality of relevance when it influences the economic decisions of users by helping them evaluate past, present or future events.' Would it not influence users in their decision making if they were informed of the fact that the company was liable to lease charges in the future for this asset? Might they not make the wrong decisions if they were not informed of these lease payments?

Court Line case

One of the most significant financial crashes of the 1970s, and particularly so in terms of its impact on the credibility of the accountancy profession, was that of the Court Line group of companies. Essentially, Court Line was involved in the 'package holiday' industry and owned ships, aircraft and hotels all over the world, while at the same time being heavily engaged in shipbuilding.

The Corporate Report (ASC) of 1975 suggested that one of the primary objectives of financial reporting should be to provide users with information such as to enable them to make correct and meaningful decisions, particularly those of an economic nature. With this objective in mind, it is important to realize that the Court Line crash was one of several notable corporate failures of the 1960s and early 1970s that questioned the very credibility of the accounting profession. Indeed, one of the conclusions that observers drew from this particular financial disaster was that, far from providing users with information that could prove useful to interested parties, the accounts of Court Line could be said to have been positively misleading, and certainly incomplete in important areas. Basically, the reporting failures relating to the Court Line case were twofold:

1 *The assets in the balance sheet*. Of the £17 million of net assets per ordinary share in the balance sheet of the Court Line group as at 30 September 1973, there was amazingly (with hindsight of course!) more than £16.5 million that could be classed as intangible (being a mixture of goodwill, deferred revenue expenditure, and costs of future holiday programmes); and

2 *The assets (and liabilities) not in the balance sheet*. While the liquidation of Court Line was progressing, it was discovered that the group had entered into non-cancellable, long

term, multi-million pound contracts for several aircraft, and it is this particular problem of omission in terms of accounting information with which we are here concerned.

During the 1970s there was no reporting requirement for companies to disclose the extent of their contractual involvement regarding the leasing of assets. It would seem that the absence of such a requirement was simply due to the fact that when one company (the lessee) leases an asset from another company (the lessor), legal ownership of the leased asset still rests with the lessor and, of course, in strict accordance with legal form, the asset will need to be shown in the balance sheet of the lessor company. The treatment makes no allowance for the fact that the usage of the asset, together with the risks and rewards attendant on such usage, can be attributed in practice to the lessee. It may thus be seen that the balance sheet of the lessee may be said to omit valuable information, both in terms of the underlying assets in use by the lessee and the liabilities associated with such leasing contracts. This problem of incompleteness of information before SSAP 21 can be seen to be a particularly serious one, in that it meant that comparability between companies purchasing assets and those leasing identical assets became meaningless, particularly when comparing their gearing and ratios involving return on capital employed (in that of course much of the borrowing and capital employed was 'off the balance sheet'). Hence, one of the prime motivators to the eventual production of an accounting standard on the subject was the need to deal with this problem of omission associated with the 'off-balance sheet' approach to the treatment of leased assets in the accounts of the lessee. SSAP 21 ('Accounting for Leases and Hire Purchase Contracts') offers a solution by adopting, in essence, a 'substance over form' approach to this problem.

The following is a quote from Ian Hay Davison (former chairman of the ASC) and is taken from the 'foreword' to SSAP 21:

> It is sometimes argued that leased assets should not be recognized on a company's balance sheet as the company does not have legal title to the asset. Whilst it is true that a lessee does not have legal ownership of the leased asset, however, he has the right to use the asset for substantially the whole of its useful economic life. These rights are for most practical purposes equivalent to legal ownership. It has long been accepted that assets held under hire purchase contracts should be recognized on the balance sheet of the hirer of the asset. SSAP 21 extends this treatment to finance leasing; it recognizes that whether an asset is owned, leased or held under a hire purchase contract, it represents an economic resource which is needed in the business and which the accounts ought to reflect in a consistent manner.

In addition to the major problem posed to the credibility of accounting information by the use of 'off-balance sheet' assets, it should also be noted here that the enormous growth of leasing, especially in view of the entry of the commercial banks into the industry, meant that it could no longer be regarded as a 'fringe' problem for the profession, and therefore SSAP 21 was issued in September 1984.

It can be seen that there was a lengthy gap between the accounting problems exposed by the Court Line crash and a subsequent standard on leasing. This was in no small measure due to powerful pressure from the leasing industry itself, which feared that any standard enforcing capitalization of leased assets in the lessee's balance sheet might precipitate governmental action to transfer the capital allowances available in respect of leased assets away from the lessor to the lessee. There was indeed ample precedent for this when one considers the situation as far as HP acquisitions are concerned. HP transactions (being essentially similar in concept to leasing transactions) have always been dealt with on a 'substance over form' basis, in that buyers capitalize the acquired asset in their own balance sheets, and show the indebtedness attendant on such a transaction in their liabilities, and (importantly) it is the buyers who in an HP transaction are entitled to claim the capital allowances. Hence, with respect to leasing, lessors felt that such a move to take away from them capital allowances would drastically affect the popularity of leasing, since they would no longer be able to pass on such tax savings to the customer (i.e. to the lessee). It can, of course, be argued that the lessee would in any case gain the taxation relief due by such a move, but it should be remembered that not all companies are in positions to take advantage of such relief against taxable profits (whereas lessors – for example, banks – most certainly are!).

In addition to such a powerful lobby against a standard there were other reasons for delay. For example, the ASC itself found difficulties with definitional problems (defining and distinguishing between different types of lease). Even lessees and their trade associations provided opposition to the idea of a standard that would require capitalization by them, as many of them had begun to realize that the false impression created by 'off-balance sheet' financing might in certain circumstances have its advantages. Leasing was one of the earlier examples of the application by the ASC of substance over form (Chapter 18).

Forms of lease agreements

Before SSAP 21, no distinction had been recognized between those leases that were long-term by nature, non-cancellable, and in effect transferring all the risks and rewards of ownership of an asset to the lessee, and those short-term leasing agreements that in fact were no more than simple rental agreements. SSAP 21 (and its parent ED 29) introduced some important distinctions in this area, and it is necessary to consider carefully some definitions before examining the requirements of the standard:

14 *A lease* is a contract between a lessor and a lessee for the hire of a specific asset. The lessor retains ownership of the asset but conveys the right to the use of the asset to the lessee for an agreed period of time in return for the payment of specified rentals. The term 'lease' as used in this statement also applies to other arrangements in which one party retains ownership of an asset but conveys the right to the use of the asset to another party for an agreed period of time in return for specified payment.

15 *A finance lease* is a lease that transfers substantially all the risks and rewards of ownership of an asset to the lessee. It should be presumed that such a transfer of risks and rewards occurs if at the inception of a lease the present value of the minimum lease payments, including any initial payment, amounts to substantially all (normally 90 per cent or more) of the fair value of the leased asset. The present value should be calculated by using the interest rate implicit in the lease ... If the fair value of the asset is not determinable, an estimate thereof should be used.

17 *An operating lease* is a lease other than a finance lease.

18 *'Fair value'* is the price at which an asset could be exchanged in an arm's length transaction less, where applicable, any grants receivable towards the purchase or use of the asset.

Activity 2

Costa plc uses three identical pieces of machinery in its factory in Leeds. These were all acquired for use on the same date by the following means:

1 machine 1 rented from Brava plc at a cost of £250 per month payable in advance and terminable at any time by either party
2 machine 2 rented from Blanca plc at a cost of eight half-yearly payments in advance of £1500
3 machine 3 rented from Sol plc at a cost of six half-yearly payments in advance of £1200
4 the cash price of this type of machine is £8000 and its estimated life four years.

Are the above machines rented by operating or finance lease?

Activity 2 feedback

Machine 1 is an operating lease as there is no transfer of the risks or rewards of ownership.

Machine 2 involves a total payment of £12 000. If this equates in present value terms to more than £7200 (i.e. 90% of £8000) and all risks and rewards of ownership are transferred then it is a finance lease.

Machine 3 involves a total payment of £7200 which on present value terms will never equate to more than £7200 therefore it is an operating lease.

Further SSAP 21 definitions

Before we look at the accounting treatment of leases we must become familiar with the following definitions. The '*interest rate implicit in the lease*' is that discount rate estimated at the time of inception of the lease which when applied to the amounts that the lessor expects to receive and retain, produces an amount (the present value) equal to the fair value of the leased asset. Note also that paragraph 16 of SSAP 21 provides that even where a lease fully meets the requirements of paragraph 15 above, the presumption that it should therefore be classed as a finance lease may in exceptional circumstances be rebutted if it can be clearly demonstrated that the lease in question does not transfer substantially all the risks and rewards of ownership to the lessee. (Correspondingly, the presumption that a lease that *fails* to meet the conditions in paragraph 15 is *not* a finance lease may in exceptional circumstances be rebutted.)

Activity 3

A lessee leases an asset on a non-cancellable lease contract with a primary term of five years from 1 January 20X1. The rental is £650 per quarter payable in advance. The lessee has the right to continue to lease the asset after the end of the primary period for as long as they wish at a peppercorn rent. In addition, the lessee is required to pay all maintenance and insurance costs as they arise. The leased asset could have been purchased for cash at the start of the lease for £10 000 and has a useful life of eight years.

Calculate the interest rate implicit in the lease.

Activity 3 feedback

From the definition of 'interest rate implicit in the lease' we can state that:

1 £10 000 (fair value) = the present value at implicit interest rate of twenty quarterly rentals payable in advance of £650
2 the present value of the first rental payable is £650 as it is paid now
3 thus £9350 = the present value at implicit interest rate of nineteen rentals of £650
4 therefore 9350/650 = 14.385 = present value at implicit interest rate of nineteen rentals of £1
5 using discount tables we can determine the interest rate as 2.95%.

Let us continue with the definitions:

18 *A hire purchase contract* is a contract for the hire of an asset which contains a provision giving the hirer an option to acquire legal title to the asset upon the fulfilment of certain conditions stated in the contract.
19 *The lease term* is the period for which the lessee has contracted to lease the asset and any further terms for which the lessee has the option to continue the asset, with or without further payment, which option it is reasonably certain at the inception of the lease that the lessee will exercise.
20 *The minimum lease payments* are the minimum payments over the remaining part of the lease term (excluding charges for services and taxes to be paid by the lessor); and
   (a) in the case of the lessee, any residual amounts guaranteed by him or by a party related to him; or
   (b) in the case of the lessor, any residual amounts guaranteed by the lessee or by an independent third party.
21 *The gross investment* in a lease at a point in time is the total of the minimum lease payments and any unguaranteed residual value accruing to the lessor.
22 *The net investment* in a lease at a point in time comprises:
   (a) the gross investment in a lease (as defined in paragraph 21); less
   (b) gross earnings allocated to future periods.
27 *Finance charge* is the amount borne by the lessee over the lease term, representing the difference between the total of the minimum lease payments (including any residual amounts guaranteed by him) and the amount at which he records the leased asset at the inception of the lease.

Accounting for leases in the lessee's books

The existence of a lease will affect the accounts of both the lessee and the lessor and SSAP 21 requires the following accounting entries for the lessee.

Finance lease

32 A finance lease should be reported in the balance sheet of a lessee as an asset and as an obligation to pay future rentals. At the inception of the lease the sum to be recorded both as an asset and as a liability should be the present

value of the minimum lease payments, derived by discounting them at the interest rate implicit in the lease.

33 In practice in the case of a finance lease the fair value of the asset will often be a sufficiently close approximation to the present value of the minimum lease payments and may in these circumstances be substituted for it.

35 Rentals payable should be apportioned between the finance charge and a reduction of the outstanding obligation for future amounts payable. The total finance charge under a finance lease should be allocated to accounting periods during the lease term so as to produce a constant periodic rate of charge on the remaining balance of the obligation for each accounting period, or a reasonable approximation thereto.

36 An asset leased under a finance lease should be depreciated over the shorter of the lease term (as defined in paragraph 19) and its useful life. However, in the case of a hire purchase contract which has the characteristics of a finance lease, the asset should be depreciated over its useful life.

In effect, the above requirements of SSAP 21 require that the fixed asset leased should be brought into the assets in the balance sheet at its fair value (or its cash purchase price in the case of a new asset) and double entry will be completed by bringing the same amount into the liabilities in the balance sheet, and as with any other fixed asset, the leased asset will be depreciated over its useful life (but limited to the number of years over which the lessee has the right to use the asset). Note also that the rental payments arising under the leasing agreement will be accounted for partly as finance charge (debit to P&L account) and partly in discharge of the liability arising from paragraph 32. The method of such allocation referred to in paragraph 35 is considered in Activity 4.

The basis to this 'substance over form' approach as laid down in SSAP 21 is best explained by SSAP itself:

12 Conceptually, what is capitalised in the lessee's accounts is not the asset itself but his rights in the asset (together with his obligation to pay rentals). However, the definition of a finance lease is such that a lessee's rights are for practical purposes little different from those of an outright purchaser. Hence, it is appropriate that lessees should include these assets in their balance sheets.

Operating lease

37 The rental under an operating lease should be charged on a straight-line basis over the lease term, even if the payments are not made on such a basis, unless another systematic and rational basis is more appropriate.

Note that before SSAP 21, this was the accounting treatment adopted by lessees with respect to *all* types of leases, whether finance or operating. HP contracts need not be considered separately:

31 Those hire purchase contracts which are of a financing nature should be accounted for on a basis similar to that set out for finance leases. Conversely, other hire purchase contracts should be accounted for on a basis similar to that set out for operating leases.

Depreciation

39 The leased asset should be depreciated on a basis compatible with that adopted for assets which are owned. FRS 15 Tangible Fixed Assets requires an asset to be depreciated by allocating the cost less estimated residual value of the asset as fairly as possible to the periods expected to benefit from its use.

The period over which a leased asset should be depreciated is the shorter of (**a**) the lease term and (**b**) the asset's useful life. The lease term is the primary period of the lease (i.e. the non-cancellable part) together with any secondary periods during which the lessee has the contractual right to continue to use the asset and which right, at the start of the lease, it is reasonable to expect him to exercise.

In most cases the residual value of leased assets at the end of the lease is likely to be small so that, even where the lessee has the right to share in the ultimate residual value, it is usual to assume for the purpose of establishing an appropriate depreciation charge that it will be nil. This will be the case whether the residual value takes the form of sale proceeds or a rebate of rentals.

Activity 4

Using the information given in Activity 3, assuming the asset has a nil residual value and assuming the asset is leased for a further two years after the primary period, show the accounting entries over the life of the lease required in the lessee's books by SSAP 21.

Activity 4 feedback

The lease falls within the definition of a finance lease therefore the 'rights in the lease' will be capitalized at fair value £10 000 and the obligation under the lease of £10 000 will be shown as a liability as shown by the following journal.

		Dr	Cr
		£	£
1.1.X1	Fixed asset	10 000	
	Creditors (lessor)		10 000

The minimum lease payments amount to $20 \times £650 = £13\,000$, the cash price was £10 000, hence the total finance charge will be £3000.

Remembering that this total finance charge should be allocated to accounting periods during the lease so as to produce a constant periodic rate of charge on the remaining balance of the obligation for each accounting period (see paragraph 35 of SSAP 21), then an appropriate method of allocation would be the actuarial method as follows:

Period	Capital sum at start of period £	Rental paid £	Capital sum during period £	Finance charge (2.95% per quarter)* £	Capital sum at end of period £
1/X1	10 000	650	9 350	276	9 626
2/X1	9 626	650	8 976	265	9 241
3/X1	9 241	650	8 591	254	8 845
4/X1	8 845	650	8 195	242	8 437
				1 037	
1/X2	8 437	650	7 787	230	8 017
2/X2	8 017	650	7 367	217	7 584
3/X2	7 584	650	6 934	205	7 139
4/X2	7 139	650	6 489	191	6 680
				843	
1/X3	6 680	650	6 030	178	6 208
2/X3	6 208	650	5 558	164	5 722
3/X3	5 722	650	5 072	150	5 222
4/X3	5 222	650	4 572	135	4 707
				627	
1/X4	4 707	650	4 057	120	4 177
2/X4	4 177	650	3 527	104	3 631
3/X4	3 631	650	2 981	88	3 069
4/X4	3 069	650	2 419	71	2 490
				383	
1/X5	2 490	650	1 840	54	1 894
2/X5	1 894	650	1 244	37	1 281
3/X5	1 281	650	631	19	650
4/X5	650	650	—	—	—
				110	
		13 000		3 000	

*The quarterly finance charge of 2.95% may be calculated in several ways: (a) by trial and error, (b) by financial pocket calculator or computer program, (c) by a mathematical formula, or (d) by reference to present value tables.

We can now apportion the annual rental of £2600 (i.e. $4 \times £650$) between a finance charge and a capital repayment as follows:

	Total rental £	Finance charge £	Capital repayments £
20X1	2600	1037*	1563
20X2	2600	843	1757
20X3	2600	627	1973
20X4	2600	383	2217
20X5	2600	110	2490
	13000	3000	10000
	(a)	(b)	(a) − (b)

*As calculated using actuarial method.

Note that the allocation of the finance charge for accounting periods by the actuarial method is not easy to calculate manually and an acceptable approximation to this method may be found in the 'sum of the digits' approach (see p. 252).

We also need to calculate a depreciation charge. The period for depreciation will be seven years as this is the lesser of useful life (8 years) and lease period (seven years). The annual depreciation charge on a straight-line basis is therefore:

$$£10000 \div 7 = £1429$$

The accounting entries in the lessee's books will be as follows assuming year-end as 31 December.

Profit and loss account charges

	Depreciation	Finance charge	Total
20X1	1429	1037	2466
20X2	1429	843	2272
20X3	1429	627	2056
20X4	1429	383	1812
20X5	1428	110	1538
20X6	1428	–	1428
20X7	1428	–	1428
	10000	3000	13000

Balance sheet entries:
Assets held under finance leases

	Cost £		Accumulated depreciation £		Net book value of assets held under finance leases £
31.12.X1	10000	–	1429	=	8571
31.12.X2	10000	–	2858	=	7142
31.12.X3	10000	–	4287	=	5713
31.12.X4	10000	–	5716	=	4284
31.12.X5	10000	–	7145	=	2855
31.12.X6	10000	–	8574	=	1426
31.12.X7	10000	–	10000	=	–

Obligations under finance leases (i.e. the capital element of future rentals payable)

	Obligations under finance leases outstanding at start of year		Capital repayment		Obligations under finance leases outstanding at year-end
	£		£		£
31.12.X1	10 000	–	1 563	=	8 437
31.12.X2	8 437	–	1 757	=	6 680
31.12.X3	6 680	–	1 973	=	4 707
31.12.X4	4 707	–	2 217	=	2 490
31.12.X5	2 490	–	2 490	=	–
31.12.X6					
31.12.X7					

Activity 5

If the lease in Activity 4 was treated as an operating lease show the entries in the lessee's books.

Activity 5 feedback

The accounting method used for operating leases is in fact the method that was generally used for all leases before SSAP 21. The method involves no capitalization of asset and no raising of a liability for obligations under leases.

The only entries in the lessee's books would be to charge the rental to the P&L account at an annual rate of £2600.

If we compare the results of Activities 4 and 5 we can quite easily see the problem SSAP 21 hoped to address.

Accounting for leases in the lessor's books

For finance leases SSAP 21 states:

38 The amount due from the lessee under a finance lease should be recorded in the balance sheet of a lessor as a debtor at the amount of the net investment in the lease after making provisions for items such as bad and doubtful rentals receivable.

39 The total gross earnings under a finance lease should normally be allocated to accounting periods to give a constant periodic rate of return on the lessor's net cash investment in the lease in each period. In the case of a hire purchase contract which has characteristics similar to a finance lease, allocation of gross earnings so as to give a constant periodic rate of return on the finance company's net investment will in most cases be a suitable approximation to allocation based on the net cash investment. In arriving at the constant periodic rate of return, a reasonable approximation may be made.

As with lessee accounting, it can be seen that SSAP 21 also adopts a 'substance over form' approach in the case of the lessor, as the guidance notes state:

71 Under a finance lease a lessor retains legal title to an asset but passes substantially all the risk and rewards of ownership to the lessee in return for a stream of rentals. In substance, under a finance lease, the lessor provides finance and expects a return thereon.

Paragraph 73 then goes on to state:

The lessor should account for leases in accordance with their economic substance. Hence, a finance lease should be accounted for on a basis similar to that for a loan, rather than as a fixed asset subject to depreciation.

Paragraph 76 states that the rentals received by the lessor from the lessee under a finance lease should be apportioned between:

1 interest earned (i.e. on the finance provided); and
2 a repayment of the capital debt.

The problem, of course, is essentially one of deciding how the total interest receivable (i.e. the finance charge) should be allocated over the term of the lease, and it should be remembered in this context that paragraph 39 of the standard (as above) states that the process of allocation should be such as to give a 'constant periodic rate of return on the lessor's net cash investment in the lease in each period'.

The 'net cash investment' in a lease at a point in time is defined in paragraph 23 of SSAP 21 as follows:

The amount of funds invested in a lease by a lessor, and comprises the cost of the asset plus or minus the following related payments or receipts:
(a) government or other grants receivable towards the purchase or use of the asset
(b) rentals received
(c) taxation payments and receipts, including the effect of capital allowances
(d) residual values, if any, at the end of the lease term
(e) interest payments (where applicable)
(f) interest received on cash surplus
(g) profit taken out of the lease.

As with lessee accounting, both the actuarial method and the 'sum of the digits' method are suitable for purposes of the process of allocation. SSAP 21 does also, however, refer to the use of certain other methods that take account of the effect of taxation, but these are somewhat more complex.

Operating leases, SSAP 21 states:

42 An asset held for use in operating leases by a lessor should be recorded as a fixed asset and depreciated over its useful life.
43 Rental income from an operating lease, excluding charges for services such as insurance and maintenance, should be recognized on a straight-line basis over the period of the lease, even if the payments are not made on such a basis, unless another systematic and rational basis is more representative of the time pattern in which the benefit from the leased asset is receivable.

Thus, SSAP 21 concludes that in respect of the lessor an operating lease should be accounted for by capitalizing the leased asset in its own balance sheet and depreciating the asset accordingly. Rentals receivable under the lease agreement should be taken to the credit of P&L account as income.

Activity 6

A lessor leases out an asset on terms which constitute a finance lease within the definition of SSAP 21. The primary period is five years commencing 1 July 20X0, and the rental payable is £3000 per annum (in arrears). The lessee has the right to continue the lease after the five-year period referred to above for an indefinite period at a peppercorn rent. The cash price of the asset in question as at 1 July 20X0 was £11 372, and one can assume a rate of interest implicit in the lease of 10%.

Show the entries in the lessor books.

Activity 6 feedback

From the information given above, it can be clearly observed that the lease in question is a finance lease within the definition of SSAP 21. The problem for the lessor is to identify and then allocate the finance charge along the lines outlined in SSAP 21.

The finance charge is simply the difference between the fair value of the asset (in this case being the cash price of the new asset), and the rental payments over the lease period, i.e. of £15 000 less £11 372, i.e. £3628.

Using the actuarial method with an interest rate of 10%, the allocation of the finance charge will be as follows:

Year-ended 30 June	Balance b/f		Finance charge (to P&L a/c) (10%)	Rental		Balance c/f (in year-end balance sheet)
	£		£	£		£
20X1	11 372	+	1 137	−(3 000)	=	9 509
20X2	9 509	+	951	−(3 000)	=	7 460
20X3	7 460	+	746	−(3 000)	=	5 206
20X4	5 206	+	521	−(3 000)	=	2 727
20X5	2 727	+	273	−(3 000)	=	Nil
			£3 628	£15 000		

The relevant extracts from the P&L accounts of the years in question will thus appear as follows:

	£ 20X1	£ 20X2	£ 20X3	£ 20X4	£ 20X5	£ Total
Rentals	3 000	3 000	3 000	3 000	3 000	15 000
Less capital repayments	1 863	2 049	2 254	2 479	2 727	11 372
Finance charges	1 137	951	746	521	273	3 628
Interest payable	(x)	(x)	(x)	(x)	(x)	
Overheads	(x)	(x)	(x)	(x)	(x)	

It should be noted here that SSAP 21 requires disclosure by lessors of their net investment in finance leases at each balance sheet date. The amounts should be described as 'finance lease receivables' and analysed in the notes to the accounts between those amounts receivable within one year and those amounts receivable thereafter.

With these requirements in mind the relevant balance sheets will then appear as follows:

	year-ended 30 June			
	20X1	20X2	20X3	20X4
Net investment in finance leases				
Current	2049	2254	2479	2727
Non-current	7460	5206	2727	–
	£9509	£7460	£5206	£2727

Taxation effect on finance lease accounting for lessors

Section 39 of SSAP 21 stated that gross earnings under a finance lease should be allocated to accounting periods to give a constant periodic rate of return on the lessor's net cash investment in the lease in each period. In Activity 6 above we have assumed the net cash investment in the lease to be the initial outflow of £11 372 less the inflow of rentals of £3000 per annum in arrears over five years. This is a very simplistic view of the cash outflows and inflows associated with a finance lease. In particular the lessor will also have a cash flow in respect of corporation tax based on rentals received less capital allowances.

Activity 7

A lessor leases an asset on a non-cancellable lease contract with a primary term of five years from 1 January 20X7. The rental is £650 per quarter payable in advance. At the end of the primary period it is expected the asset will be sold for £2373 and the proceeds passed to the lessee as a rental rebate. The cash price of the leased asset is £10 000. Tax at the rate of 35% is payable at the beginning of the fourth quarter nine months after the balance sheet date and a writing down allowance of 25% applies to the leased asset.

Show the entries in the lessor's books.

Activity 7 feedback

First we need to identify cash outflows and inflows. These will consist of: initial outflow of £10 000 to purchase asset, inflows over twenty quarters of rentals of £650, corporation tax flows associated with rentals received less capital allowances.

The tax flows can be computed as follows:

	20X7	20X8	20X9	20Y0	20Y1
Rentals	2600	2600	2600	2600	2600
Capital allowance	2500	1875	1406	1055	3164
Taxable profit at 35%	100	725	1194	1545	(564)
Tax payable	35	254	418	541	(197)

We can now use the 'actuarial method after tax' to allocate the finance charges as follows:

Period	Opening net cash investment (a) £	Cash in flow in period (b) £	Net cash investment after cash flows (c) £	Profit at 2.06% (d) £	Closing net cash investment (e) £
1/X7	10 000	650	9 350	193	9 543
2/X7	9 543	650	8 893	183	9 076
3/X7	9 076	650	8 426	174	8 600
4/X7	8 600	650	7 950	164	8 114
				714	
1/X8	8 114	650	7 464	154	7 618
2/X8	7 618	650	6 968	144	7 112
3/X8	7 112	650	6 462	133	6 595
4/X8	6 595	615 (650 – 35) tax	5 980	123	6 103
				554	
1/X9	6 103	650	5 453	112	5 565
2/X9	5 565	650	4 915	101	5 016
3/X9	5 016	650	4 366	90	4 456
4/X9	4 456	397 (650 – 253) tax	4 060	84	4 144
				387	
1/Y0	4 144	650	3 494	72	3 566
2/Y0	3 566	650	2 916	60	2 976
3/Y0	2 976	650	2 326	48	2 374
4/Y0	2 374	232 (650 – 418) tax	2 142	44	2 186
				224	
1/Y1	2 186	650	1 536	32	1 568
2/Y1	1 568	650	918	19	937
3/Y1	937	650	287	6	293
4/Y1	293	109 (650 – 541) tax	184	4	188
				61	
1/Y2	188	–	188	4	192
2/Y2	192	–	192	4	196
3/Y2	196	–	196	4	200
4/Y2	200	197 tax	3	(3)	–
				9	96 618

The percentage profit taken out in each quarter, 2.06%, is the amount to be applied to come to a final nil balance of net cash investment when all cash flows are completed. This is extremely difficult to calculate and in practice computer programs are used to find this percentage.

Profit and loss extracts

	20X7 £	20X8 £	20X9 £	20Y0 £	20Y1 £
(a) Rentals	2600	2600	2600	2600	2600
less capital repayment	(1502)	(1748)	(2005)	(2255)	(2492)
(b) Profit before tax	1098	852	595	345	108
Taxation	(35)	(253)	(418)	(541)	197
(c)	1063	599	177	(196)	305
(d) Deferred tax	(349)	(45)	210	420	(235)
(e) Profit after tax	714	554	387	224	70

Where (b) = (e)/65%

Balance sheet extract as at 31 December

	20X7 £	20X8 £	20X9 £	20Y0 £	20Y1 £
Net interest in finance lease	8498	6750	4745	2490	–*

*After eliminating rounding errors.

HP contracts

The guidance notes to SSAP 21 state that in the case of a HP contract that has the characteristics of a finance lease, it is expected from the outset that the hirer will take up the option to purchase. Thus, as with leases, SSAP 21 adopts a 'substance over form' approach and provides that most HP contracts should be accounted for on a basis similar to that set out for finance leases. (However, SSAP 21 also stipulates that in rare cases where a HP contract is not of a financing nature – for example, where the option to purchase is so highly priced that the hirer may not take it up – then such contracts should be accounted for on a similar basis to that set out for operating leases.)

Disclosure of information

In the accounts of the lessee

The Companies Act requires specific disclosure in the P&L account of amounts charged to revenue in respect of hire of plant and machinery, although a general requirement for disclosure in note form of those financial commitments not provided for in the accounts, but seen as necessary to an assessment of the company's state of affairs, might also be considered to be a relevant disclosure requirement in the context of finance leases.

However, although the law is fairly circumspect with respect to the divulgence of information concerning leases in general, and finance leases in particular, no such accusation can be levelled at SSAP 21.

The guidance notes to SSAP 21 state that 'the assets held under finance leases and the related obligations should be described in such a way as to be distinguishable from owned assets and debt respectively'. It is best left to SSAP 21 itself to state how this should be achieved:

49 The gross amounts of assets which are held under finance leases together with the related accumulated depreciation should be disclosed by each major class of asset. The total depreciation allocated for the period in respect of assets held under finance leases should be disclosed by each major class of asset.

50 The information required by paragraph 49 may, as an alternative to being shown separately from that in respect of owned fixed assets, be integrated with it such that the totals of gross amount, accumulated depreciation, net amount and depreciation allocated for the period for each major class of asset are included with similar amounts in respect of owned fixed assets. Where this alternative treatment is adopted, the net amount of assets held under finance leases included in the overall total should be disclosed. The amount of depreciation allocated for the period in respect of assets held under finance leases included in the overall total should also be disclosed.

51 The amounts of obligations related to finance leases (net of finance charges allocated to future periods) should be disclosed separately from other obligations and liabilities, either on the face of the balance sheet or in the notes to the accounts.

52 These net obligations under finance leases should be analysed between amounts payable in the next year, amounts payable in the second to fifth years inclusive from the balance sheet date, and the aggregate amounts payable thereafter. This analysis may be presented either (**a**) separately for obligations under finance leases or (**b**) where the total of these items is combined on the balance sheet with other obligations and liabilities, by giving the equivalent analysis of the total in which it is included ...

With respect to the lessee's P&L account SSAP 21 requires that:

1 the amounts charged to revenue for finance leases and HP contracts be disclosed (paragraph 53); and

2 the amounts charged to revenue in respect of operating leases analysed between amounts payable in respect of plant hire and in respect of other operating leases, be disclosed (paragraph 55).

Bearing in mind the legal requirement referred to above for the disclosure of plant hire charges, the guidance notes to SSAP 21 suggest that a note combining the P&L account requirements of both the law and the standard might appear as follows:

	£
Profit is stated after charging:	
Depreciation of owned assets	x
Depreciation of assets held under finance leases and HP contracts	x
Interest payable – bank loans and overdrafts and other loans repayable within five years	x
Finance charges payable – finance leases and HP contracts	x
Hire of plant and machinery – operating leases	x
Hire of other assets – operating leases	x

In the accounts of the lessor

Paragraph 58 requires that the net investment in:

1 finance leases; and
2 HP contracts

at each balance sheet date should be disclosed.

Paragraph 59 requires that the gross amounts of assets held for use in operating leases and the related accumulated depreciation, should be disclosed.

Paragraph 60(b) requires the disclosure of the aggregate rentals receivable in respect of an accounting period in relation to (**1**) finance leases and (**2**) operating leases.

Paragraph 60(c) requires the disclosure of the cost of assets acquired, whether by purchase or finance lease, for the purpose of letting under finance leases.

In the case of both lessees and lessors, SSAP 21 requires that disclosure should be made of the policies adopted for accounting for operating leases and finance leases. Additionally, for lessors, paragraph 60(a) requires disclosure of the policy for accounting for finance lease income.

Problems with SSAP 21

From the discussion on page 340, it may be remembered that one of the main drawbacks to the method of accounting for finance leases before SSAP 21 was that a lessee could generate revenues by the utilisation of fixed assets that were not recorded in its balance sheet. Similarly, the contractual obligations arising from the use of these (leased) assets were also omitted from the balance sheet, and this meant that comparison of such ratios as return on capital employed and gearing between companies (even those in the same industry) were often meaningless (and even positively misleading). Hence, SSAP 21 and its insistence on capitalisation in the lessee's balance sheet in respect of finance leases now enables comparisons to be achieved with some outward degree of success. Similarly, this use of a 'substance over form' approach to leasing now ensures that important omissions in respect of finance leased assets no longer occur, and that completeness (especially in terms of balance sheet information) is more generally achieved.

However, since the introduction of SSAP 21 further issues and/or problems have emerged. At page 342 we identified the SSAP 21 definition of a finance lease. This definition depended to a large extent on the 90% rule i.e. there was a presumption that a transfer of substantially all the risks and rewards of ownership passed to the lessee if 'at the inception of the lease the present value of the minimum lease payments including initial payment amounts to substantially all (normally 90% or more) of the fair value of the leased asset'. Let's look at this presumption more closely. When identifying the present value of the minimum lease payments at the inception of the lease there are several imponderables that affect the interest rate implicit in the lease, e.g. the estimated residual value.

Activity 8

A lessor issues a lease requiring rentals of £2000 per annum in advance. Within his calculations of the rentals required he has assumed a fair value for the asset leased of £10 200 and a residual value of £3000. This, using a similar calculation as that in Activity 3, implies an implicit rate of interest of 10%.

i.e.   10 200 = pv (rental payments and residual value) at implicit rate of interest

This equates at 10% as 2000 + 2000 × 3.17 + 3000 × 0.6209 = 10 203.

The lessee is aware that this lessor normally expects a 10% implicit rate of interest but he (the lessee) estimates the fair value of the leased asset at £10 200 and the residual value at £1200. Would the lessee classify this lease as a finance lease?

Feedback 8

The lessee can classify it as a finance lease if the present value of all lease payments and residual value equates to at least 90% of the fair value:

90% of fair value (10 200) = 9180
present value of lease payments and residual value at an implicit rate of 10% is
2000 + 2000 × 3.17 + 1200 × .6209 = 9085 which fails the 90% test.

The lessee would classify the lease as an operating lease.

The lessee would only classify the lease as a finance lease if he estimated the residual value at or more than £1352 (the break-even point in the above calculation).

Another estimate within the above activity is of course the fair value of the leased asset and the lessor and lessee could have different views on this, which again could affect the classification of the lease.

Activity 9

The implicit rate of interest in a lease is 10%, the residual value is estimated at £2500 and the lease payments are £2000pa in advance for 5 years. At what value does the lessee need to estimate the fair value of the leased asset to classify the lease as a finance lease?

Feedback 9

The present value of all lease payments must be greater than or equal to 90% of the fair value for classification as a finance lease.

Present value of lease payments   = 2000 + 2000 × 3.17 + 2500 × .6209
= 9892

If the lessee estimates the fair value of the asset at £11 000 (or more), 90% of which is £9900, then it can be classified as a finance lease.

Activities 8 and 9 demonstrate the scope for creative accounting within lease accounting. It would be quite easy for lessees and/or lessors to decide how they wished to classify a lease first and then ensure the estimates met their desired result. There is evidence to suggest that the spirit of SSAP 21, which requires an assessment of who has the risks and rewards associated with the asset is being ignored by some.

Leases: implementation of a new approach

A further issue concerning SSAP 21 is in relation to the definition of a liability and an asset in the recently issued Statement of Principles by the ASB. A liability is defined as an obligation to transfer economic benefits as a result of past transactions or events and an asset as rights or other access to future economic benefits controlled by an entity as a result of past transactions or events. (S of P December 1999 paragraphs 4.23 and 4.6). It could be argued that under an operating lease a lessee has an obligation to transfer future economic benefits, the future operating lease payments, and therefore a liability exists and that he also has an asset as he will control the risks and rewards associated with the asset for the period of the operating lease. Note this does not accord with the current standard SSAP 21.

In December 1999 the ASB published a discussion paper on the subject of leases entitled 'Leases: implementation of a new approach'. The paper had been developed by the G4 + 1 group. This group consists of representatives of accounting standard setters from Australia, Canada, UK, USA and New Zealand working with the IASC.

Summary of proposals of discussion paper

That the arbitrary distinction between operating and finance leases is unsatisfactory and should be abolished, to be replaced by an approach that applies the same regulations for all leases. The ASB in the paper note that many analysts recast financial statements by applying the same approach to operating and finance leases. G4 + 1 believe that recognition in a lessee's balance sheet of material assets and liabilities arising from operating leases should take place:

> The general effect of the approach proposed is that the amounts recognised as an asset and a liability by a lessee in respect of a lease of a given item would vary in amount depending on the nature of the lease.

The financial statements would thus reflect the extent to which differing lease arrangements result in financial obligations and provide financial flexibility.

The table below provides an overview of the items that would be included in the liabilities of a lessee and reported at the beginning of the lease with an asset and those that would not.

Items included in initial assets and liabilities	Item excluded from initial assets and liabilities
Minimum payments required by lease	
Amounts payable in respect of obtaining renewal options.	Rentals relating to optional renewal periods
Contingent rentals that represent consideration for the fair value of rights conveyed to lessee.	Contingent rentals relating to optional additional usage
Fair value of residual value guarantees	Residual values guaranteed where transfer of economic benefits in settlement is not probable.

(Discussion paper page 13)

The discussion paper debates the issue of recognition and measurement in relation to those leases to be included on the balance sheet.

For a lease contract the recognition point could be:

- signing a contract to lease
- purchase or manufacture by the lessor of the specific item of property that is the subject of the lease
- delivery of the property to the lessee
- rental payments falling due during the lease term.

The discussion paper suggests that recognition should take place at delivery of the property to the lessee.

For measurement of a lease we have to remember the principle that assuming an arms length transaction the cost of an acquired asset is normally measured by fair value of the consideration given. Thus the objective is to record at the beginning of the lease term the fair value of the rights and obligations that are conveyed by the lease.

Activity 10

A lessee agrees to hire a piece of equipment for 3 years at an annual rental of £10 000. The lessee returns the equipment to the lessor at end of the 3-year period. Rights and obligations of the lessee are thus:

- right to use for 3 years
- obligation to pay £10000 per annum for 3 years
- obligation to return the equipment to lessor after 3 years.

At what point should the lessee recognize an asset and at what value in accordance with the discussion paper?

Activity 10 Feedback

When the equipment is delivered to the lessee he should recognise an asset equivalent to the present value of three annual payments of £10 000 and a corresponding liability. The asset would subsequently require depreciation and impairment.

The discussion paper works through even more complicated examples involving lessee interest in residual values and various optional features, e.g. lease payments that vary with price changes and considers the measurement problems involved. It then moves on to the issue of discount rates.

Recording fair value of rights and obligations in a lease requires the discounting of future payments, thus there is a need to settle on a discount rate. The rate suggested by the discussion paper is the rate at which the lessee could borrow money for the term of the lease and with similar security to that of the lease.

The discussion paper asks for comment on 19 questions and three of these are reproduced below:

1 Do you agree that standard-setters should aim to develop a single accounting method that can be applied to leases of all kinds?
2 Do you agree that assets and liabilities should be recognised by a lessee, in relation to the rights and obligations conveyed by a lease when the lessor has substantially performed its obligation to provide the lessee with access to the leased property and should the objective be to record, at the beginning of the lease term, the fair value of the rights and obligations that are conveyed by the lease?

3 Do you agree with the proposal re the discount rate that should be applied to the rental payments?

The method of accounting treatment for leases has a profound effect on the gearing ratio of a company as the following activity demonstrates.

Activity 11

An industrial unit is leased by Company A for a 10 year period at an annual rental of £200 000pa. The discount rate implicit in the lease is assumed to be 8%. Before commencement of the lease the net assets of Company A are £5m and debt is £2m. Identify the change in the gearing ratio of Company A if the lease is recorded in accordance with

(a) SSAP 21 and
(b) Discussion paper 'Leases: implementation of a new approach'.

Assume the fair value of the industrial unit is £4m.

Activity 11 Feedback

(a) Under SSAP 21 the lease would be recorded as an operating lease and therefore left off the balance sheet as the present value of the lease payments is not equal to or greater than 90% of the fair value of the asset. Gearing would therefore remain at 40%.
(b) Under the discussion paper rules the lease would be capitalized at £1 342 000 i.e. present value at 8% of ten annual payments of £200 000 (200 000 × 6.71) and a corresponding liability shown. Net assets would rise to £6.342m and debt to £3.342m and gearing would become 53%.

Summary

The issue of SSAP 21 was the first foray by the ASC into the area of substance over form and this was occasioned by a particular corporate crash, and the need to account for transactions in accordance with economic reality rather than the contrived legal form. This concept of substance over form has been continued with the issue of FRS 5 by the ASB (see Chapter 18). However business transactions have continued to move at a pace and what might have been adequate as a standard in 1970 has been found to be lacking in the new century. The ASB's discussion paper on leases if implemented will have a profound effect on financial reports particularly in the area of gearing. This effect may lead to ever more creative accounting to circumvent the standard.

Exercises

1 Explain fully the differences between a finance lease and an operating lease.
2 Explain what is meant by the use of the words 'substance over form' as applied to SSAP 21.
3 Why might it be said that the position before the publication of SSAP 21 with respect to finance leases was unacceptable in terms of financial reporting?
4 How is a finance lease dealt with in the accounts of:
   (a) a lessee?
   (b) a lessor?

5 Are the following operating or finance leases:
   (a) A machine, fair value, £64 000 rented at a cost of £5000 per quarter payable in advance over five years. Interest rate implicit in the lease is 10%.
   (b) A machine, fair value, £56 000 rented at a cost of £6000 per quarter payable in arrears over five years. Interest rate implicit in the lease is 10%.
   (c) A machine, fair value, £60 000 rented at a cost of £15 000 per annum for an inde-terminable period which is terminable at any time by either party with no penalties.

6 At what implicit rate of interest would the lease for the machine in **5(a)** above become a finance lease?

7 In connection with SSAP 21 'Accounting for Leases and Hire Purchase Contracts':
   (a) What is the distinction between a finance lease and an operating lease? Why is this distinction important in financial reporting?
(8 marks)
   (b) You have been shown, by a non-financial director, this extract from a company's dis-closure of accounting policies.
   'Amounts receivable under finance leases are included in debtors at the amount of the net investment. Income from finance leases is credited to the profit and loss account using an actuarial method to give a constant periodic return on the net cash investment. The income includes amounts in respect of government grants grossed up at the average rate of corporation tax applicable to the lease period.'
   You are required to explain to the director the meaning of the policy.
(12 marks)
(20 marks)
(ACCA)

8 Medical Finance plc is a subsidiary of Medical Supplies plc which sells microcomputers to hospitals. On 1 October 20X1 Medical Finance plc entered into a finance lease with the Inner City Hospital under which annual rentals of £4290 will be paid for five years for the lease of equipment with a fair value of £16 500. The first payment was made on 1 October 20X1. Medical Finance plc uses the actuarial method after tax.
   An extract from a cash flow schedule prepared for the lease with Inner City Hospital shows the following:

Year ended 30.9	Net cash investment at start of period	Cash outflow cost/ tax	Cash inflow from rental	Tax	Interest paid	Profit after tax taken out of lease	Net cash invest- ment at end
	£	£	£	£	£	£	£
20X2		(16 500)	4 290		(1 445)	(205)	13 860
20X3	13 860		5 290	422	(1 160)	(167)	9 475
20X4	10 475		4 290	(13)	(815)	(116)	7 129

The rate of corporation tax used was 33% and the tax is paid or recovered in the finan-cial year following that in which it arises.
   Draft accounts are being prepared for the year-ended 30 September 20X3.

Required:
(a) Prepare the entries that would appear in the profit and loss account of Medical Finance plc for the year-ended 30 September 20X3 and in the bal-ance sheet as at that date.
(8 marks)
(b) Explain:

(i)   the major assumption used in the calculation of the net cash investment of £10 475 as at 30 September 20X3.

(ii) why there is an amount in the cash flow schedule for profit taken out of the lease.

(iii) the circumstances in which the amount due after more than one year under the lease should be disclosed on the face of the balance sheet.

(iv) the procedure for allocating gross earnings using the investment period method and any additional information that would be needed to calculate the gross earnings for the year-ended 30 September 20X3.

(12 marks)

(20 marks)

9 Arfro plc has entered into two leasing contracts as detailed below:

Contract 1 – Arfro plc as lessor. Arfro plc has acquired civil engineering plant in October 20X1 at a cost of £600 000. It was expected to have a life of five years at the end of which it could be traded in for £70 000 in part exchange for replacement plant. Depreciation on this category of plant is charged on a straight-line basis, with a full year's charge in the year of acquisition.

This plant was leased on 1 November 20X1 under an operating lease contract to Hange Ltd for a period of three years at an annual rental of £180 000, payable annually in advance on 1 November.

Contract 2 – Arfro plc as lessee. On 1 July 20X2 Arfro plc entered into a leasing contract for the supply of a technologically advanced communications system from Elsdi (19V7) plc. The contract, which is non-cancellable, is for a period of five years at an annual rental of £70 000, payable in advance on 1 July each year, starting in 20X2.

The system has been designed to meet Arfro's specification. As a consequence an open market price, which would serve as the basis of a fair value figure, is not available. Under these circumstances Arfro plc has capitalized the system on the basis of the minimum lease payments discounted at the rate of interest, 12% per annum, implicit in the lease. This same rate is also the constant periodic rate of finance charge on the balance of the obligation outstanding for each accounting period of the contract.

Depreciation is provided over the period of the lease on a straight-line basis, assuming no residual value.

Present value factors for 12%, applicable at each of the rental payment dates are

Due date	Present value factor
1 July	
20X2	1.000
20X3	0.893
20X4	0.797
20X5	0.712
20X6	0.635

In the accounts of the manufacturer/lessor, Elsdi (19V7) plc, the cost of this experimental prototype system was ascertained to be £269 200. The company's corporation tax rate is 33% and payment or recovery of corporation tax takes place nine months after the year-end on 30 June. The leased asset is eligible for writing-down allowances at the rate of 25%.

Under the special circumstances of this contract the fair value of the system is deemed to be equal to its cost. The constant periodic rate of return on the net cash investment is 10.54% per annum after tax.

Required:

Prepare extracts from the P&L accounts and balance sheets, to show the details

required by SSAP 21 'Accounting for Leases and Hire Purchase Contracts', for the year-ended 30 June 20X3, as far as this information is available, as appropriate to requirements (a), (b) and (c) below.

Your answer should contain the accompanying notes as specified in SSAP 21, except that notes covering accounting policies are not required.

Separate extracts are required for

(a)	**Arfro plc as lessor**	(6 marks)
(b)	**Arfro plc as lessee**	(10 marks)
(c)	**Elsdi (19V7) plc as lessor**	(14 marks)

Note: Marks will be awarded for workings which must be shown.

(30 marks)

10 The following problems and issues have arisen during the preparation of the draft financial statements of Dawes plc for the year to 30 September 20X7:

(a) The following schedule of the movement of plant has been drafted:

	Cost	Depreciation
	£m	£m
At 1 October 20X6 (including leased assets)	81.20	32.50
Additions at cost excluding leased assets (see 1 and 2 below)	23.00	–
Depreciation charge for year	–	19.84
Disposal (see 3 below)	(5.00)	–
Balance 30 September 20X7	99.20	52.34

1	The addition to plant is made up of:	
	Basic cost from supplier	20.00
	Value added tax	3.50
	Installation costs	1.00
	Pre-production testing	0.50
	Annual insurance and maintenance contract	1.00
	Less government grant (see 4 below)	(3.00)
		23.00

2 During the year some assets were acquired under finance leases. The fair value of these assets is represented by the movement on finance lease obligations. These increased from £21.4 million at 1 October 20X6 to £29 million at 30 September 20X7 after capital repayments during the year of £8.4 million. All finance leases for plant are for five years and none are more than three years old.

3 The disposal figure of £5 million is the proceeds from the sale of an item of plant during the year. It had cost £15 million on 1 October 20X3 and had been correctly depreciated prior to disposal. Dawes plc charges depreciation of 20% per annum on the cost of plant held at the year-end.

4 The company policy for government grants is to treat them as deferred credits in the balance sheet.

Required:

Prepare a corrected schedule of the movements on the cost and depreciation of plant, including leased assets. (7 marks)

11 Flow Ltd prepares financial statements to 31 March each year. On 1 April 1998, Flow Ltd sold a freehold property to another company, River plc. Flow Ltd had purchased the property for £500 000 on 1 April 1988 and had charged total depreciation of £60 000 on the property for the period 1 April 1988 to 31 March 1998.

River plc paid £850 000 for the property on 1 April 1998, at which date its true market value was £550 000.

From 1 April 1998 the property was leased back by Flow Ltd on a ten-year operating lease for annual rentals (payable in arrears) of £100 000. A normal annual rental for such a property would have been £50 000.

River plc is a financial institution which, on 1 April 1998, charged interest of 10.56% per annum on ten-year fixed rate loans.

Requirements:

(a) **Explain what is meant by the terms 'finance lease' and 'operating lease' and how operating leases should be accounted for in the financial statements of lessee companies.** (7 marks)

(b) **Show the journal entries which Flow Ltd will make to record**
   - **its sale of the property to River plc on 1 April 1998,**
   - **the payment of the first rental to River plc on 31 March 1999.**

   Justify your answer with reference to appropriate Accounting Standards
   (13 marks)

   (27 marks)
   CIMA (9) MAY 99

Stock and long-term contracts (SSAP 9)

After reading this chapter you should be able to:
- explain the composition of cost of stocks
- describe the five stock cost assumptions, i.e. unit cost, first in, first out (FIFO), last in, first out (LIFO), weighted average, and base stock
- show the effect on annual profit and profit trends of using different stock cost assumptions
- describe SSAP 9 and Companies Act requirements relating to stocks and work in progress
- define long-term contract, attributable profit and foreseeable losses
- describe SSAP 9 and Companies Act requirements relating to long-term contracts
- discuss whether SSAP 9 and Companies Act requirements relating to long-term contracts are compatible
- calculate amounts to be disclosed in financial statements relating to long-term contracts.

Introduction

Stocks and work in progress present several problems to the accountant. First, we have to determine the cost of the item. Secondly, we have to apply the prudence convention as appropriate. Thirdly, we have to determine the revenue recognition ('sale') point, and apply the matching convention correspondingly. These problems are particularly difficult in the case of long-term contract work in progress – a single contract lasting several years – and it is useful, following SSAP 9 itself, to treat these separately. We consider first, stock and work in progress other than long-term contract work in progress.

SSAP 9 was revised in 1988. The alterations as regards short-term stocks and work in progress were minor, and it is only with long-term contract work in progress that we need to look at the changes in any detail.

Stocks and work in progress

These comprise:

1 goods or other assets purchased for resale
2 consumable stores
3 raw materials and components purchased for incorporation into products for sale

4 products and services in intermediate stages of completion
5 finished goods.

'Cost' for the purpose of such items is defined at some length in the SSAP as follows:

17 *Cost* is defined in relation to the different categories of stocks as being that expenditure which has been incurred in the normal course of business in bringing the product or service to its present location and condition. This expenditure should include, in addition to cost of purchase (as defined in paragraph 18), such costs of conversion (as defined in paragraph 19) as are appropriate to that location and condition.

18 *Cost of purchase* comprises purchase price including import duties, transport and handling costs and any other directly attributable costs, less trade discounts, rebates and subsidies.

19 *Cost of conversion comprises*:
   (a) costs which are specifically attributable to units of production, e.g. direct labour, direct expenses and subcontracted work
   (b) production overheads (as defined in paragraph 20)
   (c) other overheads, if any, attributable in the particular circumstances of the business to bringing the product or service to its present location and condition.

20 *Production overheads*: overheads incurred in respect of materials, labour or services for production, based on the normal level of activity, taking one year with another. For this purpose each overhead should be classified according to function (e.g. production, selling or administration) so as to ensure the inclusion, in cost of conversion, of those overheads (including depreciation) which relate to production, notwithstanding that these may accrue wholly or partly on a time basis.

A moment's reflection will make it obvious that there are practical problems here. 'Direct' items should present no difficulties as figures can be related 'directly' by definition. But overhead allocation necessarily introduces assumptions and approximations – what is the normal level of activity taking one year with another? – can overheads be clearly classified according to function? – which other (non-production) overheads are 'attributable' to the present position and location of an item of stock? So for any item of stock that is not still in its original purchased state, it is a problem to determine the cost of a unit, or even of a batch. Methods in common use include job, process, batch and standard costing. All include more or less arbitrary overhead allocations.

Once we have found a figure for unit cost 'in its present location and position', the next difficulty will arise when we have to select an appropriate method for calculating the related cost where several identical items have been purchased or made at different times and therefore at different unit costs.

Consider the following transactions:

Purchases:	January	10 units at £25 each
	February	15 units at £30 each
	April	20 units at £35 each
Sales:	March	15 units at £50 each
	May	18 units at £60 each

How do we calculate stock, cost of sales, and gross profit? There are several ways of doing this, based on different assumptions as to which unit has been sold, or which unit is deemed to have been sold.

Stock cost assumptions

Five possibilities are discussed below.

Unit cost

Here we assume that we know the actual physical units that have moved in or out. Each unit must be individually distinguishable, e.g. by serial numbers. In these circumstances, impractical in most cases, we simply add up the recorded costs of those units sold to give cost of sales, and of those units left to give stock. This needs no detailed illustration.

First in, first out (FIFO)

Here it is assumed that the units moving out are the ones that have been in the longest (i.e. came in first). The units remaining will therefore be regarded as representing the latest units purchased.

Activity 1

Calculate the cost of sales and gross profit based on FIFO stock cost assumption from the data given above.

Activity 1 feedback

					Cost of sales
January		10 at £25	=	£250	
February		15 at £30	=	450	
February total		25		700	
March	−	10 at £25 (Jan.)	=	250	
	−	5 at £30 (Feb.)	=	150	400
March total		10 at £30	=	300	
April	+	20 at £35	=	700	
April total		30		1000	
May	−	10 at £30 (Feb.)	=	300	
	−	8 at £35 (Apr.)	=	280	580
May total		12 at £35		420	
					£980

Sales are 750 + 1080 = £1830
Purchases are 250 + 450 + 700 = £1400

This gives:	Sales		1830
	Purchases	1400	
	Closing stock	420	
	Cost of sales		980
	Gross profit		£850

Last in, first out (LIFO)

Here we reverse the assumption. We act as if the units moving out are the ones which came in most recently. The units remaining will therefore be regarded as representing the earliest units purchased.

Activity 2

Calculate the cost of sales and gross profit based on LIFO stock cost assumption using the given data.

Activity 2 feedback

					Cost of sales
January		10 at £25	=	£250	
February		15 at £30	=	450	
February total		25		700	
March	−	15 at £30 (Feb.)	=	450	450
March total		10	=	250	
April	+	20 at £35	=	700	
April total		30		950	
May	−	18 at £35 (Apr.)	=	630	630
		2 at £35 & 10		320	
		at £25			£1080

This gives:	Sales		1830
	Purchases	1400	
	Closing stock	320	
	Cost of sales		1080
	Gross profit		£750

Weighted average

Here we apply the average cost, weighted according to the different proportions at the different cost levels, to the items in stock. The illustration below shows the fully worked out method, involving continuous calculations. In practice, an average cost of purchases figure is often used rather than an average cost of stock figure. This approximation reduces the need for calculation to a periodic, maybe even annual, requirement.

Activity 3

Calculate the cost of sales and gross profit based on weighted average stock cost assumption.

Activity 3 feedback

				Cost of sales
January		10 at £25	=	£250	
February		15 at £30	=	450	
February total		25 at £28*		700	
March	−	15 at £28	=	420	420
March total		10 at £28	=	280	
April	+	20 at £35	=	700	
April total		30 at £32²/₃*		980	
May	−	18 at £32²/₃	=	588	588
May total		12 at £32²/₃	=	392	
					£1008

$$*\text{Working: } \frac{(10 \times 25) + (15 \times 30)}{(10 + 15)} = 28$$

$$\frac{(10 \times 28) + (20 \times 35)}{(10 + 20)} = 32\frac{2}{3}$$

This gives:

Sales		1830
Purchases	1400	
Closing stock	392	
Cost of sales		1008
Gross profit		£822

Base stock

This approach is based on the argument that a certain minimum level of stock is necessary in order to remain in business at all. Thus, it can be argued that some of the stock, viewed in the aggregate, is not really available for sale and should therefore be regarded as a fixed asset. This minimum level defined by management, remains at its original cost, and the remainder of the stock above this level is treated, as stock, by one of the other methods. In our example, the minimum level might be ten units.

> ## Activity 4
>
> Calculate the cost of sales and gross profit based on a minimum stock level of ten units and using FIFO.

Activity 4 feedback

January purchase of base stock: 10 at £25 = £250

Cost of sales

February	15 at £30	=	450	
March	− 15 at £30	=	450	450
March total	0		0	
April	+ 20 at £35	=	700	
April total	20	=	700	
May	− 18 at £35	=	630	630
May total	2 at £35	=	70	
				1080

This gives:	Sales		1830
	Purchases	1150 −	
	Closing stock	70	
	Cost of sales		1080
	Gross profit		£750

In this particular case, the gross profit is the same with this method (base stock + FIFO) as with LIFO. Can you work out why? This will not generally be the case.

So which approach or approaches are preferable or acceptable? The definition of cost already given from paragraph 17 (p. 366) does not really help. The published standard contains several appendices. Each appendix explicitly states that it 'is for general guidance and does not form part of the Statement of Standard Accounting Practice'. This means that they are not 'intended to be mandatory'. In the case of SSAP 9, however, much of their contents seems to have been generally viewed as having the same force as the SSAP itself. Appendix 1 says the following:

11 It is frequently not practicable to relate expenditure of specific units of stocks and long-term contracts. The ascertainment of the nearest approximation to cost gives rise to two problems:
  (a) the selection of an appropriate method for relating costs to stocks and long-term contracts (e.g. job costing, batch costing, process costing, standard costing)
  (b) the selection of an appropriate method for calculating the related costs where a number of identical items have been purchased or made at different times (e.g. unit cost, average cost or FIFO).

12 In selecting the methods referred to in paragraphs 11(a) and (b) above, management must exercise judgement to ensure that the methods chosen provide the fairest practicable approximation to cost. Furthermore, where standard costs are used they need to be reviewed frequently to ensure that they bear a reasonable relationship to actual costs obtaining during the period. Methods such as base stock and LIFO are not usually appropriate methods of stock valuation because they often result in stocks being stated in the balance sheet at amounts that bear little relationship to recent cost levels. When this happens, not only is the presentation of current assets misleading, but there is potential distortion of subsequent results if stock levels reduce and out of date costs are drawn into the profit and loss account.

13   The method of arriving at cost by applying the latest purchase price to the total number of units in stock is unacceptable in principle because it is not necessarily the same as actual cost and, in times of rising prices, will result in the taking of a profit which has not been realized.

14   One method of arriving at cost, in the absence of a satisfactory costing system, is the use of selling price less an estimated profit margin. This is acceptable only if it can be demonstrated that the method gives a reasonable approximation of the actual cost.

15   In industries where the cost of minor by-products is not separable from the cost of the principal products, stocks of such by-products may be stated in accounts at their net realizable value. In this case the costs of the main products are calculated after deducting the net realizable value of the by-products.

So LIFO and base stock are unacceptable because they do not bear a 'reasonable relationship to actual costs'. From a P&L account viewpoint, this is surely a strange criticism. Consider the cost of sales figures for the May sales in the FIFO and LIFO calculations above. Is it preferable to match an April cost level against an April revenue (LIFO) or, partially at least to match a February cost level against an April revenue level (FIFO)? From a balance sheet viewpoint, however, the criticism perhaps makes more sense. The balance sheet total under both LIFO and base stock (both parts considered together here) is likely to be badly out of date. Applying the latest purchase price level to all units, sometimes called next in, first out (NIFO), is also rejected.

The SSAP requirements

It is now quite clear that the calculation of the appropriate 'stock at cost' figure is by no means clear-cut. Assumptions in two respects have to be made, as discussed on p. 367. The actual 'standard accounting practice' requirement itself is very brief, and ignores all these difficulties. It is as follows:

26   The amount at which stocks are stated in periodic financial statements should be the total of the lower of cost and net realisable value of the separate items of stock or of groups of similar items.

So for each separate item we need to:

1   determine cost, discussed above
2   determine NRV, defined thus:

21   *Net realisable value*: the actual or estimated selling price (net of trade but before settlement discounts) less:

(a) all further costs to completion; and

(b) all costs to be incurred in marketing, selling and distributing.

The significance of the 'separate items' point should be noted. Suppose there are three products, A, B and C, with figures as shown in Table 22.1. The figure for stock in the accounts is £30, not the lower of £33 and £36. This is, of course, a classic example of the prudence convention.

Table 22.1 *Lower of cost and NRV*

Product	Cost	NRV	Lower
A	10	12	10
B	11	15	11
C	12	9	9
Total	33	36	30

One surprising aspect of SSAP 9 is the extraordinary devotion it shows towards HC accounting. RC is actually mentioned, but only in the context, oddly, of NRV:

> 6 Items of stock have sometimes been stated in financial statements at esti-mated replacement cost where this is lower than net realisable value. Where the effect is to take account of a loss greater than that which is expected to be incurred, the use of replacement cost is not regarded as acceptable. However, in some circumstances (e.g. in the case of materials, the price of which has fluctuated considerably and which have not become the subject of firm sales contracts by the time the financial statements are prepared) replacement cost may be the best measure of net realisable value. Also, where a company adopts the alternative accounting rules of the Companies Act 1985, items of stock may be stated at the lower of current replacement cost and net realisable value.

As already stated, using RC when it is higher than cost or NRV is also explicitly rejected in paragraph 13 (of Appendix 1).

Considerable debate has arisen over the requirement, which is quite explicit in SSAP 9 (paragraphs 19 and 20), that production overheads *are* included in 'cost' of stocks. This has been criticized on the grounds that it lacks prudence. In a sense it is less prudent to include production overheads, as to include them will obviously lead to higher stock figures in the balance sheets. It will of course not necessarily lead to a higher profit figure in any particular year, as the profit figure is only affected by the *difference* between the opening and closing stock figures, not by the absolute amounts of the opening and closing stock figures. In Appendix 1 to the standard, the requirement that production overheads should be included is defended.

> 1 Production overheads are included in cost of conversion together with direct labour, direct expenses and sub-contracted work. This inclusion is a neces-sary corollary of the principle that expenditure should be included to the extent to which it has been incurred in bringing the product 'to its present location and condition'. However, all abnormal conversion costs (such as exceptional spoilage, idle capacity and other losses), which are avoidable

2 You are given the following information in relation to Olivet Ltd.

P&L accounts	20X4 £	20X5 £
Sales	100 000	100 000
Cost of sales	50 000	60 000
	50 000	40 000
Expenses	30 000	30 000
	20 000	10 000
Dividends	10 000	10 000
	10 000	–
Balance b/d	2 500	12 500
	12 500	12 500

Balance sheets as at	20X4 £	20X5 £
Land	21 500	31 500
Buildings	20 000	39 500
Equipment	3 000	3 000
	44 500	74 000
Investments at cost	25 000	40 000
Stock	27 500	32 500
Debtors	20 000	25 000
Bank	1 500	
	118 500	171 500

Ordinary £1 shares	20 000	25 000
Share premium	6 000	7 000
Revaluation reserve	–	10 000
Profit and loss	12 500	12 500
Debentures 10%	50 000	75 000
Creditors	20 000	30 000
Proposed dividend	10 000	10 000
Bank	–	2 000
	118 500	171 500

You are required to comment on the financial position of Olivet Ltd as at 20X5. Calculate any ratios you feel necessary.

3 You are given the attached information about Fred plc, comprising summarized P&L accounts, summarized balance sheets, and some suggested ratio calculations. You should note that there may be alternative ways of calculating some of these ratios. The holder of a small number of the ordinary shares in the business has come to you for help and advice. There are a number of things he does not properly understand, and a friend of his who is an accountancy student has suggested to him that some of the ratios show a distinctly unsatisfactory position, and that he should sell his shares as quickly as possible.

Required:

(a) Write a report to the shareholder commenting on the apparent position and

prospects of Fred plc, as far as the information permits. Your report should include reference to liquidity and profitability aspects, and should advise whether, in your view, the shares should indeed be sold as soon as possible.

(12 marks)

(b) Explain the following issues to the shareholder:

(i) What is the loan redemption fund, and how has it been created?

(3 marks)

(ii) How on earth can there be £49 million of assets on the balance sheet 'not yet in use'? Surely if it is not in use it is not an asset? What are assets any-way? And coming back to that £49 million, the depreciation on these items will be artificially reducing the reported profit won't it? (6 marks)

(iii) What is all this about interest being capitalized? What does it mean, and why are they doing it? (4 marks)

(25 marks)

(ACCA)

Fred plc

Some possible ratio calculations (which can be taken as arithmetically correct).

	1992	*1991*
Current ratio	54/147 = 36.7%	56/172 = 32.6%
Acid test ratio	12/147 = 8.2%	15/172 = 8.7%
ROCE	57/249 = 22.9%	41/161 = 25.5%
ROOE	33/188 = 17.5%	24/160 = 15.0%
eps	31/190 = 16.3p	22/190 = 11.6p
Trade debtors' turnover	4/910 × 365 = 2 days	4/775 × 365 = 2 days
Trade creditors' turnover	60/730 × 365 = 30 days	60/633 × 365 = 35 days
Gross profit %	180/910 = 19.8%	142/775 = 18.3%
Operating profit %	57/910 = 6.3 p	41/775 = 5.3%
Stock turnover	42/730 × 365 = 21 days	41/633 × 365 = 24 days
Gearing	61/188 = 32.4%	1/160 = 0.6%

Fred plc

Summarized balance sheets at year-end (£m)

		1992		1991	
Fixed assets					
tangible – not yet in use		49		41	
– in use		295		237	
		344		278	
investments		1		1	
loan redemption fund		1		1	
			346		280
Current assets					
stocks		42		41	
debtors – trade	4		4		
– other	4		4		
	8		8		
bank		2		5	
cash		2		2	
		54		56	

Creditors – due within 1 year				
– trade	60		60	
– other	87		112	
		147		172
Net current liabilities			93	116
Total assets less current liabilities			253	164
Creditors – due between one and five years			61	1
Provision for liabilities and charges			4	3
Net assets			188	160
Capital and reserves				
ordinary shares of 10p each			19	19
preference shares of £1 each			46	46
share premium			1	1
profit and loss account			122	94
			188	160

Fred plc
Summarized P&L accounts for the year (£m)

		1992		1991
Sales		910		775
Raw materials and consumables		730		633
		180		142
Staff costs	77		64	
Depreciation of tangible fixed assets	12		10	
Other operating charges	38		30	
		127		104
		53		38
Other operating income		4		3
		57		41
Net interest payable		5		4
		52		37
Profit sharing – employees		2		1
		50		36
Taxation		17		12
		33		24
Preference dividends		2		2
		31		22
Ordinary dividends		3		2
		28		20

Note
Net interest payable:

	1992	1991
interest payable	12	9
interest receivable	(1)	(1)
interest capitalized	(6)	(4)
	5	4

4 You are given summarized results of an electrical engineering business, as follows. All figures are in £000.

Profit and loss account

	year-ended	
	31.12.91	*31.12.90*
Turnover	60 000	50 000
Cost of sales	42 000	34 000
Gross profit	18 000	16 000
Operating expenses	15 500	13 000
	2 500	3 000
Interest payable	2 200	1 300
Profit before taxation	300	1 700
Taxation	350	600
(Loss) profit after taxation	(50)	1 100
Dividends	600	600
Transfer (from) to reserves	(650)	500

Balance sheet

Fixed assets		
intangible	500	–
tangible	12 000	11 000
	12 500	11 000
Current assets		
stocks	14 000	13 000
debtors	16 000	15 000
bank and cash	500	500
	30 500	28 500
Creditors due within 1 year	24 000	20 000
Net current assets	6 500	8 500
Total assets less current liabilities	19 000	19 500
Creditors due after one year	6 000	5 500
	13 000	14 000
Capital and reserves		
share capital	1 300	1 300
share premium	3 300	3 300
revaluation reserve	2 000	2 000
profit and loss	6 400	7 400
	13 000	14 000

Required:
(a) Prepare a table of the following twelve ratios, calculated for both years, clearly showing the figures used in the calculations:
current ratio
quick assets ratio
stock turnover in days
debtors' turnover in days
creditors' turnover in days

gross profit %
net profit % (before taxation)
interest cover
dividend cover
ROOE (before taxation)
ROCE
gearing (12 marks)
(b) Making full use of the information given in the question, of your table of ratios, and your commonsense, comment on the apparent position of the business and on the actions of the management. (8 marks)
(20 marks)
(ACCA)

5 The Pitlochry Group is one of the leading food retailers in the UK. It ranks within the 50 largest listed British companies on the London Stock Exchange. The annual report for the year-ended 31 March 1993 includes a five-year financial summary as follows:

Five-year financial summary

year-ended 31 March	1989	1990	1991	1992	1993
	£m	£m	£m	£m	£m
Turnover	1915	3068	3326	3728	4281
% change		60	8	12	15
Profit before tax and exceptional items	72	157	187	218	261
% change		64	36	28	28
Operating profit (before investment income and interest charge)	77	144	168	201	256
% change		87	17	20	27
Market capitalization	1512	1633	1495	1737	2454
Net tangible assets					
Tangible fixed assets	444	537	736	1005	1250
Net current liabilities	(162)	(54)	(167)	(282)	(320)
Creditors (due after 1 year)	(119)	(81)	(98)	(102)	(186)
Deferred taxation	(8)	(3)	(4)	(5)	(9)
Other provisions	(2)	–	–	–	–
	153	399	467	616	735
Operating profit margin %	4	5	5.4	5.7	6.3
Market capitalization times Book value	9.9	4.1	3.2	2.8	3.3

year-ended 31 March	1989	1990	1991	1992	1993
	pence	pence	pence	pence	pence
Earnings per share	10.5	11.8	13.5	15.4	18
% change	12	14	14	17	
Dividend per share	4.10	4.80	5.60	6.53	7.80
% change	17	17	17	20	
Ordinary share prices					
high	197	222	184	231	263
low	134	153	144	159	181
Number of shareholders	15014	22969	22909	22741	22942

In the year-ended 31 March 1990 a major outlet was acquired and this has since become the principal retail identity. Over the past four years the floor area devoted to sales has tripled with the opening of 80 new stores.

In May 1993 a rights issue was made to raise £384 million which turned borrowings of £150 million into a cash balance of £198 million. The directors have adopted a growth programme suitable for a superstore involving opening 25 stores a year and penetrating complementary non-food markets. Capital expenditure for the current year is estimated at £405 million and is planned to increase to £450 million for each of the next two years.

Required:

(a) **Calculate a rate of return on capital employed and the turnover to capital employed, as percentages, using only the information provided, for each of the years included in the summary. Show clearly the workings for the calculations.**

(5 marks)

(b) **Comment on the trends shown by the data of the Pitlochry Group.**

(10 marks)

(c) **Briefly indicate additional information you would require in order to be able to use the data for inter-company comparison.** (8 marks)

(d) **Sketch a graph of turnover to capital employed and of the margin, to cover five years, and comment on the relationship as presented by the graph in the light of your calculation of rate of return on capital employed calculated in part (a). Include a comment on the growth programme outlined in the question.**

(7 marks)

(30 marks)

(ACCA)

6 Heavy Goods plc carries on business as a manufacturer of tractors. In 1994 the company was looking for acquisitions and carrying out investigations into a number of possible targets. One of these was a competitor, Modern Tractors plc. The company's acquisition strategy was to acquire companies that were vulnerable to a takeover and in which there was an opportunity to improve asset management and profitability.

The chief accountant of Heavy Goods plc has instructed his assistant to calculate ratios from the financial statements of Modern Tractors plc for the past three years and to prepare a report based on these ratios and the industry average ratios that have been provided by the trade association. The ratios prepared by the assistant accountant and the industry averages for 1994 are set out below.

Required:

(a) **Assuming the role of the chief accountant, draft a brief report to be submitted to the managing director based on the ratios of Modern Tractors plc for 1992–4 and the industry averages for 1994.** (12 marks)

(b) **Draft a brief memo to management explaining:**

(i) **in general terms why the comparison of the 1994 ratios with the ratios of previous years and other companies might be misleading; and** (3 marks)

(ii) **how specific ratios might be affected and the possible implications for the evaluation of the report.**

(5 marks)

(20 marks)

(ACCA)

		1992	1993	1994	*Industry average* 1994
Sales growth	%	30.00	40.00	9.52	8.25
Sales/total assets		1.83	2.05	1.60	2.43
Sales/net fixed assets		2.94	3.59	2.74	16.85

Sales/working capital		−21.43	−140.00	38.33	10.81
Sales/debtors		37.50	70.00	92.00	16.00
Gross profit/sales	%	18.67	22.62	19.57	23.92
Profit before tax/sales	%	8.00	17.62	11.74	4.06
Profit before interest/interest		6.45	26.57	14.50	4.95
Profit after tax/total assets	%	9.76	27.80	13.24	8.97
Profit after tax/equity	%	57.14	75.00	39.58	28.90
Net fixed assets/total assets	%	62.20	57.07	58.54	19.12
Net fixed assets/equity		3.64	1.54	1.75	0.58
Equity/total assets	%	18.29	37.07	33.45	32.96
Total liabilities/total assets	%	81.71	62.93	66.55	69.00
Total liabilities/equity		4.47	1.70	1.99	2.40
Long-term debt/total assets	%	36.59	18.54	29.27	19.00
Current liabilities/total assets	%	45.12	44.39	37.28	50.00
Current assets/ current liabilities		0.84	0.97	1.11	1.63
(Current assets − stock)/ current liabilities		0.43	0.54	0.72	0.58
Stock/total assets	%	17.07	18.54	14.63	41.90
Cost of sales/stock		8.71	8.55	8.81	4.29
Cost of sales/creditors		6.10	6.25	6.17	12.87
Debtors/total assets	%	4.88	2.93	1.70	18.40
Cash/total assets	%	15.85	21.46	25.08	9.60

Note

Total assets = (fixed assets at net book value + current assets) and net fixed assets = fixed assets at net book value.

7 Seville plc is a rapidly expanding trading and manufacturing company. It is currently seeking to extend its product range in new markets. To achieve this growth it needs to raise £800 000. The directors are considering two sources of funds:

(i) A rights issue at £2.00 per share. The shares are trading at £2.50 (1990 £2.20) per share.

(ii) A bank loan at an interest rate of 15% and repayable by instalments after two years. The bank would want to secure the loan with a charge over the company's property.

The following are extracts from the draft financial statements.

Seville plc
Draft P&L account extract year-ended 31.12.91

	1990 £000	1991 £000
Turnover	1967	1991
Operating profit	636	698
Interest payable	(45)	(55)
Profit before taxation	591	643
Taxation	(150)	(140)
Profit after taxation	441	503
Extraordinary item	(90)	–
Profit for the year	361	453

Seville plc
Draft balance sheet extract as at 31.12.91

	1990 £000	1991 £000
Fixed assets		
tangible	1132	1504
intangible	247	298
	1379	1802
Current assets		
stocks	684	679
debtors	471	511
cash in hand and at bank	80	117
Creditors: due within one year		
trade	(336)	(308)
taxation	(140)	(190)
dividends	(80)	(80)
Creditors: due after more than one year		
10% debentures, repayable 2004	(450)	(450)
finance lease	–	(100)
	1608	1981
Capital and reserves		
ordinary share capital £1 shares	800	800
revaluation reserve	144	144
profit and loss	664	1037
	1608	1981

Operating profit
Operating profit has been arrived at after charging or crediting the following:

	1990 £000	1991 £000
Depreciation	110	150
Gain on disposal of property (as part of a sale and leaseback transaction)	–	95

Extraordinary item
The extraordinary loss consists of reorganization costs in a branch where a reduction in activity involved various measures including redundancies. Attributable tax credit is £38000.

Deferred taxation
Deferred taxation has not been provided because it is not considered probable that a liability will crystallize. If deferred taxation had been provided in full then a liability for the year of £7000 would have arisen (1990 £8000).

Contingent liability
There is a contingent liability of £85000 (1990 £80000) in respect of bills of exchange discounted with bankers.

Further investigation has revealed that stock includes items subject to reservation of title of £40 000 and obsolete or slow moving items of £28 000 (1990 £28 000).

An age analysis of debtors has revealed that debts overdue by more than one year amount to £40 000 (1990 £40 000).

The auditors are yet to report and there is some discussion as to the classification of the gain on disposal and the reorganization costs.

The directors forecast that the new funds will generate an operating profit of £300 000, and that the 1991 operating profit will be repeated. If new shares are issued the dividend will increase to £150 000.

Required:

(a) Analyse the accounts based on the following ratios, from the separate points of view of potential equity holders and debt holders:
   (i)   current ratio
   (ii)   interest cover
   (iii) debt/equity ratio
   (iv)   earnings per share
   (v)   after tax return on equity
   (vi)   price/earnings ratio.
   Two different versions of each of these ratios should be calculated and used in your analysis where the input to the ratio calculation can be variously defined or where the data suggests uncertainty as to accounting treatment in the draft accounts.

   Your analysis should clearly indicate which parts of it are of particular relevance to potential equity holders and which are of particular relevance to potential debt holders. It should also comment on the limitations of each of the ratios as an evaluative tool.   (20 marks)

(b) Assuming that either funding scheme becomes effective 1 January 1992, recalculate, for each scheme, the following ratios:
   (i)   debt/equity ratio
   (ii)   interest cover
   (iii) after tax return on equity.
   For ratios (ii) and (iii), adopt the directors' forecasts. Advise the directors, with reasons, which scheme to adopt. List other factors the directors should consider.

                                                                       (10 marks)
                                                                   (30 marks)
                                                                         ACCA

(Work to the nearest £000. Corporation tax rate is 35%.)

8 Recycle plc is a listed company which recycles toxic chemical waste products. The waste products are sent to Recycle plc from all around the world. You are an accountant (not employed by Recycle plc) who is accustomed to providing advice concerning the performance of companies, based on the data which are available from their published financial statements. Extracts from the financial statements of Recycle plc for the two years ended 30 September 1997 are given below:

Profit and loss accounts – year-ended 30 September:

	1997	1996
Turnover	3000	2800
Cost of sales	(1600)	(1300)
Gross profit	1400	1500
Other operating expenses	(800)	(600)
Operating profit	600	900
Interest payable	(200)	(100)
Profit before taxation	400	800
Taxation	(150)	(250)
Profit after taxation	250	550
Proposed dividend	(200)	(200)
Retained profit	50	350
Retained profit b/fwd	900	550
Retained profit c/fwd	950	900

Balance sheets at 30 September:

	1997		1996	
	£m	£m	£m	£m
Tangible fixed assets		4100		3800
Current assets:				
Stocks	500		350	
Debtors	1000		800	
Cash in hand	50		50	
	1550		1200	
Current liabilities:				
Trade creditors	600		600	
Taxation payable	150		250	
Proposed dividend	200		200	
Bank overdraft	750		50	
	1700		1100	
Net current (liabilities)/assets		(150)		100
Long-term loans (repayable 1999)		(1000)		(1000)
		2950		2900
Capital and reserves:				
Called-up share capital (£1 shares)		2000		2000
Profit and loss account		950		900
		2950		2900

You ascertain that depreciation of tangible fixed assets for the year-ended 30 September 1997 was £1200 million. Disposals of fixed assets during the year-ended 30 September 1997 were negligible. You are approached by two individuals.

A is a private investor who is considering purchasing shares in Recycle plc. A considers that Recycle plc has performed well in 1997 compared with 1996 because turnover has risen and the dividend to shareholders has been maintained.

B is resident in the area immediately surrounding the premises of Recycle plc and is interested in the contribution made by Recycle plc to the general well-being of the community. B is also concerned about the potential environmental effect of the recycling of chemical waste. B is uncertain how the published financial statements of Recycle plc might be of assistance in addressing social and environmental matters.

Required:
(a) **Write a report to A which analyses the financial performance of Recycle plc over the two years ended 30 September 1997.**
    Assume inflation is negligible.
    Your report should specifically refer to the observations made by A concerning the performance of Recycle plc.   (25 marks)
(b) **Briefly discuss whether published financial statements satisfy the information needs of B. You should consider published financial statements IN GENERAL, NOT just the extracts which are provided in this question.**
                                                                              (5 marks)
                                                                         (30 marks)
                                                                              (CIMA)

9 H plc manufactures vehicle parts. The company sells its products to a number of independent distributors who resell the goods to garages and other retail outlets in their areas. H plc has a policy of having only one distributor in any given geographical area. Distributors are selected mainly on the basis of financial viability. H plc is keen to avoid the disruption of sales and loss of credibility associated with the collapse of a distributor.

The company is currently trying to choose between two companies which have applied to be its sole distributor in Geetown, a new sales area.

The applicants have supplied the following information:

	Applicant X			Applicant Y		
	1993	1994	1995	1993	1994	1995
Sales (£000)	1280	1600	2000	1805	1900	2000
Gross profit %	22	20	18	23	22	24
Return on capital employed %	8	12	16	14	15	16
Current ratio	1.7:1	1.9:1	2.1:1	1.7:1	1.65:1	1.7:1
Quick ratio	1.4:1	1.1:1	0.9:1	0.9:1	0.9:1	0.9:1
Gearing %	15	21	28	29	30	27

Requirements:
(a) **Explain why trends in accounting ratios could provide a more useful insight than the latest figures taken on their own.**   (4 marks)
(b) **Using the information provided above, explain which of the companies appears to be the safer choice for the role of distributor.**   (11 marks)
                                                                         (15 marks)
                                                                              (CIMA)

10 You are employed by a CIMA member who provides consultancy services to small and medium-sized businesses. You are helping her to prepare a presentation to the directors of U Ltd, a manufacturing company which is planning to expand in the near future and is hoping to attract some new investors.

As a first step, you have prepared the following table of accounting ratios:

	U Ltd year-ended 31/3/98	U Ltd year-ended 31/3/97	Industry average for year-ended 31/3/98
Return on total capital employed	16%	13%	14%
Return on equity	19%	19%	22%
Gross profit percentage	36%	37%	45%
Net profit percentage	19%	17%	25%
Current ratio	2.4:1	2.1:1	1.8:1
Quick ratio	1.5:1	1.3:1	1.0:1
Stock turnover	43 days	39 days	26 days
Debtors turnover	54 days	52 days	39 days
Gearing ratio	35%	31%	28%

Required:
(a) Explain why it might be argued that any analysis of financial statements from the shareholders' point of view ought to concentrate on profitability.

(5 marks)

(b) Your employer believes that U Ltd's return on capital employed (based on the total of long-term debt and equity) is poor, given that the company has recently been enjoying the benefit of low interest rates.

Required:
Explain how your employer could justify her opinion that U Ltd's return on capital employed is poor. (4 marks)

(c) Suggest three ways in which U Ltd might be able to improve its return on equity. Your suggestions should make the fullest possible use of the other ratios in the table. State any assumptions that you have made. (6 marks)

(15 marks)

(CIMA)

11 It has been suggested that 'cash is king' and that readers of a company's accounts should pay more attention to information concerning its cash flows and balances than to its profits and other assets. It is argued that cash is more difficult to manipulate than profit and that cashflows are more important.

Required:
(a) Explain whether you agree with the suggestion that cash flows and balances are more difficult to manipulate than profit and non-cash assets. (8 marks)

(b) Explain why it might be dangerous to concentrate on cash to the exclusion of profit when analysing a set of financial statements. (7 marks)

(15 marks)

(CIMA)

12 Below are the summarized financial statements for the years to 31 March 1996 and 1997 of Heywood Bottles plc, a company which manufactures bottles for many different drinks companies.

Note: the statements for the year to 31 March 1997 have not been audited.

Profit and loss account for the years to 31 March

	1996		1997	
	£m	£m	£m	£m
Sales		120		300
Manufacturing costs	83		261	
Depreciation	7	(90)	9	(270)
Gross profit		30		30

	£m	£m	£m	£m
Other expenses	10		28	
Interest	2	(12)	10	(38)
Profit/(loss) before tax		18		(8)
Tax		(6)		(4)
Profit/(loss) after tax		12		(12)
Dividends:				
interim paid	4		4	
final proposed	4	(8)	4	(8)
		4		(20)

Balance sheets as at 31 March

	1996		1997	
	£m	£m	£m	£m
Fixed assets:				
Land and buildings		5		5
Plant and equipment		38		58
		43		63
Current assets:				
Stock	12		18	
Debtors	25		94	
Deferred expenditure	–		6	
Bank	8		–	
	45		118	
Creditors: amounts falling due within one year				
Trade creditors	(15)		(80)	
Others	(10)		(12)	
Bank	–		(34)	
	(25)		(126)	
Net assets (liabilities)		20		(8)
Total assets less current liabilities		63		55
Creditors: amounts falling due after more than one year		(19)		(32)
Net assets		44		23
Share capital and reserves:				
Ordinary shares		25		25
Reserves:				
Capital reserves	11		10	
Profit and loss account	8	19	(12)	(2)
		44		23

Notes:

1 Plant and equipment is made up as follows:

	£m	£m
At 31 March	1996	1997
Owned plant	10	18
Leased plant	28	40

2   Creditors falling due after more than one year are leasing obligations.

The directors were disappointed in the profit for the year to 31 March 1996 and held a board meeting in April 1996 to discuss future strategy. The Managing Director was insistent that the way to improve the company's results was to increase sales and market share. As a result the following actions were implemented:

(i)   an aggressive marketing campaign through trade journals costing £12 million was undertaken. Due to expected long-term benefits £6 million of this has been included as a current asset in the balance sheet at 31 March 1997;

(ii)   a 'price promise' to undercut any other supplier's price was announced in the advertising campaign;

(iii) a major contract with Koola Drinks plc was signed that accounted for a substantial proportion of the company's output. This contract was obtained through very competitive tendering;

(iv)   the credit period for debtors was extended from two to three months.

A preliminary review by the Board of the accounts to 31 March 1997 concluded that the company's performance had deteriorated rather than improved. There was particular concern over the prospect of renewing the bank overdraft facility because the maximum agreed level of £30 million had been exceeded. The Board decided that it was time to seek independent professional advice on the company's situation.

Required:

In the capacity of a business consultant, prepare a report for the Board of Heywood Bottles plc analysing the company's performance for the year to 31 March 1997 in comparison with the previous year. Particular emphasis should be given to the effects of the implementation of the actions referred to in points (i) to (iv) above.

(15 marks)

(ACCA)

13   Arizona plc has carried on business for a number of years as a retailer of a wide variety of 'do it yourself' goods. The company operates from a number of stores around the United Kingdom.

In recent years, the company has found it necessary to provide credit facilities to its customers in order to achieve growth in turnover. As a result of this decision, the liability to the company's bankers has increased substantially.

The statutory accounts of the company for the year-ended 31 March 1998 have recently been published, and extracts are provided below, together with comparative figures for the previous two years.

Profit and loss accounts for the years ended 31 March

	1996	1997	1998
	£m	£m	£m
Turnover	1850	2200	2500
Cost of sales	(1250)	(1500)	(1750)
Gross profit	600	700	750
Other operating costs	(550)	(640)	(700)
Operating profit	50	60	50
Interest from credit sales	45	60	90
Interest payable	(25)	(60)	(110)
Profit before taxation	70	60	30
Taxation	(23)	(20)	(10)
Profit after taxation	47	40	20
Dividends	(30)	(30)	(20)
Retained profit	17	10	–

Balance sheets at 31 March

	1996	1997	1998
	£m	£m	£m
Tangible fixed assets	278	290	322
Stocks	400	540	620
Debtors	492	550	633
Cash	12	12	15
Trade creditors	(270)	(270)	(280)
Taxation	(20)	(20)	(8)
Proposed dividends	(30)	(30)	(20)
Bank overdraft	(320)	(520)	(610)
Debentures	(200)	(200)	(320)
	342	352	352
Share capital	90	90	90
Reserves	252	262	262
	342	352	352

Other information:

- Depreciation charged for the three years was as follows:

year-ended 31 March	1996	1997	1998
	£m	£m	£m
	55	60	70

- The debentures are secured by a floating charge over the assets of Arizona plc. Their repayment is due on 31 March 2008.
- The bank overdraft is unsecured. The bank has set a limit of £630 million on the overdraft.
- Over the past three years, the level of credit sales has been:

year-ended 31 March	1996	1997	1998
	£m	£m	£m
	213	263	375

Given the steady increase in the bank overdraft which has taken place in recent years, the company has recently written to its bankers to request an increase in the limit. The request was received by the bank on 15 May 1998, two weeks after the 1998 statutory accounts were published.

You are an accountant employed by the bankers of Arizona plc. The bank is concerned at the steep escalation in the level of the company's overdraft and your regional manager has asked for a report on the financial performance of Arizona plc for the last three years.

Required:

Write a report to your regional manager which analyses the financial performance of Arizona plc for the period covered by the financial statements.

Your report may take any form you wish, but should specifically address the particular concern of the bank regarding the rapidly increasing overdraft. Therefore, your report should identify aspects of poor performance which could have contributed to the increase in the overdraft.   (20 marks)

(CIMA)

Financial statement analysis

> After reading this chapter you should be able to:
> - appraise the effects of differing accounting policies on the picture given by the financial statements
> - prepare reports on the overall financial picture as revealed by the analysis of the financial statements.

Introduction

In the last chapter we provided you with a tool to analyse financial statements – ratio analysis. We also identified limitations within ratio analysis. One of these limitations was the problems encountered when companies use differing accounting policies within their financial statements. Within this chapter we will explore this problem further. The illustrations we give will, of course, need to be supplemented by further examples that you encounter from your own experience.

Effects of different accounting policies

Activity 1

Identify as many examples as possible where the choice of accounting policy could significantly affect the analysis and interpretation of published financial statements.

Activity 1 feedback

There are many examples which you may have chosen; we provide a selection for you.

- Policy on asset valuation particularly regarding land and buildings – historical cost may or may not be departed from. This will impact on profits via depreciation charges and on balance sheet structure.
- Depreciation policy will obviously impact on profits and asset values.
- Stock valuations again will impact on profits and asset values and on liquidity ratios through the cost flow assumptions made (LIFO, FIFO) and also the treatment of overhead costs.
- Long-term contract assumptions, e.g. the policy on inclusion of activity in annual turnover, and on treatment of possible future losses, and so on.
- Goodwill valuation and method of elimination from the financial statements.

- Leases allocation between operating and finance lease, method of allocating finance charges relating to both lessee and lessor.
- Research and development policy in respect of possible capitalization of development costs and policy on any resulting amortization.
- Pensions – problems associated with the type of scheme, the valuation of surplus or deficit and the allocation of these and other costs over accounting periods.
- Use of temporal or closing rate method for translation of foreign trading operations.
- Consolidation policies – definitions relating to the distinctions between subsidiary and associate, use of acquisition or merger accounting, quantification of fair values will all affect the numbers in the financial statements.
- On a more general level, the subjective judgements relating to conflicting accounting conventions and concepts, e.g. matching and prudence, will all affect the numbers. There may also be changes arising from the issue of new or revised accounting standards, which can cause major differences over time within the financial statements of any particular company or group.

It is very important that you understand the accounting implications of each of the possible different accounting policies that we outlined in the feedback above. If you do not, then you should go back to the relevant chapter and revise your knowledge of the topic or topics concerned. Once you are happy that you fully understand the principles, then the only way to make further progress is through practice, and working through artificial or real-life examples.

The next activity provides a simple illustration of what we have in mind.

Activity 2

The summarized balance sheets of three businesses in the same industry are shown below for 200X.

	A	*B*	*C*
	£000	*£000*	*£000*
Intangibles	100	–	10
Tangible fixed assets	886	582	580
Current assets	920	580	950
Current liabilities	(470)	(252)	(486)
	1436	910	1054
Long-term liabilities	(100)	(20)	(50)
	1336	890	1004
Share capital	200	40	300
Revaluation reserve	80	–	–
Retained profits	1056	850	704
	1336	890	1004

The operating profit for the three companies for the years in question was:

	282	194	148
and sales	2100	1500	1750

The companies had different treatments for the intangibles. Company A is amortizing this at £10 000 per annum and company C at £2000 per annum. Company B has written off goodwill of £40 000 to retained profits in the year. Included in the depreciation expense of company A is an extra £4000 over and above the historical cost depreciation caused by an earlier revaluation of its premises.

Appraise the financial performance and stability of each of these three companies within the limits of the information given.

Activity 2 feedback

Ratios calculated without any adjustment for differing accounting policies:

	A	B	C
	£000	*£000*	*£000*
ROCE	21.1%	21.8%	14.7%
CA:CL	1.9:1	2.3:1	1.95:1
Operating/sales	13.4%	12.9%	8.5%
Sales/CE	1.57	1.69	1.74

These ratios show B as being the most profitable company in terms of ROCE and C the least. C has the highest volume ratio at 1.74 and the lowest margin at 8.5%. A, on the other hand, has the highest margin and lowest volume turnover.

Adjustments made for differing accounting policies:

	A	B	C
	£000	*£000*	*£000*
Operating profit	282	194	148
Adjustment depreciation	4	–	–
goodwill	10	–	2
	296	194	150
Capital employed	1336	890	1004
Less revaluation reserve	(80)	–	–
Less goodwill w/o	(110)	–	(12)
	1146	890	992

Ratios calculated on adjusted figures:

ROCE	25.8%	21.8%	15.1%
Operating profit/sales	14.1%	12.9%	8.6%
S/CE	1.83	1.69	1.76

These figures, which are now more comparable, show A as the most profitable in terms of ROCE and that it has the highest volume turnover and margin ratio. C is still in third place due to its low profit margin.

This activity demonstrates the errors that could be made in analysing financial statements if the accounting policies of companies are not comparable.

Another example

Activity 3

The following information is available for companies X and Y for the year-ended 31 December 20X0. Note both companies have identical balance sheets and operating profits for the year.

	£000s
Fixed assets	250
Current assets	70
Current liabilities	(60)
	260
Long-term liabilities	(100)
	160
Share capital	100
Retained profits	60
	160
Operating profit for the year	30

Each company acquired another asset, fair value £100 000, on the 1 January 20X0 in respect of which no entries have been made in the accounts. The asset is acquired by means of a lease with rentals per quarter in advance of £6500. The term of the lease is five years and the useful life of the asset eight years.

Identify the effects on the companies' operating profits and balance sheets and any relevant ratios if the lease is treated as an operating lease by company X and a finance lease by company Y.

Assume all rentals are paid when due.

Activity 3 feedback

	X £000		Y £000	
Fixed assets	250		330	(note 2)
Current assets	44	(note 1)	44	
Current liabilities	(60)		(77.57)	(note 3)
	234		296.43	
Long-term liabilities	(100)		(166.8)	(note 3)
	134		129.63	
Share capital	100		100	
Retained profits	34		29.63	
	134		129.63	
Operating profit for the year	4		(0.37)	

Notes:

1 Cash adjusted for rental payments $4 \times 6500 = 26\,000$ and charged to operating profit assuming operating lease.

2 Under a finance lease the asset is capitalized at fair value of £100 000 and depreciation calculated for the year on a straight-line basis assuming no residual value over a five-year life – depreciation charge £20 000, NBV of asset 31 December 20X0 is therefore £80 000.

3 Activity 4 in Chapter 19 identified the finance lease calculations – as at 31 December 20X0 obligations under the finance lease are £84 370 of which £17 570 is due in less than one year.

4

	£000s
Operating profit for the year	30
Less depreciation	20
Less interest charges	10.37
	(0.37)

Ratio calculations	X	Y
ROCE	3%	loss
CA:CL	0.73:1	0.57:1
Gearing	43%	56.3%

If the lease is treated as an operating lease then all relevant ratios are more favourable than if the lease was treated as a finance lease. The ROCE is a loss, the liquidity ratio is decreased and the gearing ratio increased (when the lease is treated as a finance lease). Company Y would therefore be regarded less favourably than company X under this analysis. However, the only difference between them is the accounting treatment used for the leased asset!

Real-life vignette

British Airways plc

This company, because of FRS 5 'Reporting the Substance of Transactions' is having to make very significant changes to its published financial statements. For example, as of 1994 twenty-four aircraft previously accounted for under extendable operating lease arrangements, and therefore off the balance sheet, will need to be included as assets on the balance sheet with the corresponding liabilities also included. British Airways also, in order to avoid problems of protection policies by foreign governments, has set up 49%-owned operating companies, i.e. TAT European airlines and Deutsche BA. Under FRS 2 these were classified as associate undertakings and dealt with accordingly in the group accounts. However, under FRS 5 they will need to be classified as quasi-subsidiaries and therefore treated in the accounts as if they were subsidiary undertakings. There are obviously a whole variety of detailed effects on the numbers in the published financial statements resulting from FRS 5. Noteworthy, for example, is an increase in the value of fixed assets and related borrowings by some £1100 million!

Scottish Television plc

This company in their published statements for 1993 revalued their fixed assets back to full gross historical cost rather than continuing with the previous policy which was that fixed assets were revalued annually. The effects of this are shown in a note to the accounts, reproduced below.

Tangible fixed assets	Land and buildings		Plant and technical	
	Leasehold	Freehold	equipment	Total
Company	£000	£000	£000	£000
Cost and valuation				
At 1 January 1993 as previously stated				
at cost or valuation	354	11 846	28 681	40 881
Prior year adjustment:				
Rebasing of fixed assets to cost	240	(2 831)	(6 493)	(9 084)
At 1 January 1993 as restated at cost	594	9 015	22 188	31 797
Additions	116	1 582	3 532	5 230
Disposals	–	(39)	(700)	(739)
At 31 December 1993	710	10 558	25 020	36 288
Depreciation				
At 1 January 1993 as previously stated	–	–	20 435	20 435
Prior year adjustment:				
Rebasing of fixed assets to cost	277	3 537	(6 170)	(2 356)
At 1 January 1993 as restated	277	3 537	14 265	18 079
Disposals	–	(32)	(444)	(476)
Charge for year	23	314	2 462	2 799
At 31 December 1993	300	3 819	16 283	20 402
Net book value				
At 31 December 1993	410	6 739	8 737	15 886
Net book value				
At 31 December 1992 (restated)	317	5 478	7 923	13 718

The net book value of tangible fixed assets includes amounts totalling £1 678 000 (1992: £53 000) in respect of assets held under finance leases. The depreciation charge in respect of these assets was £350 000 (1992: £65 000).

Rebasing of fixed assets: fixed assets are included on an historical cost accounting basis. The directors consider this basis to be more appropriate than the previous policy of annual revaluation due to the subjective nature of valuations and the cost and time consuming process in preparing and accounting for annual valuations. In addition, annual revaluation is no longer required for exchequer levy purposes.

This is a change in accounting policy as previously fixed assets had been revalued annually. Comparative figures for 1992 have been restated to take account of the new policy. The effect of this change in policy in both the group and the company is to reduce the gross amount of the fixed assets at 1 January 1992 by £9 084 000, accumulated depreciation by £2 356 000 and their net book value by

£6 728 000 in the balance sheet and to reduce the depreciation charge for the year-ended 31 December 1992 by £595 000 from that previously reported. (Source Scottish Television plc published financial statements year-ended 31 December 1993.)

It is interesting to note that the gross figure for leasehold land and buildings has increased substantially whereas the figures for freehold land and buildings and equipment have reduced substantially. The effects on the depreciation balances brought forward are also of considerable interest. Clearly land and buildings of all types were previously not being depreciated, i.e. there was no expense charged to the P&L account. Plant and equipment depreciation was clearly greater than that required on a strict historical cost basis (as the balance brought forward has been reduced). This was presumably because previous depreciation was being calculated on higher revalued amounts. Note the effect this change in policy has had on the annual reported profit. The note reproduced informs us that the change in policy has increased profits for the year-ended 31 December 1992 by £595 000 and presumably those for the year-ended 31 December 1993 by a similar amount.

Naamloze Vennootschap DSM

If it appears that comparison of British companies between each other or over time becomes a very complex business when accounting policies are differing, a moment's thought will make it obvious that the situation becomes infinitely more complex when the comparison involves financial statements from different countries prepared under differing national accounting practices. The technical and subjective complexities involved in this process are well beyond the scope of this book. However, the following example provides a flavour of the problems involved.

Activity 4

Attached is an extract from a real set of published accounts, of a Dutch company, of a few years ago.

(a) For each year, calculate return, using both operating profit and net profit, on stockholders' (i.e. shareholders') equity, and a gearing ratio, under each basis.

(b) Write a brief explanation, clear to a non-accountant, about the differences between the figures under the two bases. Which basis should be used for analysis of the group's performance?

Supplementary data based on current value

The consolidated financial statements of Naamloze Vennootschap DSM are drawn up on the basis of historical cost.

Below, supplementary data on the basis of current value are given. Since there is no generally accepted method yet for presenting such data, the bases of valuation and determination of income on the basis of current value are explained insofar as they diverge from those used for the consolidated financial statements.

Fixed assets

The current value of land is generally based on appraisals, that of other tangible fixed assets is determined using price indices from external sources, making allowance for technological developments. Where lower, the recoverable value is used for valuation purposes. The value of tangible fixed assets owned by non-consolidated companies has also been restated using price indices; the effect on the equities of these companies, commensurate with the percentage of participation, is accounted for in the balance sheet.

Current assets
A revaluation is made where current inventory values diverge from the valuation in the consolidated balance sheet.

Stockholders' equity
Equity according to the consolidated balance sheet is increased by the revaluation of tangible fixed assets and inventories, after deduction of relevant deferred tax commitments and minority interests.

Operating profit
The operating profit according to the consolidated statement of income is adjusted for the additional depreciation on tangible fixed assets based on current value and for revaluation of inventories.

Net profit
The same adjustments are applied to the net profit as to the operating profit, additionally allowing for minority interests and as the gain realized through loan financing. The tax burden is not adjusted. The financing gain corresponds to the part of the revaluation adjustments in the consolidated statement of income that relates to tangible fixed assets and inventories, insofar as financed with loan capital.

For calculation of the gain realized through loan financing, use is made of the ratio of group equity to equity invested in tangible fixed assets and inventories. This ratio is determined on the basis of the consolidated balance sheet of Naamloze Vennootschap DSM at the end of the preceding financial year. In calculating the ratio, group equity is never put at less than 25% of total assets. The difference between the net result calculated on historical cost basis and the current value net result is regarded as adjustment for capital maintenance.

Consolidated statement of income

Million		1989		1988
Net sales	10772		10121	
Other operating income	397		243	
Total operating income		11169		10364
Amortization and depreciation	−602		−627	
Other operating costs	−9184		−8530	
Total operating costs		−9786		−9157
Operating profit		1383		1207
Financial income and expense		−40		−82
Profit on ordinary activities before taxation		1343		1125
Tax on profit on ordinary activities		−407		−417
Results of non-consolidated companies		98		83
Profit on ordinary activities after taxation		1034		791
Extraordinary result after taxation		345		−174
Group result after taxation		1379		617
Minority interests' share in result		1		5
Net profit		1380		622

Abridged consolidated balance sheet

Million	1989		1988	
	Historical cost	**Current value**	Historical cost	Current value
Fixed assets	**5070**	**5925**	4358	5235
Current assets	**4624**	**4625**	3988	4000
Total assets	**9694**	**10550**	8346	9235
Stockholders' equity	**3819**	**4375**	3074	3790
Minority interests in consolidated companies	**86**	**95**	79	85
Current and long-term liabilities	**5789**	**6080**	5193	5360
Total liabilities	**9694**	**10550**	8346	9235

Consolidated statement of income, restated on the basis of current value

Million	1989	1988
Operating profit		
On historical cost basis	**1383**	1207
– additional depreciation on current value basis	**–115**	–105
– difference between current value and historical cost of inventories	**20**	–65
On the basis of current value	**1288**	1037
Net profit		
On historical cost basis	**1380**	622
– additional depreciation on current value basis	**–115**	–105
– difference between current value and historical cost of inventories	**20**	–65
– gain through loan financing	**35**	50
On the basis of current value	**1320**	502

The adjustment for capital maintenance, calculated with application of DSM's customary system, was £60 million, £75 million being accounted for by tangible fixed assets, £15 million by inventories. The profit retained largely exceeds the amount of the adjustment for capital maintenance.

Activity 4 feedback

	1989	1988
Historical cost basis		
Operating profit/owners' equity	1383/3819 = 36%	1207/3074 = 39%
Net profit/owners' equity	1380/3819 = 36%	622/3074 = 20%
Gearing	3819/9694 = 39%	3074/8346 = 37%
Current value basis		
Operating profit/owners' equity	1288/4375 = 29%	1037/3790 = 27%
Net profit/owners' equity	1320/4375 = 30%	502/3790 = 13%
Gearing	4375/10 550 = 41%	3790/9235 = 41%

It can be argued that the current value figures give a truer economic comparison with other currently available alternatives. For two of the three ratios, the trends, perhaps more useful than the absolute amounts, are different. From 1988 to 1989, operating profit to owners' equity falls on a historical cost basis and rises on a current value basis. Gearing worsens on a historical cost basis and stays constant on a current value basis. Note also, as an aside, the effects of the extraordinary items in the two years. Their existence tends to suggest that the operating profit ratio is a much better long-term indicator than the net profit ratio. This makes the difference in trend direction for the operating profit ratio under the two bases all the more significant. Perhaps a much longer time series is needed.

Summary

This chapter has identified the problems caused by differing accounting policies when analysing company financial statements. It is not enough for you to know which ratios to calculate and how to calculate them, you must also look behind the information presented and use your knowledge of accounting policies, that we have hopefully given you in this text, before making any judgement on a company's financial position or profitability. As we stated in Chapter 28 a good dose of common sense is a prerequisite of any accountant. We would suggest you continue your studies in this area of analysis by reading the accounting press (e.g. *Accountancy*) and identifying where changes in accounting policies have affected the analysis of a company's performance.

Exercises

1 Identify which accounting policies would seem to have the most impact on the analysis of companies' performances.
2 You, as an accountant, are asked by your financial director, to choose suitable companies to compare your own company with. Explain, in a report to her, what would influence your choice and how you would adjust for differing accounting policies, if any.

Final thoughts

This book has explored three broad themes:

- what financial reporting is all about – the conceptual framework
- the legal framework – what the law requires accountants to do
- the regulatory framework – what rules accountants have created for themselves.

In the introductions to each of the three parts we raised issues for you to think about. We suggest that you reread these introductions on pp. 1, 175, 213 and carefully think through your answers to the questions posed.

In addition we ask you to consider the following:

- Does the regulatory framework as it currently exists in the UK lead to the production of useful information for decision makers?
- Do you believe that decision makers actually use the published financial statements?
- Where do you believe financial reporting should go from here?

Bibliography

This is not a bibliography in the full formal sense; more a helpful note on further reading. There are several aspects to consider, but the most important thing about further reading is that you actually do some. Nobody should ever rely on only one source.

You may like to read further about areas which you find either particularly difficult or particularly interesting in other textbooks. Look at two or three in a library. As regards the various detailed regulations, there can be no real substitute for looking at the original regulations themselves. You should have access to the full texts of the Statements of Standard Accounting Practice, to the full texts of the Financial Reporting Standards, and to any recent Exposure Drafts. These are available individually (very expensive) or in bound collected form (much more cheaply) from all the main accounting bodies, and are printed when first published in the official magazines of these bodies. You should also make sure you follow all the documents issued by the Accounting Standards Board as they appear, especially those relating to its Statement of Principles. The Framework published by the International Accounting Standards Committee, referred to extensively in Chapter 10, is strongly recommended.

If you wish to follow the European and international dimensions further (which any open-minded accounting student should) then look at Alexander and Archer, Alexander and Nobes or Nobes and Parker as starting points to take you further. Readers particularly interested in the income measurement and valuation debate can probably do no better than look at the now ageing book by Tom Lee, which is nevertheless still the best succinct survey and includes an excellent annotated bibliography. Nothing can quite replace reading Edwards and Bell itself.

The most important advice of all is to remember that financial accounting and reporting is continually developing. So, therefore, must you be.

Particular texts referred to here or in the text are as follows.

Alexander and Archer (eds) (1998) *1998 European Accounting Guide*, 3rd edn. Harcourt Legal, San Diego, CA.

Alexander and Nobes (1994) *A European Introduction to Financial Accounting*. Prentice-Hall, London.

Edwards and Bell (1961) *The Theory and Measurement of Business Income*. University of California Press, Berkeley, CA.

Ernst and Young UK GAAP.

Fisher (1930) *The Theory of Interest*. Macmillan, New York, 1930. (Reprinted as 'Income and capital', in Parker and Harcourt, 1969.)

Frankel (1953) *Economic Impact on Underdeveloped Societies*. Basil Blackwell, Oxford. (Reprinted as ' "Psychic" and "accounting" concepts of income and welfare', in Parker and Harcourt, 1969.)

Hendriksen E. S. (1992) *Accounting Theory*, 5th edn. Richard D. Irwin.

Hicks (1946) *Value and Capital*. Clarendon Press, Oxford. (Reprinted as 'Income' in Parker and Harcourt, 1969.)

Kaldor, N. 'The concept of income in economic theory', in Parker and Harcourt (1969).

Lee (1985) *Income and Value Measurement*. VNR, London.

Nobes and Parker (1998) *Comparative International Accounting*. Prentice-Hall, London.

Parker and Harcourt (1969) *Readings in the Concept and Measurement of Income*. Cambridge University Press, Cambridge.

Ryle (1949) *The Concept of Mind*. London. [Reprinted 1984 by University of Chicago Press, Chicago, IL.]

'Sandilands Report', Inflation Accounting Committee (MND 6225, HMSO, 1975).

Index

under normal operating conditions need, for the same reason, to be excluded.

10   The adoption of a conservative approach to the valuation of stocks and long-term contracts has sometimes been used as one of the reasons for omitting selected production overheads. In so far as the circumstances of the business require an element of prudence in determining the amount at which stocks and long-term contracts are stated, this needs to be taken into account in the determination of net realisable value and not by the exclusion from cost of selected overheads.

The Companies Act

The Companies Act 1981 introduced several explicit requirements as regards the treatment of stocks under HC accounting rules. The major items are as follows (all paragraph references are to schedule 4, 1985 Act). Stocks must be shown on the balance sheet subdivided into four categories (formats 1 and 2):

1   raw materials and consumables
2   work-in-progress
3   finished goods and goods for resale
4   payments on account.

22   Subject to paragraph 23, the amount to be included in respect of any current asset shall be its purchase price or production cost.

23   (1)   If the net realizable value of any current asset is lower than its purchase price or production cost the amount to be included in respect of that asset shall be the net realizable value.

26   (1)   The purchase price of an asset shall be determined by adding to the actual price paid any expenses incidental to its acquisition.

(2)   The production cost of an asset shall be determined by adding to the purchase price of the raw materials and consumables used the amount of the costs incurred by the company which are directly attributable to the production of that asset.

(3)   In addition, there may be included in the production cost of an asset:

(a)   a reasonable proportion of the costs incurred by the company which are only indirectly attributable to the production of that asset, but only to the extent that they relate to the period of production; and

(b)   interest on capital borrowed to finance the production of that asset, to the extent that it accrues in respect of the period of production; provided, however, in a case within paragraph (b) above, that the inclusion of the interest in determining the cost of that asset and the amount of the interest so included is disclosed in a note to the accounts.

(4)   In the case of current assets distribution costs may not be included in production costs.

Stock valuation methods acceptable under the Act are:

27   (2)   (a)   the method known as 'first in, first out' (FIFO)

(**b**) the method known as 'last in, first out' (LIFO)

(**c**) a weighted average price; and

(**d**) any other method similar to any of the methods mentioned above.

Paragraph 27 also provides that where the valuation of stock differs materially from '**the relevant alternative amount**' the amount of the difference must be disclosed in a note to the accounts. The 'relevant alternative amount' is the amount of the assets at:

1 their RC on the balance sheet date; or

2 their most recent actual purchase price or production cost before the balance sheet date.

Observe that paragraph 22 refers to 'current assets', paragraph 26 to 'assets', and paragraph 27 to 'stocks'. Paragraph 27 also applies to 'fungible assets', i.e. assets that are substantially indistinguishable from one another.

As regards stocks and work in progress other than long-term contract work in progress, there are three major differences between the Act and SSAP 9, and these should be carefully noted:

1 The Act allows the use of LIFO, as well as FIFO, weighted average, and 'any other method similar' to any of these three. It also does not totally rule out the base stock method.

2 The Act requires the disclosure of material differences between the stock figure as calculated and the relevant alternative amount as defined above. This effectively requires, in the HC accounts, a statement of what the replacement cost figure would be. This is a new requirement, and indeed the SSAP in its strict adherence to HC principles seems at odds with it. It has been suggested that the intention of this provision is to prevent hidden profits, or secret reserves, being created through extremely low stock figures.

3 The Act carefully states that production overheads *may* be included in production cost. It therefore permits both absorption costing and variable costing, whereas SSAP 9 requires absorption costing.

The general interpretation of these differences is that the Act provides a framework and the SSAP states the slightly more restrictive 'best practice'. The two are not incompatible, just a bit different. Methods permitted by the Act but not by the SSAP should not be used by accountants. That at least was the ASC's view!

Activity 5

Calculate the cost of finished goods stock in accordance with SSAP 9 from the following data relating to Unipoly Ltd for the year-ended 31 May 20X7:

	£
Direct materials cost of can opener per unit	1
Direct labour cost of can opener per unit	1
Direct expenses cost of can opener per unit	1
Production overheads per year	600 000
Administrative overheads per year	200 000
Selling overheads per year	300 000
Interest payments per year	100 000

There were 250 000 units in finished goods stock at the year-end. You may assume that there was no finished goods at the start of the year and that there was no work in progress.

The normal annual level of production is 750 000 can openers, but in the year-ended 31 May 20X7 only 450 000 were produced because of a labour dispute.

Activity 5 feedback

The direct costs of the stock are straightforward to calculate as follows:

	£
250 000 units at £1 direct material cost	250 000
250 000 units at £1 direct labour cost	250 000
250 000 units at direct £1 direct expenses cost	250 000
	750 000

SSAP 9 requires us to include production overheads only in the valuation of finished goods so overheads relating to administration, selling and interest are not relevant here.

Production overheads $600\,000 \times 250\,000/750\,000 = 200\,000$.

Adding this to direct costs gives cost of finished goods £950 000.

Long-term contract work in progress

A long-term contract is defined as follows

22 *Long-term contract*: a contract entered into for the design, manufacture or construction of a single substantial asset or the provision of a service (or of a combination of assets or services which together constitute a single project) where the time taken substantially to complete the contract is such that the contract activity falls into different accounting periods. A contract that is required to be accounted for as long-term by this accounting standard will usually extend for a period exceeding one year. However, a duration exceeding one year is not an essential feature of a long-term contract. Some contracts with a shorter duration than one year should be accounted for as long-term contracts if they are sufficiently material to the activity of the period that not to record turnover and attributable profit would lead to a distortion of the period's turnover and results such that the financial statements would not give a true and fair view, provided that the policy is applied consistently within the reporting entity and from year to year.

Such contracts involve all the difficulties discussed earlier in the context of stocks and work in progress, with also one major addition. This is the question of profit allocation over the various accounting periods. If a contract extends over, say, three years, should the contribution to profits be 0%, 0% and 100%, respectively, for the three years? Can we make profits on something before we have finished it? The realization convention might seem to argue against doing so, and the prudence convention would certainly argue against it too. But would this give a 'true and fair view' of the results for each period? And would it be of any use? All the various users want regular information on business progress. Remember the desirability of timeliness. Can we not argue that we can be 'reasonably certain', during the contract, of at least some profit – and if we can then surely the matching principle is more important than an excessive slavishness to prudence?

As so often the SSAP seeks to find a suitable middle way between the various conflicting requirements and conventions. It is at this point that the differences between the original 1975 version of SSAP 9 and the revised 1989 version become important. The original standard established the principle of recording long-term contract work in progress at cost plus 'attributable profit'. Without discussion it assumed that this resulting figure would be included in stocks on the balance sheet. The original (1975) requirement (then paragraph 27) was:

> The amount at which long-term contract work in progress is stated in periodic financial statements should be cost plus any attributable profit, less any foreseeable losses and progress payments received and receivable. If, however, anticipated losses on individual contracts exceed cost incurred to date less progress payments received and receivable, such excesses should be shown separately as provisions.

The requirement had the not insignificant disadvantage that it appeared to be illegal under the Companies Act 1985, schedule 4, paragraph 22. As we saw earlier (p. 373) this requires the normal stock figure to be 'purchase price or production cost' and this clearly cannot include any 'attributable profit'. The ASC have now got round this difficulty by requiring any figures which contain a profit element to be included under the heading of debtors instead of stocks.

The SSAP requirements are now:

28 Long-term contracts should be assessed on a contract by contract basis and reflected in the profit and loss account by recording turnover and related costs as contract activity progresses. Turnover is ascertained in a manner appropriate to the stage of completion of the contract, the business and the industry in which it operates.

29 Where it is considered that the outcome of a long-term contract can be assessed with reasonable certainty before its conclusion, the prudently calculated attributable profit should be recognised in the profit and loss account as the difference between the reported turnover and related costs for that contract.

30 Long-term contracts should be disclosed in the balance sheet as follows:
   (a) the amount by which recorded turnover is in excess of payments on account should be classified as 'amounts recoverable on contracts' and separately disclosed within debtors
   (b) the balance of payments on account (in excess of amounts (i) matched with turnover; and (ii) offset against long-term contract balances) should be classified as payments on account and separately disclosed within creditors
   (c) the amount of long-term contracts, at costs incurred, net of amounts transferred to cost of sales, after deducting foreseeable losses and payments on account not matched with turnover, should be classified as 'long-term contract balances' and separately disclosed within the balance sheet heading 'Stocks'. The balance sheet note should disclose sep-

arately the balances of: (**i**) net cost less foreseeable losses; and (**ii**) applicable payments on account

(**d**) the amount by which the provision or accrual for foreseeable losses
exceeds the costs incurred (after transfers to cost of sales) should be
included within either provisions for liabilities and charges or creditors
as appropriate.

31 Consequent upon the application of this revised standard, the corresponding
amounts in the financial statements will need to be restated on a comparable basis.

We are also given these definitions:

23 *Attributable profit*: that part of the total profit currently estimated to arise over
the duration of the contract, after allowing for estimated remedial and maintenance costs and increases in costs so far as not recoverable under the terms
of the contract, that fairly reflects the profit attributable to that part of the
work performed at the accounting date. (There can be no attributable profit
until the profitable outcome of the contract can be assessed with reasonable
certainty.)

24 *Foreseeable losses*: losses which are currently estimated to arise over the
duration of the contract (after allowing for estimated remedial and maintenance costs and increases in costs so far as not recoverable under the terms
of the contract). This estimate is required irrespective of:

(**a**) whether or not work has yet commenced on such contracts

(**b**) the proportion of work carried out at the accounting date

(**c**) the amount of profits expected to arise on other contracts.

25 *Payments on account*: all amounts received and receivable at the accounting date in respect of contracts in progress.

So in the P&L account the value of work done will be included in turnover, and the related costs will be deducted. The 'attributable profit' to date will therefore be included in the
overall profit figure. As regards the balance sheet the essence of the rather complicated
wording of the standard is as follows. The figure of turnover less payments already received
is included in debtors. Any excess payments on account, over all costs to date plus all attributable profit to date, are included in creditors. Costs incurred not yet transferred to cost of
sales, less any provisions for losses and any receipts relating to work not yet transferred to
turnover, are included in stocks. Finally, if the net figure in the previous sentence comes
out negative the figure is included in creditors or provisions.

The SSAP 'explanatory notes' supporting these formal requirements are as follows:

8 Companies should ascertain turnover in a manner appropriate to the stage
of completion of the contracts, the businesses and the industries in which they
operate.

9 Where the business carries out long-term contracts and it is considered that
their outcome can be assessed with reasonable certainty before their conclusion, the attributable profit should be calculated on a prudent basis and
included in the accounts for the period under review. The profit taken up
needs to reflect the proportion of the work carried out at the accounting date
and to take into account any known inequalities of profitability in the vari-

ous stages of a contract. The procedure to recognise profits is to include an appropriate proportion of total contract value as turnover in the profit and loss account as the contract activity progresses. The costs incurred in reaching that stage of completion are matched with this turnover, resulting in the reporting of results that can be attributed to the proportion of work completed.

10 Where the outcome of long-term contracts cannot be assessed with reasonable certainty before the conclusion of the contract, no profit should be reflected in the profit and loss account in respect of those contracts, although, in such circumstances, if no loss is expected it may be appropriate to show as turnover a proportion of the total contract value using a zero estimate of profit.

11 If it is expected that there will be a loss on a contract as a whole, all of the loss should be recognised as soon as it is foreseen (in accordance with the prudence concept). Initially, the foreseeable loss will be deducted from the work in progress figure of the particular contract, thus reducing it to net realisable value. Any loss in excess of the work in progress figure should be classified as an accrual within 'Creditors' or under 'Provisions for liabilities and charges' depending upon the circumstances. Where unprofitable contracts are of such magnitude that they can be expected to utilise a considerable part of the company's capacity for a substantial period, related administration overheads to be incurred during the period to the completion of those contracts should also be included in the calculation of the provision for losses.

The practical process for determining appropriate figures for long-term contract items requires first of all the calculation of total costs attaching to the contract to date. This should include appropriate production (or 'construction') overheads. In an appendix it is suggested that interest costs may also be included in limited circumstances:

21 In ascertaining costs of long-term contracts it is not normally appropriate to include interest payable on borrowed money. However, in circumstances where sums borrowed can be identified as financing specific long-term contracts, it may be appropriate to include such related interest in cost, in which circumstances the inclusion of interest and the amount of interest so included should be disclosed in a note to the financial statements.

Secondly, we have to calculate turnover and any related profits. There is inevitably some subjectivity here, but the appendix to the standard does its best:

23 Turnover (ascertained in a manner appropriate to the industry, the nature of the contracts concerned and the contractual relationship with the customer) and related costs should be recorded in the profit and loss account as contract activity progresses. Turnover may sometimes be ascertained by reference to valuation of the work carried out to date. In other cases, there may be specific points during a contract at which individual elements of work done with separately ascertainable sales values and costs can be identified and appropriately recorded as turnover (e.g. because delivery or customer acceptance has taken place). This accounting standard does not provide a definition of turnover in view of the different methods of ascertaining it as outlined above. However, it does require disclosure of the means by which turnover is ascertained.

24 In determining whether the stage has been reached at which it is appropriate to recognise profit, account should be taken of the nature of the business concerned. It is necessary to define the earliest point for each particular contract before which no profit is taken up, the overriding principle being that there can be no attributable profit until the outcome of a contract can reasonably be foreseen. Of the profit which in the light of all the circumstances can be foreseen with a reasonable degree of certainty to arise on completion of the contract, there should be regarded as earned to date only that part which prudently reflects the amount of work performed to date. The method used for taking up such profits needs to be consistently applied.

25 In calculating the total estimated profit on the contract, it is necessary to take into account not only the total costs to date and the total estimated further costs to completion (calculated by reference to the same principles as were applied to cost to date) but also the estimated future costs of rectification and guarantee work, and any other future work to be undertaken under the terms of the contract. These are then compared with the total sales value of the contract. In considering future costs, it is necessary to have regard to likely increases in wages and salaries, to likely increases in the price of raw materials and to rises in general overheads, so far as these items are not recoverable from the customer under the terms of the contract.

The Companies Act 1985 and long-term contracts

Two of the general requirements of the Companies Act that we have already met are of relevance here, namely:

1 all assets to be shown at purchase price or production cost (schedule 4, paragraph 26)
2 only profits realized at the balance sheet date shall be included in the P&L account (schedule 4, paragraph 12).

We have seen how the revised standard has dealt with the problem of the first requirement. But what about the second one? Could it not be argued that the standard, in requiring inclusion of profits related to contracts uncompleted and work not necessarily paid for, includes unrealized profits in the P&L account? The SSAP meets the issue absolutely head on:

44 Paragraph 91 [of schedule 4] declares that realised profits are 'such profits of a company as fall to be treated as realised profits for the purposes of those accounts in accordance with principles generally accepted with respect to the determination for accounting purposes of realised profits'. It is a 'generally accepted principle' that it is appropriate to recognise profit on long-term contracts when the outcome can be assessed with 'reasonable certainty'. The principle of recognising profit on long-term contracts under this standard, therefore, does not contravene this paragraph.

Put cynically this can be summarized as saying:

1 the law says that what we say is right

2 this is what we say

3 therefore this is right.

Long-term contracts – an illustration

Activity 6

Work carefully through the example given in Table 22.2 and the subsections below, taken from the SSAP. Think about what you are reading, and for each of the five contracts relate the figures to what you have already read and make sure that they follow from the standard. Also relate the figures to general accounting conventions, definitions and practice and make sure that they make sense.

Activity 6 feedback

Table 22.2 gives the data and the notes below explain the treatment in detail.

Project 1

P&L account – cumulative

Included in turnover	145
Included in cost of sales	(110)
Gross profit	35

Balance sheet

The amount to be included in debtors under 'amounts recoverable on contracts' is calculated as follows:

Cumulative turnover	145
less Cumulative payments on account	(100)
Included in debtors	45

In this case, all the costs incurred to date relate to the contract activity recorded as turnover and are transferred to cost of sales, leaving a zero balance in stocks.

Note: If the outcome of the contract could not be assessed with reasonable certainty, no profit would be recognized. If no loss is expected, it may be appropriate to show as turnover a proportion of the total contract value using a zero estimate of profit.

Project 2

P&L account – cumulative

Included in turnover	520
Included in cost of sales	(450)
Gross profit	70

Balance sheet

As cumulative payments on account are greater than turnover there is a credit balance, calculated as follows:

Table 22.2 Examples of long-term contract work from SSAP 9

Balance	Project number					Balance sheet total	P&L account
	1	2	3	4	5		
Recorded as turnover – being value of work done	145	520	380	200	55		1300
Cumulative payments on account	(100)	(600)	(400)	(150)	(80)		
Classified as amounts recoverable on contracts	45			50		95 DR	
Balance (excess) of payments on accounts		(80)	(20)		(25)		
Applied as an offset against long-term contract balances – see below		60	20		15		
Residue classified as payments on accounts		(20)			(10)	(30) CR	
Total costs incurred	110	510	450	250	100		
Transferred to cost of sales	(110)	(450)	(350)	(250)	(55)		(1215)
	–	60	100	–	45		
Provision/accrual for foreseeable losses charged to cost of sales				(40)	(30)		(70)
		60	100	(40)	15		
Classified as provision/accrual for losses				(40)		(40) CR	
Balance (excess) of payments on account applied as offset against long-term contract balances		(60)	(20)		(15)		
Classified as long-term contract balances			80		–	80 DR	
Gross profit or loss on long-term contracts	35	70	30	(90)	(30)		15

Cumulative turnover	520
less Cumulative payments on account	(600)
Excess payments on account	(80)

This credit balance should first be offset against any debit balance on this contract included in stocks and then any residual amount should be classified under creditors as a payment received on account as follows:

Total cost incurred to date	510
less Cumulative amounts recorded as cost of sales	(450)
	60
less Excess payments on account (above)	(80)
Included in creditors	(20)

The amount to be included in stocks is zero and the credit balance of 20 is classified as a payment received on account and included in creditors.

The balance sheet note on stocks should disclose separately the net cost of 60 and the applicable payments on account of 60.

Project 3

P&L account – cumulative

Included in turnover	380
Included in cost of sales	(350)
Gross profit	30

Balance sheet

As with Project 2, cumulative payments on account are greater than turnover and there is a credit balance calculated as follows:

Cumulative turnover	380
less Cumulative payments on account	(400)
Excess payments on account	(20)

This credit balance should first be offset against any debit balance on this contract included in stocks and the residual amount, if any, should be classified under creditors as a payment received on account.

The amount to be included in stocks under long-term contract balances is calculated as follows:

Total cost incurred to date	450
less Cumulative amounts recorded as cost of sales	(350)
	100
less Excess payments on account (above)	(20)
Included in long-term contract balances	(80)

The balance sheet note on stocks should disclose separately the net cost of 100 and the applicable payments on account of 20.

Project 4

P&L account – cumulative

Included in turnover	200
Included in cost of sales	(290)
Gross loss	(90)

Balance sheet

The amount to be included in debtors under 'amounts recoverable on contracts' is calculated as follows:

Cumulative turnover	200
less Cumulative payments on account	(150)
Included in debtors	50

The amount to be included as a provision/accrual for foreseeable losses is calculated as follows:

Total costs incurred to date		250
less Transferred to cost of sales	(250)	
Foreseeable losses on contract as a whole	(40)	
		(290)
Classified as provision/accrual for foreseeable losses		(40)

The credit balance of 40 is not offset against the debit balance of 50 included in debtors.

Project 5

P&L account – cumulative

Included in turnover	55
Included in cost of sales	(85)
Gross loss	(30)

Balance sheet

As cumulative payments on account are greater than turnover there is a credit balance, calculated as follows:

Cumulative turnover	55
less Cumulative payments on account	(80)
Excess payments on account	(25)

The credit balance should first be deducted from long-term contract balances (after having deducted foreseeable losses) and the residual balance included in creditors under payments received on account as follows:

Total costs incurred to date		100
less Transferred to cost of sales	(55)	
Foreseeable losses on contract as a whole	(30)	
		(85)
		15
less Excess payments on account (above)		(25)
Included in creditors		(10)

The balance sheet note on stocks should disclose separately the net cost of 15 and the application payments on account of 15.

Having worked through all that with the answer (i.e. Table 22.2) in front of you now let us try a full example without the answer.

Activity 7

At 31 October 20X5, Lytax Ltd was engaged in various contracts including five long-term contracts, details of which are given below:

	1 £000	2 £000	3 £000	4 £000	5 £000
Contract price	1100	950	1400	1300	1200
At 31 October 20X5:					
Cumulative costs incurred	664	535	810	640	1070
Estimated further costs to completion	106	75	680	800	165
Estimated cost of post-completion guarantee/rectification work	30	10	45	20	5
Cumulative costs incurred transferred to cost of sales	580	470	646	525	900
Progress payments					
– cumulative receipts	615	680	615	385	722
– invoiced					
– awaiting receipt	60	40	25	200	34
– retained by contractee	75	80	60	65	84

It is not expected that any contractees will default on their payments.

Up to 31 October 20X4, the following amounts had been included in the turnover and cost of sales figures.

	1 £000	2 £000	3 £000	4 £000	5 £000
Cumulative turnover	560	340	517	400	610
Cumulative costs incurred transferred to cost of sales	460	245	517	400	610
Foreseeable loss transferred to cost of sales	—	—	—	70	—

It is the accounting policy of Lytax Ltd to arrive at contract turnover by adjusting contract cost of sales (including foreseeable losses) by the amount of contract profit or loss to be regarded as recognized, separately for each contract.

Calculate the amounts to be shown in the profit and loss account and balance sheet for the year-ended 31.10.X5 in respect of the long-term contracts.

Activity 7 feedback

1 We need to establish the turnover as at 31 October 20X5. The easiest way to do this is to calculate the attributable profit at this stage of completion by reference to total costs to date applicable to cost of sales and total estimated costs to completion including rectification and guarantee work costs.

	£000
Thus total estimated costs (664 + 106 + 30)	800
Contract price	1100
Total estimated profit	300

Attributable profit to stage of completion =

$$\left(\frac{\text{cost to date transferred to cost of sales}}{\text{total estimated costs}}\right) \frac{580}{800} \times 300 = 218$$

Therefore turnover = 580 + 218 = 798

Of this turnover £560 has previously been recognized therefore the transfer to P&L account for this year is £238 which is raised through the debtor account. Progress payments received or invoiced amount to £615 + 60 + 75 = £750 therefore amounts recoverable on the contract are £48 (£798 − £750).

Costs to date taken to cost of sales is £580 of which £460 has previously been recognized thus we need to transfer £120 for the current year to match against the current year turnover of £238. Therefore profit is £118.

Left on the cost account is £664 − 580 = 84 which represents stock on long-term contracts.

Balance sheet as at 31.10.X5	£000
Current assets:	
stock: long-term contract balance	84
debtors: amounts recoverable on	48
long-term contracts	

(The retention of £75 and progress payments awaited £60 will appear under debtors.)

2

	£000
Total estimated costs (£535 + 75 + 10)	620
Contract price	950
Total estimated profit	330

Attributable profit to stage of completion
     470/620 × 330 = 250
Therefore turnover is £470 + 250 = 720

Of this turnover of £720, £340 has previously been recognized. Therefore the transfer to the P&L account for this year is £380 which is raised through the debtor account. Progress payments received or invoiced amount to (£680 + 40 + 80) £800 thus we have excess payments on account of (£720 − 800) £80.

Costs to date taken to cost of sales is £470 of which £245 had previously been recognized thus we transfer £225 for current year to match against turnover of £380. Therefore profit is £155. Left on the cost account is (£535 − 470) £65 which is stock on long-term contract. Of excess payments on account of £80, £65 can be transferred as an offset against stock on long-term contract leaving £15 excess payment on account.

Balance sheet	£000
Creditors: amounts falling due within 1 year	
payments on account	15
Note to balance sheet:	
long-term contract balances less foreseeable losses	65
less applicable payments on account	65

3

	£000
Total estimated costs £810 + 680 + 45	1535
Contract price	1400
Total estimated loss	135

all of which must be recognized immediately.

In this case turnover equals costs transferred to cost of sales £646. Of this turnover £517 has been previously recognized thus the transfer to profit and loss for this year is £129. Progress payments received or invoiced amount to (£615 + 25 + 60) £700 thus we have excess payments on account of £54.

Costs to date taken to cost of sales is £646 of which £517 has previously been recognized thus we transfer £129 for current year to match against turnover of £129. Therefore profit is zero. However, we must provide for the foreseeable loss of £135 none of which has previously been recognized, therefore we credit provision for foreseeable loss account £135 and debit the P&L account. This provision for foreseeable loss is transferable to cost account (paragraph 30c, SSAP 9) thus left on the cost account is (£810 − 646 − 135) £29 stock on long-term contract balance. Of the excess payments on account of £54, £29 can be transferred to stock account leaving £25 excess payments on account.

Balance sheet	£000
Creditors: amounts falling due within 1 year	
payments on account	25
Note to balance sheet:	
long-term contract balances less	
foreseeable losses	29
less applicable payments on account	29

4

	£000
Total estimated costs (£640 + 800 + 20)	1460
Contract price	1300
Total estimated loss	160

Turnover equals costs transferred to cost of sales £525. Of this £400 has been previously recognized thus transfer for current year is £125. Progress payments received or invoiced is (£385 + 200 + 65) £650, thus we have excess payments on account of £125.

Costs to date taken to cost of sales is £525 of which £400 has been previously recognized therefore we transfer £125 for current year to match against turnover of £125, profit zero.

Provision for foreseeable loss account already stands at £70, but now the total foreseeable loss is £160 so we must credit provision for foreseeable loss £90 and debit the P&L account. Thus, loss for current year is £90. Of the £160 balance on the provision for foreseeable loss account only £115 can be transferred to the cost account, the amount on that account. Thus provision for foreseeable loss account is left with £45 credit balance.

Balance sheet as at 31.10.X5

	£000
Creditors falling due within 1 year: payments on account	125
Provision for liabilities and charges: provision for foreseeable losses	45

5

	£000
Total estimated costs (1070 + 165 + 5)	1240
Contract price	1200
Total estimated loss	40

Turnover is costs transferred to cost of sales, £900. Of this £610 has previously been recognized thus transfer for current year, £290. Progress payments received or invoiced, £840 thus we have amounts recoverable on long-term contracts £60.

Costs to date taken to cost of sales, £900 of which £610 has been previously recognized therefore we transfer £290 for current year to match against turnover of £290, profit zero. The balance on the cost account is (£1070 – 900) £170. We must also provide for foreseeable losses of £40 so we credit provision for foreseeable losses £40 and debit the P&L account £40. The credit of £40 on the provision for foreseeable loss account can now be offset against the balance on the cost account of £170 leaving stock long-term contract balance £130.

Balance sheet

	£000
Current assets:	
Stocks: long-term contract balance	130
Debtors: amounts recoverable on long-term contracts	60

Lytax Ltd. P&L account for year-ended 31.10.X5

Turnover (238 + 380 + 129 + 125 + 290)	1162
Cost of sales (120 + 225 + 129 + 135 +125 + 90 + 290 + 40)	1154
Profit	8

Lytax Ltd. Balance sheet as at 31.10.X5

	£000
Current assets	
Stocks: Long-term contract balances (84 + 130)	214
Debtors: Amounts recoverable on long-term contracts (48 + 60)	108
Creditors: amounts falling due within one year	
Creditors	
Payments on account (15 + 25 + 125)	165
Provisions for liabilities and charges	
Provision for foreseeable losses	45

Note to balance sheet:
Long-term contract balances

	£000
Long-term contract balances less foreseeable losses (84 + 65 + 29 + 130)	308
less applicable payments on account (65 + 29)	94
	214

That example was quite difficult and required some very clear thinking as to the offsets available between provisions for losses and the balance on the cost account, and the balance of payments on account and the balance on the cost account (paragraph 30, SSAP 9).

Activity 8

A much easier example. Show how the following information for two long-term contracts should be disclosed in financial statements.

	Contract X £000	Contract Y £000
Value of work done	500	350
Cost of sales	450	400
Payments on account	525	200
Total costs to date	600	400
Foreseeable additional loss	nil	60

Activity 8 feedback

Contract X

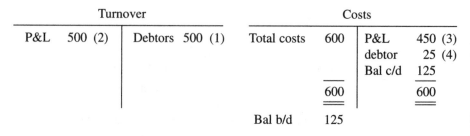

P&L

Cost of sales	450 (3)	Turnover	500 (2)
Profit	50		

Debtors

Turnover	500 (1)	Pay on account	525
Costs	25 (4)		

Contract Y

Turnover

P&L	350 (2)	Debtors	350 (1)

Costs

Total costs	400	P&L	400 (3)

P&L

Cost of sales	400 (3)	Turnover	350 (2)
Prov. for losses	60 (5)	Loss	110

Debtors

Turnover	350 (1)	Pay. on account	200
		Bal c/d	150
	350		350
Bal b/d	150		

Provision for foreseeable losses

		P&L	60 (5)

1 Raise the value of work done.
2 Transfer the value of work done as sale to P&L account.
3 Transfer proportion of total costs to P&L account as cost of sales.
4 Transfer excess payments on account to match with stock long-term contract balances.
5 Raise provision for foreseeable losses.

Profit and loss account	£000
Turnover (500 + 350)	850
Cost of sales (450 + 460)	910
Loss	60

Balance sheet
Current assets:

Stock: long-term contract balance	125
Debtors: amounts recoverable on long-term contracts	150
Provisions for liabilities and charges:	
Provision for foreseeable losses	60

Note to balance sheet:

Long-term contract balance	150
less applicable payments on account	25

The following activity is quite difficult as it involves taking account of previous years' spending on a long-term contract.

Activity 9

The following information is available in respect of a long-term contract entered into several years ago by Alpine plc.

Extract from the accounts as at 31.12 X0:

	£000s
Cumulative turnover	2280
Cumulative costs transferred to cost of sales	2400
Provision for foreseeable loss	300

Extract from the accounts as at 31.12.X1:

Cumulative costs	3840
Estimated further costs to completion	4800
Estimate of rectification work required	120
Cumulative receipts	2310
Invoices raised not paid	1200

The contract price was £7 800 000 and it is estimated that at 31.12.X1 cumulative cost of sales is £3 150 000.

Show the entries in the ledgers to account for the above contract in the year-ended 31.12.X1, and the profit and loss and balance sheet extract as at that date.

Activity 9 feedback

	£000s	£000s
Contract price		7800
Total estimated costs:		
cumulative	3840	
further costs	4800	
rectification	120	8760
Total foreseeable loss for contract		960

Contract can be estimated to be 3150/8760 = 35.96% complete

	£000
Thus turnover can be estimated to be 35.96% × 7800 =	2805
Cumulative cost of sales	3150
Loss accounted for	345
Provision for foreseeable loss required	615
	960
Provision for loss provided	300
Further provision required	315

The ledger accounts as at 31.12.X1 will be as follows:

Turnover				Costs			
X1 P&L	525	Debtors	525	X1 costs	1440	X1 P&L	750
						X1 Bal c/d	690
					1440		1440
				X1 Bal b/d	690	prov. loss	615
						Bal c/d	75
					690		690
				Bal b/d	75	debtors	75

Provision for loss				Payments on accounts			
		X1 Bal b/d	300	X0 Bal b/d	2280	receipts	2310
X1 Bal c/d	615	Foreseeable	315	X1 Bal c/d	1230	invoices	1200
	615		615	Turnover	525	Bal b/d	1230
Transfer to				Bal c/d	705		
costs	615	Bal b/d	615		1230		1230
				Transfer costs	75	Bal b/d	705
				Bal c/d	630		
					705		705
						Bal b/d	630

Profit and loss account extract for the year-ended 31.12.X1

Turnover		525
Cost of sales	750	
Further loss	315	1065
Loss on contract		540

Balance sheet extract as at 31.12.X1

Creditors: amounts falling due within one year

Payments on account	630

Summary

You should now be able to define cost of stock, long-term contract, attributable profit and foreseeable losses. You should be able to value stocks using unit cost, FIFO, LIFO, weighted average and base stock. Having completed Activities 6–9 you should be able to calculate the amounts to be disclosed in financial statements in respect of long-term contracts. You should also understand SSAP 9 and Companies Act requirements in relation to stocks and long-term contracts and discuss whether they are compatible.

Exercises

1 Explain how the four fundamental accounting concepts (SSAP 2) relate to and support the requirements of SSAP 9. What difficulties are suggested by your answer?

2 To what extent should:

(a) overheads be included in short-term work in progress valuation

(b) profits be included in long-term work in progress valuation?

Justify your recommendations.

3 P. Forte commences business on 1 January buying and selling pianos. He sells two standard types, upright and grand, and his transactions for the year are as follows:

	Upright		Grand	
	Buy	Sell	Buy	Sell
1 January	2 at £400		2 at £600	
31 March		1 at £600		
30 April	1 at £350		1 at £700	
30 June		1 at £600		1 at £1000
31 July	2 at £300		1 at £800	
30 September		3 at £500		2 at £1100
30 November	1 at £250		1 at £900	

You observe that the cost to P. Forte of the pianos is changed on 1 April, 1 July and 1 October, and will not change again until 1 January following.

Required:

(a) Prepare a statement showing gross profit and closing stock valuation, separately for each type of piano, under each of the following assumptions:

(i) FIFO

(ii) LIFO

(iii) Weighted average

(iv) RC.

(b) At a time of rising prices, (i.e. using the grand pianos as an example) comment on the usefulness of each of the methods.

4 The assistant accountant of Rolf Construction plc has been requested to prepare draft entries for the P&L account and balance sheet as at 31 March 20X4 to record the four long-term contracts which the company is currently working on. All four contracts had commenced after 1 April 20X3. The contract details are as follows:

	North Contract £000	South Contract £000	East Contract £000	West Contract £000
Costs incurred	2 400	1 500	380	7 000
Costs relating to the work certified	1 840	1 390	336	6 500
Certified value of work done	2 800	1 390	336	7 700
Attributable profit/ (foreseeable loss)	700	(48)	(108)	640
Progress payments	2 230	1 480	44	6 600
Total contract price	4 000	10 000	5 000	8 000

The following additional information was available to him:

(i) The current practice would be to take the attributable profit less foreseeable losses to the profit and loss account and to report in the balance sheet the costs incurred plus attributable profits less foreseeable losses less progress payments received and receivable.

(ii) The proposed new company policy was to apply the following disclosure criteria: long-term contracts should be disclosed in the balance sheet as follows:

(a) The amount of long-term contracts, at costs incurred, net of amounts transferred to cost of sales, after deducting foreseeable losses and applicable payments on account should be classified as long-term contract balances and separately disclosed within stocks. The balance sheet note should disclose separately the balances of:

    (i) net cost less foreseeable losses; and

    (ii) applicable payments on account.

(b) The balance of payments on account (in excess of amounts recorded as turnover and offset against long-term contracts) should be classified as payments on account and separately disclosed within creditors.

(c) The amount by which recorded turnover is in excess of payments on account should be classified as 'amounts recoverable on contracts' and separately disclosed within debtors.

(d) The amount by which the provision or accrual for foreseeable losses exceeds the costs incurred (after transfers to cost of sales) should be disclosed within either provisions for liabilities and charges or creditors as appropriate. The amount need not be separately disclosed unless material to the financial statements.

    The assistant accountant has applied the new policy and prepared the following draft entries for the profit and loss account and balance sheet:

P&L account entries

	North £000	South £000	East £000	West £000	Total £000
Turnover	2800	1390	336	7700	12 226
Costs	2400	1500	380	7000	11 280
Profit/(loss)	400	(110)	(44)	700	946

Balance sheet entries

Stocks	£822 000			
Creditors	£64 000			

Calculated as follows:

	North £000	South £000	East £000	West £000
Costs incurred	2400	1500	380	7000
Less: Cost of sales	1840	1390	336	6800
	560	110	44	200
Less: Foreseeable losses	–	(48)	(108)	–
	560	62	(64)	200

Stocks	£000	*Creditors*	£000
North	560	East	64
South	62		
West	200		
	822		64

Required:
(a) **Review the draft entries for the profit and loss account and balance sheet and amend if necessary to comply with the company's policy. Please show workings.**
(16 marks)
(b) **Briefly explain the criticisms that may be made by an analyst of the company's current and proposed policies for reporting long-term contracts in the balance sheet and profit and loss account in the light of the current debate.**
(9 marks)
(25 marks)
(ACCA)

5 Earthmovers Extraordinary plc, a company which commenced trading on 1 November 20X4 as contractors in the civil engineering industry, supply you with the following details of contracts it was engaged in at the end of its first year of business, 31 October 20X5:

	Contract A204 £000	Contract A210 £000	Contract M244 £000	Contract X101 £000
Value of work invoiced	1250	2850	2000	2400
Costs to date of last certificate	1200	2000	2300	1800
Costs since last certificate	100	–	300	200
Progress payments received	1050	2600	2000	2100
Total contract price	6500	5400	7600	4200
Estimated costs to complete	3900	2000	5400	1200

No other contracts were worked on during the year.

In accordance with the terms of the contracts, the company invoices its customers immediately it receives a certificate of the value of work done from the architect or other agent of its customer.

Calculate the amounts to be shown in the financial statements for the year-ended 31 October 20X5 in respect of the above long-term contracts.

6 Osmosis plc carries on business as a manufacturer and installer of wind turbines. The company's accounting staff are currently calculating the amounts for long-term contracts for inclusion in the draft accounts being prepared for the year-ended 30 November 1994.

The company has three contracts not completed at the year-end. These are for the manufacture and installation of wind turbines at Ascot, Bude and Cowes. The following information is available:

Ascot and Cowes contracts

	Ascot contract	Cowes contract
Contract commenced	1.12.93	1.7.94
	£000	£000
Fixed contract price	1350	2275.0
Payments on account	729	520.0
Costs incurred to date	675	577.2
Estimated cost to complete	405	1731.6
Estimated percent of work completed	60%	25%

It is company policy to match the cost of sales to turnover to date to give a profit in proportion to the turnover.

Bude contract

	1.12.92	
Contract commenced		
Information relating to	1992–3	1993–4
		Cumulative
	£000	£000
Payments on account	1581	3442.5
Costs incurred to date	1428	2652.0
Costs relating to work invoiced	1428	2550.0
Sales value of work done and invoiced	1530	3315.0

There was no expectation of any foreseeable loss on the Bude contract which was due to be completed in 1995.

Required:

(a) *Calculate* **the amounts that would appear in the balance sheet from the three contracts in accordance with the provisions of SSAP 9 'Stocks and Long-term Contracts'.**   (12 marks)

(b) *Explain* **the effect on the accounts if the auditor obtained two items of information that had not been available to the chief accountant when the contracts were being evaluated.**

The first item of information related to the cost of materials. As a result of a creditor circularization on 15 December 1994 a supplier has advised that, under the terms of their contract, the cost of materials supplied to Osmosis plc since 1 November 1994 is to be increased. This increase is because the supplier's own costs have risen by more than 10% thereby bringing into effect a price increase clause. It is estimated that the materials for the Ascot contract will increase by £67 500 of which amount £5000 relates to goods supplied to the company prior to 30 November 1994. This increase in the cost of materials does not affect the Cowes and Bude contracts. The supplier had not been aware of the increase in his own costs until dealing with and responding to the circularization letter.

The second item of information related to labour costs. A wages agreement authorized by the company on 1 December 1994 resulted in labour costs becoming £25 000 more than originally estimated.   (4 marks)

(16 marks)

(ACCA)

Taxation (SSAPs 5 and 15 and FRSs 16 and 19)

After reading this chapter you should be able to:
- describe the requirements of SSAP 5 accounting for value added tax
- describe the effect of the imputation tax system on accounting profits
- describe the requirements of FRS 16
- explain deferred tax
- describe the arguments for and against providing for deferred tax
- identify several possible methods of accounting for deferred tax
- identify the requirements of SSAP 15 'Accounting for Deferred Taxation' and the Companies Act in respect of deferred tax
- critically examine the Accounting Standards Board's approach
- identify and critically appraise the requirements of FRS 19 'Deferred Tax'.

Introduction

The amount of tax charged against profit in any period is, as we will see in Chapter 26, an important determinate of earnings per share and thus the price earnings (PE) ratio. Unfortunately, the tax charge calculated under revenue law is not simply a matter of computing a given rate of accounting profits, as taxable profits defined by revenue law are not the same as accounting profits assessed in accordance with the Companies Act and SSAPs/FRSs.

We also must consider the effect of value added tax on company accounts.

Value added tax

SSAP 5 relating to accounting for value added tax (VAT) is completely uncontroversial and is of passing interest only. The central requirements are that:

1 turnover in the P&L account should exclude VAT
2 irrecoverable VAT on fixed asset acquisition should be included with the cost of the asset; and
3 the net debit or credit carried in the balance sheet need not be separately disclosed.

Corporation tax (CT)

The tax levied on UK corporate profits is called corporation tax and it is generally due for payment nine months after the end of the accounting period. This rule applies unless the company is designated as a large company which occurs when a company's corporation tax profits for an accounting period are more than £1.5m. Such large companies will pay their CT in 4 quarterly instalments as follows:

6 months and 14 days after the start of the accounting period (AP)
9 months and 14 days after the start of the AP
14 days after the end of the AP
6 months and 14 days after the end of the AP

Activity 1

Company A and company B both have accounting periods ending 31 December 2000. Company A's taxable profits are in the region of £1m and company B's £2m. Identify the due dates, for each company, for payment of CT.

Activity 1 Feedback

Company B will be classed as a large company and will pay tax in 4 equal instalments on 14 July 2000, 14 October 2000, 14 January 2001, and 14 July 2001. Company A will not be classed as a large company and therefore will pay its CT on 14 October 2001.

The clear winner in cash flow terms is company A, the smaller company, in the above activity. The above rules were enacted as from AP ending on or after 30 June 1999 and are as a result of the modernisation of the tax system which reached its final stages in April 1999.

The old CT payment timing rules.

Prior to the modernisation of the CT system companies paid their CT 9 months after the end of the AP unless they paid dividends during the year. (Note here that the revenue , by altering the rules, have accelerated their tax cash flows from large companies). When dividends were paid during the year the revenue required advance instalments of a company's corporation tax. The advance instalment was calculated as the tax credit associated to a dividend payment and was due 14 days after the end of the quarter in which the dividend was paid. These advance payments could be deducted, within limits, from the total corporation tax bill and the remainder, known as mainstream corporation tax, was paid under the 9 month rule.

This old regime was known as the imputation tax system and, as dividends were paid by a company out of profit after tax, the revenue took the view that tax had already been deducted from these dividends. Thus the dividend in the hands of the shareholder was assessed as if tax had already been deducted at basic rate and a tax credit was imputed to the dividend received. The result was known as franked investment income. A simple example explains how this used to operate for an individual.

Example 1

Company S declares and pays a dividend of £80 to shareholder A. The basic rate of income tax is 20%. If the shareholder is a basic rate taxpayer then the tax credit imputed and the tax payable by A would be as follows:

Tax credit at 20% = $^1\!/_4$ × £80 = £20

Amount received by A before tax = £80 + £20	=	£100
Tax payable by A (basic rate tax payer)		£20
Tax deemed to have been paid		£20
Tax remaining payable by A		£0

If A paid tax at 40% then:

Tax payable by A (40% tax payer)	£40
Tax deemed to have been paid	£20
Tax remaining payable by A	£20

Of course companies could themselves be shareholders and the old rules for accounting for the imputation tax system embodied in SSAP 8 required that:

1 The total franked investment income and a tax credit based on the current income tax rate should be disclosed in the accounts in accordance with appropriate Companies Act presentation format
2 The tax credit thus credited to the P&L account would be debited 'lower down' being included within the total tax charge for the year.

The following example demonstrates how this used to operate.

Example 2

Company A receives a dividend of £20 000 from company B. Basic rate of income tax is 20%. This would be reflected in company A's books as follows:

Dividend received account

		Cash	20 000
		Taxation charge P&L	5 000
P&L	25 000		
	25 000		25 000

P &L account

Tax charge	5 000	Investment	
Profit after tax	20 000	Income	25 000
	25 000		25 000

The above treatment was required by SSAP 8 so as to provide consistency with other elements of profit appearing above the taxation charge line in the P&L account as these were also shown gross.

Activity 2

Beta plc, accounting year end 31 March 1995, paid a dividend of £80 000 on 19 February 1995. The corporation tax assessment for the company was £158 000, and was due nine months after the accounting year end. Show the liabilities for tax that would have existed in the year end accounts and the relevant ledger accounts (income tax rate 20%) under the old imputation tax system rules and SSAP 8.

Activity 2 feedback

(ACT is advance corporation tax.)

Corporation tax

31.3.95 ACT recoverable	20 000	31.3.95 P&L	158 000
31.3.95 Bal c/d	138 000		
	158 000		158 000
		1.4.95 Bal b/d (due 31.12.95)	138 000

Dividends paid

19.2.95 cash	80 000	31.3.95 P&L	80 000

ACT payable

	31.3.95 ACT rec (due 14.4.95)	20 000

ACT recoverable

31.3.95 ACT payable	20 000	31.3.95 CT	20 000

(Note the use of an ACT recoverable account.)

Limit on offset of ACT

Offset of ACT against corporation tax was limited to an amount equal to the current basic rate of income tax applied to taxable profits for the year. In Activity 2 if taxable profits were £330 000 then the limit of offset would be £66 000. Excess ACT could be recovered against the previous six years' tax bills, always remembering the offset rules, or carried forward for offset against future tax bills. This introduced the accounting problem of whether or not this unrecovered ACT would be recovered in the future. Note what prudence should have dictated here and then read on!

ACT and proposed dividends

ACT was also due on proposed dividends and was therefore shown as a liability at the year-end, but this ACT could not be offset against current year's tax only future year's tax. We therefore had a debit balance appearing on the ACT recoverable account at the year-end. The question we needed to answer in respect of this debit balance was, is it an asset? What would prudence have dictated?

SSAP 8 which was issued in 1974, 'The treatment of taxation, under the imputation system in the accounts of companies' gave us an answer to the above problem as follows:

6 For accounting purposes it is necessary to decide whether recovery of the ACT is reasonably certain and foreseeable or whether it should be written off in the profit and loss account. If the taxable income of the year under review and the amounts available from the preceding year or years are insufficient to cover

the ACT, then recoverability of ACT will depend on the extent to which income is earned in future periods in excess of dividends paid or on the existence of a deferred taxation account of adequate size. Although the relief remains available indefinitely it will be prudent to have regard only to the immediate and foreseeable future; how long this future period should be will depend upon the circumstances of each case, but it is suggested that where there is no deferred taxation account it should normally not extend beyond the next accounting period.

8 Any irrecoverable ACT (i.e. ACT the recoverability of which is not reasonably certain and foreseeable) should be written off in the profit and loss account in which the related dividend is shown.

Accounting treatment of irrecoverable ACT

SSAP 8 states:

9 There are two differing views on the presentation in the profit and loss account of irrecoverable ACT written off. One view is that irrecoverable ACT should be treated as part of the tax charge upon the company to be deducted in arriving at profits after tax: the other that the irrecoverable ACT, being a cost stemming from the payment of a dividend, should be treated as an appropriation like the dividend itself. Of the two methods the first is supported as the appropriate accounting treatment because unrelieved ACT constitutes tax upon the company or group, as opposed to tax on the shareholders, and is not an appropriation of profits. It is appreciated however that some readers or analysts of accounts may wish for their purposes to regard irrecoverable ACT in some other manner. The amount of irrecoverable ACT should therefore be separately disclosed if material.

Thus, the irrecoverable ACT affected the profit after tax figure and therefore earnings per share (eps).

Another twist

The imputation tax system allowed companies to reduce the ACT payable by the amount of tax credit on franked investment income (FII) received by the company if it was received in the same quarter as the dividend was paid. Note that this allowance did not reduce the amount of the tax bill in any way just the timing of payments. However, consider the following activity.

Activity 3

A company proposes a dividend of £28 000 at the accounting year-end, 31 March 1996, when the income tax rate is 20%. The company expects to receive dividends of £8000 from one of its investments on 2 May 1996. Which liability should the company have shown in its year-end accounts – £7000 or £5000?

Activity 3 feedback

ACT payable is $1/4 \times £28\,000 = £7000$ which is due in less than one year and would therefore appear as a liability on the balance sheet.

However, if investment dividend is received on 2 May 1996 then a tax credit of £2000 would have occurred and the company paid ACT of £5000. The liability eventually paid was thus £5000, but the liability which prudence and SSAPs (particularly SSAP 17) dictates we should declare was £7000. Strange how some companies actually reported only the £5000 as a liability!

We make no apology for working through the old regime of corporation tax and ACT as you will need to understand this when we come to the issue of transitional arrangements under the new regime.

The new tax credit rules

Although ACT has now been abolished shareholders will still receive a tax credit on their dividend income. From the 6 April 1999 the tax credit is 10% of the gross dividend and dividends will only be taxable for companies who hold investments as trading assets and for individuals paying high rate tax.

Activity 4

Alpine plc has taxable profits for the year ended 31.12.X1 of £3 000 000. Corporation tax rate is 30%. Alpine paid a dividend of £500 000 on 31.5.X1.

Calculate the tax payable and the tax payments under the previous regime, assuming ACT is 1/4 for the year in question, and under the new regime.

Activity 4 Feedback

Previous regime;

Total tax payable is $£3\,000\,000 \times 30\% = £900\,000$. ACT on dividend is $£500\,000 \times 25\% = £125\,000$. Payments are £125 000 July X1 and £775 000 September X2.

New regime;

Total tax payable is still £900 000 but payments are now £225 000 July X1, £225 000 October X1, £225 000 January X2 and £225 000 April X2. Note Alpine is classed as a large company.

FRS 16 current tax

In December 1999 the ASB finally withdrew SSAP 8, which was based upon the old tax system, by the issue of FRS 16. This deals with accounting for tax under the new tax regime with the exception of deferred tax which we will deal with later in this chapter. The new tax regime, by abolishing ACT, made accounting for tax much simpler but transitional arrangements were required for the move from one tax regime to the other and the problem of how to deal with tax credits on dividends received still needed resolving.

Transitional arrangements

These are identified in an appendix to FRS 16 and are essentially a shadow ACT system.

The shadow system is designed to ensure that ACT c/f after April 1999 is recovered only if it would have been recovered had the ACT system still existed. It was estimated that there was approximately £7bn surplus ACT still awaiting recovery when the legislation was changed. All of this £7bn will now be subject to the shadow arrangements which will allow offset against future tax bills (and actually reduce the tax bill) but only up to the amount that could have been offset if ACT had continued.

Activity 5

Apex plc has surplus ACT of £100 000 and taxable profits for the year ended 31.3.2000 of £250 000. It pays a dividend at the year end of £60 000 and received at that time a dividend of £16 000. Corporation tax rate is 30% and income tax rate 20%, implying an ACT rate of 25%. Identify the ACT set-off possible under the transitional arrangements of FRS 16.

Activity 5 Feedback

If ACT still applied Apex plc would be liable to pay in ACT

$$25\% \times £60\,000 - \text{tax credit on dividends received of } 25\% \times £16\,000 = £11\,000$$

Maximum offset of ACT would have been

$$20\% \times £250\,000 = £50\,000$$

New regulations CT liability of Apex plc year ended 31.3.2000 is

$$30\% \times 250\,000 = £75\,000$$

ACT set off possible		
Maximum offset available	£50 000	
Shadow ACT	11 000	
Therefore surplus to be set off is	39 000	(of £100 000 total surplus)
Actual MCT payable for the year is		75 000 − 39 000 = £36 000

Surplus ACT c/f is £61 000 (100 000 − 39 000) and this can be offset in future years.

The treatment of tax credits

Under SSAP 8 dividends received were grossed up by their tax credit and shown as income in the P&L account and the tax credit was shown as a deduction from the P&L account under the tax charge element. We saw this at example 2 earlier. The change in the tax regulation now requires that this method of accounting be reviewed as the majority of companies will no longer be able to recover the tax credit.

FRS 16 provides us with the following definitions:

> *Tax credit* 'The tax credit given under UK tax legislation to the recipient of a dividend from a UK company. The credit is given to acknowledge that the income out of which the dividend has been paid has already been charged to tax, rather than because any withholding tax has been deducted at source. The tax credit may

discharge or reduce the recipient's liability to tax on the dividend. Non-taxpayers may or may not be able to recover the tax credit.'

Withholding tax 'Tax on dividends or other income that is deducted by the payer of the income and paid to the tax authorities wholly on behalf on the recipient.'

There are three essential differences between tax credits and withholding tax:

- Withholding (WH) tax is a tax that has actually been paid by the recipient (or at least paid on his behalf).
- Income on which withholding tax has been suffered is treated as taxable and subject to further tax unless the amount of withholding tax is sufficient to discharge the liability; whereas in many circumstances no further tax is payable on dividends received with a tax credit. This dividend is treated as non-taxable income.
- The amount at which the dividend is measured, if it is subject to further tax, is the amount of the cash dividend received i.e. without the tax credit whereas income (dividend) subject to withholding tax is taxed on the amount received plus the withholding tax.

FRS 16 requires that 'Outgoing dividends paid and proposed, interest and other amounts payable should be recognized at an amount that:

(**a**) includes any withholding taxes; but
(**b**) excludes any other taxes, such as attributable tax credits, not payable wholly on behalf of the recipient. (para. 8 FRS 16) and

Incoming dividends, interest or other income receivable should be recognized at an amount that:

(**a**) includes any withholding taxes; but
(**b**) excludes any other taxes, such as attributable tax credits, not payable wholly on behalf of the recipient. (para. 9 FRS 16).

In addition the FRS also ensures that tax is correctly attributed between the P&L account and the STRGL as follows:

Current tax should be recognized in the profit and loss account for the period, except to the extent that it is attributable to a gain or loss that is or has been recognized directly in the STRGL. (para. 5 FRS 16)

Where a gain or loss is or has been recognized directly in the statement of total recognized gains and losses, the tax attributable to that gain or loss should also be recognized directly in that statement.' (para. 6 FRS 16)

Measurement of tax

FRS 16 requires that current tax should be measured at the amounts expected to be paid (or recovered) using the tax rates and laws that have been enacted or substantially enacted by the balance sheet date (para 14 FRS 16). Substantially enacted is where a Bill has been passed through the House of Commons and is awaiting House of Lords approval etc. at the balance sheet date or a resolution having statutory effect that has been passed under the Provisional Collection of Taxes Act 1968. This brings FRS 16 in line with IAS 12 Income Taxes.

Activity 6

The following information is available for Beta plc for the year ended 30.9 2000.

Accounting profit before taking account of dividends received or paid/proposed is £1 500 000.

Corporation tax due for the year ended 30.9.2000 is £520 000 (before taking effect of any tax paid on the company's behalf) which includes tax of £35 000 attributable to a gain recognized in the STRGL.

Dividends paid (cash) and proposed (cash) amount to £54 000 and £27 000 respectively and both were subject to withholding tax of 10%. They also have attributable tax credits of £15 000 and £7500 respectively.

The company received dividends (cash) of £72 000. These had been subject to withholding tax of 10% and have an attributable tax credit of £20 000.

The company is aware that the corporation tax rate may change from that used in the calculations above and before the due date of payment of the tax and asks for advice on how to deal with this.

Show the profit and loss account for the period ended 30.9.2000 as far as the above information permits and advise the company in respect of the change in tax rate.

Activity 6 Feedback

Abridged profit and loss account for the period ended 30.9.2000 for Beta plc

	£000	£000
Accounting profit before dividends		1500
Dividends received (gross up for WH tax but not tax credit)		80
		1580
Corporation tax (520 − 35 − 10 see note 1)		475
		1103
Dividends paid (grossed up for WH tax)	60	
Dividends proposed (but not tax credit)	30	90
		1013

Note 1:

The £35 000 tax due on the gain recognized in the STRGL will also be recognized in the STRGL. The £8000 withholding tax has been paid on behalf of the recipient company and will be deducted from the CT due as given as the figure was calculated before taking account of this.

The possibility of the change in tax rate will not be actioned by the company as FRS 16 requires that current tax should be measured at the amounts expected to be paid using the tax rates and laws that have been enacted or substantively enacted by the balance sheet date. Neither enaction or substantive enaction by the balance sheet date of 30.9.2000 is suggested by the information given above.

Disclosure requirements of FRS 16

These are quite straightforward and require a company to disclose UK or Republic of Ireland tax and foreign tax separately both for the P&L account and the STRGL.

Deferred taxation

Introduction

In the UK the amount of tax payable by a business for a particular period often bears little relationship to profit as reported by the accountants in the P&L account. The tax authorities (the Inland Revenue) take the accountant's reported profit figure as their starting point, but they make all sorts of adjustments to it. These adjustments are presented by Parliament in the Finance Acts. There is at least one Finance Act each year, sometimes two. This process enables Parliament to make fairly rapid changes (and often extremely frequent changes). The separation of taxable profit from accounting profit also means that Parliament can pursue its objectives (whatever they are!) without treading on the accountants' toes, and similarly the accountants can pursue their true and fair view unhindered by tax legislation. This separation, although common in the English-speaking world, is by no means universal. Much of mainland Europe, for example, requires tax adjustments to be incorporated in the published accounts.

The most important difference between the accountant's profit and the taxable profit concerns the treatment of depreciation. As we have seen (Chapter 16) the 'appropriate' charge for depreciation is a highly uncertain, subjective, amount. This would be unacceptable to the Revenue, who requires certainty and precision. Additionally governments have frequently felt that by varying the tax allowances, they can provide incentives to businesses to invest more, or to invest in some particular way. So the first thing that the Revenue does to the accountant's profit figure, as calculated and published, is to remove all the depreciation entries put in by the accountant. In other words the depreciation figure, which will have been deducted in arriving at the accountant's profit figure, is simply added back again (a profit on disposal that will have been added by the accountant will of course need to be removed by deduction). From the resulting figure the Revenue now deducts whatever the appropriate Finance Act tells them to, under the heading of 'capital allowances'. The implications arising from this have led to a long, complicated and sometimes badly argued debate over the last three decades.

What is deferred tax?

First let us look at the difference between taxable profits and accounting profits.

Activity 7

An asset attracting 25% capital allowances per annum costs Deftax Ltd £100. It has an expected life of five years at the end of which it is estimated it can be sold for £25. Taxation is payable at the rate of 33%. Complete the following table (note that capital allowances apply to the reducing balance of the asset).

	Year				
	1 £	2 £	3 £	4 £	5 £
accounting profit (after depreciation charge)	100	100	100	100	100
depreciation					
capital allowance					
taxable profit					
profit before tax					
taxation 33% taxable profit					
profit after tax					
profit before tax					
taxation charge calculated on accounting profits					
profit after accounting tax					

Activity 7 feedback

	Year				
	1 £	2 £	3 £	4 £	5 £
accounting profit (after depreciation charge)	100	100	100	100	100
depreciation	15	15	15	15	15
capital allowance	25	18	14	11	8
taxable profit	90	97	101	104	107
profit before tax	100	100	100	100	100
taxation 33% taxable profit	30	32	33	34	36
profit after tax	70	68	67	66	64
profit before tax	100	100	100	100	100
taxation charge if calculated on accounting profit	33	33	33	33	33
profit after accounting tax	67	67	67	67	67

The profit after tax figures, which are used for the eps and PE ratio (see Chapter 26) would indicate that in year 2 the performance of the company decreased and continued to do so for the next three years. But has the firm and the management been less successful? Arguably not! Over the five-year period the company has made the same accounting profit with the same resources each year (excluding the problems of historical cost here). Thus, the profit after accounting tax figures provides a better guide to performance of the company.

If we look carefully at the above table we note that the total tax charge is £165 over the five-year period using either method. Thus the use of capital allowances does not alter the total tax due, only the timing of those tax payments. The capital allowance has the effect of deferring tax payments in year 1, £3 and year 2, £1, and then collecting these in year 4 and 5.

So we have an eventual payment that relates to year 1 and 2 and arises as a result of the transactions and results of years 1 and 2 and it is therefore arguable that there is a liability created at year 1 and increased at year 2. We are in effect suggesting that:

1 The tax charge for year 1 and year 2 should really be £33, as this is the amount that must eventually be paid as a result of the year 1 and 2 activities.
2 There is a liability of £3 at the end of year 1, in respect of tax related to year 1 but payable in later years which increases to £4 by the end of year 2.

We can easily allow for both these considerations by creating a liability account, known as a deferred tax account. This is shown in the table below. The amount to be transferred to the credit of the deferred tax account can be formally calculated as follows.

Amount equals:

$$\text{Tax rate} \times (\text{capital allowances given} - \text{depreciation disallowed})$$

Thus for year 1:

$$33\% \times (25 - 15) = 3$$

and year 2:

$$33\% \times (18 - 15) = 1$$

	Year					
	1	2	3	4	5	Total
	£	£	£	£	£	£
Profit before tax	100	100	100	100	100	500
Taxation: payable for year	30	32	33	34	36	165
Additional charge (credit) to deferred tax account	3	1	0	(1)	(3)	0
Total tax charge	33	33	33	33	33	165
Profit after tax	67	67	67	67	67	335

Deferred tax account

	£		£	
Balance c/d 31.12.01	3	Appropriation account		
		31.12.01	3	
	3		3	
		Balance b/d 1.1.02	3	
Balance c/d 31.12.02	4	Approp. Acc. 31.12.02	1	
	4		4	
Balance c/d 31.12.03	4	Balance b/d 1.1.03	4	
	4		4	
Approp. Acc. 31.12.04	1	Balance b/d 1.1.04	4	
Balance c/d 31.12.04	3			
	4		4	
Approp. Acc 31.12.05	3	Balance b/d 1.1.05	3	

For year 4   and year 5
$33\% \times (11 - 15) = -1$ $33\% \times (8 - 15) = -3$

So the transfer for year 4 is a debit to deferred tax account of £1 (or in effect, a credit of – £1, if you find that easier to see), and a credit of £1 to the appropriation account. For year 5 we have a debit to deferred tax account of £3 and a credit of £3 to the appropriation account.

Arguments for deferred tax

From the above discussion we can note that:

1 The tax charge by including deferred tax is £67 for years 1–5, which provides a profit after tax figure which reflects the performance of the company.
2 There is a liability balance remaining at the end of each year in respect of tax related to the current or earlier years but not yet paid or due for payment. This, we also suggested, was a desirable outcome.
3 The total position viewed over the five years as a whole remains unaltered. This is to be expected as nothing we are doing, and also nothing that Parliament is doing, through capital allowances, alters the total tax eventually payable as a result of a year's profits.

All the above appears totally logical and in accord with accounting principles. So where is the problem?

Arguments against deferred tax

A problem occurs with the previous logic if a company buys assets regularly, which is a realistic assumption as companies tend to become more capital intensive. Let us demonstrate the problem with an activity.

Activity 8

In addition to the information given in Activity 7 Deftax Ltd buys an asset in year 2 for £100, one in year 3 for £120 and one in year 4 for £220 and two in year 5 for £250 and £300, respectively. All these assets also have an expected life of five years, but unlike the first asset, all these later ones have an expected scrap value of zero. Complete the table in Activity 7 using the new information and show the deferred tax account over the five-year period. Comment upon the results.

Activity 8 feedback

	Year				
	1	2	3	4	5
	£	£	£	£	£
Accounting profit	100	100	100	100	100
Depreciation	15	35	59	103	213
Capital allowance	25	43	62	103	215
Taxable profit	90	92	97	100	98
Tax charge	30	30	32	33	32
Deferred tax charge	3	3	1	0	1
Total tax	33	33	33	33	33
Profit after tax	67	67	67	67	67

To help you with the above activity we provide the workings for years 2 and 3 for the calculation of depreciation and capital allowances. Years 4 and 5 follow the same pattern.

Workings:

Year 2:

Asset 1 depreciation 75/5	=	15	
Asset 2 depreciation 100/5	=	20	
		35	

Asset 1 capital allowance 25% × 75	=	18
Asset 2 capital allowance 25% × 100	=	25
		43

Year 3:

Asset 1 depreciation	=	15	
Asset 2 depreciation	=	20	
Asset 3 depreciation 120/5	=	24	
		59	

Asset 1 capital allowance 25% × (75 − 18)	=	14
Asset 2 capital allowance 25% × (100 − 25)	=	18
Asset 3 capital allowance 25% × 120	=	30
		62

Deferred tax account

Balance c/d 31.12.01	3	3	Appropriation a/c	31.12.01
	3	3		
		3	Bal. b/d 1.1.02	
Balance c/d 3 1.12.02	6	3	Appropriation a/c	31.12.02
	6	6		
		6	Bal. b/d/ 1.1.03	
Bal. c/d 31.12.03	7	1	Appropriation a/c	31.12.03
	7	7		
		7	Bal. b/d 1.1.04	
Bal. c/d 31.12.04	7	0	Appropriation a/c	31.12.04
	7	7		
		7	Bal. b/d 1.1.05	
Bal. c/d 31.12.05	8	1	Appropriation a/c	31.12.05
	8	8		
		8	Bal. b/d 1.1.06	

Comparing the tables from Activities 7 and 8 we see that the total position over the five years is no longer the same. The total tax charge is increased by £8. This is not surprising, as it equals the liability provided for at the end of year 5 on the deferred tax account. The transfer to the deferred tax account can be seen to be the result of an amalgam of positive originating timing differences relating to depreciation. The resultant figure of profit after tax, £67 per annum, reflects the underlying profitability of the company. It does not give an impression of improved profitability because of the effect of tax allowances related to asset acquisitions. Everything appears fine so where is the problem? The problem is the £8 remaining on the deferred tax account. Does this liability actually exist?

In the long term we can suggest that:

1 If the company reaches the state where it has a constant volume of fixed assets, merely replacing its existing assets as they wear out, and also the price it has to pay for replacement fixed assets does not rise over time, then the balance of liability on the deferred tax account will remain a more or less constant figure.

2 If the company finds that it is effectively in the position of paying gradually more and more money for fixed assets each year, then the balance of liability on the deferred tax account will gradually rise, apparently without limit.

3 Only if the monetary amount of reinvestment in fixed assets actually falls will the balance of liability on the deferred tax account start to fall.

How likely is each of these three outcomes? In general 2 will tend to be the most frequent for three reasons:

1 firms have a tendency to expand
2 firms have a tendency to become more capital intensive
3 inflationary pressures tend to cause the amount of money paid for assets to increase over time.

So the most likely outcome, if full provision is to be made for deferred tax in this way, is of a liability figure on the balance sheet that is apparently ever-increasing. But what is a liability? Informally, we can say that it is an amount to be paid out in the future. We have an account representing a liability to the Inland Revenue. The balance on this account is gradually getting bigger and bigger and, as far as can reasonably be foreseen, this process is going to continue. Therefore the liability balance does not seem to be getting paid, nor, in the foreseeable future is it likely to be paid. Therefore it appears that it is not a liability at all within the meaning of the word liability! If the liability account seems all set to keep on growing, is there a probable future sacrifice?

It should be observed that one way of summarizing the two arguments as regards the liability aspect is that we can consider the position for each individual asset, or we can consider the position for all assets in the aggregate. In the former case the tax 'deferred' will all have become payable by the end of the asset's life, so deferred tax provision would seem to be necessary. In the latter case the aggregate liability is likely to go on increasing so deferred tax provision would seem to be unnecessary.

The accountants' response

Formally, three approaches have been distinguished:

1 **The flow-through approach**, which accounts only for that tax payable in respect of the period in question, i.e. timing differences are ignored.

2 **Full deferral**, which accounts for the full tax effects of timing differences, i.e. tax is shown in the published accounts based on the full accounting profit, and the element not immediately payable is recorded as a liability until reversal.

3 **Partial deferral**, which accounts only for those timing differences where reversal is likely to occur in aggregate terms (because, for example, replacement of assets and expansion is expected to exceed depreciation).

These alternatives are discussed and explained in the following activities.

Activity 9

Should the flow through approach be identified as the method to be used for accounting for tax?

Activity 9 feedback

Arguments in favour:

- Tax is assessed on taxable profits not accounting profits. The only liability for tax for the period therefore is that accordingly assessed.
- Future years' tax depends on future events and is therefore not a present liability (see definition of liability from the Statement of Principles)
- Even if current events were giving rise to future tax liabilities then, as the tax charge will be based on a complex set of future transactions, it cannot be measured with reliability and therefore should not be recognized.

Arguments against:

- As tax charges can be traced to individual transactions and events then any future tax consequences arising from these should be provided for at the outset
- Flow through method can understate an entity's liability to tax.

SSAP 11 Accounting for deferred tax issued 1975 rejected flow through as did its successor SSAP 15 issued 1978 and the revised version 1985. The latest statement from the ASB on the issue, FRED 19 Deferred Tax, still rejects the flow through approach.

Activity 10

Should the full deferral method be adopted as the method to be used for accounting for tax?

Activity 10 feedback

This was the approach recommended by the ASC in their first standard in 1975, as outlined in paragraph 9 of SSAP 11:

> The view is taken that the amount of the tax saving should not appear as a benefit of the year for which it was granted, but should be carried forward and re-credited to the profit and loss account (by way of reduction of the tax charged there-

in) in the year or years in which there are reversing time differences. The account in which these deferred tax savings are held, has, by custom, become known as the 'deferred taxation account'.

In effect, therefore, the full unreversed element is shown as a liability.

Applying this to the circumstances of Deftax Ltd, we arrive at the position in Activity 7. Thus we could well be showing a liability that will never crystallize.

Activity 11

Should partial deferral be the method adopted for accounting for tax?

Activity 11 feedback

As we have seen, the one major problem with full deferral is that the balance on the deferred tax account is likely to increase continuously where there is expansion and replacement at increased prices. If, however, timing differences are regarded in aggregate terms rather than as relating to individual assets, then this could be taken as evidence that the differences were not reversing. In short, is a liability that is never likely to become payable, a liability at all?

The ASC's second standard on deferred tax, SSAP 15 (1978), followed this approach, as explained below:

> In many businesses timing differences arising from accelerated capital allowances are of a recurring nature, and reversing differences are themselves offset, wholly or partially, or are exceeded, by new originating differences thereby giving rise to continuing tax reductions or the indefinite postponement of any liability attributable to the tax benefits received. It is therefore appropriate that in the case of accelerated capital allowances, provision be made for deferred taxation except in so far as the tax benefit can be expected with reasonable probability to be retained in the future in consequence of recurring timing differences of the same type.

Activity 12

On the assumption that the directors of Deftax Ltd foresee no reversal of timing differences for some considerable time, and using the information from Activity 7, show the taxation effect using the partial deferral method.

Activity 12 feedback

	1	*2*	*Year* *3*	*4*	*5*
	£	£	£	£	£
Profit before tax	100	100	100	100	100
Taxation	30	30	32	33	32
Deferred tax charge	0	0	0	0	0
	70	70	68	67	68

Deferred tax calculation

Year	Originating (O) timing Difference	Reversing (R) timing Difference	Net timing Difference
1	10 (25 capital allowance −15 depreciation)	–	10 (0)
2	18 (43 – 35)	–	8 (0)
3	6 (30 – 24)	3	3 (0)
4	11 (55 – 44)	11	(0)
5	28 (138 – 110)	26	2 (0)

6 onwards no net reversals.

The liability for tax will never crystallize therefore no provision for deferred tax. No net reversal appears ever to be expected.

Activity 13

A company Partax Ltd acquires a fixed asset for £100 in year 1 with residual value at end of useful life £20 and another for £200 with nil residual value in year 5. Assuming, assets are depreciated using straight line and a life of five years, that profits before tax are £250 per annum, that corporation tax is 33%, assets receive a 25% capital allowance, and that after year 5 new assets will be acquired annually, show the taxation charges using partial deferral method of provision for the first four years.

Activity 13 feedback

	Year				
	1	2	3	4	5
	£	£	£	£	£
Profit before tax	250	250	250	250	250
Depreciation	16	16	16	16	56
	266	266	266	266	306
Capital allowance	25	19	14	11	58
Taxable profit	241	247	252	255	248
Tax 33%	80	82	83	84	82
Deferred tax	2.3	–	(0.7)	(1.6)	–
Total tax	82.3	82	82.3	82.4	82

Deferred tax calculation

	Originating	Reversing	Net
1	9	–	9 O
2	3	–	3 O
3	–	3	2 R
4	–	5	5 R
5	10	8	2 O

Thereafter should be originating as assets are bought annually.

Reversals of 7 need to be provided for in total, thus a deferred tax provision of £2.3 is required at year 1 ($7 \times 33\%$). This very clearly illustrates that the deferred tax is only being 'partially' provided for.

SSAP 15 (revised) 'Accounting for Deferred Tax'

In 1983, the ASC issued an ED for a revised standard, and the standard duly appeared in 1985. It was not given a new number, but became SSAP 15 (revised) – a procedure likely to lead to considerable confusion. This broadly followed SSAP 15 and favoured partial deferral, but it did contain a 'change in emphasis' as compared with SSAP 15. The major points of SSAP 15 (revised) are discussed below:

17   Deferred tax is the tax attributable to timing differences.

18   Timing differences are differences between profits or losses as computed for tax purposes and results as stated in financial statements, which arise from the inclusion of items of income and expenditure in tax computations in periods different from those in which they are included in financial statements. Timing differences originate in one period and are capable of reversal in one or more subsequent periods.

19   A loss for tax purposes which is available to relieve future profits from tax constitutes a timing difference.

20   The revaluation of an asset (including an investment in an associated or subsidiary company) will create a timing difference when it is incorporated in the balance sheet, in so far as the profit or loss that would result from realisation at the revalued amount is taxable, unless disposal of the revalued asset and of any subsequent replacement assets would not result in a tax liability, after taking account of any expected rollover relief.

21   The retention of earnings overseas will create a timing difference only if:
     (a)   there is an intention or obligation to remit them; and
     (b)   remittance would result in a tax liability after taking account of any related double tax relief.

The crucial point is that the differences originate in one period and are capable of reversal in subsequent periods. Timing differences are explained more fully in paragraph 4:

4   The different basis of arriving at profits for tax purposes derives from three main sources. First, certain types of income are tax-free and certain types of expenditure are disallowable, giving rise to 'permanent differences' between taxable and accounting profits. Permanent differences also arise where there are tax allowances or charges with no corresponding amount in the financial statements. Secondly, there are items that are included in the financial statements of a period different from that in which they are dealt with for tax purposes, giving rise to 'timing differences'; thus revenue, gains, expenditure and losses may be included in financial statements either earlier or later than they enter into the computation of profit for tax purposes.

The three possible approaches to deferred tax, i.e. the flow-through, the full deferral and the partial deferral, are outlined and briefly appraised in paragraphs 7–9 and 12:

7   The first is called 'nil provision' or 'flow through' and is based on the principle that only the tax payable in respect of a period should be charged in that period. No provision for deferred tax would therefore be made. Those who hold this view argue that any tax liability arises on taxable profits, not accounting profits, and therefore consider that it is necessary to provide tax only on taxable profits. Further, any tax liability arising on timing differences will depend on the incidence of future taxable profits and may therefore be difficult to quantify.

8   A basis radically different from nil provision is 'full provision', sometimes called 'comprehensive allocation'. This is based on the principle that financial statements for a period should recognise the tax effects, whether current or deferred, of all transactions occurring in that period.

9   An advantage of either of these bases is that the amounts involved can be precisely quantified. However, a crucial disadvantage is that they can lead to a purely arithmetical approach in which certainty of calculation is given precedence over a reasoned assessment of what the tax effects of transactions will actually be.

12 A third basis is 'partial provision', which requires that deferred tax should be accounted for in respect of the net amount by which it is probable that any payment of tax will be temporarily deferred or accelerated by the operation of timing differences which will reverse in the foreseeable future without being replaced. Partial provision recognises that, if an enterprise is not expected to reduce the scale of its operations significantly, it will often have what amounts to a hard core of timing differences so that the payment of some tax will be permanently deferred. On this basis, deferred tax has to be provided only where it is probable that tax will become payable as a result of the reversal of timing differences. Because it is based on an assessment of what will actually be the position, partial provision is preferable to the other bases described above.

Changing tax rates and deferred tax

Corporation tax rates are changed frequently by governments and this can have an effect upon deferred tax charges.

Activity 14

A company acquires a fixed asset for £4800 in year 1. Other assets will be acquired after year 6 from which date no reversals of taxation are foreseen. The asset has a life of six years and a residual value of £1800. Capital allowances are at the rate of 25% written down and the tax rates applicable are 50% years 1–3 and 30% thereafter. Show the provisions for deferred tax (partial) if reversals take place at the prevailing tax rate. Comment on the balance on the deferred tax account as at end year 6.

Activity 14 feedback

Year	1	2	3	4	5	6
	£	£	£	£	£	£
Depreciation	500	500	500	500	500	500
Capital allowance	1200	900	675	506	380	285
Difference	700 O	400 O	175 O	6 O	120 R	215 R

thereafter originating therefore under partial provision provide for the reversals of £335.

Year	1	2	3	4	5	6
	£	£	£	£	£	£
Deferred tax charge	167.5	–	–	–	(36)	(64.5)
Balance def. tax	167.5	167.5	167.5	167.5	131.5	67

The balance on the deferred tax account at year 6 is caused by the change in the tax rate at year 5 and 6 to 30%. The provision for the reversal was provided at 50%. This balance will never become payable. We have in fact over-provided for deferred tax but we were unaware of this when we made the original provision.

Deferral vs liability method of provision

SSAP 15 has the following to say on the problem associated with Activity 14. Under the deferral method of provision for deferred tax:

> 13   The tax effects of timing differences are calculated using the tax rates current when the differences arise. No adjustments are made subsequently if tax rates change. Reversals are accounted for using the tax rates in force when the timing differences originated, although in practice the effects of reversal and new timing differences are sometimes accounted for as one item.
>
>   Those who support this method recognise that, when tax rates change, this method will not give an indication of the amount of tax payable or recoverable. Any deferred tax balance will therefore be a deferred charge or credit rather than a liability or asset.
>
>   When tax rates change, there is no need to revise the deferred tax already provided. Thus the tax charge or credit for the period relates solely to that period and is not distorted by any adjustments relating to prior periods.

Alternatively, it could be argued that the balances on the deferred tax account should be regarded as liabilities payable in the future, or as assets receivable in the future. The best available estimate of the tax rate ruling in the future when the amount is to be paid or received will generally be the current tax rate. This means that the liability balance will need to be continually revised whenever the current tax rate changes. This is known as the **liability method**. Under this method (paragraph 14):

> 14   Deferred tax provisions are revised to reflect changes in tax rates. Thus the tax charge or credit for the period may include adjustments of accounting estimates relating to prior periods. The deferred tax provision represents the best estimate of the amount that would be payable or receivable if the relevant timing differences reversed.

The ASC preferred this latter argument:

15 The liability method is the method consistent with the aim of partial provision, which is to provide the deferred tax which it is probable will be payable or recoverable.

The requirement of the standard is contained in paragraphs 24 and 25:

24 Deferred tax should be computed under the liability method.
25 Tax deferred or accelerated by the effect of timing differences should be accounted for to the extent that it is probable that a liability or asset will crystallize.

Deferred tax calculation

Under the liability method the easiest way to calculate the deferred tax charge each year is by assessing what the balance on the deferred taxation account should be at the end of each year. This is done by reference to cumulative timing differences which are calculated from the NBV of the asset as per depreciation compared with the net book value of the assets as per written down allowances. The following example illustrates this for you using both full and partial liability method of calculating deferred taxation.

Example 3

A company commences trading year 1, purchasing capital assets of £20 000, and anticipates capital expenditure of £8000, £10 000, £12 000 and £14 000, respectively, for each of the next 4 years. All assets have a life of 10 years, capital allowances are 25% per annum written down value and the tax rate for the 5 years is expected to be 30%.

Identify what the balance on the deferred taxation account should be at the end of each year.

Answer 3

Year	1	2	3	4	5
	£	£	£	£	£
Accounting balances					
Asset balance	20 000	18 000	23 200	29 400	36 400
Additions	–	8 000	10 000	12 000	14 000
Depreciation	2 000	2 800	3 800	5 000	6 400
Balance c/f	18 000	23 200	29 400	36 400	44 000
Tax balances					
Asset balance	20 000	15 000	17 250	20 437	24 328
Additions	–	8 000	10 000	12 000	14 000
Allowance	5 000	5 750	6 813	8 109	9 582
Balance c/f	15 000	17 250	20 437	24 328	28 746
Timing differences	3 000	5 950	8 963	12 072	15 254

Under full provision the deferred taxation account should have a balance of 30% of the timing difference at year 1 that is 30% × 3000 = £900. At the end of year 2 the balance should be 30% × 5950 = £1785, therefore a charge of £885 would be made to the P&L account.

Under partial provision we would need to consider whether it is probable that a liability will crystallize. As cumulative timing differences are continuing to rise it seems reasonable to assume that no provision for deferred tax should be made.

It is interesting to remember at this point that the concept of deferred taxation started from the premise that an accounting charge was required in the P&L account so as to reflect the performance of the entity in a true and fair manner. We have now arrived at the notion that we need to show a true and fair view of the liabilities in the balance sheet. The two ideas do not necessarily provide us with the same assessment for deferred taxation!

To further illustrate the provision of deferred taxation using the partial liability method, we provide two activities for you.

Activity 15

Calculate the balance on the deferred taxation account at the end of year 1 under the partial liability method assuming the same information as in Example 3 above except that at the end of year 1 the cumulative timing differences were £8000 not £3000.

Activity 15 feedback

Year	1	2	3	4	5
	£	£	£	£	£
Timing differences	8 000	5 950	8 963	12 072	15 254
Change		(2 050)	3 013	3 109	3 182
Cumulative		(2 050)	963	4 072	7 254

There is now a net reversal in cumulative timing differences at year 2 of 8000 − 5950 = 2050 and thereafter an increase. Thus, under the partial liability method at the end of year 1 the deferred tax account should show a balance of £615 (2050 × 30%).

Activity 16

Osmosis plc has been highly profitable and expanded its fixed assets base annually. At 30 November 20X4 the NBV in the balance sheet exceeded the written down values by £1.2 million, and the company has not provided for deferred tax. The pattern of capital expenditure is likely to be more irregular in the future and the following forecast has been prepared.

(ACCA)

	Capital allowances	Depreciation
	£000	£000
20X4–5	2560	2240
20X5–6	2800	2560
20X6–7	1760	2672

The corporation tax rate for 20X3–4 is 33% and the rate for future years is estimated to be 35%. Calculate the charge or credit for deferred taxation that will appear in the P&L account for the years ended 30 November 20X4 and 20X5 and the amounts that will appear in the deferred taxation account in the balance sheet as at 30 November 20X4 and 20X5.

Activity 16 feedback

Year	20X3	20X4	20X5	20X6
	£000	£000	£000	£000
Timing difference	1200	1520	1760	848
Change		320	240	(912)
Cumulative		320	560	(352)

The above shows a net reversal in cumulatives of £352 000, therefore the deferred tax balance should be 35% × 352 000 = £123 200 as at 30 November 20X4; 35% is used as next year's tax charge is estimated at this figure. The charge to the P&L account for the year-ended 30 November 20X4 is also £123 200.

Year	20X4	20X5	20X6
	£000	£000	£000
Timing difference	1520	1760	848
Change		240	(912)
Cumulative		240	(672)

The net reversal is now £672 000, therefore the deferred tax balance at the 30 November 20X5 should be 35% × 672 000, = 235 200, therefore the deferred tax charge in the P&L account for the year-ended 30 November 20X5 is £112 000 (235.2 − 123.2)

As at 30 November 20X6 the deferred tax balance would need to be 35% × 912 000, = 319 200, therefore there is a charge to the P&L account of £84 000.

If thereafter capital allowances were in excess of depreciation then the deferred tax balance as at 30 November 20X7 should be 0 and thus the charge to the P&L account would be (£319 200).

In the above activity full provision for deferred tax would have required a deferred tax balance

as at 30.11.X4 of 1200 × 35% = 420 therefore unprovided 296.8
as at 30.11.X5 of 1520 × 35% = 532 therefore unprovided 296.8
as at 30.11.X6 of 1760 × 35% = 616 therefore unprovided 296.8
as at 30.11.X7 of 912 × 35% = 319.2 therefore unprovided 0

(figures in £000s).

Crystallization of a liability

SSAP 15 (revised) states

> **26** Tax deferred or accelerated by the effect of timing differences should not be accounted for to the extent that it is probable that a liability or asset will not crystallize.

This should be contrasted with the corresponding sections of the original SSAP 15 (paragraph 27):

> Deferred taxation should be accounted for in respect of tax effects … other than any tax effects which … can be demonstrated with reasonable probability to continue in the future.

(Paragraph 29 suggested that the future should be at least three years.)

In the preamble to ED 33 (paragraph 1-5), this contrast was described as a 'significant change of emphasis'. Whether or not it really makes much difference is an open question. Paragraph 1–6 states:

> Estimates of whether or not it is probable that a liability will crystallize should be made by the board of directors on the basis of a careful and prudent appraisal of the available information and of the intentions of management.

SSAP 15 (revised) continues:

27 The assessment of whether deferred tax liabilities or assets will or will not crystallize should be based upon reasonable assumptions.

28 The assumptions should take into account all relevant information available up to the date on which the financial statements are approved by the board of directors, and also the intentions of management. Ideally this information will include financial plans or projections covering a period of years sufficient to enable an assessment to be made of the likely pattern of future tax liabilities. A prudent view should be taken in the assessment of whether a tax liability will crystallize, particularly where the financial plans or projections are susceptible to a high degree of uncertainty or are fully developed for the appropriate period.

29 The provision for deferred tax liabilities should be reduced by any deferred tax debit balance arising from separate categories of timing differences and any advanced corporation tax which is available for offset against those liabilities.

30 Deferred tax net debit balances should not be carried forward as assets, except to the extent that they are expected to be recoverable without replacement by equivalent debit balances.

Disclosure requirements (SSAP 15 (revised))

The disclosure requirements are summarized as follows:

16 It is generally accepted that, however they have been calculated, tax effects should be shown in financial statements separately from the items or transactions to which they relate. An alternative would be to treat the tax effects of timing differences as integral parts of the revenue or expenditure, assets, provisions or liabilities to which they relate, rather than showing them separately. This 'net of tax' method recognises that the value of assets and liabilities is affected by tax considerations, in particular tax deductibility. On the other hand, it fails to distinguish between a transaction and its tax consequences and therefore should not be used in financial statements.

P&L account

33 Deferred tax relating to the ordinary activities of the enterprise should be shown separately as a part of the tax on profit or loss on ordinary activities, either on the face of the profit and loss account or in a note.

34 Deferred tax relating to any extraordinary items should be shown separately as part of the tax on extraordinary items, either on the face of the profit and loss account or in a note.

35 The amount of any unprovided deferred tax in respect of the period should be disclosed in a note, analysed into its major components.

36 Adjustments to the deferred tax arising from changes in tax rates and tax allowances should normally be disclosed separately as part of the tax charge for the period. However, the effect of a change in the basis of taxation, or of a significant change in government fiscal policy, should be treated as an extraordinary item where material.

Balance sheet

37 The deferred tax balance, and its major components, should be disclosed in the balance sheet or notes.

38 Transfers to and from deferred tax should be disclosed in a note.

39 Where amounts of deferred tax arise which relate to movements on reserves (e.g. resulting from the expected disposal of revalued assets) the amounts transferred to or from deferred tax should be shown separately as part of such movements.

40 The total amount of any unprovided deferred tax should be disclosed in a note, analysed into its major components.

41 Where the potential amount of deferred tax on a revalued asset is not shown because the revaluation does not constitute a timing difference under paragraph 20, the fact that it does not constitute a timing difference and that tax has therefore not been quantified should be stated.

42 Where the value of an asset is shown in a note because it differs materially from its book amount, the note should also show the tax effects, if any, that would arise if the asset were realised at the balance sheet date at the noted value.

Companies Act and deferred tax

Schedule 4 of the Act contains several requirements affecting deferred tax. These are summarized below:

Deferred tax provisions should be included in the balance sheet under the heading 'Provisions for liabilities and charges' as part of the provision for 'Taxation, including deferred taxation.'

Paragraph 89 of the Schedule described provisions for liabilities or charges as 'any amount retained as reasonably necessary for the purpose of providing for any liability or loss which is either likely to be incurred, or certain to be incurred but uncertain as to amount or as to the date on which it will arise'.

The amount of any provisions for taxation other than deferred taxation has to be stated (para. 47 of the Schedule). Taking this requirement together with that referred to above, the balance of deferred tax will be ascertainable as the remaining figure. Tax provisions are distinguished from tax liabilities falling due within, or after more than, one year, which are shown separately under creditors in the balance sheet.

Movements on reserves and provisions must be disclosed (paragraph 46(1)). The information required (paragraph 46(2)) is:

(a) the amount of the reserves or provisions as at the date of the beginning of the financial year and as at the balance sheet date respectively
(b) any amounts transferred to or from the reserves or provisions during that year; and
(c) the source and application respectively of any amounts so transferred.

Setting off deferred tax assets against deferred tax liabilities is not regarded as contrary to paragraph 5 of the schedule (which forbids the setting off of assets and liabilities). Individual deferred tax debit balances and liabilities are elements of an aggregate deferred tax asset or liability.

Unprovided deferred tax would appear to be a contingent liability: paragraph 50(2) of the schedule therefore applies. This:

> requires information to be given with respect to the amount or estimated amount of any contingent liability not provided for, its legal nature and any valuable security provided.

Under paragraph 54:

> the basis on which the charge for UK tax is computed has to be stated. Particulars are required of any special circumstances affecting the tax liability for the financial year or succeeding financial years.

Deferred tax is not specifically referred to in the P&L account formats. The SSAP requirements in this respect have already been discussed.

A critical appraisal of the ASC's approach

SSAP 2 emphasized the role of the matching and prudence conventions (Chapter 15). However since then the issue of the Statement of Principles by the ASB has ensured accruals/matching becomes part of the 'bedrock of accounting' but prudence becomes only one aspect of the overall objective of reliability.

Before you read on you may wish to consider whether you think that these are best served by full or partial deferral, or indeed whether there is any conflict between them here.

The questions that could be asked include:

1 Is tax an expense (to be matched) or an appropriation of profits?
2 Is an accelerated tax allowance a benefit of the year reflecting a reduction 'in the effective rate of tax below the statutory rate', or is it merely a postponement of tax payments thereby providing opportunities for better performance in the future? Could this be regarded as a postponement to infinity?
3 Is it prudent to treat an accelerated tax allowance as distributable income when reversal is dependent upon events in the future?
4 Is it prudent to treat an accelerated allowance as income rather than as a liability of uncertain date of payment, or is the liability merely contingent upon certain occurrences?

An interesting comparison can be made with SSAP 4 dealing with the treatment of government grants (p. 255). Under SSAP 4 the (permanent) benefit is to 'be credited to revenue over the expected useful life of the asset'. Any immediate transfer of the whole grant to P&L is rejected as 'providing no correlation with the accounting treatment of the expenditure to which the grant relates' (paragraph 5). Yet it can be argued that any treatment of deferred tax other than full deferral is in effect crediting to P&L account not the whole amount of a grant, but the whole amount of a loan (i.e. deferral). Put like that, any proposal other than full deferral could be argued as being unacceptably imprudent.

Deferred tax is never a permanent form of corporate finance since, even ignoring the actions of Parliament and the tax authorities, any inability to maintain investment levels renders the tax payable at precisely the time when the company is least likely to be able to afford to pay it. A strong and healthy company will clearly be in a position to maintain and expand its fixed asset base. This will tend, given the existence of material capital allowances, to lead to further postponement of tax payments. If the company runs into cash and liquidity problems, then it may well be forced to cut back on its investment programme. This will tend to lead to a reduction in the deferred tax and an increase in the currently due tax payment (i.e. deferred liability is 'crystallizing'). Since the starting point for this state of affairs was that the company had run short of money, the increased tax demands are clearly coming at the worst possible time. Indeed they may finish the company off altogether.

Does the choice between full and partial matter? That is, does it have any significant effect upon reported earnings or position, with consequent effect upon the information presented to investors and other users?

It is obvious that with partial provision the tax charge will as a generality be lower than under full provision, and therefore reported earnings will be higher. It is also obvious as a generality that there will be greater *variability* in the tax charge under the partial provision method than under full provision. Some firms will charge a high percentage of the theoretical maximum potential liability and some firms will charge a small percentage or even none at all.

The important questions to consider arising from this are:

1 Are the lower tax charges under the partial provision more, or less, 'true and fair'?
2 Does the greater variability in the tax charge under the partial method reflect an inconsistent treatment of similar items (in which case it is undesirable)? Or does it reflect the appropriate treatment of different circumstances in different companies (in which case it is perfectly acceptable)?

It is clear that the ASC had and the ASB has great difficulty in formulating a coherent and acceptable standard on deferred taxation. What do you think of the regulatory position as we have described it so far?

Further changes to SSAP 15

In December 1992 the ASB made another amendment to SSAP 15 which muddied the waters of deferred taxation even more. The amendment was as a result of the UITF sixth statement relating to post-retirement health care costs. As we will see in Chapter 22, employers' pension costs are accounted for on an accruals basis not on a cash paid basis. However, employers' cash payment of pensions, not the accrued charge, is permitted as a deduction for tax purposes.

For example, if company X has charged pension costs of £50 against its profits, resulting in profit after the charge of £200, but only paid pensions in cash of £10, then the tax charge will be based on taxable profits of £240. At a rate of 33% this tax is £79 resulting in profits after tax of £121. If deferred tax using the full provision method was provided on these pension costs then profit after tax would be £134, £13 more than before. This £13 is the full provision for deferred tax on the pension provision timing difference of £40. If the partial provision method of deferred tax was used for these timing differences on pensions then the profit declared would be somewhere between £121 and £134. The partial provision method for deferred taxation may then result in there being a build up of pension liabilities without a corresponding deferred tax adjustment.

The amendment to SSAP 15 permitted companies to adopt either full or partial provision for deferred tax in relation to costs associated with pensions and post-retirement health care costs. All other deferred tax adjustments continued to require partial provision.

What was a suitable logic for capital allowances and other timing differences was not it appears suitable logic for post-retirement costs! Was this because of their (post-retirement costs) impact on the P&L account and balance sheet, we wonder? Is it really feasible to argue for partial provision in one circumstance, but full provision in another?

The future of deferred tax

The area of deferred tax remains controversial and the problems have not yet been resolved. In March 1995 the ASB issued a discussion document on the subject suggesting that full provision is the preferred method of accounting for deferred taxation.

The discussion paper explored again the three methods of providing for deferred tax: flow-through, full provision and partial provision. It argued the case for full provision in that:

- it is consistent with international and USA standards
- it is based on the position of the entity at the balance sheet date, not on an assessment of future transactions, but acknowledges that it can give rise to a deferred tax liability that may not become payable.

However, this non-payment will be due to future transactions not past. This is consistent with the ASB's definition of a liability in its statement of accounting principles – an obligation to transfer economic benefits as a result of past transactions or events.

We can also argue the case for partial provision. As partial provision provides for the probable obligation to transfer economic benefits then this is the liability that should be shown. Any other probable, possible or remote deferred tax provision should then be dealt with using SSAP 18 accounting for contingencies.

The discussion paper suggested that the apparent overstatement of the deferred taxation liability could be dealt with by the use of discounting. A further major complication for consideration.

FRED 19 deferred tax

In August 1999 the ASB issued FRED 19 based upon the replies it received to the discussion paper. In summary FRED 19 requires:

- Full provision for deferred tax

- Deferred tax to be assessed using tax rates enacted or substantially enacted (this follows FRS 16 and is a variant of the liability method discussed earlier)
- Deferred tax to be discounted if the effect of discounting is material.

Discounting is explained in an appendix to the FRED but the subject is controversial and the choice of discount rate is subjective. The use of discounting also makes the deferred tax provision more difficult to calculate and explain to the user. Given understandability is one of the qualities of financial information required by the Statement of Principles discounting may not have full support from the respondents to the FRED. The FRED acknowledges this controversy by identifying those sections that would not be included in an FRS if discounting was not supported. At least the FRED 'rejects the possibility of permitting discounting without requiring it because the option would make the results of different entities less comparable'. (para. 85 appendix V)

Summary

Within this chapter we have considered some problem areas of accounting for taxation. These are:

1 the accounting treatment of tax under the new tax regime
2 transitional arrangements from old to new tax required
3 the accounting treatment of deferred taxation.

We have investigated the SSAP and FRS requirements in respect of these problem areas and noted the variety of answers that are used in company financial reports. We leave you with the question 'Does the required accounting treatment of taxation in published financial reports lead to a true and fair view?'

FRS 19 deferred tax

Introduction

FRS 19 Deferred Tax was published by the ASB in December 2000 just as this book was in press. The following paragraphs cover the main point of the FRS which is based on FRED 19. FRS 19 also supersedes SSAP 15 for those accounting periods ending on or after 23 January 2002.

Discounting

FRS 19 has made several changes from FRED 19 the most interesting of these being in the area of discounting. The FRED stated that it 'rejected the possibility of permitting discounting without requiring it because the option would make the results of different entities less comparable'. The ASB seem to have changed their minds in respect of comparability as discounting is now made optional as paragraph 42 clearly states: 'Reporting entities are permitted but not required to discount deferred tax assets and liabilities to reflect the time value of money.'

It appears their decision in this area is based on the fact that as long as full disclosure is given in the accounts in respect of the effect of the discounting on the financial statements then there would not be a serious loss of comparability if not all entities discounted deferred tax.

The FRS also states that the unwinding of the discounting rate should be shown under the deferred tax charge not, as first suggested in the FRED, as a finance cost. It is worth noting here that the unwinding of discounting in relation to provisions and liabilities (see Chapter 23, p. 477) *is* shown as part of financing costs. The ASB justify this change, and the apparent lack of consistency with FRS 12, as follows: 'However, even though the unwinding of the discount on a deferred tax liability(or asset) can be regarded in principle as a financing item, the FRS does not require it to be shown as part of the financing section in the profit and loss account. The reason is that profit and loss account formats require all of the tax consequences of pre-tax profits to be shown separately, below the subtotal "profits on ordinary activities before taxation." The unwinding of a discount on a deferred tax balance, whether viewed conceptually as part of the tax expense or as a finance item, is not part of profits before tax. Hence, it is shown after the subtotal of profits before tax.'

Example 1 (adapted from appendix 1 FRS 19)

Given that the original cost of fixed assets of an entity is £3300, depreciation to date £1000 and capital allowances to date on fixed assets £2186 calculate the deferred tax provision required under FRS 19.

Answer 1
Full provision for deferred tax is required which is calculated as

$$30\% \times (2186 - 1000) = £356.$$

Example 2

Further to the information given in Example 1 the following is available. It is assumed that the reversal of timing differences will occur as follows and that government bond post tax rates are as per column 4.

Year	Reversal of Timing difference	Deferred tax liability (at 30%)	Gov. bond post tax rate (%)
col. 1	col. 2	col. 3	col. 4
1	22	7	4.7
2	91	27	4.4
3	143	43	4.2
4	207	62	4.0
5	131	39	3.9
6	148	44	3.8
7	186	56	3.8
8	89	27	3.7
9	117	35	3.7
10	52	16	3.7
	1186	356	

Calculate the discounted deferred tax provision required under FRS 19.

Answer 2
FRS 19 requires us to discount at a rate equivalent to the post tax yields to maturity that could be obtained at the balance sheet date on government bonds with maturity dates, and in currencies similar to those of deferred tax assets and liabilities. These we will assume

are those given in column 4 above. When discounted the deferred tax liability becomes £290 (i.e. $7/(1.047)^1 + 27/(1.044)^2 + 43/(1.042)^3 + 62/(1.04)^4$, etc.) The liability has in fact been discounted by £66.

Unwinding of the discounting

The FRS requires us to show, in the performance statement, 'changes in the amount of discount deducted in arriving at the deferred tax balance' (para. 60(a)(ii)) and in the balance sheet 'the impact of discounting on and discounted amount of the deferred tax balance' (para. 61(b)). Thus we need to be able to calculate the unwinding of the discounting. Using the example above and discounting the deferred tax liabilities from the end of year 1 onwards gives a discounted deferred tax figure of £295 compared to an undiscounted figure of £349, a discounting effect of £54. Comparing this with the discounting effect at year 0 of £66 identifies an unwinding of £12. Another way to calculate this unwinding is to multiply the discounted deferred tax liabilities by the bond rate again.

Year	Discounted deferred tax	Bond rate %	unwinding
col. 1	col. 2	col. 3	col. 3 × co. 2
1	7	4.7	0.3
2	25	4.4	1.1
3	38	4.2	1.6
4	53	4.0	2.2
5	33	3.9	1.3
6	35	3.8	1.3
7	43	3.8	1.6
8	20	3.7	0.8
9	25	3.7	0.9
10	11	3.7	0.4
	290		11.5

This £12 will be shown as an increase to the deferred tax provision due to the unwinding of the discounting.

FRS 19 requirements

The standard requires full provision to be made for deferred tax assets and liabilities arising from timing differences between the recognition of gains and losses in the financial statements and their recognition in a tax computation. It clearly states in the FRS that transactions or events that give the entity an obligation to pay more or less tax in the future must have occurred by the balance sheet date and this is in accordance with the ASB's definition of an asset or liability.

The FRS requires deferred tax to be recognized on timing differences attributable to:

- accelerated capital allowances
- accruals for pension costs and other post-retirement benefits that will be deductible for tax purposes only when paid
- elimination of unrealised intragroup profits on consolidation
- unrelieved tax losses

- other sources of short-term timing differences

and prohibits the recognition of deferred tax on timing differences arising when:

- a fixed asset is revalued without there being any commitment to sell the asset
- the gain on sale of an asset is rolled over into replacement assets
- the remittance of a subsidiary, associate or joint venture's earnings would cause tax to be payable, but no commitment has been made to the remittance of the earnings. (FRS 19 Summary para. (b)(a and b))

There is one interesting exception to the above requirements and that is:

(c) As an exception to the general requirement not to recognise deferred tax on revaluation gains and losses, the FRS requires deferred tax to be recognised when assets are continuously revalued to fair value, with changes in fair value being recognised in the profit and loss account. (FRS 19 Summary para.(c))

Deferred tax presentation and disclosure in financial statements

Deferred tax liabilities are required to be shown as provisions for liabilities and charges and deferred tax assets as debtors. The exact requirements in respect of disclosure are quoted below and we also show the disclosure illustration included in Appendix 11 to the FRS.

60 The notes to the financial statements should disclose the amount of deferred tax charged or credited within:
  (a) tax on ordinary activities in the profit and loss account, separately disclosing material components, including those attributable to:
      (i) changes in deferred tax balances (before discounting, where applicable) arising from:
        - the origination and reversal of timing differences;
        - changes in tax rates and laws; and
        - adjustments to the estimated recoverable amount of deferred tax assets arising in previous periods.
      (ii) where applicable, changes in the amounts of discount deducted in arriving at the deferred tax balance.
  (b) tax charged or credited directly in the statement of total recognised gains and losses for the period, separately disclosing material components, including those listed in (a) above.

61 The financial statements should disclose:
  (a) the total deferred tax balance (before discounting, where applicable), showing the amount recognised for each significant type of timing difference separately;
  (b) the impact of discounting on, and the discounted amount of, the deferred tax balance; and
  (c) the movement between the opening and closing net deferred tax balance, analysing separately:
      (i) the amount charged or credited in the profit and loss account for the period;

      (**ii**) the amount charged or credited directly in the statement of total recognised gains and losses for the period; and

      (**iii**) movements arising from the acquisition or disposal of businesses.

62 The financial statements should disclose the amount of a deferred tax asset and the nature of the evidence supporting its recognition if:

    (**a**) the recoverability of the deferred tax asset is dependent on future taxable profits in excess of those arising from the reversal of deferred tax liabilities; and

    (**b**) the reporting entity has suffered a loss in either the current or preceding period in the tax jurisdiction to which the deferred tax asset relates.

1 Tax on profit on ordinary activities
(a) Analysis of charge in period

	200Y		200X	
	£m	£m	£m	£m
Current tax:				
UK corporation tax on profits of the period	**40**		26	
Adjustments in respect of previous periods	**4**		(6)	
		44		20
Foreign tax		**12**		16
Total current tax (note 1(b))		**56**		36
Deferred tax:				
Origination and reversal of timing differences	**67**		60	
Effect of increased tax rate on opening liability	**12**		–	
Increase in discount	**(14)**		(33)	
Total deferred tax (note 2)		**65**		27
Tax on profit on ordinary activities		**121**		63

(b) Factors affecting tax charge for period

The tax assessed for the period is lower than the standard rate of corporation tax in the UK (31 per cent). The differences are explained below:

	200Y	200X
	£m	£m
Profit on ordinary activities before tax	**361**	327
Profit on ordinary activities multiplied by standard rate of corporation tax in the UK of 31% (200X: 30%)	**112**	98
Effects of:		
Expenses not deductible for tax purposes (primarily goodwill amortisation)	**22**	10
Capital allowances for period in excess of depreciation	**(58)**	(54)
Utilisation of tax losses	**(17)**	(18)
Rollover relief on profit on disposal of property	**(10)**	–
Higher tax rates on overseas earnings	**3**	6
Adjustments to tax charge in respect of previous periods	**4**	(6)
Current tax charge for period (note 1(a))	**56**	36

2 Provision for deferred tax

	31.12.200Y	21.12.200X
	£m	£m
Accelerated capital allowances	**426**	356
Tax losses carried forward	**–**	(9)
Undiscounted provision for deferred tax	**426**	347
Discount	**(80)**	(66)
Discounted provision for deferred tax	**346**	281
Provision at start of period	**281**	
Deferred tax charge in profit and loss account for period (note 1)	**65**	
Provision at end of period	**346**	

Summary

FRS 19 requires:

- full provisioning for deferred tax
- deferred tax to be assessed using tax rates enacted or substantially enacted by the balance sheet date.

In addition reporting entities are permitted but not required to discount deferred tax assets and liabilities to reflect the time value of money. If discounting is adopted as a policy then all deferred tax balances must be discounted where the impact of discounting is material.

Exercises

1 Outline the major arguments in favour of always providing for deferred tax where the amounts would be material.
2 Outline the major arguments in favour of only providing for deferred tax when 'it is probable that a liability will crystallize' (SSAP 15, paragraph 24). Are there any difficulties with this approach?
3 Explain and distinguish between:
   (a) the flow-through approach
   (b) full deferral
   (c) partial deferral.
4 Explain and distinguish between:
   (a) the deferral method
   (b) the liability method.
   Do you agree with the choice made by the ASC?
5 'Comparability requires that either all companies provide in full for deferred tax, or that it is always ignored. Therefore SSAP 15 and the concept of partial deferral, must be unacceptable.' Consider.
6 Draft a memorandum to your client, a non-accountant, outlining what deferred tax is and why there are problems in suggesting the appropriate treatment.

7 With regard to SSAP 15 'Accounting for Deferred Taxation':
   (a) Under what circumstances may a company assume that timing differences will not reverse and how might the existence of these circumstances be substantiated? (8 marks)
   (b) What additional information must be disclosed in a note to the accounts with regard to deferred taxation? (4 marks)
   (c) Comment on the possible justification for a note such as that in (b) above. (8 marks)
   (20 marks)
   (ACCA)

8 In connection with SSAP 15 'Accounting for Deferred Taxation':
   (a) Write a description of accounting for deferred taxation which includes all of the main items in the standard. The description should be appropriate for inclusion in the statement of accounting policies in a company's annual financial report, in accordance with SSAP 2 'Disclosure of Accounting Policies'. (6 marks)
   (b) Prepare an example of a note on deferred taxation which includes all of the main items in the standard. The note should be appropriate for inclusion in a company's financial statements and you should use your own figures to illustrate your answer. (You need not show comparative figures and you may assume that the company is not part of a group of companies.) (8 marks)
   (c) Do you consider that the liability method adopts a balance sheet rather than a profit and loss account perspective? Contrast this with the deferral method. State your reasons. (6 marks)
   (20 marks)
   (ACCA)

9 At 31 October 1992 Dex Ltd had claimed capital allowances in excess of depreciation by £250 000. The company has no deferred tax balance but the director asks the accountant to check this position given the projections for capital allowances and depreciation for the next four years as follows (corporation tax rate 50%):
   31.10.93 £70 000 (O), 31.10.94 £80 000 (O), 31.10.95 £20 000 (O), 31.10.96 £50 000 (R).
   (corporate tax rate 50%.)

10 You, the trainee accountant, are having to prepare the draft entries for deferred tax for the 30 September 1992 year-end accounts. The following information is available to you.
   As at 30 September 1992 excess capital allowances over depreciation amounted to £1.696 million. Estimates for the next four years are as follows:

	year-ended 30.9.XX			
	1993	1994	1995	1996
	£000	£000	£000	£000
Capital allowances	312	328	416	600
Depreciation	584	605	626	592

Thereafter capital allowances are expected to exceed depreciation. Show all the entries relating to deferred tax **required for the year-end accounts** 30 September 1992. Tax rate 50%.

11 The draft accounts of Orchaos plc have been prepared as at 31 December 1992 and showed a profit of £28 million.
   The fixed assets had a NBV of £136.6 million and consisted of offices, new plant and equipment. The offices had been acquired on 1 January 1992 under a twenty-year lease for £30 million. The new plant had been acquired on 1 January 1992 for £10 million and

the company had received a government grant of £2.5 million which it has credited to the plant fixed asset account. The equipment had been acquired in earlier years at a cost of £130 million and had a written-down value of £102.9 million at 31 December 1992. The company planned to undertake substantial further investment in fixed assets in 1997.

Capital allowances of £35.4 million have been allowed. The offices did not qualify for any tax allowances. The new plant had an estimated useful life of 25 years and qualified for a 25% writing-down allowance on the net cost.

The company prepared the following estimates for the four years ended 31 December 1996:

year-ended 31 December	Depreciation	Capital allowances
	£m	£m
1993	11.0	18.92
1994	19.8	12.32
1995	19.8	10.12
1996	17.6	14.84

Assume a corporation tax rate of 35%.

Required:

(a) Explain

  (i) the extent to which tax deferred or accelerated by the effect of timing differences should be accounted for; and

  (ii) the procedure for determining the amount to be quantified.

(6 marks)

(b) (i) Prepare the balance sheet entry for Orchaos plc as at 31 December 1992 for deferred taxation to comply with the provisions of SSAP 15 'Accounting for Deferred Taxation'

  (ii) explain the effect on the deferred tax computation for Orchaos plc as at 31 December 1992 if the company has suffered its first loss following a year in which it had incurred substantial costs in relocating with the result that the accounts showed a loss adjusted for tax purposes of £28 million. (14 marks)

(c) Assuming that the new plant attracted a 25% writing-down allowance on the full cost of £10 million:

  (i) explain how this would affect the calculation of deferred tax; and

  (ii) calculate the tax effect of the timing difference as at 31 December 1992. (4 marks)

(d) Critically discuss the statement that SSAP 15 'Deferred Taxation' does not necessarily result in the accounts of different companies in the same industry being comparable. (6 marks)

(30 marks)

(ACCA)

12 You are the management accountant of Construct Ltd, a private company which has as its main business activity the construction of houses for sale in the domestic sector. For its year ended 31 December 1998, the company charged depreciation of £700 000 and claimed capital allowances of £600 000. For the next five years, the capital allowances and depreciation for Construct Ltd are expected to be as follows:

	Capital Allowances	Depreciation
Year ending	£000	£000
31 December 1999	500	700
31 December 2000	450	720
31 December 2001	600	740
31 December 2002	800	780
31 December 2003	950	820

At 1 January 1998, the next book value of fixed assets which qualified for capital allowances exceeded their tax written-down value by £1.4 million. Construct Ltd follows the provisions of SSAP 15 – *Accounting for deferred tax* – and accordingly a provision for deferred tax of £225 000 was made in the 1997 financial statements. The rate of corporation tax which is appropriate for Construct Ltd is 31%.

Requirements:

(a) **Calculate the charge or credit to the profit and loss account for deferred tax for the year ended 31 December 1998 and the balance on the deferred tax account at 31 December 1998**

    (i) **under the accounting policy followed by Construct Ltd;** (6 marks)

    (ii) **under the full provision method.** (4 marks)

(b) **Explain why the Accounting Standards Board is currently reviewing SSAP 15 and may well produce a revised Financial Reporting Standard which requires the use of the full provision method.** (10 marks)

(20 marks)

CIMA (9) MAY 99

22

Pensions costs (SSAP 24, FRS 17)

After reading this chapter you should be able to:
- explain the different types of pension schemes
- explain the problems associated with accounting for pension costs
- describe the SSAP 24 'Accounting for Pension Costs' requirements
- describe the Companies Act requirements in relation to pension costs
- describe the FRS 17 'Retirement Benefits' requirements
- outline the current recommendations in relation to pension scheme accounts
- analyse the current discussion in respect of pension costs in employer financial statements.

Introduction

Pensions are, of course, amounts paid to employees after they have retired from active work. In essence, an agreement exists that on retirement an employee will receive regular payments until death. The amount of these payments per year will be related to the earnings of the employee whilst in work. The number of years for which the pension will actually be paid is obviously in the lap of the gods.

SSAP 24 'Accounting for Pension Costs' was issued in May 1988 and as the SSAP states accounting for pension costs is important as regards the effect on reported results.

1 The provision of a pension is part of the remuneration package of many employees. Pension costs form a significant proportion of total payroll costs and they give rise to special problems of estimation and of allocation between accounting periods. Accordingly, it is important that standard accounting practice exists concerning the recognition of such costs in the employers' financial statements. This Statement deals with the accounting for, and the disclosure of, pension costs and commitments in the financial statements of enterprises that have pension arrangements for the provision of retirement benefits for their employees.

Types of pension schemes

Pension schemes can take a variety of different forms; they can be either funded or unfunded, defined contribution or defined benefit.

Funded or unfunded

An unfunded pension scheme is where the employer business itself undertakes to pay the pensions directly from its own resources as they fall due. With a funded scheme resources are accumulated in a separate legal entity (i.e. there is a separate fund). This separate fund may be a unique creation for the one employer, or it may be operated by a specialist assurance company running many such schemes. The two types of scheme have obvious differences in terms of financial management and in terms of the book-keeping entries. With a funded scheme money leaves the employer over the years of the employment and goes into the external fund. With an unfunded scheme no pensions money leaves the employer at all until the employment has ceased and the actual pension begins to be paid. However, the accounting problem is more concerned with what to do with the debits than with what to do with the credits. The credit may be to cash (with a funded scheme, common in the UK) or to a provision account (with an unfunded scheme, common in a number of continental European countries for example).

The SSAP dismisses the funding distinction rapidly:

> **65** A *funded scheme* is a pension scheme where the future liabilities for benefits are provided for by the accumulation of assets held externally to the employing company's business.
>
> **5** Pension schemes may also be classified by the way in which they are financed, namely funded schemes or schemes where the benefits are paid directly by the employer. The same accounting principles apply to both types of scheme.

Defined contribution or benefit

Another distinction between different types of pension scheme relates to the way in which the legal obligations under the scheme are defined. In the simplest of terms a pension scheme can be envisaged as a 'pot'. Money is put into the pot (contributions) and money is taken out of the pot (pensions). A pension scheme can be defined in terms of what goes into the pot or it can be defined in terms of what comes out of it. More formally we can define the contributions, and the benefits will in the long run be varied according to what is available in the pot. Or we can define the benefits per period to be paid from the pot and the contributions are varied as necessary to ensure that those benefits can be paid:

> **3** Pension schemes to which this Statement applies may basically be divided into defined contribution schemes and defined benefit schemes. In a defined contribution scheme, the employer will normally discharge his obligation by making agreed contributions to a pension scheme and the benefits paid will depend upon the funds available from these contributions and investment earnings thereon. The cost to the employer can, therefore, be measured with reasonable certainty. A number of pension schemes in the United Kingdom and Ireland, including many smaller ones, are defined contribution schemes.
>
> **4** In a defined benefit scheme, however, the benefits to be paid will usually depend upon either the average pay of the employee during his or her career or, more typically, the final pay of the employee. In these circumstances, it is impossible to be certain in advance that the contributions to the pension

scheme, together with the investment return thereon, will equal the benefits to be paid. The employer may have a legal obligation to provide any unforeseen shortfalls in funds or, if not, may find it necessary to meet the shortfall in the interests of maintaining good employee relations. Conversely, if a surplus arises the employer may be entitled to a refund of, or reduction in, contributions paid into the pension scheme. Thus, in this type of scheme the employer's commitment is generally more open than with defined contribution schemes and the final cost is subject to considerable uncertainty. The larger UK and Irish schemes are generally of the defined benefit kind and these cover the great majority of members of schemes.

Problems

Evaluation of cost

The first difficulty is how to evaluate the cost associated with an agreement to pay a regular sum of money until someone's totally unknown date of death. For an individual this is a non-starter, but collectively and using the laws of averaging it is possible to do so within acceptable limits. This is the job of 'actuarial' experts and forms the basis of the insurance and pensions 'industry'. The use of statistical techniques based on projections of historic data produces adequate approximations. This aspect of the pensions problem is not addressed by SSAP 24. It is not an accounting problem, any more than the valuation of a building is itself an accounting problem.

Matching principle

The accounting problems are quite large enough by themselves. The basic matching principle requires that the costs associated with an employee should be matched in and over the accounting periods which benefit from his or her employment. This means that the entire expense of providing an employee with a pension should have been charged before the day of retirement.

It is naturally with defined benefit schemes, the common UK type, that the actuarial difficulties and uncertainties arise:

8 In defined benefit schemes, the choice of assumptions and the choice of valuation method can each have a major effect on the contribution rate calculated at each valuation. The choice of assumptions can be as significant as the choice of method.

9 The assumptions which the actuary must make in carrying out his valuation will be about matters such as future rates of inflation and pay increases, increases to pensions in payment, earnings on investments, the number of employees joining the scheme, the age profile of employees and the probability that employees will die or leave the company's employment before they reach retiring age. The actuary will view the assumptions as a whole; he will make assumptions which are mutually compatible, in the knowledge that, if experience departs from the assumptions made, the effects of such departures may well be offsetting, notably in the case of investment yields and increases in prices and earnings.

12   The funding methods developed by actuaries are designed to build up assets in a prudent and controlled manner in advance of the retirement of the members of the scheme, in order that the obligations of the scheme may be met without undue distortion of the employer's cash flow. The actuary's main concern is that the present and estimated future contribution levels should be at least sufficient to provide security for the payment of the promised benefits.

13   A range of actuarial methods is available for determining the level of contributions needed to meet the liabilities of the pension scheme. Some methods will tend to lead to higher levels of funding in the scheme than others.

14   In practice, it is common for actuaries to aim at a level contribution rate as a proportion of pensionable pay in respect of current service. The contribution rate thus determined depends on the particular actuarial method used and the assumption made regarding new entrants to the scheme. In broad terms, in projecting a stable contribution rate, accrued benefits methods rely on the assumption that the flow of new entrants will be such as to preserve the existing average age of the work-force; prospective benefits methods, on the other hand, normally look only to the existing work-force and seek a contribution rate that will remain stable for that group despite its increasing age profile until the last member retires or leaves. In a mature scheme both types of method may in practice achieve stable contribution rates but the size of the fund under a prospective benefits method will tend to be larger than under an accrued benefits method because it is intended to cover the ageing of the existing work-force.

There are obvious difficulties in applying the accruals convention to a situation so fraught with uncertainty as the above. Until recently many companies simply did not attempt the problem. Pension costs were often accounted for on a cash basis. This means that the whole matching problem is ignored and any payments relating to pensions are simply charged to P&L accounts as they fall due. This approach is no longer acceptable.

Activity 1

Well plc operate a funded defined benefit pension scheme. The company makes a contribution to the scheme of 6% of its annual payroll in any one year. In 1995 a formal actuarial valuation of the scheme takes place and a shortfall of £4.5 million is identified. This shortfall is to be made good in the next three years, commencing 1995 in equal instalments. The annual payroll and profit before pension costs for the company is as follows:

	Payroll £m	Profit £m
1992	16.7	2
1993	17.1	2.3
1994	17.3	2.3
1995	17.4	2.4

and profits and payroll for the next three years are estimated to increase by 2% and 1% per annum.

If pension costs were accounted for as cash is paid to the scheme, show the effect on profits.

Activity 1 feedback

The activity is intended to show the effect on profits of accounting for pension costs on a cash basis:

	Profit before pensions £m	Regular pension cost £m	Additional payment or shortfall £m	Profit after pensions £m
1992	2	1		1
1993	2.3	1.03		1.27
1994	2.3	1.04		1.26
1995	2.4	1.04	1.5	(0.14)
1996	2.45	1.05	1.5	(0.1)
1997	2.50	1.06	1.5	(0.06)
1998	2.55	1.075	—	1.475

The above activity demonstrates the drastic effect that pension costs can have on a company's profit situation if these pension costs are accounted for on a cash basis. An equally dramatic effect can occur if surpluses on pension schemes are accounted for in the same way. When an actuary values a pension scheme and finds it in surplus then a 'pension holiday' is normally taken by the employer, i.e. no regular contributions are made by the employer to the scheme until the surplus is depleted.

SSAP 24 requirements

The accounting of pension costs on a cash basis is, of course, not in accordance with the matching principle and SSAP 24 states:

16 From the point of view of the employee a pension may be regarded as deferred remuneration; from the point of view of the employer it is part of the cost incurred in obtaining the employee's services. The accounting objective therefore requires the employer to recognise the cost of providing pensions on a systematic and rational basis over the period during which he benefits from the employees' services. Many companies have, until now, simply charged the contributions payable to the pension scheme as the pension cost in each accounting period. In future, in order to comply with this Statement, it will be necessary to consider whether the funding plan provides a satisfactory basis for allocating the pension cost to particular accounting periods.

17 In the case of a defined contribution scheme the employer's obligation at any time is restricted to the amount of the contributions payable to date. The pension cost is, therefore, the amount of the contributions payable in respect of the particular accounting period.

18 The selection of the actuarial method and assumptions to be used in assessing the pension cost of a defined benefit scheme is a matter of judgement for the actuary in consultation with his client, taking account of the circumstances of the specific company and its work-force. This Statement requires that the actuarial valuation method and assumptions used for accounting pur-

poses should satisfy the accounting objective. In order that full provision may be made over the employees' service lives for the expected costs of their pensions, the effect of expected future increases in earnings, including merit increases, up to the assumed retirement date or earlier date of withdrawal or death in service, should be recognised. Account will also need to be taken of expected future increases in deferred pensions and pensions in payment where the employer has an express or implied commitment to grant such increases. The calculation of benefit levels should be based on the situation most likely to be experienced and not on a contingent event not likely to occur. The actuarial method selected should be used consistently and should be disclosed. If there is a change of method this fact should be disclosed and the effect quantified. The actuarial assumptions and the actuarial method taken as a whole should be compatible and should lead to the actuary's best estimate of the cost of providing the pension benefits promised.

19 If the funding plan does not provide a satisfactory basis for determining the pension cost charge, separate actuarial calculations will be required.

It is clear from paragraph 18 that a number of variations may have to be incorporated into the accounting treatment:

20 The total cost of pensions in a year can notionally be divided into the regular cost, which is the consistent ongoing cost recognized under the actuarial method used, and variations from the regular cost. Where a stable contribution rate for regular contributions, expressed as a percentage of pensionable earnings, has been determined, that rate will provide an acceptable basis for calculating the regular cost under the stated accounting objective so long as it makes full provision for the expected benefits over the anticipated service lives of employees.

21 Variations from the regular cost may arise from:
   (a) experience surpluses or deficiencies
   (b) the effects on the actuarial value of accrued benefits of changes in assumptions or method
   (c) retroactive changes in benefits or in conditions for membership
   (d) increases to pensions in payment or to deferred pensions for which provision has not previously been made.

These different types of variation are discussed at some length in the SSAP. The general principle is that such adjustments (whether plus or minus) should be spread over the remaining service lives (i.e. working lives) of the current employees. If the adjustment relates to those already retired then the relevant remaining service life must be zero, and the adjustment will be taken in full in the current year.

Activity 2

Using the data given in Activity 1 and given that the average remaining service life of current employees is nine years when the fund is valued, show the profits for the company in accordance with SSAP 24 up to 1998.

Activity 2 feedback

Under SSAP 24 the deficit identified of £4.5 million on the scheme, even though it is paid in cash over three years, must be accounted for over the estimated average remaining service life.

	Profit before pensions £m	Contributions £m	Charge to profits £m	Profit after pensions £m
1992	2	1	1	1
1993	2.3	1.03	1.03	1.27
1994	2.3	1.04	1.04	1.26
1995	2.4	2.54	1.54	0.86
1996	2.45	2.55	1.55	0.9
1997	2.50	2.56	1.56	0.94
1998	2.55	1.075	1.575	0.975

(Deficit of £4.5 million is charged at £0.5 million per annum, commencing in 1995.)

By matching pension costs we avoid drastic changes in profit.

The accounting objective explored

The formal accounting objective of the SSAP as a whole is stated very briefly:

> **77** The accounting objective is that the employer should recognise the expected cost of providing pensions on a systematic and rational basis over the period during which he derives benefit from the employee's services. The ways in which this is to be achieved are detailed in paragraphs 78 to 92.

It is interesting to compare this with the less formal and more explanatory paragraph 16 quoted earlier on p. 438. The first sentence in paragraph 16 refers to 'the employee's services'. The second sentence specifically related to the accounting objective refers on the other hand to 'the employees' services'. Paragraph 77 is a formal restatement of the second sentence from paragraph 16, but with the first sentence totally removed. What is the precise meaning of 'the employees' services'?

For defined contribution schemes there is no difficulty of course and the formal standard requirement is brief:

> **78** For defined contribution schemes the charge against profits should be the amount of contributions payable to the pension scheme in respect of the accounting period.

For defined benefit schemes both the situation and the standard requirements are more complicated:

> **79** For defined benefit schemes the pension cost should be calculated using actuarial valuation methods which are consistent with the requirements of this Statement. The actuarial assumptions and method, taken as a whole, should be compatible and should lead to the actuary's best estimate of the cost of

providing the pension benefits promised. The method of providing for expected pension costs over the service lives of employees in the scheme should be such that the regular pension cost is a substantially level percentage of the current and expected future pensionable payroll in the light of the current actuarial assumptions.

80 Subject to the provisions of paragraphs 81 to 83, variations from the regular cost should be allocated over the expected remaining service lives of current employees in the scheme. A period representing the average remaining service lives may be used if desired.

81 The provisions of paragraph 80 should not be applied where, and to the extent that, a significant change in the normal level of contributions occurs because contributions are adjusted to eliminate a surplus or deficiency resulting from a significant reduction in the number of employees covered by the enterprise's pension arrangements. Except where such treatment would be inconsistent with SSAP 6 in relation to an extraordinary item, any reduction in contributions arising in these circumstances should be recognised as it occurs. Amounts receivable may not be anticipated; for example, the full effect of a contribution holiday should not be recognised at the outset of the holiday, but rather spread over its duration.

82 In strictly limited circumstances prudence may require that a material deficit be recognised over a period shorter than the expected remaining service lives of current employees in the scheme. Such circumstances are limited to those where a major event or transaction has occurred which has not been allowed for in the actuarial assumptions, is outside the normal scope of those assumptions and has necessitated the payment of significant additional contributions to the pension scheme.

83 Where a refund that is subject to deduction of tax in accordance with the provisions of the UK Finance Act 1986, or equivalent legislation, is made to the employer, the enterprise may depart from the requirements of paragraph 80 and account for the surplus or deficiency in the period in which the refund occurs.

Note in particular the statement in paragraph 79 that refers to pension costs (plural) over the service lives (plural) of employees in the scheme (plural), and to a substantially level percentage of the current *and expected future* payroll (emphasis added). Some have argued that this wording allows for expected changes in the pension scheme, such as an expected future influx of younger members, to be taken into account in calculating this year's charge. The alternative intended meaning is that the charge should be based on expectations of future happenings affecting the current members of the pension scheme. One would assume that the latter was intended, for two reasons: first, because the singular employee in the first sentence of paragraph 16 implies so and secondly, because it seems difficult to argue that the matching principle (this year's costs against this year's benefits) is consistent with allowing events with no past or present costs or past or present benefits to affect current results. But the wording of paragraphs 77 and 79 certainly allows either interpretation. Clarity of punctuation is just as important as clarity of thought!

The essence of paragraphs 80–83 is simple enough. Adjustments, whether representing extra costs or reductions in costs, should be spread forward over the entire period affected as regards the effect on reported profits. Notice the reluctance to allow prudence great weight in paragraph 82.

'One-off' and voluntary (*ex gratia*) payments and increases, however, do need to be dealt with immediately:

> **84**   Where *ex gratia* pensions are granted the capital cost, to the extent not covered by a surplus, should be recognised in the profit and loss account in the accounting period in which they are granted.

> **85**   Where allowance for discretionary or *ex gratia* increases in pensions is not made in the actuarial assumptions, the capital cost of such increases should, to the extent not covered by a surplus, be recognised in the profit and loss account in the accounting period in which they are initially granted.

Activity 3

State the accounting treatment in accordance with SSAP 24 for the following:

1 A pension scheme, where regular contributions of £2 million were made by the employer, was found on actuarial valuation to be in deficit to the amount of £0.3 million representing *ex gratia* pensions to six employees who had never joined the pension scheme.
2 A significant number of employees are made redundant in one year resulting in a fall in regular contributions to be made to the pension scheme.

Activity 3 feedback

1 The deficit of £0.3 million is due entirely to an *ex gratia* payment and therefore this should be accounted for in the year in question not spread over average remaining life – paragraph 84.
2 If the redundancies are not due to an extraordinary event then the change in regular contribution should be recognized as it occurs and not spread over average remaining life – paragraph 81.

Balance sheet effects of matching pension costs

It inevitably follows that, because we are dealing with the debits on a 'systematic and rational basis', whatever the amounts actually payable by the employer in the year, there will be balances left over – in effect accruals and prepayments.

> **86**   If the cumulative pension cost recognised in the profit and loss account has not been completely discharged by payment of contributions or directly paid pensions, the excess should be shown as a net pension provision. Similarly, any excess of contributions paid or directly paid pensions over the cumulative pension cost should be shown as a prepayment.

Activity 4

From the data in Activity 2 identify the balance sheet effect of accounting for pension costs in accordance with SSAP 24.

Activity 4 feedback

The balance sheet effect is that an accrual for pension costs will occur of the cumulative difference between contributions and charges to profit as follows. (This could easily be seen by drawing up double entry accounts.)

	Contributions	*Charge to P&L*	*Cumulative differences – prepayment*
	£m	*£m*	*£m*
1995	2.54	1.54	1
1996	2.55	1.55	2
1997	2.56	1.56	3
1998	1.075	1.575	2.5

The accrual will gradually decrease to zero over the estimate of average remaining life. In this case by 2003.

Users of accounts need to be aware of the effects on balance sheet assets and liabilities and thereby key ratios of the accounting regulations in respect of surpluses and deficits on pension funds. Note that surpluses will create prepayments and deficits accruals.

Activity 5

Max plc has a funded defined benefit scheme to which a regular contribution of £5 million is made. An actuarial valuation of the fund identifies a surplus of £26 million and Max is recommended by the actuary to take a pension holiday for four years and thereafter for three years reduce the contribution to £3 million. The average remaining service life of current employees is ten years.

Show the charge to the P&L account, and the effect on the balance sheet, over the relevant years, in accounting for the above in accordance with SSAP 24.

Activity 5 feedback

The surplus of £26 million must be spread over the average remaining life of ten years, i.e. £2.6 million per annum.

Year	*Regular contribution*	*Surplus variation*	*Total contribution*	*Charge to P&L*	*Provision balance sheet*
1	5	(5)	–	2.4	2.4
2	5	(5)	–	2.4	4.8
3	5	(5)	–	2.4	7.2
4	5	(5)	–	2.4	9.6
5	5	(2)	3	2.4	9
6	5	(2)	3	2.4	8.4
7	5	(2)	3	2.4	7.8
8	5	–	5	2.4	5.2
9	5	–	5	2.4	2.6
10	5	–	5	2.4	–
	50	26	24	24	

Scope and disclosure requirements

The scope and applicability of SSAP 24 is wide:

73 This Statement applies where the employer has a legal or contractual commitment under a pension scheme or one implicit in the employer's actions, to provide, or contribute to, pensions for his employees. It also addresses discretionary and ex gratia increases in pensions and ex gratia pensions. The same principles apply irrespective of whether the scheme is funded or unfunded.

74 This Statement applies to defined contribution schemes and defined benefit schemes.

75 Although this Statement primarily addresses pensions, its principles may be equally applicable to the cost of providing other post-retirement benefits.

76 This Statement does not apply to either state social security contributions or redundancy payments.

With an area like pensions, with its considerable uncertainty and scope both for different methods and for different assumptions within those methods, it is particularly important for a full understanding of the accounts that there is very full disclosure of what has been done. There is less to disclose in the case of a defined contribution scheme:

87 The following disclosures should be made in respect of a defined contribution scheme:

(a) the nature of the scheme (i.e. defined contribution)

(b) the accounting policy

(c) the pension cost charge for the period

(d) any outstanding or prepaid contributions at the balance sheet date.

However, with a defined benefit scheme the disclosure requirements of SSAP 24 are long and detailed:

88 The following disclosures should be made in respect of a defined benefit scheme:

(a) the nature of the scheme (i.e. defined benefit)

(b) whether it is funded or unfunded

(c) the accounting policy and, if different, the funding policy

(d) whether the pension cost and provision (or asset) are assessed in accordance with the advice of a professionally qualified actuary and, if so, the date of the most recent formal actuarial valuation or later formal review used for this purpose. If the actuary is an employee or officer of the reporting company, or of the group of which it is a member, this fact should be disclosed

(e) the pension cost charge for the period together with explanations of significant changes in the charge compared to that in the previous accounting period

(f) any provisions or prepayments in the balance sheet resulting from a difference between the amounts recognised as cost and the amounts funded or paid directly

    (**g**) the amount of any deficiency on a current funding level basis, indicating the action, if any, being taken to deal with it in the current and future accounting periods

    (**h**) an outline of the results of the most recent formal actuarial valuation or later formal review of the scheme on an ongoing basis.
This should include disclosure of:
- (**i**) the actuarial method used and a brief description of the main actuarial assumptions
- (**ii**) the market value of scheme assets at the date of their valuation or review
- (**iii**) the level of funding expressed in percentage terms
- (**iv**) comments on any material actuarial surplus or deficiency indicated by (**iii**) above

    (**i**) any commitment to make additional payments over a limited number of years

    (**j**) the accounting treatment adopted in respect of a refund made in accordance with the provisions of paragraph 83 where a credit appears in the financial statements in relation to it

    (**k**) details of the expected effects on future costs of any material changes in the group's and/or company's pension arrangements.

89 Where a company or group has more than one pension scheme disclosure should be made on a combined basis, unless disclosure of information about individual schemes is necessary for a proper understanding of the accounts. For the purposes of paragraph 88(g) above, however, a current funding level basis deficiency in one scheme should not be set off against a surplus in another.

As far as the UK is concerned (including foreign subsidiaries as consolidated) the SSAP formally applies in respect of accounting periods beginning on or after 1 July 1988.

Deferred taxation

The accrual or prepayment which appears in the balance sheet of an entity, as described in Activities 4 and 5, is the cumulative timing difference at that point in time between the cash paid as contributions and the charge made to the P&L account using the matching concept. Companies are able to charge pension cash payments as an expense in the calculation of taxable profits. The fact that the accounting profit recognizes pension costs on a matched basis therefore gives rise to this timing difference being recognized under SSAP 15 'Accounting for Deferred Tax'.

SSAP 15 requires the recognition of deferred tax on a partial liability method, that is we need to identify whether the liability will crystallize in the future. The assessment of a deficit or surplus on the pension fund at a year-end, described in paragraph 79 of SSAP 24, is based on the provision of pension benefits promised to date. It does not take into account the possible future beneficiaries of the scheme who do not currently exist. The partial liability method of determining deferred tax requires us to look into the future and see if the timing difference will reverse or not – an assessment of future transactions. You saw this occurring in respect of depreciation and capital allowances when an assessment of future capital expenditure had to be made.

We therefore arrive at a position where pension surplus or deficits are assessed on the basis of past transactions, but deferred tax is assessed on the basis of future transactions! An anomaly would exist in the accounts if the pension deficit is recognized as a liability, but the timing difference in relation to deferred tax is not recognized as an asset. The problem, however, is that this anomaly occurs in respect of all deferred tax provided on a partial liability method not just for pensions.

However, SSAP 15, as stated in Chapter 21, was amended in December 1992 to allow deferred tax in relation to pension costs to be recognized on a full provision basis.

Companies Act requirements

Paragraph 50, subsection 4 of schedule 4, Companies Act 1985, requires a company to give details of any pension commitments provided for in the company's balance sheet and also of any such commitments for which no provision has been made. Particulars of pension commitments to past directors of the company must be disclosed separately.

Paragraph 50(6) of schedule 4 requires that disclosure under paragraph 50(4) should separately include details of commitments undertaken on behalf of, or for the benefit of, any holding company or fellow subsidiary of the company and any subsidiary of the company.

Paragraph 56(4) of schedule 4 requires companies to disclose the total pension costs incurred in the year on behalf of all employees of the company, together with separate disclosure of social security costs incurred on their behalf. These requirements apply to group accounts, but not to banking, insurance and shipping companies.

June 1995 discussion in respect of pension costs

Problems still remain in the pension area even after SSAP 24. For instance, spreading surpluses and deficits over the average remaining life seems quite straightforward, but first we must estimate what the average is (will all companies arrive at the same estimate given identical information?), then we must decide on a method of spreading. We have used straight-line for spreading surpluses and deficits, but as you know from a study of depreciation and SSAP 12 this may not be the only or the most suitable way of assessing 'benefit' received from employees.

Secondly, are users of financial statements aware of the effect that the spreading of surpluses and deficits has on balance sheet assets and liabilities and thereby the effect on key ratios?

Thirdly, how standard are the actuarial techniques used in valuing pension funds? SSAP 24 gives very little guidance on actuarial methods and assumptions.

Fourthly, should pension costs be calculated using expected final salary or current salary?

Fifthly, current regulation has not prevented pension funds being plundered!

In an attempt to address some of these problems the ASB commissioned two reports on SSAP 24:

- Technical release from the Financial Reporting and Auditing Group (FRAG) of the ICAEW – 'Review for major practical problems of SSAP 24'.
- A paper from the Pensions Research Advisory Group (PRAG) SSAP 24 Working Party – 'Review of SSAP 24'.

Both reports suggested that there are too many options available to preparers of accounts in relation to pension costs and that disclosure requirements do not necessarily ensure proper explanations are provided to users.

In response to the above the ASB issued a discussion paper in June 1995 which attempted to identify solutions to the problems of SSAP 24.

Problem one – amortization methods

The ASB in the discussion paper suggests two methods of spreading, amortizing, the surplus/deficit over the remaining life:

- straight-line method
- percentage of pay method – this allocates a smaller proportion to the earlier years but then the amount increases rapidly.

The paper concludes that the method chosen should be straight-line. Since any amortization method is arbitrary, the simpler, more straightforward method should be chosen. In addition, this method is more prudent in dealing with deficits in that it takes account of a larger proportion in the earlier years than does the percentage of pay method.

Problem two – disclosure

The discussion paper states that many of the problems with current practice for accounting of pensions may be exacerbated by the inadequacy of pension cost information in financial statements. The present disclosure requirements do not explain adequately how the pension cost has been calculated, or the interrelationship between the pension cost, the surplus or deficiency and the balance sheet figures; instead they focus on disclosing funding information.

The suggested disclosure is as follows:

37 The following separate assumptions should be disclosed:
- rate of increase in salaries
- rate of increase in pensions in payment
- rate of return on investments
- rate of increase in dividend income
- rate of interest applied to discount liabilities (which is normally the rate of return on investments).

The reasons for and effect of changes in the assumptions should be explained, including the effect on the current period's profit and loss charge and any surplus or deficiency. In addition there should be an explanation of the method used to determine the asset values.

Profit and loss charge or credit
38 The profit and loss charge or credit should be analysed into:
- normal pension cost
- amortisation of the unrecognised surplus or deficiency
- interest element arising on the total of the recognised and unrecognised surplus or deficiency
- past service cost.

Balance sheet reconciliation

39 The surplus or deficiency measured for the calculation of the pension cost should be reconciled to the balance sheet liability or prepayment. This reconciliation should include an analysis of the movements on the surplus or deficiency in the period, that part of the surplus or deficiency not recognised at the balance sheet date, and the totals of the scheme assets and of the liability for pension benefits at the balance sheet date.

Movement in the unrecognised surplus or deficiency

40 The amount of the unrecognised surplus or deficiency should be analysed to show the opening unrecognised surplus or deficiency, any surplus, deficiency and past service awards arising in the period, the amortisation of the surplus or deficiency and the unrecognised surplus or deficiency at the end of the period.

Problem three – actuarial techniques

This is addressed by suggesting that an accrued benefits method should be used by actuaries in determining how the obligation for pension benefits accumulates over the lives of the employees rather than a prospective benefits method. The accrued benefits method is built on the principle that for an individual the incremental addition to the obligation in each period will be greater nearer retirement because of the time value of money.

The prospective benefits method is built on the principle that the obligation accumulates evenly over the employees' working lives.

The ASB prefers the accrued benefits method as it reflects the economic reality better, that because of the time value of money the cost of providing a pension increases nearer retirement.

Interestingly, the Board suggests a major alternative to the actuarial-based measurement method that is currently used in the UK – market-based measurement. This method, which is used in the USA, is based on the principle that the employer should account for the obligation as it exists now and would measure the liabilities and scheme assets at current market prices. The actuarial measurement approach is based on the principle that the employer's obligation is perceived as emerging over the long term and therefore current market prices will not be representative of the eventual outcome. What is required is an estimate of the present value of the long-term cash flows associated with the liability for pension benefits and the scheme assets.

The Board's preference is for an actuarial-based approach.

Problem four – salary assumption

In relation to this problem the Board take the view that the employer should account for a pension cost based on the estimated final salary on which the pension benefit will be based.

Combining accrued benefits method with final salary produces a projected unit method which is the method currently used by two-thirds of the top 100 companies in the UK!

July 1998 discussion in respect of pension costs

A further discussion paper entitled 'Aspects of accounting for pension costs' was issued by the ASB in July 1998. This discussion paper describes the progress of the initial discussion and takes on board the international work on pension costs. The paper addresses four key issues:

- Measurement basis for the assets held in a pension scheme.
- Discount rate to be applied to a pension liability.
- Recognition of actuarial gains and losses.
- Treatment of past service costs.

Measurement basis of pension scheme assets

The international work on pension schemes proposes the use of market value for pension scheme assets, rather than actuarial values, which is the current UK proposal under the 1995 discussion paper. The new discussion paper suggests a move to market values in the interests of international harmonization and the belief, now, that market values are the most objective and reliable measure of scheme assets. The ASB goes even further than this and within the discussion paper actually promotes international harmonization as follows:

> **1.1.5** The question is whether the use of actuarial values rather than market values is a sufficiently significant issue to warrant the UK treatment being different from international practice. The Board believes that it is not.

Discount rate for pension obligations

On this issue the Board does not pursue international harmonization. The Board disagrees with IAS 19 that requires pension obligations to be discounted at the market rate of fixed rate bonds thus not reflecting any element of risk. The Board believes that the obligations should be discounted at a rate that reflects risk. The rate used for the discounting would therefore be higher than that suggested by the IASC thus the liability would be reduced under the Board's proposed method. The reason given for the use of a risk discount rate is that entities generally fund liabilities from investments in matched assets which will not be risk free.

Recognition of actuarial gains and losses

Actuarial gains and losses arise due to:

- Differences between the actual and expected returns on scheme assets.
- The effect of changes in the discount rate applied to the liability.
- Unexpectedly high or low increases in salaries or the cost of other benefits, e.g. medical care.
- Changes in estimate of future increases in salaries or in the cost of other benefits according to the discussion paper.

Under SSAP 24 these gains and losses are spread over the service life remaining of employees (see Activity 2 of this chapter). The discussion paper proposes three further alternative methods for the recognition of these actuarial gains and losses as follows:

- Immediate recognition as an exceptional item in the profit and loss account.
- Immediate recognition in the statement of total recognized gains and losses (see Chapter 26 on FRS 3) thus avoiding the profit and loss account.
- Immediate recognition in the statement of total recognized gains and losses but subsequent recycling to the profit and loss account.

The following activity illustrates the differences between these four available methods.

Activity 6

The normal contribution by Spine plc to the pension scheme is £2.4m per annum. An actuarial valuation of the scheme has identified a deficit of £10m which is to be paid into the scheme in two equal instalments of £5m in the next and the following year. The average remaining service life of the employees is ten years. Show the charges to the profit and loss account and statement of recognized gains and losses (STRGL) under the four methods proposed by the discussion paper in respect of recognition of actuarial gains and losses.

Activity 6 feedback

SSAP 24 method

The profit and loss account would show a charge of £3.4m per annum for the next ten years i.e. the normal charge of £2.4m plus £1m being the spread of the deficit.

1st Alternative

The profit and loss account would show an exceptional charge in the next year of £10m together with the normal charge of £2.4m. In the next nine years the charge would be £2.4m per annum.

2nd Alternative

The profit and loss account would show an annual charge of £2.4m for the next ten years. The STRGL would be charged with £10m in the next year. The main disadvantage with this method is the possibility of creative accounting in that preparers of accounts may deliberately underestimate the annual charge to the profit and loss account as any deficit only hits the STRGL.

3rd Alternative

The profit and loss account will show a charge of £3.4m every year, the annual charge of £2.4m and the recycling of £1m every year from the STRGL. This is the same effect as the current SSAP 24 method. The STRGL would show an initial charge of £10m and then a £1m credit every year from the recycling to profit and loss account.

The discussion paper asks for comments as to the preferred method and if any methods are completely unacceptable.

Treatment of past service costs

Past service costs arise when there is an increase in the benefits promised under a pension scheme. For example, pension scheme regulations may be amended to pay a benefit to a spouse where none was previously paid. Thus both current and former employees will now potentially receive a benefit that has not previously been provided for. This will lead to the necessity to recognize and provide for this benefit. The question of how to account for these past service costs then arises. The cost of the change could be recognized, according to the discussion paper, as follows:

- Recognize all past service costs immediately in the profit and loss account.
- Recognize past service costs relating to former employees immediately in the profit and loss account and spread forward those relating to current employees (SSAP 24 method).
- Offset past service costs against any surplus arising and recognize as a cost in the profit and loss account only any excess.

These three methods would have markedly different effects on the profit figures declared by a company.

The Board favours the first method identified above but again asks for comments as to the preferred method.

FRED 20, November 1999

Yet another stage in this long saga was reached in the late 1999, when the ASB issued an exposure draft, FRED 20, entitled Retirement Benefits. This contains some significant changes in the ASB thinking as compared with both SSAP 24 and with the 1995 discussion paper. It follows and extends the direction implied by the 1998 discussion paper of moving towards the use of market values and falling into line behind the IASC (and US) approach, but it goes rather further than this. Indeed it is an interesting paradox that the ASB uses consistency with the IASC standard as a justification for the chosen direction, and then explicitly states that its proposals go beyond and depart from the international standard, by implication because the ASB regards itself as ahead of international thinking.

The main changes from SSAP 24 are as follows:

1 *Measuring pension scheme assets*
   The FRED proposes that pension scheme assets should be valued using market values, rather than on the actuarial basis required by SSAP 24. The justification for this is primarily the pragmatic one that this method seems to have gained general acceptance internationally. The ASB also points out that experience of using market values by the actuarial profession has increased over recent years.

2 *Measuring pension scheme liabilities*
   The FRED proposes a move away from using the expected rate of return on the scheme assets, as in SSAP 24, as the discount rate for scheme liabilities, to the use instead of a discount rate that reflects the characteristics of the liabilities (leading in general to the use of what is known as an AA corporate bond rate, again consistent with the IASC standard). In idealistic logic, under a market value approach, the scheme liabilities would, like the assets, be measured at market value. However since in general there is no active market for pension scheme liabilities, the fair value will have to be estimated by actuarial means.

   The FRED proposes that an accrued benefits method of valuing defined benefit liabilities should be used. Under this method, the estimated total cost of the defined benefit is allocated to each period, the liability arising from the costs to date is discounted, and the discount then unwinds over the employee's service life. The effect of this is that there will be a higher annual cost at the end of an employee's service life than at the beginning, because the effect of discounting the cost lessens as the employee approaches retirement. The ASB states that this does reflect the economic reality of the situation, as the cost of providing a defined benefit does increase as retirement nears. The FRED proposes that the defined benefit liability should be the best estimate of the present value of the amount that will actually be paid out. This means in particular that the liability should be estimated based on the expected final salary immediately prior to retirement, not on current salaries at the time of the valuation of the liability.

3 *Recognition of actuarial gains and losses*

SSAP 24 requires actuarial gains and losses, i.e. variations around regular cost, to be recognised gradually over the remaining service lives of the employees. The IASC, in IAS 19, towards which so far the ASB has been actively seeking to harmonise, has a very complicated requirement involving what is called a corridor approach. Under this system, actuarial gains or losses within a 10% 'corridor' around the greater of the gross assets and the gross liabilities in the scheme need not be recognised, and any gains or losses outside this band may be spread forward over the expected average remaining working lives of the employees. Although more rapid recognition is possible under IAS 19, the effect of all this is to allow massive nonrecognition of actuarial gains and losses.

The interesting and difficult question is whether allowing this non-recognition is a good thing or a bad thing. It is income-smoothing on a heroic scale, i.e. it represents a deliberate attempt to defer the reporting of news, whether good or bad, until later periods, and then to spread that effect as thinly as possibly over as many periods as possible. This does not seem consistent with the information-giving function of financial reporting. However, it can also be validly argued that to recognise the effect of possibly very large actuarial gains or losses in reported earnings in one year, when they may well reverse in later years, and in any event are not the result of business operations in the normal sense of the term, may well distort the picture, and produce apparent volatility which will frighten markets and other users.

The ASB believes that it has solved this problem in the UK, because the UK, unlike IASC GAAP, requires the presentation of two performance statements under FRS 3, i.e. a profit and loss account to show the results of operations, and the statement of total recognised gains and losses to show the effects of other asset and liability valuation changes. This means that the ASB can safely require that the whole of any actuarial gains and losses can be recognised immediately *in the statement of total recognised gains and losses*, without producing sharp fluctuations in the profit and loss account and reported earnings.

This is in fact the proposal under FRED 20, i.e. that actuarial gains and losses should be recognised immediately in the statement of total recognised gains and losses. This would lead to the balance sheet showing a pension asset or liability equal to the recoverable surplus or deficit in the scheme.

There are international discussions going on about the whole issue of whether one or two performance statements are desirable. It seems likely that the IASC will develop a proposal for changes towards the FRS 3 approach, but possibly significantly different in detail. The ASB might then feel a need to revise FRS 3 towards this new approach. These developments could affect the arguments in this pensions debate. The story is not yet over.

Pension scheme accounts

So far in this chapter we have been considering the treatment of pension costs in the accounts of the employer. Since most pension schemes in the UK are funded schemes, it follows that a large number of pension schemes exist as separate entities. These pension schemes require their own accounts and have their own accounting problems. These problems are of a fairly specialist nature, but are worth a brief exploration. The ASC issued its first SORP (SORP 1) on pension scheme accounts in 1986, which goes into very considerable detail as to recommended disclosure requirements.

The starting point for considering pension funds is to remember what they exist for. In essence, they exist to ensure, as efficiently as possible, that employees of a business can rely on receiving pensions on retirement, independently of the success or otherwise of the business which currently employs them. The pension scheme needs to report to those concerned (especially the actual members of the scheme) on the health of the scheme within the framework of the above overall purpose:

1 The objectives of a pension scheme's annual report are to inform members and other users as to:
(a) the general activity, history and development of the scheme
(b) the transactions of the scheme and the size of its fund
(c) the progress of the scheme towards meeting its potential liabilities and obligations to members; and
(d) the investment policy and performance of the scheme.
To be of value to the users, this information should be provided on a timely basis.

The SORP suggests that the annual report of a pension scheme should contain four main elements:

2 In order to achieve these objectives and to present a balanced report on the pension scheme as a whole, the annual report should be made available as soon as possible after the accounting date and should comprise:
(a) A trustees' report. This is primarily a review of, or comment on:
  (i) membership statistics and major changes in benefits, constitution or legal requirements
  (ii) the financial development of the scheme as disclosed in the accounts
  (iii) the actuarial position of the scheme as disclosed in the actuary's statement; and
  (iv) the investment policy and performance of the scheme, including details of any delegation of investment management responsibilities by the trustees.
(b) Accounts. These are a stewardship report, designed to give a true and fair view of the financial transactions of the scheme during the accounting period and of the disposition of its net assets at the period end. An auditors' report on the accounts should be attached if the accounts have been audited.
(c) An actuary's statement. This is a statement by an actuary based on his investigation into, and report on, the ability of the current fund of the

pension scheme to meet accrued benefits and the adequacy of the fund and future contribution levels to meet promised benefits when due.

(**d**) An investment report. Investment policy and performance are important aspects of the stewardship function and accordingly the trustees' report in amplification of the accounts should contain or have appended additional information on investments held and investment income earned and comment on investment policy and performance.

3 As explained in paragraph 2, the information required of the investment report may instead be included in the trustees' report. The accounts and the actuary's statement are, however, two separate expert reports, having fundamentally different objectives. The former is a record of the origin and current size and disposition of the fund and the latter is a statement based on an investigation into, and report on, the present and future ability of the scheme to meet the accrued and prospective obligations to its members. These two reports require to be read in conjunction with each other, but neither should form a part of, or be subsumed into, the other.

Notice the different nature of each of these four sections. The first is an overall summary – a verbal report on the state of the scheme as a whole. The second is intended as a straightforward summary of transactions – a stewardship report in the old-fashioned sense of the term. The third section, the actuary's statement, is quite different and is an overtly forward-looking appraisal by experts as to whether in their view the scheme will have the liquid funds available in the future to meet the cash disbursements due in the future. The final section should contain details as stated of the current investment portfolio.

The basis which should underlie the accounts of a pension scheme is suggested as follows:

32 The accounts should normally be prepared on the basis of the accruals concept.

33 All the assets and liabilities of the scheme at the period end should be included in the net assets statement in order to show the current size and disposition of the fund. The only exceptions to this are:

(**a**) the liabilities to pay pensions and other benefits in the future, which will be reported upon separately in the actuary's statement

(**b**) insurance policies purchased to match the pension obligations of specific individual members (see paras 61 and 62); and

(**c**) additional voluntary contributions separately invested from the assets of the principal scheme.

34 The carrying amount of investments should be the market value of the date of the net assets statement, where such a value is available, or else at the trustees' estimate thereof.

35 The carrying amount of all other assets and liabilities recognised in the net assets statement should be based on normal accounting conventions.

The SORP continues to prescribe suggested contents of these in considerable detail.

Review of SORP 1

The requirements of SORP 1 have been brought into question in the aftermath of such high-profile cases as that of Maxwell. This has led to a review of both SORP 1 and the auditing guidelines in respect of the pension funds. The resulting revised SORP 1 'Financial Reports of Pension Schemes 1996' is more prescriptive. Auditing guidelines are expected to be tightened and new legislation may impose further responsibilities on trustees.

The enquiry instituted by the government after the Maxwell scandal resulted in the Goode Report. This report made many recommendations, several emphasizing the need for pension legislation to be underpinned by codes of practice. It also recommended a review of SORP 1 to incorporate such issues as cash flow statements and presentation of total return on investments.

Several critics of the Goode Report have suggested that it didn't go far enough and that it should have suggested a fundamental change to pensions law. We await the government's White Paper in respect of pension schemes.

Summary

The problems in respect of SSAP 24 will have to be dealt with not least because of the impact of pension costs on financial statements. The method of accounting chosen will impact on the view of users in respect of the financial position and profitability of a company.

The two options proposed in the discussion paper, actuarial based or market based, will both still permit different assumptions to be made by companies in respect of, for example, rate of return on investments resulting in differences in pension costs identified.

Perhaps there is a third method available to account for pensions – cash accounting! However, using a cash method we would have to contend with the impact of contribution holidays and cash injections on financial statements. Whatever method is eventually chosen there is a need for increased disclosure as suggested by the discussion document. There is also a need to ensure that the accounting method chosen reflects the conceptual framework and other ASB statements and that special cases are not made to deviate from these as was done for deferred tax on post-retirement benefits!

Addendum

The ASB issued FRS 17, Retirement Benefits, in November 2000. In broad terms, though not in all the detail, FRS 17 is consistent with FRED 20. This means that, in one important respect, FRS 17 is significantly different from the corresponding IASC Standard, IAS 19. The FRS requires actuarial gains and losses to be recognized, immediately they occur, in the statement of total recognized gains and losses. IAS 19 (revised) requires actuarial gains and losses to be recognized in the profit and loss account to the extent that they exceed 10 per cent of the greater of the gross assets or gross liabilities in the scheme. Recognition of actuarial gains and losses exceeding the 10 per cent corridor may be spread forward over the expected average remaining working lives of the employees participating in the scheme. Recognition of actuarial gains and losses within the 10 per cent corridor is allowed under IAS 19, but not required.

The FRS notes (in Appendix III) that the structure for reporting financial performance is more developed in the UK and the Republic of Ireland than under IASs: a second performance statement - the statement of total recognized gains and losses - was introduced by FRS 3 'Reporting Financial Performance' in 1992, whereas no such statement is used in practice under IASs. The implication is clearly given that the IASC can be expected to 'catch up'. Since Sir David Tweedie was chairman of the ASB when FRS 17 was issued, and is now chairman of IASC, convergence can perhaps be expected!

This whole area is in fact tied up with the ongoing discussions internationally about the possibility (probability) of a single performance statement, replacing both the profit and loss account and the statement of total recognized gains and losses in their current form (and necessitating a complete rethink of FRS 3).

Retirement benefits are a complicated area, and in a sense somewhat specialist. Since the key issues have been discussed in principle in the chapter, we concentrate here on the main statements and wording of FRS 17 itself. The requirements are required to be phased in before or by accounting periods ending on or after 22 June 2003 (please do not write in and ask us why!). FRS 17 applies to all enterprises, in effect, except those applying the FRSSE.

The Standard gives a series of definitions, as follows.

Actuarial gains and losses

Changes in actuarial deficits or surpluses that arise because:

(**a**) events have not coincided with the actuarial assumptions made for the last valuation (experience gains and losses) or
(**b**) the actuarial assumptions have changed.

Current service cost

The increase in the present value of the scheme liabilities expected to arise from employee service in the current period.

Curtailment

An event that reduces the expected years of future service of present employees or reduces for a number of employees the accrual of defined benefits for some or all of their future service. Curtailments include:

(**a**) termination of employees' services earlier than expected, for example as a result of closing a factory or discontinuing a segment of a business, and

(**b**) termination of, or amendment to the terms of, a defined benefit scheme so that some or all future service by current employees will no longer qualify for benefits or will qualify only for reduced benefits.

Defined benefit scheme

A pension or other retirement benefit scheme other than a defined contribution scheme.

Defined contribution scheme

A pension or other retirement benefit scheme into which an employer pays regular contributions fixed as an amount or as a percentage of pay and will have no legal or constructive obligation to pay further contributions if the scheme does not have sufficient assets to pay all employee benefits relating to employee service in the current and prior periods.

Expected rate of return on assets

The average rate of return, including both income and changes in fair value but net of scheme expenses, expected over the remaining life of the related obligation on the actual assets held by the scheme.

Interest cost

The expected increase during the period in the present value of the scheme liabilities because the benefits are one period closer to settlement.

Past service cost

The increase in the present value of the scheme liabilities related to employee service in prior periods arising in the current period as a result of the introduction of, or improvement to, retirement benefits.

Projected unit method

An accrued benefits valuation method in which the scheme liabilities make allowance for projected earnings. An accrued benefits valuation method is a valuation method in which the scheme liabilities at the valuation date relate to:

(**a**) the benefits for pensioners and deferred pensioners (i.e. individuals who have ceased to be active members but are entitled to benefits payable at a later date) and their dependants, allowing where appropriate for future increases, and

(**b**) the accrued benefits for members in service on the valuation date.

The accrued benefits are the benefits for service up to a given point in time, whether vested rights or not.

Retirement benefits

All forms of consideration given by an employer in exchange for services rendered by employees that are payable after the completion of employment.

Scheme liabilities

The liabilities of a defined benefit scheme for outgoings due after the valuation date.

Settlement

An irrevocable action that relieves the employer (or the defined benefit scheme) of the primary responsibility for a pension obligation and eliminates significant risks relating to the obligation and the assets used to effect the settlement. Settlements include:

(**a**) a lump-sum payment to scheme members in exchange for their rights to receive specified pension benefits

(**b**) the purchase of an irrevocable annuity contract sufficient to cover vested benefits; and

(**c**) the transfer of scheme assets and liabilities relating to a group of employees leaving the scheme.

Vested rights

These are:

(**a**) for active members, benefits to which they would unconditionally be entitled on leaving the scheme;

(**b**) for deferred pensioners, their preserved benefits;

(**c**) for pensioners, pensions to which they are entitled.

Vested rights include where appropriate the related benefits for spouses or other dependants.

Defined contribution schemes are, of course, relatively simple. The cost of a defined contribution scheme is equal to the contribution payable to the scheme for the accounting period. The cost should be recognized within operating profit in the profit and loss account.

Defined benefit schemes are very much more complicated, and FRS 17 takes 62 paragraphs to deal with them. The rules for measurement are dealt with first.

Assets in a defined benefit scheme should be measured at their fair value at the balance sheet date.

Defined benefit scheme liabilities should be measured on an actuarial basis using the projected unit method. The scheme liabilities comprise:

(**a**) any benefits promised under the formal terms of the scheme; and

(**b**) any constructive obligations for further benefits where a public statement or past practice by the employer has created a valid expectation in the employees that such benefits will be granted.

The benefits should be attributable to periods of service according to the scheme's benefit formula, except where the benefit formula attributes a disproportionate share of the total benefits to later years of service. In such cases, the benefit should be attributed on a straight-line basis over the period during which it is earned.

The assumptions underlying the valuation should be mutually compatible and lead to the best estimate of the future cash flows that will arise under the scheme liabilities. The assumptions are ultimately the responsibility of the directors (or equivalent) but should be set upon advice given by an actuary. Any assumptions that are affected by economic conditions (financial assumptions) should reflect market expectations at the balance sheet date.

The actuarial assumptions should reflect expected future events that will affect the cost of the benefits to which the employer is committed (either legally or through a constructive obligation) at the balance sheet date.

Defined benefit scheme liabilities should be discounted at a rate that reflects the time value of money and the characteristics of the liability. Such a rate should be assumed to be the current rate of return on a high quality corporate bond of equivalent currency and term to the scheme liabilities.

Full actuarial valuations by a professionally qualified actuary should be obtained for a defined benefit scheme at intervals not exceeding 3 years. The actuary should review the most recent actuarial valuation at the balance sheet date and update it to reflect current conditions.

In summary, therefore, the key points regarding the measurement of defined benefit scheme assets and liabilities are as follows:

- Defined benefit scheme assets are measured at fair value.
- Defined benefit scheme liabilities are measured using the projected unit method.
- Defined benefit scheme liabilities are discounted at the current rate of return on a high-quality corporate bond of equivalent term and currency to the liability.
- Full actuarial valuations should be obtained at intervals not exceeding 3 years and should be updated at each balance sheet date.

The issue of recognition can be considered under two headings: recognition in the balance sheet and recognition in the performance statements. As regards the balance sheet, the surplus/deficit in a defined benefit scheme is the excess/shortfall of the value of the assets in the scheme over/below the present value of the scheme liabilities. The employer should recognize an asset to the extent that it is able to recover a surplus either through reduced contributions in the future or through refunds from the scheme. The employer should recognize a liability to the extent that it reflects its legal or constructive obligation.

A surplus in the scheme gives rise to an asset of the employer to the extent that:

(**a**) the employer controls its use, i.e. has the ability to use the surplus to generate future economic benefits for itself, either in the form of a reduction in future contributions or a refund from the scheme; and

(**b**) that control is a result of past events (contributions paid by the employer and investment growth in excess of rights earned by the employees).

In practice, it is probable that a reduction in future contributions by the employer to the pension scheme will be the reason for any asset of the employer. The ASB is insistent that the right to reduce future contributions is an asset, notwithstanding the fact that the employer neither owns nor controls the surplus in the scheme itself. Remember that it is not the surplus being capitalized; it is the right to reduce future contributions (which right exists because of the surplus): an important distinction.

In determining the asset to be recognized, the amount that can be recovered through reduced contributions in the future is the present value of the liability expected to arise from future service by current and future scheme members less the present value of future employee contributions. No growth in the number of active scheme members should be assumed but a declining membership should be reflected if appropriate. The amount that can be recovered should be based on the assumptions used under the FRS, not the funding assumptions. The present value of the reduction in future contributions is determined using the discount rate applied to measure the defined benefit liability.

The amount to be recovered from refunds from the scheme should reflect only refunds that have been agreed by the pension scheme trustees at the balance sheet date.

Any unpaid contributions to the scheme should be presented in the balance sheet as a creditor due within 1 year. The defined benefit asset or liability should be presented separately on the face of the balance sheet:

(**a**) in balance sheets of the type prescribed for companies in Great Britain by the Companies Act 1985, Schedule 4, format 1: after item J *Accruals and deferred income* but before item K *Capital and reserves*; and

(**b**) in balance sheets of the type prescribed for companies in Great Britain by the Companies Act 1985, Schedule 4, format 2: any asset after ASSETS item D *Prepayments and accrued income* and any liability after LIABILITIES item D *Accruals and deferred income*.

Where an employer has more than one scheme, the total of any defined benefit assets and the total of any defined benefit liabilities should be shown separately on the face of the balance sheet.

The deferred tax relating to the defined benefited asset or liability should be offset against the defined benefit asset or liability and not included with other deferred tax assets or liabilities.

As regards recognition in the performance statements, the change in the defined benefit asset or liability (other than that arising from contributions to the scheme) should be analysed into the following components:

- Periodic costs:
  - the current service cost;
  - the interest cost;
  - the expected return on assets;
  - actuarial gains and losses.
- Non-periodic costs:
  - past service costs; and
  - gains and losses on settlements and curtailments.
- The requirements for each of these six components are as follows:
  - The current service cost should be based on the most recent actuarial valuation at the

beginning of the period, with the financial assumptions updated to reflect conditions at that date. It should be included within operating profit in the profit and loss account (except insofar as the related employee remuneration is capitalized in accordance with another accounting standard). Any contribution from employees should be set off against the current service cost.

- The interest cost should be based on the discount rate and the present value of the scheme liabilities at the beginning of the period. The interest cost should, in addition, reflect changes in the scheme liabilities during the period.

- The expected return on assets is based on long-term expectations at the beginning of the period and is expected to be reasonably stable. For quoted corporate or government bonds, the expected return should be calculated by applying the current redemption yield at the beginning of the period to the market value of the bonds held by the scheme at the beginning of the period. For other assets (for example, equities), the expected return should be calculated by applying the rate of return expected over the long term at the beginning of the period (given the value of the assets at that date) to the fair value of the assets held by the scheme at the beginning of the period. The expected return on assets should, in addition, reflect changes in the assets in the scheme during the period as a result of contributions paid into and benefits paid out of the scheme. The expected rate of return should be set by the directors (or equivalent) having taken advice from an actuary.

- The net of the interest cost and the expected return on assets should be included as other financial costs (or income) adjacent to interest.

- Actuarial gains and losses arising from any new valuation and from updating the latest actuarial valuation to reflect conditions at the balance sheet date should be recognized in the statement of total recognized gains and losses for the period.

- Past service costs should be recognized in the profit and loss account on a straight-line basis over the period in which the increases in benefit vest. To the extent that the benefits vest immediately, the past service cost should be recognized immediately. Any unrecognized past service costs should be deducted from the scheme liabilities and the balance sheet asset or liability adjusted accordingly.

- Losses arising on a settlement or curtailment not allowed for in the actuarial assumptions should be measured at the date on which the employer becomes demonstrably committed to the transaction and recognized in the profit and loss account covering that date. Gains arising on a settlement or curtailment not allowed for in the actuarial assumptions should be measured at the date on which all parties whose consent is required are irrevocably committed to the transaction and recognized in the profit and loss account covering that date.

All this detail concerning the recognition issue under defined benefit schemes can be summarized as follows:

- An asset is recognized to the extent that an employer can recover a surplus in a defined benefit scheme through reduced contributions and refunds. A liability is recognized to the extent that the deficit reflects the employer's legal or constructive obligation.

- The resulting defined benefit asset or liability is presented separately on the face of the balance sheet after other net assets.

- The change in the defined benefit asset or liability (other than that arising from contributions to the scheme) is analysed into the following components:

(i)   the current service cost
(ii) the interest cost
(iii) the expected return on assets
(iv) actuarial gains and losses
(v)   past service costs (if any)
(vi) settlements and curtailments (if any).

■ The current service cost and interest cost are based on the discount rate at the beginning of the period. The expected return on assets is based on the expected rate of return at the beginning of the period. The current service cost is shown within the appropriate statutory heading for pension costs in the profit and loss account. The interest cost and expected return on assets are shown as a net amount of other finance costs (or income) adjacent to interest.

■ The expected return is calculated by applying the expected rate of return over the long term to the market value of scheme assets at the beginning of the year, adjusted for any contributions received and benefits paid during the year. Although the expected rate of return will vary according to market conditions it is expected that the amount of the return will normally be relatively stable.

■ Actuarial gains and losses are recognized immediately in the statement of total recognized gains and losses. They are not recycled into the profit and loss account in subsequent periods.

■ Past service costs are recognized in the profit and loss account over the period until the benefits vest. If the benefits vest immediately, the past service cost is recognized immediately.

■ Gains and losses arising on settlements and curtailments are recognized immediately in the profit and loss account.

The Standard contains some further details that only the practitioner is likely to need to explore. The disclosure requirements for defined contribution schemes are the following:

■ the nature of the scheme (i.e. defined contribution);
■ the cost for the period; and
■ any outstanding or prepaid contributions at the balance sheet date.

The disclosure requirements relating to defined benefit schemes are extensive, and set out in detail in the FRS. They may be summarized as follows:

■ the main assumptions underlying the scheme;
■ an analysis of the assets in the scheme into broad classes and the expected rate of return on each class;
■ an analysis of the amounts included (a) within operating profit, (b) within other finance costs and (c) within the statement of total recognized gains and losses;
■ a 5-year history of (a) the difference between the expected and actual return on assets, (b) experience gains and losses arising on the scheme liabilities and (c) the total actuarial gain or loss;
■ an analysis of the movement in the surplus or deficit in the scheme over the period and a reconciliation of the surplus/deficit to the balance sheet asset/liability.

Full application of FRS 17 will lead to the withdrawal of SSAP 24, and UITF Abstracts 6 and 18.

Exercises

1 Why is a special SSAP dealing specifically with pension costs necessary?

2 Explain the requirements of SSAP 24.

3 It is important to distinguish between the problem of providing pensions for today's employees and the problem of ensuring that the pension fund can meet all expected future demands. SSAP 24 fails to make clear this distinction. Do you agree?

4 The following information is available on a company pension scheme.

(a) The scheme is a funded defined benefit scheme with annual contributions by the employer of £3 million.

(b) In year 10 the actuarial valuation identified a surplus of £18 million, £6 million of which was due to an extraordinary item.

(c) The actuary recommends that the surplus be eliminated by a pension holiday for four years and a reduced contribution of £2 million for six years.

(d) The average remaining service life of employees is ten years.

Show the annual charge to the P&L account and the balance sheet entry in respect of years 10–20.

5 At present your company operates a defined benefit pension scheme and charges the annual contributions payable to this pension scheme as the pension cost in each accounting period.

You are required

(a) **to write a report for your managing director explaining any change required by SSAP 24** (5 marks)

(b) **to summarize the necessary disclosures in respect of a defined benefit pension scheme.** (10 marks)

(15 marks)

(CIMA AFA)

6 **In connection with SSAP 24 'Accounting for Pension Costs':**

(a) **what is the objective of accounting for pension costs as required by SSAP 24?** (4 marks)

(b) **what are the advantages and disadvantages of the approach in SSAP 24 of charging pension contributions to the P&L account, as compared to charging the amounts actually paid?** (10 marks)

(c) The actuarial valuation at 30 June 1990 of the funded pension scheme of Jems plc showed a surplus of £360 million. The actuaries recommended that the company eliminate the surplus by taking a contribution holiday in 1991 and 1992 and then paying contributions of £30 million per annum for eight years. After that the standard contribution would be £60 million per annum. The average remaining service life of employees in the scheme at 30 June 1990 was ten years. The credit provision in the balance sheet for the year-ended 30 June 1993 was calculated as follows:

	£m
Surplus at 30.6.90	360
Regular payments 3 years × £60m	(180)
Contributions paid 1 × £30m	30
Contributions deferred £360m/10 years × 7	(252)
Provision in balance sheet	(42)

You are required to write a brief note, addressed to a non-financial director, explaining why it is necessary to have a provision of £42 million in the balance sheet.

(6 marks)

(20 marks)

(ACCA)

23

Post-balance sheet events and provisions and contingencies (SSAP 17, FRS 12)

After reading this chapter you should be able to:
- explain post-balance sheet events, adjusting events and non-adjusting events
- describe the requirements of SSAP 17 and Companies Act relating to post-balance sheet events
- list examples of adjusting and non-adjusting post-balance sheet events
- define contingencies
- describe the requirements of FRS 12 and Companies Act relating to provisions, contingent liabilities and contingent assets
- show how to treat contingency events within financial statements.

Introduction

Accounts of all undertakings are prepared at an arbitrary date – the balance sheet date – which is a convenient cut-off point. However, accounts, no matter how sophisticated the information technology, are never prepared, audited and approved by directors in a few days. Generally there is a time lag of a number of months between the balance sheet date and the 'signing off' of the accounts by the directors. During this period numerous events can occur that may or may not have an influence on the information we are providing, by the final accounts, for users. This is the area SSAP 17 deals with. Equally there may be conditions existing at the balance sheet date with uncertain outcomes and this is the subject of FRS 12. It is important to remember at this stage the primary characteristics that make accounting information useful according to the ASB – namely relevance, i.e. information which influences decisions, and reliability, i.e. information which is free from error or bias.

Post-balance sheet events (SSAP 17)

Numerous events can and do occur between the balance sheet date and the date the accounts are approved. The question is which events are relevant to users needs.

Activity 1

As the recently qualified accountant of Aveler plc, a food retailer with balance sheet date 31 December 20X1, you notice the following items occurring before the accounts are approved by the directors:

1 The sale, during the period from 31 December 20X1 to the date the accounts are approved by the directors, of 1000 tins of baked beans.
2 The purchase, during the period from 31 December 20X1 to the date the accounts are approved by the directors, of 750 tins of baked beans.
3 The incurrence of other expenses, during the period from 31 December 20X1 to the date the accounts are approved by the directors, amounting to £125.
4 Notification that a customer who owes the company £10 000 as at 31 December 20X1 has gone into liquidation on 17 January 20X2.
5 A fire on 4 January 20X2 destroys all the stock in one warehouse.
6 The receipt of a letter from the company's insurers stating that it is unclear whether Aveler was actually insured for loss of stock by fire.

Which of the above items are relevant to the accounts for the period ending 31 December 20X1?

Activity 1 feedback

Items **1–3** are events which relate purely to the next financial period and therefore are not relevant to users for the period in question.

Item **4** is a relevant event as if account is not taken of this information then the debtors balance will be overstated as at 31 December 20X1. In other words the debtors value will be unreliable.

Items **5** and **6** are related. Item **5** is a disaster occurring in the next financial period and therefore should be accounted for in that period in which the loss occurred. As far as the period ending 31 December 20X1 is concerned the stock still existed at the balance sheet date. However, you should perhaps question whether or not the fact of the fire is not a relevant piece of information to be given to users. Item **6** has a decidedly uncertain outcome, i.e. the event has not yet occurred, and will be subject to FRS 12.

Adjusting and non-adjusting events

In the above activity we have suggested that events occurring after the balance sheet date can be divided into three groups:

1 those that provide additional evidence of conditions existing at the balance sheet date (item **4**)
2 those that provide evidence of conditions that did not exist at the balance sheet date, but whose disclosure is arguably necessary for a proper understanding of the financial position (item **5**)
3 those that relate purely to the new financial period (items 1–3).

(Note item **6** is not defined as an event in this context.)

SSAP 17 is concerned with the first two of these, which it defines respectively as **adjusting** and **non-adjusting post-balance sheet events**. The formal definitions are:

18 *Post-balance sheet events* are those events, both favourable and unfavourable, which occur between the balance sheet date and the date on which the financial statements are approved by the board of directors.

19 *Adjusting events* are post balance sheet events which provide additional evidence of conditions existing at the balance sheet date. They include events which because of statutory or conventional requirements are reflected in financial statements.

20 *Non-adjusting events* are post balance sheet events which concern conditions which did not exist at the balance sheet date.

The date of approval referred to in paragraph 18 is the date of the board meeting that approves the accounts. In the case of group accounts, it will be the board meeting of the holding company.

22 A material post balance sheet event requires changes in the amounts to be included in financial statements where:
   (a) It is an adjusting event; or
   (b) It indicates that application of the going concern concept to the whole or a material part of the company is not appropriate.

Examples of adjusting events

The appendix to the standard gives some examples of likely adjusting events:

The following are examples of post balance sheet events which normally should be classified as adjusting events:
   (a) *Fixed assets.* The subsequent determination of the purchase price or of the proceeds of sale of assets purchased or sold before the year-end.
   (b) *Property.* A valuation which provides evidence of a permanent diminution in value.
   (c) *Investments.* The receipt of a copy of the financial statements or other information in respect of an unlisted company which provides evidence of a permanent diminution in the value of a long-term investment.
   (d) *Stocks and work-in-progress.*
      (i)   The receipt of proceeds of sales after the balance sheet date or other evidence concerning the net realizable value of stocks.
      (ii) The receipt of evidence that the previous estimate of accrued profit on a long-term contract was materially inaccurate.
   (e) *Debtors.* The renegotiation of amounts owing by debtors, or the insolvency of a debtor.
   (f) *Dividends receivable.* The declaration of dividends by subsidiaries and associated companies relating to periods prior to the balance sheet date of the holding company.
   (g) *Taxation.* The receipt of information regarding rates of taxation.
   (h) *Claims.* Amounts received or receivable in respect of insurance claims which were in the course of negotiation at the balance sheet date.
   (i) *Discoveries.* The discovery of errors or frauds which show that the financial statements were incorrect.

It is important not to forget the point that any post-balance sheet event that suggests that the going concern assumption is not applicable should be treated as an adjusting event;

> **8** Some events occurring after the balance sheet date, such as a deterioration in the operating results and in the financial position, may indicate a need to consider whether it is appropriate to use the going concern concept in the preparation of financial statements. Consequently these may fall to be treated as adjusting events.

Treatment of non-adjusting events in accounts

By contrast, non-adjusting events obviously do not require adjustment in the figures in the accounts. But they may nevertheless require disclosure in the accounts, by way of note, to ensure that the accounts taken as a whole are not misleading:

> **23** A material post balance sheet event should be disclosed where:
> **(a)** it is a non-adjusting event of such materiality that its non-disclosure would affect the ability of the users of financial statements to reach a proper understanding of the financial position; or
> **(b)** it is the reversal or maturity after the year-end of a transaction entered into before the year-end, the substance of which was primarily to alter the appearance of the company's balance sheet.
> **24** In respect of each post balance sheet event which is required to be disclosed under paragraph 23, the following information should be stated by way of notes in financial statements:
> **(a)** the nature of the event; and
> **(b)** an estimate of the financial effect, or a statement that it is not practicable to make such an estimate.
> **25** The estimate of the financial effect should be disclosed before taking account of taxation, and the taxation implications should be explained where necessary for a proper understanding of the financial position.

Examples of non-adjusting events

Examples of non-adjusting events are also given in the Appendix. The following are examples of post-balance sheet events which normally should be classified as non-adjusting events:

1 mergers and acquisitions
2 reconstructions and proposed reconstructions
3 issues of shares and debentures
4 purchases and sales of fixed assets and investments
5 losses of fixed assets or stocks as a result of a catastrophe, such as fire or flood
6 opening new trading activities or extending existing trading activities
7 closing a significant part of the trading activities if this was not anticipated at the year-end
8 decline in the value of property and investments held as fixed assets, if it can be demonstrated that the decline occurred after the year-end

9 changes in rates of foreign exchange
10 government action, such as nationalization
11 strikes and other labour disputes
12 augmentation of pension benefits.

Redrafting of accounts for post-balance sheet events

Activity 2

Pass plc drew up its accounts for the year-ending 31 December 20X1 as follows:

Draft P&L account (summarized)

	£000s
Profit on ordinary activities before tax	412
Tax on profit on ordinary activities	104
Profit on ordinary activities after tax	308
Dividends proposed	192
Retained profits for the year	116

Draft balance sheet as at 31.12.X1

	£000s	£000s
Fixed assets		3656
Current assets	1106	
Creditors falling due within one year	1044	
Net current assets		62
Total assets less current liabilities		3718
Creditors falling due after one year		320
		3398
Capital and reserves		
Called up share capital		1700
Share premium		1298
P&L account		400
		3398

Before the accounts were approved by the directors the following items were discovered:

1 Included in fixed assets are two buildings with NBVs respectively of £60 000 and £80 000. The £60 000 building was sold on the 17 December 20X1 at a price to be determined by independent valuers. On the 9 January 20X2 the price was agreed at £69 000. The £80 000 building was sold on 4 January 20X2 at a price of £63 000.

2 Items of stock included in current assets at £20 000 as at 31 December 20X1 were sold on 2 January 20X2 for £18 500 and other items of stock valued at £10 000 were sold on 10 January 20X2 for £17 000 to a customer who subsequently went into liquidation on 19 January 20X2. It was noted that as at 31 December 20X1 this customer owed Pass plc £11 500.

3 On the 2 January 20X2 a fire occurred at one of the company's warehouses where stock, included in the balance sheet at £20 000 was severely damaged. On the 10 March 20X2 the company received a cheque from the insurers for £26 000.

4 On the 11 March 20X2 150 employees of the 175-strong workforce took strike action. The strike is anticipated to be of a short-term nature.

You are required to redraft the above accounts taking into account the above items where necessary for the approval of the directors.

Activity 2 feedback

1 The £60 000 building was sold on 17 December 20X1 and therefore should not appear in the balance sheet as at 31 December 20X1. Thus, it is an adjusting event whereby fixed assets will be reduced by £60 000 and a profit on sale of £9000 will be taken to the P&L account (whether the profit is shown as ordinary, exceptional or extraordinary will depend on FRS 3, Chapter 26). The £80 000 building was not sold until 4 January 20X2 and therefore the sale is non-adjusting. However, the fact that the building was sold at a valuation of £63 000, i.e. £17 000 less than NBV is an adjusting event as the valuation provides evidence as to the permanent diminution in value of the asset as at 31 December 20X1. (It is assumed that the four days between balance sheet date and sale date has not been sufficient time for new circumstances to arise which would have caused the loss.) Thus fixed assets must be reduced by £17 000 and the loss taken to the P&L account for the year 20X1.

2 Again the event of actual sale of stock on 2 January 20X2 is a non-adjusting event but the fact that the stock only had a net realizable value of £18 500 is an adjusting event and closing stock and profits must accordingly be reduced by £1500.

The sale of stock on 10 January 20X2 and the subsequent non-recovery of debt relating to that sale are both non-adjusting events. However, account must be taken of the fact that £11 500 of debt as at 31 December 20X1 has become irrecoverable on 19 January 20X2 and debtors and profits must be reduced accordingly.

3 The fire is a non-adjusting event and no account will be taken of it in redrafting the accounts. However, a note to the accounts is required in accordance with SSAP 17 disclosure of non-adjusting events.

4 This is again a non-adjusting event, but consideration will need to be given as to whether a note to the accounts is required. Perhaps as the strike is anticipated to be of a short-term nature no note need be given but this will be decided in accordance with the characteristic of relevance. In other words, would non-disclosure affect the ability of the users of the financial statements to reach a proper conclusion.

Redrafted P&L account for the year-ended 31.12.X1

	£000s
Profit on ordinary activities before tax	401
(412 + 9 item 1, −17 item 1, − 1.5 item 2, −1.5 item 2)	
Tax on profit on ordinary activities (assume no change)	104
	297
Dividends proposed	192
	105

Redrafted balance sheet as at 31.12.X1

	£000s	£000s
Fixed assets (3656 – 60 item 1, –17 item 1)		3579
Current assets (1106 – 1.5 item 2, –1.5 item 2, +69 item 1)	1172	
Creditors falling due within one year	1044	
Net current assets		128
Total assets less current liabilities		3707
Creditors falling due after one year		320
		3387
Capital and reserves		
Called up share capital		1700
Share premium		1298
P&L account (105 + 284)		389
		3387

Window dressing and SSAP 17

We must return to paragraph 23(b) of SSAP 17 which we quoted earlier and consider this in more detail as it refers to what is commonly known as 'window-dressing'.

The limitation of this requirement is interesting. There is no requirement to reverse or remove the transaction from the published accounts, even if it is obviously a purely artificial one designed to alter the appearance of the published balance sheet. Disclosure by way of note is enough to justify an unqualified report from the auditors – assuming, of course, that the accounts can still be regarded as showing a true and fair view.

Distinction between adjusting and non-adjusting

In practice, the distinction between an adjusting and non-adjusting event must be carefully considered. For example, the material bankruptcy of a debtor that occurs two months after the balance sheet date (before the accounts are approved) would be an adjusting event if the debt was in existence at the balance sheet date. However, if the debt had arisen shortly after the balance sheet date then the bankruptcy would be a non-adjusting event, requiring no alteration to the accounts, but disclosure by way of note if material. But if, in this latter situation, the likely loss is so great as to put at risk the viability of the firm, and so question the going concern convention, then the bankruptcy would need to be treated as an adjusting event after all. The introduction to the appendix (which does not have a force of a standard) states that:

> In exceptional circumstances, to accord with the prudence concept, an adverse event which would normally be classified as non-adjusting may need to be reclassified as adjusting. In such circumstances, full disclosure of the adjustment would be required.

The explanatory note to the standard also states:

> **4** Events which occur after the date on which the financial statements are approved by the board of directors do not come within the scope of this Standard. If such events are material the directors should consider publishing the relevant information so that users of financial statements are not misled.

The standard also requires that:

> **26** The date on which the financial statements are approved by the board of directors should be disclosed in the financial statements.

The Companies Act 1985

As discussed on p. 229, schedule 4, paragraph 3(b) requires that:

> **(b)** all liabilities and losses which have arisen or are likely to arise in respect of the financial year to which the accounts relate or a previous financial year shall be taken into account, including those which only become apparent between the balance sheet date and the date on which it is signed on behalf of the board of directors.

Adjusting post-balance sheet 'liabilities and losses' are therefore given statutory enforcement (but not 'gains'). Additionally, the directors' report is required to contain:

1 particulars of any important event affecting the company since the year-end (or its subsidiaries)
2 an indication of likely future developments
3 an indication of the activities in the field of research and development.

Notice that this directors' report requirement (1 above) refers to all items, without distinguishing between adjusting and non-adjusting.

Accounting for provisions, contingent liabilities and contingent assets

SSAP 18

The issue of accounting for contingencies was first dealt with under SSAP 18. This statement provided a definition of a contingency as follows:

> **14** Contingency is a condition which exists at the balance sheet date, where the outcome will be confirmed only on the occurrence or non-occurrence of one or more uncertain future events. A contingent gain or loss is a gain or loss dependent on a contingency.

It also made a distinction between a contingency and a provision. With a provision the only difficulty is the estimation of the actual amount implied by the outcome. The outcome itself is not in question. This month's estimated electricity bill is a provision. No one doubts that a bill will come!

1   It is not intended that uncertainties with accounting estimates should fall within the scope of this statement, for example, the lives of the fixed assets, the amount of bad debts, the net realisable value of inventories, the expected outcome of long term contracts or the valuation of properties and foreign currency balances. The recommended treatment of contingent gains and losses was that

- ■ Contingent losses if remote should be ignored:
  - – if possible should be disclosed by note
  - – if probable accrued.

Interestingly, the standard gave no guidance on the distinction between these three words: probable, possible, remote.

The following activity illustrates the problem in distinguishing between them.

Activity 3

PPR plc a retailer of washing machines has a year-end 31 December. During December a washing machine was sold to a customer who carried out the plumbing for the washing machine himself. On 24 December the machine failed to operate correctly resulting in the customer's house suffering severe damage due to flooding. The customer, together with several relatives, had to spend Christmas in a hotel as his home was uninhabitable. The customer is planning to sue PPR plc for a considerable amount of damages. Would you as an accountant for PPR accrue a loss for the damages pending, make a note of the loss, or ignore it completely?

Activity 3 feedback

The above scenario is an example of a contingent loss, i.e. the condition existed at the balance sheet date as the washing machine had been sold and the flooding had occurred by that date, but the outcome will presumably only be confirmed when the claim for damages is settled. The treatment of the contingent loss in the accounts is therefore dependent upon whether we view the loss as probable, possible or remote. How do we decide this? Ask a lawyer? Possibly. However, if the claim results in a court case how many directors would consider prejudicing that case by declaring it 'probable' in the accounts? Not many we would suggest! In other words, the declaration of a contingency as probable, possible or remote requires a subjective judgement and SSAP 18 gives us no definitions of these three words.

A standard English dictionary provides us with the following definitions: *probable* – likely to be or to happen but not necessarily so; *possible* – feasible but less than probable; capable of being true under some interpretation or in some circumstances; *remote* – distant, slight, faint.

If in the above activity the customer was suing for £100 000 in damages then if this was termed a probable contingent loss the company would accrue £100 000 into its accounts, i.e. profits for the year would be reduced by £100 000 and a contingency for £100 000 would appear on the balance sheet under provisions for liabilities and charges. A director wishing to keep his or her profits for the year high may well wish to persuade the preparers of the accounts that the contingency was only possible or remote thus we enter the area of 'creative accounting'. Remember the ASB state in their Statement of Principles that accounts must be reliable and to be reliable the information contained in financial statements must be neutral, that is free from bias. However, prudence must also be exercised, according to the ASB, for information to be reliable, but doesn't prudence imply a bias? The question remains as to whether this statement from the ASB will provide us with an answer to the above area of creative accounting.

The Companies Act and contingencies

The 1985 Companies Act contains several requirements concerning *contingent liabilities* (and only contingent *liabilities*), and other likely payments that are not all contingencies within the meaning of SSAP 18. These are as follows (schedule 4, paragraph 50):

50 (**1**) Particulars shall be given of any charge on the assets of the company to secure the liabilities of any other person, including, where practicable, the amount secured.

(**2**) The following information shall be given with respect to any other contingent liability not provided for:

(**a**) the amount or estimated amount of that liability

(**b**) its legal nature; and

(**c**) whether any valuable security has been provided by the company in connection with that liability and if so, what.

(**3**) There shall be stated, where practicable:

(**a**) the *aggregate* amount or estimated amount of contracts for capital expenditure, so far as not provided for; and

(**b**) the aggregate amount or estimated amount of capital expenditure authorized by the directors which has not been contracted for.

(**4**) Particulars shall be given of:

(**a**) any pension commitments included under any provision shown in the company's balance sheet; and

(**b**) any such commitments for which no provision has been made; and where any such commitment relates wholly or partly to pensions payable to past directors of the company separate particulars shall be given of that commitment so far as it relates to such pensions.

(**5**) Particulars shall also be given of any other financial commitments which:

(**a**) have not been provided for; and

(**b**) are relevant to assessing the company's state of affairs.

(**6**) Commitments within any of the preceding sub-paragraphs undertaken on behalf of or for the benefit of:

(**a**) any holding company or fellow subsidiary of the company; or

(**b**) any subsidiary of the company;

shall be stated separately from the other commitments within that sub-paragraph (and commitments within paragraph (a) shall also be stated separately from those within paragraph (b)).

The requirements of SSAP 18 were therefore wider than those of the Act.

Redrafting of accounts involving contingencies under SSAP 18

Activity 4

Ssaps plc, a construction company, drew up its accounts for the year-ended 31 December 20X1 as follows:

Draft P&L account (summarized)	£m
Profit on ordinary activities before tax	832
Tax on ordinary activities	256
Profit on ordinary activities after tax	576
Dividends proposed	232
Retained profit for the year	344

Draft balance sheet as at 31.12.X1

	£m	£m
Fixed assets		5321
Current assets	2231	
Creditors falling due within one year	1832	
Net current assets		399
Total assets less current liabilities		5720
Creditors falling due after one year	1231	
Provisions for liabilities and charges	56	1287
		4433
Capital and reserves		2532
Share premium		1103
P&L account		798
		4433

Consideration needs to be given as to the treatment of the following items and where necessary amendments made to the draft accounts:

1 Concrete producers within the UK are subject to orders made by the Restrictive Trade Practices Court which prohibit them from entering into arrangements to share markets or fix target prices for products. It has been discovered that employees of Ssaps have entered into prohibited arrangements. It is possible that contempt proceedings may be taken against the company but it is impossible to indicate the levels of any penalties that may be imposed.

2 Ssaps has guaranteed a loan of £1 million taken out by one of its subsidiary companies. In March 20X2 the subsidiary placed itself into liquidation and there would appear to be insufficient funds to repay the loan. Ssaps has also guaranteed a loan of £2 million for another subsidiary which has a good trading position.

3 There is an outstanding legal action concerning the delivery of defective concrete to a customer of Ssaps. The lawyers for Ssaps estimate that it is probable that they could achieve a settlement out of court for £90 000, but if the case goes to court the award could be in the region of £75 000–£150 000.

4 Ssaps at the year-end had discounted £600 000 bills of exchange without recourse. At the 15 March 20X2 £150 000 were still outstanding and are due to mature in one month's time.

5 It is estimated that of the guarantees and undertakings in respect of the commitments of haulage contractors for the financing of truck mixer chassis there will be a possible liability of £1 million.

Activity 4 feedback

1 This would appear to be a possible contingent liability and therefore a note must be shown to the accounts.

2 It is very likely that the guarantee for £1 million will be called in therefore the accounts must be amended. The other loan guaranteed would appear to be remote and therefore no provision or note is required.

3 This is a difficult one to judge but it would seem reasonable to provide for £90 000 in the accounts as a probable liability.

4 The bills of exchange are without recourse therefore no liability will follow on the company.

5 This would appear to be an example of a possible liability and therefore a note is required to the accounts.

Redrafted P&L account	*£m*
Profit on ordinary activities before tax	830.91
Tax	256
Profit on ordinary activities after tax	574.91
Dividends proposed	232
Retained profit for the year	342.91

Redrafted balance sheet as at 31.12.X1

	£m	*£m*
Total assets less current liabilities		5720
Creditors greater than one year	1231	
Provisions for liabilities and charges	57.09	1288.09
		4431.91
Capital and reserves		
Called up share capital		2532
Share premium		1103
P&L account		796.91
		4431.91

In the above activity it is worth noting, first, that accruing a contingency into the accounts did have an effect on the profit of a company, but that detailed disclosure of the contingency was not required; thus the item was not brought to the attention of users! Secondly, that the accrual made was of an estimated nature and that once the liability was realized any excess in the provision account was released to profits of future years.

The provisions problem

The standard presentation balance sheet format for a set of financial statements includes a line 'provisions for liabilities and charges'. The items under this heading can cover such things as deferred tax (see Chapter 21), pensions provisions (see Chapter 22), warranties, restructuring costs, onerous contracts, environmental liabilities and many others. In addition provisions for bad debts, for depreciation, and general accruals and prepayments are included elsewhere in the balance sheet. All of these have an effect on the profit and loss account. At the time the debate took place in respect of fair value in acquisition accounting which resulted in FRS 7 only some of these provisions were covered by specific standards: depreciation, deferred tax and pensions. FRS 7 (see Chapter 24 for further details) does not allow provisions or accruals for future operating losses or for reorganization or integration costs to be included as part of the value of the fixed assets acquired. These provisions, states FRS 7, are the responsibility of the acquirer and fall to be treated by the acquirer in his/her accounts after the acquisition. Even after the issue of FRS 7 it still left a potentially large charge to the profit and loss account in terms of provisions that was not covered by any standard – the area was wide open to abuse. As an example, BT in its financial statements for the year-ended 31 March 1998 showed total provisions on the balance sheet of £1426m of which £112 m were referred to as other. The ASB issued a discussion paper on the subject in November 1995 and a FRED was produced, incorporating a review of SSAP 18, in June 1997. This FRED became a standard in September 1998, FRS 12 'Provisions, Contingent Liabilities and Contingent Assets'. The ASB identified the need for a standard in this area as follows:

The need for a standard

1   Although provisions, and the movements on them, are often material to the entity's financial position and performance, there is little published guidance on their accounting and disclosure. Recently, several concerns have been expressed. First, if recognition of a provision is based on the *intention* to incur expenditure rather than on an *obligation* to do so, recognition would not reflect a change in the economic position of the entity, since only an external commitment can affect the financial position at the balance sheet date. A second concern relates to the specific costs that may be included within any provision: under present practice several future years expenditure, including items related to ongoing operations, may be aggregated into one large provision that is reported as an exceptional item (sometimes referred to as 'big bath' accounting). Finally, the lack of a complete framework of disclosure requirements for provisions means that disclosures have, in some cases, been unhelpful for those seeking to ascertain the significance of the provision and any movements in the year.

(para. 1 appendix 111)

The problem of big bath accounting is identified in the following activity.

Activity 5

A company, with annual expected future profits of £2.5m, decides to recognize the possibility of an exceptional provision for reorganization costs for future years of £2m in the current year when its expected profits are £4.5m. In the event the charges for reorganization costs are £0.5m next year, £0.5m the following year and thereafter no further costs are expected to arise. Show the effect of the proposed accounting treatment for the reorganization costs on the profit of the company for the current and future years. Comment on this treatment.

Activity 5 feedback

	Year 1	Year 2	Year 3	Year 4
Provision b/f	0	2.0	1.5	0
Expense	0	(0.5)	(0.5)	0
P&L	2.0	0	(1.0)	0
Provision c/f	2.0	1.5	0	0
Profits	4.5	2.5	2.5	2.5
Provision	(2.0)	0	1.0	0
Profit after prov.	2.5	2.5	3.5	2.5

The company has been able to move £1m profits from year 1 to year 3 by the accounting method used for provisions and in addition has avoided the need to charge £0.5m to year 2 profit, this was in effect provided for from year 1 which was a good year for profits. In effect the company has taken a big bath in year 1 when it had substantial profits and has protected future years' profits.

The ASB address this issue in FRS 12 by setting out general requirements for provisions and by specifying their application to a number of commonly occurring circumstances.

FRS 12 objectives and definitions

The ASB identifies the objectives of FRS 12 as to ensure that:

(a) provisions are recognised and measured on a consistent basis and that sufficient information is disclosed in the notes to the financial statements to enable users to understand their nature, timing and amount; and

(b) contingencies are recognised and measured on a consistent basis and that sufficient information is disclosed in the notes to the financial statements to enable users to understand their nature and amount and the uncertainties expected to affect their ultimate outcome.

Thus the Board has issued a standard on an issue that was previously not covered by a standard, provisions, and have also superseded SSAP 18 in respect of contingencies. The Board's intention is also to inject some consistency into this area of accounting to ensure comparability over time and between companies.

The standard provides us with several definitions:

Constructive obligation

An obligation that derives from an entity's actions where:

(**a**) by an established pattern of past practice, published policies or a sufficiently specific current statement, the entity has indicated to other parties that it will accept certain responsibilities; and

(**b**) as a result, the entity has created a valid expectation on the part of those other parties that it will discharge those responsibilities.

Contingent asset

A possible asset that arises from past events and whose existence will be confirmed only by the occurrence of one or more uncertain future events not wholly within the entity's control.

Contingent liability

(**a**) a possible obligation that arises from past events and whose existence will be confirmed only by the occurrence of one or more uncertain future events not wholly within the entity's control; or

(**b**) a present obligation that arises from past events but is not recognised because:

    (**i**) it is not probable that a transfer of economic benefits will be required to settle the obligation; or

    (**ii**) the amount of the obligation cannot be measured with sufficient reliability.

Legal obligation

An obligation that derives from:

(**a**) a contract (through its explicit or implicit terms);

(**b**) legislation; or

(**c**) other operation of law.

Liabilities

Obligations of an entity to transfer economic benefits as a result of past transactions or events.

Obligating event

An event that creates a legal or constructive obligation that results in an entity having no realistic alternative to settling that obligation.

Onerous contract

A contract in which the unavoidable costs of meeting the obligations under it exceed the economic benefits expected to be received under it.

Provision

A liability of uncertain timing or amount.

Restructuring

A programme that is planned and controlled by management, and materially changes either:

(**a**) the scope of a business undertaken by an entity; or

(**b**) the manner in which that business is conducted.

It also makes a distinction between a provision and a contingency as did SSAP 18 but it seems that the distinction has changed as probable contingencies now become provisions but only where these meet the definition of a liability. Indeed it now seems that provisions are a subset of liabilities not a separate item on the balance sheet, although the FRS does not identify a change to the standard format of balance sheet presentation.

13 The FRS distinguishes between:
  (a) provisions – which are recognised as liabilities (assuming that a reliable estimate can be made) because they are present obligations where it is probable that a transfer of economic benefits will be required to settle the obligations; and
  (b) contingent liabilities – which are not recognised as liabilities because they are either:
    (i) possible obligations, as it has yet to be confirmed whether the entity has an obligation that could lead to a transfer of economic benefits; or
    (ii) present obligations that do not meet the recognition criteria in the FRS because either it is not probable that a transfer of economic benefits will be required to settle the obligation, or a sufficiently reliable estimate of the amount of the obligation cannot be made.

Accounting treatment for provisions, contingent liabilities and contingent assets

The accounting treatment is dependent upon the recognition of each of the above. A provision is only recognized when an entity has a present obligation (legal or constructive) as a result of a past event. It is probable that a transfer of economic benefits will be required to settle the obligation; and a reliable estimate can be made of the amount of the obligation. If these conditions are not met then no provision is recognized. A contingent liability is not recognized but a note is required similar to that which was required for possible contingencies under SSAP 18. Contingent assets are also not recognized but a probable one would require a note as it did under SSAP 18. It sounds as though all that FRS 12 has done is to reclassify probable contingencies as provisions but this is not true. The standard has made it much more difficult for a company to accrue a provision into the accounts as it now requires a demonstration of legal or constructive obligation before such an accrual can be made.

Activity 6

Review the items in Activity 4 and determine under FRS 12 how these would be treated in the accounts of Ssaps plc.

Activity 6 feedback

Item 1: This would be treated as a possible contingency and a note made to the accounts as no legal obligation yet exists.

Item 2: A provision is required as there is a legal obligation as a result of a past event and it is probable that there will be a need to transfer economic benefits of £1m.

Item 3: A provision is again required as on the basis of evidence available there is a present obligation which can be estimated at £90 000.

Item 4: No legal obligation therefore no liability

Item 5: There is no present obligation as a result of a past event therefore no liability. In the feedback to the above activity a liability (provision) was determined first of all by reference to whether or not there was a legal or constructive present obligation. Then by whether or not this had resulted from a past event and lastly by determining if it was probable that a transfer of economic benefits would be required and a best estimate of these made. The standard provides a very useful decision chart for determining the existence of a provision and this is reproduced in Figure 23.1 on p. 482.

Further examples

The following activities provide further examples of accounting for provisions, contingent liabilities and contingent assets.

Activity 7

A car manufacturer provides warranties at the point of sale of the car to cover manufacturing defects that become apparent within three years of sale. Past experience shows that warranties equate to £150 000 per annum. What if anything should be provided in the manufacturer's accounts for the warranties?

Activity 7 feedback

The manufacturer has a legal obligation, the warranty, which has resulted from a past event, the sale of the car. It is probable that a transfer of economic benefits will occur, £150 000 per annum. Thus a provision is required in the accounts of £150 000.

Activity 8

A leisure company causes severe damage to the habitat of wildlife in a country where there is no legal protection for the wildlife. The company has a high profile in the support of wildlife as it makes large contributions to the World Wildlife Fund and campaigns vigorously on their behalf. To rectify the damage to the habitat a charge of £1m is likely. What if anything should be provided in the leisure company's accounts?

Activity 8 feedback

The leisure company has a constructive obligation, its policy on wildlife, as a result of a past event, the damage to the habitat. Thus a provision is required of £1m in the accounts.

Activity 9

The Board of Alex plc takes a decision on 24 March to close down one of its divisions. The

Board also agrees the detailed plan for closure put forward on 24 March. No further action is taken on the closure and the year-end for Alex plc is 31 March. What should Alex plc provide in the accounts in respect of the closure?

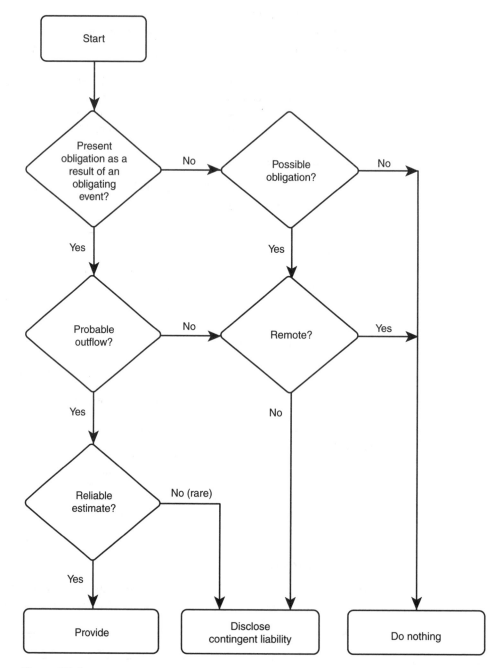

Figure 23.1

Activity 9 feedback

There is no constructive obligation as an obligating event has not yet occurred. The Board of Alex plc can change their mind in regard to the closure. A constructive obligation will only exist when the closure is communicated in detail to employees and customers. A problem exists here though as the point of recognition of the constructive obligation is dependent upon a subjective judgement – at what point will the company make a sufficiently specific statement as to the closure. No provision will be made in the accounts as at 31 March.

FRS 12 tells us that a constructive obligation to restructure arises only when an entity:

77   (a)   has a detailed formal plan for the restructuring identifying at least:
   - (i)   the business or part of a business concerned;
   - (ii)   the principal locations affected;
   - (iii)   the location, function, and approximate number of employees who will be compensated for terminating their services;
   - (iv)   the expenditures that will be undertaken; and
   - (v)   when the plan will be implemented; and

    (b)   has raised a valid expectation in those affected that it will carry out the restructuring by starting to implement that plan or announcing its main features to those affected by it.

This still leaves us with a subjective judgement to make!

Activity 10

A company has for many years made a provision for repair and maintenance of its assets. Should the company continue to do so after the issue of FRS 12.

Activity 10 feedback

The answer is no. The company has no constructive or legal obligation as a result of a past obligating event. The company should only charge to the profit and loss account the amount actually expensed on repairs and maintenance.

An example similar to that above is self-insurance and FRS 12 deals with this issue as follows:

Self-insurance

An entity that operates a chain of retail outlets decides not to insure itself in respect of the risk of minor accidents to its customers: instead it will 'self insure'. Based on its past experience, it expects to pay £100 000 a year in respect of these accidents. Should provision be made for the amount expected to arise in a normal year?

Present obligation as a result of a past obligating event –
there is no present obligation.

Conclusion –
No provision is recognised. There is no present obligation because there is no other party involved in insuring the risks.

Measurement of a provision under FRS 12

Provisions are required by the standard to be recognised at a 'best estimate' value. This requires evaluation of what a 'rational' entity would pay to settle the obligation. This again requires subjective judgement and FRS 12 suggests the use of a statistical method of estimation, 'expected value', taken from probability theory.

The provision is also required to be measured at its present value. This therefore means that provisions may require discounting if they are not payable immediately. The FRS identifies the discount rate to be used as a:

> pre-tax rate that reflects current market assessments of the time value of money and risk specific to the liability. The discount rate should not reflect risks for which future cash flow estimates have been adjusted.

The measurement of the provision is becoming even more subjective! There is a further problem with discounting future liabilities and that is that the discount will unwind. For example, a liability of £100 due in two years time, using a 10% discount rate, will be shown on the balance sheet now as £82.64, after a year the liability will be shown as £90.91. What do we do with the difference of £8.27 which represents the unwinding of the discounting? The FRS states that

> the unwinding of the discount should be included as a financial item adjacent to interest but should be shown separately from other interest on the face of the profit and loss account or in a note.

Thus the £8.27 becomes a charge to the profit and loss account. Does this then provide a true and fair view? We leave this for your discussion.

> The standard is effective for accounting periods ending on or after 23 March 1999. Earlier adoption is encouraged but not required.

Summary

You should now be able to decide how to treat a post-balance sheet event in a set of company accounts in accordance with SSAP 17 and you should be aware of window dressing in relation to SSAP 17. In relation to provisions you should now realize that the area is controversial and requires a deal of subjective judgement. Many people have argued that FRS 12 contravenes prudence, one of the concepts encaptured in SSAP 2. Prudence in SSAP 2 is defined as requiring that a provision is made for all known liabilities which leads many to believe that this requires the recognition of all future expenses. This is illogical, in our opinion, and prudence is actually a state of being free from bias, not being overly pessimistic. It will be interesting to see how reporting under FRS 12 develops and what impact the unwinding of the discounting will have on accounts.

Exercises

1 Outline the circumstances in which post-balance sheet events affect the contents of financial statements. In what different ways are those contents affected? Give examples to illustrate your points.

2 Outline the recommended treatment of provisions, contingent liabilities and contingent assets, clearly defining and illustrating the meaning of each term.

3 Give examples of each of the following:
   (a) an adjusting post-balance sheet event
   (b) a contingent liability
   (c) a contingent asset
   (d) a provision
   (e) a non-adjusting post-balance sheet event
   (f) a contingency that is also a non-adjusting post-balance sheet event.

4 'Financial statements should be prepared on the basis of conditions existing at the balance sheet date.' SSAP 17, 'Accounting for Post Balance Sheet Events'.
   (a) Recognizing the possibility of time lags in establishing what conditions actually exist at the balance sheet date, how does SSAP 17 seek to ensure that financial accounts are prepared in accordance with this rule?   (10 marks)
   (b) How does SSAP 17 seek to ensure that financial accounts prepared in accordance with this rule are not misleading?   (10 marks)
   Your answer should include *three* examples relating to (a) and a further three examples relating to (b).   **(20 marks)**
   (ACCA)

5 State, with reasons, how you would account for the following items:
   (a) The directors of a company have discovered a painting in a cupboard and have sent it to an auction house, who have confirmed that it should sell for £1 million in the following month's auction.   (3 marks)
   (b) A claim has been made against a company for injury suffered by a pedestrian in connection with building work by the company. Legal advisers have confirmed that the company will probably have to pay damages of £200 000 but that a claim can be made against the building subcontractors for £100 000.   (3 marks)
   (c) A company uses 'recourse factoring' whereby the company agrees with the factor to repurchase any debts not paid to the factor within 90 days of the sales invoice date. During the year the factored credit sales of the company were £2 million, of which £1.8 million had been paid to the factor, £150 000 was unpaid but due within 90 days and £50 000 was unpaid for more than 90 days.   (3 marks)
   (d) The manufacturer of a snooker table has received a letter from a professional snooker player, who was defeated in the final of a major snooker competition, threatening to sue the manufacturer for £1 million, being his estimate of his loss of earnings through failing to win the competition, on the grounds that the table was not level.   (3 marks)
   (12 marks)
   (ACCA)

6 State with reasons how you would account for the following items under FRS 12.
   (a) A company leases all its computer hardware on an operating lease which has three years to run. The hardware becomes obsolete during the current year as it is incapable of running the new systems required by the company for its digital sales system. The company has to purchase new hardware but finds it impossible to sell the existing hardware nor can it cancel the lease.
   (b) The government has introduced, during the current year, new health and safety regulations which are legally binding on all companies. In order to operate within the new regulations the company will need to retrain most of its

staff. No retraining has taken place before the year-end but it is expected to cost £100 000 for retraining in the next year.

7 (i) FRS – *Provisions, contingent liabilities and contingent assets* requires that a company should recognise provisions in the balance sheet, but not contingent liabilities. State one example of a provision and one example of a contingent liability and explain why each should be classified in this manner.

(6 marks)

(ii) FRS 12 rquires that a provision should be recognised when:
■ an entity has a present obligation as a result of a past event,
■ it is probable that a transfer of economic benefits will be required to settle the obligation, and
■ a reliable estimate can be made of the amount of the obligation.

Unless these conditions are met, no provision should be recognised.

It has been suggested that the criteria in FRS 12 for the recognition of provisions have been designed to make it more difficult to manipulate the financial statements, but in doing so they ignore the concept of prudence.

Explain whether you agree with this suggestion. (5 marks)

You may find it useful to refer to the following definitions from FRS 12:

Provision	'a liability that is our uncertain timing or amount, to be settled by the transfer of economic benefits'
Contingent liability	'either (i) a possible obligation arising from past events whose existence will be confirmed only by the occurrence of one or more uncertain future events not wholly within the entity's control; or (ii) a present obligation that arises from past events but is not recognised because it is not probable that a transfer of economic benefits will be required to settle the obligation or because the amount of the obligation cannot be measured with sufficient reliability'

CIMA(S) MAY 00
(adapted)

24

Group accounts and associated companies (FRSs 2, 6, 7, 8, 9)

After reading this chapter you should be able to:
- explain a business combination
- outline the need for group accounts
- consider the mechanics of preparing group accounts
- state the requirements of Companies Act in relation to group accounts
- describe the requirements of FRS 2 'Accounting for Subsidiary Undertakings'
- define an associated undertaking
- describe the requirements of Companies Act and FRS 9 'Associated and Joint Ventures'
- explain merger accounting
- outline the requirements of FRS 6 'Acquisitions and Mergers' and FRS 7 'Fair Values in Acquisition Accounting'
- practice the preparation of group accounts involving inter-company trading, unrealized profits, pre-acquisition profits and inter-company balances
- describe the issues surrounding FRS 8 'Related Party Transactions'.

Introduction

Most people are vaguely familiar from their daily newspapers with such words as 'takeover', 'merger', etc., but few have need to understand how such business combinations are actually structured. There are two basic possibilities:

1 A new company may be formed in order to absorb one or more existing companies. The essential feature here is that the new company would physically take over the assets and liabilities of the companies absorbed, and the latter would then cease to exist.
2 A limited company may be taken over by another limited company, but in this case the company being taken over would continue to exist (and would still, of course, keep its own assets and liabilities).

It is important here to recognize that in case **2** the acquiring company obtains control over the actions of the company taken over, as opposed to simply acquiring the assets of that company (case **1**). In effect, with case **2** the purchasing company is acquiring an investment rather than a collection of sundry assets, and the cost of this investment would itself appear in the purchasing company's balance sheet as an asset (in much the same way as individuals purchase investments (shares) in limited companies).

The twin elements in this transaction are an acquiring (or holding) company, and a company (or companies) being acquired (subsidiaries), and these form the basis for an examination of the structure of groups of companies.

Activity 1

A plc, an engineering firm, owns buildings and plant and machinery with a NBV of £500 000. B plc buys these assets on 1 January 200X from A at a cost of £650 000 and leases them back to A on an operating lease.

C plc, on the 1 January 200X purchases 55% of the ordinary voting shares of A plc on the open market.

Which company, B plc or C plc, has control of A plc?

Activity 1 feedback

B plc owns the assets A plc is using but in no way does B plc control the decisions of A plc's directors. Presumably A plc could gain the use of assets from another company if necessary. C plc owns A shares therefore has controlling voting power over who is appointed to the board of directors and thus controls A plc.

Need for group accounts

Before we consider the form that group accounts take, let us briefly examine the separate accounts of H Ltd (a holding company) and of S Ltd, of which H Ltd holds 55% of the ordinary voting shares.

In H company's balance sheet the shareholding (interest) in S will simply appear as an investment at HC. However, as with any other asset in a balance sheet, the use of HC as the basis of valuation would not normally give the shareholders of H Ltd any indication of the value of the subsidiary or of the underlying assets.

In relation to the holding company's P&L account the only reference to the subsidiary would be 'dividends received from S Ltd' (assuming there were any) and, of course, this would give no indication of the subsidiary's profitability.

As far as the group is concerned the holding company's accounts give no meaningful information about the group's activities, hence a way has to be found to prepare information about the related activities of H Ltd and S Ltd in a consolidated (combined) format.

Several accounting alternatives have been developed to accommodate this need to report fully on the activities of groups of companies.

Method 1 – the parent company approach

With this method of accounting the assumption is made that the group accounts are being prepared to be primarily of use by the shareholders of the controlling parent company, and the minority interests are credited with their share of the net tangible assets of the subsidiary, but this does not include any share of premium on acquisition.

This approach is, in fact, the usual method of consolidation to be followed where a subsidiary is acquired. A simple example is given below.

Big Ltd acquired the whole of the issued ordinary share capital of Little Ltd at a price of £1.50 per share for cash as at 30 June, at which date their respective balance sheets were as follows:

	Big Ltd (£)	Little Ltd (£)
Investment in Little Ltd	75 000	
Land and buildings	100 000	25 000
Plant	40 000	20 000
Sundry other assets	20 000	15 000
	235 000	60 000
£1 ordinary shares	150 000	50 000
Reserves	85 000	10 000
	235 000	60 000

As at this date, the estimated fair values of Little Ltd assets were:

Land and buildings	30 000
Plant	22 000
Sundry other assets	15 000
Total	£67 000

In Big's balance sheet, the investment in Little is shown at £1.50 × 50 000 shares i.e. £75 000). In the group's balance sheet the subsidiary's assets would be best brought in at fair value amounting to £67 000, and of course we would need to account for the difference between this figure and the cost of the investment in Little of £75 000 as goodwill on consolidation (£8000). The consolidated balance sheet would look like this:

Land and buildings	130 000
Plant	62 000
Goodwill on consolidation	8 000
Sundry other assets	35 000
	235 000
Ordinary share capital	150 000
Reserves	85 000
	235 000

It should be noted in passing that goodwill may perhaps be thought of as an intangible fixed asset, but should certainly not be regarded as a current asset. Further, the complexity of the conceptual and practical accounting issues surrounding the very existence (or non-existence) of goodwill in company accounts, in general, gave rise to separate standards of accounting practice on goodwill (SSAP 22 and then FRS 10) (see Chapter 16).

Goodwill (premium) on acquisition

From previous chapters you should, by now, be aware of the inadequacies of historic cos as a measure of asset value. It will be realized that the net book value (NBV) of an asset (or collection of assets) in the balance sheet of a company will not necessarily bear any relationship to the market value of these assets or of that company.

Obviously, when one company acquires shares in another company, then the price it is willing to pay for these shares will be computed by reference to the underlying value of the assets of the company to be acquired, and not of course of their book value as shown in the balance sheet. One would normally expect the assets of the company being acquired to be revalued on the basis of the fair value of those assets for consolidation purposes. Further, since one company is acquiring control of another company (i.e. as opposed to simply buying a small (minority) shareholding), then the price to be paid for that controlling interest is very often a price in excess of the total of the fair value of the net assets of the subsidiary. Fair value is the price at which an asset could be purchased in an arm's length transaction.

For accounting purposes this excess is termed 'goodwill' (or 'premium') on acquisition.

Obviously this 'difference' referred to above needs to be accounted for (if only to ensure that double entry is maintained!) and it is usual for the total of such premium (goodwill) on acquisition of all group subsidiaries to be shown as an asset in the group balance sheet. Note that FRS 10 refers to this goodwill arising on acquisition of a subsidiary as 'purchased goodwill', whereas other texts can be seen to use the term 'premium on acquisition' to describe this figure. We shall, therefore, regard these terms as interchangeable for our purposes here.

Discount on acquisition can also occur. This relates to the possibility of one company acquiring control of another at a discounted price (i.e. as opposed to at a premium). In practice, this is not so far-fetched as it might at first sight appear, in that an acquiring company may for various reasons (e.g. empire building) be quite willing to purchase a company with a recent history of trading losses, together with a forecast future of losses. This 'discount' on the purchase price (i.e. the surplus of the fair value of tangible assets acquired over purchase consideration) at the date of acquisition may be thus thought of as compensation for anticipated future losses to the acquiring group. (One might also reasonably assume that in the medium-term future the group would hope to turn this subsidiary into profitability.) Again, this figure of discount will need to be accounted for in the group balance sheet, but remember it will constitute a credit balance rather than an asset. It is, in effect, a form of capital reserve. Alternatively, this 'discount' may arise because the asset values agreed on acquisition may not be deemed to be 'fair values' by the acquiring company, and may be revalued downwards on consolidation.

It must be emphasized at this stage that the calculation of the goodwill or discount on acquisition should be made after a fair valuation has been made of the net assets acquired. In practice, in many cases no revaluation occurs and it is then assumed that the book value reflects the fair value, as is the case with the illustrations used later in this chapter. Note also that for purposes of computation of goodwill or discount on acquisition we usually take the fair value of net assets as being equal to the proportion of the subsidiary's ordinary share capital plus reserves as at date of acquisition. We will deal with the issue of fair value when we look at FRS 7. We have already looked at the accounting for goodwill in Chapter 16.

Method 2 – equity accounting

This particular method is only appropriate where there is no 'control' as defined earlier. In other words it is not a method to be used where we have a subsidiary company situation, but is only to be used where one company has a significant interest in another, and in this connection the words 'associated company' rather than 'subsidiary company' are appropriate.

A fuller discussion of the equity accounting method and its use for dealing with associated companies is given later in this chapter, together with a consideration of SSAP 1 and FRS 9 (being the accounting standard on associated companies).

Method 3 – proportional consolidation

Using this method we simply add together the various components of each company's balance sheet (assets and liabilities) on the basis of H Ltd's proportionate interest in S Ltd in order to arrive at the 'group' picture.

Activity 2

H Ltd acquired 80% of the equity share capital of S Ltd for cash at 31 December at a price of £1.50 per share, and their respective balance sheets as at 31 December were as follows:

	H Ltd (£)	S Ltd (£)
Investment in S Ltd		
(i.e. 8000 shares × 80% × £1.50)	9 600	
Plant and machinery	50 000	4 000
Sundry current assets	25 000	6 000
	84 600	10 000
Represented by:		
£1 ordinary shares	40 000	8 000
Reserves	44 600	2 000
	84 600	10 000

Combine both balance sheets as outlined above to produce a 'group' position.

Activity 2 feedback

	£	
Plant and machinery	53 200	(50 000 + 80% × 4000)
Goodwill on consolidation	1 600	(9600 – 80% × (8000 + 2000))
Sundry current assets	29 800	(25 000 + 80% × 6000)
	84 600	

	£
Ordinary share capital	
(Note 1)	40 000
Reserves	44 600
	84 600

Note that as with any consolidation, only the holding company's share capital constitutes the capital of the group. The subsidiary's own share capital reflects internal financing within the group, and is simply a reflection of the investment in the subsidiary as shown in the assets of the holding company's individual balance sheet. In essence, these two items are 'netted off' (contra'd) as part of the 'goodwill on acquisition' calculation.

Proportional consolidation is not *used in practice* because of the *significance of the concept of 'control'*. When one company acquires control of another company (even though as in this case H does not acquire the whole of S's equity share capital), then H can determine the future action of S and can dictate the way in which S should utilize all (i.e. 100%) of its assets. This is the reality of the relationship between H and S (i.e. control), and is quite different from the impression given in our balance sheet produced above, which implies that the group controls only 80% of S's various assets. Nor, of course, does this method give any indication of the existence of an external (minority) interest in S Ltd.

Method 1 again – the Parent Company Approach (or acquisition method)

The parent company approach used in the UK became known as acquisition accounting and we provide an activity below for you to practice this method again.

ACTIVITY 3

Large plc acquired the whole of the issued ordinary share capital of Small Ltd. at a price of £3.50 per share for cash as at 30 September, at which date their respective balance sheets were as follows:

	Large plc (£)	Small Ltd. (£)
Investment in Small Ltd	115 500	–
Land and buildings	210 000	43 000
Plant and equipment	75 000	22 000
Net current assets	63 500	18 000
	464 000	83 000
£2 ordinary shares	246 000	66 000
Reserves	218 000	17 000
	464 000	83 000

The estimated fair values at 30 September above of Small Ltd assets were:

Land and Buildings	49 000
Plant and equipment	19 000
Net current assets	18 000
	86 000

Prepare the consolidated balance sheet of Large plc as at 30 September using acquisition accounting.

Activity 3 feedback

This activity is similar to the example provided under method 1 earlier.

	£
Goodwill on acquisition is calculated as follows:	
Paid for 33 000 shares of Small Ltd. at £3.50 each	115 500
Bought all of Small Ltd's net assets at fair value	86 000
Goodwill on acquisition	29 500

Consolidated balance sheet Large plc 30 September	
Goodwill on acquisition	29 500
Land and buildings	259 000
Plant and equipment	94 000
Net current assets	81 500
	464 000
£2 Ordinary shares	246 000
Reserves	218 000
	464 000

Note that in the above consolidated balance sheet the share capital shown is only that of Large plc as the shares of Small Ltd are all held by Large. Also note that the reserves of Small, £17 000, that existed when Large made the acquisition seem to have disappeared. In fact these reserves have been 'capitalised' to the 'cost of control'. This is explained by the fact that the fair value of Small's net assets is the equivalent of the ordinary shares and reserves of Small as follows:

Fair value Small's net assets	86 000
Represented by:	
£2 ordinary shares	66 000
Reserves	17 000
Revaluation reserve at acquisition	3 000
	86 000

The earlier calculation of goodwill can now be written as:

Cost of control (i.e. paid for acquisition)		115 500
Bought 100% Small's shares		66 000
Bought 100% Small's reserves	17 000	
	3 000	20 000
		86 000
Goodwill on acquisition		29 500

From our discussion so far we can highlight several issues as follows:

■ the need to define control, subsidiary and associated company
■ the need to decide on the most appropriate method of accounting to use for subsidiary and associated companies
■ the need to deal with the goodwill that may or may not be generated from the method chosen
■ the need to define fair value.

Definition of subsidiary

The Companies Act 1989 changed the definition of a subsidiary from that of the 1985 Act. The 1985 Act stated that:

> one company [S Ltd] will be classed as a subsidiary of another company [H Ltd] if:
>
> 1 H Ltd is a member of S Ltd and controls the composition of the board of directors of S Ltd or
> 2 H Ltd holds more than half the nominal value of the equity share capital of S Ltd.
> 3 S Ltd is a subsidiary of a third company S1 Ltd which is itself a subsidiary of H Ltd.

The 1989 Act states that a parent company should be defined as one which either:

1 holds a majority of the voting rights in a subsidiary undertaking; or
2 is a member of the subsidiary and has the right to appoint or remove a majority of its directors; or
3 has the right to direct the operating and financial policies of the subsidiary by the terms of the memorandum or articles of the subsidiary or by a control contract authorized by the subsidiary's memorandum or articles; or
4 is a member of the subsidiary and controls a majority of the voting rights of the subsidiary, either alone or under a voting agreement entered into with other shareholders; or
5 holds a participating interest in the subsidiary (i.e. an interest in its shares held on a long-term basis for the purpose of securing a contribution to the parents' activities by the exercise of control or influence over the subsidiary), and actually exercises a dominant influence over the subsidiary or manages the affairs of itself and the subsidiary on a unified basis; or
6 is the parent company of an undertaking which under the criteria set out above is itself the parent undertaking of another undertaking (i.e. a sub-subsidiary).

Activity 4

Explain the differences between the definitions given in the Companies Act of 1985 and 1989.

Activity 4 feedback

The changes in the definitions of a subsidiary are mainly to reflect a substance over form approach, i.e. the Companies Act 1989 emphasizes dominant influence not the legal structure. This emphasis on dominant influence is designed to prevent the use of artificial off-balance sheet financing devices. Note that another major change was from holdings of equity share capital to holdings of voting rights. Note also that subsidiary company has now become subsidiary undertaking.

The change from the Companies Act 1985 to 1989 can perhaps best be illustrated by the following examples.

Activity 5

State whether the following would be a subsidiary:

(a) under Companies Act 1985
(b) under Companies Act 1989.

1 Company A holds 69% of the equity of company B representing 42.3% of the voting rights.
2 Company C holds 30% of the ordinary shares of company D and all the preference shares. Company D is controlled by its preference shareholders.

Activity 5 feedback

1 Subsidiary 1985 Act; not a subsidiary 1989 Act
2 not subsidiary 1985 Act; subsidiary 1989 Act.

FRS 2 'Accounting for Subsidiary Undertakings'

The changes made by the Companies Act 1989 to accounting for subsidiaries and the problems that existed with the original ASC's statement – SSAP 14 – made it necessary for the ASB to review accounting for subsidiaries. In July 1992 FRS 2 was issued.

FRS 2 provides us with definitions of some of the terms used by the Companies Act 1989 in defining a subsidiary undertaking:

> 7 *Dominant influence:*
>   Influence that can be exercised to achieve the operating and financial policies desired by the holder of the influence, notwithstanding the rights or influence of any other party.
>   (a) In the context of paragraph 14(c) and section 258(2)(c) *the right to exercise a dominant influence* means that the holder has a right to give directions with respect to the operating and financial policies of another undertaking with which its directors are obliged to comply, whether or not they are for the benefit of that undertaking [*From 10A Sch 4(1)*]
>   (b) *The actual exercise of dominant influence* is the exercise of an influence that achieves the result that the operating and financial policies of the undertaking influenced are set in accordance with the wishes of the holder of the influence and for the holder's benefit whether or not those wishes are explicit. The actual exercise of dominant influence is identified by its effect in practice rather than by the way in which it is exercised. [*FRS defining phrase used in s 258(4)(a)*]

12 *Managed on a unified basis:*

Two or more undertakings are managed on a unified basis if the whole of the operations of the undertakings are integrated and they are managed as a single unit. Unified management does not arise solely because one undertaking manages another [*FRS defining phrase used in s 258(4)(b)*]

15 *Participating interest:*

An interest held by an undertaking in the shares of another undertaking which it holds on a long-term basis for the purpose of securing a contribution to its activities by the exercise of control or influence arising from or related to that interest [*from s 260*]

(a) A holding of 20% or more of the shares of an undertaking shall be presumed to be a participating interest unless the contrary is shown.

(b) An interest in shares includes an interest which is convertible into an interest in shares, and includes an option to acquire shares or any interest which is convertible into shares.

(c) An interest held on behalf of an undertaking shall be treated as held by that undertaking.

Dominant influence is a key factor in deciding whether one company is in control of another. For example, one company actually having power of veto over another would indicate control and dominant influence.

Mixed groups

Complex holdings of shares exist between companies and it can be difficult sometimes to identify holding and subsidiary companies. We must remember the Companies Act definition that a company is the parent company of an undertaking which under the criteria set out above is itself the parent undertaking of another undertaking.

Activity 6

In the examples given below identify the parent subsidiary relationships.

1 H owns 75% of the voting shares of S which in turn owns 40% of the voting shares of S1. H also owns directly 15% of the voting shares of S1.

2 H owns 100% of the voting shares of S which in turn owns 30% of S1. H also owns 75% of S2 which in turn owns 25% of S1.

3 H owns 60% of the voting shares of S which in turns owns 20% of the voting shares of S1. H also owns directly 20% of the voting shares of S1.

Activity 6 feedback

The relationships are easier to see if a diagram is drawn.

1

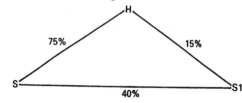

(a) S is a subsidiary of H (75% ownership) S1 is not a subsidiary of S (assuming no information in respect of dominant influence).

(b) H directly owns 75% × 40% of S1 + 15% of S1
    = 30% + 15%
    = 45% which would imply no subsidiary relationship.

(c) However H controls S thus controls 40% of S1 plus 15%.

(d) Therefore S1 is a subsidiary of H and will be consolidated with a minority interest of 55%.

2

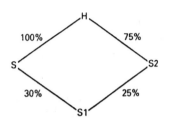

(a) S and S2 are subsidiaries of H.

(b) H directly owns 100% × 30% + 75% × 25% of S1
    = 30% + 18.75%
    = 48.75% only.

(c) However, H controls 30% + 25% = 55%.

(d) Thus S1 is a subsidiary of H and will be consolidated with a minority interest of 51.25%.

3

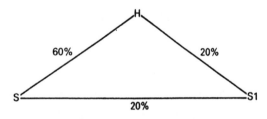

(a) S is a subsidiary of H.

(b) H owns 60% × 20% + 20% of S1 = 32% of S1.

(c) H controls 20% + 20% of S1 = 40%.

(d) Thus, S1 is *not* a subsidiary of H (assuming no indication of dominant influence) and will not be consolidated.

Minority Interest (MI)

In Activity 6 we considered examples of holdings where the holding company held less than 100% of the shares of the acquired company. When preparing the consolidated balance sheet we will have to consider how to deal with the part we do not own. This part is referred to as the minority interest but the minority interest will include more than just the shares as this minority will also have earned, and therefore own, a proportion of the reserves equivalent to the shareholding. The example below illustrates consolidation where a minority interest exists.

Example

Alpha plc bought 75% of the shares of Beta Ltd for cash at a price of £4 per share when the balance sheets of the two companies were as follows:

	Alpha (£)	Beta (£)
Fixed assets (before investment in beta)	400 000	75 000
Net current assets	75 000	12 000
	475 000	87 000
Share capital	350 000	60 000
Reserves	125 000	27 000
	475 000	87 000

The nominal value of Alpha and Beta shares is respectively £2 and £2.50 and the fair value of Beta's fixed assets at acquisition is £83 000 and the net current assets £12 000.

The first point to note in the above example is that Alpha has not yet recorded the purchase of 75% of Beta in its books. This must be done prior to consolidation and thus Alpha's balance sheet will become:

Fixed assets	400 000
Investment in Beta (18 000 shares at £4 ps)	72 000
Net current assets	3 000
	475 000
£2 share capital	350 000
Reserves	125 000
	475 000

We can now calculate goodwill on acquisition (or cost of control):

Cost of Alpha's control of Beta is		72 000
For which Alpha bought:		
75% of share capital of beta	45 000	
75% of reserves of £27 000	20 250	
75% of revaluation to f. v.	6 000	71 250
Goodwill on acquisition		750

At this point it is worth calculating the minority interest holding at date of acquisition. The minority interest is obviously 25% of the shares and reserves of Beta but also includes 25% of the revaluation reserve created on recording Beta's assets at fair value. Thus minority interest is:

25% of share capital of Beta	15 000
25% of reserves at acquisition	6 750
25% of fair value reserve	2 000
Minority interest at date of acquisition	23 750

The consolidate balance sheet can now be prepared as follows:

Goodwill on acquisition	750
Fixed assets	483 000
Net current assets	15 000
	498 750
£2 share capital	350 000
Reserves	125 000
Minority interest	23 750
	498 750

Note that the minority interest is recorded as a one line entry on the consolidated balance sheet.

Pre-acquisition profits and acquisition accounting

Throughout the foregoing examples the profits earned by S Ltd before its acquisition by H Ltd have been regarded as non-distributable and have been set against the cost of investment account for purposes of consolidation (see Activity 3). These profits are usually referred to as pre-acquisition profits. Further, only S's profits made since the date of acquisition (i.e. the post-acquisition profits) can be included in group reserves in the group balance sheet and regarded as distributable. However, it should be noted that any dividend paid by S Ltd after its acquisition by H Ltd but out of pre-acquisition profits would be set against the cost of the investment in S Ltd for consolidation purposes. This treatment is, in fact, an application of the concept of capital maintenance. It should be noted that the acquisition of a subsidiary by a holding company is a capital transaction, and the cost of H's investment in S Ltd is, in effect, the price paid to acquire the net assets plus goodwill as at the date of that acquisition. This, as we explained at Activity 3, is equivalent to acquiring the issued equity share capital plus reserves of S Ltd. Hence, any group distribution of the reserves of S Ltd in existence as at the date of acquisition would effectively be a distribution of capital, and would be contrary to English law. Note, however, that as far as the minority interest is concerned, any distinction between pre- and post-acquisition profits attributable to minority would serve no useful purpose, since it is the group's capital maintenance with which we are solely concerned.

This general approach to group accounting is called **acquisition accounting**, and it always assumes control by a holding company of a subsidiary.

Remember that in the introductory paragraph to this chapter the words 'takeover' and 'merger' were used, and whereas one might associate a takeover of one company by another with an acquisition accounting approach, there exists an alternative approach to be adopted for the merger form of business combination. Not surprisingly, this approach is known as **merger accounting**. In fact, merger accounting was initially only popular in the United States and was originally only to be applied in situations where two (or more) companies came together in a 'pooling of interests', in which neither party is dominant. This is discussed further on pp. 531–541.

Acquisition accounting later than date of acquisition

Activity 7

1 H Ltd purchased 80% of the equity share capital of S Ltd for cash at 31 December year 1 at a price of £1.50 per share, when the balance on S Ltd's reserves stood at £2000.
2 The consolidation is required to be made at 31 December year 2, at which point the individual balance sheets of the two companies are as follows:

	H Ltd (£)	S Ltd (£)
Investment in S Ltd	9 600	
Plant and machinery	60 000	5 000
Sundry current assets	35 000	6 000
	104 600	11 000
Represented by:		
£1 ordinary shares	40 000	8 000
Reserves	64 600	3 000
	104 600	11 000

Activity 7 feedback

The consolidated balance sheet as at 31 December year 2 would then be as follows:

	£
Plant and machinery	65 000
Goodwill on acquisition (note 1)	1 600
Sundry current assets	41 000
	107 600
Represented by:	
£1 ordinary shares	40 000
Group reserves (note 2)	65 400
Minority interests (note 3)	2 200
	107 600

Notes

1

	£	£
Cost of investment in S Ltd		9 600
acquired ordinary shares at 31 December year 1		
(80% × 8000)	6 400	
acquired reserves at 31 December	1 600	8 000
(being 80% of balance of £2000 on reserves of		
S Ltd at 31 December)		
Goodwill on acquisition)		1 600

2 Reserves of H Ltd at 31 December year 2   64 600
  Reserves of S Ltd accruing to group since
  date of acquisition to 31 December year 2   800
  $(3000 - 2000) \times 80\%$

                                              65 400

3 Share capital at 31 December year 2 of S Ltd accruing
  to minorities $(20\% \times 8000)$ 1 600
  Reserves at 31 December year 2 of S Ltd accruing
  to minorities $(20\% \times 3000)$ 600

                                               2 200

Inter-company trading and the elimination of unrealized profits

When one member of a group, S Ltd, buys from an external supplier goods at a price (say) of £100, and sells those goods to a fellow group company S1 Ltd at a price of £140, then S Ltd can legitimately show a profit of £40 in its own P&L account. However, on consolidation of the accounts of S Ltd and S1 Ltd it should be recognized that this sale from S Ltd to S1 Ltd cannot give rise to a profit as far as the group P&L account is concerned as the sale is in effect an internal group transfer. In order for the group to realize a profit, a sale must be made to a customer outside the group. This is shown diagrammatically in Figure 24.1. (The arrows represent sales either within or outside the group as indicated. R = realized group sales; UR = unrealized group sales.)

Note again that although internal group sales reflect unrealized profit as far as the *group* is concerned, there is nonetheless a realized profit to be had from such transactions as far as the P&L accounts *individual* companies within the group are concerned.

Referring to the previous example if the individual accounts of S Ltd and S1 Ltd are combined for consolidation purposes without further adjustment, then group profit will show £40 and group stock will stand at £140. In other words, group profit will be overstated by £40 and also the stock of the group will be stated at £40 in excess of cost to the group (as opposed to cost to S Ltd).

FRS 2 on the subject of inter-group transactions has this to say:

  39   To the extent that they are reflected in the book value of assets to be included in the consolidation, profits or losses on any intragroup transactions should

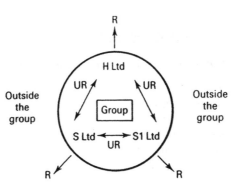

Figure 24.1
Group sales.

be eliminated in full. Amounts in relation to debts and claims between undertakings included in the consolidation should also be eliminated. The elimination of profits or losses relating to intragroup transactions should be set against the interests held by the group and the minority interest in respective proportion to their holdings in the undertaking whose individual financial statements recorded the eliminated profits or losses. All profits or losses on transactions that would be eliminated if they were between undertakings included in the consolidation should also be eliminated if one party is a subsidiary undertaking excluded because of its different activities (paragraph 25(c)). [*FRS requirement in relation to 4A Sch 6. The Act allows partial elimination but the FRS requires elimination in full.*]

Activity 8

A plc owns 75% of the shares in B plc bought when the reserves of B were £200 000. The individual balance sheet of A and B as at 30 June 200X are given below. During the year B has sold goods to A at a profit margin of 25% on cost. £50 000 of these goods lie in A's closing stock as at 30 June 200X. Also B owes C an outside supplier £2000 and C owes A £5000 as at 30 June 200X.

Prepare the consolidated balance sheet as at 30 June 200X.

	Individual balance sheets 30.6.0X	
Assets	*A*	*B*
	£000s	£000s
Land and plant	1000	200
Stock	600	400
Debtors	200	40
Investment in B	275	–
	2075	640
Liabilities		
Creditors	30	16
	2045	624
Represented by:		
Ordinary £1 shares	1000	100
Reserves	1045	524
	2045	624

Activity 8 feedback

Consolidated balance sheet as at 30.6.0X

Assets	*£000s*
Goodwill (note 1)	50
Land and Plant	1200
Stock (1000 – 10)	990
Debtors (240 – 2)	238
	2478

Liabilities

Creditors (46 − 2)	44	
	2434	
Represented by:		
Ordinary £1 shares	1000	
Reserves (note 2)	1280.5	
	2280.5	
Minority interest (note 3)	153.5	
	2434	

Note 1

Cost of investment in B		275
less ordinary shares acquired	75	
reserves acquired 75% × 200	150	225
Goodwill on acquisition		50

Note 2

Reserves A	1045
reserves post-acquired B	
75% (524 − 10 − 200)	235.5
	1280.5

Note 3

Minority interest	
25% ordinary shares	25
25% reserves = 25% × 514)	128.5
	153.5

The reconciliation of inter-company balances

It is commonplace for companies within a group to shuffle liquidity and stocks between themselves as and when required, and indeed this is one of the advantages of a group structure. Obviously with reference to such transactions, the indebtedness to/from member companies will need to be recorded in the individual companies' books of account as appropriate. Hence, each company will carry balances in its own year-end balance sheet reflecting the indebtedness to/from other companies within the group. In relation to the group's position as regards the outside world, these balances are internal balances, and will therefore not require to be shown in the group balance sheet. They are in fact cancelled on consolidation across the individual balance sheets of group members.

Occasionally, however, it is not possible to cancel out such inter-company balances, and this may often be due to a transfer of goods or cash between group companies straddling the financial year-end.

A consolidation adjustment is required at the year-end to adjust for goods or cash in transit between two companies before we can carry out the consolidation of accounts. The adjustment assumes that we account for the transit item as though it had reached its destination.

Activity 9

The financial year-end of two companies A Ltd and B Ltd within the same group is 31 December. On 29 December A Ltd dispatches goods to B Ltd to invoice value of £40 000 and charges B Ltd's ledger account accordingly. B Ltd does not receive either goods or invoice until 4 January. Prepare the consolidation adjustment in B's books and note any other adjustment that may be required on consolidation.

Activity 9 feedback

The adjustment will bring the goods into B's books as at 31 December.

B Ltd's ledger books	Dr	Cr
Goods in transit (stock)	£40 000	
A Ltd current account		£40 000

On consolidation the respective inter-company balances in the current accounts which are now in agreement will cancel out.

However, we must remember that this stock of £40 000 in transit will contain an element of unrealized profit and this will need eliminating on consolidation.

The regulations governing the presentation of group accounts

From the legal viewpoint the Companies Act 1948 was the principal act governing the publication of group accounts, but this has, of course, now been consolidated within the Companies Act 1985. However, in addition to this Act, we as accountants must attach equal importance in our coverage of this area to FRS 2. The important features of both of the above sources of regulation are covered below, together with relevant section or schedule references being to the Companies Act 1985.

There is a general requirement within company law that requires that not only individual companies, but also groups of companies, to comply with the various disclosure provisions of the Companies Act 1985. In particular, section 227(1) states that 'the directors shall, as well as preparing individual accounts for the year, also prepare group accounts'. Section 227(2) then states that those group accounts should include both a consolidated balance sheet and a consolidated P&L account, and it will of course be realized that these group accounts may (and usually will) be incorporated into the holding company's own accounts. (Note also that there are circumstances in which exemption is granted from consolidation of a subsidiary's accounts within the group, and this is dealt with on p. 506–508.)

In addition to company law recognition of the form of group accounts, it should also be noted that FRS 2 states that consolidated accounts should be the normal form of group accounts, and that the basis of consolidation should be disclosed in the notes to the accounts as an accounting policy of the group.

You may be aware that company law allows certain categories of company, defined by the Companies Act as 'small' or 'medium-sized' to file only a modified (i.e. a somewhat less detailed) version of its annual accounts with the Registrar of Companies. Although the detailed provisions of this area are not appropriate to our study of groups, it should be noted that the Act allows a *holding* company to file modified accounts for itself, but only where the group itself would in law be regarded as small (or medium sized).

Further, just as the above applies to the accounts of the holding company, so it extends this provision to the accounts of the group. In other words in circumstances where a group would qualify as small (or medium-sized) if it were an individual company, then the group accounts themselves may be modified accordingly.

Consistency within the group

FRS 2 has the following to say on this:

40 Subject to paragraph 41 below, uniform group accounting policies should be used for determining the amounts to be included in the consolidated financial statements, if necessary by adjusting for consolidation the amounts which have been reported by subsidiary undertakings in their individual financial statements. [*4A Sch 3(1)*]

41 In exceptional cases, different accounting policies may be used. Where the directors of the parent undertaking depart from the Act's general requirement to use the same group accounting rules to value or otherwise determine the assets and liabilities to be included in the consolidated financial statements, schedule 4A paragraph 3(2) requires disclosure of the particulars, which should include the different accounting policies used. [*4A s 3(2)*]

Difficulty can also occur in achieving the same accounting periods for all companies in the group. FRS 2 has this to say:

42 The financial statements of all subsidiary undertakings to be used in preparing the consolidated financial statements should, wherever practicable, be prepared to the same financial year-end and for the same accounting period as those of the parent undertaking of the group.

43 Where the financial year of a subsidiary undertaking differs from that of the parent undertaking of the group, interim financial statements should be prepared to the same date as those of the parent undertaking of the group for use in the preparation of the consolidated financial statements. If it is not practicable to use such interim financial statements, the financial statements of the subsidiary undertaking for its last financial year should be used, providing that year-ended not more than three months before the relevant year-end of the parent undertaking of the group. In this case any changes that have taken place in the intervening period that materially affect the view given by the group's financial statements should be taken into account by adjustments in the preparation of the consolidated financial statements [*FRS preference of alternatives permitted by 4A Sch 2(2)*].

44 The following information should be given for each subsidiary undertaking which is included in the consolidated financial statements on the basis of information prepared to a different date or for a different accounting period from that of the parent undertaking of the group: [*Subject to section 231, 5 Sch 19 requires disclosures for different financial year-ends*] (**a**) the name of the subsidiary undertaking;

(**b**) the accounting date or period of the subsidiary undertaking; and

(**c**) the reason for using a different accounting date or period for the subsidiary undertaking.

Activity 10

H Ltd's (a holding company) year-end is 30 June 200X whereas its subsidiary S Ltd's year-end is 31 March 200X. It is not practicable for the subsidiary to prepare interim financial statements. However, it is known that S Ltd has incurred a huge trading loss in the three months to 30 June 200X.

At what date would the consolidated statements be prepared and what factors would need disclosing?

Activity 10 feedback

The accounts would be prepared as at 30 June 200X using the subsidiary accounts for the year-ended 31 March 200X and making necessary adjustments within the consolidation for the loss. Disclosure according to paragraph 44 of FRS 2 would be required.

Exemptions from consolidation

Let us see what FRS 2 says for this:

76 The Act requires that all the subsidiary undertakings of a parent undertaking are to be included in the consolidated financial statements for that group, subject to the exceptions permitted or required by section 229(2)–(4). The circumstances in which the Act permits or requires a subsidiary undertaking to be excluded from consolidation are the following:

Permissive exclusions

(**a**) 'if its inclusion is not material for the purpose of giving a true and fair view; but two or more undertakings may be excluded only if they are not material taken together'; or

(**b**) 'where the information necessary for the preparation of group accounts cannot be obtained without disproportionate expense or undue delay'; or

(**c**) 'where severe long-term restrictions substantially hinder the exercise of the rights of the parent company over the assets or management of that undertaking'; or

(**d**) 'where the interest of the parent company is held exclusively with a view to subsequent resale and the undertaking has not previously been included in consolidated group accounts prepared by the parent company';

Required exclusion

(**e**) 'where the activities of one or more subsidiary undertakings are so different from those of other undertakings to be included in the consolidation that their inclusion would be incompatible with the obligation to give a true and fair view'.

FRS 2 elaborates on the conditions for exclusion.

Materiality requires no further mention (according to FRS 2) as FRSs only deal with material items in the first place! As for disproportionate expense and undue delay FRS 2 states that exclusion on these grounds cannot be justified.

FRS 2 also limits exclusion on the grounds of severe long-term restrictions to those cases where the effect of the restrictions is that the parent undertaking does not control the subsidiary. It also requires that severe long-term restrictions be identified by their effect in practice.

Activity 11

Company C with two subsidiaries in foreign countries learns that the trading of S1 is to be severely restricted by the government of the country in which it operates. There is a remote possibility that the same could happen to S2. Should both subsidiaries be excluded from consolidation?

Activity 11 feedback

S1 should be excluded on the grounds of severe long-term restrictions, but not S2.

FRS 2 defines two sets of circumstances only in which an interest is considered to be held exclusively with a view to subsequent resale:

1 immediate intention to sell and the expectation of a sale within approximately one year
2 if it was acquired as a result of the enforcement of a security.

As far as exclusion on the grounds of different activities is concerned FRS 2 states that these are so exceptional that it would be misleading to link them in general to any particular contrast of activities. It goes on to say:

> For example, the contrast between Schedule 9 and 9A companies (banking and insurance companies and groups) and other companies or between profit and not-for-profit undertakings is not sufficient of itself to justify non-consolidation. The different activities of undertakings included in the consolidation can better be shown by presenting segmental information rather than by excluding from consolidation the subsidiary undertakings with different activities.

Note that a parent undertaking is also exempt from preparing consolidated financial statements where it itself is a wholly owned subsidiary undertaking. It is interesting to note that the Companies Act allows five circumstances for exemption but that FRS 2 limits this to three.

Accounting treatment of excluded subsidiaries

The particular treatment required is dependent on the reasons for exclusion, and FRS 2 lays down the following rules:

Severe long-term restrictions
27 A subsidiary undertaking excluded on the grounds set out in paragraph 25(a) [severe long-term restrictions] should be treated as a fixed asset investment. If restrictions were in force at its acquisition date, the subsidiary undertaking should be carried initially at cost; if restrictions came into force at a later date,

the subsidiary undertaking should be carried at a fixed amount calculated using the equity method at that date. While the restrictions are in force, no further accruals should be made for the profits or losses of that subsidiary undertaking, unless the parent undertaking still exercises a significant influence over it. If this is the case, it should treat the subsidiary undertaking as an associated undertaking using the equity method. The carrying amount of subsidiary undertakings subject to severe long-term restrictions should be reviewed and written down for any permanent diminution in value. In assessing diminution in value, each subsidiary undertaking should be considered individually. Any intragroup amounts due from subsidiary undertakings excluded on the grounds of severe long-term restrictions should also be reviewed and written down, if necessary.

28 When the severe restrictions cease and the parent undertaking's rights are restored, the amount of the unrecognized profit or loss that accrued during the period of restriction for that subsidiary undertaking should be separately disclosed in the consolidated profit and loss account of the period in which control is resumed. Similarly, any amount previously charged for permanent diminution that needs to be written back as a result of restrictions ceasing should be separately disclosed.

Held exclusively with a view to subsequent resale

29 A subsidiary undertaking that is excluded from consolidation on the grounds set out in paragraph 25(b) [held exclusively with a view to subsequent resale] should be recorded in the consolidated financial statements as a current asset at the lower of cost and net realisable value.

Different activities [4A Sch 18]

30 A subsidiary undertaking excluded on the grounds set out in paragraph 25(c) [different activities] should be recorded in the consolidated financial statements using the equity method, as required by the Act.

FRS 2 also requires certain disclosures in consolidated statements for subsidiaries excluded from consolidation as follows:

(a) particulars of the balances between the excluded subsidiary undertakings and the rest of the group

(b) the nature and extent of transactions of the excluded subsidiary undertakings with the rest of the group

(c) or an excluded subsidiary undertaking carried other than by the equity method, any amounts included in the consolidated financial statements in respect of:
  (i) dividends received and receivable from that undertaking; and
  (ii) any write-down in the period in respect of the investment in that undertaking or amounts due from that undertaking

(d) or subsidiary undertakings excluded because of different activities, the separate financial statements of those undertakings. Summarized information may be provided for undertakings that individually, or in combination with those with similar operations, do not account for more than 20% of any one or more of operating profits, turnover or net assets of the group. The group amounts should be measured by including all excluded subsidiary undertakings.

Changes in composition of a group

FRS 2 changes the point at which an undertaking becomes or ceases to be a subsidiary undertaking from that given in SSAP 14. There is now a single triggering date which is the date control of the undertaking passes, and this, according to FRS 2, is a matter of fact and cannot be backdated or otherwise altered.

Subsidiaries can be acquired in stages, for example a purchase of 20% of equity of a company in 19X0 could be followed by a further purchase of 40% in 19X2 which then passes control to the parent undertaking. The problem with acquisition in stages is: when is the undertaking first consolidated and at what value should we include its assets and liabilities?

FRS 2 provides this answer:

> Where a subsidiary undertaking is acquired in stages, its net identifiable assets and liabilities are to be included in the consolidation at their fair values on the date it becomes a subsidiary undertaking, rather than at the date of the earlier purchases. Using other methods to compute the amounts to be included in the consolidation would fail to give a full picture of the assets and liabilities acquired that now comprise part of the group's resources.

Activity 12

P acquired 20% of S1 for £100 000 when the fair value of its net assets were £400 000. P acquired a further 40% of S for £400 000 when the fair value of its net assets were £700 000. What is the value of goodwill arising on consolidation of S1?

Activity 12 feedback

According to FRS 2 goodwill is the difference between the fair value of the group's share of net assets on the date the undertaking becomes a subsidiary and the total acquisition cost of the interests held. Therefore:

	£
Acquisition cost	500 000
Group share of fair value 60% × 700 000	420 000
Goodwill	80 000

If in Activity 12 goodwill had been calculated at each stage of acquisition, i.e.

Acquisition cost	100 000
Group shares (20% × 400 000)	80 000
Goodwill	20 000
Acquisition cost	400 000
Group share (40% × 700 000)	280 000
Goodwill	120 000
Total goodwill	140 000

FRS 2 permits this method of calculation of goodwill in the rare cases where using the required method would be misleading.

When a group disposes of part of an interest in a subsidiary undertaking a profit or loss on disposal will obviously arise but how do we calculate this? According to FRS 2:

> it should record any profit or loss arising calculated as the difference between the carrying amount of the net assets of that subsidiary undertaking attributable to the group's interest before the reduction and the carrying amount attributable to the group's interest after the reduction together with any proceeds received. The net assets compared should include any related goodwill not previously written off through the profit and loss account. Where the undertaking remains a subsidiary undertaking after the disposal, the minority interest in that subsidiary undertaking should be increased by the carrying amount of the net identifiable assets that are now attributable to the minority interest because of the decrease in the group's interest. No amount for goodwill that arose on acquisition of the group's interest in that subsidiary undertaking should be attributed to the minority interest.

Activity 13

The value of a subsidiary's net assets at 31 March 200X is £400 000. At this date the parent, which held a 100% share in the subsidiary, disposes of 40% for £200 000. On the original acquisition of the subsidiary, goodwill of £80 000 arose which was eliminated against the reserves. Calculate the profit or loss on disposal.

Activity 13 feedback

	£
Group share of net assets before disposal including goodwill (100% × (400 000 + 80 000))	480 000
Group share of net assets after disposal including goodwill (60% × (400 000 + 80 000))	288 000
Disposal proceeds	200 000
	488 000
Profit on disposal	8 000

Note that if goodwill had not been included in the above example the profit on disposal would have been £40 000! The difference of £32 000 is 40% of the goodwill that avoided the P&L account.

We can usefully refresh our memory of group accounts and work through a full example.

Activity 14

The balance sheets of Alexander and Britton on 30 June 1996 were as follows:

	Alexander		Britton	
	£000s	£000s	£000s	£000s
Fixed assets				
Land and buildings	108		64	
less Depreciation	20	88	32	32
Plant and machinery	65		43	
less Depreciation	25	40	29	14
		128		46
Investments				
Shares in Britton		35		–
Current assets				
Stock	25		27	
Debtors	48		21	
Bank	22		6	
	95		54	
Creditors < 1 year				
Creditors	112	(17)	34	20
		146		66
Represented by				
Ordinary £1 share		100		50
Capital reserves		10		
Revenue reserves		36		16
		146		66

1 Alexander acquired 37 500 shares in Britton in 1992 when there had been a debit balance on the revenue reserve of £3000.
2 During the year-ended 30 June 1996 Alexander purchased a machine from Britton for £5000 which had yielded a profit on selling price of 30% to that company. Depreciation on the machine had been charged in the accounts at 20% on cost.
3 Britton purchases goods from Alexander providing Alexander with a gross profit on invoice price of $33\frac{1}{3}\%$. On 30 June 1996 the stock of Britton included an amount of £8000 being goods purchased from Alexander for £9000.
Required
Prepare the consolidated balance sheet of Alexander and its subsidiary as at 30 June 1996.

Activity 14 feedback

	£000
(a) Cost of control	35
shares of net assets	
75% (50 – 3)	35.25
Negative goodwill	0.25
(b) Inter-group transfer of machine – unrealized profit	1500
excess depreciation charged 20% × 1500	300
Britton's accounts unrealized profit	1200

(c) Inter-group stock transfer – unrealized profit

$33^1/_3\% \times £9000$	3000
Reduction in value	1000
Alexander's accounts unrealized profit	2000

Consolidated balance sheet as at 30 June 1996

Fixed assets		*£000*
Land and buildings		120
Plant and machinery		52.8
		172.8
Current assets		
Stock	50	
Debtors	69	
Bank	28	
	147	
Creditors < 1 year		
Creditors	146	1
		173.8
Represented by:		
Ordinary £1 shares		100
Capital reserves		10.25
Revenue reserves $(36 - 2 + 75\% \, (19 - 1.2))$		47.35
		157.6
Minority interest $(25\% \, (66 - 1.2))$		16.2
		173.8

Consolidated profit and loss account

It is worthwhile at this point considering the preparation of a consolidated profit and loss account for a group. The principles of preparation are the same as those for the balance sheet. Thus the aspect of control over profits is highly important. A simple example demonstrates the preparation of a consolidated profit and loss account.

Example

The individual profit and loss accounts of High plc and Low Ltd as at 31 December 200X are as follows:

	High plc (£)	Low Ltd (£)
Turnover	100 000	50 000
Cost of sales	75 000	30 000
Gross profit	25 000	20 000
Distribution expenses	4 000	3 000
Administration expenses	7 000	8 000
	14 000	9 000

Investment income:		
Dividends received		
and receivable from Low Ltd	2 250	
	16 250	
Taxation	7 000	3 000
	9 250	6 000
Retained profits b/f	22 000	4 000
	31 250	10 000
Dividends paid and proposed	5 250	3 000
	26 000	7 000

The share capital of Low Ltd consists of 100 000 ordinary £1 shares of which High bought 75 000 on 1 January 200X for £9000. Goodwill on acquisition is to be amortized over 20 years. The fair value of Low's assets at date of acquisition equated to net book values and the only reserves existing when High bought in were retained profits. During the year High sold goods to Low for £12 000 which included a profit of £2000. As at 31.12.0X half of these goods still remain in Low's stocks. The dividends paid and proposed by Low are all paid out of current profits.

		£
First we need to identify the goodwill on acquisition:		£
Cost of High's control of Low		90 000
Bought 75% of Low's shares	75 000	
Bought 75% of Low's retained profits	3 000	78 000
Goodwill		12 000
Amortization per annum		600
Next we need to sort inter company trading:		
Reduce High's sales by		12 000
Reduce High's profits by		1 000
Reduce Low's stock by		1 000

Consolidated profit and loss account for the year ended 31.12.0X		
Turnover (150 000 − 12 000)		138 000
Cost of sales (105 000 − 12 000 + 1000)		94 000
		44 000
Distribution expenses	7 000	
Administration expenses	15 000	
Amortization of goodwill	600	22 600
		21 400
Taxation		10 000
Consolidated profit on ordinary activities after tax		11 400
Less minority interest (25% × 6000 − Low's profit after tax)		1 500
Consolidated profit for the financial year		9 900
(of which £9250 is dealt with in Holding company's own P&L)		
Profits b/f (all of Law's are pre-acquisition)		22 000

Dividends paid	4 000	
Proposed	1 250	5 250
		26 650

Note that the allocation of profit to minority interest for the year takes place after calculating consolidated profit after tax and that the inter-company transactions in relation to Low's dividends paid and proposed to High are eliminated.

Acquisition part way through a year

When the acquisition of a subsidiary occurs part way through the year then a proportion of that year's profits of the subsidiary will be regarded as pre-acquisition. When preparing the consolidated profit and loss account for the year of acquisition it is appropriate to only bring in the post acquisition amount at each line of consolidation (i.e. turnover, cost of sales, etc.) on a time basis.

Preparation of consolidated accounts involving more than one subsidiary

These are relatively straightforward if you remember the rules already explained. We include an activity here of a consolidation involving several companies to test your understanding and application of the techniques of consolidation as required by FRS 2.

Activity 15

A plc acquired 5m £1 shares of B Ltd 5 years ago when the reserves of B stood at £6m. B Ltd. acquired 2.25m £1 shares in C Ltd 4 years ago when the accumulated reserves of C were £1/2m. A plc also acquired 3m £1 share of D Ltd 2 years ago when D's reserves were £0.3m. At the date of acquisition the net book value of all assets equated to fair value. There has been no issue of shares in any of the above companies throughout the 5-year period. The following balance sheets relate to the group companies as at 31.12.200X.

	A	B	C	D
	£m	£m	£m	£m
Fixed assets	45	5	1.5	2
Investment in B	16	–	–	–
Investment in C	–	4.5	–	–
Investment in D	4	–	–	–
Net current assets	32	18	2.5	1
	97	27.5	4	3
Share capital	18	7.5	3	4
Reserves	79	20	1	(1)
	97	27.5	4	3

Prepare the consolidated balance sheet of A group as at 31.12.200X assuming all goodwill has an indefinite life and no impairment has occurred since acquisition.

Activity 15 feedback

B and D are subsidiaries of A with controlling interests of 66.6% and 75% respectively. C is a subsidiary of B at an ownership of 75% but as B is a subsidiary of A then C is also a subsidiary of A at a controlling interest of 50%. A diagram aids understanding here:

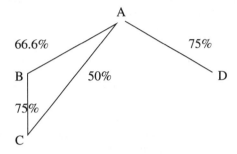

The goodwill calculations at acquisition are:

	B	C	D
Cost of control	16	4.5	4
Shares bought	5	2.25	3
Reserves bought	4	0.375	0.225
	9	2.625	3.225
Goodwill	7	1.875	0.775
Group share	7	1.25	0.775

Minority calculations are:

	B	C	D
Total net assets	23	4	3
M.I. % share	33.3	50	25
M.I.	7.67	2	0.75 Total 10.42

Consolidated balance sheet as at 31 December 200X

	£m
Goodwill	9.025
Fixed assets	53.5
Net current assets	53.5
	116.025
Share capital	18
Reserves [79 + (20 − 6)2/3 + (1 − 0.5)1/2 + (−1 − 0.3)3/4]	87.605
Minority interest	10.42
	116.025

Accounting for the results of associates and joint ventures (FRS 9)

Accounting for the results of associated companies was first dealt with in SSAP 1 which was issued in January 1971 as the first standard of the ASC. The standard was revised in April 1982. Essentially the standard required, that where an investment held by a company in another resulted in that other company being described as an associate company then, equity accounting was to be used to show the results of the associated company. The definition of an associated company as given by SSAP 1 (revised) was as follows:

13   An associated company is a company not being a subsidiary of the investing group or company in which:

(a) the interest of the investing group or company is effectively that of a partner in a joint venture or consortium and the investing group or company is in a position to exercise a significant influence over the company in which the investment is made; or

(b) the interest of the investing group or company is for the long term and is substantial and, having regard to the disposition of other shareholdings, the investing group or company is in a position to exercise a significant influence over the company in which the investment is made.

14   Where the interest of the investing group or company is not effectively that of a partner in a joint venture or consortium but amounts to 20 per cent or more of the equity voting rights of a company, it should be presumed that the investing group or company has the ability to exercise significant influence over that company unless it can clearly be demonstrated otherwise.

Revision of SSAP 1

SSAP 1 came up for review in July 1994 when the ASB issued a discussion paper on the subject of accounting for associates. The Board carried out the review because it felt that preparers of accounts were able to take 'a too literal interpretation of the definition of an associated company, which was applied to the form of the reporting entity's interest in another entity rather than the substance' (para. 3 appendix 11 FRS 9). What this statement meant was that the Board felt that preparers were using the 20% rule rather than identifying significant influence. In other words a holding of 19.5% would be accounted for as a simple investment regardless of whether the investing company had significant influence or not.

SSAP 1, at the time of the review, had been in existence for 23 years and over that time the business world had developed considerably bringing with that development new relationships between entities. In particular SSAP 1 (revised) did not cover the identification of and accounting for joint ventures.

The Board also felt that SSAP 1 needed reviewing because it:

Encouraged but did not require additional disclosures where significant interests were included by equity accounting. There was little evidence of additional disclosures being made.   (para. 3 appendix 111)

FRS 9 'Associates and Joint Ventures'

FRS 9 was issued in November 1997, effective for accounting periods ending on or after 23 June 1998, and sets out the definitions and accounting treatments for associates and joint ventures, two types of interest that a reporting entity may have in other entities. It also deals with joint arrangements that are not entities. Joint arrangements do not constitute an entity where the arrangement is such that it does not carry on a trade or business of its own.

The standard lists the type of investments an entity can have as follows:

- simple investment
- associate
- joint venture
- joint arrangement that is not an entity
- subsidiary.

Definitions of investment types

FRS 9 provides us with the following definitions:

Associate

An entity (other than a subsidiary) in which another entity (the investor) has a *participating interest* and over whose operating and financial policies the investor *exercises a significant influence*.

Participating interest

An interest held in the shares of another entity on a long-term basis for the purpose of securing a contribution to the investor's activities by the exercise of control or influence arising from or related to that interest. The investor's interest must, therefore, be a beneficial one and the benefits expected to arise must be linked to the exercise of its significant influence over the investee's operating and financial policies. An interest in the shares of another entity includes an interest convertible into an interest in shares or an option to acquire shares.

Companies legislation provides that a holding of 20 per cent or more of the shares of an entity is to be presumed to be a participating interest unless the contrary is shown. The presumption is rebutted if the interest is either not long-term or not beneficial.

Exercise of significant influence

The investor is actively involved and is influential in the direction of its investee through its participation in policy decisions covering aspects of policy relevant to the investor, including decisions on strategic issues such as:

(a) the expansion or contraction of the business, participation in other entities or changes in products, markets and activities of its investee; and
(b) determining the balance between dividend and reinvestment.

Companies legislation provides that an entity holding 20 per cent or more of the voting rights in another entity should be presumed to exercise a significant influence over that other entity unless the contrary is shown. For the purpose of applying this presumption, the shares held by the parent and its subsidiaries in that entity should be aggregated. The presumption is rebutted if the investor does not fulfil the criteria for the exercise of significant influence set out above.

Entity

A body corporate, partnership, or unincorporated association carrying on a trade or business with or without a view to profit. The reference to carrying on a trade or business means a trade or business of its own and not just part of the trades or businesses of entities that have interests in it.

Joint venture

An entity in which the reporting entity holds an interest on a long-term basis and is *jointly controlled* by the reporting entity and one or more other venturers under a contractial arrangement.

Joint control

A reporting entity jointly controls a venture with one or more other entities if none of the entities alone can control that entity but all together can do so and decisions on financial and operating policy essential to the activities, economic performance and financial position of that venture require each venturer's consent.

Interest held on a long-term basis

An interest that is held other than exclusively with a view to subsequent resale. An interest held exclusively with a view to subsequent resale is:

(a) an interest for which a purchaser has been identified or is being sought, and which is reasonably expected to be disposed of within approximately one year of its date of acquisition; or

(b) an interest that was acquired as a result of the enforcement of a security, unless the interest has become part of the continuing activities of the group or the holder acts as if it intends the interest to become so.

Investee

An entity in which the investor has invested.

Joint arrangement that is not an entity

A contractual arrangement under which the participants engage in joint activities that do not create an entity because it would not be carrying on a trade or business of its own. A contractual arrangement where all significant matters of operating and financial policy are predetermined does not create an entity because the policies are those of its participants, not of a separate entity.

Activity 16

Serp plc, a building firm, is involved in the following arrangements with other building entities:

■ an interest in a project Castle Residential with Locking Ltd and Crawford Ltd. The project involves the renovation of the castle building to provide resident accommodation. The participants have equal shares in the project and are to share profits equally. Invoices are sent to Cork plc by each of the participants for their work done.

- a 30% interest in Alpha Ltd to the Board of which Serp appoints two directors.
- a 70% interest in Beta Ltd.
- an equal interest with X Ltd in Gamma Ltd. The consent of Serp plc and X Ltd is required to all decisions on financial and operating policies of Gamma Ltd essential to its activities, economic performance and financial position.
- a 15% interest in Wimp plc.
- a 22% interest in Alpine plc which is seen as a short-term investment.

Identify what type, in accordance with FRS 9, each of these arrangements is.

Activity 16 feedback

Castle Residential is a joint arrangement as the project is not in itself an entity. Alpha Ltd is an associate as we can presume significant influence from two directors. Beta Ltd is a subsidiary if we assume 70% interest implies 70% voting rights. Gamma Ltd is a joint venture as it is jointly controlled by Serp and X.

Wimp and Alpine are trade investments as the former investment does not demonstrate any significant influence and the latter is for a short term.

Accounting for types of investment

Having identified what type of relationship an interest in an investee constitutes the method of accounting then needs to be determined. This method of accounting needs to be able to provide a true and fair view of the investment in the consolidated accounts to users and to fit with current principles developed by the Board. One of the objectives of reviewing FRS 9, according to the Board, was to improve information given about associates and joint ventures, particularly where they played a significant part in the reporting entity's operations. The equity method, by including only the net assets and results had been criticized as failing to show the full amount of resources and obligations arising from the investor's involvement. The FRS specifies the accounting treatment in consolidated statements for investments as follows:

- subsidiaries – acquisition accounting
- joint arrangements that are not entities – each party should account for its own share of assets, liabilities and cash flows in the joint arrangement
- joint ventures – gross equity method
- associates – equity method.

Equity method

The equity method of accounting for associates is amplified as follows in the FRS:

Equity method
A method of accounting that brings an investment into its investor's financial statements initially at its cost, identifying any goodwill arising. The carrying amount of the investment is adjusted in each period by the investor's share of the results of its investee less any amortisation or write-off for goodwill, the investors share

of any relevant gains or losses, and any other changes in the investee's net assets including distributions to its owners, for example by dividend. The investor's share of its investee's results is recognised in its profit and loss account. The investor's cash flow statement includes the cash flows between the investor and its investee, for example relating to dividends and loans.

This is in fact the same method as that specified by SSAP 1. An alternative method for accounting for associates could have been considered, that of proportional consolidation. However, proportional consolidation was rejected by the ASB on the grounds that the investor does not control its interest in individual assets, liabilities and cash flows (which is what proportional consolidation implies) but controls its investment, as a single asset, in the investee.

Gross equity method

This is defined by the standard as:

> A form of equity method under which the investor's share of the aggregate gross assets and liabilities underlying the net amount included for the investment is shown on the face of the balance sheet and, in the profit and loss account, the investor's share of the investee's turnover is noted."   (para 4 FRS 9)

This is in fact an expanded version of equity accounting and requires an extra line to be shown on the profit and loss account in respect of turnover, and two lines to be shown on the balance sheet identifying share of gross assets and share of gross liabilities.

Illustration of associate and joint venture accounting

The accounting for joint ventures and associates is illustrated by Appendix IV Example 1 of FRS 9.

Example 1 – The normal presentation

Consolidated profit and loss account

The format is illustrative only. The amounts shown for 'Associates' and 'Joint ventures' are subdivisions of the item for which the statutory prescribed heading is 'Income from interests in associated undertakings'. The subdivisions may be shown in a note rather than on the face of the profit and loss account.

	£m	£m
Turnover: group and share of joint ventures	*320*	
Less: share of joint ventures' turnover	*(120)*	
Group turnover		200
Cost of sales		(120)
Gross profit		80
Administrative expenses		(40)
Group operating profit		40

Share of operating profit in		
Joint ventures	30	
Associates	24	
		54
		94
Interest receivable (group)		6
Interest payable		
Group	(26)	
Joint ventures	(10)	
Associates	(12)	
		(48)
Profit on ordinary activities before tax		52
Tax on profit on ordinary activities*		(12)
Profit on ordinary activities after tax		40
Minority interests		(6)
Profit on ordinary activities after taxation and minority interest		34
Equity dividends		(10)
Retained profit for group and its share of associates and joint ventures		24

*Tax relates to the following:	Parent and subsidiaries	(5)
	Joint ventures	(5)
	Associates	(2)

Consolidated balance sheet

	£m	£m	£m
Fixed assets			
Tangible assets		480	
Investments			
Investments in joint ventures:			
Share of gross assets	130		
Share of gross liabilities	(80)		
		50	
Investments in associates		20	
			550
Current assets			
Stock		15	
Debtors		75	
Cash at bank and in hand		10	
		100	
Creditors (due within one year)		(50)	
Net current assets			50

Total assets less current liabilities	600
Creditors (due after more than one year)	(250)
Provisions for liabilities and charges	(10)
Equity minority interest	(40)
	300

Capital and reserves	
Called up share capital	50
Share premium account	150
Profit and loss account	100
Shareholders' funds (all equity)	300

Goodwill arising on acquisition of an associate or joint venture

As with the acquisition of a subsidiary, goodwill will arise on the acquisition of an associate or joint venture. This goodwill is to be identified in the same way as for a subsidiary, by attributing fair value to the assets and liabilities acquired and comparing them to the fair value of the consideration paid. This goodwill is then to be amortized as required by FRS 10 to the profit and loss account but shown as part of the investee's results. The goodwill identified is not shown as an intangible fixed asset as for subsidiaries but is shown as part of the carrying amount of the investment but separately disclosed. The following activity demonstrates the methods of equity accounting and gross equity accounting.

Activity 17

X Ltd acquired 600 £1 ordinary shares in Y Ltd at a price of £1.50 per share on 31 December 20X1, at which point the profit and loss account of Y Ltd had a credit balance of £800. The respective balance sheets of X Ltd and Y Ltd as at 31 December 20X2 are summarized below:

	X Ltd £	Y Ltd £
Fixed assets	15 000	3 200
Investment in Y Ltd	900	
Current assets	1 000	1 800
	16 900	5 000
Share capital	8 000	2 000
Retained profits	8 900	3 000
	16 900	5 000

X Ltd also has a subsidiary company Z Ltd and it is proposed to prepare consolidated accounts for the X Ltd group for the year-ended 31 December 20X2. You are required to draft the initial consolidated balance sheet of the group as at 31 December 20X2 before the inclusion of the results of Z Ltd, but after the inclusion of Y Ltd assuming firstly that the investment in Y Ltd is an associate and secondly a joint venture. Amortize goodwill over a life of 20 years.

Activity 17 feedback

Y as an associate.
Consolidated balance sheet as at 31 December 20X2

	£	£
Fixed assets		15 000
Investment in Y Ltd share of net assets	1 500	
goodwill (see note 1)	57	1 557
Net current assets		1 000
		17 557
Share capital		8 000
Reserves (see note 2)		9 557
		17 557

Y as a joint venture
Consolidated balance sheet as at 31 December 20X2

	£	£
Fixed assets		15 000
Investments in joint ventures:		
share of gross assets	1 500	
goodwill (see note 1)	57	
share of gross liabilities	0	1 557
Net current assets		1 000
		17 557
Share capital		8 000
Reserves		9 557
		17 557

Notes

1. Goodwill calculation

Cost of investment	900
Assets acquired 30% × 2800	840
Goodwill	60
Amortization per annum	3

2. Reserves calculation reserves of X Ltd

	8 900
30% of post-acquisition Y (2200)	660
amortization goodwill	(3)
	9 557

The following activity brings together acquisition accounting, equity accounting, gross equity accounting and accounting for joint arrangements. You might like to refer to the following extract from the summary of FRS 9 before commencing the next activity.

Type of investment	Treatment in consolidated financial statements
Subsidiaries	The investor should consolidate the assets, liabilities, results and cash flows of its subsidiaries.
Joint arrangements	Each party should account for its own share of the assets, liabilities and cash flows in the joint arrangement, measured according to the terms of that arrangement, for example pro rata to their respective interests.
Joint ventures	The venturer should use the gross equity method showing in addition to the amounts included under the equity method, on the face of the balance sheet, the venturer's share of the gross assets and liabilities of its joint ventures, and, in the profit and loss account, the venturer's share of their turnover distinguished from that of the group. Where the venturer conducts a major part of its business through joint ventures, it may show fuller information provided all amounts are distinguished from those of the group. Appendix IV sets out an optional columnar presentation.
Associates	The investor should include its associates in its consolidated financial statements using the equity method. In the investor's consolidated profit and loss account the investor's share of its associates' operating result should be included immediately after group operating result. From the level of profit before tax, the investor's share of the relevant amounts for associates should be included within the amounts for the group. In the consolidated statement of total recognised gains and losses the investor's share of the total recognised gains and losses of its associates should be included, shown separately under each heading, if material. In the balance sheet the investor's share of the net assets of its associates should be included and separately disclosed. The cash flow statement should include the cash flows between the investor and its associates. Goodwill arising on the investor's acquisition of its associates, less any amortisation or write-down, should be included in the carrying amount for the associates but should be disclosed separately. In the profit and loss account the amortisation or write-down of such goodwill should be separately disclosed as part of the investor's share of its associates' results.
Simple investments	The investor includes its interests as investments at either cost or valuation.

Activity 18

The following information is available in respect of Serp plc and the other entities for the year-ended 31st March 20X8 (see Activity 16).

Profit and Loss account for the year-ended 31.3.X8

	Serp plc £000	Gamma Ltd £000	Alpha Ltd £000	Beta Ltd £000
Turnover	9 000	6 000	15 000	10 000
Cost of sales	3 900	2 200	8 000	5 000
Gross profit	5 100	3 800	7 000	5 000
Administration and distrib.	900	1 200	2 100	1 100
Operating profit	4 200	2 600	4 900	3 900
Dividends received	50			
Interest payable	150	170	–	1 100
Profit before tax	4 100	2 430	4 900	2 800
Taxation	1 750	1 100	2 100	1 100
Profit after tax	2 350	1 330	2 800	1 700

1 Serp plc has not received any dividends from any of its investments except for those from Wimp plc and Alpine plc.
2 Net assets of Alpha at acquisition, 1 April 20X3 were £18 000 000 and of Beta purchased 1 April 20X4 £15 000 000.
3 Serp bought its share in Gamma at 1 April 20X7.
4 Information in respect of Castle residential project is as follows:

Profit and loss memorandum accounts as at 31.3.X8

	Serp plc £000	Locking £000	Crawford £000
Turnover	2000	700	1500
Cost of sales	950	400	600
Gross profit	1050	300	900
Administration and distribution	300	20	100
Operating profit	750	280	800
Interest payable	50	–	100
Profit before tax	700	280	700
Taxation	170	–	100
Profit for the year	530	280	600

The above figures in respect of Serp are included in Serp's profit and loss account but no adjustment has been made in repect of the turnover and costs reported by Locking and Crawford on the project.

Balance Sheets as at 31.3.X8 for Serp plc and other entities

	Serp plc £000	Gamma £000	Alpha £000	Beta £000

Tangible fixed assets		16 500	10 130	30 000	27 500
Investments in:	Beta	12 000			
	Gamma	2 500			
	Alpha	5 700			
	Wimp, Alpine	5 000			
Current assets		3 200	1 000	4 000	2 500
Creditors amounts due one year		(2 900)	(800)	(2 700)	(900)
		42 000	10 330	31 300	29 100
Creditors amounts due greater than one year		(2 200)	(4 000)	(7 500)	(9 000)
		39 800	6 330	23 800	20 100
Share capital		10 000	5 000	4 000	8 000
Reserves		29 800	1 330	19 800	12 100
		39 800	6 330	23 800	20 100

The accounting policy of Serp plc is to write goodwill off over a period of 15 years.

Required:
Prepare the consolidated accounts for the Serp group for the year-ended 31.3.X8.

Activity 18 feedback

1 The joint arrangement has to be accounted for in Serp's accounts in accordance with the terms of that arrangement, i.e. equal shares.

	Project £000	Equalization £000	Equal shares £000
Turnover	4200	(600)	1400
Cost of sales	1950	(300)	650
Gross profit	2250	(300)	750
Admin. & Distrib.	420	(160)	140
Operating profit	1830	(140)	610
Interest payable	150	0	50
Profit before tax	1680	(140)	560
Taxation	270	(80)	90
Profit after tax	1410	(60)	470

Goodwill calculations:		£000
Joint venture Gamma	purchase price	2 500
	50% × 5000	2 500
	Goodwill	0
Subsidiary Beta	purchase price	12 000
	70% × 15m	10 500
	Goodwill	1 500

Amortization per annum £100 bought 1.4.X4 thus already amortized £300.

Associate Alpha	purchase price	5 700
	30% × 18m	5 400
	Goodwill	300

Amortization per annum £20 bought 1.4.X3 thus already amortized £80.

Consolidated profit and loss account for Serp group for the year-ended 31.3.X8

	£000	£000
Turnover: group and share of joint ventures	21 400	
Less: share of joint venturer's turnover	3 000	
Group turnover (9000 − 600 equal + 10 000 subsid)		18 400
Cost of sales (3900 − 300 equal + 5000 sub)		8 600
Gross profit		9 800
Administration and distribution costs (900 − 160 + 1100)		1 840
Group operating profit		7 960
Share of operating profit in:		
Joint venture	1 300	
Associate	1 470	
Amortization goodwill	20 1 450	2 750
		10 710
Dividends received trade investments		50
		10 760
Interest payable:		
group (150 + 1100)	1 250	
associate	−	
joint venture	85	1 335
Profit on ordinary activities before tax		9 425
Tax:		
group (1750 + 1100 − 80)	2 770	
joint venture (50% × 1100)	550	
associate (30% × 2100)	630	3 950
Profit on ordinary activities after tax		5 475
Minority interest (30% × 1700)		510
		4 965
Equity dividends		−
Retained profit for group and its share of associate and joint ventures		4 965

Consolidated balance sheet for Serp group as at 31.3.X8

Fixed assets	
Intangible (1500 − 300 − 100)	1 100
Tangible (16 500 + 27 500)	44 000

Investments
investments joint ventures:

share of gross assets (50% × 11 130)	5 565	
share of gross liabilities (50% × 4800)	2 400	3 165

investments in associates:

share of net assets (30% × 23 800)	7 140	
goodwill (300 − 100)	200	7 340
trade investments		5 000
		60 605

Current assets (3200 + 2500)	5 700	
Creditors amounts due within one year (2900 + 900 + 60)	3 860	1 840
		62 445
Creditors amounts due after one year (2200 + 9000)		11 200
		51 245
Equity minority interest (30% × 20 100)		6 030
		45 215

Called up share capital	10 000
Reserves	35 215
	45 215

Reserves:

Serp	29 800	
Less equalization	60	29 740
Alpha (5800 × 30%)	1 740	
Amortization goodwill	100	1 640
Gamma		665
Beta (5100 × 70%)	3 570	
Amortization goodwill	400	3 170
		35 215

Disclosure requirements FRS 9

The initial disclosure requirements are quite straightforward and are reproduced below from FRS 9:

51 The following disclosures should be made in addition to the amounts required on the face of the primary financial statements under the equity method or the gross equity method.

For all associates and joint ventures

52 The names of the principal associates and joint ventures should be disclosed in the financial statements of the investing group, showing for each associate and joint venture:

(a) the proportion of the issued shares in each class held by the investing group, indicating any special rights or constraints attaching to them;

   (**b**) the accounting period or date of the financial statements used if they dif-
           fer from those of the investing group; and

   (**c**) an indication of the nature of its business.

53 Any notes relating to the financial statements of associates and joint ventures,
       or matters that should have been noted had the investor's accounting policies
       been applied, that are material to understanding the effect on the investor of its
       investments should be disclosed, in particular noting the investor's share in con-
       tingent liabilities incurred jointly with other venturers or investors and its share
       of the capital commitments of the associates and joint ventures themselves.

54 If there are significant statutory, contractual or exchange control restrictions
       on the ability of all associate or joint venture to distribute its reserves (other
       than those shown as non-distributable), the extent of the restrictions should
       be indicated.

55 The amounts owing and owed between an investor and its associates or its
       joint ventures should be analysed into amounts relating to loans and amounts
       relating to trading balances. This disclosure may be combined with those
       required by FRS 8 'Related Party Disclosures'.

56 A note should explain why the facts of any particular case rebut either the
       presumption that an investor holding 20 per cent or more of the voting rights
       of another entity exercises significant influence over the operating and finan-
       cial policies of that entity or the presumption that an investor holding 20 per
       cent or more of the shares of another entity has a participating interest.

In addition to the above disclosure FRS 9 also requires supplementary facts if certain thresholds are exceeded. These are as follows:

■ where the aggregate of the investor's share in its associate or joint venture exceeds 15%
  of the group's gross assets or gross liabilities or turnover or operating results (three year
  average) then a note showing the investor's share in turnover (not required for joint venture), fixed assets, current assets, creditors amounts less than one year and creditors
  amounts greater than one year is required.

■ where the thresholds as above are exceeded at a 25% level then a note showing the
  investor's share in turnover, profit before tax, profit after tax, fixed assets, current assets
  creditors less than one year and creditors greater than one year is required.

Activity 19

Show for the Serp group (Activity 18) the additional threshold disclosures required by FRS 9, if any.

Activity 19 feedback

In the Serp example the shares are as follows:

	Joint venture	*Associate*
Gross assets	£5565 < 15%	£10 200 < 15%
Gross liabilities	£2400 > 15% < 25%	£3060 >15% < 25%
Turnover	£3000 >15% < 25%	£4500 >15% < 25%
Operating results	£650 > 15% < 25%	£840 >15% < 25%

The group gross assets are £50 800, gross liabilities are £15 000, turnover is £18 400 and operating results £4050 where any amounts included in the group by way of equity accounting for associates and gross equity accounting for joint ventures are excluded. Disclosure is therefore required in respect of exceeding the 15% threshold but not the 25% for both joint venture and associate.

Additional disclosure for joint venture
Share of assets:

share of fixed assets	5065	
share of current assets	500	5565

Share of liabilities:

less than one year	400	
greater one year	2000	2400
		3165

Additional disclosure for associate

Share of turnover of associate	4500

Share of assets:

share of fixed assets	9000	
share of current assets	1200	10 200

Share of liabilities:

less than one year	810	
greater one year	2250	3060
		7140

Effects of FRS 9

FRS 9 has already had an impact on financial statements. Three examples of its impact are given below:

- Thames Water has reclassified most of its associates as joint ventures.
- Norcross has reclassified an associate as a trade investment on the grounds that a 40% share does not give them a significant influence.
- Persimmon has reclassified an associate as a participation in a joint arrangement which is not an entity! The financial statements for the year-ending 31 December 1996 have been amended by reclassifying investments of £8.546m as tangible fixed assets of £0.096m, current assets of £8.123m, current liabilities of (£0.327m), and for 31 December 1997 tangible fixed assets of £0.096m, current assets £7.016 and current liabilities (£0.176m). This change could have affected liquidity ratios but given that Persimmon has net current assets of £423m 1996 and £391m 1997 the effect is marginal. In 1997 the ratio of current assets to current liabilities was 3.7 and without the reclassification it would have been 3.65, a marginal change.
- Interestingly John Laing for the financial statements year-ended 31 December 1997 included unincorporated joint ventures in the group accounts using proportional consolidation!

Merger accounting

This chapter has so far reviewed three forms of accounting for business combinations. First, the method that deals with the acquisition by a holding company of control of one or more subsidiaries was considered, and this was referred to as 'acquisition accounting' and recognized in FRS 2. Secondly, 'equity accounting' and thirdly 'gross equity accounting' was examined, and this was covered by FRS 9.

SSAP 23 (issued May 1985) entitled 'Accounting for Acquisitions and Mergers' formally recognized the use of a fourth approach for accounting for certain types of business combination, merger accounting, and it is this method which will be covered in the next section of this chapter.

'Acquisition' is the name given to the process whereby a 'hunter–predator' company stalks another with the aggressive purpose of takeover. 'Mergers' suggests the voluntary blending of activity between consenting parties. In reality, the distinction between the two may be purely semantic.

Sensibly, the Companies Act 1948 did not draw a distinction between the two operations; section 50 (now section 130 of the 1985 Act) (in effect) made it clear that the free reserves of an acquired company were to be placed to the share premium account in the balance sheet of the acquirer and treated for all purposes as part of the capital fund. It did not matter if the shares were acquired for cash or in return for shares, as Justice Harmen made clear in the Ropner Holdings Case (1952), which is summarized as follows.

	Balance sheets of Ropner Holdings Ltd	
	Before acquisition	*After acquisition*
	(£m)	*(£m)*
Ropner Holdings:		
Share capital	1	3
Share premium	–	5
	1	8
Assets	1	8
Shipping company A:		
Share capital	1	
Free reserves	2	Same
	3	(Only the *ownership*
		of capital has changed)
Assets	3	
Shipping company B:		
Share capital	1	
Free reserves	3	Same
	4	(Only the *ownership*
		of capital has changed)
Assets	4	

Ropner Holdings Ltd was incorporated to acquire the assets of two shipping companies by means of exchanges of shares at nominal value. Accordingly, the directors issued 2 000 000 shares, equivalent to the combined share capitals of the companies acquired. The free reserves of the subsidiaries were converted to a capital reserve in the hands of the holding company.

The Ropner Holdings case thus emphasized that companies should grow because of the efficiency of their management to make profits and not by the simple expedient of 'buying distributable profits' in companies more efficient than themselves. In the boom years from 1945 to 1979, several cash-rich companies grew by acquisition into conglomerates whose diverse activities made little economic sense. The stringent financial climate of 1980 onwards forced most of them to carry out severe rationalization of their activities.

The 'Ropner' principle was disliked by business people who wished to distribute large dividends to shareholders and it became the practice, in the case of 'mergers', to ignore the principle and treat pre-merger profits in subsidiary companies as still retaining their free character and be distributable as dividend. This convenient door was slammed shut by the case of *Shearer v. Bercain Ltd* (1980), which firmly restated the 'Ropner' principle.

Following the decision, it was suggested in accountancy circles that the strict legal position was unduly harsh. It is against this historical and semi-political business background that the current legislation, allowing pre-acquisition free reserves of 'merged' companies to remain distributable as dividend, should be read.

Merger accounting first appeared in ED 3 (1971), although for various reasons (and in particular doubts as to the legality of merger accounting) it never became a standard. ED 3 proposed a distinction between an acquisition and a merger. Essentially, it stated that an acquisition takes place when one company takes over another (i.e. where control of one company passes to another), whereas a merger occurs when two or more companies come together and each company involved continues to have some identity. In other words, a merger reflects a pooling of interests (and resources) in which two or more companies merge their previously separate businesses into one integrated unit and in which the combined new ownership's interests mirror the relative interests of the original entities.

The distinction recognized in ED 3 between acquisition accounting and merger accounting was to prove important due to the sometimes quite dramatic differences resulting from the application of each method that is examined later in this chapter.

Although ED 3 never materialized into an official standard, the Companies Act 1981, permitting the use of merger accounting in certain specific situations, was the catalyst for SSAP 23, the implications of which shall now be considered.

For the purposes of SSAP 23, the main criterion to determine which method of accounting should be applied was whether or not the combination was based principally on a share for share exchange (as opposed to, for example, a cash offer):

> **3** Merger accounting is considered to be an appropriate method of accounting when two groups of shareholders continue, or are in a position to continue, their shareholdings as before but on a combined basis. Acquisition accounting is therefore required when there is a transfer of the ownership of at least one of the combining companies, and substantial resources leave the group as consideration for that transfer. Conversely, when only limited resources leave the group, merger accounting may be used.

As will be seen from paragraph 11(d) of SSAP 23 (reproduced below), the 'limited resources' (e.g. cash) referred to above should be restricted to no more than 10% of the fair value of the consideration given for the assets acquired.

Definition of merger

SSAP 23 was quite specific in its definition of what constituted a merger as opposed to an acquisition:

11 A business combination may be accounted for as a merger if all of the following conditions are met:

(**a**) the business combination results from an offer to the holders of all equity shares and the holders of all voting shares which are not already held by the offeror; and

(**b**) the offeror has secured, as a result of the offer, a holding of (i) at least 90% of all equity shares (taking each class of equity separately) and (ii) the shares carrying at least 90% of the votes of the offeree; and

(**c**) immediately prior to the offer, the offeror does not hold (i) 20% or more of all equity shares of the offeree (taking each class of equity separately), or (ii) shares carrying 20% or more of the votes of the offeree; and

(**d**) not less than 90% of the fair value of the total consideration given for the equity share capital (including that given for shares already held) is in the form of equity share capital; not less than 90% of the fair value of the total consideration given for voting non-equity share capital (including that given for shares already held) is in the form of equity and/or voting non-equity share capital.

Note that the use of the word 'may' in paragraph 11 meant that even if the conditions for merger accounting were met in full, the use of the merger accounting method in a merger situation was not compulsory, and acquisition accounting may be adopted.

Any business combination that does *not* satisfy the conditions as laid down in *paragraph 11* above had to be accounted for as an acquisition.

Companies Act 1989

Now let us turn and look at what the 1989 Act has to say on mergers.

A merger according to the Act occurs when

1 at least 90% of the nominal value of the relevant shares in the undertaking are acquired

2 and these shares are acquired as a result of an arrangement providing for the issue of equity shares by the parent undertaking

3 and the fair value of any consideration other than equity shares does not exceed 10% of the nominal value of the equity shares issued.

Relevant shares are defined as those carrying unrestricted rights to participate both in distributions and in the assets of the undertaking upon liquidation. Normally equity shares will be relevant shares.

Comparison of Companies Act and SSAP 23

Now we have two definitions for a merger, Companies Act and SSAP 23, but are they the same?

> ## Activity 20
>
> Compare the two definitions and identify any differences between them. Use an example to illustrate your point.

Activity 20 feedback

The first major difference is part C of SSAP 23 which restricts the use of merger accounting where an existing holding of 20% or more occurs. Thus, if company A held 21% of the equity shares of company B at 1 January 1992 and then acquired the other 79% on 2 January 1992 in a share for share exchange under SSAP 23 this could not be accounted for as a merger but under the Companies Act it could. Note if the original holding had only been 19% then even under SSAP 23 we could use merger accounting.

The second major difference concerns the cash element of any consideration given for the equity shares. Note SSAP 23 allows 10% of the fair value of total consideration to be in cash whereas the Companies Act only allows 10% of nominal value of equity shares issued to be in the form of cash. For example, if company A bought all the equity shares of company B by the issue of 100 £1 A shares and £12 cash where the fair value of A shares was £1.50 then in accordance with SSAP 23 £12 would be compared to 10% of the fair value of $100 \times £1.50 = £150$ which is £15. As £12 is less than £15 we could use merger accounting in accordance with SSAP 23. For the Companies Act £12 would be compared to 10% of the nominal value, i.e. 10% of £100. As £12 is greater than £10, we therefore could not use merger accounting in accordance with the Companies Act.

SSAP 23 problems

As we can see from Activity 20 SSAP 23 needed revising because of the Companies Act 1989, but there was already great dissatisfaction in the accounting world with SSAP 23 as there were too many ways companies could circumvent its rules. It also used the words '*may* account for as a merger'. This use of the word '*may*' we have seen in another standard SSAP 13 'Accounting for Research and Development'.

Various schemes had been invented by companies to circumvent SSAP 23 including vendor placings, vendor rights and disposing of the original stake under a sale and buy back agreement.

Revision to SSAP 23

ED 48 was issued in February 1990 by the ASC as a proposed revision to SSAP 23.

However, due to the demise of the ASC, ED 48 was not progressed until May 1993 when FRED 6 'Acquisitions and Mergers' was issued. This was finally converted into a standard, FRS 6, in September 1994.

FRS 6 provides definitions for when a business combination can be considered a merger and when it has to be considered as an acquisition. It also, within its prescribed accounting treatment, removes the word '*may*'. Thus, all business combinations that meet the definition for merger must be accounted for using merger accounting.

A merger is defined as:

A business combination that results in the creation of a new reporting entity formed from the combining parties, in which the shareholders of the combining entity come together in a partnership for the mutual sharing of the risks and benefits of the combined entity, and in which no party to the combination in substance obtains control over any other, or is otherwise seen to be dominant, whether by virtue of the proportion of its shareholders' rights in the combined entity, the influence of its directors or otherwise.

An acquisition is defined as any other business combination that is not a merger.

In addition, the standard sets out conditions that must be met for merger accounting to be used:

6   *Criterion 1* – No party to the combination is portrayed as either acquirer or acquired, either by its own board or management or by that of another party to the combination.

7   *Criterion 2* – All parties to the combination, as represented by the boards of directors or their appointees, participate in establishing the management structure for the combined entity and in selecting the management personnel, and such decisions are made on the basis of a consensus between the parties to the combination rather than purely by exercise of voting rights.

8   *Criterion 3* – The relative sizes of the combining entities are not so disparate that one party dominates the combined entity by virtue of its relative size.

9   *Criterion 4* – Under the terms of the combination or related arrangements, the consideration received by equity shareholders of each party to the combination, in relation to their equity shareholding, comprises primarily equity shares in the combined entity; and any non-equity consideration, or equity shares carrying substantially reduced voting or distribution rights, represents an immaterial proportion of the fair value of the consideration received by the equity shareholders of that party. Where one of the combining entities has, within the period of two years before the combination, acquired equity shares in another of the combining entities, the consideration for the acquisition should be taken into account in determining whether this criterion has been met.

10   For the purpose of paragraph 9, the consideration should not be taken to include the distribution to shareholders of

   (**a**)   an interest in a peripheral part of the business of the entity in which they were shareholders and which does not form part of the combined entity; or

   (**b**)   the proceeds of the sale of such a business, or loan stock representing such proceeds.

   A peripheral part of the business is one that can be disposed of without having a material effect on the nature and focus of the entity's operations.

11   *Criterion 5* – No equity shareholders of any of the combining entities retain any material interest in the future performance of only part of the combined entity.

12   For the purposes of paragraphs 6–11 above any convertible share or loan stock should be regarded as equity to the extent that it is converted into equity as a result of the business combination.

Each of the above criteria are further explained in the explanation to the standard. In particular, criterion 4 outlaws the use of vendor placings and rights and other such schemes as follows:

69 Criterion 4 is concerned with the extent to which equity shareholders of the combination entities receive any consideration other than equity shares (as defined in paragraph 2 above) in the combined entity. Cash, other assets, loan stock and preference shares are all examples of non-equity consideration.

70 As stated in the note on legal requirements (Appendix 1), companies legislation provides that one of the conditions for merger accounting is that the fair value of any consideration other than the issue of equity shares (as defined in companies legislation) did not exceed 10 per cent of the nominal value of the equity shares issued. Criterion 4 requires a further condition to be met, that all but an immaterial proportion of the fair value of the consideration received must be in the form of equity shares (as defined in paragraph 2); this definition of equity, which is that adopted in FRS 4 'Capital Instruments', is narrower than that of companies legislation, and is used to avoid the possibility of criterion 4 being met by the use of shares that, although within the statutory definition of equity, have characteristics that are closer to non-equity.

71 The FRS requires that all arrangements made in conjunction with the combination must be taken into account. Equity shareholders will be considered to have disposed of their shareholding for cash where any arrangement is made in connection with the combination that enabled them to exchange or redeem the shares they received in the combination for cash (or other non-equity consideration); for example, a vendor placing or similar arrangement should be treated as giving rise to non-equity consideration. However, a normal market selling transaction, or privately arranged sale, entered into by a shareholder is not made in conjunction with the combination and does not prevent the criterion being met.

The explanation for criterion 3 provides further details on the relative size issue:

67 Where one party is substantially larger than the other parties it would be presumed that the larger party can or will dominate the combined undertaking. This will not be consistent with treating such a business combination as a merger as the combined entity will not be a substantially equal partnership.

68 A party would be presumed to dominate if it is more than 50 per cent larger than each of the other parties to the combination, judged by reference to the ownership interests; that is, by considering the proportion of the equity of the combined entity attributable to the shareholders of each of the combining parties. However, this presumption may be rebutted if it can be clearly shown that there is no such dominance; other factors, such as voting or share agreements, blocking powers or other arrangements, can mean that a party to the combination has more influence, or conversely less influence, than is indicated by its relative size. Circumstances that rebut the presumption of dominant influence based on relative sizes would need to be disclosed and explained.

Companies Act and FRS 6

FRS 6 states that:

> **5** A business combination should be accounted for by using merger accounting if:
>   **(a)** the use of merger accounting for the combination is not prohibited by companies legislation; [*4A Sch 10*] and
>   **(b)** the combination meets all the specific criteria set out in paragraphs 6–11 below and thus falls within the definition of a merger.
> Acquisition accounting should be used for all other business combinations, except as provided in paragraphs 13 and 14.

We have identified the legal rules in respect of merger accounting on p. 531.

Activity 21

Identify any differences between the Companies Act and FRS 6 definitions of when merger accounting can be used. Which is the more prescriptive? (You may find an actual copy of FRS 6 useful in completing this activity.)

Activity 21 feedback

FRS 6 makes no mention of acquiring a specific proportion of relevant shares, but the Companies Act indicates that there could be a minority interest of not more than 10%. However, the explanation to criterion 5 does state that this criterion would be failed if any material minority of shareholders left in one of the combining parties had not accepted the terms of the combination offer. It also references us to the 10% rule in company legislation. There does appear to be the implication that criterion 5 is more restrictive than the Companies Act.

The Companies Act requires that the arrangement provides for the issue of equity shares. FRS 6 also refers to equity shares but its definition of equity shares is consistent with that in FRS 4 'Capital Instruments' which is narrower than that in companies legislation. Thus, again, FRS 6 is more restrictive than the Companies Act.

The Companies Act also allows the fair value of any consideration other than equity shares to be up to a maximum of 10% of the nominal value of the equity shares issued. Criterion 4 refers to an immaterial proportion of the fair value that can be received in other than equity shares as defined under FRS 4. Again FRS 6 is more restrictive, that is, if we assume that immaterial is something less than 10%.

Given that the ASB has been at pains to restrict the use of merger accounting then presumably it has some advantages in the financial performance and position it portrays of the group over and above that of acquisition accounting. Whether these advantages are to the benefit of the external user or not is another question.

Differences between acquisition accounting and merger accounting

The main differences between the two methods can be examined under the headings of:

1 goodwill
2 share premium
3 pre-acquisition profits.

Goodwill

With a merger, there is no change in ownership and we merely have a pooling of resources, a consolidated balance sheet produced for a merger situation will simply combine the existing balance sheets, and the assets will therefore remain at the book values at which they appear in the original balance sheets of the separate companies, that is to say no goodwill is recognized in the new balance sheet (since none is in fact acquired).

However, with acquisition accounting the net assets of the company acquired will usually be revalued as at the date of acquisition, and, of course, the difference between the purchase consideration and this asset revaluation will give rise to goodwill (premium) on acquisition.

Share premium

With an acquisition where a company issues shares to acquire another company the cost of the investment is recorded in the acquirer's balance sheet and, of course, any shares issued in consideration are recorded at market value, i.e. nominal value plus share premium created. However, with a merger situation, shares issued in the share-for-share exchange involved are recorded at nominal value, i.e. no share premium is created.

FRS 6 states:

> 18 The difference, if any, between the nominal value of the shares issued plus the fair value of any other consideration given, and the nominal value of the shares received in exchange should be shown as a movement on other reserves in the consolidated financial statements. Any existing balance on the share premium account or capital redemption reserve of the new subsidiary undertaking should be brought in by being shown as a movement on other reserves. These movements should be shown in the reconciliation of movements in shareholders' funds.

Pre-acquisition profits

For acquisition accounting purposes and in accordance with the concept of capital maintenance, the distributable profits of any acquired company are frozen, i.e. are not legally regarded as available for distribution by the group.

On the other hand, with merger accounting and in keeping with the spirit of a pooling of resources, the reserves of each participant company are merely pooled, i.e. those that were distributable before the merger remain distributable after the merger.

FRS 6 states:

17   The results and cash flows of all the combining entities should be brought into the financial statements of the combined entity from the beginning of the financial year in which the combination occurred; adjusted so as to achieve uniformity of accounting policies. The corresponding figures should be restated by including the results for all the combining entities for the previous period and their balance sheets for the previous balance sheet date, adjusted as necessary to achieve uniformity of accounting policies.

It is obvious when one considers the above differences why merger accounting has proven popular, especially in the United States. Following from above, it can be seen that with merger accounting the balance sheet of the new company does not carry a goodwill figure that might have to be amortized against profits. Nor is there a non-distributable share premium account arising in the merged balance sheet, and also the distributable reserves of the group are enlarged as opposed to the situation which would have prevailed under the acquisition accounting method.

It is appropriate here to consider an example of the application of merger accounting and also to contrast it with acquisition accounting.

Activity 22

Two companies A plc and M plc have the following respective balance sheets as at 30 June 19XX:

	A plc £	M plc £
Issued ordinary shares (£1)	9 000	6 000
Revenue reserves	2 000	3 000
	11 000	9 000
Represented by:		
plant and machinery	6 000	7 000
net current assets	5 000	2 000
	11 000	9 000

A plc acquired the whole of the share capital of M plc on the basis of a one-for-one share exchange as at the above date, at which point the market values of their respective share were:

A plc	£4
M plc	£4

The fair values of M plc's tangible assets as at 30 June 19XX were:

Plant and machinery	£8000
Net current assets	£2500

Prepare the consolidated balance sheet for A plc using both acquisition and merger basis.

Activity 22 feedback

Consolidated balance sheet as at 30 June 19XX

	Acquisition £		*Merger* £
Issued ordinary shares (£1)	15 000	(note 1)	15 000
Share premium	18 000	(note 2)	–
Revenue reserves	2 000	(note 3)	5 000
	35 000		20 000
Represented by:			
plant and machinery	14 000	(note 4)	13 000
goodwill on acquisition	13 500	(note 4)	–
	27 500		13 000
Net current assets	7 500	(note 4)	7 000
	35 000		20 000

Notes

1 Based on a one-for-one exchange A plc will need to issue a further 6000 £1 shares (i.e. 9000 + 6000 = 15 000).
2 Issued at a price of £4 per share the share premium on the issue of A plc shares for acquisition accounting purposes will be £3 per share (i.e. 6000 × £3 = £18 000).
3 For acquisition accounting purposes (but not for merger accounting) the reserves of M plc of £3000 as at the date of acquisition will be frozen.

4 Cost of investment (i.e. 6000 shares at £4 each) 24 000
less fair value of net assets acquired (i.e. £8000 + £2500) (10 500)
  13 500

Despite the simplicity of this example the differences are amply illustrated:

1. Under acquisition accounting a non-distributable share premium account arises.
2. Under merger accounting the reserves of M plc at the date of acquisition are regarded as distributable by the group.
3. For acquisition accounting the assets of M plc are recorded at fair values, whereas for merger accounting purposes book values prevail.

FRS 6 disclosure requirements

The objective of FRS 6 was to:

- ensure that merger accounting was only used for those situations when a merger occurred
- ensure the use of acquisition accounting for all other business combinations
- ensure that in both cases relevant information concerning the effects of the combination was provided to users.

Having covered the first two of these objectives already FRS 6 meets the third by identifying disclosure requirements as follows.

For all business combinations
- names of combining entities
- accounting method used for combination
- date of combination.

For mergers
- analysis of profit and loss account and SORG into
  - those amounts relating to each entity for the previous year and up to the date of merger
  - those amounts relating to the combined entity after merger
- composition and fair value of consideration given
- aggregate book value of each party to the merger at date of merger
- adjustments made to the accounts of any party to the merger to ensure consistency of accounting practices for the combined entity
- statement of adjustments to reserves resulting from the merger.

For acquisitions
- composition and fair value of consideration given
- a table showing:
  - book values of each party before acquisition adjustments
  - fair value amounts and adjustments on acquisition amount of goodwill arising
- post-acquisition profits of the combined entity are to be shown separately as a component of continuing operations
- P&L account after acquisition should show costs incurred in reorganizing, restructuring and integrating the acquired entity
- cash flow should show cash and cash equivalents paid on acquisition net of any balances taken over
- for material acquisitions the profit after tax and minority interests of the acquired entity should be disclosed for the current year up to the date of acquisition and for the previous year showing turnover, operating profit, exceptional items, profit before tax, tax, minority interests and extraordinary items.

FRS 7 'Fair Values in Acquisition Accounting'

We have already seen that under acquisition accounting the identifiable assets and liabilities of the acquired entity have to be included in the consolidation at fair value; the difference between fair value and cost of acquisition being identified as goodwill. But what is fair value?

Until the publication of FRS in September 1994 there had been no guidance on this, although the ASC had been considering the problem before its demise.

The need for a standard on the subject of fair values is obvious in that post-acquisition profits are open to manipulation if fair value is not consistently applied.

Activity 23

A plc acquires B plc as at 31 May 1996. The book value of B plc's net assets are £4 million and the market value of the consideration given by A plc is £5 million. No guidance is available from the ASB on the definition of fair value. One accountant involved in the acquisition suggests the fair value of the net assets of B plc is £4.2 million; another suggests that as a provision £0.2 million is agreed to be required for costs subsequent to the acquisition, and because he takes a different view on the fair value of the other net assets, the fair value is only £3.8 million.

Identify the figure for goodwill from each of the scenarios above and any effects on future profits after acquisition given goodwill is to be amortized over ten years.

Activity 23 feedback

	Scenario 1 £m	Scenario 2 £m
Goodwill	0.8	1.2
P&L charge for goodwill	0.08	0.12
Depreciation	higher than 2	less than 1
Provision for costs	0.2	nil

The different views of fair value have a material impact on the profits of the combined entity after acquisition.

FRS 7 therefore had to deal with the above two abuses, i.e.

- undervaluing assets so that depreciation is reduced and goodwill is exaggerated
- setting up provisions for future costs so that goodwill is exaggerated but future profits are not affected.

It did so by defining fair values as:

> the amount at which an asset or liability could be exchanged in an arm's length transaction between informed and willing parties other than in a forced or liquidation sale.

It also restricted the assets and liabilities to be considered as part of this fair value to those that were capable of being disposed of or settled separately, without disposing of a business entity; thus provisions for future costs were not part of this fair value.

This is made even more apparent by the following paragraph from FRS 7:

> 7 As a consequence of the above principles, the following do not affect fair values at the date of acquisition and therefore fall to be treated as post-acquisition items:
>
> (a) changes resulting from the acquirer's intentions or future actions
>
> (b) impairments, or other changes, resulting from events subsequent to the acquisition
>
> (c) provisions or accruals for future operating losses or for reorganisation and integration costs expected to be incurred as a result of the acquisition, whether they relate to the acquired entity or to the acquirer.

The fair value of tangible fixed assets is explained in paragraph 9 of FRS 7:

9 The fair value of a tangible fixed asset should be based on:
   (a) market value, if assets similar in type and condition are bought and sold on an open market; or
   (b) depreciated replacement cost, reflecting the acquired business's normal buying process and the sources of supply and prices available to it.

The fair value should not exceed the recoverable amount of the asset.
And intangible assets, paragraph 10

10 Where an intangible asset is recognised, its fair value should be based on its replacement cost, which is normally its estimated market value.

Acquisition accounting does lead to some changes being required to the assets and liabilities that will need to be recognized as part of fair value. Two examples are pension surpluses or deficits that would, without acquisition having taken place, have been recognized over future years, and contingent assets that were not previously recognized in accordance with SSAP 18, but now need to be recognized as it is expected that the amounts expended on its purchase will be recovered.

FRS 7 also deals with the cost of the acquisition as the value placed on this will also affect goodwill and therefore post-acquisition profits and/or distributable profits.

The cost of acquisition is

26 The amount of cash paid and the fair value of other purchase consideration given by the acquirer, together with the expenses of the acquisition as described in paragraph 28. Where a subsidiary undertaking is acquired in stages, the cost of acquisition is the total of the costs of the interests acquired, determined as at the date of each transaction.

27 Where the amount of purchase consideration is contingent on one or more future events, the cost of acquisition should include a reasonable estimate of the fair value of amounts expected to be payable in the future. The cost of acquisition should be adjusted when revised estimates are made, with consequential corresponding adjustments continuing to be made to goodwill until the ultimate amount is known.

The main problems here stem from the necessity to place a fair value on capital instruments issued as part of the purchase consideration. If the capital instruments are quoted then the market price on the date of acquisition is taken as fair value. For unquoted capital instruments FRS 7 states that the fair value is to be estimated by taking account of:

- the value of similar securities that are quoted
- the present value of the future cash flows of the instrument issued
- any cash alternative to the issue of the securities
- the value of any underlying security into which there is an option to convert.

Interestingly there was a dissenting view by a member, Mr Main, of the ASB on the issue of FRS 7. He dissents from the standard due to the prescribed treatment of costs that an acquirer incurs in converting the acquired entity into the business unit it envisages. In other words Mr Main believes that changes resulting from the acquirer's intentions or future actions that were envisaged at acquisition should form part of the fair value acquired; FRS 7 says these are to be treated as post-acquisition costs.

> ## Activity 24
>
> Identify possible reasons for Mr Main's belief that such costs as identified above should form part of the fair value of the acquirer's assets and liabilities.

Activity 24 feedback

Mr Main's reasons are stated in an appendix to FRS 7 and we quote these as follows:

2   Mr Main believes that it is very rare for a company to acquire another without intending to make changes to the acquired business to enable it to operate efficiently. Such changes may include, on the one hand, investment in, and reorganisation of, the assets being acquired to enable products or services to be provided efficiently, and, on the other hand, reductions of excessive manpower, buildings or equipment to enable an adequate profit to be earned.

3   Mr Main believes that the need for such changes and the likely cost of executing them are invariably known to the acquirer at the time the acquisition is made, and that the normal practice of management when considering a proposed acquisition for approval is to aggregate the acquisition price with these costs of bringing the acquired entity into a state acceptable to the buyer, in order to arrive at the investment total against which the expected earnings are judged.

4   The requirement of the FRS will prevent a company from recognising in the financial statements at the time of acquisition the costs of the intended changes. It is only when such costs are committed irrevocably that they are to be included in the financial statements, and even then, to the extent that these costs are not capital expenditure, they cannot be included as part of the investment cost of the acquisition.

7   Mr Main believes that the concerns over past abuses could be met, without overturning long-standing practice, by a standard that provided a stricter definition of what costs should be permitted to be included in acquisition provisions, together with more detailed note disclosure of the provisions made. Provisions would be restricted to costs to be incurred within twelve months of the acquisition, and would exclude any costs relating to the acquiring entity's own activities. Provisions for future losses would also be prohibited. Notes to the financial statements would be required to disclose the separate elements of the provisions involved and the actual expenditure subsequently charged against the provisions. Surplus provisions would be required to be adjusted against goodwill rather than be released to the profit and loss account. He believes that the disclosure requirements in the related FRS 6 would provide sufficient information on the effects of an acquisition without the need for the radical change in practice introduced in FRS 7.

Related party transactions

So far in this chapter we have dealt with accounting for business combinations, subsidiaries, associates and joint ventures. However, what we have not considered is that the parties in these business combinations often enter into transactions with each other that unrelated parties would not undertake. For example:

- assets and liabilities may be transferred between parties at values above or below market value
- one party may make a loan to another at a beneficial interest rate or without taking into account the full risk involved
- services carried out by one party for another may be charged for at a reduced rate.

One of our basic assumptions within accounting is that transactions are carried out at arm's length between independent parties. If they are not then users of financial statements will be misled if they are not provided with information in respect of these related party transactions. However, we need to decide how much information to provide and also to define when parties are related.

The first attempt to issue a standard in respect of related parties was made by the ASC in 1989 when they issued ED 46. This did not progress to a standard and the ASB did not revive the topic until 1994 when FRED 8 'Related Party Disclosures' was issued. The revival of interest in the topic occurred at the time of the Robert Maxwell affair where several Maxwell companies were involved in related party transactions. The FRED was converted to FRS 8 in October 1995.

FRS 8 'Related Party Disclosures'

FRED 8 identified the need for disclosure of related party transactions as follows:

> The common practice of companies in organising their businesses through the medium of other companies in the same group, associated undertakings and other related entities has caused transactions between related parties to become a routine and necessary part of the operations of many business enterprises. Related parties may nevertheless enter into transactions that unrelated parties either would not undertake, or would undertake only on different terms. Reporting control relationships and related party transactions draws the attention of users of financial statements to the possibility that those statements may have been affected by the relationship.

This theme is maintained by FRS 8 in its explanation for the issue of the standard:

> In the absence of information to the contrary, it is assumed that a reporting entity has independent discretionary power over its resources and transactions and pursues its activities independently of the interests of its individual owners, managers and others. Transactions are presumed to have been undertaken on an arm's length basis, i.e. on terms such as could have been obtained in a transaction with an external party, in which each side bargained knowledgeably and freely, unaffected by any relationship between them.
>
> These assumptions may not be justified when related party relationships exist, because the requisite conditions for competitive, free market dealings may not be present. Whilst the parties may endeavour to achieve arm's length bargaining the very nature of the relationship may preclude this occurring. Sometimes the nature of the relationship between the parties is such that the disclosure of the relationship alone will be sufficient to make users aware of the possible implications of related party transactions. For this reason, transactions between a subsidiary undertaking, 90 per cent or more of whose voting rights are controlled within the group, and other members and investees of the same group are not required to be disclosed in the separate financial statements of that subsidiary undertaking.

Related parties

FRS 8 defines related parties as follows:

(**a**) Two or more parties are related parties when at any time during the financial period:

   (**i**)   one party has direct or indirect control of the other party; or

   (**ii**)   the parties are subject to common control from the same source; or

   (**iii**)   one party has influence over the financial and operating policies of the other party to an extent that the other party might be inhibited from pursuing at all times its own separate interests; or

   (**iv**)   the parties, in entering a transaction, are subject to influence from the same source to such an extent that one of the parties to the transaction has subordinated its own separate interests.

The FRS also takes on board the substance over form issue by stating that:

(**b**) For the avoidance of doubt, the following are related parties of the reporting entity:

   (**i**)   its ultimate and intermediate parent undertakings, subsidiary undertakings, and fellow subsidiary undertakings

   (**ii**)   its associates and joint ventures

   (**iii**)   the investor or venturer in respect of which the reporting entity is an associate or a joint venture

   (**iv**)   directors of the reporting entity and the directors of its ultimate and intermediate parent undertakings; and

   (**v**)   pension funds for the benefit of employees of the reporting entity or of any entity that is a related party of the reporting entity.

Unless there is evidence to the contrary the following are also presumed to be related parties of the reporting entity unless it can be demonstrated that neither party has influenced the financial and operating policies of the other in such a way as to inhibit the pursuit of separate interests:

(**c**) (**i**)   the key management of the reporting entity and the key management of its parent undertaking or undertakings

   (**ii**)   a person owning or able to exercise control over 20 per cent or more of the voting rights of the reporting entity, whether directly or through nominees

   (**iii**)   each person acting in concert in such a way as to be able to exercise control or influence over the reporting entity; and

   (**iv**)   an entity managing or managed by the reporting entity under a management contract.

Additionally, because of their relationship with certain parties that are, or are presumed to be, related parties of the reporting entity, the following are also presumed to be related parties of the reporting entity:

   (**i**)   members of the close family of any individual falling under parties mentioned in (**a**)–(**c**) above; and

(ii) partnerships, companies, trusts or other entities in which any individual or member of the close family in (**a**)–(**c**) above has a controlling interest.

Information to be disclosed

The FRS requires the disclosure of all material related party transactions and that the following information is provided:

- names of related parties
- description of relationship between the parties
- description of the transactions
- amounts involved
- amounts due at balance sheet date
- any other elements of the transactions necessary for an understanding of the financial statements
- amounts written off in the period in respect of debts due to or from related parties.

The FRS only provides one example of 'any other element':

the need to give an indication that the transfer of a major asset had taken place at an amount materially different from that obtainable on normal commercial terms.

This is notably different from the original FRED which stated that an example of 'any other element' was:

a material difference between the fair value and the transacted amount where material transfers of assets, liabilities or services have taken place.

It even provided a definition of fair value:

the amount at which an asset or liability could be exchanged in a transaction between informed and willing parties, other than in a forced or liquidation sale.

Comments were invited by the ASB in respect of this issue of fair value, in particular whether the requirement should be made specific and not left as part of any other elements. The problem with this issue is that it may not be that easy to identify the fair value of the transaction as in most cases the transaction would not have taken place without the parties being related, so there is no comparison available. We would be entering the realms of 'guesstimates'. As we can see the FRS solved the problem by excluding the suggestion that fair values be provided!

The scope of the standard is also interesting in that it does not require disclosure of related party transactions:

(**a**) in consolidated financial statements, of any transactions or balances between group entities that have been eliminated on consolidation

(**b**) in a parent's own financial statements when those statements are presented together with its consolidated financial statements

(**c**) in the financial statements of subsidiary undertakings, 90 per cent or more of whose voting rights are controlled within the group, of transactions with entities that are part of the group or investees of the group qualifying as related parties, provided that the consolidated financial statements in which that subsidiary is included are publicly available

(**d**) of pension contributions paid to a pension fund; and

(**e**) of emoluments in respect of services as an employee of the reporting entity.

Item (**c**) above was a change from FRED 8 where the exemption had only been available for wholly owned subsidiaries on the grounds that the consolidated financial statements were publicly available. However, in the consolidated statements the related party transactions are not disclosed as they are eliminated on consolidation. The ASB, it appears, believe that

> the nature of the relationship is such that disclosure of the fact that the exemption has been invoked is sufficient to alert the reader of the financial statements to the possible existence of the related party transaction.

The problem with the above is that the reader will not have any information in respect of the amount of these related party transactions!

Summary

Within this chapter we have looked at ways of accounting for a company's investment in another undertaking; as a trade investment, as an associate, as a joint arrangement which is not an entity, as a joint venture, as an acquisition or as a merger. We have formulated consolidated accounts using all of these methods and considered their implications. We have looked in detail at the accounting requirements for the consolidation of subsidiary under-takings using acquisition accounting in accordance with FRS 2 and FRS 7. We have iden-tified the new regulations in respect of the use of merger accounting, FRS 6 and noted that the ASB has issued a standard to replace SSAP 1 on equity accounting and accounting for joint ventures, FRS 9. We also identified the issues surrounding related party transactions FRS 8.

The whole area of accounting for business combinations is highly complex and we have not been able deal with all aspects here. For example, we have not dealt with disposal of previously acquired entities, nor increased holdings in the same entity. However, we hope we have provided you with a great deal of food for thought, and you may like to consider whether you believe the current regulation actually does provide a true and fair view!

It is also worth noting here that the ASB in December 1998 issued a discussion paper entitled 'Business Combinations'. This discussion paper has not yet been converted into a FRED but it proposed that:

- a single method of accounting for all business combinations should be used
- the method proposed for use was acquisition accounting NOT merger accounting
- where it is difficult to identify an acquirer in a business combination that either one company should be designated as acquirer based on some criteria or a fresh-start method of accounting should be used.

We do not propose to explain the fresh-start method here, except to say that it would require *both* companies in the business combination to value assets at fair value. If this discussion paper ever reaches FRS status and that FRS incorporates its suggestions we will then be using:

- acquisition accounting for subsidiaries
- equity accounting for associated companies

- gross equity accounting for joint ventures
- proportional consolidation for joint arrangements
- fresh-start method accounting where acquirer cannot be indentified and merger accounting will not be in use.

Is this a suitable point to question whether the characteristic of understandability can be applied to group accounts?

At this point we provide a further activity for you to practise your consolidation skills. The provision of an activity at the summary stage in a chapter is most unusual in this text but it is essential that you learn to apply the techniques of consolidation.

Activity 25

On 1 April 1995 Hardy plc acquired 4 million of Sibling plc's ordinary shares, paying £4.50 each. At the same time it also purchased, at par, £500 000 of its 10% redeemable preference shares. At the date of acquisition the retained profits of Sibling plc were £8 400 000.

Reproduced below are the draft balance sheets of the two companies at 31 March 1998:

	Hardy plc		Sibling plc	
	£000	£000	£000	£000
Fixed assets				
Land and buildings		22 000		12 000
Plant and equipment		20 450		10 220
Investment in Sibling plc				
– equity		18 000		–
– preference		500		–
		60 950		22 220
Current assets				
Stock	9 850		6 590	
Debtors	11 420		3 830	
Cash at bank	490		–	
	21 760		10 420	
Creditors: amounts falling due within one year				
Creditors	5 600		3 810	
Bank overdraft	–		570	
Provision for taxation	2 470		1 980	
Provision for dividends				
– ordinary	800		500	
– preference	–		200	
	(8 870)		(7 060)	
Net current assets		12 890		3 360
Creditors: amounts falling due after more than one year				
10% Debentures 2001		(12 000)		(4 000)
Net assets		61 840		21 580

Share capital and reserves		
Ordinary shares of £1 each	10 000	5 000
10% Redeemable preference shares		2 000
Profit and loss reserve	51 840	14 580
	61 840	21 580

Extracts from the profit and loss account of Sibling plc, before intra-group adjustments, for the year to 31 March 1998 are:

	£000
Profit before tax	5400
Taxation	(1600)
	3800

The following information is relevant:

(i) Included in the land and buildings of Sibling plc is a large area of development land at its cost of £5 million. Its fair value at the date Sibling plc was acquired was £7 million and by 31 March 1998 this had risen to £8.5 million. The group valuation policy for development land is that it should be carried at fair value and not depreciated.

(ii) Also at the date of Sibling plc's acquisition the plant and equipment included plant that had a fair value of £4 million in excess of its carrying value. This plant had a remaining life of 5 years. The group calculates depreciation on a straight-line basis. The fair value of Sibling plc's other net assets approximated to their carrying values.

(iii) During the year Sibling plc sold goods to Hardy plc for £1.8 million. Sibling plc adds a 20% mark-up on cost to all its sales. Goods with a transfer price of £450 000 were included in Hardy plc's stock at 31 March 1998.

  The balance on the current accounts of the parent and subsidiary was £240 000 on 31 March 1998.

(iv) Hardy plc has not accounted for any dividends receivable from Sibling plc.

(v) Consolidated goodwill is written off on a straight-line basis over a five-year life.

Required:

(a) Prepare the consolidated balance sheet of Hardy plc at 31 March 1998.

(17 marks)

(b) Calculate the minority interest in the adjusted profit of Sibling plc for the year to 31 March 1998. (4 marks)

(c) Explain why FRS 7 'Fair Values in Acquisition Accounting' considers it important to consolidate the fair values of assets and liabilities of an acquired subsidiary at the date of acquisition. (4 marks)

(25 marks)

(ACCA 98)

Activity 25 feedback

(a) Consolidated balance sheet of Hardy plc as at 31 March 1998:

	£000	£000
Fixed assets		
Land and buildings (w i)		37 500
Plant and equipment (w i)		32 270
		992
		70 762
Current assets		
Stock (w ii)	16 365	
Debtors (11 420 + 3 830 – 240)	15 010	
Cash and bank	490	
	31 865	
Creditors: amounts falling due within one year		
Bank overdraft	570	
Creditors (5 600 + 3 810 – 240)	9 170	
Creditors – dividends payable to minority – ordinary	100	
– preference	150	
Taxation (2 470 +1 980)	4 450	
Provision for dividends – Hardy plc	800	
	15 240	
Net current assets		16 625
Creditors: amounts falling due after more than one year		
10% Debentures 2001		(16 000)
Minority interests (w vi)		(6 421)
Net assets		64 966
Share capital and reserves		
Ordinary shares of £1 each		10 000
Reserves:		
Revaluation (w v)		1 200
Profit and loss reserve (w iii)		53 766
		64 966

Workings (Note: all figures in £000)

		Land and buildings	Plant
(i)	Balance from question – Hardy plc	22 000	20 450
	– Sibling plc	12 000	10 220
	Revaluation of land	3 500	
	Revaluation of plant		4 000
	Deduct additional depreciation		
	(20% × 4 000 for three years)		(2 400)
		37 500	32 270

(ii) Stock

Amounts per question (9 850 + 6 590)	16 440
	(75)
	16 365

(iii)

Consolidated profit and loss reserve

	Hardy plc	Sibling plc		Hardy plc	Sibling plc
Unrealised profit (w ii)		75	B/f	51 840	14 580
Additional depreciation (w i)		2 400			
Adjusted profit c/f		12 105			
		14 580			
Minority interest			Adjusted profit b/f		12 105
(20% × 12 105 (w vi)		2 421			
Pre-acq profit (80% × 8 400)		6 720	Profit of S	2 964	
Post-acq profit (80% × 3 705)		2 964	Ordinary divis – S	400	
Goodwill amortisation (w iv)	1 488		Preference divis – S	50	
Balance c/f	53766		(w vii)		
	55 254	12 105		55 254	12 105

(iv)

Cost of control

Investments at cost – equity	18 000	Ordinary shares (80% × 5 000)	4 000
– preference	500	Pref shares (25% × 2 000)	500
		Pre-acq profit (w iii)	6 720
		Revaluation reserve (w v)	4 800
		Goodwill	2 480
	18 500		18 500

Goodwill of £2 480 is depreciated at 20% per annum for three years = £1 488

(v)

Revaluation reserve

Minority – 20%	1 500	Plant	4 000
Pre-acq (2 000 + 4 000) × 80%	4 800	Land	3 500
Post-acq (8 500 – 7 000) × 80%	1 200		
	7 500		7 500

(vi)

Minority interest

Balance c/f	6 421	Ordinary shares (20% × 5000)	1 000
		Pref shares (75% × 2 000)	1 500
		Accumulated profit (w iii)	2 421
		Revaluation	1 500
	6 421		6 421

(vii)   Proposed dividends – Sibling plc
Minority (current liability) – ordinary (20% × 500)   100
                              – preference (75% × 200)   150   250

Group – ordinary (80% × 500)   400
         – preference (25% × 200)   50   450

Total (500 ordinary + 200 preference)   700

(b) See working (iii)
(c) See pages 541–544.

Exercises

1 State the definition of 'subsidiary undertaking', and construct (using appropriate assumptions) a mixed group structure bringing together a holding company, a subsidiary, and a sub-subsidiary.
2 To what extent are groups allowed to present modified accounts for filing?
3 What is the accounting treatment laid down in FRS 2 for subsidiaries excluded from consolidation on the grounds of:
   (a) dissimilar activities?
   (b) lack of effective control?
4 What is the definition of 'associated undertaking' and how will an associate be dealt with in the balance sheet of a group with subsidiaries?
5 State the circumstances in which a business combination will be accounted for using merger accounting as opposed to acquisition accounting.
6 Explain the effects on a group's P&L account and balance sheet of the use of merger accounting as opposed to acquisition accounting in order to account for business combinations.
7 You have recently been appointed chief accountant of Jasmin (Holdings) plc and are about to prepare the group balance sheet at 31 March 1994.
   The following points are relevant to the preparation of those accounts.
   (a) Jasmin (Holdings) plc owns 90% of the ordinary £1 shares and 20% of the 10% £1 preference shares of Kasbah plc. On 1 April 1993 Jasmin (Holdings) plc paid £96 million for the ordinary £1 shares and £1.6 million for the 10% £1 preference shares when Kasbah's reserves were a credit balance of £45 million.
   (b) Jasmin (Holdings) plc sells part of its output to Kasbah plc. The stock of Kasbah plc on 31 March 1994 includes £1.2 million of stock purchased from Jasmin (Holdings) plc at cost plus one third.
   (c) The policy of the group is to revalue its tangible fixed assets on a yearly basis. However the directors of Kasbah plc have always resisted this policy preferring to show tangible fixed assets at historical cost. The market value of the tangible fixed assets of Kasbah plc at 31 March 1994 is £90 million. The directors of Jasmin (Holdings) plc wish you to follow the requirements of FRS 2 'Accounting for Subsidiary Undertakings' in respect of the value of tangible assets to be included in the group accounts.
   (d) The ordinary £1 shares of Fortran plc are split into 6 million 'A' ordinary £1 shares and 4 million 'B' ordinary £1 shares. Holders of 'A' shares are assigned one vote and holders of 'B' ordinary shares are assigned two votes per share. On 1 April 1993 Jasmin (Holdings) plc acquired 80% of the 'A' ordinary shares and 10% of the 'B' ordinary shares when the profit and loss reserve of Fortran plc was £1.6 million and the revaluation reserve was £2 million. The 'A' ordinary shares and 'B' ordinary shares carry equal rights to share in the company's profit and losses.

(e) The fair values of Kasbah plc and Fortran plc were not materially different from their book values at the time of acquisition of their shares by Jasmin (Holdings) plc.

(f) Goodwill arising on acquisition is amortized over five years.

(g) Kasbah plc has paid its preference dividend for the current year but no other dividends are proposed by the group companies. The preference dividend was paid shortly after the interim results of Kasbah plc were announced and was deemed to be a legal dividend by the auditors.

(h) Because of its substantial losses during the period, the directors of Jasmin (Holdings) plc wish to exclude the financial statements of Kasbah plc from the group accounts on the grounds that Kasbah plc's output is not similar to that of Jasmin (Holdings) plc and that the resultant accounts therefore would be misleading. Jasmin (Holdings) plc produces synthetic yarn and Kasbah plc produces garments.

Relevant balance sheets as at 31 March 1994 are set out below:

	£000 Jasmin (Holdings) plc	£000 Kasbah plc	£000 Fortran plc
Tangible fixed assets	289 400	91 800	7 600
Investments			
shares in Kasbah (at cost)	97 600		
shares in Fortran (at cost)	8 000		
	395 000		
Current assets			
stock	285 600	151 400	2 600
cash	319 000	500	6 800
	604 600	151 900	9 400
Creditors: amounts falling due within one year	289 600	238 500	2 200
Net current assets	315 000	(86 600)	7 200
Total assets less current liabilities	710 000	5 200	14 800
Capital and reserves			
Called up share capital			
ordinary £1 shares	60 000	20 000	10 000
10% £1 Preference shares		4 000	
Revaluation reserve	40 000		1 200
Profit and loss reserve	610 000	(18 800)	3 600
Total assets less current liabilities	710 000	5 200	14 800

Required:

(a) **List the conditions for exclusion of subsidiaries from consolidation for the directors of Jasmin (Holdings) plc and state whether Kasbah plc may be excluded on these grounds.** (4 marks)

(b) **Prepare a consolidated balance sheet for Jasmin (Holdings) Group plc for the year-ending 31 March 1994. (All calculations should be made to the nearest thousand pounds.)** (18 marks)

(c) **Comment briefly on the possible implications of the size of Kasbah plc's losses for the year for the group accounts and the individual accounts of Jasmin (Holdings) plc.**
(3 marks)
(25 marks)
(ACCA)

8 Greenhouse plc is engaged in the paper making industry and has one subsidiary Airedale plc and several autonomous manufacturing units. Greenhouse plc owns 60% of the voting shares of Airedale plc which were acquired on 1 September 1992, when the P&L account balance of Airedale was £1.4 million. The draft P&L accounts for the year-ended 31 August 1994 including discontinued activities were:

	Greenhouse plc		Airedale plc	
	£000	£000	£000	£000
Turnover		15 050		12 340
Cost of sales		(12 679)		(10 622)
Gross profit		2 371		1 718
Dividend income (net)		280		64
		2 651		1 782
Loss on disposal of unit (net of all provisions for losses)	180			
Distribution costs	1 042		824	
Administrative expenses	766		307	
		(1 988)		(1 131)
Net profit before tax		663		651
Corporation tax		(268)		(96)
Net profit after tax before dividends		395		555

(a) During the year Greenhouse plc had closed down one of its largest manufacturing units. The following details relate to the closure of this unit up to the date of its discontinuance in July 1994, and are included in the profit and loss account of Greenhouse plc.

		£000
Turnover		1300
Cost of sales		(1225)
Gross profit		75
Distribution costs		(100)
Administrative expenses		(285)
Operating loss		(310)
Provision for losses at 1.9.93		
– operational loss	50	
– loss on disposal	70	
	120	
Loss on disposal of unit	(300)	
		(180)
		(490)
Taxation relief		82
Loss on discontinued activities		(408)

(b) Greenhouse plc is currently developing a new paper making machine which will become operational in 1996. The auditors have agreed that the project has commercial viability and are happy that the outcome of the project will be successful and be beneficial to the company. The current year's expenditure of £36 000 has been included in administrative expenses.

Airedale plc has been attempting to create a chemical product which will neutralize the caustic effects of the wastepaper it produces. This would enable it to reduce the costs of disposal of the wastepaper. Currently this research has proved to be unsuccessful. The costs of this research amounting to £72 000 have been charged to cost of sales.

It is the group policy to defer research and development expenditure to future periods wherever this is possible within the terms of SSAP 13, 'Accounting for Research and Development'.

(c) Greenhouse plc proposes to declare a final dividend of 5p per ordinary share. Airedale plc has already paid an interim dividend of 10p per ordinary share on 1 May 1994 and does not propose to pay a final dividend. The issued share capital of Greenhouse plc is 600 000 ordinary shares of 50p each and of Airedale plc is 200 000 ordinary shares of £1 each. Greenhouse plc accounts for dividends received on a cash basis.

(d) The P&L account balances at 1 September 1993 were £1.75 million for Greenhouse plc and £1.6 million for Airedale plc.

(e) Airedale plc occasionally trades with its parent company. During the year Greenhouse plc had purchased goods amounting to £275 000 from Airedale plc, and Airedale plc had purchased goods from Greenhouse plc amounting to £450 000. These transactions had occurred early in the financial year and none of these goods remained in stock at the financial year-end. Inter-company sales are charged at cost plus 25% profit.

(f) The ACT fraction to be used in this question is 20/80.

Required:

(a) Prepare the consolidated P&L account for the year-ended 31 August 1994 for Greenhouse plc, in a form suitable for publication under the Companies Act 1989 and Format 1 of FRS 3, 'Reporting Financial Performance'. Earnings per share should be calculated but the notes to the accounts are not required. (22 marks)

(b) Calculate the figure for the group's P&L account which would appear in the consolidated balance sheet of Greenhouse plc as at 31 August 1994.

(3 marks)

(25 marks)

(Calculations may be rounded to the nearest thousand pounds except for earnings per share.) (ACCA)

9 **Prepare the consolidated balance sheet of the Sadex plc group of companies at 30 June 1991.**

Note: (1) Calculations should be made to the nearest £1000. (2) Marks are awarded for workings. These must be shown.

(44 marks)

(ACCA)

Sadex plc, a manufacturing company, holds a number of long-term investments, including:

(1) *£1 ordinary shares in Ignat plc*

On 11 November 1989 Sadex had acquired 1 800 000 of the 3 000 000 shares in issue at that date (together with the voting rights), at a cost of £4.268 million. Subsequently, in March 1990, Ignat distributed a previously declared 1 for 5 scrip (bonus) issue from pre-acquisition reserves, by utilizing the share premium account. On 30 September 1990 Ignat made a 1 for 9 rights issue at 125p per share, all of which was taken up by Sadex at a cost of £300 000.

At the date on which Sadex acquired its initial holding, (11 November 1989), the reserves of Ignat had comprised:

	£000
Share premium account	670
Other reserves	Nil
Profit and loss account	70 (debit balance)

The book values of Ignat's assets at the date of acquisition were the same as their fair values with the exceptions that:

(a) the fair values of land and buildings were £500 000 and £610 000, respectively, compared with their book values which were £300 000 and £410 000, respectively. The fair values were not recorded in the accounts. Ignat depreciates buildings at the rate of 5% per annum on their written-down book values at the end of the year

(b) certain items of stock with a book value of £562 000 had a fair value of £742 000. The whole of this stock had been sold by 30 June 1991.

(2) *£1 ordinary shares in Ramed Ltd (cost £1.684 million)*

Sadex had acquired a 30% holding of the equity shares on 30 September 1990 and treats Ramed as an associated company. At 1 July 1990, the capital and reserves of Ramed had consisted of:

	£000
Ordinary share capital (called up and fully paid)	2200
Revaluation reserves	730
Other reserves	140
P&L account	230

Ramed's profits for the year-ended 30 June 1991 were earned evenly throughout the period.

Summarized balance sheets of Sadex plc, Ignat plc and Ramed Ltd at 30 June 1991

	Sadex plc		Ignat plc		Ramed Ltd	
	£000	£000	£000	£000	£000	£000
Fixed assets						
Intangible						
Development costs						72
Tangible						
Land and buildings	1 926		854		1 900	
Plant and machinery	3 645		2 662		1 053	
Equipment and vehicles	1 082		1 574		994	
		6 653		5 090		3 947
Investments						
Shares in group undertaking	4 568					
Loan to group undertaking	630					

	Sadex plc		Ignat plc		Ramed Ltd	
Participating interest	1 684					
Loan to undertaking in which the company has a participating interest	340					
Other investments	208		127		229	
		7 430		127		229
		14 083		5 217		4 248
Current assets						
Stocks	2 432		1 605		1 866	
Debtors						
Trade debtors	2 912		2 458		2 107	
Amounts owed by group undertaking	737					
Amounts owed by undertaking in which the company has a participating interest	208					
Other debtors	956		112		85	
Bank and cash	104		92		100	
	7 349		4 267		4 158	

	Sadex plc		Ignat plc		Ramed Ltd	
	£000	£000	£000	£000	£000	£000
Creditors: amounts falling due within 1 year						
Trade creditors	2 991		1 864		1 515	
Bills of exchange payable			350		117	
Other creditors, including taxation and social security	2 715		1 503		1 643	
	5 706		3 717		3 275	
Net current assets		1 643		550		883
Total assets less current liabilities		15 726		5 767		5 131
Creditors: amounts falling due after more than 1 year						
Debenture loans	5 000					
Convertible loan stock					900	
Trade creditors	119		52			
Other creditors	1 243		630		340	
		(6 362)		(682)		(1 240)

Provisions for liabilities and charges					
Deferred taxation	608		73		99
Other provisions	269		212		172
		(877)		(285)	(271)
		8487		4800	3620
Capital and reserves					
Called up share capital	6500		4000		2200
Share premium account	820		170		
Revaluation reserve					730
Other reserves	306		110		220
P&L account	861		520		470
	8487		4800		3620

Additional information:

1 The called up share capital of each of the companies consists of ordinary shares of £1 per share.

2 Goodwill on consolidation is amortized at the rate of 20% per annum on a straight-line basis, with a full year's write-off in the year in which the acquisition takes place. This policy is applied in respect of holdings in both subsidiary and associated under-takings.

3 The amount owed by Ignat for goods and services supplied by Sadex (£737000) is included in trade creditors within Creditors: amounts falling due within 1 year.

4 Amounts owed by Ramed for goods and services supplied by Sadex, £148000 are included in trade creditors, and proposed dividends, £60000, are included in other cred-itors within Creditors: amounts falling due within 1 year.

5 Sadex has advanced loans of £630000 to Ignat and £340000 to Ramed. These sums are shown under Creditors: amounts falling due after more than 1 year.

6 At 30 June 1991, the closing stock of Sadex included goods obtained from Ignat at a transfer price of £860000, being cost plus one-third. It is the policy of Sadex to pro-vide for unrealized profit in full without taking minority interests into consideration.

10 Goliath plc has adopted a strategy of growth by acquisition and over the last two years has bought the following:

1 On 1 April 1991 280000 £1 ordinary shares in Sampson Limited for cash of £316000. At the date of acquisition the balance on reserves was £75000 credit.

2 On 1 April 1992 80000 £1 ordinary shares in Adam Limited for cash of £40000. This holding gives Goliath significant influence but not control.

3 On 1 April 1992 140000 debentures in Sampson Limited for cash of £140000.

The summarized balance sheets, as at 31 March 1993, of the three companies are as fol-lows:

	Goliath plc	Sampson Ltd	Adam Ltd
	£000	*£00*	*£000*
Tangible fixed assets	2440	660	50
Investments	496	–	–
Net current assets	234	150	3
10% debentures	(300)	(350)	–
	2870	460	53

Issued ordinary £1 shares	1000	350	20
Reserves	1870	110	33
	2870	460	53

The summarized P&L accounts for the year-ended 31 March 1993, of the three companies are as follows:

	Goliath plc £000	Sampson Ltd £000	Adam Ltd £000
Turnover	5500	1650	770
Operating profit	600	150	13
After charging directors' fees	70	20	12
Depreciation	75	30	2
Investment income from Sampson Ltd			
dividend proposed	40	–	–
debenture interest	14	–	–
From Adam Ltd			
dividend proposed	2.4	–	–
Interest payable	(30)	(35)	–
Profit before tax	626.4	115	13
Taxation	(200)	(52)	(3)
Profit after tax	426.4	63	10
Dividend proposed	(170)	(50)	(6)
Retained	256.4	13	4

You may assume that the results are all of continuing operations.

Required:

(a) A consolidated P&L account for the Goliath Group for the year-ended 31 March 1993, including all relevant notes to the accounts (so far as the information is available). You may assume that the company takes advantage of the Companies Act permission not to publish its own P&L account. The notes to the accounts should include a statement of movement on reserves.

(30 marks)

(b) A consolidated balance sheet as at 31 March 1993, including all relevant notes to the accounts (so far as the information is available). (10 marks)

(40 marks)

(ACCA)

11 You are given the following information:

1 On 1 January 1989 ABC plc acquired 80% of the ordinary share capital and voting rights of DEF Ltd.

2 DEF Ltd acquired 75% of the ordinary share capital and voting rights of GHI Ltd on 1 January 1987.

3 The summarized balance sheets of these three companies at 31 December 1990 were as follows:

	ABC plc £m	DEF Ltd £m	GHI Ltd £m
Tangible fixed assets	1840	863	520
Investment in subsidiary			
(at cost)	1452	500	–
Stock	350	212	108

Debtors		213	127	82
Bank		234	26	19
		4089	1728	729
Trade creditors		162	101	52
Taxation payable		112	47	27
Dividends payable		100	50	40
Ordinary share capital		500	200	100
Retained profits		3215	1330	510
		4089	1728	729

4 At the dates of share purchases the following information is known:

Company	Date	Ordinary share capital £m	Retained profits £m
DEF Ltd	1.1.1987	200	560
DEF Ltd	1.1.1989	200	800
GHI Ltd	1.1.1987	100	240
GHI Ltd	1.1.1989	100	320

5 During 1990 the following intra-group trading took place:

Selling company	Buying company	Sales at transfer price £m	Profit on sales
DEF Ltd	ABC plc	280	40% on cost

25% of these transfers are held as stock at 31 December 1990.

6 With the following exceptions, the fair value of the assets of investee companies closely approximated their book value at the relevant acquisition dates:

Company	Asset	Book value £m	Fair value
		£m	
DEF Ltd	Stock*	147	197
DEF Ltd	Equipment†	200	400

*All of this stock had been sold by 31 December 1989. †This equipment was purchased in 1988 and is depreciated over its five-year life on a straight-line basis. It is still held by DEF Ltd.

7 DEF Ltd has levied a management charge of £10 million per annum on GHI Ltd for services which it provides. In 1990 GHI Ltd has neither paid this charge nor accrued it as outstanding.

8 No dividends receivable have been accrued by parent companies.

9 Group accounting policies are as follows:

  (a) only goodwill pertaining to the parent company is included in the consolidated financial statements

  (b) goodwill is written off on a straight-line basis over five years

  (c) in the year of purchase, a full year's depreciation is provided in respect of fixed assets.

You are required

  (a) to prepare the consolidated balance sheet of ABC plc at 31 December 1990 for presentation to the shareholders (35 marks)

  (b) to explain why the fair value of a company's assets is used in the preparation of consolidated financial statements. (5 marks)

(40 marks)
(CIMA)

12 'The consolidation of financial statements hides rather than provides information.'
You are required to discuss this statement. (15 marks)
(CIMA)

13 Lavinia plc has made the following acquisitions:

(a) Many years ago the company subscribed at par for 7200 £1 ordinary shares in May Ltd, a company being newly floated. No further issues have been made to date.

(b) Some years later, Lavinia plc acquired 9000 £1 ordinary shares in Herbert Ltd for £37 200. At that time Herbert Ltd's shareholders' funds were as shown below.

(c) On 31 December 1992 May Ltd acquired 5000 £1 ordinary shares in John Ltd for £40 000. It is clearly established that Lavinia plc exerts a dominant influence over John Ltd.

Herbert Ltd
at date of acquisition by Lavinia plc.
Shareholders' funds

	£
£1 ordinary shares	15 000
Share premium	7 000
P&L	10 000
	32 000

Lavinia plc adopts the following accounting policies:

Depreciation
The cost of intangible assets is written off on a straight-line basis over the expected useful life of the asset.

Goodwill
On the acquisition of subsidiary businesses the purchase consideration is allocated over the underlying net assets at their fair values. Goodwill arising is capitalized and amortized over the 60 months following acquisition on a straight-line basis.

You ascertain the following information:

1 Herbert Ltd owns certain licences and rights which, although not recorded, had a fair value on date of acquisition of £30 000 and have a life of ten years of which five years were outstanding at 1 April 1992.

2 Having taken independent advice Lavinia plc has decided to provide for a group litigation liability of £2000. The whole of this liability was incurred by John Ltd in the recent past.

3 At acquisition John Ltd held certain stocks at a book value of £1000 but which were considered to have a fair value of only £200. John Ltd does not intend to recognize this difference in its records. Since acquisition before the year-end, of these stock items, items with a book value of £750 and a fair value of £150 have been sold to customers.

4 Lavinia plc has not recorded dividends receivable.

5 During the year John Ltd sold goods to Herbert Ltd for £2000 making a profit of £500 and to May Ltd for £4000 making a profit of £1500. These goods had all been sold to customers by the end of the year but Herbert Ltd and May Ltd had yet to settle their accounts.

The draft accounts of the four companies, before any adjustments required by the foregoing, are as follows:

Balance sheets as at 31 March 1993

	Lavinia plc £	May Ltd £	Herbert Ltd £	John Ltd £
Sundry assets	85 000	35 000	47 000	30 000
Current liabilities	21 000	16 000	8 000	10 000
	64 000	19 000	39 000	20 000
£1 ordinary shares	24 000	9 000	15 000	8 000
Share premium	11 000		7 000	4 000
Profit and loss	29 000	10 000	17 000	8 000
	64 000	19 000	39 000	20 000

P&L for the year-ended 31 March 1993

	£	£	£	£
Turnover	176 000	65 000	109 000	55 000
Cost of sales	90 000	33 000	56 000	28 000
Gross profit	86 000	32 000	53 000	27 000
Other net operating expenses	64 000	23 000	39 000	20 000
Operating profit	22 000	9 000	14 000	7 000
Income receivable	3 000	1 000	2 000	1 000
Interest payable	8 000	2 000	3 000	2 000
Profit before taxation	17 000	8 000	13 000	6 000
Taxation	8 000	3 000	5 000	2 000
Profit after taxation	9 000	5 000	8 000	4 000
Dividends				
paid	2 500	2 000	1 000	500
proposed	2 500	2 500	1 667	500
Retained	4 000	500	5 333	3 000

Required:
For Lavinia Group plc prepare
(a) The group P&L account for the year-ended 31 March 1993. (14 marks)
(b) The group balance sheet as at 31 March 1993 in as much detail as the question allows. (16 marks)
(30 marks)
Work to the nearest £000. Ignore taxation. Notes to the accounts are not required.
(ACCA)

14 Playmore plc acquired 60% the ordinary share capital of School Ltd on 1 October 1996. The purchase cost of the shares was satisfied by issuing 200 000 ordinary £1 shares of Playmore plc at £1.75 per share. Issue costs of £20 000 were incurred. The companies' financial statements for the year-ended 30 November 1996 were as follows:

Balance sheets at 30 November 1996

	Playmore plc £000	School Ltd £000
Tangible fixed assets	700	140
Investment in School Ltd	350	–
	1050	140
Current assets		
Stock	60	180
Debtors	95	85
Cash	75	45
	230	310
Creditors: amounts falling due within one year	(160)	(100)
Net current assets	70	210
Total assets less current liabilities	1120	350
Creditors: amounts falling due after one year	(420)	(70)
	700	280
Ordinary £1 shares	300	40
Share premium account	150	60
Profit and loss reserve	250	180
	700	280

Profit and loss accounts for the year-ended 30 November 1996

	Playmore plc £000	School Ltd £000
Turnover	1260	708
Cost of sales	(644)	(426)
Gross profit	616	282
Distribution costs	(248)	(42)
Administrative expenses	(130)	(84)
Operating profit	238	156
Interest payable	(28)	(12)
Income from School Ltd	18	–
Profit before taxation	228	144
Tax on profit	(113)	(54)
Profit after taxation	115	90
Dividends paid	(15)	(30)
Retained profit for year	100	60

The following information is relevant to the preparation of the group financial statements.

(a) At the date of acquisition the value of the tangible fixed assets of School Ltd at open market price was £200000. The estimated net realizable value of these assets was £160000. Because of the proximity of the acquisition to the financial year-end, no depreciation adjustment is to be made in the group accounts, and the carrying value of the tangible fixed assets in School Ltd's accounts at the date of acquisition is deemed to be the year-end value. All other assets and liabilities of School Ltd were stated at their fair values at the time of acquisition.

(b) The issue costs of £20 000 incurred on the issue of ordinary share capital had been charged to the profit and loss account of Playmore plc under the heading of 'Administrative expenses'.

(c) School Ltd paid an ordinary dividend of 10p per share on 1 November 1996. No further dividends were declared for the year-ending 30 November 1996. ACT on the dividends paid in the year had been accounted for by both companies.

(d) Goodwill arising on acquisition is to be amortised against the profit and loss account over a six year period on the straight-line basis. A full year's charge is to be included in administrative expenses for the year-ending 30 November 1996.

(e) There were no intercompany transactions during the financial year and it is assumed that the profit of School Ltd accrues evenly over the year. School Ltd had not issued any shares since the acquisition by Playmore plc.

(f) The company's policy is to account for preacquisition dividends by treating them as a return of the cost of the investment in the subsidiary.

Required:

(a) Prepare a consolidated balance sheet and profit and loss account for the Playmore Group plc for the year-ending 30 November 1996. (Notes to the accounts are not required: workings should be to the nearest £000.)

(21 marks)

(b) Explain how the fair value might be estimated where the purchase consideration is in the form of share capital and no suitable market price exists (for example where the shares issued are those of an unquoted company).

(4 marks)

(25 marks)

(ACCA)

15 Was FRS 9 necessary? Discuss.

16 Hill plc is a small company that has recently achieved a listing on the Alternative Investment Market. The company's management are ambitious and intend to expand rapidly. On 1 April 1997 Hill plc acquired all of the ordinary share capital of Glen Ltd by way of a share exchange. Hill plc issued four of its own shares for every three shares in Glen Ltd. The market value of Hill plc's shares on 1 April 1997 was £5 each. The share issue has not yet been recorded in Hill plc's books. The summarized financial statements of both companies for the year to 30 September 1997 are:

Profit and loss accounts:

	Hill plc		Glen Ltd	
	£000	£000	£000	£000
Turnover		1000		1000
Cost of sales		(630)		(660)
Gross profit		370		340
Operating expenses		(120)		(100)
Operating profit		250		240
Taxation		(50)		(40)
Profit after tax		200		200
Dividends – interim	(40)		–	
Dividends – final (proposed)	(40)	(80)	(60)	(60)
Retained profit for the year		120		140

Balance sheets:

	Hill plc		Glen Ltd	
	£000	£000	£000	£000
Fixed assets		440		670
Current assets				
Stock	240		280	
Debtors	170		210	
Bank	20		40	
	430		530	
Creditors: amounts falling due within one year				
Creditors	170		160	
Taxation	50		40	
Dividends	40		60	
	(260)		(260)	
Net current assets		170		270
		610		940
Debentures		–		(150)
Net assets		610		790
Capital and reserves				
Ordinary shares of £1 each		200		150
Profit and loss account		410		640
		610		790

The following information is relevant:

1 The fair values of Glen Ltd's land and stock were in excess of their book values at the date of acquisition by £125 000 and £25 000, respectively. The fair values of the other net assets were equal to their book values. All of the stock at the date of acquisition had been sold prior to 30 September 1997.

2 Consolidated goodwill is to be written off to cost of sales over five years. A full year's charge is made in the year of acquisition.

3 Hill plc includes only post-acquisition dividends, calculated on a time apportioned basis, in its consolidated reserves. It has not accounted for the proposed dividend of Glen Ltd. All profits accrue evenly throughout the year.

Required:

Prepare for Hill plc:

(a) Using acquisition accounting:

(i) a consolidated profit and loss account for the year to 30 September 1997;
Note: you are not required to analyse the profit and loss account between continuing operations and acquisitions.

(ii) a consolidated balance sheet as at 30 September 1997.   (11 marks)

(b) Using merger accounting: the consolidated reserves at 30 September 1997.
(4 marks)
(15 marks)
(ACCA)

17 The summarized balance sheets of Bacup plc, Townley plc and Rishworth plc as at 31 March 1997 are as follows.

	Bacup	Townley	Rishworth
Fixed assets:	£000	£000	£000
Tangible fixed assets	3820	4425	500
Development expenditure	–	200	–
Investments	1600	–	–
	5420	4625	500
Current assets:			
Stock	2740	1280	250
Debtors	1960	980	164
Cash at bank	1260	–	86
	5960	2260	500
Creditors: amounts falling due within one year:			
Trade creditors	(1620)	(2870)	(142)
Bank overdraft	–	(2260)	–
Taxation	(400)	(150)	(58)
Proposed dividends	(500)	(200)	–
	(2520)	(5480)	(200)
Net current assets (liabilities)	3440	(3220)	300
Net assets	8860	1405	800
Share capital and reserves:			
Ordinary shares of 25p each	4000	500	200
Reserves:			
Share premium	800	125	
Profit and loss account			
at 31 March 1996	2300	380	450
Retained for year	1760	400	150
	8860	1405	800

The following information is relevant:
(i) Investments

Bacup plc acquired 1.6 million shares in Townley plc on 1 April 1996 paying 75p per share. On 1 October 1996 Bacup plc acquired 40% of the share capital of Rishworth plc for £40 0000.

(ii) Group accounting policies

Development expenditure should be written off as incurred. The development expenditure in the balance sheet of Townley plc relates to a project that was commenced on 1 April 1995. At the date of acquisition the value of the capitalized expenditure was £80 000. No development expenditure of Townley plc has yet been depreciated.

Goodwill

All goodwill is written off on a straight-line basis over a five-year life. Time apportionment is used where goodwill arises part way through an accounting period.

(iii) Intra-group trading

The stock of Bacup plc includes goods at a transfer price of £200 000 purchased from Townley plc after the acquisition. The stock of Rishworth plc includes goods at a transfer

price of £125 000 purchased from Bacup plc. All stock transfers were at cost plus 25%.
   The debtors of Bacup plc include an amount owing from Townley plc of £250 000. This does not agree with the corresponding amount in the books of Townley plc due to a cash payment of £50 000 made on 29 March 1997, which had not been received by Bacup plc at the year-end.

(iv) Share premium
The share premium account of Townley plc arose prior to the acquisition by Bacup plc.

Required:

(a) A consolidated balance sheet of the Bacup plc group as at 31 March 1997.

(18 marks)

(b) Norden Manufacturing plc has been approached by Mr Long, a representative of Townley plc. Mr Long is negotiating for Norden plc to supply Townley plc with goods on six-month credit. Mr Long has pointed out that Townley plc is part of the Bacup plc group and provides the consolidated balance sheet to support the credit request.

Required:
Briefly discuss the usefulness of the group balance sheet for assessing the credit-worthiness of Townley plc and describe the further investigations you would advise Norden Manufacturing plc to make.

(7 marks)

(25 marks)

(ACCA 97)

18 The balance sheets of A plc and its investee companies B Ltd and D Ltd, and of B Ltd's investee company C Ltd at 31 March 1998 (the accounting date for all four companies) are given below:

	A plc		B Ltd		C Ltd		D Ltd	
Fixed assets:	£m	£m	£m	£m	£m	£m	£m	£m
Tangible assets	450		220		250		250	
Investments	850		280		–		–	
		1300		500		250		250
Current assets:								
Stocks	200		145		120		120	
Debtors	100		90		90		80	
	300		235		210		200	
Current liabilities:								
Trade creditors	50		40		40		40	
Taxation	20		15		12		10	
Dividends	15		10		10		10	
Bank overdraft	50		40		30		30	
	135		105		92		90	
Net current assets		165		130		118		110
10% debentures		(200)		(90)		(80)		(80)
		1265		540		288		280

Capital and reserves:				
Share capital (£1 shares)	700	400	200	180
Share premium account	200	80	40	40
Profit and loss account	365	60	48	50
	1265	540	288	270

Notes to the financial statements:

1 Investments by A plc and B Ltd were as follows:

   ■ On 31 March 1996, A plc bought 300 million shares in B Ltd for £500 million. On the same date, A plc acquired all the debentures of B Ltd at par. The profit and loss account of B Ltd showed a balance of £52 million at that date. Apart from its investment in the shares of C Ltd, the net assets of B Ltd at 31 March 1996 had a fair value which was the same as their book value. The investment in the shares of C Ltd at 31 March 1996 had a fair value of £240 million.

   ■ On 31 March 1993, B Ltd bought 160 million shares in C Ltd for £200 million. On the same date, B Ltd acquired all the debentures of C Ltd at par. The profit and loss account of C Ltd showed a balance of £10 million at that date and a balance of £40 million at 31 March 1996. At 31 March 1993 and 31 March 1996, all of the net assets of C Ltd had a fair value which was the same as their book value.

   ■ On 31 March 1997, A plc bought 72 million shares in D Ltd for £140 million. On the same date, A plc acquired all the debentures of D Ltd at par. The profit and loss account of D Ltd showed a balance of £50 million at that date. At 31 March 1997, all of the net assets of D Ltd had a fair value which was the same as their book value. The board of directors of D Ltd had nine members and, because of the influence A plc was able to exercise over D Ltd through its trading relationship (see note 3 below), six of the nine were appointees of A plc, including the chairman and the managing director.

   ■ On 15 April 1996, A plc acquired a 9% stake in E Ltd for £40 million. Another corporate investor holds 65% of the shares in E Ltd.

2 Premiums on acquisition are amortized over their estimated useful economic life of ten years. Debenture interest is payable every six months on 31 March and 30 September each year. The payments are made to the registered holders of debentures on the 25th of the month in which they take place.

3 D Ltd's main business is the manufacture of a component used by A plc (but not by B Ltd or C Ltd). The turnover of D Ltd for the year-ended 31 March 1998 was £150 million, and £120 million of this represented sales to A plc, which were invoiced at cost plus 20%. At 31 March 1998, the stocks of A plc included £30 million in respect of goods purchased from D Ltd. At 31 March 1998 the debtors of D Ltd and the creditors of A plc included £20 million in respect of goods purchased from D Ltd by A plc.

4 A plc and B Ltd deal with investment income on an accruals basis. All shares in issue in all companies are equity shares.

Requirements:

(a) Explain how B Ltd, C Ltd, D Ltd and E Ltd will be dealt with in the consolidated balance sheet of A plc at 31 March 1998. Give reasons for your answer in each case. You may assume that equity shares in all companies carry one vote per share at general meetings.   (10 marks)

(b) Prepare the consolidated balance sheet of the A plc group at 31 March 1998. You should perform all calculations to the nearest £0.1 million.   (30 marks)

(40 marks)

(CIMA 98)

19 You are the accountant responsible for the Rag group consolidation. The profit and loss accounts of Rag plc, Tag Ltd and Bobtail Ltd for the year ended 31 March 1999 are given below.

	Rag plc £000	Tag Ltd £000	Bobtail Ltd £000
Turnover (*Note 1*)	65 000	50 000	100 000
Cost of sales	(35 000)	(28 000)	(82 000)
Gross profit	30 000	22 000	18 000
Other operating expenses	(15 000)	(11 000)	(9 000)
Operating profit	15 000	11 000	9 000
Investment income (*Note 2*)	3 000	1 200	–
Interest payable	(3 200)	(1 800)	(1 200)
Profit before taxation	14 800	10 400	7 800
Taxation	(3 600)	(2 800)	(2 400)
Profit after taxation	11 200	7 600	5 400
Proposed dividends	(6 000)	(4 000)	(3 000)
Retained profit	5 200	3 600	2 400
Retained profit – 1 April 1998	20 000	15 000	12 000
Retain profit – 31 March 1999	25 200	18 600	14 400

Notes to the profit and loss accounts:
Note 1
Rag plc supplies a component which is used by both Tag Ltd and Bobtail Ltd. Because of the close relationships between the three companies, the component is supplied at a mark-up of only 10% on cost. Details of inter-company sales of the product for the year to 31 March 1999 were as follows:

- Rag plc to Tag Ltd   £8 million
- Rag plc to Bobtail Ltd   £4 million

Details of the stocks of the component supplied by Rag plc which were included in the books of Tag Ltd and Bobtail Ltd at the beginning and end of the year were:

Stocks of the component in the books at 31 March	1999 £000	1998 £000
Tag Ltd	2200	1980
Bobtail Ltd	1100	990

Note 2
Details of inter-company shareholdings are as follows:

- On 15 July 1992 Rag plc purchased 4.5 million of the issued £1 equity shares of Tag Ltd for £4 million. The balance sheet of Tag Ltd at 15 July 1992 showed the following:

	£000
Share capital	6 000
Share premium	3 000
Profit and loss account	7 000
	16 000

■ On 8 October 1993, Tag Ltd purchased 2 million of the issued £1 equity shares of Bobtail Ltd for £7.4 million. The balance sheet of Bobtail Ltd at 8 October 1993 showed the following

	£000
Share capital	5 000
Share premium	3 000
Profit and loss account	8 000
	16 000

The policy of Rag plc is to amortise goodwill over 20 years with a full year's write-off in the year of acquisition. At the dates they joined the Rag group, the fair values of the net assets of Tag Ltd and Bobtail Ltd were the same as their book values.

Note 3
Both Rag plc and Tag Ltd recognise investment income on an accruals basis. The profit and loss accounts of Rag plc and Tag Ltd show dividend income as being the **cash** dividend receivable.

Your assistant is responsible for preparing the draft consolidated financial statements for your review. She is aware that Tag Ltd will be dealt with as a 75% subsidiary but is unsure of the way of dealing with Bobtail Ltd.

Requirements:
(a) Write a memorandum to your assistant which
   ■ **explains how Bobtail Ltd will be incorporated into the consolidated financial statement of Rag plc;**
   ■ **describes and justifies any disclosures which are required in the notes to the consolidated financial statements regarding the investment in Bobtail Ltd.**

   Your memorandum should refer to relevant provisions of company law and Financial Reporting Standards to support your explanations. (10 marks)
(b) Prepare a working schedule for the consolidated profit and loss account of Rag plc for the year endd 31 March 1999. You should start with the turnover and end with the retained profit at the end of the year.
   Do NOT prepare notes to the consolidated profits and loss account. (30 marks)
   (40 marks)
   CIMA FRP MAY 99

20 AB, a public limited company, manufactures goods for the aerospace industry. It acquired an electronics company CG, a public limited company on 1 December 1999 at an agreed value of £65 million. The purchase consideration was satisfied by the issue of 30 million shares of AB, in exchange for the whole of the share capital of CG. The directors of AB have decided to adopt merger accounting principles in accounting for the acquisition, but the auditors have not as yet concurred with the use of merger accounting in the financial statements.

The following summary financial statements relate to the above companies as at 31 May 2000.

Profit and loss accounts for the year ended 31 March 2000

	£000	£000
	AB	CG
Turnover	45 000	34 000
Cost of sales	(31 450)	25 280)
Gross profit	13 550	8 720

Distribution and administrative expenses	(9 450)	(3 820)
Operating profit	4 100	4 900
Interest payable	(200)	(400)
Profit before taxation	3 900	4 500
Taxation	(1 250)	(1 700)
Dividends (proposed)	(250)	
Retained profit for the year	2 400	2 800

Balance sheets at 31 May 2000

	£000	£000
	AB	CG
Tangible fixed assets	36 000	24 500
Cost of investment in CG	(30 000)	
Net current assets	29 000	17 500
Creditors: amounts due after more than one year	(2 000)	(4 000)
Total assets less liabilities	93 000	38 000
Capital and reserves		
Ordinary shares of £1	55 000	20 000
Share premium account	3 000	6 000
Revaluation reserve	10 000	
Profit and loss account	25 000	12 000
	93 000	38 000

The following information should be taken into account when preparing the group accounts:

(i) The management of AB feel that the adjustments required to bring the following assets of CG to their fair values at 1 December 1999 are as follows:

Fixed assets to be increased by £4 million;
Stock to be decreased by £3 million (this stock has been sold by the year end);
Provision for bad debts to be increased by £2 million in relation to specific accounts;
Depreciation is charged at 20% per annum on a straight line basis on tangible fixed assets;
The increase in the provision for bad debts was still required at 31 May 2000. No further provisions are required on 31 May 2000.

(ii) CG has a fixed rate bank loan of £4 million which was taken out when interest rates were 10% per annum. The loan is due for repayment on 30 November 2001. At the date of acquisition the company could have raised a loan at an interest rate of 7%. Interest is payable yearly in arrears on 30 November.

(iii) CG acquired a corporate brand name on 1 July 1999. The company did not capitalise the brand name but wrote the cost off against reserves in the Statement of Total Recognised Gains and Losses. The cost of the brand name was £18 million. AB has consulted an expert brand valuation firm who have stated that the brand is worth £20 million at the date of acquisition based on the present value of notional royalty savings arising from ownership of the brand. The auditors are satisfied with the reliability of the brand valuation. Brands are not amortised by AB but are reviewed annually for impairment, and as at 31 May 2000, there has been no impairment in value. Goodwill is amortised over a 10 year period with a full charge in the year of acquisition.

(iv) AB incurred £500 000 of expenses in connection with the acquisition of CG. This figure comprised £300 000 of professional fees and £200 000 of issue costs of the shares. The acquisition expenses have been included in administrative expenses.

Required:
(a) **Prepare consolidated profit and loss accounts for the year ended 31 May 2000 and consolidated balance sheets as at 31 May 2000 for the AB group utilising:**
   (i) **Merger accounting;**
   (ii) **Acquisition accounting.** (19 marks)
(b) **Discuss the impact on the group financial statements of the AB group of utilising merger accounting as opposed to acquisition accounting. (Candidates should discuss at least three effects on the financial statements.)** (6 marks)
(25 marks)
ACCA FRE JUNE 2000

21 The balance sheets of Left plc and Right plc at 31 December 1999, the accounting date for both companies, were as follows:

	Left plc £000	Right plc £000
Tangible fixed assets	60 000	40 000
Stocks	10 000	9 000
Other current assets	12 000	10 000
Current liabilities	(9 000)	(8 000)
Quoted debentures	(15 000)	(12 000)
	58 000	39 000
Equity share capital (£1 shares)	30 000	20 000
Share premium account	10 000	5 000
Profit and loss account	18 000	14 000
	58 000	39 000

On 31 December 1999, Left plc purchased all the equity shares of Right plc. The purchase consideration was satisfied by the issue of 6 new equity shares in Left plc for every 5 equity shares purchased in Right plc. At 31 December 1999 the market value of a Left plc share was £2.25 and the market value of a Right plc share was £2.40. Relevant details concerning the values of the net assets of Right plc at 31 December 1999 were as follows:

- The fixed assets had a fair value of £43.5 million.
- The stocks had a fair value of £9.5 million
- The debentures had a market value of £11 million.
- Other net assets had a fair value that was the same as their book value.

The effect of the purchase of shares in Right plc is NOT reflected in the balance sheet of Left plc that appears above.
Requirements:
(a) **Prepare the consolidated balance sheet of the Left plc group at 31 December 1999 assuming the business combination is accounted for**
   - **as an acquisition; and**
   - **as a merger.** (14 marks)
(b) **Discuss the extent to which the business combination satisfies the requirements of FRS 6 – *Acquisitions and mergers* for classification as a merger. You should indicate the other information you would need to enable you to form a definite conclusion.** (6 marks)
(20 marks)
CIMA(9) MAY 00

22 The balance sheets of Sea plc and its subsidiaries River Ltd and Stream Ltd at 31 March 2000 – accounting reference-date for all three companeis – are given below.

	Sea plc		River Ltd		Stream Ltd	
	£000	£000	£000	£000	£000	£000
Fixed assets						
Intangible assets					5000	
Tangible assets	41000		30000		20000	
Investiments	17000					
		58000		30000		25000
Current assets						
Stocks	8000		6000		4000	
Debtors	7000		5250		3500	
Cash	2000		500		300	
	17000		11750		7800	
Current liabilities						
Trade creditors	3000		2200		1500	
Taxation	3200		2300		1600	
Proposed dividend	2200		1800		1200	
	8400		6300		4300	
Net current assets		8600		5450		3500
Long-term loans		(20000)				(8052)
Provisions for liabilities and charges						(1000)
		46600		35450		19448
Capital and reserves						
Called-up share capital (£1 shares)		20000		17000		12000
Share premium account		15000				1500
Profit and loss account		11600		18450		5948
		46600		35450		19448

Notes to the balance sheets

1 Sea plc subscribed for 100% of the share capital of River Ltd on the date of its incorporation. No changes have taken place to the issued share capital of River Ltd since that date.

2 River Ltd supplies a component that is used by Sea plc in its manufacturing process. River Ltd applies a 20% mark-up to the cost of manufacture of the component to arrive at the selling price to Sea plc. At 31 March 2000 the stocks of Sea plc included £600000 in respect of components purchased from River Ltd.

3 Inter-company trading is meant to cease on 25 March each year to enable agreement of intercompany balances at the year end. On 24 March 2000, Sea plc made a payment of £200000 to River Ltd in respect of components purchased in February 2000. This payment cleared the balances due for purchases up to February 2000. Purchases of the component from 1 March to 24 March 2000 by Sea plc amounted to £180000. This amount was included in the creditors of Sea plc and the debtors of River Ltd at 24 March 2000. On 30 March 2000, contrary to normal practice, River Ltd despatched goods having an invoiced price of £150000 and entered the transaction in its books. The transaction was not recorded by Sea plc in its balance sheet that is given above.

4 The debtors of Sea plc include the dividend receivable from Riber Ltd. Apart from dividend transfers and the purchase of components by Sea plc from River Ltd there are no other intercompany transactions.

5 Following protracted negotiations, the Directors of Sea plc concluded an agreement whereby Sea plc acquired 9 million £1 shares in Stream Ltd on 31 March 2000. The terms of the acquisition were that Sea plc would issue 2 new £1 shares for every 3 shares acquired in Stream Ltd. On 31 March 2000 the market value of a £1 share in Sea plc was £3. The share issue by Sea plc on 31 March 2000 is not reflected in the balance sheet of Sea plc that appears above. The proposed dividend of Stream Ltd that is included in its balance sheet at 31 March 2000 is payable to those shareholders whose names appear on the register on 30 March 2000.

6 The intangible fixed assets of Stream Ltd at 31 March 2000 consist of the estimated value of a brand that is associated with the company. This estimate has been made by the Directors and no reliable external estimate of the market value of the brand is available.

7 Relevant details of tangible fixed assets of Stream Ltd at 31 March 2000 are:

Description	Balance sheet carrying value £000	Market value £000	Depreciated replacement cost £000	Recoverable amount £000
Property	10 000	12 000	Not given	13 500
Plant	10 000	Not given	11 000	14 000

8 Stocks of Stream Ltd at 31 March 2000 comprise:
   - Obsolete stock (balance sheet value £500 000). This stock has a replacement cost of £400 000 and a net realisable value of £300 000.
   - The balance of stock (balance sheet value £3 500 000). This stock has a replacement cost of £3 800 000 and a net realisable value of £4 200 000.

9 The long-term loan of Stream Ltd is a zero-coupon bond that was issued on 1 April 1995 for net proceeds of £5 million. It is redeemable on 31 March 2005 for a single payment of £12 969 000. If the bond had been issued on 31 March 2000 then the effective finance cost would have been 8%.

10 The provision of £1 million in the balance sheet of Stream Ltd is against the reorganisation costs expected to be incurred in integrating the company into the Sea plc group. These costs would not be necessary if Stream Ltd were to remain outside the group. Although the plan was agreed by the Board of Directors before 31 March 2000, it was not made known to those affected by the plan until after 31 March 2000.

11 No amortisation of the goodwill on acquisition of Stream Ltd is necessary until the year ending 31 March 2001.

Requirements:
(a) Calculate the goodwill that arises on the acquisition of Stream Ltd by Sea plc on 31 March 2000. You should ensure that each component of the calculation is fully explained. (16 marks)
(b) Prepare the consolidated balance sheet of the Sea plc group at 31 March 2000.
(19 marks)
(35 marks)
CIMA(9) MAY 00

23 T and W are farmers. T owns a piece of land which he has never been able to cultivate successfully. W owns a powerful tractor. They have entered into a joint venture agreement in which they will use T's land and W's tractor to raise a crop. They will account for this venture in joint venture accounts in their own business records.

T can charge £800 to the joint venture for the use of the land and W can charge £1000 for the use of the tractor.

W paid £900 for the seed and £80 for diesel fuel for the tractor. The land turned out to be difficult to clear and W had to pay £2000 for an attachment for the tractor. It was agreed that W could retain the tractor attachment at the end of the venture and that it should be valued at £1400 at that time.

The crop was sold for £19 000 to a large supermarket chain. The supermarket paid T by means of a bill of exchange. T discounted the bill for £18 600. T was responsible for the finance charge on discounting the bill, which could not be charged to the joint venture.

The profit on the joint venture was shared equally by T and W. The venture was dissolved by a cheque from T to W.

Requirements:

(a) **Prepare a memorandum joint venture account for the transactions described above and the subsequent appropriation of profit.** (5 marks)

(b) **Prepare joint venture accounts for T and W.** (6 marks)

(c) **Show how the bill of exchange would be accounted for in T's books and describe the information that might have to be disclosed in T's financial statements in respect of the bill.** (4 marks)

(15 marks)
CIMA(5) MAY 00

24 FRS 8 – *Related Party Disclosures* – was issued in October 1995. Prior to its existence, there were specific requirements for related-party disclosures contained in the 1985 Companies Act and the Listing Rules of the London Stock Exchange.

On 1 April 1997, Ace plc owned 75% of the equity share capital of Deuce Ltd and 80% of the equity share capital of Trey Ltd. On 1 April 1998, Ace plc purchased the remaining 25% of the equity shares of Deuce Ltd. In the two years ended 31 March 1999, the following transactions occurred between the three companies.

(i) On 30 June 1997 Ace plc manufactured a machine for use by Deuce Ltd. The cost of manufacture was £20 000. The machine was delivered to Deuce Ltd for an invoiced price of £25 000. Deuce Ltd paid the invoice on 31 August 1997. Deuce Ltd depreciated the machine over its anticipated useful economic life of five years, charging a full year's depreciation in the year of purchase.

(ii) On 30 September 1998, Deuce Ltd sold some goods to Trey Ltd at an invoiced price of £15 000. Trey Ltd paid the invoice on 30 November 1998. The goods had cost Deuce Ltd £12 000 to manufacture. By 31 March 1999, Trey Ltd had sold all the goods outside the group.

(iii) For each of the two years ended 31 March 1999, Ace plc provided management services to Deuce Ltd and Trey Ltd. Ace plc did not charge for these services in the year ended 31 March 1998 but in the year ended 31 March 1999 decided to impose a charge of £10 000 per annum to each company. The amounts of £10 000 are due to be paid by each company on 31 May 1999.

Requirements:

(a) **Explain why related-party disclosures are needed and why FRS 8 was considered necessary given the existing requirements of the 1985 Companies Act and the Listing Rules of the London Stock Exchange.** (6 marks)

(b) **Summarise the related-party disclosures which will be required in respect of transactions (i) to (iii) above for *both* of the years ended 31 March 1998 and 31 March 1999 in the financial statements of Ace plc, Deuce Ltd and Trey Ltd.** (14 marks)

You may assume that Ace plc presents consolidated financial statements for *both* of the years dealt with in the question.

(20 marks)
CIMA9 MAY 99

25

Foreign currency translation (SSAP 20)

After reading this chapter you should be able to:
- explain the necessity for foreign currency conversion and currency translation
- describe the SSAP 20 regulations in respect of foreign currency transactions for individual companies
- examine the position where foreign currency investments and borrowings are matched
- describe the SSAP 20 regulations in respect of translation of the accounts of foreign branches and subsidiaries
- translate accounts of foreign companies
- describe the disclosure requirements of SSAP 20 and the Companies Act in respect of foreign currency translation.

Introduction

Business is increasingly international. Whenever a business has any dealings abroad, then it will be involved in 'foreign' currencies. Since it must keep its accounting records and prepare accounting reports in its own 'home' currency, then figures expressed in foreign money units need to be re-expressed in 'home' units (assumed to be pounds sterling). If foreign currency exchange rates remain absolutely constant, i.e. if the value of one currency in terms of the other does not change, then no difficulties arise. But this is not the case, and as we all know exchange rates can and do fluctuate very considerably over relatively short periods of time!

Currency conversion

Currency conversion is required when a foreign currency transaction is completed within an accounting period. A transaction, foreign or otherwise, can be regarded as comprising two events:

1. the purchase or sale of an asset or the incurring of an expense or item of income
2. the receipt or payment of monies for these assets, expenses or items of income.

These events need to be recorded in a company's books as they occur.

Activity 1

A UK company sells goods to a Swiss company on 1 May 20X2 for SwFr750 000. Payment is received on 1 August 20X2. Exchange rate 1 May 20X2 is £1 = SwFr3.5544, 1 August 20X2 is £1 = SwFr3.7081.

The year-end for the company is 30 September 20X2. Record the above transaction in the company books and name the balance on the debtor account.

Activity 1 feedback

Remembering the transaction is two events we need to record the sale of goods immediately, but we must record the event in £s not SwFrs.

Sales account	Debtors – (Swiss company)
1.5.X2 Debtors 211 006	1.5.X2 Sales 211 006

750 000 ÷ 3.5544 (exchange rate 1 May 20X2) = £211 006. When payment is received on 1 August 20X2 it will be in the form of SwFr50 000 which we must convert to £s at the exchange rate at that time = 750 000 ÷ 3.7081 = £202 260.

Event will be recorded as

		£	£
Dr	Cash	202 260	
Cr	Debtor		202 260

Thus there is a balance on the debtor account of £8746 which is obviously a loss on exchange which will need to be reported in the P&L account for ordinary activities.

Similarly, if the exchange rate had decreased from May to August a profit on exchange would have occurred which again would be reported as profit on ordinary activities.

Currency translation

The above activity involved a transaction that was completed by the year-end but we need to consider how to deal with foreign transactions that are not completed by the year-end.

Activity 2

Let us assume in Activity 1 that the company's year-end is 30 June 20X2 when the exchange rate is £1 = SwFr3.6573. Record the transaction in the company's books.

Activity 2 feedback

The initial sale will be recorded as before but at the year-end 30 June 20X2 the debtors account will show a balance of £211 006 which is not correct because if the debt was paid at this date we would receive SwFr 50 000 = £205 069 which is the value of the debt at 30 June 20X2, thus we translate the debtor account at the year-end at the exchange rate ruling:

Debtor

1.5.X2 Sales	211 006	30.6.92 P&L – Loss on exchange 30.6.X2 Balance c/d	5937 205 069
	211 006		211 006
1.7.X2 Balance b/d	205 069	1.8.X2 Cash 30.6.X3 P&L – Loss on exchange	202 260 2809

and the balancing figure of £5937 is the loss on exchange identified as at 30 June 20X2 which will be debited to the P&L account. When the debt is finally paid on 1 August 20X2 a further exchange loss of £2809 is identified for the next year. Notice the total loss of £8746 is now split over the two years – £5937 in year-ended 30 June 20X2 and £2809 in year-ended 30 June 20X3.

The above currency translation follows the concept of prudence as we are taking account of the loss as soon as we are aware of it. However, what would we have done if on 30 June 20X2 the exchange rate was £1 = SwFr3.4973?

This time at the year-end the debtor would translate as 750 000 ÷ 3.4973 = £214 451 giving a profit on exchange of £3445 and on 1 August 20X2 when debt is finally paid a loss of £12 191. The gain of £3445 is an unrealized gain and prudence would dictate that we should not recognize this gain. Let us see what SSAP 20 says on the issue.

SSAP 20 requirements for individual companies' foreign currency transactions

SSAP 20 states:

> **49** All exchange gains or losses on settled transactions and unsettled short term monetary items should be reported as part of the profit or loss for the year from ordinary activities (unless they result from transactions which themselves would fall to be treated as extraordinary items, in which case the exchange gains or losses should be included as part of such items).

Thus, the SSAP is telling us to recognize an unrealized gain in the accounts (in the activity above this was £3445), but the Companies Act tell us that only profits realized at the balance sheet date should be included in the P&L account!

In a statement accompanying the release of SSAP 20 the ASC outlined the arguments in favour of their requirement as follows:

1 Realized profits are what accountants say they are (this is quite correct, it's what paragraph 91 of schedule 4, 1985 Act says).
2 Where exchange gains arise on short-term monetary items their ultimate cash realization can normally be assessed with reasonable certainty and they are therefore realized in accordance with the prudence concept defined in SSAP 2.
3 It provides symmetry with losses.

Translation of long-term monetary items

SSAP 20 states:

> **50** Exchange gains and losses on long term monetary items should also be recognised in the profit and loss account; however, it is necessary to consider on the grounds of prudence whether, in the exceptional cases outlined in paragraph 11, the amount of the gain, or the amount by which exchange gains exceed past exchange losses on the same items, to be recognised in the profit and loss account should be restricted.

Paragraph 11 tells us that the exceptional cases are when there are doubts as to the convertibility or marketability of the currency in question.

Thus, on the translation of a long-term loan any gain on exchange can be taken to the P&L account even though it is not realized as long as there are no doubts as to the convertibility or marketability of the currency. Given the rather 'fluid' times over recent years in respect of exchange rates we could of course have no doubts as to convertibility one week, but have a great deal of doubt the next!

SSAP 20 does not argue that exchange gains on unsettled long-term monetary items are realized but that:

> **3** exchange gains can be determined no less objectively than exchange losses at the balance sheet date and that it would be illogical to deny that favourable movements in exchange rates had occurred whilst accounting for adverse movements ... this symmetrical treatment of exchange gains and losses on long term monetary items is necessary to show a true and fair view of the results of a company which is involved in foreign currency operations.

It is interesting to note from the above statement that symmetry is required for a true and fair view rather than prudence! Also it is worth noting that SSAP 20 does not invoke the true and fair override but invokes the ruling that departure from the accounting principles is allowed if there are special reasons. The special reason is the need to show a true and fair view.

Investments matched by borrowings

A company that has made a foreign equity (shareholding) investment is exposed to an exchange risk on that investment. However, it is possible for the investing company to protect itself by raising loans in the foreign country denominated in the foreign currency, and using the money from these borrowings to make the investment. From the point of view of the home (investing) company it has:

1 an asset, exposed to an exchange risk
2 a liability, also exposed to an exchange risk.

Since the asset and liability, in principle equal in amount, are in effect part of one overall transaction, and since the exchange risks are equal and opposite, the effects of exchange rate movements on these items should simply be cancelled out.

Normally, however, a foreign currency investment, a long-term non-monetary item, would not be translated in the accounts at the year-end but the loan, a long-term monetary item would be translated. SSAP 20 does allow us to translate foreign currency investments where a loan is used as a 'hedge'.

The formal SSAP provision is as follows:

> **51** Where a company has used foreign currency borrowings to finance, or provide a hedge against its foreign equity investments and the conditions set out in this paragraph apply, the equity investments may be denominated in the appropriate foreign currencies and the carrying amounts translated at the end of each accounting period at closing rates for inclusion in the investing company's financial statements. Where investments are treated in this way, any exchange differences arising should be taken to reserves and the exchange gains or losses on the foreign currency borrowings should then be offset, as a reserve movement, against these exchange differences. The conditions which must apply are as follows:
>
> **(a)** in any accounting period, exchange gains or losses arising on the borrowings may be offset only to the extent of exchange differences arising on the equity investments
>
> **(b)** the foreign currency borrowings, whose exchange gains or losses are used in the offset process, should not exceed, in the aggregate, the total amount of cash that the investments are expected to be able to generate, whether from profits or otherwise; and
>
> **(c)** the accounting treatment adopted should be applied consistently from period to period.

Activity 3

A company whose year-end is 31 March takes out two loans on 1 August one for 5 000 000 pesetas and one for FF200 000 when exchanges rates were £1 = 180 pesetas = FF10. The French franc loan is used to make an equity investment of $30 000; £1 = $1.60. At the same time another equity investment is purchased of 100 000 Australian dollars (A$), £1 = A$1.9. How would the above be shown in the company's books at the year-end when £1 = 186 pesetas = FF9.7 = $1.5 = A$1.95.

Activity 3 feedback

Initially, when the loans and investments are taken up they will need to be recorded in the books in £s as follows:

Loan pesetas	Loan FF
1/8 cash 27 778 (5 000 000 ÷ 180)	1/8 Cash 20 000 (200 000 ÷ 10)

Investment $	Investment A$
1/8 cash 18 750 (30 000 ÷ 1.60)	1/8 cash 52 632 (100 000 ÷ 1.9)

Long-term monetary items, i.e. pesetas loan and French franc loan will be translated at year-end exchange rate, but can the investments be translated at year-end? The answer is only if they are hedged. In this case it is only clear that the dollar investment is hedged therefore only this investment can be translated at year-end as follows:

Loan pesetas			Loan FF		
31/3 gain P&L 896	1/8 27 778		31/3 Bal c/d 20 619	1/8	20 000
31/3 Bal c/d 26 882				31/3	loss
				reserves	619

Investment $			Reserves for currency		
1/8	18 750		Loan FF 619	Inv $1250	
31/3	gain	31/3 bal c/d	Bal c/d 631		
reserves	1 250	20 000			

Thus, the loss on the FF loan avoids the P&L account and is taken to reserves to offset against the gain on the dollar investment. Note, that if the loss on the loan is greater than the gain on the investment the excess loss must be taken to the P&L account; and also that by translating the dollar investment at the year-end net assets of the company have increased.

Note that paragraph 51 of SSAP 20 does not state that the foreign currency investment and hedged loan must be in the same currency. It is perfectly clear that where investments and loans are in the same currency the loss on one will offset the gain on the other due to the change in the currency rate. However, the logic of hedging using different currencies is rather unclear as you cannot be certain the risk will be covered. It is interesting to note, in Activity 3, that if the French loan and dollar investment had not been treated as hedging transactions then the P&L account would have borne a further loss of £619!

The argument for taking gains and losses on translated investments to reserves is as follows according to SSAP 20:

19 The results of the operations of a foreign enterprise are best reflected in the group profit and loss account by consolidating the net profit or loss shown in its local currency financial statements without adjustment (other than for normal consolidation adjustments). If exchange differences arising from the retranslation of a company's net investment in its foreign enterprise were introduced into the profit and loss account, the results from trading operations, as shown in the local currency financial statements, would be distorted. Such differences may result from many factors unrelated to the trading performance or financing operations of the foreign enterprise; in particular, they do not represent or measure changes in actual or prospective cash flows. It is therefore inappropriate to regard them as profits or losses and they should be dealt with as adjustments to reserves.

So, because the gain or loss on the investment does not represent changes in cash flow, it must be taken to reserves. Compare this with a foreign currency loan, which on translation at year-end shows a gain. This can be taken to P&L account but it does not represent a change in cash flow and if the loan is not due for another nine years it can hardly be said to be prospective. SSAP 20 uses the following argument.

10 In order to give a true and fair view of results, exchange gains and losses on long term monetary items should normally be reported as part of the profit or loss for the period in accordance with the accruals concept of accounting;

treatment of these items on a simple cash movements basis would be inconsistent with that concept. Exchange gains on unsettled transactions can be determined at the balance sheet date no less objectively than exchange losses; deferring the gains whilst recognizing the losses would not only be illogical by denying in effect that any favourable movement in exchange rates had occurred but would also inhibit fair measurement of the performance of the enterprise in the year. In particular, this symmetry of treatment recognizes that there will probably be some interaction between currency movements and interest rates and reflects more accurately in the profit and loss account the true results of currency involvement.

Read that three times, and remember the requirement of SSAP 2 that when a conflict occurs between prudence and matching (or accruals), prudence should prevail.

Summary of individual company transactions

1 *Settled transactions*: gain or loss is obviously realized and reflected in cash flows.
2 *Unsettled transactions*: short-term monetary items translate at year-end exchange rate and gain or loss although unrealized is taken to P&L as it is 'reasonably certain'.
3 Long-term monetary items treated the same as short term so as to give symmetry.
4 Investments if they are hedged can be translated at year-end, gains or losses taken to reserves and offset by gain or loss on hedged loan.

Translation methods

When translating any particular item we can take two basic possible views:

1 We can use the exchange rate ruling when the item was created (historic rate).
2 We can use the exchange rate ruling when the item is being reported (current, or closing, rate).

Since we can apply this choice to each item one at a time, it is clear that many different combinations are possible. Four that have been suggested are outlined below.

Single rate (closing rate)

This is based on the idea that the holding company has a net investment in the foreign operation, and that what is at risk from currency fluctuations is this net financial investment. All assets, liabilities, revenues and expenses will be translated at the closing (balance sheet date) rate. Exchange differences will arise if the closing rate differs from the previous year's closing rate, or from the date when the transaction occurred.

Mixed rate (current/non-current)

Here current assets and liabilities would be translated at the closing rate, whereas fixed assets and non-current liabilities would be translated at the rate ruling when the item was established (i.e. current items are translated at current rates and fixed items are translated at fixed rates).

Mixed rate (monetary/non-monetary)

This proposal would translate monetary assets and liabilities at the closing rate, and all non-monetary assets and liabilities at the rate ruling when the item was established. There is an analogy here with the arguments for CPP accounting (p. 88). Monetary items are automatically expressed in current monetary units (so use the current rate for them) and non-monetary items are expressed in out-of-date monetary units (so use the out-of-date rate for them).

Mixed rate (temporal)

This is based on the idea that the foreign operations are simply a part of the group that is the reporting entity. Some of the individual assets and liabilities of the group just 'happen' to be abroad. The valuation basis used to value the assets and liabilities determines the appropriate exchange rate. Those assets recorded on a HC basis would be translated at the historic rate – the rate ruling when the item was established. Assets recorded on a current value basis would be translated at the current (closing) rate. Revenues and expenses should theoretically be correspondingly translated at the rate ruling on the date when the amount shown in the accounts was established, i.e. assuming an even spread of trading at the average rate for the year.

It is important to avoid the assumption that the temporal method means using historic exchange rates. The words temporal and historic are sometimes, quite wrongly, used interchangeably in this context. 'Temporal' means literally 'at the time', i.e. consistent with the underlying valuation basis. So the temporal method *does* mean using historic exchange rates *when applied to HC accounts*. This broadly reduces the temporal to the monetary/non-monetary method. But the temporal method means using current exchange rates *when applied to current value (e.g. CC) accounts*. This would broadly reduce the temporal to the single-rate method.

Recent proposals

There has been much controversy over the appropriate method to use. The two favoured possibilities are the closing rate and the temporal methods. No less than three EDs were issued, EDs 16, 21 and 27. ED 21 allowed a free choice between the two, but the SSAP, as we shall see, defines the circumstances for each. The Americans have had equally drastic changes of heart, swinging from compulsory temporal (which did mean historic, as current value accounts are not accepted in the United States as the main published accounts) in SFAS 8, to a position close to SSAP 20 in SFAS 52.

SSAP 20

The essential rule is that foreign currency items should enter the books at the exchange rate ruling on the date of the transaction:

46   Subject to the provisions of paragraphs 48 and 51, each asset, liability, revenue or cost arising from a transaction denominated in a foreign currency should be translated into the local currency at the exchange rate in operation on the date on which the transaction occurred; if the rates do not fluctuate significant-

ly, an average rate for a period may be used as an approximation. Where the transaction is to be settled at a contracted rate, that rate should be used. Where a trading transaction is covered by a related or matching forward contract, the rate of exchange specified in that contract may be used.

To explain this last point, if a company buys from abroad and agrees to pay, say, $10000 in six weeks' time, then the company can enter into a foreign exchange contract through a bank to buy $10000 in six weeks' time at a predetermined rate of exchange. This rate of exchange is both known and contractually unalterable, and should be used instead of the 'current' rate:

47 Subject to the special provisions of paragraph 51, which relate to the treatment of foreign equity investments financed by foreign currency borrowings, no subsequent translations should normally be made once non-monetary assets have been translated and recorded.

Non-monetary assets may, of course, be depreciated, reduced in value, and so on like any other asset. But they should not be retranslated. Notice the 'HC' mentality implied by paragraph 47.

48 At each balance sheet date, monetary assets and liabilities denominated in a foreign currency should be translated by using the closing rate or, where appropriate, the rates of exchange fixed under the terms of the relevant transactions. Where there are related or matching forward contracts in respect of trading transactions, the rates of exchange specified in those contracts may be used.

Activity 4

Home Ltd established a 100%-owned subsidiary, Away Ltd on 1 January year 8 by subscribing £25000 of shares in cash when the exchange rate was twelve 'tickets' to the £.

Away Ltd raised a long-term loan of £100000 tickets locally on 1 January year 8 and immediately purchased equipment costing 350000 tickets, which was expected to last ten years with no residual scrap value. It was to be depreciated under the straight-line method.

Below are shown the accounts of Away Ltd in the foreign currency for year 8, during which the relevant exchange rates were:

	Tickets to £
1 January	12
Average for year	11
Average for period in which closing stock acquired	10.5
31 December	10

P&L account for year 8

	In tickets
Sales	450000
less Cost of sales	(360000)
Gross profit	90000
less Depreciation	(35000)
Other expenses	(15000)
Net profit	40000

Balance sheet as at 31 December year 8

Share capital	300 000
Retained profits	40 000
	340 000
Equipment at cost	350 000
less depreciation	35 000
	315 000
Stock at cost	105 000
Net monetary current assets	20 000
less long-term loan	(100 000)
	340 000

Translate the accounts for the subsidiary using both the closing rate and temporal rate and identify what to do with the exchange differences.

Activity 4 feedback

P&L account for year 8	£'s – closing rate	£'s – temporal	
Sales	45 000	40 909	(11)
less Cost of sales	36 000	32 727	(11)
Gross profit	9 000	8 182	
less Depreciation	(3 500)	(2 917)	(12)
Other expenses	(1 500)	(1 364)	(11)
Net profit	4 000	3 901	

Balance sheet as at 31 December year 8			
Share capital	25 000	25 000	
Retained profits	4 000	3 901	
	29 000	28 901	
Equipment at cost	35 000	29 167	(12)
less Depreciation	3 500	2 917	(12)
	31 500	26 250	
Stock at cost	10 500	10 000	(10.5)
Net monetary current assets	2 000	2 000	(10)
less Long-term loan	(10 000)	(10 000)	(10)
	34 000	28 250	
Suspense – exchange difference	(5 000)	651	
	29 000	28 901	

Notes

1 The closing-rate P&L account is translated at the closing rate. SSAP 20 prefers this, but also permits the closing-rate P&L account to be translated at the average rate. (By contrast ED 27 required the average rate to be used!)

2 The share capital figure in the closing-rate results is translated at the original rate. This permits any profits on translation to be highlighted, and attributed to the current year.

So what do we do with the exchange difference?

Under the temporal method, the loss on exchange of £651 may be considered as a single figure. Prudence would suggest writing it off through the P&L account. But suppose it had been a gain on exchange. Presumably it could be credited to the P&L account if it is realized. Or should prudence prevail anyway here. What do you think?

Under the closing-rate method, the issue is more complicated. Differences have arisen in respect of each type of balance sheet item because the opening balances (representing the net investment in the overseas subsidiary by the holding company) have been retranslated back into sterling at the closing rate. The total gain of £5000 can be broken down as in Table 27.1. Should any of these three items go through the P&L account? ED 21 suggested that the £833 should, whereas the long-term items should be dealt with through reserves. Again, what do you think? Perhaps we should begin to look at SSAP 20, to find out the ASC's view.

Table 27.1 *Translation of exchange differences*

Item	Closing rate	Opening rate	Difference
Opening fixed assets	$\dfrac{350\,000}{10}$	$\dfrac{350\,000}{12}$	£5834 (credit)
Opening net current assets	$\dfrac{50\,000}{10}$	$\dfrac{50\,000}{12}$	£833 (credit)
$(300\,000 + 100\,000 - 350\,000)$			
Opening long-term loan	$\dfrac{100\,000}{10}$	$\dfrac{100\,000}{12}$	£1667 (debit)
			£5000 (credit)

Consolidated financial statements

In most cases the foreign business will be carrying out its activities on a day-to-day basis as a separate, autonomous semi-independent unit. The holding company will not be involved in the day-to-day transactions of the subsidiary. It may be looking forward to receiving regular dividends, but it will regard its investment as in the net worth of the foreign enterprise as a whole, and not in its individual assets. In its day-to-day operations the foreign enterprise is not dependent on the reporting currency of the investing company, and therefore not dependent on fluctuations in the exchange rate. Since the foreign subsidiary is regarded in effect as a single asset by the investing company, it arguably follows that its results should be translated at a single rate.

So, the SSAP says:

52 When preparing group accounts for a company and its foreign enterprises, which includes the incorporation of the results of associated companies or foreign branches into those of an investing company, the closing rate/net investment method of translating the local currency financial statements should normally be used.

This makes some sense, particularly as by multiplying every item in the foreign currency accounts by the same exchange factor the internal relationship between the items is preserved unchanged. But it can be criticized in that to take *historic* value figures and translate them by a *current* exchange rate produces a meaningless number – *current* cost plus closing rate would make more sense. In a statement accompanying the issue of SSAP 20, the ASC defended its proposal (paragraph 7):

(**a**) the holding company's investment is normally in the net worth of a business operation rather than in its individual assets and liabilities

(**b**) the method of translation ensures that the translated results and relationships do not differ significantly from those reported prior to translation

(**c**) the method acknowledges the fact that operations which are conducted in currencies and in economic environments other than those of the parent are essentially different from the parent's own operations; and

(**d**) translation of the historical cost accounts at closing rates is merely a restatement of assets and liabilities for the purposes of consolidation and does not constitute a revaluation.

Subparagraph (**d**) is an absurdly weak statement, but undoubtedly the use of a single rate does avoid major distortions, given the underlying HC basis, and closing rate is the only feasible single rate to use.

So the balance sheet items should all be translated at the closing rate – the rate ruling at the balance sheet date. As regards the P&L account:

54 The profit and loss account of a foreign enterprise accounted for under the closing rate/net investment method should be translated at the closing rate or at an average rate for the period. Where an average rate is used, the difference between the profit and loss account translated at an average rate and at the closing rate should be recorded as a movement on reserves. The average rate used should be calculated by the method considered most appropriate for the circumstances of the foreign enterprise.

In the accompanying statement the ASC explained this change from ED 27 as follows:

15 Commentators on the exposure draft were evenly divided between those who agreed with the proposal to translate the profit and loss account of a foreign subsidiary at an average rate for the period and those with a preference for the closing rate. The standard now offers a choice between the two methods. Although it is considered that the closing rate is more likely to satisfy the stated objective that translated results and relationships should not differ significantly from those reported prior to translation, it is acknowledged

that the use of this method may require the restatement of previously reported interim periods.

How is that for clarity of purpose and commitment to standardization?

Exchange differences arising from the closing rate method should be recorded as movement on reserves (a different treatment to that suggested by ED 21). The ASC's argument
for this we saw earlier (p. 582, paragraph 19).

The temporal method

The standard does recognize that in some exceptional cases overseas activities are not carried on as separate semi-independent units dependent on the local currency. The overseas
activity may be carried on as an extension of the home company's business and not as a
separate business:

> **55** In those circumstances where the trade of the foreign enterprise is more
> dependent on the economic environment of the investing company's
> currency than that of its own reporting currency, the temporal method should
> be used.

In explanation of this:

> **22** However, there are some cases in which the affairs of a foreign enterprise
> are so closely interlinked with those of the investing company that its results
> may be regarded as being more dependent on the economic environment of
> the investing company's currency than on that of its own reporting curren-
> cy. In such a case the financial statements of the foreign enterprise should
> be included in the consolidated financial statements as if all its transactions
> had been entered into by the investing company itself in its own currency.
> For this purpose the temporal method of translation should be used; the
> mechanics of this method are identical with those used in preparing the
> accounts of an individual company.

So the 'mechanics' are:
1 fixed assets and stocks – translate at actual rate at date of the transaction (assuming the
   HC basis).
2 Monetary assets and liabilities – translate at current (closing) rate.
3 P&L account – depreciation at the rate used for the corresponding fixed asset on the balance sheet, sales and other expenses at the actual rate, usually approximated by the average rate for the year.

Whether the temporal or closing rate should be used in any particular situation is a question of 'fact' depending on the circumstances. Borderline situations will no doubt arise, but
it should be emphasized that the standard does not allow a *choice* of methods; it allows for
two methods for two different defined circumstances. It is not expected that the temporal
method will be used by many companies.

> **23** All the available evidence should be considered in determining whether the
> currency of the investing company is the dominant currency in the economic

environment in which the foreign enterprise operates. Amongst the factors to be taken into account will be:

(a) the extent to which the cash flows of the enterprise have a direct impact upon those of the investing company

(b) the extent to which the functioning of the enterprise is dependent directly upon the investing company

(c) the currency in which the majority of the trading transactions are denominated

(d) the major currency to which the operation is exposed in its financing structure.

24 Examples of situations where the temporal method may be appropriate are where the foreign enterprise:

(a) acts as a selling agency receiving stocks of goods from the investing company and remitting the proceeds back to the company

(b) produces a raw material or manufactures parts or sub-assemblies which are then shipped to the investing company for inclusion in its own products

(c) is located overseas for tax, exchange control or similar reasons to act as a means of raising finance for other companies in the group.

Once this decision has been taken:

56 The method used for translating the financial statements of each foreign enterprise should be applied consistently from period to period unless its financial and other operational relationships with the investing company change.

Exchange gains and losses arising from foreign exchange cover operations, as discussed earlier, may be offset against each other through reserves under certain conditions. This applies both at the individual company stage and at the consolidation stage:

57 Where foreign currency borrowings have been used to finance, or provide a hedge against, group equity investments in foreign enterprises, exchange gains or losses on the borrowings, which would otherwise have been taken to the profit and loss account, may be offset as reserve movements against exchange differences arising on the retranslation of the net investments provided that:

(a) the relationships between the investing company and the foreign enterprises concerned justify the use of the closing rate method for consolidation purposes

(b) in any accounting period, the exchange gains and losses arising on foreign currency borrowings are offset only to the extent of the exchange differences arising on the net investments in foreign enterprises

(c) the foreign currency borrowings, whose exchange gains or losses are used in the offset process, should not exceed, in the aggregate, the total amount of cash that the net investments are expected to be able to generate, whether from profits or otherwise; and

(d) the accounting treatment is applied consistently from period to period.

Exchange differences arising from the use of the temporal method, which is in effect identical to treating the transactions of the foreign company as the transactions of the home company, will be taken to the P&L account unless there are doubts as to the convertibility or marketability of the currency.

Activity 5

Below are the final accounts for the year to 31 March year 5 of Otters Ltd, an overseas wholly owned subsidiary of Seals Ltd of London.

The relevant exchange rates of the two currencies were as follows:

	Tails to £	
1 January year 1	16.00	(when ordinary shares issued)
1 April year 1	16.20	(when land and buildings bought)
1 January year 1	16.50	(when debentures issued)
1 September year 3	18.00	(when fixtures, etc. bought)
31 March year 4	19.80	
Average for January – March year 4	19.70	(when opening stock bought)
31 March year 5	20.10	
Average for January – March year 5	20.05	(when closing stock bought)
Average for year to 31 March year 5	20.00	

Notes

1 Retained profits from previous years were £10 240 (under temporal) and £9950 (under closing) rate methods.
2 Paid dividend was £7394 as received in London.

Trading and P&L account for year to 31 March year 5

	Tails 000s	Tails 000s
Sales		10 000
less cost of sales		
Opening stock	1800	
Purchases	7700	
	9500	
less closing stock	2000	7500
Gross profit		2500
less wages and salaries	600	
Sundry expenses	380	
Building depreciation	100	
Fixtures depreciation	100	
Debenture interest	120	1300
Net profit		1200
less overseas tax		600
		600
Profits undistributed in previous years		200
		800

less dividends (remitted to London)		
paid	150	
proposed	300	450
Retained profits at end of year		350

Balance sheet as at 31 March year 5

		Tails 000s
Ordinary shares		3000
Retained profits		350
		3350
8% debenture		1500
Current liabilities:		
creditors	2000	
overseas tax	600	
proposed dividend	300	2900
		7750
Land and buildings:		
cost	2500	
less depreciation	500	2000
Fixtures etc.:		
cost	500	
less depreciation	250	250
Current assets:		
stock	2000	
debtors	2000	
cash at bank	1500	5500
		7750

Translate the accounts of Otters Ltd using both the closing rate and temporal rate, identify the exchange gain or loss and its accounting treatment according to SSAP 20.

Activity 5 feedback

Temporal method

P&L account for year to 31 March year 5

	Tails 000s	*Tails 000s*	*(Rate)*		*£*
Sales		10 000	(20)		500 000
less cost of sales					
Opening stock	1 800		(19.7)	91 371	
Purchases	7 700		(20)	385 000	
	9 500			476 371	
less closing stock	2 000	7 500	(20.05)	99 751	376 620
Gross profit		2 500			123 380

less wages and salaries	600		(20)	30 000	
Sundry expenses	380		(20)	19 000	
Building depreciation	100		(16.2)	6 173	
Fixtures depreciation	100		(18)	5 556	
Debenture interest	120	1 300	(20)	6 000	66 729
Net profit		1 200			56 651
less overseas tax		600	(20)		30 000
		600			26 651
Profits undistributed in previous years		200	Calc.		10 240
		800			36 891
less dividends (remitted to London)					
paid	150		Act.	7 394	
proposed	300	450	(20.10)	14 925	22 319
Retained profits at end of year		350			14 572

Balance sheet as at 31 March year 5

	Tails 000s	Tails 000s	Rate	£	£
Ordinary shares		3 000	(16)		187 500
Retained profits		350	Calc.		14 572
		3 350			202 072
8% debenture		1 500	(16.5)		90 909
Current liabilities					
creditors	2 000		(20.1)	99 502	
overseas tax	600		(20.1)	29 851	
proposed dividend	300	2 900	(20.1)	14 925	144 278
		7 750			437 259
Land and buildings					
cost	2 500		(16.2)	154 321	
less depreciation	500	2 000	(16.2)	30 864	123 457
Fixtures etc.					
cost	500		(18)	27 778	
less depreciation	250	250	(18)	13 889	13 889
Current assets					
stock	2 000		(20.05)	99 751	
debtors	2 000		(20.1)	99 502	
cash at bank	1 500	5 500	(20.1)	74 627	273 880
					411 226
Suspense – difference on translation					26 033
		7 750			437 259

The gain of £26 033 will be added to the P&L account for ordinary activities.

Closing rate method

P&L account for year to 31 March year 5

		Tails 000s	Rate		£
Sales		10 000	(20.1)		
less cost of sales					
Opening stock	1 800		(20.1)		
Purchases	7 700		(20.1)		
	9 500				
less closing stock	2 000	7 500	(20.1)		
Gross profit		2 500			
less wages and salaries	600		(20.1)		
Sundry expenses	380		(20.1)		
Building depreciation	100		(20.1)		
Fixtures depreciation	100		(20.1)		
Debenture interest	120	1 300	(20.1)		
Net profit		1 200	(20.1)		59 701
less overseas tax		600	(20.1)		29 851
		600			29 850
Profits undistributed in previous years		200	Calc.		9 950
		800			39 800
less dividends (remitted to London)					
paid	150		Act.	7 394	
proposed	300	450	(20.1)	14 925	22 319
Retained profits at end of year		350			17 481

Balance sheet as at 31 March year 5

		Tails 000s	(Rate)	£
Ordinary shares		3 000	(20.1)	149 254
Retained profits		350	Calc.	17 481
		3 350		166 735
8% debenture		1 500	(20.1)	74 627
Current liabilities				
creditors	2 000		(20.1)	
overseas tax	600		(20.1)	
proposed dividend	300	2 900	(20.1)	144 278
		7 750		385 640

Land and buildings						
cost	2 500			(20.1)	124 378	
less depreciation	500	2 000		(20.1)	24 876	99 502
Fixtures, etc.						
cost	500			(20.1)	24 876	
less depreciation	250	250		(20.1)	12 438	12 438
Current assets						
stock	2 000			(20.1)	99 502	
debtors	2 000			(20.1)	99 502	
cash at bank	1 500	5 500		(20.1)	74 627	273 631
						385 571
Suspense – difference on translation						69
		7 750				385 640

The gain of £69 will be identified as a foreign currency reserve.

Disclosure requirements

59 The methods used in the translations of the financial statements of foreign enterprises and the treatment accorded to exchange differences should be disclosed in the financial statements.

60 The following information should also be disclosed in the financial statements:

(a) for all companies, or groups or companies, which are not exempt companies, the net amount of exchange gains and losses on foreign currency borrowings less deposits, identifying separately:

(i) the amount offset in reserves under the provisions of paragraphs 51, 57 and 58; and

(ii) net amount charged/credited to the profit and loss account

(b) for all companies or groups of companies, the net movement on reserves arising from exchange differences.

This is straightforward. Exempt companies are certain banking, insurance and shipping companies exempt from certain of the 1985 Act disclosure requirements.

The Companies Act 1985

In addition to the general requirement to disclose accounting policies (schedule 4, paragraph 36) the Act specifically states (fourth schedule, paragraph 58(i)):

Where sums originally denominated in foreign currencies have been brought into account under any items shown in the balance sheet or profit and loss account, the basis on which those sums have been translated into sterling shall be stated.

Paragraph 46 of the schedule requires disclosure about movements on any reserves, i.e.:

1 the amount of the reserve at the beginning of the year
2 the amount of the reserve at the balance sheet date
3 the amounts transferred to or from the reserves
4 the source and application of any amounts so transferred.

The standard recommends that exchange gains and losses should be incorporated into the P&L formats of schedule 4 as follows:

Gains or losses arising from trading transactions should normally be shown as 'other operating income or expense' while those arising from arrangements which may be considered as financing should be disclosed separately as part of 'Other interest receivable/payable and similar income/expense'. Exchange gains or losses which arise from events which themselves fall to be treated as extraordinary items should be included as part of such items.

Summary

A fascinating topic, but not an easy one. It is made more difficult by the questionable logic of parts of the SSAP!

A brief review of these are:

1 the reporting of an exchange gain on an unsettled transaction, thus an unrealized gain, as part of the profit for the year thus providing symmetry with losses!
2 the recognition of unrealized gains on long-term monetary items in the profit and loss account as long as there are no doubts as to the convertibility or marketability of the currency
3 the hedging of foreign currency borrowings and foreign currency investments especially when the loan and investment are in different foreign currencies
4 the choice of temporal v. closing rate method for the translation of foreign branches and subsidiaries
5 the choice allowed by SSAP 20 as to using either the average rate or the closing rate for the translation of the P&L account of a foreign subsidiary.

Exercises

1 'The translation of foreign currency transactions and financial statements should produce results which are generally compatible with the effects of rate changes on a company's cash flows and its equity and should ensure that the financial statements present a true and fair view of the results of management actions. Consolidated statements should reflect the financial results and relationships as measured in the foreign currency financial statements prior to translation' (SSAP 20, paragraph 2).
   To what extent do the proposals of the SSAP achieve this objective?

2 A loan is made to a foreign company of $20 000, costing £10 000 during year 1. The loan is denominated in dollars. At the end of year 1 the loan is translated as £9500, at the end of year 2 as £10 500, and during year 3 it is repaid, the proceeds being converted to £10 600.

Required:
(a) Show the accounting entries for each year.
(b) State how you would deal with the gains or losses on exchange for each year, at that time.
(c) Justify your answers.

3 According to SSAP 20, when should:
(a) closing rate method
(b) temporal method
be used and why? Do you agree?

4 Explain the differences in treatment and effect of the two methods (temporal and closing rate) in the context of:
(a) HC accounts.
(b) RC or CC accounts.

5 'SSAP 20 preserves a proper balance between prudence and the need to show a true and fair view'. Discuss.

6 With regard to SSAP 20 'Foreign Currency Translation':
(a) Explain the closing rate/net investment method.   (7 marks)
(b) Explain the temporal method.   (7 marks)
(c) What factors should be taken into account in deciding whether the temporal method should be adopted? Give two examples of situations where this method may be the most appropriate.   (11 marks)
                                                                         (25 marks)
                                                                            (ACCA)

7 **(a) Outline the two major methods of accounting for foreign currency translation, explaining clearly the objectives upon which they are based.**
                                                                           (12 marks)
(b) Should exchange differences appear in the profit and loss account or be charged direct to reserves? State the reason for your answer.
                                                                            (8 marks)
                                                                         (20 marks)
                                                                            (ACCA)

8 Home has a wholly owned subsidiary S which it acquired on 1 January 20X3.
The balance sheet of S as at 1 January 20X3 and 31 December 20X3 are as follows in FC units:

		1.1.X3 FC units		31.12.X3 FC units
Fixed assets		450		330
Stock	240		360	
Debtors	120		240	
	360		600	
		1.1.X3 FC units		31.12.X3 FC units
Creditors	210	150	240	360
		600		690
Ordinary share capital		600		600
Retained profits		–		90
		600		690

and the P&L account for the year 31.12.X3.

Sales		1500
Cost of sales (240 + 1200 – 360)	1080	
Depreciation	120	1200
Net profit		300
Taxation		150
		150
Proposed dividend		60
		90

Translate the accounts of S using both the closing rate and temporal rate given

1 January 20X3 £1 = 3FC
30 June 20X3 £1 = 2.5FC
31 December 20X3 £1 = 2FC

9 In connection with SSAP 20 'Foreign Currency Translation':
   (a) What is the difference between foreign currency conversion and foreign currency translation?   (3 marks)
   (b) What are the stated objectives of foreign currency translation and what possible alternative objectives are there?   (7 marks)
   (c) Why does the standard suggest that in areas of hyper-inflation the local currency financial statements should first be adjusted for current price levels before translation?   (5 marks)
   (d) Why does the standard allow, subject to certain conditions, exchange gains and losses on foreign currency borrowings to be recorded as movements on reserves rather than in the P&L account?   (5 marks)
                                                                   (20 marks)
                                                                        (ACCA)

10 Somco plc, whose registered office is in London, conducts operations and transactions both in the UK and overseas.
    During the year-ended 31 December 1989, the company was involved in various transactions in foreign currencies. Relevant exchange rates, except where given separately in the individual circumstances, were as scheduled below:

At		Rolads (R) R = £1	Nidars (N) N = £1	Krams (K) K = £1	Sarils (S) S = £1
31 December	1988	1.6	0.52	6.9	2210.0
27 February	1989			7.0	
4 March	1989		0.65		
25 May	1989	1.5		6.7	
25 August	1989		0.50		
2 September	1989				2224.0
11 November	1989	1.8			
31 December	1989	2.0	0.54	7.5	2250.0
Average for	1989	1.7			

The transactions concerned are identified by the letters (A) to (F) and are detailed thus:
   (A) Somco plc bought equipment (as a fixed asset) for 130 000 nidars on 4 March 1989 and paid for it on 25 August 1989 in sterling.
   (B) On 27 February 1989 Somco plc sold goods which had cost £46 000 for £68 000 to

a company whose currency was krams. The proceeds were received in krams on 25 May 1989.

(C) On 2 September 1989 Somco plc sold goods which had cost £17 000 for £24 000 to a company whose currency was sarils. The amount was outstanding at 31 December 1989 but the proceeds were received in sarils on 7 February 1990 when the exchange rate was S2306.0 = £1. The directors of Somco plc approved the final accounts on 28 March 1990.

(D) Somco plc borrowed 426 000 rolads on 25 May 1989 and repaid it in sterling on 11 November 1989.

(E) On 9 November 1988 Somco plc had acquired an equity investment at a cost of 196 000 krams when the rate of exchange was K7.3 = £1. This investment was hedged by a loan of 15 000 nidars, at an exchange rate of N0.56 = £1, obtained on the same day.

(F) Somco plc has an overseas wholesale warehouse which is financed locally in rolads and is treated as an independent branch for accounting purposes.

The net investment in the branch was R638 600 on 1 January 1989 and R854 700 on 31 December 1989. During the year 1989 the branch had made a net profit of R423 400, of which R207 300 had been remitted to the UK parent company; these had realized £116 727.

In accounting for the branch, Somco plc uses the average annual rate in translating P&L account items.

Required:

For each of the above independent transactions:

(a) Calculate the gross profit or loss (if any) and the foreign currency gain or loss which would be included in the company's final accounts for the year-ended 31 December 1989. (12 marks)

(b) State how each of the gains or losses in (a) would be accounted for by Somco plc to comply with the requirements of SSAP 20 'Foreign Currency Translation' and SSAP 17 'Post Balance Sheet Events', as appropriate.
   Give brief reasons to justify the treatment which you have adopted. (15 marks)

(c) Additionally, in respect of (F) only, prepare the branch current account in the UK head office ledger, in both foreign currency and sterling and, as a separate calculation, show the composition of the foreign currency retranslation difference. (9 marks)
   All calculations should be to the nearest £1.

(36 marks)
(ACCA)

11 Your managing director has been studying the accounts of two similar groups with overseas subsidiaries. He is puzzled by the different notes on accounting policies relating to foreign exchange transactions which read as follows:

Company 1 'Overseas assets and liabilities are translated at the closing rates of exchange. Results for the year are translated at the average rate of exchange. Gains and losses arising in translation are dealt with in accordance with SSAP 20.'

Company 2 'The accounts of overseas subsidiaries are translated using the temporal method applied in accordance with SSAP 20. Results for the year are translated using average rate.'

You are required to write a report for your managing director

(a) explaining the concepts on which the closing rate and temporal methods are based (6 marks)

(b) **discussing the factors which will be considered when a group is choosing between the closing rate and temporal methods.**

(9 marks)

(15 marks)

(CIMA)

12 You are the group accountant in the T Group which has just acquired its first foreign subsidiary. The T Group has financed the acquisition of this new overseas subsidiary by foreign currency borrowing. Your managing director has asked you to explain how the financial statements of this foreign subsidiary will be translated into £ sterling.

You are required to write a memorandum to your managing director explaining
(a) **the choice of foreign currency translation methods** (3 marks)
(b) **the treatment of foreign exchange differences** (8 marks)
(c) **the disclosure required of the foreign exchange translation method and of the treatment of foreign exchange differences.** (4 marks)

(15 marks)

(CIMA)

13 During the year-ended 31 December 19X7, FC plc, a UK registered company operating in several overseas locations, carried out the following transactions denominated in foreign currencies:

(i) Transactions with a French supplier of raw materials were as follows:

		French francs
1.1.X7	Balance outstanding	50 000
1.5.X7	Purchases	280 000
1.8.X7	Payment	(300 000)
1.11.X7	Purchases	320 000
31.12.X7	Balance outstanding	350 000

(ii) In 19X6, FC plc purchased an 8% equity investment in a Belgian customer for 3 600 000 Belgian francs. The rate of exchange ruling at the date of purchase was £1 = BF64. As a hedge against future exchange rate fluctuations, FC plc financed this investment with the proceeds of a German DM-denominated loan of DM180 000 raised on the same date, when the rate of exchange was £1 = DM3.15. In 19X7, a dividend of BF38 000 was payable to FC plc. This amount had not been remitted at 31 December 19X7. Sales to this customer are billed in sterling amounts.

(iii) The company is the owner of a hotel situated in an Italian resort. This hotel is treated as an independent branch operation. The local management is responsible for all income and expenditure in local currency (lira) with surplus cash being remitted to the UK from time to time.

The following financial statements, received from the hotel management, summarize the operations during 19X7:

Balance sheets

	31.12.X7	31.12.X6
	Lira (000)	*Lira (000)*
Property and fittings	520 000	520 000
Net current assets	106 000	84 000
	626 000	604 000

Loan from Italian bank	400 000	400 000
Head office capital account	100 000	100 000
Surplus retained	126 000	104 000
	626 000	604 000

P&L account for the year-ended 31 December 1987

	Lira (000)
Income from hire of rooms and sundry services	746 000
less operating expenses	483 000
	263 000
less local taxes	91 000
	172 000
less remittances to FC plc	150 000
Surplus retained	22 000

The company received £69 450 from the branch during the year. No cash was in transit at the year-ends. FC plc accounts for its foreign currency transactions in accordance with the provisions of SSAP 20, with P&L accounts being translated at the average rate for the year. The company considers that its accounting for foreign currency transactions reflects their economic substance as far as possible within the provisions of SSAP 20.

Exchange rates prevailing during 19X7 were as follows:

Value of pound sterling (£) against:

	French franc (FF)	Belgian franc (BF)	German mark (DM)	Italian lira (lira)
At 1.1.X7	9.60	62.50	3.12	2050
1.5.X7	9.45	–	–	–
1.8.X7	9.50	–	–	–
1.11.X7	9.50	–	–	–
31.12.X7	9.65	60.10	3.05	2130
Average for period	–	–	–	2080

You are required to
(a) **prepare the journal entries necessary to reflect the foreign exchange aspects of the above transactions in the books of FC plc for the year-ended 31 December 19X7** (20 marks)
(b) **state the amounts which would appear in the balance sheet of FC plc at 31 December 19X7 in respect of the above items, including comparatives where possible** (10 marks)
(c) **explain how the specific exchange differences arising during the year would be dealt with in FC plc's financial statements.** (5 marks)
(35 marks)
(CIMA)

Reporting financial performance (SSAP 25, FRS 3 and 14, FRED 22)

After reading this chapter you should be able to:
- explain the contents of FRS 14 'Earnings per Share'
- calculate various earnings per share
- explain the concepts of all-inclusive income and current operating performance
- outline the past attempts made by the ASC to deal with these concepts
- consider the ASB solution to these problems – FRS 3 'Reporting Financial Performance'
- explain the contents of SSAP 25 'Segmental Reporting'
- look at the position of SSAP 25 within relation to the above objectives
- appraise the requirements of FRED 22.

Introduction

Earnings per share (eps) is found by dividing profit attributable to the ordinary shareholders by the number of ordinary shares in issue. As an absolute, however, it has no meaning or relevance. If we are told that company A has an eps of 6p whereas company B has an eps of 25p, we are unable to compare the performance of the two because we know nothing about their relative size, or more specifically, about the number or value of shares in issue. For the same reasons the quoted share price of the two companies provides no basis for comparison of the stockmarket's perceptions of either.

Thus analysts and investors require a basis of comparison and an indicator of confidence in particular companies. Such an indicator is the price/earnings (PE) ratio, which is simply calculated by dividing the share price by the eps, thereby relating company performance to external perception.

The calculation and use of the PE ratio is illustrated in the following example, where the PE ratio for company X is calculated to be 7.5 and for company Y, 12. In which company would you invest?

Company	X	Y
Price per share (*a*)	150p	96p
Earnings per share (*b*)	20p	8p
PE ratio (*a/b*)	7.5	12

Company X has a higher share price and greater eps, but company Y is expected to perform better in the future. Why? The normal action of supply and demand has bid up the share price of Y relative to current earnings, and the market is therefore saying something about its confidence in Y relative to X. Obviously a very high PE would indicate such extravagant expectations that there may be some element of risk, but generally a high PE is a good indicator of market support. People are willing to pay more for something they think more highly of.

If the PE ratio is used in this way, being quoted in the financial press and elsewhere, it matters greatly that its derivation is consistent and comparable. There are no problems with the price of the share, but what of earnings?

For many years SSAP 3, 'Earnings per Share', provided the 'standard' treatment for calculating and disclosing this ratio. This was superseded by FRS 14 'Earnings per Share', issued in October 1998, and effective for accounting periods ending on or after 23 December 1998. As the ASB notes in an explanatory appendix to FRS 14, the new Standard has been developed essentially as part of a process of 'international development'. It is based very closely on the new International Standard, IAS 33. The ASB notes that IAS 33 is generally close to the longstanding UK approach enshrined in SSAP 3. In other words, the changes between SSAP 3 and FRS 14 are not significant, and it is explicitly stated in the appendix that the ASB 'were it not for international developments on the matter, would not be revising UK guidance on the subject at this time'.

Essentially, therefore, FRS 14 represents a tidying-up of UK 'guidance' rather than any major change. Reaction to the ASB exposure draft, FRED 16, which was very closely based on IAS 33 was that there should:

> be a greater degree of customisation of the international standard than had been presented in the FRED to minimise inconsistencies with existing UK law and standards and to allow the proposals to sit more comfortably within the UK reporting framework. This view was accepted by the Board, within the restrictions of its decision not to make unnecessary changes to the IASC requirements.

The objective of FRS 14 is stated in paragraph 1, and indicates the focus on the number of shares, rather than on earnings.

> The objective of this FRS is to improve the comparison of the performance of different entities in the same period and of the same entity in different accounting periods by prescribing methods for determining the number of shares to be included in the calculation of earnings per share and other amounts per share and by specifying their presentation.

Paragraph 2 gives a number of definitions, as follows.

Equity instrument
Any instrument that evidences an ownership interest in an entity, i.e. a residual interest in the assets of the entity after deducting all of its liabilities.

Fair value
The amount at which a financial instrument could be exchanged in an arm's length transaction between informed and willing parties, other than in a forced or liquidation sale.

Financial instrument
Any contract that gives rise to both a financial asset of one entity and a financial liability or equity instrument of another entity.

Ordinary share

An instrument falling within the definition of equity shares as defined in FRS 4 'Capital Instruments'.

Ordinary shares participate in the net profit for the period only after any other types of shares such as preference shares. An entity may have more than one class of ordinary shares. Ordinary shares of the same class will have the same rights to receive dividends.

Potential ordinary share

A financial instrument or a right that may entitle its holder to ordinary shares.

Examples of potential ordinary shares are:

(a) debt or equity instruments, including preference shares, that are convertible into ordinary shares;

(b) share warrants and options;

(c) rights granted under employee share plans that may entitle employees to receive ordinary shares as part of their remuneration and similar rights granted under other share purchase plans; and

(d) rights to ordinary shares that are contingent upon the satisfaction of certain conditions resulting from contractual arrangements, such as the purchase of a business or other assets, i.e. contingently issuable shares.

Warrants or options

Financial instruments that give the holder the right to purchase or subscribe for ordinary shares.

Basic earnings per share

The requirements of the FRS are simple and clear.

> **9** Basic earnings per share should be calculated by dividing the net profit or loss for the period attributable to ordinary shareholders by the weighted average number of ordinary shares outstanding during the period.
>
> **10** For the purpose of calculating basic earnings per share, the net profit or loss for the period attributable to ordinary shareholders should be the net profit or loss for the period after deducting dividends and other appropriations in respect of non-equity shares.

The straightforward situation where the number of shares in issue is constant is illustrated in Activity 1 below.

Activity 1

The summarized P&L account for EPS plc for the year ended 20X1 is as follows:

	£000	£000
Profit before taxation		1000
Taxation (including deferred adjustment)		400
		600

Preference dividend	50
Ordinary dividend	100
	150
	450

The number of ordinary shares in issue is 2 million.
  Calculate the basic eps.

Activity 1 feedback

From the definition of eps

$$\text{Basic eps} = \frac{\text{Profit after tax less preference dividend}}{\text{Number of ordinary shares}}$$

$$= \frac{60\,000\,000 - 5\,000\,000}{2\,000\,000}$$

$$= 27.5\text{p per share}$$

The tax problem

A difficulty arises, affecting the comparability of the eps between different companies, from the mechanism of the tax system in the UK. When a company pays a dividend then it must also pay advance corporation tax (ACT) to the government. This ACT will usually be set off against the total 'mainstream' corporation tax of one or more future years. In other words the level of dividends paid affects the timings of tax payments, but not the total tax payment, and therefore not the total tax charges. But in some circumstances tax paid may not be recoverable in this way. When this happens, the amount of the tax charges, and therefore the amount of the 'earnings' as defined in FRS 14, would be altered purely by the dividend policy. Since the whole point of 'eps' is to focus on profitability rather than distribution, this is perhaps unsatisfactory.

Two alternative methods of calculating eps have been suggested. The *net basis* includes all the elements of the taxation charge in the P&L accounts. In other words, it uses the actual tax charge, and therefore the actual profits after tax figures from the accounts. The *nil basis* attempts to arrive at what the earnings would be if distributions (i.e. dividends) were nil. It thus excludes the variable elements of the total tax charge and includes only the constant elements.

These different elements were well described in the old SSAP 3 as follows.

6 The tax charge will always include some elements which are constant in that they will not vary with the proportion of the profit distributed by way of dividend; the charge may, however, include other elements which do vary according to the amount of profit distributed and which would be absent if no distributions were made. These components may be classified as follows:
     Constant
     Corporation tax on income
     Tax attributable to dividends received

Overseas tax unrelieved because the rate of overseas tax exceeds the rate of UK corporation tax.
Variable
Irrecoverable ACT
Overseas tax unrelieved because dividend payments restrict the double tax credit available.

Activity 2

The profit before tax for the year ended 20X2 for EPS plc was £1 226 330 and the company paid preference dividends of £50 000. The number of shares in issue remained at 2 million. The taxation charge for the year was £320 000 made up as follows:

	£
Corporation tax on profit of the year	272 000
Deferred taxation	(12 000)
Irrecoverable ACT written off	60 000

Calculate the net and nil eps.

Activity 2 feedback

The *net eps* figure is calculated using all the elements of the taxation charge.
Therefore the profit after tax figure we use is:

	£
£1 226 330 − £320 000	= 906 330
The preference dividend is	50 000
Thus the numerator of the eps calculation	= 856 330

$$\text{Net eps} = \frac{85\,633\,000}{2\,000\,000} = 42.8\text{p per share}$$

The nil eps figure is calculated by excluding the variable elements of the tax charge i.e. the irrecoverable ACT.
Thus, the numerator for the eps calculation is now:

$$856\,330 + 60\,000 = £916\,330$$

$$\text{Net eps} = \frac{91\,633\,000}{2\,000\,000} = 45.8\text{p per share}$$

FRS 3 discussed this issue at some length, concluding that the nil basis is on balance preferable as it takes 'account of all the relevant points', but 'emphasised the desirability' (whatever that means) of also disclosing the nil basis if 'materially different' (whatever that means!). FRS 14, however, is silent on the whole matter, and automatically, in paragraphs 9 and 10 already quoted, requires the net basis of calculation. Appendix II notes that:

> On the basis that this figure may be derived from other disclosures, respondents agreed that there were no circumstances in which earnings per share on the nil basis needed to be disclosed.

The number of shares problem

So far, we have assumed that the number of equity shares in issue is given, and presents no problem. The problems arising when this assumption is relaxed can be considered under two headings:

1 where there are changes in the equity share capital during the financial year under consideration

2 where there are in existence at the end of the period securities with no current claim on equity earnings. but which will give rise to such a claim in the future.

We and FRS 14 deal with these problems one at a time.

Changes in equity share capital during the year

14 For the purpose of calculating basic earnings per share, the number of ordinary shares should be the weighted average number of ordinary shares outstanding during the period.

The simple situation is where there has been an issue during the year at full market price. This is straightforward. The issue of new shares at 'full' price does not distort the relationship between 'earnings' and 'resources' so a weighted average calculation is all that is required.

Activity 3

Fullmar plc had issued share capital on 31 December X1 as follows:

500 000 7% £1 preference shares
4 000 000 25p ordinary shares

Profit after tax for the year ended 31 December X1 was £435 000. On 1 October X1 Fullmar had issued 1 million 25p ordinary shares at full market price.
Calculate the eps for Fullmar plc for the year ended 31 December X1.

Activity 3 feedback

The number of ordinary shares in issue on 1 January X1 was 3 million and 1 million were issued on 1 October X1. Thus the time weighted average number of ordinary shares in issue for the year was

$$3\,000\,000 \times \frac{9}{12} + 4\,000\,000 \times \frac{3}{12} = 3\,250\,000$$

The earnings for the year attributable to the ordinary shareholders is £435 000 – 35 000 preference dividend = £400 000. Therefore

$$\text{eps} = \frac{40\,000\,000}{3\,250\,000} \text{ p per share} = 12.3\text{p per share}$$

Life is not quite so simple if the number of shares has been changed at a price different from the market price.

21   The weighted average number of ordinary shares outstanding during the period and for all periods presented should be adjusted for events, other than the
conversion of potential ordinary shares, that have changed the number of
ordinary shares outstanding, without a corresponding change in resources.

22   Ordinary shares may be issued, or the number of shares outstanding may be
reduced, without a corresponding change in resources. Examples include:

(a) a bonus issue;

(b) a bonus element in any other issue or buy-back, for example a bonus
element in a rights issue to existing shareholders or a put warrant, involving the repurchase of shares at significantly more than their fair value;

(c) a share split; and

(d) a share consolidation.

23   In a bonus issue or a share split, ordinary shares are issued to existing shareholders for no additional consideration. Therefore, the number of ordinary
shares outstanding is increased without an increase in resources. The number of ordinary shares outstanding before the event is adjusted for the proportionate change in the number of ordinary shares outstanding as if the event
had occurred at the beginning of the earliest period reported.

This is also entirely logical. More shares have been issued at no 'cost'. The earnings of
the business during the year can only be regarded as relating to the shares at the end of the
year, i.e. to all the shares including the new ones. No distortion arises, as no resources were
passed into the business when the new shares were created.

Activity 4

Using the same data as in Activity 3 but assuming that the shares issued on October X1 were
a capitalization issue calculate the eps for the year.

Activity 4 feedback

We now have a capitalization issue not a full market price issue of shares and therefore we
assume 4 million shares in issue for the whole of the year. (Note this assumption would be
the same no matter at what point during the year the capitalization was made.)

The number of shares in issue can also be calculated from the following:

$$3\,000\,000 \times \frac{9}{12} \times \frac{4}{3} + 4\,000\,000 \times \frac{3}{12}$$

$$\text{(bonus factor)}$$

$$= 3\,000\,000 + 1\,000\,000 = 4\,000\,000$$

Remember this for more complicated examples

$$\text{eps} = \frac{40\,000\,000}{4\,000\,000} = 10\text{p per share}$$

We need to think about the implications of such changes for meaningful comparison with
prior year's figures.

53   If the number of ordinary or potential ordinary shares outstanding is changed

by events, other than the conversion of potential ordinary shares, without a corresponding change in resources – for example, those referred to in paragraph 22 – the calculation of basic and diluted earnings per share for all periods presented should be adjusted retrospectively. If these changes occur after the balance sheet date but before the date of approval of the financial statements, the calculations per share for the financial statements and those of any prior period should be based on the new number of shares. When calculations per share reflect such changes in the number of shares, that fact should be stated. In addition, basic and diluted earnings per share of all periods presented should be adjusted for the effects of a business combination that is merger accounted under FRS 6.

Activity 5

If the eps for the year ended 31 December X0 for Fullmar plc was 8p how would this figure have to be adjusted for the bonus issue in 20X1 if at all?

Activity 5 feedback

Paragraph 21 of FRS 14 tells us that when a bonus issue of shares is made the eps figures for previous years must be adjusted. Thus we assume the bonus issue was also in existence in 20X0 and adjust the eps figure accordingly.

The bonus issue represents a 1 for 3 share issue, i.e. the number of shares has increased by one-third, therefore we must have four-thirds times the original number of shares (remember this is the denominator of our calculation) and the eps will be multiplied by three-quarters, i.e.

$$8p \times \frac{3}{4} = 6p$$

Rights issue at less than full market price

Paragraph 24 states the procedure.

In a rights issue, the exercise price is often less than the fair value of the shares. Therefore, such a rights issue includes a bonus element as indicated in paragraph 22(b) above. The number of ordinary shares to be used in calculating basic earnings per share for all periods before the rights issue is the number of ordinary shares outstanding before the issue, multiplied by the following factor:

$$\frac{\text{Fair value per share immediately before the exercise of rights}}{\text{Theoretical ex-rights fair value per share}}$$

The theoretical ex-rights fair value per share is calculated by adding the aggregate fair value of the shares immediately before the exercise of the rights to the proceeds from the exercise of the rights, and dividing by the number of shares outstanding after the exercise of the rights. Where the rights themselves are to be publicly traded separately from the shares before the exercise date, fair value for the purposes of this calculation is established at the close of the last day on which the shares are traded together with the rights.

This is complicated! A rights issue combines the characteristics of a capitalization issue and a full market price issue. New resources are passing into the business so a higher earnings figure, related to these new resources should be expected. But at the same time there is a bonus element in the new shares, which should be treated like a capitalization issue. To the extent that the rights issue provides new resources, i.e. equates to an issue at full market price, we need to calculate the average number of shares weighted on a time basis. To the extent that the rights issue includes a discount or bonus element we need to increase the number of shares deemed to have been in issue for the whole period. The theoretical ex rights price can be calculated as follows:

1 Calculate the total market value of the equity before the rights issue (actual cum rights price × number of shares).
2 Calculate the total proceeds expected from the right issue (issue price × number of shares).
3 Add these two amounts, and divide by the total number of shares involved altogether (i.e. by the total number after the rights issue).

Activity 6

Trig plc as at the 30 June X1 has 600 000 £1 ordinary shares in issue with a current market value of £2 per share. On the 1 July X1 Trig plc makes a four for six rights issue at £1.75 and all rights are taken up. Earnings for the year after tax and preference dividends are £81 579 and the previous year's eps was declared as 9p. Calculate the eps figure that should be shown in the financial statements for the year ended 31 December X1.

Activity 6 feedback

We first need to calculate the theoretical ex rights price of the shares:

Market value of equity before rights	=	600 000 × £2	= 1 200 000
Proceeds from rights issue	=	400 000 × £1.75	= 700 000
		1 000 000	1 900 000

$$\text{Theoretical ex rights price} = \frac{1\,900\,000}{1\,000\,000} = £1.90$$

Secondly, we calculate the weighted average number of shares:

$$600\,000 \times \frac{1}{2} \times \frac{2}{1.9} \; + \; 1\,000\,000 \times \frac{1}{2} = 815\,789$$
(time weighting)   (time weighting)

$$\text{Therefore eps for year ending 31 December X1} = \frac{8\,157\,900}{815\,789} = 10\text{p per share}$$

Thirdly, we need to recalculate the previous year's eps

$$9 \times \frac{1.9}{2} = 8.55\text{p per share}$$

A reduction has occurred in the previous year's eps as we have inserted the bonus element of the rights issue.

Diluted earnings per share

Where there are securities existing at the year end that will have a claim on equity earnings from some time in the future, then it is clear that at this future time the claim of each currently existing share will, other things equal, be reduced (or diluted). It is likely to be useful information to current shareholders and others to give them a picture of what the eps would be if this dilution takes place. This is done by recalculating the current year's eps as if the dilution had already occurred.

The formal requirement is:

27 For the purpose of calculating diluted earnings per share, the net profit attributable to ordinary shareholders and the weighted average number of shares outstanding should be adjusted for the effects of all dilutive potential ordinary shares.

28 The calculation of diluted earnings per share is consistent with the calculation of basic earnings per share while giving effect to all dilutive potential ordinary shares that were outstanding during the period.

29 For the purpose of calculating diluted earnings per share, the number of ordinary shares should be the weighted average number of ordinary shares calculated in accordance with paragraphs 14 and 21, plus the weighted average number of ordinary shares that would be issued on the conversion of all the dilutive potential ordinary shares into ordinary shares. Potential ordinary shares should be deemed to have been converted into ordinary shares at the beginning of the period or, if not in existence at the beginning of the period, the date of the issue of the financial instrument or the granting of the rights by which they are generated.

30 Such financial instruments or rights include, but are not restricted to, the following examples, in respect of which specific guidance is provided in the paragraphs as indicated:

(**a**) convertible debt or equity instruments;

(**b**) share warrants and options (paragraphs 35–38);

(**c**) rights granted under employee or other share purchase plans (paragraphs 39–44); and

(**d**) rights to ordinary shares that are contingent upon the satisfaction of certain conditions resulting from contractual arrangements, such as the purchase of a business or other assets, i.e. contingently issuable shares (paragraphs 45–52).

Activity 7

All the information given in Activity 1 on p. 604 applies. In addition to the 2 million ordinary shares already in issue, however, there exists convertible loan stock of £500 000 bearing interest at 10%. This may be converted into ordinary shares between 20X3 and 20X6 at a rate of one ordinary share for every £2 of loan stock. Corporation tax is taken for convenience as 50%. Calculate the fully diluted eps.

Activity 7 feedback

The fully diluted eps is found as follows. If the conversion is fully completed then there will be two effects:

1 The share capital will increase by 250 000 shares (1 share for every £2 of the £500 000 loans).
2 The profit after tax will increase by the interest on the loan no longer payable less the extra tax on this increase. The interest at 10% on £500 000 is £50 000, but the extra tax on this profit increase would be 50% of £50 000, i.e. £25 000.

So profit after tax, and therefore 'earnings', will increase by 50 000 − 25 000 = £25 000. Fully diluted eps will therefore be:

$$\frac{600\,000 + 25\,000 - 50\,000}{2\,000\,000 + 250\,000}$$

$$= \frac{575\,000}{2\,250\,000}\,\text{p}$$

$$= 25.6\text{p per share}$$

Remember that the fully diluted eps is a hypothetical calculation. It assumes total conversion into equity participation. The extent to which this assumption is likely in any particular circumstance is irrelevant.

As already stated, FRS 14 continues to give detailed comment on the technicalities of those rights mentioned in paragraph 30b, c and d.

A further problem concerns the effect of distribution on the earnings number:

53 For the purpose of calculating diluted earnings per share, the amount of net profit or loss for the period attributable to ordinary shareholders, as calculated in accordance with paragraph 10, should be adjusted by the post-tax effect of:
   (a) any dividends on dilutive potential ordinary shares that have been deducted in arriving at the net profit attributable to ordinary shareholders as calculated in accordance with paragraph 10;
   (b) interest recognised in the period for the dilutive potential ordinary shares; and
   (c) any other changes in income or expense that would result from the conversion of the dilutive potential ordinary shares.
56 For the purpose of calculating diluted earnings per share, the net profit attributable to ordinary shareholders and the weighted average number of shares should be adjusted for the effects of dilutive potential ordinary shares. Potential ordinary shares should be treated as dilutive when, and only when, their conversion to ordinary shares would decrease net profit or increase net loss per share from continuing operations.

It is perhaps useful at this point to look at an example of a calculation of eps involving more than one type of share issue. The following example appears complicated but only requires a clear thought process and a knowledge of FRS 14 requirements.

Activity 8

Part of a listed company's consolidated profit and loss account is shown below:

Chasewater Public Limited Company
Consolidated P&L account (extract) for the year ended 30 June 20X5

	£	£
Group net profit before taxation		500 000
Taxation		270 000
Group net profit after taxation		230 000
Minority interests in subsidiaries		20 000
Attributable to shareholders in Chasewater Plc		210 000
Extraordinary items (after taxation)		11 000
Net profit for year		221 000
Dividends (net) -		
Preference	25 000	
Ordinary	100 000	
		125 000
Retained earnings for year		96 000

Notes

1 Issued share capital (fully paid), 1 July 20X4: 250 000 10% cumulative preference shares of £1 each, and 4 million ordinary shares of 25p each.
2 Loan capital, 1 July 20X4: £500 000 7% convertible debentures (convertible into 200 ordinary shares per £100 debenture, with proportionate increases for subsequent bonus issues, and for the bonus element in subsequent rights issues).
3 Changes during the year ended 30 June 20X5:

1 October 20X4	Rights issues of ordinary shares (ranking for dividend 20X4–5): 1 for 4 at £0.90 per share: market price before issue, £1.00
1 January 20X5	Conversion of £100 000 of 7% convertible debentures
1 March 20X5	Bonus issue of ordinary shares, 1 for 3

4 Basic earnings per share for the year ended 30 June 20X4 was 4.0p.
5 Corporation tax, 52%; income tax basic rate, 30%.

You are required:
  (a) **to compute the company's basic earnings per share for the current year, and its comparative BEPS for the previous year; and**
  (b) **to compute the company's fully diluted earnings per share for the current year only.**

Activity 8 feedback

On reading the question you should have noted the following:

1 a rights issue on 1 October 20X4 of 1 million shares
2 a conversion of debentures on 1 January 20X5 to 200 000 shares plus the bonus element of the rights issue
3 a bonus issue on 1 March 20X5.

A quantity of convertible debentures still remain in issue.

First, we calculate the earnings for the eps calculation. This is straightforward:

	£
Profit after tax after extraordinary items	221 000
Preference dividend	25 000
Earnings for basic eps calculation	196 000

Secondly, as a rights issue has taken place we need to calculate the adjusting factor, i.e.:

$$\frac{\text{actual cum rights}}{\text{theoretical ex rights}}$$

Market value of equity before rights =	$4\,000\,000 \times £1$	=	4 000 000
Proceeds of rights issue =	$1\,000\,000 \times 90\text{p}$ =		900 000
	5 000 000		4 900 000

$$\text{Theoretical ex rights price} = \frac{4\,900\,000}{5\,000\,000} = 98\text{p}$$

Adjusting factor = 100/98 (this represents the bonus element of the rights issue).

Thirdly, we need to calculate the time weighted average number of shares and remember to include the bonus issue for the whole of the year and multiply the proportion of capital in issue before rights by the above factor of 100/98. Note the conversion of debentures on 1 January 20X5 will be to

$$200\,000 \times \frac{100}{98} \text{ shares} = 204\,082 \text{ shares}$$

and that the bonus issue will be calculated as follows:

Number of shares in issue before bonus =
$4\,000\,000 + 1\,000\,000$ rights $+ 204\,082$ conversion $= 5\,204\,082$

$$\text{Bonus issue at 1 for 3} = \frac{5\,204\,082}{7} = 743\,440$$

Number of shares in issue after bonus = 6 938 776
Time weighted number of shares =

$$\left[4000 \times \frac{3}{12} \times \frac{100}{98} + 5\,000\,000 \times \frac{3}{12}\ 5\,204\,082 \times \frac{2}{12} \right]$$

$$\frac{4}{3} \text{ (bonus factor)} + 6\,938\,776 \times \frac{4}{12}$$

$$= (1\,020\,408.1 + 1\,250\,000 + 867\,347)\,\frac{4}{3} + 2\,312\,925.3$$

$$= 3\,137\,755.1 \times \frac{4}{3} + 2\,312\,925.3 = 6\,496\,598.6$$

The fourth, fifth and sixth steps are as follows:

$$\text{Basic eps 20X5} = \frac{19\,600\,000}{6\,496\,598.6} = 3.02\text{p}$$

$$\text{Revised eps 20X4} = 4\text{p} \times \frac{3}{4} \text{ (bonus factor)} \times \frac{98}{100} \text{ (rights factor)} = 2.94\text{p}$$

Fully diluted eps also needs to be calculated to see if there is a 5% dilution:

	£
Basic earnings	196 000
Add back debenture interest assuming full conversion took place at the 1 July 20X4	
$\frac{6}{12} \times 7\% \times 500\,000 + 6\,\frac{6}{12} \times 7\% \times 4\,000\,000 =$	31 500
Corporate tax adjustment for non-payment of debenture interest	(16 380)
Diluted earnings	211 120

The weighted number of shares will need recalculating assuming all convertible debentures converted on 1 July 20X4, i.e. 1 million shares issued. Note the bonus issue will now be 2 083 333 shares on 1 March 20X5, and the rights issue 1 250 000 shares on 1 October 20X4.

Time weighted number of shares =

$$\left[5\,000\,000 \times \frac{3}{12} \times \frac{100}{98} + 6\,250\,000 \times \frac{5}{12}\right]\frac{4}{3} + 8\,333\,333 \times \frac{4}{12}$$

$$= 7\,950\,680$$

$$\text{Diluted eps} = \frac{21\,112\,000\text{p}}{7\,950\,680} = 2.66\text{p}$$

Disclosure requirements of FRS 14

These are quite straightforward.

69 An entity should present basic and diluted earnings per share on the face of the profit and loss account for each class of ordinary share that has a different right to share in the net profit for the period. An entity should present basic and diluted earnings per share with equal prominence for all periods presented.

70 An entity should present basic and diluted earnings per share, even if the amounts disclosed are negative (i.e. a loss per share).

Additional disclosures

71   An entity should disclose the following:

(**a**) the amounts used as the numerators in calculating basic and diluted earnings per share, and a reconciliation of those amounts to the net profit or loss for the period; and

(**b**) the weighted average number of ordinary shares used as the denominator in calculating basic and diluted earnings per share, and, excepting figures given in respect of different classes of ordinary share, a reconciliation of these denominators to each other.

The ASB recognizes that companies may wish to disclose additional (not alternative) calculations of eps on different bases. Paragraphs 73–75 allow them to do so, but only with full explanations, and reconciliation to the required bases.

All inclusive and current operating performance concepts

The issue to understand is that there are two arguments concerning the function of the P&L account. The first possibility is that the P&L account should show everything that has happened in the year – the all-inclusive concept. The second possibility is that the P&L account should include only normal recurring activities of the business – the current operating performance concept. If extraordinary or prior year transactions occur during the financial year then the inclusion of them in the current P&L could mislead the user when estimating the possibility and magnitude of future results. Current operating performance concept suggests that these extraordinary and prior year transactions should be dealt with as adjustments to retained earnings. This is reserve accounting!

The ASC rejected reserve accounting and was concerned that all transactions of the year should be recorded through the P&L account. However, it proposed that this be done in a way that would highlight the items that were not normal recurring activities of the business.

It gave four reasons for this view in the 1986 version of the now deleted SSAP 6:

(**a**) by segregating extraordinary items for separate disclosure, the profit on ordinary activities can be shown as an element of the all-inclusive profit for the financial year

(**b**) inclusion and separate disclosure of extraordinary and prior year items will enable the P&L account for the year to give a better view of a company's profitability and progress

(**c**) exclusion, being a matter of subjective judgement, could lead to a loss of comparability between the reported results of companies

(**d**) exclusion could result in extraordinary and prior year items being overlooked in any consideration of results over a series of years.

The ASC accepted that simply to put every transaction, of whatever type, into the P&L account without any separate disclosure would lead to distortion and misinterpretation. To this end, it required companies to distinguish between those items that are derived from the ordinary activities of the business from those that are not. Unless the latter were deemed to be prior year items (see below) they were extraordinary items and should be shown separately in the P&L account after the results derived from ordinary activities.

The ASC therefore supported an all-inclusive concept, but in such a way that the benefits of the current operating performance concept were taken on board. Also as the eps was used by users in their assessment of the company's performance through the PE ratio the calculation of eps was to be carried out before extraordinary items, that is, only using ordinary activities.

It is clear that the determination of operating profit depended upon the definition of 'ordinary activities of the business'.

> **28** Ordinary activities are any activities which are usually, frequently or regularly undertaken by the company and any related activities in which the company engages in furtherance of, incidental to, or arising from those activities. They include, but are not confined to, the trading activities of the company.
>
> (SSAP 6)

The definition of extraordinary items logically followed from this:

> **30** Extraordinary items are material items which derive from events or transactions that fall outside the ordinary activities of the company and which are therefore expected not to recur frequently or regularly. They do not include exceptional items nor do they include prior year items merely because they relate to a prior year.
>
> (SSAP 6)

To cut a long story short, the ASC spent much time and effort in trying to tighten up the definition, in practice, of what was or was not extraordinary. This used to be particularly significant because at one time eps used to be defined as based on profit after 'exceptional' but before 'extraordinary' items, despite the difficulties of deciding whether a particular event caused the one or the other.

This decision was subjective and as such it may well have been relatively easy for a company to make out a case for all profits being exceptional and all losses extraordinary thus showing the best possible eps, as at this point in time the definition of eps had not been changed.

ASB solution

The market, over the years, has tended to look to the eps for a single measure of performance and the ASB took the view that the market must be re-educated and forced to look at a variety of data to arrive at a conclusion on a company's performance. In our view this is highly commendable. Users must look at all relevant data. Alan Cook, the ASB's technical director is quoted as saying 'when people ask you what single figure they should look at, it is like asking which part of the TV screen they should be looking at, when they should be looking at the whole screen'.

David Tweedie the chair of ASB is quoted as saying:

> A company's results cannot realistically be encapsulated in a single number such as earnings per share or profit before tax. For a proper understanding of the position a much wider perspective is needed – we must move emphasis away from concentrating on a single performance indicator towards highlighting a whole range of important components of financial performance.

FRS 3 'Reporting Financial Performance'

Let us now take a look at the ASB solution to the eps and extraordinary item problem – FRS 3 – issued in October 1992.

The objective of FRS 3

This is to require reporting entities falling within its scope to highlight a range of important components of financial performance to aid users in understanding the performance achieved by a reporting entity in a period and to assist them in forming a basis for their assessment of future results and cash flows.

This objective is met by requiring entities to use a layered format for the P&L account which will highlight important components of the financial performance as follows:

1 results of continuing operations
2 results of discontinued operations
3 profits or losses on the sale or termination of an operation or restructuring and profits or losses on the disposal of fixed assets
4 extraordinary items.

FRS 3 illustrates this diagramatically as follows:

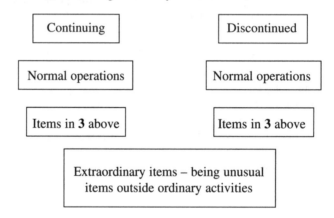

Profit and loss for continuing and discontinued operations

The ASB are asking us to show separately the profit and loss from continuing operations and from discontinuing operations. This is a complete change from the way P&L accounts have previously been drafted. The objective of this is to, 'highlight the results of continuing operations by removing and reporting separately the results of those material operations which have been sold or terminated', so that users can clearly see the profits from continued operations. All this is highly commendable but is it possible to distinguish between continuing and discontinued operations? What is an operation? FRS 3 defines discontinued operations as:

4 *Discontinued operations:*
   Operations of the reporting entity that are sold or terminated and that satisfy all of the following conditions:
   (a) The sale or termination is completed either in the period or before the earlier of three months after the commencement of the subsequent period and the date on which the financial statements are approved.

(**b**) If a termination, the former activities have ceased permanently.

(**c**) The sale or termination has a material effect on the nature and focus of the reporting entity's operations and represents a material reduction in its operating facilities resulting either from its withdrawal from a particular market (whether class of business or geographical) or from a material reduction in turnover in the reporting entity's continuing markets.

(**d**) The assets, liabilities, results of operations and activities are clearly distinguishable, physically, operationally and for financial reporting purposes.

Operations not satisfying all these conditions are classified as continuing.

This definition, in practice, requires an assessment of the effect on the nature and focus of operations of sales or terminations.

Activity 9

Identify whether the following cases would be treated as a discontinuance or not under FRS 3:

- a furniture company has traditionally served the cheaper end of the domestic furniture market. It terminates this business and moves into office furniture
- a hotel company has traditionally served the lower end of the market. It sells off these hotels and moves into the luxury end of the market
- a furniture company sells its business in Torquay and purchases one in the same market sector in Bournemouth
- a hotel company sells its hotels in the UK and buys hotels in the USA.

Activity 9 feedback

The first two and the last are examples of discontinuance as they change the nature and focus of the business from:

- domestic furniture to office furniture
- cheaper end of the market to the luxury
- UK to USA.

The third is not a discontinuance as it still operates in a similar location.

The FRS doesn't state whether moving from England to Scotland would be a discontinuance and nor could it. The decision will have to be based on a consideration of the circumstances for each company!

The FRS adds at paragraph 43:

> to be classified as discontinued a sale or termination should have resulted from a strategic decision either to withdraw from a particular market, either class of business or geographically or to curtail materially its presence in a continuing market (downsizing).

Disclosure of results of continuing and discontinued operations

Once we have defined our continuing and discontinuing operations the next question is 'How much detail is required to be shown on the face of the P&L account?'

Remember we still have to comply with the format statements as given by Companies Act, but we can clarify, delete or add to this. FRS 3 asks as a minimum for the analysis of continuing operations, acquisitions (as a component of continuing) and discontinuing operations for turnover and operating profit. Other statutory items required between these two can be given by way of note if not shown on the face of the P&L account.

FRS 3 further asks that the following items are to be shown separately on the face of the P&L account after operating profit and before interest:

- profits or losses on the sale or termination of an operation
- costs of a fundamental reorganisation or restructuring
- profits or losses on the disposal of fixed assets.

Exceptional items, i.e. those that fall *within* the operating activities of the business, other than those identified above, are to be included in the format heading to which they relate and disclosed in the notes. They can be shown on the face of the P&L account if it is necessary in order to show a true and fair view. In other words we have a subjective decision in respect of how much detail we show on the P&L account for exceptional items.

Extraordinary profit or loss should be shown on the P&L account in total, with an analysis in the notes of each individual item or all individual items may be shown on the P&L account. The taxation in respect of extraordinary items is also required on the face of the P&L account.

Extraordinary items are defined by FRS 3 paragraph 6 as material items possessing a high degree of abnormality which arise from events or transactions that fall outside the ordinary activities of the reporting entity and which are not expected to recur. They do not include exceptional items nor do they include prior period items merely because they relate to a prior period. Interestingly the notes to FRS 3 state that as extraordinary items are extremely rare no examples are provided.

David Tweedie is on record as stating that the ASB has effectively outlawed extraordinary items!

FRS 3 also requires the eps to be shown on the face of the P&L account under the new definition, but allows entities to show other eps calculated on another level of earnings on the P&L account as long as it is no more prominent than the required eps. A reconciliation between the two is required in the notes to the accounts, as is the reason for showing the alternative eps.

Activity 10

Devise a format for a P&L account and relative notes, in accordance with the Companies Act, that will meet the requirements of FRS 3 as to continued and discontinued operations, exceptional and extraordinary items.

Activity 10 feedback (taken from the illustration given in FRS 3)

P&L account example 1

	1993 £m	1993 £m	1992 as restated £m
Turnover			
Continuing operations	550		500
Acquisitions	50		
	600		
Discontinued operations	175		190
		775	690
Cost of sales		(620)	(555)
Gross profit		155	135
Net operating expenses		(104)	(83)
Operating profit			
Continuing operations	50		40
Acquisitions	6		
	56		
Discontinued operations	(15)		12
Less 1992 provision	10	51	52
Profit on sale of properties in continuing operations		9	6
Provision for loss on operations to be discontinued			(30)
Loss on disposal of discontinued operations	(17)		
Less 1992 provision	20		
		3	
Profit on ordinary activities before interest		63	28
Interest payable		(18)	(15)
Profit on ordinary activities before taxation		45	13
Tax on profit on ordinary activities		(14)	(4)
Profit on ordinary activities after taxation		31	9
Minority interests		(2)	(2)
[Profit before extraordinary items]		29	7
[Extraordinary items] (included only to show positioning)		–	–
Profit for the financial year		29	7
Dividends		(8)	(1)
Retained profit for the financial year		21	6

Earnings per share	**39p**	**10p**
Adjustments	*x*p	*x*p
[to be itemized and an adequate description to be given]		
Adjusted earnings per share	*y*p	*y*p

[Reason for calculating the adjusted earnings per share to be given]

Note required in respect of P&L account example 1

	1993			1992 (as restated)		
	Contin-uing	Discon-tinued	Total	Con-tinuing	Discon-tinued	Total
	£m	£m	£m	£m	£m	£m
Cost of sales	455	165	620	385	170	555
Net operating expenses						
distribution costs	56	13	69	46	5	51
administrative						
expenses	41	12	53	34	3	37
other operating income	(8)	0	(8)	(5)	0	(5)
	89	25	114	75	8	83
Less 1992 provision	0	(10)	(10)			
	89	15	104			

The total figures for continuing operations in 1992 include the following amounts relating to acquisitions: costs of sales £40 million and net operating expenses of £4 million (namely distribution costs £3 million, administrative expenses £3 million and other operating income £2 million).

Note that in the feedback to the above activity the P&L account still carries a column showing comparison figures for the previous year. These comparative figures require a restatement as all that can be included in continuing operations are those operations that are continuing in the current year, otherwise the figures would not be comparable.

Prior year adjustments

In certain circumstances it may be arguable that an event has occurred or an event has been recognized which, in retrospect, clearly relates to earlier years. Such items should perhaps be best included by altering the balance brought forward on the P&L account from last year. Otherwise the current results would be distorted by an item not properly relating to the current year. This logic was recognized by the ASC in SSAP 6 and FRS 3 broadly repeats the original requirements.

> **29** Prior period adjustments should be accounted for by restating the comparative figures for the preceding period in the primary statements and notes and adjusting the opening balance of reserves for the cumulative effect. The cumulative effect of the adjustments should also be noted at the foot of the

statement of total recognized gains and losses of the current period. The effect of prior period adjustments on the results for the preceding period should be disclosed where practicable.

FRS 3 defines prior period adjustments as:

Material adjustments applicable to prior periods arising from changes in account- ing policies or from the correction of fundamental errors. They do not include normal recurring adjustments or corrections of accounting estimates made in prior periods.

This definition clearly states that prior year adjustments are not those items which are the correction of estimates previously made. For example, the estimate in respect of an insur- ance claim pending made at the end of year 1 may require amending in year 2 as more infor- mation becomes available, but this would not be a prior year adjustment. FRS 3 has this to say on the correction of accounting estimates:

61 Estimating future events and their effects requires the exercise of judgement and will require reappraisal as new events occur, as more experience is acquired or as additional information is obtained. Because a change in esti- mate arises from new information or developments, it should not be given retrospective effect by a restatement of prior periods. Sometimes a change in estimates may have the appearance of a change of accounting policy and care is necessary to avoid confusing the two.

Changes in accounting policies

These are defined as prior year adjustments and require the amounts for the current and corresponding periods to be restated on the basis of the new policies. However, it is impor- tant to differentiate between changes in accounting policies and changes in accounting esti- mates. It is also worth noting that a change in accounting policy can only be made if the new policy will provide a truer and fairer presentation of the result and of the financial posi- tion of a reporting entity.

Fundamental errors

These are not items we would expect to see occurring, but when they do they clearly are prior year adjustments. FRS 3 states:

63 In exceptional circumstances it may be found that financial statements of prior periods have been issued containing errors which are of such signifi- cance as to destroy the true and fair view and hence the validity of those financial statements. The corrections of such fundamental errors and the cumulative adjustments applicable to prior periods have no bearing on the results of the current period and they are therefore not included in arriving at the profit or loss for the current period. They are accounted for by restat- ing prior periods, with the result that the opening balance of retained prof- its will be adjusted accordingly, and highlighted in the reconciliation of movements in shareholders' funds. As the cumulative adjustments are recognised in the current period, they should also be noted at the foot of the statement of total recognised gains and losses of the current period.

We refer to the statement of total recognized gains and losses later.

Activity 11

In preparing the financial statements for the year ended 31 December 20X5 Alpha plc discovers the following; all of which are material in the context of the company's results:

- development expenditure that met the required criteria of SSAP 13 was previously capitalized and amortized. Alpha now believe that writing off all expenditure on development work would give a fairer presentation of the results
- a debt that was previously considered to be collectable as at 31 December 20X4 now requires writing off
- the estimate of costs payable in respect of litigation was £250 000 as at 31 December 20X4. This has now materialized at £280 000
- the directors of Alpha are of the view that depreciating vehicles by the reducing balance method rather than the straight-line method as previously used will present a fairer view of the financial performance of the company.

All of the above items relate to the prior period but which should be treated as prior year adjustments under FRS 3?

Activity 11 feedback

- The development item is a prior year adjustment as it constitutes a change in accounting policy
- the write-off of the bad debt is simply a change in the estimate of bad debts and therefore not a prior year adjustment
- the litigation cost is again just a change in the provision for the liability, a change in estimate, and therefore not a prior year adjustment
- the last item in relation to depreciation may appear to be a change in accounting policy but in fact SSAP 12 states that this isn't the case. A change in the method of providing depreciation is not a change in accounting policy but a change in the estimates of the amount to be provided. Therefore this is not a prior year adjustment.

Statement of total recognized gains and losses (SORG)

We have already referred to this in connection with prior year adjustments.
According to FRS 3 (summary paragraph f)

> It is a primary financial statement that enables users to consider all recognised gains and losses of a reporting entity in assessing its overall performance. It therefore includes the profit or loss for the period together with all other movements on reserves reflecting recognised gains and losses attributable to shareholders. The statement is not intended to reflect the realisation of gains recognised in previous periods nor does it deal with transfers between reserves, which should continue to be shown in the notes to the financial statements.

Note the use of the word 'primary' in the above statement. This means the SORG ranks on a par with the other primary statements, P&L account and balance sheet.

Activity 12

What other recognized gains and losses could there be other than those recognized in the P&L account?

Activity 12 feedback

The other gains and losses will be any movements on reserves which reflect changes in the recognized net assets of the reporting entity other than those resulting from capital contributed or repaid. Thus we are concerned with revaluations of assets and foreign currency adjustments. FRS 3 provides an example of a statement of total recognized gains and losses as follows:

Statement of total recognized gains and losses

	20X3	20X2 as restated
	£m	£m
Profit for the financial year	29	7
Unrealized surplus on revaluation of properties	4	6
Unrealized (loss)/gain on trade investment	(3)	7
	30	20
Currency translation differences on foreign currency net investments	(2)	5
Total recognized gains and losses relating to the year	28	25
Prior year adjustment	(10)	
Total gains and losses recognized since last annual report	18	

The prominence of this statement should ensure that users are aware of movements on reserves and do not have to search the notes to the accounts for such information as used to be the case.

Activity 13

The figures in the example of a SORG provided above are based on the same information as the layered P&L example we provided earlier.
Explain why the profit for the financial year of £29m in the SORG is before dividends.
Explain the meaning of the final figure on the SORG of £18 million.

Activity 13 feedback

The £29 million is before dividends because the statement is required to reflect all gains attributable to the shareholders. The dividends are part of that gain, we just happen to pay it to them in cash!

The £18 million represents the change in net assets between the opening and closing balance sheets excluding transactions involving shareholders, e.g. contribution of extra share capital.

Historical cost profits and losses

FRS 3 requires two further statements to be provided so that users of financial statements have enough information on which to base their decision making. The first of these is the note of historical cost profits and losses. It is a memorandum item, not a primary statement, and is provided in order to permit comparison between entities which have revalued assets and those that haven't. The note is required whenever there is a material difference between the historical profit and loss and that declared in the financial statements. It appears immediately following the profit and loss account or the SORG.

Activity 14

Identify two reasons why the reported profit and loss and the historical profit and loss may be different.

Activity 14 feedback

The differences occur when entities revalue assets.
Thus adjustments will be required for:

- the difference between the profit or loss on sale of an asset calculated on the revalued amount as included in the P&L account and that based on a depreciated historical cost
- the difference between the depreciation calculated on the revalued amount of all assets and that based on historical cost.

The following example is provided in FRS 3:

Note of historical cost profits and losses

	20X3	20X2 as restated
	£m	£m
Reported profit on ordinary activities before taxation	45	13
Realization of property revaluation gains of previous years	9	10
Difference between historical cost depreciation charge and the actual depreciation charge of the year calculated on the revalued amount	5	4
Historical cost profit on ordinary activities before taxation	59	27
Historical cost profit for the year retained after taxation, minority interests, extraordinary items and dividends	35	20

The final statement required by FRS 3 is 'reconciliation of movements in shareholders' funds'. The following example is again provided by FRS 3:

Reconciliation of movements in shareholders' funds

	20X3	20X2 as restated
	£m	£m
Profit for the financial year	29	7
Dividends	(8)	(1)
	21	6
Other recognized gains and losses relating to the year (net)	(1)	18
New share capital subscribed	20	
Goodwill written-off	(25)	
Net addition to shareholders' funds	15	24
Opening shareholders' funds (originally £375m before deducting prior year adjustment of £10m)	365	340
Closing shareholders' funds	380	365

The purpose of this statement is to reflect the other changes between opening and closing net assets that are not reflected in the P&L account or the SORG, such as new share capital.

Profit or loss on the disposal of an asset

FRS 3 requires the identification in the P&L account of profits and losses on the sale of assets (p. 620). But which profit is this? The difference between depreciated historical cost or depreciated revalued cost? FRS 3 (paragraph 21) states:

> the profit or loss on the disposal of an asset should be accounted for in the profit and loss account of the period in which the disposal occurs as the difference between the net sale proceeds and the net carrying amount, whether carried at historical amount or at valuation.

This is why the note in respect of historical cost profits and losses is so important.

This was also a change to previous requirements. Previously directors had the option of calculating the profit or loss by reference to historical or revalued cost.

Activity 15

An asset purchased five years ago at a cost of £10 000 has an estimated life of ten years and an even pattern of usage with no estimated residual value. Two years ago the asset was revalued to £14 000. It is now sold for £9000. Show the entries in the P&L account and the note of historical cost profit and losses if

- the asset was not revalued in the books
- the asset was revalued in the books.

Activity 15 feedback

	£	
Historical cost carrying value at sale	5 000	
Sale proceeds	9 000	
Profit on sale	4 000	shown in P&L account, no item required in note of historical cost profit
Revalued carrying value at sale	10 000	
Sale proceeds	9 000	
Loss on sale	1 000	shown in P&L account

Realization of property revaluation gains of previous years £7000 (14 000 – (10 000 – 3000)) shown in note of historical cost profits and losses.

Segmental reporting

FRED 1, the exposure draft prior to FRS 3, did discuss whether to restrict the application of the discontinued category to a material segment or business segment and decided against this for the following reasons:

- it would not necessarily achieve the objectives of removing from the results of continuing operations, those material operations that would not be present in the next period
- there would be the significant problem of devising an effective definition for material or business segment without resorting to a lengthy list of examples of its practical application.

Does this imply an operation is something less than a business segment and where does it leave SSAP 25 'Segmental Reporting' which does not provide a lengthy list of examples for the definition of a segment?

FRS 3 makes only one reference to segmental reporting and surprisingly no reference at all to SSAP 25.

> **53** It is important for a thorough understanding of the results and financial position of a reporting entity that the impact of changes on material components of the business should be highlighted. To assist in this objective, if an acquisition, a sale or a termination has a material impact on a major business segment the FRS requires that this impact should be disclosed and explained.

Segmental reporting or disaggregation was discussed in the *Corporate Report* of 1975.

Corporate Report and segmental reporting

The *Corporate Report* states:

> The problem of disaggregation (i.e. the analysis of general corporate information between separate divisions or classes of business which are individually of economic significance, sometimes called segment or site reporting) arises in the context of the degree of disclosure appropriate in basic financial statements. The problem is found at its most extreme in organisations of vast size and spread such as nationalised industries and multinational companies.

Our suggestion is that the basis of division activities selected should be the one which in the opinion of the management will most fairly represent the range and significance of the entity's activities. The division could be based on groups of products or services, group companies, operating or geographic divisions, markets served or any combination of these items which would assist fair presentation.

We consider it desirable that the following information (the preparation of which may involve some arbitrary apportionments) should be disclosed about each main class of activity:

(**a**) Turnover
(**b**) Value added
(**c**) Profits or losses before tax
(**d**) Capital employed
(**e**) Employment information

The basis of division into classes of activity should be stated as should, where appropriate, other bases for internal and special purpose reporting. There should also be disclosed, insofar as they will assist in forming a view of the entity's financial position and will not be damaging to its interest, significant changes during the year in principal products, services or markets as classified in the corporate report.

Probably the most frequently used basis of segmentation is by industry or product line. With many of the present day 'conglomerate' organisations where different and disparate businesses come together into group ownership such a breakdown is obviously of crucial importance to a user who wishes to deal with one particular component. Another basis that may be of considerable importance is by geographical area. Multinational companies that merely produce total figures are unlikely to satisfy the users of any one particular country – certainly the non-shareholder users. Regional reporting within a country might also be highly useful in some circumstances.

The Companies Act requires the following:

55 (**1**) If in the course of the financial year the company has carried on business of two or more classes that, in the opinion of the directors, differ substantially from each other, there shall be stated in respect of each class [describing it] –
   (**a**) the amount of the turnover attributable to that class; and
   (**b**) the amount of the profit or loss of the company before taxation which is in the opinion of the directors attributable to that class.
(**2**) If in the course of the financial year the company has supplied markets that, in the opinion of the directors, differ substantially from each other, the amount of the turnover attributable to each such market shall also be stated.
In this paragraph 'market' means a market delimited by geographical bounds.

Paragraph 55(5) of schedule 4 states that where, in the opinion of the directors, the disclosure of any information required by paragraph 55 would be seriously prejudicial to the interests of the company, that information need not be disclosed but the fact that any such information has not been disclosed must be stated.

In addition, certain further requirements for quoted companies are set out in the

'Admission of Securities of Listing'. Section 5, chapter 2, paragraph 21(c) of that publication requires:

A geographical analysis of both net turnover and contribution to trading results of those trading operations carried on by the company (or group) outside the UK and the Republic of Ireland.

No analysis of the contribution to trading results is required unless the contribution to profit or loss from a specific area is 'abnormal' in nature. 'Abnormal' is defined as substantially out of line with the normal ratio of profit to turnover.

SSAP 25 'Segmental Reporting'

Pressures for an extension of segmental reporting have further increased in recent years, as businesses become ever larger and more international. Responding to this the ASC issued a SSAP in June 1990. This repeats the various requirements of the Companies Act as stated above, which apply to all companies, and proposes further requirements on 'publicly accountable entities' only.

A 'publicly accountable entity' is one which:

4 (a) is a public limited company or has a public limited company as a subsidiary; or
 (b) is a banking or insurance company or group (as defined for the purposes of Part VII of the Companies Act 1985); or
 (c) exceeds the criteria, multiplied in each case by 10, for defining a medium sized company under section 248 of the Companies Act 1985, as amended from time to time by statutory instrument.

However, a subsidiary that is not a public limited company or a banking or insurance company need not comply with these provisions if its parent provides segmental information in compliance with this accounting standard.

5 All entities are encouraged to apply the provisions of this accounting standard in all financial statements intended to give a true and fair view of the financial position and profit or loss.
6 Where, in the opinion of the directors, the disclosure of any information required by this accounting standard would be seriously prejudicial to the interests of the reporting entity, that information need not be disclosed: but the fact that any such information has not been disclosed must be stated. This repeats the exemption contained in paragraph 55(5) of Schedule 4 to the Companies Act 1985 in the wider context of this accounting standard.

In essence the requirements are for disclosure of segmental information on both a class of business and a geographical basis. We are given the following definitions:

30 A class of business is a distinguishable component of an enterprise that provides a separate product or service or a separate group of related products or services.
31 A geographical segment is a geographical area comprising an individual country or group of countries in which a company operates.
23 Common costs are costs that relate to more than one segment.

The important parts of the proposed standard accounting practice are:

34 If an entity has two or more classes of business, or operates in two or more geographical segments which differ substantially from each other, it should define its classes of business and geographical segments in its financial statements, and it should report with respect to each class of business and geographical segment the following financial information:

(**a**) turnover, distinguishing between

   (**i**) turnover derived from external

   (**ii**) turnover derived from other segments

(**b**) result, before accounting for taxation, minority interests and extraordinary items; and

(**c**) net assets.

The reporting entity should disclose the geographical segmentation of turnover by origin. It should also disclose turnover to third parties by destination or state where appropriate that this amount is not materially different from turnover to third parties by origin.

Segment result will normally be disclosed before taking account of interest. However, where all or part of the entity's business is to earn and/or incur interest, or where interest income or expense is central to the business, interest should normally be included in arriving at the segment result. Net assets will normally be non-interest bearing operating assets less the non-interest bearing operating liabilities, but to the extent that the segment result is disclosed after accounting for interest the corresponding interest-bearing assets or liabilities should also be included.

37 The total of the amounts disclosed by segment should agree with the related total in the financial statements. If it does not, the reporting entity should provide a reconciliation between the two amounts. Reconciling items should be properly identified and explained.

38 Comparative figures for the previous accounting period should be provided. If, however, on the first occasion on which an entity provides a segmental report the necessary information is not readily available, comparative figures need not be provided.

39 The directors should re-define the segments when appropriate. If a change is made to the definitions of the segments or to the accounting policies that are adopted for reporting segmental information, the nature of the change should be disclosed. The reason for the change and its effect should be stated. The previous year's figures should be re-stated to reflect the change.

These proposed requirements raise a few questions. An obvious problem is to define the appropriate segments in any particular circumstance. This should be done bearing in mind the purpose of segmental information which is to:

1 ... provide information to assist the readers of financial statements:

(**a**) to appreciate more thoroughly the results and financial position of the enterprise by permitting a better understanding of the enterprise's past performance and thus a better assessment of its future prospects; and

(**b**) to be aware of the impact that changes in significant components of a business may have on the business as a whole.

8 In identifying separate reportable segments, the directors should have regard to the overall purpose of presenting segmental information (as set out in paragraph 1) and the need of the user of the financial statements to be informed where an entity carries on operations in different classes of business or in different geographical areas that:

(a) earn a return on investment that is out of line with the remainder of the business; or

(b) are subject to different degrees of risk; or

(c) have experienced different rates of growth; or

(d) have different potentials for future development.

12 When deciding whether or not an entity operates in different classes of business, the directors should take into account the following factors:

(a) the nature of the products or services

(b) the nature of the production processes

(c) the markets in which the products or services are sold

(d) the distribution channels for the products

(e) the manner in which the entity's activities are organized

(f) any separate legislative framework relating to part of the business, for example, a bank or an insurance company.

13 Although it is possible to identify certain characteristics that differentiate between classes of business, no single set of characteristics is universally applicable nor is any single characteristic determinative in all cases. Consequently, determination of an entity's classes of business must depend on the judgement of the directors.

15 A geographical analysis should help the user of the financial statements to assess the extent to which an entity's operations are subject to factors such as the following:

(a) expansionist or restrictive economic climates

(b) stable or unstable political regimes

(c) exchange control regulations

(d) exchange rate fluctuations.

16 It is not practicable to define a method of grouping that will reflect all the differences between international business environments and that would apply to all entities. The selected grouping should reflect the purpose of presenting segmental information (as set out in paragraph 1) and the factors noted in paragraphs 8 and 15. Although geographical proximity may indicate similar economic trends and risks, this will not necessarily be the case.

A second significant difficult is that the SSAP appears to require the allocation of all elements to particular segments. Thus common costs and net assets which relate to more than one segment should be allocated.

Common costs

23 Common costs are costs relating to more than one segment. They should be treated in the way that the directors deem most appropriate in pursuance of the objectives of segmental reporting. Entities may apportion some common costs for the purposes of internal reporting and, in such cases, it may be reasonable for such costs to be similarly apportioned for external reporting purposes. If the apportionment would be misleading, common costs should not be apportioned in the segmental disclosures but should be deducted from the total of the segment results. Costs that are directly attributable to individual reportable segments are not common costs for the purpose of this accounting standard and therefore should be allocated to those segments, irrespective of the fact that they may have been borne by a different segment or by the Head Office.

Segment net assets

24 The net assets of each reportable segment should be disclosed. In most cases these will be the non-interest bearing operating assets less the non-interest bearing operating liabilities. However, to the extent that the segment result is disclosed after accounting for interest as described in paragraph 22, the corresponding interest bearing operating assets and liabilities should also be included.

25 Segment operating assets and liabilities may include assets and liabilities relating exclusively to one segment and also an allocated portion of assets and liabilities that relate jointly to more than one segment. Assets and liabilities used jointly by more than one segment should be allocated to the segments on a reasonable basis. Assets and liabilities that are not used in the operations of any segment should not be allocated to segments. Operating assets of a segment should not normally include loans or advances to, or investments in, another segment unless interest therefrom has been included in arriving at the segment result on the basis set out in paragraph 22.

22 In the majority of entities, different classes of business or geographical segments are financed by different proportions of interest bearing debt and equity. The interest earned or incurred by individual segments is therefore a result of the entity's overall financial policy rather than a proper reflection of the results of the various segments. Consequently, comparisons of profit between segments or between different years for the same segment are likely to be meaningless if interest is included in arriving at the result. For these reasons, it will normally be appropriate for segment results to be disclosed before taking account of interest. However, where all or part of the entity's business is to earn and/or incur interest (as in the financial sector, for example), or where interest income or expense is central to the business (as in the contracting or travel businesses, for example), interest should normally be included in arriving at the segment result.

It is clear that the SSAP throws up a number of practical difficulties. It is forced, like the Companies Act before it, to allow directors to determine what is appropriate for their business – and by implication to assume that auditors can and will properly monitor this. The assumption that this will be adequate ought to be entirely valid. Time will tell.

Activity 16

Given below is the segmental analysis of turnover and operating profit contained in the press release of the preliminary announcement of 1991 results for RMC group plc.

Segmental analysis of turnover and operating profit

(a) Geographical

	Turnover		Operating profits	
	1991	1990	1991	1990
	£m	£m	£m	£m
UK	903.6	1028.3	34.9	89.7
Germany	926.7	699.9	90.4	71.7
Other EU countries	700.2	620.7	55.1	56.9
Countries outside the EU	267.2	240.4	14.2	13.6
	2797.7	2589.3	194.6	231.9

(b) By business

	1991	1990	1991	1990
	£m	£m	£m	£m
Ready mixed concrete and aggregates	1758.0	1776.1	134.9	177.7
Cement, lime and concrete products	621.8	390.4	46.9	32.0
Merchanting, DIY, waste control, leisure and others	417.9	422.8	12.8	22.2
	2797.7	2589.3	194.6	231.9

Operating profit is stated after charging depreciation of £117.5 million (1990 £101.3 million).

1 What extra insight into the company does this information give over and above that of knowing total turnover and operating profit?
2 What further information would you describe as desirable in order to make further comment.

Activity 16 feedback

1 The total turnover figure on an historical costs basis has increased but operating profit has decreased from 1990 to 1991. The geographical analysis shows us that:

	Turnover % change 1990–1	Operating Profit % change 1990–1
UK	−12%	−61%
Germany	+32%	+26%
Other EU countries	+13%	−3%
Countries outside the EU	+11%	+4%

Therefore the decrease in the operating profit is due entirely to the UK market which accounts for one third of the turnover.

The business segment analysis shows us that:

Ready mixed concrete and aggregates	−1%	−24%
Cement, lime and concrete products	+59%	+47%
Merchanting, DIY, waste control, leisure and others	−1%	−42%

Therefore, the decrease in the operating profit is due to the ready mixed concrete segment and the DIY segment.

2 Further information required would be that described in SSAP 25, i.e. net assets disclosed by geographical and business segment to determine return on capital employed and sales to capital employed.

Summary

This chapter has been concerned with one of the most controversial areas of current financial reporting. How to report information on an entity's financial performance to users, which is true and fair, in order to assist their decision making process. The eps, which is used as a market indicator, is dependent on the definition given to earnings. At the base of these issues is the equation of how income should be measured and recognized for an entity. FRS 3 is based on the concept of changes in wealth, recognized as the difference between opening and closing net assets on a balance sheet, to measure performance rather than historical cost profit. Interestingly chapters four and five of the Statement of Principles issued by the ASB deal with recognition and measurement and chapter six with presentation. These have not yet gone through the due process, but FRS 3 which uses the same concepts is approved ahead of this!

Problems still exist within the interpretation of FRS 3:

- do extraordinary items exist? Companies are beginning to report them
- entities are able to calculate and represent on the face of the profit and loss account a variant of eps; some entities are creative in their interpretation of equal prominence
- the interpretation of operations is not clear cut and FRS 3 and SSAP 25 are not integrated
- directors are able within their presentation of the layered profit and loss account to divert the users' attention to the good news
- are the users capable of understanding this mass of information that is now provided – three primary statements, four if we include cash flow, three further notes to the accounts and a plethora of eps figures?

Inconclusive international discussion on the whole question of performance statements is ongoing. A suggestion which seems to be meeting with some favour is that there should be one single performance statement incorporating all the elements of both the profit and loss account and the statement of recognised gains and losses with carefully segregated sections and subheadings. The final outcome is not yet clear.

However FRS 3 does have one thing in its favour – *all* information is provided, the user just needs to learn to use it correctly and be aware of the motives of directors in the preparation of this information.

Addendum: FRED 22

Introduction

The ASB published FRED 22 (revision of FRS 3) Reporting Financial Performance in December 2000. The FRED makes extensive changes to FRS 3 to reflect the international shift in views towards reporting comprehensive income, i.e. reporting *all recognized* gains and losses in a single statement instead of splitting these gains and losses between the performance statement and the STRGL

The combined single statement of financial performance

This is the key requirement within FRED 22. The statement will have, it is proposed, three sections:

- operating
- financing and treasury
- other gains and losses.

An example of the proposed statement is given in the FRED and we reproduce it below

Statement of financial performance (Example 2)

	Continuing operations	Acquisitions	Discontinued operations	Total	Total 2000
	2001	2001	2001	2001	restated
Operating	£m	£m	£m	£m	£m
Turnover	600	50	175	825	690
Cost of sales	(445)	(40)	(165)	(650)	(555)
Gross profit	155	10	10	175	135
Other expenses	(95)	(4)	(25)	(124)	(83)
Operating income/profit	60	6	(15)	51	52
Financing and treasury					
Interest on debt				(26)	(15)
Financing relating to pension provision				20	11
Financing and treasury income/profit				(6)	(4)
Operating and financing income before taxation				45	48
Taxation on operating and financing income				(5)	(10)
Operating and financing income after taxation				40	38
Minority interests				(5)	(4)
Income from operating and financing activities for the period				35	34

Other gains and losses

Revaluation gain on disposal of properties in continuing operations	6	4
Revaluation of fixed assets	4	3
Actuarial gain on defined benefit pension scheme	276	91
Profit on disposal of discontinued operations	3	–
Exchange translation differences on foreign currency net investments	(2)	5
Other gains and losses before taxation	287	103
Taxation on other gains and losses	(87)	(33)
Other gains and losses after taxation	200	70
Minority interests	(30)	(10)
Other gains and losses of the period	170	60
Total gains and losses of the period	205	94

The division of gains and losses between the three sections is further explained in paras. 18–26.

The operating section

18 Gains and losses may be excluded from the operating section of the performance statement only if they are permitted or required to be taken to another section by the [draft] FRS, other accounting standards or UITF Abstracts.

19 Income from operating activities focuses on what a reporting entity earns for its output (revenue) and what it sacrifices to obtain that output (expenses) in its dealings with its customers. To provide information on the operating margins the entity achieves, the expenses charged in the operating section should comprise all costs incurred in carrying out the entity's operations. This section should therefore include allocations reflecting the consumption of economic benefits of long-term items, for example the depreciation and impairment of fixed assets or the current service cost representing the increase in the actuarial liability expected to arise from employee service in the current period.

20 For most entities, the bulk of gains and losses recognised during a period will fall into this section. The presumption is that gains and losses recognised during the period arise from an entity's operating activities. Only by exception will certain gains and losses (those that arise from the financing of the entity, or represent holding gains or losses on long-term items) be reported in one of the other sections of the performance statement, as specified by accounting standards. Thus, the operating section will exclude the gains and losses arising from the financing of the operations of the entity, although it will include gains and losses arising from operating activities that are financial in nature (see paragraph 23).

The financing and treasury section

21 Only gains and losses specified by the [draft] FRS, other accounting standards or UITF Abstracts should be reported in the financing and treasury section of the performance statement.

22 The recognised gains and losses that should appear in this section are:
   (a) interest payable and receivable;
   (b) the unwinding of the discount on long-term items, e.g. pensions;
   (c) income from investments held as part of treasury activities;
   (d) gains and losses arising on the repurchase or early settlement of debt (as determined in accordance with FRS 4 'Capital Instruments'); and
   (e) any other recognised gain or loss identified for inclusion by another accounting standard or by a UITF Abstract.

   The basis on which gains and losses arising on financial activities have been reported in the operating section of the performance statement should be disclosed and this should be applied consistently from period to period.

23 This section of the performance statement contains those gains and losses arising from the financing of the entity's operations. This does not mean that all items of a financial nature will be reported here. Where some or all of an entity's trade with its external customers is financial in nature, gains and losses arising from those activities will be reported in the operating section of the performance statement.

   Reporting entities that are part of special industries, such as banking and insurance companies, will adapt the formats required by the [draft] FRS. Other entities will need to consider the extent to which their operating results should incorporate their financial activities.

24 The items included in the financing and treasury section as specified in paragraph 22 should be disclosed in the notes if not presented on the face of the performance statement.

Other gains and losses

25 Only gains and losses specified by the [draft] FRS or other accounting standards or UITF Abstracts should be reported in other gains and losses within the performance statement.

26 The recognised gains and losses that should appear in this section are:
   (a) revaluation gains and losses on fixed assets (as determined in accordance with FRS 15 'Tangible Fixed Assets');
   (b) gains and losses on disposal of properties in continuing operations (as determined in accordance with FRS 15);
   (c) actuarial gains and losses arising on defined benefit schemes (as determined in accordance with FRS 17 'Retirement Benefits');
   (d) profits and losses on disposal of discontinuing operations;
   (e) exchange translation differences on foreign currency net investments (as determined in accordance with SSAP 20 'Foreign currency translation');
   (f) revaluation gains and losses arising on investment properties (as determined in accordance with SSAP 19 'Accounting for investment properties');
   (g) on the lapse of an unexercised warrant, the amount previously recognised in respect of that warrant (as determined in accordance with FRS 4 'Capital Instruments'); and
   (h) any other recognised gain or loss as determined in accordance with or identified by another accounting standard or a UITF Abstract.

Further issues within FRED 22

The illustration of the performance statement shown above does not include a line showing the dividends for the period. This is deliberate as the ASB now take the view that dividends are transactions with owners not expenses of the entity and therefore should be excluded from the performance statement. This exclusion of dividends from the financial performance statement (FPS) is also in accordance with international practice (see IAS 1) but as it is contrary to UK companies legislation the ASB have a problem. The Board have raised with the Department of Trade and Industry the possibility of a change in the law. Dividends will however have to be shown on the face of the FPS as a memo item as follows:

Memorandum items

Earnings per share	39p	41p
Adjustments [to be itemised and described]	Xp	Xp
Adjusted earnings per share	Yp	Yp
Diluted earnings per share	Zp	Zp
Dividend per share: equity	3.0p	1.8p
preference	0.6p	0.6p
Dividend for the period: equity	£6.7m	£0.7m
preference	£1.3m	£1.3m
Prior period adjustment recognised during the period	(£10m)	

The FRED also puts forward the need for a new primary statement 'Reconciliation of ownership interests', an example of this follows.

	2001	2000 as restated
	£m	£m
Recognised gains and losses relating to the period	205	94
Dividends	(8)	(2)
	197	92
New share capital subscribed	20	1
Net addition to ownership interests	217	93
Opening shareholders' funds (originally £517m before deduction of £10m prior period adjustment)	508	415
Closing ownership interests	725	508

Comprehensive notes to the FPS are specified by the FRED, including a rather useful table of exceptional items which have been reported over the past 5 years. An example of this is given in Appendix 1 to the FRED which we reproduce below.

Five-year information on exceptional items

	2001	2000	1999	1998	1997
	£m	£m	£m	£m	£m
Exceptional items					
Restructuring costs					
Redundancy payments	(5)				
Loyalty bonuses	(1)				
IT integration and upgrade costs	(2)			(2)	
Rebranding	(3)				
Inventory obsolescence write-down	(1)	(4)		(3)	
VAT refund				21	
Total exceptional items reported	(12)	(4)	0	16	0

The FRED also highlights a possible inconsistency between the requirements of SSAP 19 and the logic of FRED 22 in respect of the recognition of gains and losses on investment properties i.e. the fair value changes. The logic behind FRED 22 would suggest that such gains and losses should be taken to the operating section of the performance statement when investment properties are the main activity of the entity. SSAP 19 however requires such gains to be taken to the STRGL which would correspond to the other gains and losses section of the FRED 22 FPS. The logic of SSAP 19 has, in our opinion always been suspect, and it is certainly not in accordance with international practice which requires these gains and losses to be taken through income. As it currently stands the FRED proposes that investment property gains and losses are taken under the other section of the FPS but the ASB is considering revising SSAP 19 to include them under the operating income section and the FRED would then follow suit.

Summary

The main points of the FRED are:

- A single statement of financial performance to be presented as a primary statement.
- FPS to be divided into three sections:
    operating
    financing and treasury
    other gains and losses.
- Recycling, in a future period, of gains and losses between sections of the FPS is not permitted.
- Dividends are excluded from the FPS as they are not an expense of the entity (they will be shown as a memorandum item).
- Several memorandum items are required to be shown on the face of the FPS including eps, dividends, and prior period adjustments.
- Reconciliation of ownership interests is required as a primary statement.
- Notes to the FPS are required in respect of reserve movements, exceptional items over the past 5 years.
- Two optional notes are also proposed:
    tax effects of items in other gains and losses
    historical cost gains and losses.

■ Extraordinary items are still regarded as extremely rare.

It will be interesting to see if this FRED ever becomes a FRS. Watch this space.

Exercises

1 Calculate from the following information:
  (a) the basic eps
  (b) the fully diluted eps.
  The capital of the company is as follows:
  ■ £500 000 in 7% preference shares of £1 each
  ■ £1 000 000 in ordinary shares of 25p each
  ■ £1 250 000 in 8% convertible unsecured loan stock carrying conversion rights into ordinary shares as follows: on 31 December 120 shares for each £100 nominal of loan stock.
  The P&L account for the year ended 31 December showed:
  (a) profit after all expenses, but before extraordinary items, loan interest and corporation tax – £1 200 000. Extraordinary items – £100 000 (expense)
  (b) corporation tax is to be taken as 35% of the profits shown in the accounts after all expenses and after loan interest.

2 FRS 3 'Reporting Financial Performance' is based on the 'all inclusive' concept of income rather than the 'current operating' income concept.
  Required:
  Discuss the merits of both the 'all inclusive' income and the 'current operating' income concepts.
  (Note: the current operating income approach is sometimes referred to as reserve accounting).

3 **(a)** How does FRS 3 'Reporting Financial Performance' define a prior year adjustment?
  (4 marks)
  (b) Set out below is a draft statement of total recognized gains and losses for Triathlon plc for the year ended 31 March 1996 and the comparative figures for the year ended 31 March 1995 unamended.

	1996	1995
	£000	£000
Total recognized gains and losses relating to the year	400	350

  Two fundamental errors have just been discovered which consist of unreported profits that had been omitted from the above statement. In the year ended 31 March 1994 there was an unreported profit before tax of £80 000 (tax £40 000) and in the year ended 31 March 1995 an unreported profit before tax of £100 000 (tax £45 000).
  You are required to amend the above statement in order to account for these two fundamental errors. (6 marks)
  (c) State, with reasons, whether you consider the following events, which are all material, should be accounted for as prior year adjustments:
  (i) A company changes its accounting policies in order to comply with a new SORP (Statement of Recommended Practice).
  (ii) An error in the valuation of the closing stock in the financial statements issued two years previously has been discovered.
  (iii) The directors of a company engaged in a long-term contract which had previously been valued in the financial statements at cost plus attributable profit (in accordance with SSAP 9 'Stocks and Work in Progress') are now of the opinion that there will be a loss on the contract as a whole.

(iv)   A computer, which had been purchased three years previously for £100 000 and was being depreciated at 15% per annum on the straight-line basis, has been sold for £15 000.

(v)   A company has leased premises for five years and the terms of the lease state that the tenant is responsible for all the repairs during the lease. The lease has expired and the landlord has requested a sum of £1 million for repairs necessary to restore the property to its former condition. The company has agreed to pay this sum because it has failed to repair the property during the lease period.

(10 marks)

(20 marks)

(ACCA adapted)

4   You are required to answer the following questions in accordance with SSAP 25 'Segmental Reporting'.

(a)   What is the purpose of segmental reporting?   (4 marks)

(b)   What criteria should be used to identify separate reportable segments?

(6 marks)

(c)   What information should be disclosed for each report segment?

(6 marks)

(d)   Outline the main difficulties with the disclosure for segmental information and outline the arguments against the disclosure of segmental information.

(4 marks)

(20 marks)

(ACCA)

5   **Discuss the advantages and disadvantages of earnings per share as a measure of corporate performance.**   **(15 marks)**

(CIMA)

6   Brachol plc is preparing its accounts for the year ended 30 November 1992.

The following information is available from the previous year's balance sheet. At 30 November 1991 there were credit balances on the share premium account of £2 025 000 and the revaluation reserve of £4 050 000 and the P&L account of £2 700 000. During 1992 the following transactions occurred:

1   One million shares of £1 each were issued in exchange for net assets that had a fair value of £3 755 000.

2   A factory property that had been revalued from £500 000 to £1 310 000 in 1990 was sold for £2 525 000.

3   A fixed asset investment was revalued from £1 305 000 to £900 000.

4   There was a currency translation loss of £270 000 arising on a foreign currency net investment.

5   A warehouse property was revalued from £1 000 000 to £1 540 000.

A prior period adjustment of £1 350 000 was required which had arisen from a change in accountancy policy that had overstated the previous year's profit. The P&L account for the year ended 30 November 1992 showed a profit attributable to members of the company of £810 000 and a dividend of £675 000.

Required:

(a) (i)   draft a note showing the movements on reserves as at 30 November 1992

(ii)   draft a statement of total recognized gains and losses to show the net deduction from or addition to net assets as at 30 November 1992.

(6 marks)

(b)   Explain briefly

(i)   the purpose of the statement of total recognized gains and losses; and

(ii) the extent to which a user of the accounts will be better able to make decisions by referring to a statement of total recognized gains and losses rather than the statement of movements on reserves that is produced to comply with the Companies Act 1985. (7 marks)

(c) **Explain briefly**
  (i) the nature of the adjustments that would be required to reconcile the profit on ordinary activities before tax to the historical cost profit
  (ii) the possible use that can be made of such information by a potential investor. (7 marks)

(20 marks)
(ACCA)

7 The information you need to answer this question is given below:

Required:

Prepare, for Arfro plc, separate schedules of segmental data for the year ended 30 June 1993, analysed

(a) geographically and

(b) by class of business

in each case showing, for each significant segment, turnover, result and net assets in the form and detail prescribed by the Companies Act 1985 and SSAP 25 'Segmental Reporting'.

Figures for any insignificant segment, as defined by SSAP 25, should be combined with those of a reportable segment.

All calculations should be rounded to the nearest £1,000.

(37 marks)
(ACCA)

Arfro plc – selected data for the year ended 30 June 1993

The financial accountant has produced the following figures for Arfro plc for the year ended 30 June 1993.

Geographical analysis

	Turnover – total by origin	Turnover – third party by destination	Net operating assets
	%	%	%
UK	75	45	44
Europe (other than UK)	15	30	37
Far East	5	15	12
Other	5	10	7
	100	100	100

Class of business analysis

	Turnover – total by origin	Net operating assets
	%	%
Raw materials production	10	5
Manufacturing	60	70
Merchandising	25	20
Distribution	5	5
	100	100

Other information

Item	Amount £000	Basis of allocation to segments
Turnover – total	47 980	Given percentages (see note above)
– inter segment	13 060	Allocated below
– third party	34 920	*Derived*
Apportioned costs	24 010	*Pro rata* total turnover (see note below)
Apportioned costs	8 000	*Pro rata* net operating assets (see note below)
Allocated costs	3 000	Allocated below
Common costs	6 824	Not allocated but accounted for in total only
Net interest payable	469	
Net assets – allocated	19 860	Given percentages (see note above)
– unallocated	5 154	Accounted for in total only

Note: Separate calculations are needed for geographical analysis and for analysis by class of business, as shown in the preceding tables.

Segment profit/loss, operating profit and profit before tax have not been given and are to be derived.

Direct allocations

	Turnover inter-segment £000	Allocated costs £000
Geographical analysis (by origin)		
UK	9 761	1 980
Europe (other than UK)	2 604	670
Far East	431	200
Other	264	150
	13 060	3 000
Class of business analysis		
Raw materials production	562	–
Manufacturing	11 431	2 000
Merchandising	1 067	1 000
Distribution	–	–
	13 060	3 000

8 The information you need to answer this question is given below.

Required:

(a) Calculate the figures for basic earnings per share and fully diluted earnings per share which would be disclosed in the final accounts for Arfro plc for the year ended 30 June 1993 (actual) and 30 June 1994 (forecast). Detailed workings of the respective earnings figures and of the numbers of shares used as the divisors, must be shown but the accompanying notes required by SSAP 3, Earnings per share, are not required. (20 marks)

(b) Calculate the revised basic earnings per share figure for the year ended 30 June 1992 which would be disclosed as the corresponding previous year figure in the final accounts for the year ended 30 June 1993. (2 marks)

(c) Tabulate the capital employed figures, corresponding to those given for 1 July 1992, at 30 June 1993 (actual) and 30 June 1994 (forecast) after accounting for the matters contained in Appendix. (8 marks)

(30 marks)
(ACCA)

Details of capital structure and related matters of Arfro plc
At 1 July 1992, the capital employed by Arfro plc consisted of

	£	£
Called-up share capital, fully paid		
5 000 000 8% preference shares of 100p per share		5 000 000
28 000 000 ordinary shares of 50p per share		14 000 000
		19 000 000
Reserves		
share premium	1 700 000	
other reserves	870 000	
profit and loss	2 714 000	
		5 284 000
Shareholders' funds		24 284 000
Long-term loans		
10% debentures 1993/8		3 000 000
(interest payable 31.12, 30.6)		
Capital employed		27 284 000

On 1 October 1992, Arfro plc issued the shares of a previously declared 1 for 4 rights issue of ordinary shares at 135p per share, all of which had been taken up. The purpose of the issue was to provide cash for the buy back of some of the company's own preference shares.

Middle market price of ordinary shares on the last day of quotation cum rights was 225p per share. The rights shares ranked for dividend in the first year of issue.

Part of the proceeds of the rights issue was used on this same day to buy back 1 500 000 of Arfro's own 8% preference shares on the open market at 170p per share, for cancellation. These shares had been initially issued at 130p per share. The premium payable on buy back was appropriated from share premium account to the full extent permitted by the Companies Act 1985.

On 1 January 1993 Arfro plc issued options, exercisable on or before 30 June 2000, to senior executives to subscribe for 1 000 000 ordinary shares of 50p per share at a price of 190p per share. None of these options were exercised during the year ended 30 June 1993 or forecast to take place before 1997.

On 31 March 1993 Arfro plc bought back £2 000 000 10% own debentures at 96 cum. int. which were immediately cancelled.

Other information
1 It is the policy of Arfro plc to utilize share premium account to the fullest extent permitted by current legislation. Items affecting reserves which do not result in share premium account entries are dealt with through other reserves.
2 Basic earnings per share for the year ended 30 June 1992 was 7.804p per share.
3 The closing price of 2.5% Consolidated stock was assumed to be £27.75 on 30 June 1992 and £26.25 on 30 June 1993.
4 The company was liable for corporation tax at 33%.

5

	year ended 30 June	
	1993	1994
	(actual)	(forecast)
	£	£
Profit before interest and tax	5 034 000	5 777 000
Tax on profit on ordinary activities	1 627 000	1 945 000
Extraordinary items	Nil	Nil
6 Proposed dividends (per share)		
8% preference shares	8p	8p
Ordinary shares	3p	4p
Interim dividends	Nil	Nil

9 FRS 3 'Reporting Financial Performance' became effective for accounting periods ending on or after 22 June 1993.

The objective of financial statements is to provide information about the financial position and performance of an enterprise that is useful to a wide range of users.

The ASB's 'Statement of Principles for Financial Reporting' states: 'Financial reporting gives an account of the results of stewardship of management to enable users to assess the past performance of management and to form a basis for developing future expectations about financial performance'.

In relation to the income statement there are basically two potentially conflicting views of what is the most useful form of presentation of information:

(i) The concept of 'comprehensive income' or 'all-inclusive income' in which the underlying principle is that all gains and losses, irrespective of their nature, are relevant and should be reported in the period in which they occur.

Effectively this is a statement of the change in the owners' equity, other than by injections and withdrawals of capital.

(ii) The 'current operating performance concept' or 'maintainable earnings concept' in which the emphasis is on ordinary, normal, recurring earnings. Only those gains and, more particularly losses, which have occurred, and are likely to occur, or 'be maintained' in the future should be reported as income for the period.

Required:

(a) Discuss the contribution of FRS 3 to the debate over whether the 'comprehensive income' or 'current operating performance' concept is preferable.

(6 marks)

(b) Describe how the following requirements of FRS 3 improve the informational content of financial statements:

(i)   the analysis of results between continuing and discontinued activities;

(ii)   the treatment of extraordinary and exceptional items;

(iii)   the calculation of the profit or loss on disposal of a fixed asset;

(iv)   the inclusion of a 'Statement of Total Recognised Gains and Losses';

(v)   the 'Note of Historical Cost Profits and Losses'. (12 marks)

(c) Describe the criticisms that have been made of FRS 3 in relation to the areas in (b) above. (7 marks)

(25 marks)

(ACCA 97)

10 You are the management accountant of Prompt plc, a UK company which prepares financial statements to 31 March each year. The financial statements for the year ended 31 March 1998 are due to be formally approved by the board of directors on 15 June 1998.

Your assistant has prepared a first draft of the financial statements. These show a turnover of £200 million and a profit before taxation of £18 million. Your assistant has identified a number of transactions ((a), (b) and (c) below) for which he is unsure of the correct accounting treatment. For each transaction, he has indicated the treatment followed in the draft financial statements. You have reviewed the transactions highlighted by your assistant.

Required:

Draft a memorandum to your assistant which explains the correct accounting treatment for each transaction. Where the treatment adopted by your assistant in the draft financial statements is incorrect, your memorandum should indicate the reasons for this. For each transaction, your memorandum should refer to relevant provisions of company law and accounting standards.

Transaction (a)

During the year ended 31 March 1998, Prompt plc entered into an arrangement with a finance company to factor its debts. Each month 90% of the value of the debts arising from credit sales that month was sold to the factor, who assumed legal title and responsibility for collection of all debts. Upon receipt of the cash by the factor, the remaining 10% was paid to Prompt plc less a deduction for administration and finance costs. Any debtor who did not pay the factor within three months of the debt being factored was transferred back to Prompt plc and the amounts advanced by the factor recovered from Prompt plc. In preparing the draft financial statements, your assistant has removed the whole of the factored debts from trade debtors at the date the debts are factored. The net amount receivable from the factor has been shown as a sundry debtor. (5 marks)

Transaction (b)

On 15 March 1998, Prompt plc decided to close one of its three factories. This decision was taken because the product (called product X) which was manufactured at the factory was considered obsolete. A gradual run down of the operation commenced on 15 April 1998 and was expected to be complete by 15 June 1998. The factory produced monthly operating statements detailing turnover, profits and assets, and the turnover for the year ended 31 March 1998 was £35 million. Closure costs (including redundancy) were estimated to be £2.5 million. Your assistant has made no entries in the draft financial statements in respect of the closure since it took place in the year ending 31 March 1999. (12 marks)

Transaction (c)

On 30 June 1997, Prompt plc issued 100 million £1 debentures. The issue costs were £100 000. The debentures carry no interest entitlement but are redeemable on 30 June 2007 at a price of £259 million. Your assistant has included the nominal value of the debentures (£100 million) as part of shareholders' funds since they represent long-term finance for the company. The issue costs of £100000 have been charged to the profit and loss account for the year, and your assistant suggests that the difference between the issue price and the redemption price should be dealt with in 2007 when the debentures are redeemed. (8 marks)

(25 marks)

(CIMA)

11   The following financial statements relate to Globelink International plc for the year ended 30 November 1996.

Group profit and loss account for the year ended 30 November 1996

	£000	£000
Turnover		
Continuing operations		
Ongoing	214277	
Acquisitions	7573	
	221850	
Discontinued operations	54853	
		276703
Cost of sales		(220398)
Gross profit		56305
Distribution costs	21886	
Administrative expenses	21421	
		(43307)
		12998
Other operating income		894
Income from interests in associated undertakings		3575
Operating profit		
Continuing operations		
Ongoing	16590	
Acquisitions	1585	
	18175	
Discontinued operations	(708)	
		17467
Profit on disposal of fixed assets	1170	
Discontinued operations		
Loss on sale of operations	(3168)	
		(1998)
		15469
Income from investments	1648	
Interest payable	(1432)	
		216
Profit on ordinary activities before taxation		15685
Tax on profit on ordinary activities		(4747)
Profit on ordinary activities after taxation		10938
Minority interests		(404)
Profit attributable to members of the parent company		10534
Dividends		(2815)
Retained profit for the year		7719

Group balance sheet at 30 November 1996

	£000
Fixed assets	
Intangible assets	2 680
Tangible assets	43 940
Investments in associated undertakings	26 670
	73 290
Current assets	
Stock	33 962
Debtors	26 470
Cash at bank and in hand	11 468
	71 900
Creditors: *amounts falling due within one year*	(32 530)
Net current assets	39 370
Total assets less current liabilities	112 660
Creditors: *amounts falling due after more than one year*	(16 338)
Accruals and deferred income	
Deferred government grants	(3 530)
Minority interests	(812)
	91 980
Capital and reserves	
Called up share capital	39 600
Share premium account	645
Revaluation reserve	12 725
Profit and loss account	39 010
	91 980

The following information is relevant to the financial statements of Globelink International plc.

(a) The group manufactures and sells printing machinery within the United Kingdom and Asia.

   (i) Sales to Asian customers account for 32% of total group turnover.

   (ii) Sales originating from Asian subsidiaries account for 34% of the total group turnover including intercompany sales.

   (iii) Discontinued activities totally relate to United Kingdom business and operations.

   (iv) Items (i) and (ii) above relate solely to continuing activities.

(b) Total intercompany sales from continuing activities were £16.5 million during the year. Asian subsidiary companies originated 20% of these sales.

(c) Asian subsidiaries contributed 24% of the continuing operating profit before taking into account common costs and the profit before tax of associated undertakings. Any apportionment of the common costs of £2.4 million was deemed to be misleading by the directors and therefore no apportionment was to take place. The associated undertakings are all operating from the United Kingdom.

(d) The group has 25% of its tangible and intangible fixed assets located in Asia and 30% of its current assets. No government grants have been received in Asia. The creditors falling due after more than one year relate to a loan obtained by the UK parent company. Additionally, the directors felt that it was not possible to allocate 'creditors falling due within one year' of £7.8 million between the segments. After adjusting for this amount, 30% of the balance related to activities in Asia.

(e) The directors have decided that for the purpose of the disclosure requirements of FRS 3 'Reporting Financial Performance', the acquisitions in the year do not have a material impact on a business segment as they relate to UK operations. However they consider that the discontinued operations have a material impact on the UK operations.

Required:

(a) **Prepare a segmental report by geographical area for Globelink International plc in accordance with SSAP 25 'Segmental Reporting', FRS 3 'Reporting Financial performance' and the Companies Act 1985 as amended by Companies Act 1989. (All calculations should be to the nearest £000.)**

(21 marks)

(b) **Briefly describe FOUR limitations of SSAP 25 'Segmental Reporting'.**

(4 marks)

(25 marks)

(ACCA)

12 FRS 14 has made no significant changes to the earlier requirements of FRS 3. Discuss.

13 Earnit plc is a listed company. The issued share capital of the company at 1 April 1999 was as follows:

- 500 million equity shares of 50p each.
- 100 million £1 non-equity shares, redeemable at a premium on 31 March 2004. The effective finance cost of these shares for Earnit plc is 10% per annum. The carrying value of the non-equity shares in the financial statements at 31 March 1999 was £110 million.

Extracts from the consolidated profit and loss account of Earnit plc for the year ended 31 March 2000 showed:

	£ million
Turnover	250
Cost of sales	(130)
Gross profit	120
Other operating expenses	(40)
Operating profit	80
Exceptional gain	10
Interest payable	(25)
Profit before taxation	65
Taxation	(20)
Profit after taxation	45
Appropriations of profit (see note)	(26)
Retained profit	19

Note – appropriations of profit:
- to non-equity shareholders — 11
- to equity shareholder — 15

26

The company has a share option scheme in operation. The terms of the option are that optionholders are permitted to purchase 1 equity share for every option held at a price of

£1.50 per share. At 1 April 1999, 100 million share options were in issue. On 1 October 1999, the holders of 50 million options exercised their option to purchase, and 70 million new options were issued on the same terms as the existing options. During the year ended 31 March 2000, the average market price of an equity share in Earnit plc was £2.00.

There were no changes to the number of shares or share options outstanding during the year ended 31 March 2000 other than as noted in the previous paragraph.

Requirements:

(a) **Compute the basic and diluted earnings per share of Earnit plc for the year ended 31 March 2000. Comparative figures are *not* required.**

(10 marks)

(b) **Explain to a holder of equity shares in Earnit plc the usefulness of both of the figures you have calculated in part (a).** (10 marks)

(20 marks)

CIMA(9) MAY 00

14 Both SSAP 25 – *Segmental reporting* and *FRS 3 – Reporting financial performance* require additional analysis of some of the figures in the profit and loss account.

Explain the purpose of the analyses required by SSAP 25 and FRS 3 and explain how these would assist a shareholder who wished to evaluate the company's performance.

(8 marks)

CIMA(5) May 00

Cash flow statements
(FRS 1) (revised 1996)

After reading this chapter you should be able to:
- describe the difference between funds flow and cash flow
- explain why the ASB found it necessary to require cash flow rather than funds flow statements
- describe the requirements of FRS 1 'Cash Flow Statements' (revised)
- prepare cash flow statements
- identify any problems in relation to cash flow statements.

Introduction

SSAP 10 'Statements of Source and Application of Funds', was issued in July 1975 and has been considered for revision on two occasions since. Research had revealed dissatisfaction with SSAP 10 in several areas. In June 1990, prior to the 'wind up' of the ASC, ED 54 'Cash Flow Statements' was issued because, according to the ASC, the changing economic environment had led to increasing sophistication in the requirements of users of financial statements, particularly financial analysts. In September 1991 the ASB issued their statement on cash flow – FRS 1. This was then revised in October 1996.

Cash flow reporting

The traditional accounting process is, as we have seen in Part One, an uncertain and complex process. Not only is profit determination complex, it is potentially misleading. In any accounting year, there will be a mixture of complete and incomplete transactions. Transactions are complete when they have led to a final cash settlement and these cause no profit-measurement difficulties.

Considerable problems arise, however, in dealing with incomplete transactions, where the profit or loss figure can only be estimated by means of the accruals concept, whereby revenue and costs are:

> matched with one another so far as their relationship can be established or justifiably assumed, and dealt with in the profit and loss account of the period to which they relate.

Thus, the profit for the past year is dependent on the validity of many assumptions about the *future*, e.g. the future life of assets is estimated in order to calculate the depreciation charge for the past year.

The greater the volume of incomplete transactions, the greater the degree of estimation and, accordingly, the greater the risk that investors could turn out to have been misled if actual outcomes deviate from estimates.

To explore the differences between cash flow and profit reporting, consider the following.

Activity 1

Below are two short statements about the same business in the same year. Summarize in words what each statement is telling us, and suggest reasons for the differences between them.

A.   *£000s*

Sales	410
less cost of sales	329
	81
less other expenses	36
	45
less depreciation	13
	32
less taxation provided	13
	19
less dividend provided	8
Retained profit	11

B.   *£000s*

Sales received	387
less payments for goods for sale	333
	54
less other expenses paid	32
	22
less capital expenditure	20
	2
less taxation paid	14
	(12)
less dividend paid	7
Increase in borrowing	(19)

Activity 1 feedback

Clearly statement A is a P&L and appropriation account. It shows the revenues and expenses, calculated on the traditional bases, the taxation charged relating to the year, and the dividends which it has been decided should be paid out to shareholders in relation to that year. It shows a profit and implies (though we do not know the size of the business) a successful year.

Statement B is a statement of cash movements in the year – a summary of the cash book, but analysed into the various reasons the cash has moved. The individual differences between the two statements will be due to changes in accruals, prepayments and the like. Overall, statement B shows a reduction in the cash resources of the business before the payment of the dividend, and obviously shows an even bigger contraction in the cash resources of the business after the dividend payout in the year. Statement B surely implies an unsuccessful year.

People often talk about 'cash flows' or claim to be in favour of 'cash flow statements' or 'cash flow reporting' without being too precise about what they mean. In fact, different people are likely to mean significantly different things, and it is very important that we are able to separate out the various situations and arguments one from the other.

At one level, it can be suggested that cash flow reporting, actual and budgeted, should *completely* replace both P&L account (on whatever basis) and balance sheet. The argument for this (ignoring barter situations) is that only cash represents and demonstrates an increase or decrease in the business resources, and that this suggests both that only cash *should* be reported, and that only cash need be reported. This argument is surely untenable. Users need information about changes in the command of a business organization over resources, over goods and services or the power to obtain goods and services.

At a second level, it can be suggested that some form of cash flow statement on the lines of statement B in the above activity, since it obviously gives information which is potentially useful and which is additional to and different from the information in the P&L account, should be required, as an additional statement, in the final reporting package. This is surely logical. Indeed, it is arguably precisely because a P&L account for the year is not a good indicator of the cash flow position for the year, and because a cash flow statement for the year is not a good indicator of the profit and loss position for the year, that the argument for including both is so powerful.

The final level which we should perhaps consider is the debate about the content and role of the funds flow statement. The funds flow statement as traditionally prepared for many years was conceptually speaking an extremely odd animal. It tried to adjust away some, but not all, of the accrual adjustments used in the creation of the P&L account to start with. Historically, the reason for much of this obscurity was that the funds flow statement, being an additional statement not required by the law, was deliberately designed not to give additional information, merely to rearrange already available information in a different form. We are now happily past this state of affairs, and can surely concentrate on being useful.

For example, consider the traditional-type funds flow statement which is shown in statement C.

C. *Summarized funds flow statement*

	£000	£000
Source		
Profit before taxation		2978
Adjustments for items not involving the movement of funds – depreciation		272
Generated from operations		3250
Disposal of fixed assets		890
		4140

Application

Dividends paid		1296
Tax paid		1298
Expenditure on fixed assets		1352

Increase in working capital

Land for development, work in progress and stock	5663	
Debtors	14	
Creditors	(182)	
		5495
		9441
Movement in liquid funds – increase in bank borrowings		(5301)
		4140

This can be readily altered into an approximate cash flow statement by adjusting profit for changes in working capital. Increases in stock represent outflows of cash that have not been recouped by sale, increases in debtors are effectively a form of loan to customers, whereas increases in creditors are a form of loan to the company. In short, they are incomplete transactions, and their elimination avoids the problems of asset valuation inherent therein. Thus:

	£000
Funds from operations	3250
less increase in working capital	5495
Negative cash flow from operations	(2245)

For ease of analysis cash flow statements calculated in this way are often shown as in statement D with operational flows and movements in cash being included as sources or outflows as appropriate.

D. *Summarized cash flow statement*

	£000	%
Sources		
Disposal of assets	890	14
Increase in borrowings	5301	86
	6191	100
Outflows		
Dividends paid	1296	21
Tax paid	1298	21
Fixed assets	1352	22
Negative cash flow on operations	2245	36
	6191	100

It is clear that although this company appears to be profitable, the company has in fact spent more cash than it has received in its trading operations, yet it has continued to pay dividends, invest in fixed assets and pay (without choice, presumably) tax. These excessive outflows have only been possible because of extreme levels of short-term borrowing.

Cash flow analysis has its deficiencies.

Activity 2

Suggest some deficiencies of this form of cash flow analysis.

Activity 2 feedback

It does not smooth cash payments and receipts, and is likely to exhibit a lumpy pattern over time. However, trends may be easier to determine and analyse from aggregation of several years' flows, say three years. Cash flows so calculated are also historic statements, and if we hypothesize that user decisions are future oriented, we should perhaps attempt to provide more relevant information by forecasting future flows as well as reporting actual past flows. Although forecasts are, by definition, subjective, the assumptions on which they are based may be evaluated and reported on by auditors. And cash flow forecasts remain free from allocations and accruals. Companies presently produce cash budgets for internal decision-making; could they be summarized and reported for external decision-making? They may be relevant, but would they be reliable? And is a forecast of future cash flows an adequate indicator of future wealth and well-offness?

Funds flow or cash flow?

What is funds flow? Unfortunately SSAP 10 did not provide a definitive answer to this as it gave no definition of funds. There are many definitions of funds from cash through to working capital, the emphasis varying as we move from cash to accrual based funds.

Activity 3

An extract from the balance sheet of A plc as at 31 December 20X2

	£000s 31.12.X2	£000s 31.12.X1
Stock	4300	4600
Debtors	2600	1300
Cash and bank	1200	2500
	8100	8400
Creditors	6500	7900
	1600	500

Identify the change in funds.

Activity 3 feedback

If we look solely at cash we could state that A plc had experienced a decrease in cash of £1 300 000 over the year. On the other hand, looking at working capital provides a much better position, an increase of £1 100 000 over the year. But which figure should users of accounts have regard to when taking decisions?

FRS 1 does provide us with a definition of cash flow – an increase or decrease in an amount of cash or cash equivalent resulting from a transaction. FRS 1 (revised) amended this to an increase in an amount of cash.

Funds, on the other hand, takes a broader approach. The essential difference between the philosophy of FRS 1 and that of SSAP 10 is that SSAP 10 took this broader view – with the emphasis on the working capital as in Activity 3, while FRS 1 takes the narrower view and would focus more on the actual cash position – i.e. the cash and bank figure as in Activity 3.

Advantages of cash flow over funds flow

The ASB states the following in FRS 1:

51 The Board believes that the information provided by a cash flow statement has the following advantages over that provided by a working capital based funds flow statement:

(a) Funds flow data based on movements in working capital can obscure movements relevant to the liquidity and viability of an entity. For example, a significant decrease in cash available may be masked by an increase in stock or debtors. Entities may, therefore, run out of cash while reporting increases in working capital. Similarly, a decrease in working capital does not necessarily indicate a cash shortage and a danger of failure.

(b) As cash flow monitoring is a normal feature of business life and not a specialized accounting technique, cash flow is a concept which is more widely understood than are changes in working capital.

(c) Cash flows can be a direct input into a business valuation model and, therefore, historical cash flows may be relevant in a way not possible for funds flow data.

(d) A funds flow statement is based largely on the difference between two balance sheets. It reorganizes such data, but does not provide new data. The cash flow statement and associated notes required by the FRS may include data not disclosed in a funds flow statement.

So does a cash flow statement have the relevant characteristics of useful information (Chapter 10)? Let us see if you can answer the question.

Activity 4

State whether you believe, given your knowledge so far, that cash flow is understandable, relevant, reliable and complete.

Activity 4 feedback

1 *Understandable*: paragraph 51(b) above states that the ASB believe it is understandable. Certainly cash is a concept that most people understand, whereas accrual accounting takes us a few years to learn and even more years to understand the need for it!

2 *Relevant*: cash certainly is relevant as without it a business cannot operate. Companies may be able to show a healthy profit but have a very poor cash position as they are relying on borrowed funds.

3 *Reliable*: cash is the end product of a transaction. It is realized! Whereas funds based on profit require us to estimate a point of realization of revenue prior to receipt of cash and the ultimate realization of cash can be in doubt. Cash is certainly free from bias.

4 *Complete*: paragraph 51(d) would appear to imply that cash flow statements complement balance sheets and profit and loss but as to whether they complete the picture of the company as required by users is another matter. Is anything that is historical information providing a complete picture? The ASB admit that the cash flow statement is incomplete as follows:

> **50** A cash flow statement shows information about the reporting entity's cash flows in the reporting period, but this provides incomplete information for assessing future cash flows. Some cash flows result from transactions that took place in an earlier period and some cash flows are expected to result in further cash flows in a future period. Accordingly, cash flow statements should normally be used in conjunction with the profit and loss accounts and balance sheets when making an assessment of future cash flows.

It is useful to remember at this stage that the cash flow statement was issued at the same time as some major companies were facing collapse – Polly Peck and many travel companies. We are not suggesting that preparing cash flow information would have prevented the companies from collapse, far from it, but it may have provided the user with relevant information and the collapse might not have been such a surprise. For the year to 31 December 1989 Polly Peck's accounts showed a healthy source and application funds flow of £172 million whereas a cash flow statement would have shown an outflow of £130 million!

In fact, it could be said that having to provide cash flow information may well have made companies think again about their plans. Remember cash is the 'life blood' of organizations and without it they cannot operate. According to David Tweedie the chairman of the ASB 'cash is a very difficult figure to fiddle'. The ASB in their statement on the need for cash flow information, which is reproduced below for you, suggest that cash flow provides an indication of the quality of the profit earned – an interesting word to use!

> **48** Historical cash flow information may assist users of financial statements in making judgements on the amount, timing and degree of certainty of future cash flows; it gives an indication of the relationship between profitability and cash generating ability, and thus of the quality of the profit earned. In addition, analysts and other users of financial information often, formally or informally, develop models to assess and compare the present value of the future cash flows of entities. Historical cash flow information could be useful to check the accuracy of past assessments and indicate the relationship between the entity's activities and its receipts and payments.

One of the important differences between funds flow and cash flow, given in ED 54, is that a funds flow statement is based largely on the difference between two balance sheets; it reorganizes the data but does not provide any new data; a cash flow statement will. Let us move on and look at these new data.

Requirements of FRS 1 (revised)

Scope

FRS 1 applies to all financial statements except those for

1 small entities as defined by the Companies Act
2 entities which would have come under category **1** above had they been companies incorporated under companies legislation
3 90% or more owned subsidiaries (where the information will be provided in the group accounts)
4 building societies (for two years from effective date)
5 mutual life assurance companies
6 pension funds
7 open-ended investment funds.

Activity 5

The exclusions quoted above do not include particular industry groups such as banking and insurance. Why not?

Activity 5 feedback

The answer is simple. If movements of cash are regarded as necessary information for users of plcs such as ICI, Hanson and BT then they are as equally important for banks and insurance companies. There is no business for which cash flow is not relevant in some form as a restraint or as an opportunity. Witness the difficulties of MMI (Municipal Mutual Insurance).

Format

An entity's cash flow statement has now to consist of eight standard headings as prescribed by paragraph 7 of the revised standard:

> 7 An entity's cash flow statement should list its cash flows for the period classified under the following standard headings:
> - operating activities
> - returns on investments and servicing of finance
> - taxation
> - capital expenditure and financial investment
> - acquisitions and disposals
> - equity dividends paid
> - management of liquid resources
> - financing.

The first six headings should be in the sequence set out above. Operating cash flows can be presented by either the direct method (showing the relevant constituent cash flows) or the indirect method (calculating operating cash flows by adjustment to the operating profit reported in the profit and loss account). The cash flows relating to the management of liquid resources and financing can be combined under a single heading provided that the cash flows relating to each are shown separately and separate subtotals are given.

Several examples of cash flow statements for different entities are given as an appendix to the revised FRS. We reproduce the one for a single company below:

Example 1 **XYZ Limited. Cash flow statement for the year-ended 31 December 1996**
Reconciliation of operating profit to net cash inflow from operating activities

	£000	*£000*
Operating profit		6022
Depreciation charges		899
Increase in stocks		(194)
Increase in debtors		(72)
Increase in creditors		234
Net cash inflow from operating activities		6889

Cash flow statement

Net cash inflow from operating activities		6889
Returns on investments and servicing of finance (note 1)		2999
Taxation		(2922)
Capital expenditure		(1525)
		5441
Equity dividends paid		(2417)
		3024
Management of liquid resources (note 1)		(450)
Financing (note 1)		57
Increase in cash		2631

Reconciliation of net cash flow to movement in net debt (note 2)

Increase in cash in the period	2631	
Cash to repurchase debenture	149	
Cash used to increase liquid resources	450	
Change in net debt		3230
Net debt at 1.1.96		(2903)
Net funds at 31.12.96		327

Notes are also required to the cash flow statement as follows:
Notes to the cash flow statement
Note 1 – gross cash flows
Returns on investments and servicing of finance

Interest received	3011
Interest paid	(12)
	2999

Capital expenditure

Payments to acquire intangible fixed assets	(71)
Payments to acquire tangible fixed assets	(1496)
Receipts from sales of tangible fixed assets	42
	(1525)

Management of liquid resources

Purchase of treasury bills	(650)
Sale of treasury bills	200
	(450)

Financing

Issue of ordinary share capital	211
Repurchase of debenture loan	(149)
Expenses paid in connection with share issues	(5)
	57

Note 2 – analysis of changes in net debt*

	At 1 Jan 1996 £000	Cash flows £000	Other changes £000	At 31 Dec 1996 £000
Cash in hand, at bank	42	847		889
Overdrafts	(1784)	1784		
		2631		
Debt due within 1 year	(149)	149	(230)	(230)
Debt due after 1 year	(1262)		230	(1032)
Current asset investments	250	450		700
Total	(2903)	3230	–	327

The cash flow statement for a group is more complicated than that for a company as it includes an additional item 'acquisitions and disposals'. This can be seen as line 5 on the example below, which is again taken from FRS 1 (revised), showing a figure of £17 824 net cash outflow.

In this example all changes in net debt are cash flows.

Example 2 **XYZ group plc. Cash flow statement for the year-ended 31 December 1996**

	£000	£000
Cash flow from operating activities (note 1)		16 022
Returns on investments and servicing of finance* (note 2)		(2239)
Taxation		(2887)
Capital expenditure and financial investment (note 2)		(865)
Acquisitions and disposals (note 2)		(17 824)
Equity dividends paid		(2 606)
Cash outflow before use of liquid resources and financing		(10 399)
Management of liquid resources (note 2)		700
Financing (note 2)		
– Issue of shares	600	
– Increase in debt	2347	
		2 947
Decrease in cash in the period		(6 752)

Reconciliation of net cash flow to movement in net debt (note 3)

Decrease in cash in the period	(6752)
Cash inflow from increase in debt and lease financing	(2347)
Cash inflow from decrease in liquid resources	(700)
Change in net debt resulting from cash flows	(9 799)
Loans and finance leases acquired with subsidiary	(3 817)
New finance leases	(2 845)
Translation difference	643
Movement in net debt in the period	(15 818)
Net debt at 1.1.96	(15 215)
Net debt at 31.12.96	(31 033)

Notes to the cash flow statement

Note 1 – reconciliation of operating profit to operating cash flows

	£000	Continuing £000	Discontinuing £000	Total £000
Operating profit		20 249	(1616)	18 633
Depreciation charges		3 108	380	3 488
Share of profit of associate	(1420)			
Dividend from associate	350			
Profit of associate less dividends received		(1070)		(1 070)

*This heading would include any dividends received other than those from equity account-ed entities included in operating activities.

Cash flow relating to previous year restructuring provision (note 4)		(560)	(560)
Increase in stocks	(11 193)	(87)	(11 280)
Increase in debtors	(3 754)	(20)	(3 774)
Increase in creditors	9 672	913	10 585
Net cash inflow from continuing operating activities	17 012		
Net cash outflow in respect of discontinued activities		(990)	
Net cash inflow from operating activities			16 022

Note 2 – analysis of cash flows for headings netted in the cash flow statement

	£000	£000
Returns on investments and servicing of finance		
Interest received	508	
Interest paid	(1 939)	
Preference dividend paid	(450)	
Interest element of finance lease rental payments	(358)	
Net cash outflow for returns on investments and servicing of finance		(2 239)
Capital expenditure and financial investment		
Purchase of tangible fixed assets	(3 512)	
Sale of trade investment	1 595	
Sale of plant and machinery	1 052	
Net cash outflow for capital expenditure and financial investment		(865)
Acquisitions and disposals		
Purchase of subsidiary undertaking	(12 705)	
Net overdrafts acquired with subsidiary	(5 516)	
Sale of business	4 208	
Purchase of interest in a joint venture	(3 811)	
Net cash outflow for acquisitions and disposals		(17 824)
Management of liquid resources*		
Cash withdrawn from 7 day deposit	200	
Purchase of government securities	(5 000)	
Sale of government securities	4 300	
Sale of corporate bonds	1 200	
Net cash inflow from management of liquid resources		700

XYZ Group PLC includes as liquid resources term deposits of less than a year, government securities and AA rated corporate bonds.

Financing

Issue of ordinary share capital	600
Debt due within a year:	
increase in short-term borrowings	2006
repayment of secured loan	(850)
Debt due beyond a year:	
new secured loan repayable in 2000	1091
new unsecured loan repayable in 1998	1442
Capital element of finance lease rental payments	(1342)
	2347

Net cash inflow from financing   2947

Note 3 – analysis of net debt

	At 1 Jan 1996 £000	Cash flow £000	Acquisition* excl. cash and overdrafts) £000	Other non-cash changes £000	Exchange movement £000	At 31 Dec 1996 £000
Cash in hand, at bank	235	(1250)			1392	377
Overdrafts	(2528)	(5502)			(1422)	(9452)
		(6752)				
Debt due after 1 yr	(9640)	(2533)	(1749)	2560	(792)	(12154)
Debt due within 1 yr	(352)	(1156)	(837)	(2560)	1465	(3440)
Finance leases	(4170)	1342	(1231)	(2845)		(6904)
		(2347)				
Current asset investments	1240	(700)				540
Total	(15215)	(9799)	(3817)	(2845)	643	(31033)

Note 4 – cash flow relating to exceptional items

The operating cash outflows include under discontinued activities an outflow of £560 000, which relates to the £1 600 000 exceptional provision for a fundamental restructuring made in the 1995 accounts.

Note 5 – major non-cash transactions

(a) During the year the group entered into finance lease arrangements in respect of assets with a total capital value at the inception of the leases of £2 845 000.

(b) Part of the consideration for the purchases of subsidiary undertakings and the sale of a business that occurred during the year comprised shares and loan notes, respectively. Further details of the acquisitions and the disposal are set out below.

*This column would include any net debt (excluding cash and overdrafts) disposed of with a subsidiary undertaking.

Note 6 – purchase of subsidiary undertakings

	£000
Net assets acquired:	
Tangible fixed assets	12 194
Investments	1
Stocks	9 384
Debtors	13 856
Taxation recoverable	1 309
Cash at bank and in hand	1 439
Creditors	(21 715)
Bank overdrafts	(6 955)
Loans and finance leases	(3 817)
Deferred taxation	(165)
Minority shareholders' interests	(9)
	5 522
Goodwill	16 702
	22 224
Satisfied by:	
Shares allotted	9 519
Cash	12 705
	22 224

The subsidiary undertakings acquired during the year contributed £1 502 000 to the group's net operating cash flows, paid £1 308 000 in respect of net returns on investments and servicing of finance, paid £522 000 in respect of taxation and utilized £2 208 000 for capital expenditure.

Note 7 – sale of business

	£000
Net assets disposed of:	
Fixed assets	775
Stocks	5386
Debtors	474
	6635
Loss on disposal	(1227)
	5408
Satisfied by:	
Loan notes	1200
Cash	4208
	5408

The business sold during the year contributed £200 000 to the group's net operating cash flows, paid £252 000 in respect of net returns on investments and servicing of finance, paid £145 000 in respect of taxation and utilized £209 000 for capital expenditure.

Preparation of cash flow statements

Operating activities

First, we need to identify the net cash inflow from operating activities. The standard explains this as follows:

11 Cash flows from operating activities are in general the cash effects of transactions and other events relating to operating or trading activities, normally shown in the profit and loss account in arriving at operating profit. They include cash flows in respect of operating items relating to provisions, whether or not the provision was included in operating profit. Dividends received from equity accounted entities should be included as operating cash flows where the results are included as part of operating profit.

12 A reconciliation between the operating profit reported in the profit and loss account and the net cash flow from operating activities should be given either adjoining the cash flow statement or as a note. The reconciliation is not part of the cash flow statement: if adjoining the cash flow statement, it should be clearly labelled and kept separate. The reconciliation should disclose separately the movements in stocks, debtors and creditors related to operating activities and other differences between cash flows and profits. The reconciliation should also show separately the difference between dividends received and results taken into account for equity accounted entities.

There are two methods available to arrive at the net cash inflow from operating activities. The first is the direct method which shows cash receipts and payments, particularly those from customers, those to suppliers and those to employees; in other words cash accounting. The second is the indirect method which starts with the operating profit and adjusts it for non-cash charges and credits which will include reversing accruals and pre-payments. FRS 1 requires the indirect method as the ASB does not believe that the benefits to the users of the direct method outweigh the costs of preparing it.

Activity 6

Why would it be costly for companies to prepare net cash inflow from operating activities using the direct method?

Activity 6 feedback

Companies operate an accounting system that is geared towards accrual accounting. The direct method would require a company to either use an accounting system which directly records and analyses the cash flow in relation to each transaction, thus operating two accounting systems, or to adjust sales, cost of sales and other items in the profit and loss account for non-cash items, changes in working capital and other items which relate to investing or financing activities – a time-consuming business.

Returns on investments and servicing of finance

These are receipts resulting from the ownership of an investment and payments to providers of finance, non-equity shareholders and minority interests.

14 Cash inflows from returns on investments and servicing of finance include:
- (**a**) interest received, including any related tax recovered; and
- (**b**) dividends received, net of any tax credits (except dividends from equity accounted entities whose results are included as part of operating profit).

15 Cash outflows from returns on investments and servicing of finance include:
- (**a**) interest paid (even if capitalised), including any tax deducted and paid to the relevant tax authority;
- (**b**) cash flows that are treated as finance costs under FRS 4 (this will include issue costs on debt and non-equity share capital);
- (**c**) the interest element of finance lease rental payments;
- (**d**) dividends paid on non-equity shares of the entity; and
- (**e**) dividends paid to minority interests.

One item that was originally included in this list under FRS 1 original was dividends paid to equity shareholders. This now has its own separate heading, 'equity dividends paid'.

Activity 7

Is it logical to have dividend payments in with financing costs (as shown on the cash flow statement)?

Activity 7 feedback

The P&L account treats dividend payments as an appropriation of profit not as a cost of servicing finance such as interest paid to debenture holders. The cash flow statement continues this distinction between the two.

Capital expenditure and financial investment

19 The cash flows included in 'capital expenditure and financial investment' are those related to the acquisition or disposal of any fixed asset other than one required to the classified under 'acquisitions and disposals' as specified in paragraphs 22–24 of the FRS and any current asset investment not included in liquid resources dealt with in paragraphs 26–28. If no cash flows relating to financial investment fall to be included under this heading the caption may be reduced to 'capital expenditure'.

20 Cash inflows from 'capital expenditure and financial investment' include:
- (**a**) receipts from sales or disposals of property, plant or equipment; and
- (**b**) receipts from the repayment of the reporting entity's loans to other entities or sales of debt instruments of other entities other than receipts forming part of and acquisition or disposal or a movement in liquid resources, as specified respectively in paragraphs 22–24 and 26–28 of the FRS.

21 Cash outflows from 'capital expenditure and financial investment' include:
   (a) payments to acquire property, plant or equipment; and
   (b) loans made by the reporting entity and payments to acquire debt instruments of other entities other than payments forming part of an acquisition or disposal or a movement in liquid resources, as specified respectively in paragraphs 22–24 and 26–28 of the FRS.

Acquisitions and disposals

22 The cash flows included in 'acquisitions and disposals' are those related to the acquisition or disposal of any trade or business, or of an investment in an entity that is or, as a result of the transaction, becomes or ceases to be either an associate, a joint venture, or a subsidiary undertaking.

23 Cash inflows from 'acquisitions and disposals' include:
   (a) receipts from sales of investments in subsidiary undertakings, showing separately any balances of cash and overdrafts transferred as part of the sale;
   (b) receipts from sales of investments in associates or joint ventures; and
   (c) receipts from sales of trades or businesses.

24 Cash outflows from 'acquisitions and disposals' include:
   (a) payments to acquire investments in subsidiary undertakings, showing separately any balances of cash and overdrafts acquired;
   (b) payments to acquire investments in associates and joint ventures; and
   (c) payments to acquire trades or businesses.

Management of liquid resources

26 The 'management of liquid resources' section should include cash flows in respect of liquid resources defined in paragraph 2. Each entity should explain what it includes as liquid resources and any changes in its policy. The cash flows in this section can be shown in a single section with those under 'financing' provided that separate subtotals for each are given.

27 Cash inflows in management of liquid resources include:
   (a) withdrawals from short-term deposits not qualifying as cash in so far as not netted under paragraph 9(b); and
   (b) inflows from disposal or redemption of any other investments held as liquid resources.

28 Cash outflows in management of liquid resources include :
   (a) payments into short-term deposits not qualifying as cash in so far as not netted under paragraph 9(b); and
   (b) outflows to acquire any other investments held as liquid resources.

Activity 8

Two companies A and B both have spare cash of £1 million. Company A leaves this cash in its current account with the bank. Company B puts the cash on short-term deposit, with maturity in four months. What effect would this have on the cash flow of company A and B?

Activity 8 feedback

For company A there would be no effect. The £1 million cash will already have been reported through its cash inflow from operating activities.

Company B will record the £1 million as part of its management of liquid resources and therefore as a cash outflow. Thus company A would show an increase in cash of £1 million more than company B. Is this fair? Well it does reflect the cash position. FRS 1 (revised) has this to say on the issue:

9 The adoption of a strict cash approach and introduction of the section for cash flows relating to the management of liquid resources have the following advantages. The approach:

(**a**) avoids an arbitrary cut-off point in the definition of cash equivalents;

(**b**) distinguishes cash flows arising from accumulating or using liquid resources from those for other investing activities; and

(**c**) provides information about an entity's treasury activities that was not previously available to the extent that the instruments dealt in fell within the definition of cash equivalents.

Financing

29 Financing cash flows comprise receipts or repayments of principal from or to external providers of finance. The cash flows in this section can be shown in a single section with those under 'management of liquid resources' provided that separate subtotals for each are given.

30 Financing cash inflows include:

(**a**) receipts from issuing shares or other equity instruments; and

(**b**) receipts from issuing debentures, loans, notes and bonds, and from other long-term and short-term borrowings (other than overdrafts).

31 Financing cash outflows include:

(**a**) repayments of amounts borrowed (other than overdrafts);

(**b**) the capital element of finance lease rental payments;

(**c**) payments to reacquire or redeem the entity's shares; and

(**d**) payments of expenses or commissions on any issue of equity shares.

Practical examples

A simple example first of all.

Activity 9

The balance sheet of Axbrit plc for the year-ended 31 March 20X2 is as follows:

	20X2 £000s	20X1 £000s
Fixed assets	230	160
less depreciation	60	44
	170	116

Current assets		
Stock	25	20
Debtors	15	18
Cash	27	21
	67	59
Creditors payable within one year		
Creditors	27	21
Taxation	16	12
Dividend	20	18
	63	51
Net current assets	4	8
Creditors payable after one year		
10% debentures	32	30
Net assets	142	94
Represented by		
Ordinary share capital £1 shares	33	27
Share premium account	30	24
P&L account	79	43
	142	94

Prepare the cash flow statement for the year-ended 31 March 20X2 given that no fixed assets were sold during the year, ignoring ACT and given that the increase in debentures took place on 1 April 20X1.

Activity 9 feedback

The first item we need to calculate is net cash inflow from operating activities:

	£000s
Operating profit	75.2
Depreciation	16
Increase in stocks	(5)
Decrease in debtors	3
Increase in creditors	6
	95.2
Operating profit is calculated as follows:	
Increase in profit and loss	36
Add interest on loans	3.2
Taxation	16
Dividend	20
	75.2

Cash flow statement for the year-ended 31.3.X2

Net cash inflow from operating activities (note 1)	95.2
Returns on investments and servicing of finance	(3.2)

Tax paid	(12)
Capital expenditure	(70)
	10
Equity dividends paid	(18)
Management of liquid resources	(8)
Financing (note 1)	14
Increase in cash	6

Notes to the cash flow

Several notes are required to the cash flow statement as identified on p. 660. For the example at Activity 9 note 1 would be required to show gross cash flows. This is not difficult to prepare and we do not bother with its reproduction here.

Also a note reconciling the movement of cash in the period with the movement in net debt should be provided and an analysis from opening to closing component amounts. For Activity 9 these notes would appear as follows:

Reconciliation of net cash flow to movement in net debt

	£000s
Increase in cash in the period	6
Cash from issue of debentures	(2)
Change in net debt	4
Net debt at 1.4.X1	(9)
Net debt at 31.3.X2	(5)

Analysis of changes in net debt

	At 1.4.X1 £000	Cash flows £000	Other changes £000	At 31.3.X2 £000
Cash in bank	21	6		27
Debt due after one year	(30)	(2)		(32)
	(9)	4		(5)

A more complicated example follows.

Activity 10

From the P&L account and balance sheets of Thomas Manufacturing plc given below prepare the cash flow statement for the year-ended 31 December 20X5.

Thomas Manufacturing plc
P&L account for the year-ended 31.12.X5

	£000	£000
Turnover		5000
Change in stocks of finished goods and work in progress		500
Own work capitalized		150
Other operating income		50
Raw materials and consumables	(2000)	
Other external charges	(750)	
		(2750)
Staff costs		(1500)
Depreciation and other amounts written off tangible and intangible assets		(400)
Other operating charges		(100)
		950
Income from fixed asset investments (dividends)		20
Other interest receivable		5
		975
Interest payable and similar charges		(160)
Profit on ordinary activities before taxation		815
Tax on profit on ordinary activities		(325)
Profit on ordinary activities after taxation		490
Extraordinary income	70	
Extraordinary charges	(90)	
Extraordinary loss	(20)	
Tax on extraordinary loss	8	
		(12)
Profit for the financial year		478
Dividends:		
Paid	(100)	
Proposed	(150)	
		(250)
Retained profit for the financial year		228

Balance sheet as at 31.12.X5

31.12.X4

Net £000	Cost £000		Cost £000	Depreciation etc. £000	Net £000
		Fixed assets			
100	200	Intangible assets	350	200	150
800	1500	Tangible assets	2500	775	1725
100	100	Investments	200	–	200
1000	1800		3050	975	2075

	Current assets	
1000	Stocks	1600
1000	Debtors	1200
50	Investments	–
250	Cash at bank and in hand	30
2300		2830
	Creditors: amounts falling due within 1 year	
–	Bank loans	(257)
(500)	Trade creditors	(600)
(200)	Taxation	(210)
(100)	Proposed dividend	(150)
(43)	ACT on proposed dividend	(64)
(843)		(1281)

1457	*Net current assets*	1549
2457	*Total assets less current liabilities*	3624

		Financed by creditors: amounts falling due after more than 1 year	
980		Debenture loans	790
		Provisions for liabilities and charges	
100		Deferred tax	129
		Capital and reserves	
		Called-up share capital:	
	1000	Ordinary shares (£1)	1500
	200	Share premium account	300
	–	Revaluation reserve	500
	177	P&L account	405
1377			2705
2457			3624

Notes:

1 As at 1 January 20X5, freehold land was revalued from £500 000 to £1 000 000.

2 During the year-ended 31 December 20X5, plant and machinery costing £300 000, written down to £50 000 at 31 December 20X4, was sold for £75 000. These book gains and losses were adjusted into the depreciation charge in the P&L account.

3 'Own work capitalized' refers to development work carried forward as an 'intangible asset'.

4 Debentures with a nominal value of £190 000 were redeemed at par during the year.

5 Ordinary shares were issued for cash during the year; there were no redemptions or purchases of the company's own shares.

6 The investments shown as current assets at 31 December 20X4 were realized during the year at £50 000.

7 During 20X5, the mainstream corporation tax charge for 20X4 was settled and paid in the sum of £180 000.

8 Corporation tax rate 40%; income tax basic rate 30%. Corporation tax payable nine months after the year-end.

Activity 10 feedback

Notes to the cash flow statement:

1 Reconciliation of operating profit to net cash inflow from operating activities.

	£000s
Operating profit (815 – 25 + 160)	950
Extraordinary items	(20)
Depreciation charge	425
Profit on sale of tangible fixed assets	(25)
Increase in stocks	(600)
Increase in debtors	(200)
Increase in creditors	100
Net cash inflow from operating activities	630

Cash flow statement for the year-ended 31.12.X5	£000s	£000s
Net cash inflow from operating activities	650	
Outflow from extraordinary items	(20)	630
Return on investments and servicing of finance		
interest received	25	
interest paid	(160)	
Net cash outflow from returns on investment and servicing of finance		(135)
Taxation		
Corporate tax paid		(257)
Capital expenditure		
Payments to acquire intangible fixed assets	(150)	
Payments to acquire tangible fixed assets	(900)	
Receipts from sales to tangible fixed assets	75	
Net cash outflow from investing activities		(975)
		(737)
Equity dividends paid		(200)
		(937)
Management of liquid resources		
Increase in loans	257	
Sales of investments	50	307
Financing		
Issue of ordinary share capital	600	
Repurchase of debentures	(190)	
Net cash inflow from financing		410
Decrease in cash		(220)

The need for FRS 1 (revised)

The need for the preparation of a cash flow statement has now been widely accepted by accounting professionals and companies alike. The revised FRS has dealt with many of the problems that the original standard had not, least of which was the controversial requirement to show cash flow in terms of cash and cash equivalents. The removal of cash equivalents however gave rise to the need to identify the management of liquid resources. These liquid resources are a key element in identifying how an entity manages their cash position, and therefore its appearance on the cash flow statement is to be welcomed.

Summary

Within this chapter we have attempted to show you how to draw up a cash flow statement using the indirect method and we have highlighted some of the problems associated with it. Remember the issue of cash accounting was discussed earlier, in some detail, in Chapter 9. It may be worthwhile for you to reread that chapter. On the whole the revised cash flow statement is an improvement on its predessor.

Exercises

1 The draft P&L account and source and application of funds statement of Metamorphose is set out below for the year-ended 30 November 1997.
   You are required to:
   (a) Prepare a detailed cash flow statement for the year-ended 30 November 1997.
   (5 marks)
   (b) Comment on the usefulness of both cash flow statements and source and application of funds statements in financial reporting.
   (15 marks)

Metamorphose
Draft P&L account year-ended 30.11.97

	£	£
Credit sales		20 000
Opening stock	3000	
Purchases	4000	
	7000	
Closing stock	2000	
Cost of goods sold		5 000
Gross profit		15 000
Depreciation	2000	
Loss on sale of asset	1500	
Wages	5000	
		8 500
Net profit		6 500
Taxation		3 000
		3 500
Dividends		3 000
Retained profit		500

Metamorphose
Draft source and application of funds statement year-ended 30.11.97

	£	£
Adjusted profit		10 000
Proceeds on sale of asset		2 000
		12 000
Loan		4 000
		16 000
Purchase of machine	3000	
Taxation	4000	
Dividends	2000	
		9 000
		7 000
Increase/(decrease) in working capital		
Decrease in stock	(1000)	
Increase in debtors	5000	
Decrease in creditors	2000	
	6000	

	£	
Closing cash	2400	
Opening cash	1400	
		1000
		7 000

(20 marks)
(ACCA)

2   'Cash is a very difficult figure to fiddle' (David Tweedie). Does FRS 1 fully support this statement?

3   The balance sheet of CF plc for the year-ended 31 December 1994, together with comparative figures for the previous year, is shown below (all figures £000)

	1994		*1993*	
Fixed assets	270		180	
Less depreciation	(90)		(56)	
	180		124	
Current assets				
Stock	50		42	
Debtors	40		33	
Cash	–		11	
		90		86
Current liabilities				
Trade and operating				
creditors	(33)		(24)	
Taxation	(19)		(17)	
Dividend	(28)		(26)	
Bank overdraft	(10)		–	

	(90)	(67)
Net current assets	–	19
Net assets	180	143
Represented by		
Ordinary share capital £1 shares	25	20
Share premium	10	8
P&L account	65	55
Shareholders' funds	100	83
15% debentures, repayable 1998	80	60
Capital employed	180	143

You are informed that: there were no sales of fixed assets during 1994; the company does not pay interim dividends; and new debentures and shares issued in 1994 were issued on 1 January.

Required:

(a) **Show your calculation of the operating profit of CF plc for the year-ended 31 December 1994.** (4 marks)

(b) **Prepare a cash flow statement for the year, in accordance with FRS 1 'Cash Flow Statements', including 'Note 1' as required by that standard, i.e. the reconciliation of operating profit to net cash inflow from operating activities.** (10 marks)

(c) **State the headings of the three other notes which you would be required to include in practice under FRS 1.** (2 marks)

(d) **Comment on the implications of the information given in the question plus the statements you have prepared, regarding the financial position of the company.** (6 marks)

(e) **FRS 1 supports the use of the indirect method of arriving at the net cash inflow from operating activities, which is the method you have used to prepare 'Note 1' required in part (b) of this question.**
What is the direct method of arriving at the net cash inflow from operations? State, with reasons, whether you agree with the FRS 1 acceptance of the indirect method. (3 marks)
(25 marks)
(ACCA)

4 The following are the financial statements, with an extract from the notes, of Plath plc:
Plath plc
P&L account for the year-ended 31.3.92

	£m
Turnover	1162
Cost of sales	(866)
Gross profit	296
Distribution costs	(47)
Administrative expenses	(110)
Operating profit	139
Interest received	79
Interest paid	(55)
Profit before taxation	163

	Taxation	(24)
	Profit for the financial year	139
	Dividends	(49)
	Retained profit for the financial year	90

Plath plc
Balance sheet as at 31.3.92

31.3.91		
£m		£m
	Fixed assets	
234	Intangible assets	277
600	Tangible assets	1 023
68	Investments	69
902		1369
	Current assets	
128	Stocks	246
353	Debtors	460
20	Investments	–
124	Cash at bank and in hand	250
625		956
	Creditors: amounts falling due within one year	
185	Bank loans and overdrafts	388
311	Trade creditors	244
25	Taxation	42
22	Proposed dividend	49
543		723
82	*Net current assets*	233
984	*Total assets less current liabilities*	1602
	Creditors: amounts falling due after more	
555	*than one year*	756
	Provisions for liabilities and charges	
2	Deferred taxation	3
427		843
	Capital and reserves	
24	Called up share capital	29
377	Share premium	447
–	Revaluation reserve	251
26	Profit and loss	116
427		843

Notes

1 Debentures were issued at a premium of 5%. The premium was credited to the P&L account.

2 The trading profit is after charging depreciation on the tangible fixed assets of £22 million and amortization on the intangible fixed assets of £7 million.

3 The sale of the short-term investments realized £25 million.

4 During the year-ended 31 March 1992, plant and machinery, costing £1464 million, written down to £244 million at 31 March 1994, was sold for £250 million.

5 During the year-ended 31 March 1992 25 million 20p shares were issued at a premium of £2.80.

Required:

(a) **Prepare a cash flow statement of Plath plc for the year-ended 31 March 1992 in compliance with FRS 1. Include the following notes to the cash flow statements:**

1 **Reconciliation of operating profit to net cash inflow from operating activities.**

2 **Analysis of cash flows or headings netted in the cash flow statement.**

3 **Analysis of net debt.** (25 marks)

(b) **Explain the treatment of the depreciation charge and of the dividends paid.**

(5 marks)

(c) **Comment on the usefulness of the statement prepared for part (a).**

(10 marks)

(40 marks)

(Work to the nearest £ million.) (ACCA)

5 In November 1996 the Accounting Standards Board issued FRS 1 (Revised) – *Cash Flow Statements*. The appendix to FRS 1 contains a number of examples of cash flow statements drawn up in accordance with the new Standard. The examples given present the cash flows under a number of standard headings, as shown below.

		£000
(i)	Cash flow from operating activities	X
(ii)	Returns on investments and servicing of finance	X
(iii)	Taxation	X
(iv)	Capital expenditure and financial investment	X
(v)	Acquisitions and disposals	X
(vi)	Equity dividends paid	X
(vii)	Management of liquid resources	X
(viii)	Financing	X
	Decrease in cash in the period	X

Requirements:

(a) **Describe the cash flows which are reported under EACH of the headings (i) to (viii), given above.** (10 marks)

(b) **Summarise the changes which FRS 1 (Revised) made to the old FRS 1, and explain why each change was considered necessary by the Accounting Standards Board.** (10 marks)

(20 marks)

6 The draft balance sheets for the years to 31 March 1998 and 1997 of Ladway plc are shown below:

	1998		1997	
Fixed assets	£m	£m	£m	£m
Intangible assets – goodwill		450		410
Tangible assets		2480		1830
		2930		2240

Current assets

Stock	920		763	
Debtors	642		472	
Cash	–		34	
	1562		1269	

Creditors: amounts falling due within one year

Creditors	680		518	
Accrued interest	4		–	
Bank overdraft	63		–	
Proposed dividends	210		180	
Taxation	176		185	
Deferred credit – government grants	50		40	
	(1183)		(923)	

Net current assets		379		346
Creditors: amounts falling due after more than one year				
8% Debenture 2003		(200)		–
Provisions for liabilities and charges				
Government grants	210		160	
Deferred tax	52		30	
Environmental provision	76	(338)	24	(214)
Net assets		2771		2372

Share capital and reserves

Ordinary shares of £1 each		500		400
10% Preference capital		350		350
		850		750

Reserves:

Share premium account	90		70	
Revaluation reserve	170		–	
Profit and loss account	1661	1921	1552	1622
		2771		2372

The draft profit and loss account for Ladway plc for the year to 31 March 1998 is as follows:

		£m
Turnover		3655
Cost of sales:		
Depreciation of:		
– tangibles	366	
– goodwill	36	
Other costs	2522	(2924)
Gross profit for period		731
Other operating income:		
– government grant		50
		781

Distribution costs	75	
Administration	56	
Environmental provision	67	(198)
		583
Interest		
– Debenture		(12)
Profit before tax		571
Taxation		(177)
Profit for the period after tax		394
Dividends:		
ordinary		
– interim	40	
– final	210	
preference	35	(285)
Retained profit for the period		109

The following information is relevant:
Tangible fixed assets:
- **(i)** these include land which was revalued giving a surplus of £170 million during the period;
- **(ii)** the company's motor vehicle haulage fleet was replaced during the year. The fleet originally cost £42 million and had been written down to £11 million at the time of its replacement. The gross cost of the fleet replacement was £180 million and a trade in allowance of £14 million was given for the old vehicles;
- **(iii)** the company acquired some new plant on 1 July 1997 at a cost of £120 million from Bromway plc. An arrangement was made on the same day for the liability for the plant to be settled by Ladway plc issuing at par an 8% debenture dated 2003 to Bromway plc. The value by which the debenture exceeded the liability for the plant was received from Bromway plc in cash.

Environmental provision:
The provision represents an estimate of the cost of environmental improvements relating to the company's mining activities.

Ordinary share issues:
During the year Ladway plc made a bonus issue from the share premium account of one for every ten shares held. Later Ladway plc made a further share issue for cash.

Required:
(a) A cash flow statement for Ladway plc for the year to 31 March 1998 prepared in accordance with FRS 1 'Cash Flow Statements (revised 1996)'.

(20 marks)

The revision of FRS 1 'Cash Flow Statements' by the Accounting Standards Board includes a requirement for companies to disclose a note that reconciles the movement of cash in the period with the movement in **net debt**. This statement is not part of the cash flow statement but usually adjoins it.

Required:

(b) Describe the composition of the reconciliation to net debt, and discuss the relevance and usefulness of this information to users of financial statements.

(5 marks)

(25 marks)

7 The following draft financial statements relate to the Duke Group plc.

Draft Group Balance Sheet at 31 May 2000

	2000 £m	1999 £m
Fixed assets:		
Intangible assets – goodwill	90	83
Tangible assets	1239	1010
Investments	780	270
	2109	1363
Current assets:		
Stocks	750	588
Debtors	660	530
Cash at bank and in hand	45	140
	1455	1258
Creditors: amounts falling due within one year	(1501)	(1213)
Net current assets	(46)	45
Total assets less current liabilities	2063	1408
Creditors: amounts falling due after more than one year	(1262)	(930)
Minority interests – equity	(250)	(150)
	551	328
Capital and reserves:		
Called up share capital:		
– ordinary shares of £1	100	70
– 7% redeemable preference shares of £1 each	136	130
Share premium account	85	15
Revaluation reserve	30	10
Profit and loss account	200	103
	551	328

Draft Group Profit and Loss Account for the year ended 31 May 2000

	£m	£m
Turnover – continuing operations	5795	
– acquisitions	1515	
Cost of sales		7310
		(5920)
Gross profit		1390
Distribution and administrative expenses		(772)
Share of operating profit in associate		98

Operating profit – continuing operations		598
– acquisitions		118
		716
Profit on sale of tangible fixed assets		15
Interest receivable	34	
Interest payable	(22)	
		12
Profit on ordinary activities before taxation		743
Tax on profit on ordinary activities		(213)
(including tax on income from associated undertakings £15 million)		
Profit on ordinary activities after taxation		530
Minority interest – equity		(97)
Profit attributable to members of the parent company		433
Dividends	135	
Other non-equity appropriations	6	(141)
Retained profit for the year		292

Group Statement of Total Recognised Gains and Losses for the year ended 31 May 2000

	£m
Profit attributable to members of the parent company	433
Surplus on revaluation of fixed assets	20
Exchange difference on retranslation of foreign equity investment	(205)
Exchange difference on loan to finance foreign equity investment	10
	258

Reconciliation of Shareholders' Funds for the year ended 31 May 2000

Total recognised gains and losses	258
Dividends	(135)
Other movements:	
New shares issued	100
Total movements during the year	223
Shareholders' funds at 1 June 1999	328
Shareholders' funds at 31 May 2000	551

The following information is relevant to the Duke Group plc.
(i) Duke acquired an 80 per cent holding in Regent plc on 1 June 1999. The fair values of the assets of Regent on 1 June 1999 were as follows:

	£m
Tangible fixed assets	60
Stocks	30
Debtors	25
Cash at bank and in hand	35
Trade creditors	(20)
Corporation tax	(30)
	100

The purchase consideration was £97 million and comprised 20 million ordinary shares of £1 in Duke, valued at £4, and £17 million in cash. The group amortizes goodwill over ten years.

(ii) The tangible fixed asset movement for the period comprised the following amounts at net book value:

	£m
Balance at 1 June 1999	1010
Additions (including Regent)	278
Revaluations of properties	20
Disposals	(30)
Depreciation	(39)
Balance at 31 May 2000	1239

(iii) There have been no sales of fixed asset investment in the year. The investments included under fixed assets comprised the following items:

	£m 2000	£m 1999
Investment in associated company	300	220
Trade investment (including purchase of foreign equity investment of £400m equivalent during year to 31 May 2000)	480	50
	780	270

(iv) Interest receivable included in debtors was £15m as at 31 May 1999 and £17m as at 31 May 2000.

(v) Creditors: amounts falling due within one year comprised the following items:

	£m 2000	£m 1999
Trade creditors (including interest payable £9m (2000) Nil (1999))	1193	913
Corporation tax	203	200
Dividend	105	100
	1501	1213

(vi) Duke had alllotted 10 million ordinary shares of £1 at a price of £2 upon the exercise of directors' options during the year.

(vii) Included in creditors: amounts payable after more than one year is a bill of exchange for £100 million (raised 30 June 1999) which was given to a supplier on the purchase of fixed assets and which is payable on 1 July 2001.

(viii) The exchange differences included in the Statement of Total Recognised Gains and Losses relate to a transaction involving a foreign equity investment. A loan of £300 million was taken out during the year to finance a foreign equity investment in Peer of £400 million. Both amounts are after retranslation at 31 May 2000.

(ix) The preference share dividends are always paid in full on 1 July each year and at 31 May 2000 the preference shares have a par value of £130 million.

Required:

(a) **Prepare a group cash flow statement using the indirect method for the Duke Group plc for the year ended 31 May 2000 in accordance with the requirements of FRSI (Revised) 'Cash Flow Statements'.**

Your answer should include the following:
(i)   a reconciliation of operating profit to operating cash flows;
(ii) an analysis of cash flows for any headings netted in the cash flow statement.
      The notes regarding the acquisition of the subsidiary and a reconciliation
      of net cash flow to movement in net debt are not required.   (24 marks)
(b) Discuss the nature of the additional information which is provided by the Group
    Cash Flow Statement of the Duke group in (a) above as compared to the Group
    Profit and Loss Account and Group Balance Sheet of Duke.   (6 marks)
    (30 marks)
    ACCA FRE JUNE 2000

8 L plc processes tea and coffee, and manufactures health foods. The company's latest trial
   balance at 31 March 2000 is as follows:

	£000	£000
Administrative expense	3 000	
Bank	300	
Cost of sales – tea	3 000	
Cost of sales – coffee	9 000	
Cost of sales – health foods	7 000	
Creditors		1 700
Debtors	2 800	
Deferred taxation		900
Distribution costs	4 000	
Interest	4 950	
Interim dividend paid	1 000	
Loans (repayable 2005)		45 000
Profit and loss		86 000
Reorganization costs	3 100	
Sales – tea		18 000
Sales – coffee		11 000
Sales – health foods		15 000
Share capital		77 000
Stock at 31 March 2000	2 400	
Tangible fixed assets	214 000	
Taxation	50	
	254 600	254 600

(i)   The company closed its coffee-processing factory during the year. According to the trial
      balance, additional operating costs associated with this reorganisation have amounted
      to £3.1 million so far. The directors expect that they will have to pay a further £2.4 mil-
      lion in order to complete this closure.
(ii) Administrative expenses and distribution costs can be allocated as follows:

	Administration	Distribution
Tea	30%	40%
Coffee	20%	10%
Health foods	50%	50%

(iii) L plc guarantees that all of its health food products are made from organic ingredients.
      Just before the year end it was discovered that some of its range included soya protein
      which had been genetically modified. The company was forced to recall these products
      from supermarkets and other retail outlets and to offer refunds to customers. The final

cost of this event will not be determined with any accuracy before the financial statements have been finalised, but it is likely to be between £300 000 and £700 000. The directors are of the opinion that this cost is material.

(iv)   Several of L plc's customers claim to have suffered a severe allergic reaction to a new range of health foods introduced by the company during the year. These customers are seeking compensation which is material in amount. L plc does not accept responsibility and the company's lawyers have advised that the company has a reasonably strong case.

(v)   The balance on the taxation account is the amount remaining after the settlement of the tax charge for the year ended 31 March 1999. The directors have estimated the charge for the current year at £2.0 million.

(vi)   The provision for deferred tax is to be increased by £350 000. The company is making no provision for potential liabilities in respect of deferred taxation of £1.4 million.

(vii)   The directors have proposed a final dividend of £1.2 million.

(viii)   During the year the company purchased tangible fixed assets costing £19 million. Depreciation for the year has been included in the expenses in the trial balance and amounts to £4.9 million. During the year the company sold £9.1 million tangible fixed assets which had a net book value of £12.0 million. The loss on disposal has already been taken into account in calculating the relevant costs in the trial balance.

L plc's balance sheet at 31 March 1999 was as follows:

	£000	£000
Fixed assets		
Tangible assets		211 900
Current assets		
Stock	2 100	
Trade debtors	2 300	
Bank	1 200	
	5 600	
Creditors: amounts due within one year		
Trade creditors	2 300	
Taxation	7 700	
Proposed dividend	1 600	
	11 600	
Net current liabilities		(6 000)
		205 900
Creditors: amounts due after one year		
Loans		42 000
		163 900
Provision for liabilities and charges		
Deferred taxation		900
		163 000
Share capital		77 000
Profit and loss		86 000
		163 000

Requirements:

(a) **Prepare L plc's cash flow statement for the year ended 31 March 2000. This should be in the form prescribed by FRS 1.**

(Note: It is also possible to produce this statement from the information provided in the trial balance and opening balance sheet.)

(19 marks)

(b) **The comparative figures in L plc's balance sheet would have made it clear that the cash balance had changed from £1.2 million to £0.3 million. This might suggest that the cash flow statement is unnecessary.**

Explain whether the cash flow statement provides useful information.

(4 marks)

(23 marks)

CIMA(S) MAY 2000

28

Interpretation of financial statements

After reading this chapter you should be able to:
- identify the needs of users wishing to make use of accounting information
- explain the technique of ratio analysis and calculate appropriate ratios
- explain what each of the ratios means, and discuss their limitations
- identify additional information that users may require to aid their analysis
- briefly discuss multivariate analysis.

Introduction

We have been concerned in several chapters of this book with the provision of financial information to users which presents a true and fair view of the entity. We have assumed that users intend to use this information to gain some insight as to the reporting entity's stability, performance, future prospects and/or whatever else may interest them. We have paid little attention so far to how users can use this information or which tools of analysis they require in order to use it.

Accounting information and users

Financial statements provide valuable information for both the owners of the business and for any potential owners/investors. Within Chapter 2 we identified the users of accounting information and their differing needs.

The following activity provides a useful piece of revision.

Activity 1

Identify the users of accounting information and their needs/objectives.

Activity 1 feedback

- *Investors/owners* – is the money invested in the business making a suitable return for them or could it earn more if invested elsewhere? Is the business a safe investment, that is, is it likely to become insolvent/bankrupt? Should the investors invest more money in the business?

- *Suppliers* – is the business able to pay for the goods bought on credit? Will the business continue to be a recipient of the goods the supplier produces?
- *Customers* – is the business able to supply the goods the customer requires and when it requires them? Will the business continue in operation so that guarantees on goods purchased will be met?
- *Lenders* – is there adequate security for the loan made? Does the business make a sufficient profit and have enough cash available to make the necessary payments to the lender of interest and capital?
- *Employee* – does the business make sufficient profit and have enough cash available to make the necessary payments to the employees? Will the business continue in operation at its current level so that the employee has secure employment?
- *Government* – to calculate taxation due. To aid decision making in respect of the economy as a whole 'and as controller of the well being of United Kingdom plc'.
- *Public* – the majority of their needs is in respect of employment, pollution and health and safety which is not particularly, as yet, provided by financial statements, but note our comments in Chapter 9 in respect of environmental accounting.

From the feedback to the above activity it is possible to identify three general areas of interest in which users' needs and objectives may lie.

- *Financial status* – can the business pay its way, is it in fact *liquid*?
- *Performance* – how successful is the business, is it making a reasonable profit, is it utilising its assets to the fullest, is it in fact *profitable* and *efficient*?
- *Investment* – is the business a suitable investment for shareholders or would returns be greater if they invested elsewhere, is it a good *investment*?

Benchmarking

These three general areas of interest require answers to questions which are subjective in nature, not objective. For instance, how do we judge whether a profit is reasonable? We could do so by comparing current profit to profit made in previous years or to profit made by other businesses. In other words we use benchmarks against which we compare current performance, financial status and investment potential. However, we need to take great care in carrying out this benchmarking so that we do not invalidate the results.

Consider, for example, your opinion of the disco you attended last night. You may think it was the best disco you have ever attended; your friend may think it was the worst night out he or she ever had. This is because the experiences/benchmarks you each have are different and you are making a subjective judgement on how the current disco compares with those you previously attended. Thus, in setting benchmarks against which we can compare a company we must be aware of the limitations of this comparison.

First we need to identify benchmarks/indicators we can use, then consider their limitations.

Four possible benchmarks are:

- past period achievements
- budgeted achievements
- other business' achievements
- averages of business' achievements in the same area.

> ## Activity 2
>
> Identify for each indicator above its uses and limitations.

Activity 2 feedback

- Past periods.
  Uses – to identify whether current activity is better or worse than previous periods.
  Limitations – external factors may have influenced activity levels, e.g. public awareness of environmental issues may have necessitated a change in manufacturing process leading to increased costs.
- Budgets.
  Uses – has current activity matched planned activity?
  Limitations – the budget may not be a valid standard of performance, e.g. underlying assumptions may have been unrealistic or set at too high a level.
- Other businesses.
  Uses – is our business performing as well?
  Limitations – businesses may not be truly comparable with regard to size and type, e.g. grocery sole trader compared to supermarket; manufacturer compared to retailer.
  External factors may affect one business, e.g. lengthy strike.
  Accounting policies and bases on which accounting information is prepared may be different, e.g. stock valuations, depreciation, historic cost or revalued amount, treatment of research and development, treatment of goodwill.
- Industry averages have uses and limitations very similar to those of other businesses. Additionally, an average is simply that – an average which takes account of the best and the worst.

Each of the four benchmarks identified are commonly used in assessing business status, performance and potential, but interpretation of accounts is highly subjective and requires skilled judgement, bearing in mind the limitations of these benchmarks.

Technique of ratio analysis

Financial statements identify for us a multitude of figures, for example, profit before tax, gross profit, total of fixed assets, net current assets.

However, these figures do not mean very much unless we can compare them to something else. For example, looking at a set of financial statements for a high street retailer may tell us that profit before tax is £3 million, but will not tell us if this is a good profit. It will probably be more than the profit of a sole trader in the same industry but does it mean the high street retailer is performing better?

> ## Activity 3
>
> You have £1150 to invest and discover that type 1 investment will provide interest of £68 per annum and type 2 investment will provide a single interest payment of £341 after five years.
>   Which investment would you choose, assuming no compound interest and no change in the value of the pound?

Activity 3 feedback

Investment 1 provides a return of 68/1150 = 5.91% per annum. Investment 2 a return of 68.2/1150 = 5.93% per annum. Thus investment 2 provides the highest return.

In the above we compared the return with the amount invested and expressed the figures in the same units – percentage per annum. We were then able to identify which investment provided the better return.

The next section identifies which figures in a set of financial statements it would be useful to compare to evaluate financial status, performance and investment potential of a business. The financial statements used are those of Serendipity plc which are reproduced below.

Serendipity plc P&L accounts

	year-ended 31.12.X4		year-ended 31.12.X5	
	£000	£000	£000	£000
Sales		584		972
Opening stock	31		47	
Purchases	405		700	
	436		747	
Closing stock	47		62	
		389		685
Gross profit		195		287
Wages and salaries	78		101	
Depreciation	16		31	
Debenture interest	–		8	
Other expenses	54		62	
		148		202
Net profit before tax		47		85
Taxation		16		39
Net profit after tax		31		46
Proposed dividend		16		23
Retained profit for year		15		23

Serendipity balance sheet as at

	31.12.X4		31.12.95	
	£000	£000	£000	£000
Fixed assets		280		428
Current assets				
stock	47		62	
debtors	70		156	
bank	39		16	
	156		234	

Creditors less than 1 year		
creditors	39	109
taxation	16	39
proposed dividends	16	23
	71	171
Net current assets	85	63
creditors greater than 1 year		
10% debentures	–	80
	365	411
Financed by		
ordinary share capital	272	295
retained profits	93	116
	365	411

Before beginning any ratio analysis it is useful to look at the accounts and identify any changes from one year to the next.

Activity 4

Compare and contrast each item on the balance sheet and P&L of Serendipity plc with the figure for the previous year. Note five points of interest from this comparison.

Activity 4 feedback

You should have identified five from the following:
- sales have increased in X5
- cost of sales has increased
- expenses have increased
- profit after tax has increased by 50%
- fixed assets have increased substantially
- net current assets have reduced
- shares and debentures have been increased in X5.

Having identified various points of interest we are now ready to carry out the ratio analysis.

Performance

The first ratio to be considered is return on capital employed (ROCE)

$$ \text{ROCE} = \frac{\text{profit before taxation and long-term loan interest}}{\text{net assets (or capital employed including long-term loan)}} $$

This ratio identifies how much profit the business has made from the capital invested in it and answers the question: would the owners be better off selling the business and placing the proceeds on a bank deposit account?

Activity 5

Calculate the ROCE for Serendipity plc for X4 and X5.

Activity 5 feedback

	X4	X5
ROCE	47/365 = 12.87%	93/491 = 18.9%

This ratio has increased from X4 to X5 indicating an increase in profitability of the business from the increased investment.

But where has this increased profitability come from? Is it because the business has increased sale prices or reduced expenses, that is, increased net profit margins, or is it because the business has increased the volume of trade compared to the capital employed?

These two questions can be expressed as ratios as follows:

$$\text{net profit margin} = \frac{\text{profit before tax and long-term interest}}{\text{sales}}$$

$$\text{volume of trade} = \frac{\text{sales}}{\text{capital employed}}$$

Calculating these two ratios for Serendipity plc we have

	X4	X5
net profit margin	47/584 = 8%	93/972 = 9.6%

Net profit margin has increased indicating benefit gained from control of expenses or increased sale prices

volume of trade	584/365 = 1.6 times	972/491 = 1.98 times.

This indicates that Serendipity plc is earning more sales per pound of net assets or capital employed in X5 than X4.

The three ratios we have looked at so far have the following relationship:

$$\text{ROCE} = \text{margin} \times \text{volume}$$
$$\frac{P}{CE} = \frac{P}{S} \times \frac{S}{CE}$$

This relationship can be shown as a family tree

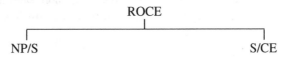

This family tree can be expanded and will provide a framework for ratio analysis. For example:

net profit/sales = gross profit/sales − expenses/sales

or, in brief

$$\frac{GP}{S} - \frac{E}{S}$$

Sales/capital employed can be inverted to capital employed/sales that is the value of assets held per pound of sales, and then expanded to

fixed assets/sales + net current assets/sales

or, in brief

$$\frac{FA}{S} + \frac{NCA}{S}$$

Activity 6

Calculate these four further ratios for Serendipity plc and interpret them.

Activity 6 feedback

	X4	X5
Gross profit margin	195/584 = 33.3%	287/972 = 29.5%

This demonstrates a reduction in gross profit probably due to a decrease in sale prices which has generated more sales or an increase in cost of goods sold

	X4	X5
Expenses/sales	148/584 = 25.3%	194/972 = 20%

This has decreased from X4 to X5 indicating a better control of expenses.

	X4	X5
FA/S	280/584 = 0.48	428/972 = 0.44

If we invert the above then for X4 we have 2.08 and for X5 2.27, that is, fixed assets have generated 2.08 times their value in sales in X4 and 2.27 times their value in sales in X5. Fixed assets are earning more sales.

	X4	X5
NCA/S	85/584 = 0.15	63/972 = 0.06

Inverting gives X4 6.87 and X5 15.4.

Net current assets are also earning more sales in X5 than X4.

The family tree of ratios, or pyramid, now looks like this:

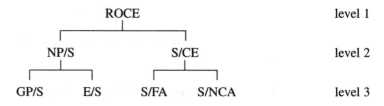

ROCE	level 1
NP/S S/CE	level 2
GP/S E/S S/FA S/NCA	level 3

The pyramid can be extended to level 4 by comparing individual expenses to sales and breaking down the fixed assets and net current assets into their constituent parts.

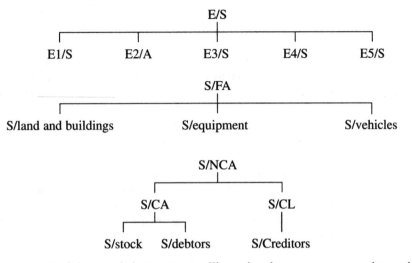

However, as stock is recorded at cost not selling price then a more appropriate ratio than S/stock would be cost of goods sold/stock, and as creditors relates to goods purchased on credit it would be better to look at credit purchases/creditors. Lastly S/debtors would be more appropriate as credit sales/debtors.

Example 1 demonstrates the calculation and interpretation of these level 4 ratios.

Example 1

The following information is provided for Anne Ltd as at 31 December 20X4:

	£000s
Cost of goods sold	220
Average stock for the year	50
Trade creditors	86
Credit purchases	216
Trade debtors	96
Credit sales	284

Cost of goods sold/stock = 220/50 = 4.4, that is, 4.4 times the average stock level has been used in cost of goods sold for the year. This could be written much simpler as: stock is turned over every 83 days, i.e. 365/4.4 = 83 days.

The ratio is therefore

$$\frac{\text{average stock}}{\text{cost of goods sold}} \times 365$$

The debtors and creditors' ratios are written as:

$$\frac{\text{trade debtors}}{\text{credit sales}} \times 365$$

which will tell us on average how long it takes debtors to pay

$$\frac{\text{trade creditors}}{\text{credit purchases}} \times 365$$

which will tell us how long on average it takes the business to pay its creditors.

The information provided above does not give a figure for credit sales or credit purchases; therefore we will have to use total sales and total purchases as an approximation

$$\text{debtors' period} = 96 \times 365/284 = 123 \text{ days}$$
$$\text{creditors' period} = 86 \times 365/216 = 145 \text{ days}$$

Whether or not these level 4 ratios should be calculated when carrying out a ratio analysis will depend upon the information produced at previous levels. For example, when considering Serendipity plc we noted a marked improvement in the efficiency of net current assets, therefore, calculating the fourth level ratios may tell us where this improvement came from.

Activity 7

Calculate stock, debtor and creditor turnover periods for Serendipity plc and interpret them.

Activity 7 feedback

	X4	*X5*
Stock turnover	$(31 + 47)/2 \times 365/389$	$(47 + 62)/2 \times 365/685$
	36.6 days	29 days

Thus stock is being turned over quicker in X5, demonstrating greater efficiency.

Debtors' turnover period	$70/584 \times 365$	$156/972 \times 365$
	44 days	58 days

Thus, debtors have been allowed (or have taken), 14 more days on average in X5 than X4 in which to pay their debts to the business. This could possibly indicate that Serendipity plc is losing control of its debtor collection or that it has purposely allowed debtors more time to pay so as to encourage more sales.

Creditors' turnover period	$39/405 \times 365$	$109/700 \times 365$
	35 days	57 days

(note cost of goods sold could be used as a substitute for purchases if the financial statements do not provide a figure for purchases). This indicates Serendipity plc is taking longer to pay its suppliers – 22 days longer. This may damage relations with suppliers if Serendipity does not take care, but also demonstrates how Serendipity is using creditors to finance its business operations. A balance has to be struck within this dichotomy.

Within the analysis of Serendipity plc at level 3 there was also a benefit gained from control of expenses. Therefore fourth level analysis here would also be beneficial.

Activity 8

Calculate ratios of wages, depreciation and other expenses to sales and interpret them for Serendipity plc.

Activity 8 feedback

	X4	*X5*
Wages/sales	78/584 = 13.3%	101/972 = 10.4%

Indicating that the amount of wages expended to generate £1 of sales has been reduced.

Depreciation/sales	16/584 = 2.7%	31/972 = 3.2%

Depreciation has marginally increased as a proportion of sales. This may be due to an increase in assets.

Other expenses/sales	54/584 = 9.3%	62/972 = 6.4%

Other expenses have also been controlled as a percentage of sales. These three ratios, as we saw earlier, when combined gave an increase in profit margin – increased *profitability*. The pyramid also demonstrates that the ratios on the left-hand side show profitability and those on the right show efficiency in the use of assets.

Before moving on to consider financial status within ratio analysis we need to take another look at the first ratio on the pyramid – ROCE. Capital employed consists of shareholder funds, that is share capital and reserves, and long-term debt, for example, debentures. In the example of Serendipity plc ROCE was

X4	12.87%
X5	18.9%

However, the debentures in X5 only required a return to be paid to the holders of 10% even though the capital invested, £10 000, earned 18.9%. The earnings over and above the 10% will then accrue to the shareholders and their return will be increased beyond the 18.9% that the total capital earned. This phenomenon can be demonstrated by calculating the ratio of return on shareholders funds:

$$\text{ROOE} = \frac{\text{profit before tax, but after long-term debt interest}}{\text{shareholders' equity (or owners' equity)}}$$

X4	*X5*
47/365 = 12.88%	85/411 = 20.68%

The shareholders have increased their earnings in the business partly due to the benefit gained by borrowing at a lower rate of return than the business is earning. However, the converse can also occur! Note that ROCE and ROOE were both the same in X4 as there was no long-term debt.

Activity 9

Given the following information calculate ROCE and ROOE for Knight Ltd for X4 and X5.

	X4	X5
	£	£
Profit before tax	80	85
Interest charged	10	10
Capital employed	1250	1280
Long-term debt	100	100

Activity 9 feedback

ROCE	90/1250 = 7.2%	95/1280 = 7.4%
ROOE	80/1150 = 7%	85/1180 = 7.2%

The return on capital employed made in each year is 7.2% and 7.4%, but the return payable to the long-term debt holders is 10% in both years. Therefore the return available to the shareholders *reduces* to 7% and 7.2%.

Financial status

It is essential for a business to be able to pay its debts as and when they fall due, otherwise its chances of remaining in operation become remote. Thus there is a need to analyse the assets available to meet liabilities. This can be done in the short, medium and long term.

For the short term we use the quick assets ratio or acid test

$$\frac{\text{current assets less stock}}{\text{current liabilities}}$$

for the medium term the current ratio

$$\frac{\text{current assets}}{\text{current liabilities}}$$

and for the long term the gearing ratio

$$\frac{\text{long term debt}}{\text{shareholders' funds}}$$

Another ratio, interest cover, can also be calculated

$$\frac{\text{net profit before interest and tax}}{\text{total interest charges}}$$

This last ratio shows the safety margin between profits generated, out of which interest must be paid, and the amount of the interest itself.

Activity 10

Calculate four liquidity ratios for Serendipity plc and interpret them.

Activity 10 feedback

	X4		*X5*	
Acid test	$\dfrac{156 - 47 = 109}{71}$	71	$\dfrac{234 - 62 = 172}{171}$	171
expressed as	1.5:1		1:1	

The ratio has decreased from X4 to X5 quite considerably but there are still plenty of liquid assets. The ratio will need careful monitoring to control this downward trend.

Current ratio	156/71 = 2.2:1	234/171 = 1.4:1

Again this ratio has been substantially reduced but still appears adequate. Monitoring of this downward trend is again required.

Gearing ratio	not relevant	80/411 = 19.5%

This is low and we would consider this company low geared. If a company is high geared then it may have difficulty meeting the required interest payments.

Interest cover	not relevant	(85 + 8)/8 = 12

In X5 the profit covered the required interest payment twelve times indicating no immediate problem for Serendipity plc. Notice how consideration of all four ratios helped to build up a picture of the financial status of Serendipity plc.

Investment potential

Before looking in detail at investment ratios it is useful to carry out some practical research.

Activity 11

Obtain a fairly recent copy of the *Financial Times*, or the equivalent in your own country. Look up the London share information service found in the *FT* and make a note of the data provided for each company. Also read the 'UK company news' either in the *FT* or any other quality newspaper and note down any ratios or indicators used to evaluate the companies.

Activity 11 feedback

Your list possibly included the following:
- book value per share compared with market value per share
- net dividend
- dividend cover
- earnings per share
- gross dividend yield
- price earnings ratio.

We will look at each of these ratios in turn.

Book value per share

This is the ordinary shareholders funds/number of shares. This book value is the value each share would have if the company's assets and liabilities were sold at their balance sheet (book) value. The market value is the price a potential shareholder is willing to pay to acquire a share in the company. Comparing these two values identifies whether the market values the company at more or less than its book value.

Net dividend

This is the amount of dividend declared in any one year per share which equals paid and proposed dividends divided by the number of shares. People invest in shares for one of two reasons: either to earn dividends or to earn capital growth in the value of the share, or both. The level of dividend and its comparison with previous years is generally regarded as an important indicator of future expectations. However, one danger with this comparison is that dividends are not necessarily just paid out of the current year's earnings but can be paid out of retained earnings. It is therefore important to look at dividend cover in any one year.

Dividend cover

$$\frac{\text{Net profit available to ordinary shareholders}}{\text{Total ordinary dividend}}$$

Activity 12

The following information is available in respect of Kit plc

	X4	X5
	£	£
Ordinary shares issued £1	1 875 000	1 875 000
8% preference shares £1	660 000	660 000
Dividend ordinary shares	225 000	187 500
Net profit after tax	257 500	231 900

Calculate dividend per share in pence for both preference and ordinary shares, and dividend cover.

Activity 12 feedback

Dividend per share in pence preference	8p	8p
Dividend per share ordinary	12p	10p
Dividend cover	257 500/277 800	231 900/240 300
	0.93	0.97

Thus the dividend per share has reduced from X4 to X5, but the dividend cover has improved. However, this dividend cover is less than one which indicates that the company is not earning enough in either year to pay the dividend and is therefore using past earn-

ings retained to fund the dividend payment. This may be a dang
investors.

Earnings per share

This is another indicator used widely by the investment community. It represe   .nt
of profit the company has earned during the year for each ordinary share.

For the example of Kit plc the earnings per share in X4 is 204 700/1 875 000 = 10.9p and
X5 is 179 100/1 875 000 = 9.6p. Note that we considered earnings per share in Chapter 26.

Gross dividend yield

This is calculated from the formula

$$\frac{\text{gross dividend}}{\text{market price of ordinary share}}$$

Shareholders may be willing to accept a low gross dividend yield if there is a greater than
average capital growth in share value expected or if the company is a safe investment. Gross
dividend is calculated by grossing up the dividend declared in the accounts for basic rate
taxation as dividends are always declared and paid net of basic income tax.

For example, in the case of Kit plc if the basic rate of tax is 20% then the gross dividend
is:

	X4	X5
	225 000/80%	187 500/80%
	281 250	234 375
or per share	15p	12.5p

If the market value per share for Kit was £1.75 in X4 and £1.82 in X5, then the gross dividend yield is

15/175	12.5/182
8.6%	6.9%

Price/earnings ratio PE ratio

The formula for this is

$$\frac{\text{market price per share}}{\text{earnings per share}}$$

For Kit this is

175/10.9	182/9.6
16.1	19

Like the dividend yield the PE ratio will change as the market price per share changes. It
represents the market's view of the growth potential of the company, its dividend policy

and the degree of risk involved in the investment. In general a high PE indicates the market has a high/good opinion of these factors, a low PE a low/poor opinion of these factors. Another way of looking at the PE is that it represents the number of years' earnings it is necessary to have at the current rate to recover the price paid for the share. For Kit this was nineteen years at the X5 rate of earnings.

Limitations of ratio analysis

We discussed three of these in Activity 2, changes in environment, absence of comparable data, different accounting policies, but we can identify others.

Non-monetary factors

Non-monetary factors are not reflected in ratio analysis. Thus, such factors as the quality of the product or service are not reflected, nor whether labour relations are good or bad. In fact no regard is had to the goodwill of the business.

Historic cost accounting

The historical nature of accounts must always be borne in mind as our interpretation of the business is based on this historical information, but this may not be the best guide as to the future performance, financial status and investment potential.

Short-term fluctuations

Ratio analysis does not identify short-term fluctuations in assets and liabilities as our appraisal is based on a balance sheet which provides values of assets and liabilities as at a point in time. By using these year-end figures we may, for example, present a better view of liquidity than has been the case throughout the year. Remember the possibilities of window dressing that we referred to in Chapter 23.

Changes in the value of money

We all know how inflation affects the value of the pound in our pocket and this is no different for a business. In fact inflation and price changes could make the whole of our ratio analysis invalid.

Activity 13

The following sales figures are available for David plc

	X0	X1
	£000	£000
	700	800

The price of goods sold had been subject to an increase of 10% at the beginning of X1.
What is the magnitude of the increase in volume of trade?

Activity 13 feedback

Sales have increased by £100 000 from X0 to X1 but £70 000 of this is due to the price increase, inflation in the price of goods sold. Volume of sales has only increased by £30 000, that is, 4% not 14%.

Additional information

Ratio analysis is a tool that aids the user in building up an overall picture of the condition/state of a business entity. Other information can help to fill in more of this picture.

Activity 14

Identify additional information that you would like when undertaking a ratio analysis of a company.

Activity 14 feedback

- Inflation effects on the company
- does the balance sheet represent the position of the business throughout the year or just at the year-end
- cash flow throughout the year
- forecast business plans in the form of budgets and cash flows
- information in respect of the quality of goods and services and other factors affecting the assessment of goodwill in the business
- industrial averages of ratios
- differences in accounting policies between businesses.

Much of the above information will not be available to all users. For example, it would be very difficult, probably impossible, for a potential investor to obtain detailed information in respect of future plans of the business apart from that disclosed in the directors' report in the financial statements.

Multivariate analysis

The ratio analysis we have considered so far is univariate analysis. This is where one ratio is considered at a time and then all ratios, once calculated, are assessed together and the analyst makes a considered judgement on the state of the entity. On the other hand multivariate analysis combines some of the ratios together in a specified manner by applying weightings to each of the ratios. The result is an index number that is compared to previous years, other companies and industrial averages.

Multivariate analysis has been widely used in predicting corporate failure. In 1968 Professor Altman combined five ratios to produce what he named a Z score. Companies with Z scores above 2.99 he found had not failed whereas those below 1.81 had. His research was undertaken in the manufacturing sector of the United States and it is important to remember that this may not apply to companies outside the USA or to those outside the particular sector he considered. It is also worth noting the date of his research as, since then, the world economy and business practices have changed considerably.

Taffler and Tisshaw carried out similar work in the UK but have not published the details of this as it is used as a working model and they need to retain the commercial interest.

There may well be other Z scores used by groups of analysts, but our view is that the use of univariate analysis with additional information and a good deal of commonsense should enable you to make a reasonable assessment of a company's financial status, performance, potential and position in the market.

The following activity gives a ratio analysis example.

Activity 15

The following are extracts from an industrial performance analysis for two groups, Alpha Group plc and Omega Group plc.

The two groups operate in different industrial sectors and have accordingly adopted different operating and financial strategies.

Alpha Group plc	1991–2 £000	1990–1 £000	1989–90 £000
Profit and loss data			
turnover	20 915	19 036	16 929
operating profit	1 386	1 189	943
depreciation	299	264	214
income from investments	23	20	14
interest payable	95	66	60
Balance sheet data			
intangible fixed assets	636	660	484
tangible fixed assets	7 213	5 605	4 654
investments	234	201	148
	8 083	6 466	5 286
Stocks	1 405	1 312	1 217
Trade debtors	65	54	57
Cash	97	62	43
Other current assets	1 000	550	700
Total current assets	2 567	1 978	2 017
Trade creditors	1 651	1 521	1 381
Overdraft	150	–	160
Short-term loans	300	151	200
Other current liabilities	1 371	1 271	1 008
Total current liabilities	3 472	2 943	2 749
Total assets less current liabilities	7 178	5 501	4 554
Creditors: amounts falling due after more than 1 year	904	604	239
Provisions for liabilities and charges	180	159	158
Minority interests	150	132	130
	5 944	4 606	4 027

Ordinary shares	3 000	3 000	3 000
Preference shares, redeemable 1995	2 000	–	–
Reserves	944	1 606	1 027
	5 944	4 606	4 027

Omega Group plc

	1991–2	1990–1	1989–90
	£000	£000	£000
Profit and loss data:			
turnover	19 540	15 260	16 320
operating profit	620	340	220
depreciation	240	220	220
income from investments	20	20	20
interest payable	720	660	720
Balance sheet data:			
intangible fixed assets	–	–	–
tangible fixed assets	1 620	1 360	1 360
investments	220	280	240
	1 840	1 640	1 600
Stocks	3 870	2 540	2 040
Trade debtors	2 660	1 920	2 040
Cash	800	480	400
Other current assets	4 000	4 000	3 580
Total current assets	11 330	8 940	8 060
Trade creditors	2 700	1 620	1 020
Overdraft	60	180	–
Short-term loans	1 800	1 200	1 820
Other current liabilities	1 140	840	740
Total current liabilities	5 700	3 840	3 580
Total assets less current liabilities	7 380	6 740	6 080
Creditors: amounts falling due after more than 1 year	5 400	5 100	4 660
Provisions for liabilities and charges	260	300	360
Minority interests	200	180	200
	1 520	1 160	860
Ordinary shares	600	600	600
Preference shares redeemable 1995	200	200	200
Reserves	720	360	60
	1 520	1 160	860

Required:

(a) **A set of five key ratios of use in monitoring the operational performance of the two groups over three years. Show clearly your workings and justify the definitions of the inputs to your ratio calculations.**
(10 marks)

(b) **A set of three key ratios of use in monitoring the financial structure of the two groups over three years. Show clearly your workings and justify the definitions of the inputs to your ratio calculations.** (5 marks)

(c) **Identify the contrasting operating and financing strategies of the two groups as revealed by your ratio analysis.** (6 marks)

(d) **For each group suggest an industrial sector for which such a strategy would give a best fit. Give reasons for your suggestions.** (4 marks)

(e) **List five ways in which financial statements could be improved in order to make them more useful as the basis for input to ratio analysis. Identify the constraints on implementation of these improvements.** (5 marks)

(30 marks)
(ACCA)

Activity 15 feedback

(**a**) There are more than five ratios that will monitor operational performance. We provide six for you.

ROCE

	Alpha plc	Omega plc
1989–90	957/4914 = 19.5%	240/7900 = 3.0%
1990–1	1209/5652 = 21.4%	360/8120 = 4.4%
1991–2	1409/7628 = 18.5%	640/9240 = 6.9%

Return is calculated by adding operating profit and investment income.

Capital employed is calculated by adding overdraft and short-term loans to total assets less current liabilities, as the interest payable in the P&L data is not separated into long- and short-term interest payable.

Profit to sales

1989–90	1 157/16 929 = 6.8%	440/16 320 = 2.7%
1990–1	1 453/19 036 = 7.6%	560/15 260 = 3.7%
1991–2	1 685/20 915 = 8.1%	860/19 540 = 4.4%

The nearest figure to gross profit we can achieve from the data is operating profit and depreciation, so this figure is used in the above calculation.

Asset utilization – sales to capital employed

1989–90	16 929/4 766 = 3.55	16 320/7 660 = 2.13
1990–1	19 036/5 451 = 3.49	15 260/7 840 = 1.95
1991–2	20 915/7 394 = 2.83	19 540/9 020 = 2.16

Note that capital employed is the figure used in the ROCE calculation less the amount of investments, as sales income is not generated from investments.

Stock turnover

1990–91	1265/19 036 = 24 days	2290/15 260 = 54 days
1991–2	1359/20 915 = 23 days	3160/19 540 = 59 days

Average stock is used in the above calculations. Stock has to be compared to sales here as we have no information in respect of cost of sales.

Debtors' turnover

1989–90	57/16 929 = 1 day	2040/16 320 = 46 days
1990–1	54/19 036 = 1 day	1920/15 260 = 46 days
1991–2	65/20 915 = 1 day	2660/19 540 = 50 days

Note that average debtors figures could have been used in the above calculations.

Creditors' turnover

1989–90	1381/16 929 = 30 days	1020/16 320 = 23 days
1990–1	1521/19 036 = 29 days	1620/15 260 = 39 days
1991–2	1651/20 915 = 29 days	2700/19 540 = 50 days

Again average creditors figures could have been used in the above calculations. The sales figures have to be used as we do not have information in respect of cost of sales.

(b) Key ratios to monitor financial structure are as follows:

Gearing

1989–90	757/4157 = 18.2%	7040/860 = 818%
1990–1	914/4738 = 19.3%	6980/1140 = 612%
1991–2	3534/4094 = 86.3%	7720/1520 = 508%

Debt is taken to be preference shares, long-term creditors, provisions, overdraft and short-term loans in the above calculations.

Current ratio

1989–90	2017/2749 = 0.7	8060/3580 = 2.3
1990–1	1978/2943 = 0.7	8940/3840 = 2.3
1991–2	2567/3472 = 0.7	11 240/5700 = 2.0

Acid test

1989–90	800/2749 = 0.3	6020/3580 = 1.7
1990–1	666/2943 = 0.2	6400/3840 = 1.7
1991–2	1162/3472 = 0.3	7460/5700 = 1.3

(c) The ratio analysis carried out above identifies the following:

- Alpha has a much higher ROCE than Omega, but Alpha's is falling, whereas Omega's is rising.
- Alpha has a higher margin on operating profits than Omega. However Omega's has nearly doubled in three years.
- Alpha's asset utilization is better than Omega's but Omega's is rising, whereas Alpha's is falling.
- Alpha appears to operate almost entirely by cash sales whereas Omega allows 50 days for debtor's payment.
- Creditor periods are one month for Alpha but two months for Omega. Note Omega's does match its credit given period.
- Alpha's gearing is low when compared to Omega's, but an increase occurred in 1991–2 when preference shares were issued to finance expansion. Omega's gearing is very high although it has started to fall.
- Not much change has occurred for both companies throughout the period in their liquid-

ity. Alpha's is lower than Omega's but as it has been at this low level for three years then one would assume the business is viable. Omega's liquidity is high and therefore too many resources are tied up in current assets.

Overall Alpha benefits from high margins, high asset turnover and good use of working capital. The preference share issue has increased gearing but this is not at danger levels and could be expected to decrease as profits increase from the additional resources. Omega has low margins and low asset turnover and maintains high working capital in debtors and slow-moving stocks. Omega's high gearing makes it sensitive to interest changes.

(d) Alpha, given its debtor strategy, high margin and high turnover may well be in the food retailing sector. Omega may be a manufacturer in the engineering industry or something similar.

(e) Improvements to financial statements. We have discussed these throughout this chapter and elsewhere in this book. Summarizing we would suggest that:

■ more relevant and reliable information is required that enables predictions to be made

■ that historical cost is not a suitable base, deprival value may be more relevant

■ that the change in the value of the pound over a period does not permit useful comparisons to be made

■ that the information is not timely enough

■ that different accounting policies used by companies distort the comparison.

The constraints on the implementation of these improvements are centred around the problems of:

■ providing sensitive commercial information within the public domain

■ the subjectivity involved in measurement if historical cost is abandoned

■ identifying accounting policies that would reflect a true and fair view of all entities

■ identifying a conceptual accounting framework.

Summary

Within this chapter we returned again to the users of financial statements and their needs. We identified a tool, ratio analysis, in an attempt to meet these needs. It also became apparent that the construction of a picture in relation to a company's performance, financial status and well being, and future potential, was an intricate mix of ratio analysis, additional information and a good dose of commonsense on the part of the analyst.

We also briefly considered multivariate analysis. The questions at the end of this chapter will provide you with practice in honing your analytical skills.

Exercises

1 Obtain a set of accounts for a supermarket and a manufacturer. You can do this by accessing your university library or using the service provided by the *Financial Times*.

Compare and contrast the nature of the current assets and liabilities of your two companies.

2 You are given the following information in relation to Olivet Ltd.

P&L accounts	20X4	20X5
	£	£
Sales	100 000	100 000
Cost of sales	50 000	60 000
	50 000	40 000
Expenses	30 000	30 000
	20 000	10 000
Dividends	10 000	10 000
	10 000	–
Balance b/d	2 500	12 500
	12 500	12 500

Balance sheets as at	20X4	20X5
	£	£
Land	21 500	31 500
Buildings	20 000	39 500
Equipment	3 000	3 000
	44 500	74 000
Investments at cost	25 000	40 000
Stock	27 500	32 500
Debtors	20 000	25 000
Bank	1 500	
	118 500	171 500

Ordinary £1 shares	20 000	25 000
Share premium	6 000	7 000
Revaluation reserve	–	10 000
Profit and loss	12 500	12 500
Debentures 10%	50 000	75 000
Creditors	20 000	30 000
Proposed dividend	10 000	10 000
Bank	–	2 000
	118 500	171 500

You are required to comment on the financial position of Olivet Ltd as at 20X5. Calculate any ratios you feel necessary.

3 You are given the attached information about Fred plc, comprising summarized P&L accounts, summarized balance sheets, and some suggested ratio calculations. You should note that there may be alternative ways of calculating some of these ratios. The holder of a small number of the ordinary shares in the business has come to you for help and advice. There are a number of things he does not properly understand, and a friend of his who is an accountancy student has suggested to him that some of the ratios show a distinctly unsatisfactory position, and that he should sell his shares as quickly as possible.

Required:

(a) Write a report to the shareholder commenting on the apparent position and

prospects of Fred plc, as far as the information permits. Your report should include reference to liquidity and profitability aspects, and should advise whether, in your view, the shares should indeed be sold as soon as possible.

(12 marks)

(b) **Explain the following issues to the shareholder:**
(i) **What is the loan redemption fund, and how has it been created?**

(3 marks)

(ii) **How on earth can there be £49 million of assets on the balance sheet 'not yet in use'? Surely if it is not in use it is not an asset? What are assets anyway? And coming back to that £49 million, the depreciation on these items will be artificially reducing the reported profit won't it?** (6 marks)

(iii) **What is all this about interest being capitalized? What does it mean, and why are they doing it?** (4 marks)

(25 marks)

(ACCA)

Fred plc
Some possible ratio calculations (which can be taken as arithmetically correct).

	1992	1991
Current ratio	54/147 = 36.7%	56/172 = 32.6%
Acid test ratio	12/147 = 8.2%	15/172 = 8.7%
ROCE	57/249 = 22.9%	41/161 = 25.5%
ROOE	33/188 = 17.5%	24/160 = 15.0%
eps	31/190 = 16.3p	22/190 = 11.6p
Trade debtors' turnover	4/910 × 365 = 2 days	4/775 × 365 = 2 days
Trade creditors' turnover	60/730 × 365 = 30 days	60/633 × 365 = 35 days
Gross profit %	180/910 = 19.8%	142/775 = 18.3%
Operating profit %	57/910 = 6.3 p	41/775 = 5.3%
Stock turnover	42/730 × 365 = 21 days	41/633 × 365 = 24 days
Gearing	61/188 = 32.4%	1/160 = 0.6%

Fred plc

Summarized balance sheets at year-end (£m)

	1992	1991
Fixed assets		
tangible – not yet in use	49	41
– in use	295	237
	344	278
investments	1	1
loan redemption fund	1	1
	346	280
Current assets		
stocks	42	41
debtors – trade	4	4
– other	4	4
	8	8
bank	2	5
cash	2	2
	54	56

Creditors – due within 1 year					
– trade	60		60		
– other	87		112		
		147		172	
Net current liabilities			93		116
Total assets less current liabilities			253		164
Creditors – due between one and five years			61		1
Provision for liabilities and charges			4		3
Net assets			188		160
Capital and reserves					
ordinary shares of 10p each			19		19
preference shares of £1 each			46		46
share premium			1		1
profit and loss account			122		94
			188		160

Fred plc
Summarized P&L accounts for the year (£m)

		1992		*1991*
Sales		910		775
Raw materials and consumables		730		633
		180		142
Staff costs	77		64	
Depreciation of tangible fixed assets	12		10	
Other operating charges	38		30	
		127		104
		53		38
Other operating income		4		3
		57		41
Net interest payable		5		4
		52		37
Profit sharing – employees		2		1
		50		36
Taxation		17		12
		33		24
Preference dividends		2		2
		31		22
Ordinary dividends		3		2
		28		20

Note
Net interest payable:

interest payable		12	9
interest receivable		(1)	(1)
interest capitalized		(6)	(4)
		5	4

4 You are given summarized results of an electrical engineering business, as follows. All figures are in £000.

Profit and loss account

	year-ended	
	31.12.91	*31.12.90*
Turnover	60 000	50 000
Cost of sales	42 000	34 000
Gross profit	18 000	16 000
Operating expenses	15 500	13 000
	2 500	3 000
Interest payable	2 200	1 300
Profit before taxation	300	1 700
Taxation	350	600
(Loss) profit after taxation	(50)	1 100
Dividends	600	600
Transfer (from) to reserves	(650)	500

Balance sheet

Fixed assets		
intangible	500	–
tangible	12 000	11 000
	12 500	11 000
Current assets		
stocks	14 000	13 000
debtors	16 000	15 000
bank and cash	500	500
	30 500	28 500
Creditors due within 1 year	24 000	20 000
Net current assets	6 500	8 500
Total assets less current liabilities	19 000	19 500
Creditors due after one year	6 000	5 500
	13 000	14 000
Capital and reserves		
share capital	1 300	1 300
share premium	3 300	3 300
revaluation reserve	2 000	2 000
profit and loss	6 400	7 400
	13 000	14 000

Required:
(a) Prepare a table of the following twelve ratios, calculated for both years, clearly showing the figures used in the calculations:
current ratio
quick assets ratio
stock turnover in days
debtors' turnover in days
creditors' turnover in days

gross profit %
net profit % (before taxation)
interest cover
dividend cover
ROOE (before taxation)
ROCE
gearing   (12 marks)

(b) **Making full use of the information given in the question, of your table of ratios,**
    and your commonsense, comment on the apparent position of the business and
    on the actions of the management.   (8 marks)
                                                                                (20 marks)
                                                                                (ACCA)

5   The Pitlochry Group is one of the leading food retailers in the UK. It ranks within the 50
    largest listed British companies on the London Stock Exchange. The annual report for the
    year-ended 31 March 1993 includes a five-year financial summary as follows:

Five-year financial summary

year-ended 31 March	1989	1990	1991	1992	1993
	£m	£m	£m	£m	£m
Turnover	1915	3068	3326	3728	4281
% change		60	8	12	15
Profit before tax and exceptional items	72	157	187	218	261
% change		64	36	28	28
Operating profit (before investment income and interest charge)	77	144	168	201	256
% change		87	17	20	27
Market capitalization	1512	1633	1495	1737	2454
Net tangible assets					
Tangible fixed assets	444	537	736	1005	1250
Net current liabilities	(162)	(54)	(167)	(282)	(320)
Creditors (due after 1 year)	(119)	(81)	(98)	(102)	(186)
Deferred taxation	(8)	(3)	(4)	(5)	(9)
Other provisions	(2)	–	–	–	–
	153	399	467	616	735
Operating profit margin %	4	5	5.4	5.7	6.3
Market capitalization times Book value	9.9	4.1	3.2	2.8	3.3

year-ended 31 March	1989	1990	1991	1992	1993
	pence	pence	pence	pence	pence
Earnings per share	10.5	11.8	13.5	15.4	18
% change	12	14	14	17	
Dividend per share	4.10	4.80	5.60	6.53	7.80
% change	17	17	17	20	
Ordinary share prices					
high	197	222	184	231	263
low	134	153	144	159	181
Number of shareholders	15014	22969	22909	22741	22942

In the year-ended 31 March 1990 a major outlet was acquired and this has since become the principal retail identity. Over the past four years the floor area devoted to sales has tripled with the opening of 80 new stores.

In May 1993 a rights issue was made to raise £384 million which turned borrowings of £150 million into a cash balance of £198 million. The directors have adopted a growth programme suitable for a superstore involving opening 25 stores a year and penetrating complementary non-food markets. Capital expenditure for the current year is estimated at £405 million and is planned to increase to £450 million for each of the next two years.

Required:

(a) **Calculate a rate of return on capital employed and the turnover to capital employed, as percentages, using only the information provided, for each of the years included in the summary. Show clearly the workings for the calculations.**
(5 marks)

(b) **Comment on the trends shown by the data of the Pitlochry Group.**
(10 marks)

(c) **Briefly indicate additional information you would require in order to be able to use the data for inter-company comparison.** (8 marks)

(d) **Sketch a graph of turnover to capital employed and of the margin, to cover five years, and comment on the relationship as presented by the graph in the light of your calculation of rate of return on capital employed calculated in part (a). Include a comment on the growth programme outlined in the question.**
(7 marks)

(30 marks)

(ACCA)

6 Heavy Goods plc carries on business as a manufacturer of tractors. In 1994 the company was looking for acquisitions and carrying out investigations into a number of possible targets. One of these was a competitor, Modern Tractors plc. The company's acquisition strategy was to acquire companies that were vulnerable to a takeover and in which there was an opportunity to improve asset management and profitability.

The chief accountant of Heavy Goods plc has instructed his assistant to calculate ratios from the financial statements of Modern Tractors plc for the past three years and to prepare a report based on these ratios and the industry average ratios that have been provided by the trade association. The ratios prepared by the assistant accountant and the industry averages for 1994 are set out below.

Required:

(a) **Assuming the role of the chief accountant, draft a brief report to be submitted to the managing director based on the ratios of Modern Tractors plc for 1992–4 and the industry averages for 1994.** (12 marks)

(b) **Draft a brief memo to management explaining:**
   (i) **in general terms why the comparison of the 1994 ratios with the ratios of previous years and other companies might be misleading; and** (3 marks)
   (ii) **how specific ratios might be affected and the possible implications for the evaluation of the report.** (5 marks)

(20 marks)

(ACCA)

		1992	1993	1994	Industry average 1994
Sales growth	%	30.00	40.00	9.52	8.25
Sales/total assets		1.83	2.05	1.60	2.43
Sales/net fixed assets		2.94	3.59	2.74	16.85

Sales/working capital		−21.43	−140.00	38.33	10.81
Sales/debtors		37.50	70.00	92.00	16.00
Gross profit/sales	%	18.67	22.62	19.57	23.92
Profit before tax/sales	%	8.00	17.62	11.74	4.06
Profit before interest/interest		6.45	26.57	14.50	4.95
Profit after tax/total assets	%	9.76	27.80	13.24	8.97
Profit after tax/equity	%	57.14	75.00	39.58	28.90
Net fixed assets/total assets	%	62.20	57.07	58.54	19.12
Net fixed assets/equity		3.64	1.54	1.75	0.58
Equity/total assets	%	18.29	37.07	33.45	32.96
Total liabilities/total assets	%	81.71	62.93	66.55	69.00
Total liabilities/equity		4.47	1.70	1.99	2.40
Long-term debt/total assets	%	36.59	18.54	29.27	19.00
Current liabilities/total assets	%	45.12	44.39	37.28	50.00
Current assets/ current liabilities		0.84	0.97	1.11	1.63
(Current assets − stock)/ current liabilities		0.43	0.54	0.72	0.58
Stock/total assets	%	17.07	18.54	14.63	41.90
Cost of sales/stock		8.71	8.55	8.81	4.29
Cost of sales/creditors		6.10	6.25	6.17	12.87
Debtors/total assets	%	4.88	2.93	1.70	18.40
Cash/total assets	%	15.85	21.46	25.08	9.60

Note

Total assets = (fixed assets at net book value + current assets) and net fixed assets = fixed assets at net book value.

7 Seville plc is a rapidly expanding trading and manufacturing company. It is currently seeking to extend its product range in new markets. To achieve this growth it needs to raise £800 000. The directors are considering two sources of funds:

(i) A rights issue at £2.00 per share. The shares are trading at £2.50 (1990 £2.20) per share.

(ii) A bank loan at an interest rate of 15% and repayable by instalments after two years. The bank would want to secure the loan with a charge over the company's property.

The following are extracts from the draft financial statements.

Seville plc
Draft P&L account extract year-ended 31.12.91

	1990 £000	1991 £000
Turnover	1967	1991
Operating profit	636	698
Interest payable	(45)	(55)
Profit before taxation	591	643
Taxation	(150)	(140)
Profit after taxation	441	503
Extraordinary item	(90)	–
Profit for the year	361	453

Seville plc
Draft balance sheet extract as at 31.12.91

	1990 £000	1991 £000
Fixed assets		
tangible	1132	1504
intangible	247	298
	1379	1802
Current assets		
stocks	684	679
debtors	471	511
cash in hand and at bank	80	117
Creditors: due within one year		
trade	(336)	(308)
taxation	(140)	(190)
dividends	(80)	(80)
Creditors: due after more than one year		
10% debentures, repayable 2004	(450)	(450)
finance lease	–	(100)
	1608	1981
Capital and reserves		
ordinary share capital £1 shares	800	800
revaluation reserve	144	144
profit and loss	664	1037
	1608	1981

Operating profit
Operating profit has been arrived at after charging or crediting the following:

	1990 £000	1991 £000
Depreciation	110	150
Gain on disposal of property (as part of a sale and leaseback transaction)	–	95

Extraordinary item
The extraordinary loss consists of reorganization costs in a branch where a reduction in activity involved various measures including redundancies. Attributable tax credit is £38 000.

Deferred taxation
Deferred taxation has not been provided because it is not considered probable that a liability will crystallize. If deferred taxation had been provided in full then a liability for the year of £7000 would have arisen (1990 £8000).

Contingent liability
There is a contingent liability of £85 000 (1990 £80 000) in respect of bills of exchange discounted with bankers.

Further investigation has revealed that stock includes items subject to reservation of title of £40 000 and obsolete or slow moving items of £28 000 (1990 £28 000).

An age analysis of debtors has revealed that debts overdue by more than one year amount to £40 000 (1990 £40 000).

The auditors are yet to report and there is some discussion as to the classification of the gain on disposal and the reorganization costs.

The directors forecast that the new funds will generate an operating profit of £300 000, and that the 1991 operating profit will be repeated. If new shares are issued the dividend will increase to £150 000.

Required:

(a) **Analyse the accounts based on the following ratios, from the separate points of view of potential equity holders and debt holders:**
   (i)   **current ratio**
   (ii) **interest cover**
   (iii) **debt/equity ratio**
   (iv) **earnings per share**
   (v)   **after tax return on equity**
   (vi) **price/earnings ratio.**
   Two different versions of each of these ratios should be calculated and used in your analysis where the input to the ratio calculation can be variously defined or where the data suggests uncertainty as to accounting treatment in the draft accounts.

   Your analysis should clearly indicate which parts of it are of particular relevance to potential equity holders and which are of particular relevance to potential debt holders. It should also comment on the limitations of each of the ratios as an evaluative tool.   (20 marks)

(b) **Assuming that either funding scheme becomes effective 1 January 1992, recalculate, for each scheme, the following ratios:**
   (i)   **debt/equity ratio**
   (ii) **interest cover**
   (iii) **after tax return on equity.**
   For ratios (ii) and (iii), adopt the directors' forecasts. Advise the directors, with reasons, which scheme to adopt. List other factors the directors should consider.

                                                                      (10 marks)
                                                                      (30 marks)
                                                                      ACCA

(Work to the nearest £000. Corporation tax rate is 35%.)

8 Recycle plc is a listed company which recycles toxic chemical waste products. The waste products are sent to Recycle plc from all around the world. You are an accountant (not employed by Recycle plc) who is accustomed to providing advice concerning the performance of companies, based on the data which are available from their published financial statements. Extracts from the financial statements of Recycle plc for the two years ended 30 September 1997 are given below:

Profit and loss accounts – year-ended 30 September:

	1997	1996
Turnover	3000	2800
Cost of sales	(1600)	(1300)
Gross profit	1400	1500
Other operating expenses	(800)	(600)
Operating profit	600	900
Interest payable	(200)	(100)
Profit before taxation	400	800
Taxation	(150)	(250)
Profit after taxation	250	550
Proposed dividend	(200)	(200)
Retained profit	50	350
Retained profit b/fwd	900	550
Retained profit c/fwd	950	900

Balance sheets at 30 September:

	1997 £m	1997 £m	1996 £m	1996 £m
Tangible fixed assets		4100		3800
Current assets:				
Stocks	500		350	
Debtors	1000		800	
Cash in hand	50		50	
	1550		1200	
Current liabilities:				
Trade creditors	600		600	
Taxation payable	150		250	
Proposed dividend	200		200	
Bank overdraft	750		50	
	1700		1100	
Net current (liabilities)/assets		(150)		100
Long-term loans (repayable 1999)		(1000)		(1000)
		2950		2900
Capital and reserves:				
Called-up share capital (£1 shares)		2000		2000
Profit and loss account		950		900
		2950		2900

You ascertain that depreciation of tangible fixed assets for the year-ended 30 September 1997 was £1200 million. Disposals of fixed assets during the year-ended 30 September 1997 were negligible. You are approached by two individuals.

A is a private investor who is considering purchasing shares in Recycle plc. A considers that Recycle plc has performed well in 1997 compared with 1996 because turnover has risen and the dividend to shareholders has been maintained.

B is resident in the area immediately surrounding the premises of Recycle plc and is interested in the contribution made by Recycle plc to the general well-being of the community. B is also concerned about the potential environmental effect of the recycling of chemical waste. B is uncertain how the published financial statements of Recycle plc might be of assistance in addressing social and environmental matters.

Required:
(a) Write a report to A which analyses the financial performance of Recycle plc over the two years ended 30 September 1997.
   Assume inflation is negligible.
   Your report should specifically refer to the observations made by A concerning the performance of Recycle plc. (25 marks)
(b) Briefly discuss whether published financial statements satisfy the information needs of B. You should consider published financial statements IN GENERAL, NOT just the extracts which are provided in this question.

(5 marks)
(30 marks)
(CIMA)

9 H plc manufactures vehicle parts. The company sells its products to a number of independent distributors who resell the goods to garages and other retail outlets in their areas. H plc has a policy of having only one distributor in any given geographical area. Distributors are selected mainly on the basis of financial viability. H plc is keen to avoid the disruption of sales and loss of credibility associated with the collapse of a distributor.

The company is currently trying to choose between two companies which have applied to be its sole distributor in Geetown, a new sales area.

The applicants have supplied the following information:

	Applicant X			Applicant Y		
	1993	*1994*	*1995*	*1993*	*1994*	*1995*
Sales (£000)	1280	1600	2000	1805	1900	2000
Gross profit %	22	20	18	23	22	24
Return on capital employed %	8	12	16	14	15	16
Current ratio	1.7:1	1.9:1	2.1:1	1.7:1	1.65:1	1.7:1
Quick ratio	1.4:1	1.1:1	0.9:1	0.9:1	0.9:1	0.9:1
Gearing %	15	21	28	29	30	27

Requirements:
(a) Explain why trends in accounting ratios could provide a more useful insight than the latest figures taken on their own. (4 marks)
(b) Using the information provided above, explain which of the companies appears to be the safer choice for the role of distributor. (11 marks)
(15 marks)
(CIMA)

10 You are employed by a CIMA member who provides consultancy services to small and medium-sized businesses. You are helping her to prepare a presentation to the directors of U Ltd, a manufacturing company which is planning to expand in the near future and is hoping to attract some new investors.

As a first step, you have prepared the following table of accounting ratios:

	U Ltd year-ended 31/3/98	U Ltd year-ended 31/3/97	Industry average for year-ended 31/3/98
Return on total capital employed	16%	13%	14%
Return on equity	19%	19%	22%
Gross profit percentage	36%	37%	45%
Net profit percentage	19%	17%	25%
Current ratio	2.4:1	2.1:1	1.8:1
Quick ratio	1.5:1	1.3:1	1.0:1
Stock turnover	43 days	39 days	26 days
Debtors turnover	54 days	52 days	39 days
Gearing ratio	35%	31%	28%

Required:

(a) Explain why it might be argued that any analysis of financial statements from the shareholders' point of view ought to concentrate on profitability.

(5 marks)

(b) Your employer believes that U Ltd's return on capital employed (based on the total of long-term debt and equity) is poor, given that the company has recently been enjoying the benefit of low interest rates.

Required:

Explain how your employer could justify her opinion that U Ltd's return on capital employed is poor. (4 marks)

(c) Suggest three ways in which U Ltd might be able to improve its return on equity. Your suggestions should make the fullest possible use of the other ratios in the table. State any assumptions that you have made. (6 marks)

(15 marks)

(CIMA)

11 It has been suggested that 'cash is king' and that readers of a company's accounts should pay more attention to information concerning its cash flows and balances than to its profits and other assets. It is argued that cash is more difficult to manipulate than profit and that cashflows are more important.

Required:

(a) Explain whether you agree with the suggestion that cash flows and balances are more difficult to manipulate than profit and non-cash assets. (8 marks)

(b) Explain why it might be dangerous to concentrate on cash to the exclusion of profit when analysing a set of financial statements. (7 marks)

(15 marks)

(CIMA)

12 Below are the summarized financial statements for the years to 31 March 1996 and 1997 of Heywood Bottles plc, a company which manufactures bottles for many different drinks companies.

Note: the statements for the year to 31 March 1997 have not been audited.

Profit and loss account for the years to 31 March

	1996 £m	1996 £m	1997 £m	1997 £m
Sales		120		300
Manufacturing costs	83		261	
Depreciation	7	(90)	9	(270)
Gross profit		30		30

Other expenses	10		28	
Interest	2	(12)	10	(38)
Profit/(loss) before tax		18		(8)
Tax		(6)		(4)
Profit/(loss) after tax		12		(12)
Dividends:				
interim paid	4		4	
final proposed	4	(8)	4	(8)
		4		(20)

Balance sheets as at 31 March

	1996		1997	
	£m	£m	£m	£m
Fixed assets:				
Land and buildings		5		5
Plant and equipment		38		58
		43		63
Current assets:				
Stock	12		18	
Debtors	25		94	
Deferred expenditure	–		6	
Bank	8		–	
	45		118	
Creditors: amounts falling due within one year				
Trade creditors	(15)		(80)	
Others	(10)		(12)	
Bank	–		(34)	
	(25)		(126)	
Net assets (liabilities)		20		(8)
Total assets less current liabilities		63		55
Creditors: amounts falling due after more than one year		(19)		(32)
Net assets		44		23
Share capital and reserves:				
Ordinary shares		25		25
Reserves:				
Capital reserves	11		10	
Profit and loss account	8	19	(12)	(2)
		44		23

Notes:

1 Plant and equipment is made up as follows:

	£m	£m
At 31 March	1996	1997
Owned plant	10	18
Leased plant	28	40

2 Creditors falling due after more than one year are leasing obligations.

The directors were disappointed in the profit for the year to 31 March 1996 and held a board meeting in April 1996 to discuss future strategy. The Managing Director was insistent that the way to improve the company's results was to increase sales and market share. As a result the following actions were implemented:

(i) an aggressive marketing campaign through trade journals costing £12 million was undertaken. Due to expected long-term benefits £6 million of this has been included as a current asset in the balance sheet at 31 March 1997;

(ii) a 'price promise' to undercut any other supplier's price was announced in the advertising campaign;

(iii) a major contract with Koola Drinks plc was signed that accounted for a substantial proportion of the company's output. This contract was obtained through very competitive tendering;

(iv) the credit period for debtors was extended from two to three months.

A preliminary review by the Board of the accounts to 31 March 1997 concluded that the company's performance had deteriorated rather than improved. There was particular concern over the prospect of renewing the bank overdraft facility because the maximum agreed level of £30 million had been exceeded. The Board decided that it was time to seek independent professional advice on the company's situation.

Required:

In the capacity of a business consultant, prepare a report for the Board of Heywood Bottles plc analysing the company's performance for the year to 31 March 1997 in comparison with the previous year. Particular emphasis should be given to the effects of the implementation of the actions referred to in points (i) to (iv) above.

(15 marks)

(ACCA)

13 Arizona plc has carried on business for a number of years as a retailer of a wide variety of 'do it yourself' goods. The company operates from a number of stores around the United Kingdom.

In recent years, the company has found it necessary to provide credit facilities to its customers in order to achieve growth in turnover. As a result of this decision, the liability to the company's bankers has increased substantially.

The statutory accounts of the company for the year-ended 31 March 1998 have recently been published, and extracts are provided below, together with comparative figures for the previous two years.

Profit and loss accounts for the years ended 31 March

	1996	1997	1998
	£m	£m	£m
Turnover	1850	2200	2500
Cost of sales	(1250)	(1500)	(1750)
Gross profit	600	700	750
Other operating costs	(550)	(640)	(700)
Operating profit	50	60	50
Interest from credit sales	45	60	90
Interest payable	(25)	(60)	(110)
Profit before taxation	70	60	30
Taxation	(23)	(20)	(10)
Profit after taxation	47	40	20
Dividends	(30)	(30)	(20)
Retained profit	17	10	–

Balance sheets at 31 March

	1996	1997	1998
	£m	£m	£m
Tangible fixed assets	278	290	322
Stocks	400	540	620
Debtors	492	550	633
Cash	12	12	15
Trade creditors	(270)	(270)	(280)
Taxation	(20)	(20)	(8)
Proposed dividends	(30)	(30)	(20)
Bank overdraft	(320)	(520)	(610)
Debentures	(200)	(200)	(320)
	342	352	352
Share capital	90	90	90
Reserves	252	262	262
	342	352	352

Other information:

- Depreciation charged for the three years was as follows:

year-ended 31 March	1996	1997	1998
	£m	£m	£m
	55	60	70

- The debentures are secured by a floating charge over the assets of Arizona plc. Their repayment is due on 31 March 2008.
- The bank overdraft is unsecured. The bank has set a limit of £630 million on the overdraft.
- Over the past three years, the level of credit sales has been:

year-ended 31 March	1996	1997	1998
	£m	£m	£m
	213	263	375

Given the steady increase in the bank overdraft which has taken place in recent years, the company has recently written to its bankers to request an increase in the limit. The request was received by the bank on 15 May 1998, two weeks after the 1998 statutory accounts were published.

You are an accountant employed by the bankers of Arizona plc. The bank is concerned at the steep escalation in the level of the company's overdraft and your regional manager has asked for a report on the financial performance of Arizona plc for the last three years.

Required:

Write a report to your regional manager which analyses the financial performance of Arizona plc for the period covered by the financial statements.

Your report may take any form you wish, but should specifically address the particular concern of the bank regarding the rapidly increasing overdraft. Therefore, your report should identify aspects of poor performance which could have contributed to the increase in the overdraft. (20 marks)

(CIMA)

29

Financial statement analysis

After reading this chapter you should be able to:
- appraise the effects of differing accounting policies on the picture given by the financial statements
- prepare reports on the overall financial picture as revealed by the analysis of the financial statements.

Introduction

In the last chapter we provided you with a tool to analyse financial statements – ratio analysis. We also identified limitations within ratio analysis. One of these limitations was the problems encountered when companies use differing accounting policies within their financial statements. Within this chapter we will explore this problem further. The illustrations we give will, of course, need to be supplemented by further examples that you encounter from your own experience.

Effects of different accounting policies

Activity 1

Identify as many examples as possible where the choice of accounting policy could significantly affect the analysis and interpretation of published financial statements.

Activity 1 feedback

There are many examples which you may have chosen; we provide a selection for you.

- Policy on asset valuation particularly regarding land and buildings – historical cost may or may not be departed from. This will impact on profits via depreciation charges and on balance sheet structure.
- Depreciation policy will obviously impact on profits and asset values.
- Stock valuations again will impact on profits and asset values and on liquidity ratios through the cost flow assumptions made (LIFO, FIFO) and also the treatment of overhead costs.
- Long-term contract assumptions, e.g. the policy on inclusion of activity in annual turnover, and on treatment of possible future losses, and so on.
- Goodwill valuation and method of elimination from the financial statements.

- Leases allocation between operating and finance lease, method of allocating finance charges relating to both lessee and lessor.
- Research and development policy in respect of possible capitalization of development costs and policy on any resulting amortization.
- Pensions – problems associated with the type of scheme, the valuation of surplus or deficit and the allocation of these and other costs over accounting periods.
- Use of temporal or closing rate method for translation of foreign trading operations.
- Consolidation policies – definitions relating to the distinctions between subsidiary and associate, use of acquisition or merger accounting, quantification of fair values will all affect the numbers in the financial statements.
- On a more general level, the subjective judgements relating to conflicting accounting conventions and concepts, e.g. matching and prudence, will all affect the numbers. There may also be changes arising from the issue of new or revised accounting standards, which can cause major differences over time within the financial statements of any particular company or group.

It is very important that you understand the accounting implications of each of the possible different accounting policies that we outlined in the feedback above. If you do not, then you should go back to the relevant chapter and revise your knowledge of the topic or topics concerned. Once you are happy that you fully understand the principles, then the only way to make further progress is through practice, and working through artificial or real-life examples.

The next activity provides a simple illustration of what we have in mind.

Activity 2

The summarized balance sheets of three businesses in the same industry are shown below for 200X.

	A £000	B £000	C £000
Intangibles	100	–	10
Tangible fixed assets	886	582	580
Current assets	920	580	950
Current liabilities	(470)	(252)	(486)
	1436	910	1054
Long-term liabilities	(100)	(20)	(50)
	1336	890	1004
Share capital	200	40	300
Revaluation reserve	80	–	–
Retained profits	1056	850	704
	1336	890	1004

The operating profit for the three companies for the years in question was:

	282	194	148
and sales	2100	1500	1750

The companies had different treatments for the intangibles. Company A is amortizing this at £10 000 per annum and company C at £2000 per annum. Company B has written off goodwill of £40 000 to retained profits in the year. Included in the depreciation expense of company A is an extra £4000 over and above the historical cost depreciation caused by an earlier revaluation of its premises.

Appraise the financial performance and stability of each of these three companies within the limits of the information given.

Activity 2 feedback

Ratios calculated without any adjustment for differing accounting policies:

	A	*B*	*C*
	£000	*£000*	*£000*
ROCE	21.1%	21.8%	14.7%
CA:CL	1.9:1	2.3:1	1.95:1
Operating/sales	13.4%	12.9%	8.5%
Sales/CE	1.57	1.69	1.74

These ratios show B as being the most profitable company in terms of ROCE and C the least. C has the highest volume ratio at 1.74 and the lowest margin at 8.5%. A, on the other hand, has the highest margin and lowest volume turnover.

Adjustments made for differing accounting policies:

	A	*B*	*C*
	£000	*£000*	*£000*
Operating profit	282	194	148
Adjustment depreciation	4	–	–
goodwill	10	–	2
	296	194	150
Capital employed	1336	890	1004
Less revaluation reserve	(80)	–	–
Less goodwill w/o	(110)	–	(12)
	1146	890	992

Ratios calculated on adjusted figures:

ROCE	25.8%	21.8%	15.1%
Operating profit/sales	14.1%	12.9%	8.6%
S/CE	1.83	1.69	1.76

These figures, which are now more comparable, show A as the most profitable in terms of ROCE and that it has the highest volume turnover and margin ratio. C is still in third place due to its low profit margin.

This activity demonstrates the errors that could be made in analysing financial statements if the accounting policies of companies are not comparable.

Another example

Activity 3

The following information is available for companies X and Y for the year-ended 31 December 20X0. Note both companies have identical balance sheets and operating profits for the year.

	£000s
Fixed assets	250
Current assets	70
Current liabilities	(60)
	260
Long-term liabilities	(100)
	160
Share capital	100
Retained profits	60
	160
Operating profit for the year	30

Each company acquired another asset, fair value £100 000, on the 1 January 20X0 in respect of which no entries have been made in the accounts. The asset is acquired by means of a lease with rentals per quarter in advance of £6500. The term of the lease is five years and the useful life of the asset eight years.

Identify the effects on the companies' operating profits and balance sheets and any relevant ratios if the lease is treated as an operating lease by company X and a finance lease by company Y.

Assume all rentals are paid when due.

Activity 3 feedback

	X £000		Y £000	
Fixed assets	250		330	(note 2)
Current assets	44	(note 1)	44	
Current liabilities	(60)		(77.57)	(note 3)
	234		296.43	
Long-term liabilities	(100)		(166.8)	(note 3)
	134		129.63	
Share capital	100		100	
Retained profits	34		29.63	
	134		129.63	
Operating profit for the year	4		(0.37)	

Notes:

1 Cash adjusted for rental payments 4 × 6500 = 26 000 and charged to operating profit assuming operating lease.

2 Under a finance lease the asset is capitalized at fair value of £100 000 and depreciation calculated for the year on a straight-line basis assuming no residual value over a five-year life – depreciation charge £20 000, NBV of asset 31 December 20X0 is therefore £80 000.

3 Activity 4 in Chapter 19 identified the finance lease calculations – as at 31 December 20X0 obligations under the finance lease are £84 370 of which £17 570 is due in less than one year.

4

		£000s
Operating profit for the year		30
Less depreciation		20
Less interest charges		10.37
		(0.37)

Ratio calculations	X	Y
ROCE	3%	loss
CA:CL	0.73:1	0.57:1
Gearing	43%	56.3%

If the lease is treated as an operating lease then all relevant ratios are more favourable than if the lease was treated as a finance lease. The ROCE is a loss, the liquidity ratio is decreased and the gearing ratio increased (when the lease is treated as a finance lease). Company Y would therefore be regarded less favourably than company X under this analysis. However, the only difference between them is the accounting treatment used for the leased asset!

Real-life vignette

British Airways plc

This company, because of FRS 5 'Reporting the Substance of Transactions' is having to make very significant changes to its published financial statements. For example, as of 1994 twenty-four aircraft previously accounted for under extendable operating lease arrangements, and therefore off the balance sheet, will need to be included as assets on the balance sheet with the corresponding liabilities also included. British Airways also, in order to avoid problems of protection policies by foreign governments, has set up 49%-owned operating companies, i.e. TAT European airlines and Deutsche BA. Under FRS 2 these were classified as associate undertakings and dealt with accordingly in the group accounts. However, under FRS 5 they will need to be classified as quasi-subsidiaries and therefore treated in the accounts as if they were subsidiary undertakings. There are obviously a whole variety of detailed effects on the numbers in the published financial statements resulting from FRS 5. Noteworthy, for example, is an increase in the value of fixed assets and related borrowings by some £1100 million!

Scottish Television plc

This company in their published statements for 1993 revalued their fixed assets back to full gross historical cost rather than continuing with the previous policy which was that fixed assets were revalued annually. The effects of this are shown in a note to the accounts, reproduced below.

Tangible fixed assets	Land and buildings		Plant and technical	
	Leasehold	Freehold	equipment	Total
Company	£000	£000	£000	£000
Cost and valuation				
At 1 January 1993 as previously stated at cost or valuation	354	11 846	28 681	40 881
Prior year adjustment:				
Rebasing of fixed assets to cost	240	(2 831)	(6 493)	(9 084)
At 1 January 1993 as restated at cost	594	9 015	22 188	31 797
Additions	116	1 582	3 532	5 230
Disposals	–	(39)	(700)	(739)
At 31 December 1993	710	10 558	25 020	36 288
Depreciation				
At 1 January 1993 as previously stated	–	–	20 435	20 435
Prior year adjustment:				
Rebasing of fixed assets to cost	277	3 537	(6 170)	(2 356)
At 1 January 1993 as restated	277	3 537	14 265	18 079
Disposals	–	(32)	(444)	(476)
Charge for year	23	314	2 462	2 799
At 31 December 1993	300	3 819	16 283	20 402
Net book value				
At 31 December 1993	410	6 739	8 737	15 886
Net book value				
At 31 December 1992 (restated)	317	5 478	7 923	13 718

The net book value of tangible fixed assets includes amounts totalling £1 678 000 (1992: £53 000) in respect of assets held under finance leases. The depreciation charge in respect of these assets was £350 000 (1992: £65 000).

Rebasing of fixed assets: fixed assets are included on an historical cost accounting basis. The directors consider this basis to be more appropriate than the previous policy of annual revaluation due to the subjective nature of valuations and the cost and time consuming process in preparing and accounting for annual valuations. In addition, annual revaluation is no longer required for exchequer levy purposes.

This is a change in accounting policy as previously fixed assets had been revalued annually. Comparative figures for 1992 have been restated to take account of the new policy. The effect of this change in policy in both the group and the company is to reduce the gross amount of the fixed assets at 1 January 1992 by £9 084 000, accumulated depreciation by £2 356 000 and their net book value by

£6 728 000 in the balance sheet and to reduce the depreciation charge for the year-ended 31 December 1992 by £595 000 from that previously reported. (Source Scottish Television plc published financial statements year-ended 31 December 1993.)

It is interesting to note that the gross figure for leasehold land and buildings has increased substantially whereas the figures for freehold land and buildings and equipment have reduced substantially. The effects on the depreciation balances brought forward are also of considerable interest. Clearly land and buildings of all types were previously not being depreciated, i.e. there was no expense charged to the P&L account. Plant and equipment depreciation was clearly greater than that required on a strict historical cost basis (as the balance brought forward has been reduced). This was presumably because previous depreciation was being calculated on higher revalued amounts. Note the effect this change in policy has had on the annual reported profit. The note reproduced informs us that the change in policy has increased profits for the year-ended 31 December 1992 by £595 000 and presumably those for the year-ended 31 December 1993 by a similar amount.

Naamloze Vennootschap DSM

If it appears that comparison of British companies between each other or over time becomes a very complex business when accounting policies are differing, a moment's thought will make it obvious that the situation becomes infinitely more complex when the comparison involves financial statements from different countries prepared under differing national accounting practices. The technical and subjective complexities involved in this process are well beyond the scope of this book. However, the following example provides a flavour of the problems involved.

Activity 4

Attached is an extract from a real set of published accounts, of a Dutch company, of a few years ago.

(a) For each year, calculate return, using both operating profit and net profit, on stockholders' (i.e. shareholders') equity, and a gearing ratio, under each basis.

(b) Write a brief explanation, clear to a non-accountant, about the differences between the figures under the two bases. Which basis should be used for analysis of the group's performance?

Supplementary data based on current value

The consolidated financial statements of Naamloze Vennootschap DSM are drawn up on the basis of historical cost.

Below, supplementary data on the basis of current value are given. Since there is no generally accepted method yet for presenting such data, the bases of valuation and determination of income on the basis of current value are explained insofar as they diverge from those used for the consolidated financial statements.

Fixed assets

The current value of land is generally based on appraisals, that of other tangible fixed assets is determined using price indices from external sources, making allowance for technological developments. Where lower, the recoverable value is used for valuation purposes. The value of tangible fixed assets owned by non-consolidated companies has also been restated using price indices; the effect on the equities of these companies, commensurate with the percentage of participation, is accounted for in the balance sheet.

Current assets
A revaluation is made where current inventory values diverge from the valuation in the consolidated balance sheet.

Stockholders' equity
Equity according to the consolidated balance sheet is increased by the revaluation of tangible fixed assets and inventories, after deduction of relevant deferred tax commitments and minority interests.

Operating profit
The operating profit according to the consolidated statement of income is adjusted for the additional depreciation on tangible fixed assets based on current value and for revaluation of inventories.

Net profit
The same adjustments are applied to the net profit as to the operating profit, additionally allowing for minority interests and as the gain realized through loan financing. The tax burden is not adjusted. The financing gain corresponds to the part of the revaluation adjustments in the consolidated statement of income that relates to tangible fixed assets and inventories, insofar as financed with loan capital.

For calculation of the gain realized through loan financing, use is made of the ratio of group equity to equity invested in tangible fixed assets and inventories. This ratio is determined on the basis of the consolidated balance sheet of Naamloze Vennootschap DSM at the end of the preceding financial year. In calculating the ratio, group equity is never put at less than 25% of total assets. The difference between the net result calculated on historical cost basis and the current value net result is regarded as adjustment for capital maintenance.

Consolidated statement of income

Million	1989		1988	
Net sales	10772		10121	
Other operating income	397		243	
Total operating income		11169		10364
Amortization and depreciation	−602		−627	
Other operating costs	−9184		−8530	
Total operating costs		−9786		−9157
Operating profit		1383		1207
Financial income and expense		−40		−82
Profit on ordinary activities before taxation		1343		1125
Tax on profit on ordinary activities		−407		−417
Results of non-consolidated companies		98		83
Profit on ordinary activities after taxation		1034		791
Extraordinary result after taxation		345		−174
Group result after taxation		1379		617
Minority interests' share in result		1		5
Net profit		1380		622

Abridged consolidated balance sheet

Million	1989 Historical cost	1989 Current value	1988 Historical cost	1988 Current value
Fixed assets	5070	5925	4358	5235
Current assets	4624	4625	3988	4000
Total assets	9694	10550	8346	9235
Stockholders' equity	3819	4375	3074	3790
Minority interests in consolidated companies	86	95	79	85
Current and long-term liabilities	5789	6080	5193	5360
Total liabilities	9694	10550	8346	9235

Consolidated statement of income, restated on the basis of current value

Million	1989	1988
Operating profit		
On historical cost basis	1383	1207
– additional depreciation on current value basis	–115	–105
– difference between current value and historical cost of inventories	20	–65
On the basis of current value	1288	1037
Net profit		
On historical cost basis	1380	622
– additional depreciation on current value basis	–115	–105
– difference between current value and historical cost of inventories	20	–65
– gain through loan financing	35	50
On the basis of current value	1320	502

The adjustment for capital maintenance, calculated with application of DSM's customary system, was £60 million, £75 million being accounted for by tangible fixed assets, £15 million by inventories. The profit retained largely exceeds the amount of the adjustment for capital maintenance.

Activity 4 feedback

	1989	1988
Historical cost basis		
Operating profit/owners' equity	1383/3819 = 36%	1207/3074 = 39%
Net profit/owners' equity	1380/3819 = 36%	622/3074 = 20%
Gearing	3819/9694 = 39%	3074/8346 = 37%
Current value basis		
Operating profit/owners' equity	1288/4375 = 29%	1037/3790 = 27%
Net profit/owners' equity	1320/4375 = 30%	502/3790 = 13%
Gearing	4375/10 550 = 41%	3790/9235 = 41%

It can be argued that the current value figures give a truer economic comparison with other currently available alternatives. For two of the three ratios, the trends, perhaps more useful than the absolute amounts, are different. From 1988 to 1989, operating profit to owners' equity falls on a historical cost basis and rises on a current value basis. Gearing worsens on a historical cost basis and stays constant on a current value basis. Note also, as an aside, the effects of the extraordinary items in the two years. Their existence tends to suggest that the operating profit ratio is a much better long-term indicator than the net profit ratio. This makes the difference in trend direction for the operating profit ratio under the two bases all the more significant. Perhaps a much longer time series is needed.

Summary

This chapter has identified the problems caused by differing accounting policies when analysing company financial statements. It is not enough for you to know which ratios to calculate and how to calculate them, you must also look behind the information presented and use your knowledge of accounting policies, that we have hopefully given you in this text, before making any judgement on a company's financial position or profitability. As we stated in Chapter 28 a good dose of common sense is a prerequisite of any accountant. We would suggest you continue your studies in this area of analysis by reading the accounting press (e.g. *Accountancy*) and identifying where changes in accounting policies have affected the analysis of a company's performance.

Exercises

1   Identify which accounting policies would seem to have the most impact on the analysis of companies' performances.
2   You, as an accountant, are asked by your financial director, to choose suitable companies to compare your own company with. Explain, in a report to her, what would influence your choice and how you would adjust for differing accounting policies, if any.

Final thoughts

This book has explored three broad themes:

- what financial reporting is all about – the conceptual framework
- the legal framework – what the law requires accountants to do
- the regulatory framework – what rules accountants have created for themselves.

In the introductions to each of the three parts we raised issues for you to think about. We suggest that you reread these introductions on pp. 1, 175, 213 and carefully think through your answers to the questions posed.

In addition we ask you to consider the following:

- Does the regulatory framework as it currently exists in the UK lead to the production of useful information for decision makers?
- Do you believe that decision makers actually use the published financial statements?
- Where do you believe financial reporting should go from here?

Bibliography

This is not a bibliography in the full formal sense; more a helpful note on further reading. There are several aspects to consider, but the most important thing about further reading is that you actually do some. Nobody should ever rely on only one source.

You may like to read further about areas which you find either particularly difficult or particularly interesting in other textbooks. Look at two or three in a library. As regards the various detailed regulations, there can be no real substitute for looking at the original regulations themselves. You should have access to the full texts of the Statements of Standard Accounting Practice, to the full texts of the Financial Reporting Standards, and to any recent Exposure Drafts. These are available individually (very expensive) or in bound collected form (much more cheaply) from all the main accounting bodies, and are printed when first published in the official magazines of these bodies. You should also make sure you follow all the documents issued by the Accounting Standards Board as they appear, especially those relating to its Statement of Principles. The Framework published by the International Accounting Standards Committee, referred to extensively in Chapter 10, is strongly recommended.

If you wish to follow the European and international dimensions further (which any open-minded accounting student should) then look at Alexander and Archer, Alexander and Nobes or Nobes and Parker as starting points to take you further. Readers particularly interested in the income measurement and valuation debate can probably do no better than look at the now ageing book by Tom Lee, which is nevertheless still the best succinct survey and includes an excellent annotated bibliography. Nothing can quite replace reading Edwards and Bell itself.

The most important advice of all is to remember that financial accounting and reporting is continually developing. So, therefore, must you be.

Particular texts referred to here or in the text are as follows.

Alexander and Archer (eds) (1998) *1998 European Accounting Guide*, 3rd edn. Harcourt Legal, San Diego, CA.

Alexander and Nobes (1994) *A European Introduction to Financial Accounting*. Prentice-Hall, London.

Edwards and Bell (1961) *The Theory and Measurement of Business Income*. University of California Press, Berkeley, CA.

Ernst and Young UK GAAP.

Fisher (1930) *The Theory of Interest*. Macmillan, New York, 1930. (Reprinted as 'Income and capital', in Parker and Harcourt, 1969.)

Frankel (1953) *Economic Impact on Underdeveloped Societies*. Basil Blackwell, Oxford. (Reprinted as ' "Psychic" and "accounting" concepts of income and welfare', in Parker and Harcourt, 1969.)

Hendriksen E. S. (1992) *Accounting Theory*, 5th edn. Richard D. Irwin.

Hicks (1946) *Value and Capital*. Clarendon Press, Oxford. (Reprinted as 'Income' in Parker and Harcourt, 1969.)

Kaldor, N. 'The concept of income in economic theory', in Parker and Harcourt (1969).

Lee (1985) *Income and Value Measurement*. VNR, London.

Nobes and Parker (1998) *Comparative International Accounting*. Prentice-Hall, London.

Parker and Harcourt (1969) *Readings in the Concept and Measurement of Income*. Cambridge University Press, Cambridge.

Ryle (1949) *The Concept of Mind*. London. [Reprinted 1984 by University of Chicago Press, Chicago, IL.]

'Sandilands Report', Inflation Accounting Committee (MND 6225, HMSO, 1975).

Index